Business Law

AUSTRALIA
The Law Book Company
Sydney

CANADA AND U.S.A.
The Carswell Company
Toronto, Ontario

INDIA
N.M. Tripathi (Private) Ltd.
Bombay
and
Eastern Law House (Private) Ltd.
Calcutta
M.P.P. House
Bangalore
Universal Book Traders
Delhi

ISRAEL
Steimatzky's Agency Ltd.
Tel Aviv

PAKISTAN
Pakistan Law House
Karachi

CHARLESWORTH'S

BUSINESS LAW

FIFTEENTH EDITION

by

PAUL DOBSON

LL.B., of Lincoln's Inn, Barrister;
Wedlake Saint Professor and Head of Department of Law
at the Polytechnic of West London

and

CLIVE M. SCHMITTHOFF

LL.M., LL.D. (London), DR.JUR. (Berlin), DRES.h.c.,
Hon.F.I.Ex.; of Gray's Inn, Barrister;
Visiting Professor in International Business Law
at the City University;
Hon. Professor of Law at the University of Kent at Canterbury;
Hon. Professor of Law at the Ruhr-Universität Bochum;
Emeritus Professor of the City of London Polytechnic

LONDON
SWEET & MAXWELL LTD.
1991

First Edition	(1929)	By His Honour Judge Charlesworth
Second Edition	(1931)	” ” ”
Third Edition	(1934)	” ” ”
Second Impression	(1935)	
Third Impression	(1936)	
Fourth Edition	(1938)	” ” ”
Fifth Edition	(1942)	” ” ”
Sixth Edition	(1945)	” ” ”
Second Impression	(1946)	
Third Impression	(1947)	
Fouth Impression	(1947)	
Fifth Impression	(1948)	
Sixth Impression	(1948)	
Seventh Edition	(1949)	” ” ”
Second Impression	(1951)	
Eighth Edition	(1955)	” ” ”
Second Impression	(1957)	
Ninth Edition	(1960)	By Clive M. Schmitthoff and David A. G. Sarre
Second Impression	(1961)	
Tenth Edition	(1963)	” ” ”
Eleventh Edition	(1967)	” ” ”
Second Impression	(1969)	
Third Impression	(1971)	
Twelfth Edition	(1972)	” ” ”
Second Impression	(1974)	
Third Impression	(1974)	
Translated into French	(1976)	
Thirteenth Edition	(1977)	” ” ”
Second Impression	(1979)	
Fourteenth Edition	(1984)	” ” ”
Fifteenth Edition	(1991)	By Paul Dobson and Clive M. Schmitthoff

Published by
Sweet & Maxwell,
South Quay Plaza,
183 Marsh Wall, London E14 9FT
Computerset by
M.F.K. Typesetting Ltd., Hitchin, Hertfordshire
Printed and bound in Great Britain by
Richard Clay (The Chaucer Press) Limited, Bungay, Suffolk

A CIP catalogue record
for this book is available
from the British Library

ISBN 0-420-486402

PREFACE

Sometime in about 1988 Clive Schmitthoff got me to agree to co-edit this, the fifteenth edition, with him. The book covers a very wide area of English Law and the full enormity of what I had undertaken was borne in upon me only when I fell to considering how to produce this edition after Clive's untimely death in September 1990. Even with the notes of developments since the last edition which Clive had meticulously made and kept, I could not have done it without greatly extending the practice, established in recent editions by Clive and his friend and co-editor, David Sarre, of using eminent specialist editors for specific parts of the book. Their help is gratefully acknowledged. They are:

Professor John Birds (Insurance)
Christopher M.C. Cashmore (Carriage)
Nigel Clayton (Negotiable Instruments)
Allison Coleman (Trade Secrets, Patents and Trade Marks)
Sionaidh Douglas-Scott (Conflict of Laws)
Alison Firth (Copyright)
Bernadette Griffin (International Trade)
Stephen Griffin (Guarantees)
Michael Griffiths (Bankruptcy)
Diana Iller (Employment Law)
Richard Kidner (Bailment, Pawn and Lien)
Hilary Panford (Agency)
Pamela Salisbury (Partnership)
Murray Smith (Arbitration)
Professor John A. Usher (Competition)

In a work of the breadth of this one, the new developments which have been incorporated are far too numerous to list in total. Some of them are: the Consumer Protection (Cancellation of Contracts Concluded away from Business Premises) Regulations 1987, the provisions of the Consumer Protection Act 1987 on Product Liability, Product Safety and Misleading Price Indications, the repeal of section 40 of the Law of Property Act 1925, the Minors' Contracts Act 1987, the Copyright, Designs and Patents Act 1988 and the 1990 edition of Incoterms. All of that is quite apart from the onward march of case law. A number of improvements have been made with the contents of certain chapters (including those on Agency and Employment Law) being re-arranged into a more readable format and with an expansion of coverage in other areas, including the additon to the chapter on Patents and Trade Marks of a passage on Trade Secrets. Two chapters have been completely re-written, namely the Conflicts of Laws chapter to take in the Contracts (Applicable Law) Act 1990, the Civil Jurisdiction and Judgments Act 1991 and other developments, and the Bankruptcy chapter which, of course, takes in the Insolvency Act 1986.

I record the gratitude which I, like I think many others, feel towards Clive for the encouragement and assistance he gave to us as young writers and I would like to think that he and Judge Charlesworth would have approved the change of the title of the work to the more modern *Charlesworth's Business Law*.

I have endeavoured to state the law as it was on August 1, 1991.

PAUL DOBSON

Woodford Green,
August 1991

CONTENTS

TABLE OF CASES

TABLE OF EUROPEAN CASES

TABLE OF STATUTES

PART 1: CONTRACT

CHAPTER 1

NATURE OF CONTRACT

DEFINITION OF CONTRACT

A CONTRACT is an agreement which will be enforced by the law.

This definition is satisfied when the following elements are present:

1. There must be an agreement. Since nobody can agree with himself (though he may resolve to do or not to do an act), there must be at least two parties to an agreement. One of them will make an offer, and the other will indicate acceptance. When offer and acceptance correspond in every respect, there is agreement between the parties.

2. The parties must intend their agreement to result in legal relations. This means that the parties must intend that if one of them fails to fulfil a promise undertaken by the agreement, he shall be answerable for that failure in law.

It is evident that not all agreements are intended to produce legal consequences. If, for example, John agrees to lend his cycle to his friend Paul but later refuses to let him have it, an action for damages will not lie against John because the two friends did not contemplate, when entering into the agreement, that it should be enforceable in law. Similarly, if a father fails to pay his son the promised pocket money, it is obvious that the son cannot sue the father. The former agreement is of purely social character, the latter is a domestic arrangement. Neither of these agreements qualifies as a contract.

3. English law is not content with these two requirements. It requires further that either consideration must be present or that the contract should be in a deed.

4. The parties must have capacity to contract.

5. The reality of the contract must not be affected by circumstances which render the contract unenforceable, voidable, void or illegal.

All these elements of a valid contract will be considered in detail in the following chapters, with the exception of the second one, *i.e.* the intention of creating legal relations, which it is convenient to treat here.

Intention of Creating Legal Relations

It has already been seen that the intention to create legal relations is an element necessary for the formation of a contract. Both parties must have this intention but what matters is not what they had in mind when concluding the contract, but whether reasonable persons would draw the conclusion from their words and actions that they want to be legally bound. If the parties indicate expressly or impliedly that they do not wish their agreement to be binding on them, the law would accept and respect their intention. In the absence of an express statement that the parties do not intend to be legally bound, there is a clear difference of approach to domestic agreements and commercial agreements. With the former, the courts are more likely to infer that no legal relationship was intended, whereas in the case of a commercial agreement there is normally a presumption that the parties intended to be legally bound.

Domestic agreements

Engagements of purely domestic or social nature are often not intended to be binding in law but are intended to rely on bonds of mutual trust and affection.

A husband who was a Civil Servant in Ceylon (now Sri Lanka) came to England with his wife. When his leave was nearing its end and he had to return to Ceylon, he promised his wife who, on the doctor's advice had to remain in England, a household allowance of £30 a month until she joined him in Ceylon. Later the parties separated and the wife sued for the allowance. *Held*, domestic agreements such as these were outside the realm of contract altogether: *Balfour* v. *Balfour* [1919] 2 K.B. 571.

A husband and a wife, whose marriage was unhappy, hoped that their relationship would improve if the husband bought her a car. The husband acquired a car on hire-purchase terms and agreed that the registration book should be put into the wife's name and that she should have possession of the car. In spite of this arrangement, the marriage continued to be unhappy and the parties separated. *Held*, applying the rule in *Balfour* v. *Balfour, ante*, the husband, and not the wife, was entitled to the car because the arrangement between them was of purely domestic character: *Spellman* v. *Spellman* [1961] 1 W.L.R. 921.

A mother who lived in Trinidad wanted her daughter to study for the English Bar and after completion of her studies to practise as a lawyer in Trinidad. At a time when mother and daughter were very close, the mother bought a house in London to enable the daughter to reside there during her studies. Later differences arose and the mother claimed possession of the house. *Held*, that the arrangements in relation to the house were made without contractual intent and that the mother was entitled to possession of the house: *Jones* v. *Padavatton* [1969] 1 W.L.R. 328.

On the other hand, even if the parties are in a domestic or social relationship but intend their agreement to have legal consequences, an enforceable contract is concluded.

A husband had formed an attachment to another woman and the spouses intended to separate. They negotiated in the husband's car about some arrangement for the future. Before the wife left the car she insisted that the husband gave her a written statement according to which in consideration of her paying the mortgage on the family home (which was in the name of her husband) he should transfer that house into her sole ownership. The wife paid the mortgage and asked for the transfer of the house. *Held*, the rule in *Balfour* v. *Balfour* did not apply. In that case the parties reached their agreement when they lived in amity but in the present case they negotiated at arms' length as they had decided to separate and reasonable persons would regard their agreement as intended to be binding in law. The wife was entitled to the house: *Merritt* v. *Merritt* [1970] 1 W.L.R. 1211.

Brian and his two brothers Peter and Barrie were directors of a family company engaged in the building trade. Serious disputes arose between the three brothers and, as the company needed additional finance, it took up a loan from a finance house. That loan was secured by way of a mortgage on the company's property. The three brothers had large individual loan accounts with the company and agreed in writing between themselves that if one of them voluntarily resigned his directorship, his loan account with the company should be forfeited immediately and the money be used towards the repayment of the loan given by the finance company. Brian voluntarily resigned his directorship. *Held*, Brian's argument that the agreement between the three brothers was only of domestic character was not sound and therefore the rule in *Balfour* v. *Balfour* did not apply. Owing to the dissensions between the brothers the family relationship had already been destroyed and nothing but the biological tie remained. The written agreement between the brothers was intended to create legal relations and Brian could not recover his loan account, but the company could not rely on the contract between the brothers because it was a stranger thereto (see p. 192, *post*): *Snelling* v. *John G. Snelling Ltd.* [1973] 1 Q.B. 87.

The parties, a widow, her grandmother, and the widow's lodger, agreed to "go shares" with respect to a newspaper competition. Sellers J. *held* that they intended to create legal relations, *viz.* to form an informal syndicate and that the recipient of the prize money had to share it with the others: *Simpkins* v. *Pays* [1955] 1 W.L.R. 975.

Commercial agreements

In a commercial agreement, the parties will normally intend there to be a legal relationship, *i.e.* that if one of them breaks the agreement, the other shall have the right to succeed in legal proceedings to enforce the agreement.

At a time when the English national football team was winning the World Cup, the Esso Petroleum Company ran a promotion campaign in which a customer who bought four gallons of petrol would be given a free "World Cup coin." Signs were displayed at Esso garages saying "Free World Cup Coins" and "One coin will be given away with every four gallons." Esso claimed that no contract was made between the garage proprietor and the customer in relation to the World Cup coins, claiming that, since the coins had such a small intrinsic value, the proprietor could not have intended to create a legally binding relationship. *Held*, rejecting Esso's argument, that it had been intended that a customer who accepted the garage's offer by buying four gallons of petrol would thereby become entitled in law to have his World Cup coin. That was so, even though the low value of the coin would probably mean that he would never actually bring a court case to enforce that right. Therefore there was a legally binding contract to supply a World Cup coin to the customer in return for him agreeing to buy four gallons of petrol: *Esso Petroleum Co. Ltd.* v. *Customs and Excise Commissioners* [1976] 1 W.L.R. 1.

The parties may, however, expressly agree that their agreement, although couched in legal terms, shall not be binding in law but shall be binding "in honour only."

The R. Company made an agreement with the C. Company whereby they were appointed agents for the sale of paper supplied by the C. Company. One clause in the agreement was, "This arrangement is not entered into as a formal or legal agreement and shall not be subject to legal jurisdiction in the law courts." *Held*, no contract was made between the parties: *Rose & Frank Co.* v. *Crompton Bros. Ltd.* [1925] A.C. 445.

A condition expressly negativing the intention of creating legal relations is not contrary to public policy, but is binding.

A. sued the promoters of a football pool for £4,335 which he claimed to have won. The pool was subject to a condition that it was not to be legally enforceable. *Held*, the claim failed: *Appleson* v. *Littlewood Ltd.* [1939] 1 All E.R. 464.

Comfort letters

In commercial dealings where one party, A., has to decide whether to allow credit to another party, B., it may be that a third party, C., who has an interest in the credit being allowed to B., writes a "comfort letter" to A. in order to encourage A. to allow B. the credit. It is possible, of course that the comfort letter amounts to a fully binding guarantee of B.'s debt. If it does not, then the question may still arise as to whether the comfort letter was intended to create a legally binding agreement, albeit not a guarantee, between C. and A. The answer will depend upon the context in which the comfort letter was written and upon its wording.

Metals was a company wholly owned by the defendants. It was set up to trade on the London Metal Exchange and it needed an increase in funds in order to do this. Negotiations were conducted with a merchant bank for the bank to provide these funds to Metals. During the negotiations, the defendants rejected a request that they give a guarantee for the repayment by Metals of the funds; they did, however, give to the bank a comfort letter in which the defendants stated, "it is our policy to ensure that the business [of Metals] is at all times in a position to meet its liabilities to [the bank]." Subsequently Metals became insolvent and unable to repay the bank, which sued the defendants, relying upon the comfort letter as creating a legally binding obligation. *Held*, in the context (that the defendants had already refused to give a guarantee) the statement in the comfort letter was only a statement of the defendants' policy at the time and did not amount to a promise as to their future conduct. It therefore had no contractual effect: *Kleinwort Benson Ltd.* v. *Malaysia Mining Corpn Berhad* [1989] 1 W.L.R. 379.

Collective agreements

The Trade Union and Labour Relations Act 1974, s.18(1) to (3), as amended, provides that a collective agreement between a trade union and an employer (or an employers' association) is conclusively presumed not to have been intended by the parties to be legally enforceable, except if the following two conditions are satisfied:

(a) the agreement is in writing, and
(b) it contains a statement that the parties intend it to be a legally enforceable contract.

Terms prohibiting or restricting the right to strike

Whether or not the collective agreement constitutes a legally enforceable contract between the parties to it, some of its terms may be incorporated into individual contracts of employment. However, even on the individual level terms which prohibit or restrict the right of an employee to engage in a strike or other industrial action, are unenforceable, except if those terms are incorporated into the individual contract and the collective agreement itself satisfies the following four conditions:

(a) it is in writing, and
(b) contains a provision expressly stating that those terms may be incorporated into the contract of employment with the employee, and
(c) the collective agreement is reasonably accessible to the employee at his place of work and can be consulted during working hours, and
(d) each of the contracting trade unions is an "independent trade union," *i.e.* a trade union which is not under the control of the employer (section 18(4)).

The statutory provisions on trade disputes are discussed later (pp. 193–194).

At common law

At common law a collective agreement is not normally enforceable because it is usually not intended to create legal relations (*Ford Motor Co.* v. *Amalgamated Union of Engineering and Foundry Workers* [1969] 2 Q.B. 303).

Ex gratia payments

The promise of an *ex gratia* payment is ambiguous; it might mean that, without recognising a pre-existing legal liability, the promise should create an enforceable legal obligation.

E., a pilot employed by S., was promised an *ex gratia* payment on termination of his services. He left the employment of S. *Held*, the promise of an *ex gratia* payment was enforceable in law: *Edwards* v. *Skyways Ltd.* [1964] 1 W.L.R. 349.

Without prejudice negotiations

It happens sometimes that the parties attempt to settle a dispute in "without prejudice" negotiations. In order to encourage such attempts to settle disputes by agreement, there is a general rule that "without prejudice" negotiations are not admissible in evidence; nor can access to them be ordered by the court on "discovery" during a pre-trial process (*Rush & Tompkins* v. *Greater London Council* [1988] 3 W.L.R. 939). This rule against admissibility and discoverability does not depend upon the use of the words "without prejudice" but applies to all negotations, written or oral, genuinely aimed at settlement. There is, however, an important and obvious exception to the rule, where the court has to decide whether the negotiations have resulted in a binding settlement (*Walker* v. *Wilsher* (1889) 23 Q.B.D. 335). If agreement is reached on some issues but not on all, the question is whether the agreement was merely a step in the negotiations intended to be binding only on the condition that final settlement will be reached on all outstanding points, or whether the intention was that the agreement, as far as it went, should be binding in any event, and the settlement of the outstanding issues should be left to further negotiations or judicial decision.

A work accident had occurred in which a fitter was injured. The fitter's solicitor and the agent for the employers' insurers agreed in "without prejudice" negotiations that the liability of the employers should not exceed 50 per cent. but they could not reach agreement on the valuation of the fitter's claim. The fitter started proceedings and the employers (who were the defendants for procedural reasons) denied liability. *Held*, the 50/50 agreement reached in the "without prejudice" negotiations was intended to be binding although the parties had not reached agreement on the quantum of the plaintiff's claim: *Tomlin* v. *Standard Telephones and Cables Ltd.* [1969] 1 W.L.R. 1378.

Too vague agreements

The agreement may be so vague as to show that the parties did not intend to be bound in law.

The company agreed with V. that, on the expiration of V.'s existing contract, they would favourably consider an application by V. for a renewal of his contract. *Held*, the agreement was not intended to bind the company to renew their contract with V. and imposed no obligation on them to renew it: *Montreal Gas Co.* v. *Vasey* [1900] A.C. 595.

A husband who had left his wife agreed to pay her £15 a week "as long as he had it." *Held*, that although husband and wife could enter into a legally binding agreement, the vague terms which were used indicated an intention not to create legal obligations: *Gould* v. *Gould* [1970] 1 Q.B. 275 (Lord Denning M.R. gave a strong dissenting judgment).

The parties agreed that the buyers should acquire land of approximately 51½ acres at £500,000. Of the purchase price, £250,000 was to be paid upon first completion, £125,000 12 months later, and the balance of £125,000 thereafter, and on occasion of each completion "a proportionate part of the land" should be transferred to the buyers. *Held*, the power to release "a proportionate part of the land" was an element of substance which left the whole contract uncertain: *Bushwall Properties Ltd.* v. *Vortex Properties Ltd.* [1976] 1 W.L.R. 591.

An agreement to agree on some future date may likewise be too vague, see p. 27, *post*. But if an agreement intended to create legal relations contains a term which is meaningless, that term may be disregarded by the court and the contract is binding, see p. 28, *post.*

CHAPTER 2

FORMATION OF CONTRACT

THE essence of contract is that there should be an **agreement** between the contracting parties. This agreement is normally constituted by one party making an **offer** and the other indicating its **acceptance**. The acceptance must correspond to the offer in all material aspects.

The negotiations between the parties need not always lead to a contract. Inquiries may be made or offers invited but no offer may be made or, if one is made, it need not be accepted.

Before the concepts of offer and acceptance can be considered in detail, it is necessary to distinguish certain statements preliminary to the offer from the offer itself.

STATEMENTS PRELIMINARY TO AN OFFER

An offer must be distinguished from

(a) an invitation to make an offer, and
(b) a declaration of intention.

Invitation to make an offer

An invitation to make an offer is not an offer which is capable of being turned into a contract by acceptance. An advertisement is normally only intended to be an invitation to treat, *i.e.* to negotiate. Further, a shopkeeper who displays goods in his window with a ticket on them stating a price, does not make an offer, but merely invites the public to make an offer to buy the goods at the price stated. Therefore, if a customer enters the shop, tenders the price and demands the article, the shopkeeper is not bound to sell it to him. The demand of the customer is the offer which the shopkeeper is free to accept or reject as he pleases.

Goods were sold in B.'s shop under the self-service system. Customers selected their purchases from shelves on which goods were displayed, put them into a wire basket supplied by B. and took them to the cash desk where they paid the price. *Held*, the contract was made, not when the customer put the goods in the basket, but when the cashier accepted the offer to buy and received the price: *Pharmaceutical Society* v. *Boots Cash Chemists* (*Southern*) [1953] 1 Q.B. 401.

P. advertised in the column "Classified Advertisements" of the periodical *Cage and Aviary Birds* "Quality British ... bramblefinch hens." T. ordered a bramblefinch hen and enclosed his cheque, and P. supplied him with the bird. The Protection of Birds Act 1954, s.6(1) makes it an offence to sell, *offer for sale*, or have in his possession for sale these birds, except in specified cases. P. was accused of having committed the offence of *offering for sale* a bramblefinch hen, by inserting the advertisement into the periodical. *Held*, P. was not guilty because the advertisement was not an offer to sell. "When one is dealing with advertisements and circulars, unless they indeed come from manufacturers, there is business sense in their being construed as invitations to treat and not offers for sale": *per* Lord Parker C.J. in *Partridge* v. *Crittenden* [1968] 1 W.L.R. 1204.

Note that if P. had been accused of *having in his possession for sale* the bird, he would have been convicted.

British Car Auctions were in business as auctioneers of motor cars. Their standard conditions provided that no contractual relationship should ensue between the auctioneers and the buyer but that any contract resulting from the auction should be directly between the seller and the buyer. British Car Auctions auctioned a Morris 1100 car which undoubtedly was unroadworthy. They were accused under section 68 of the Road Traffic Act 1960 which made it an offence "to offer to sell" an unroadworthy car. *Held*, at an auction the bidder, and not the auctioneer, made the offer and that offer was accepted by the fall of the auctioneer's hammer (see p. 352, *post*). The charge was dismissed: *British Car Auctions Ltd*. v. *Wright* [1972] 1 W.L.R. 1519.

A prospectus to subscribe to the shares or debentures of a company is often in the nature of an invitation to make an offer; the application for shares or debentures is the offer and the allotment by the company is the acceptance.

Declaration of intention

A declaration by a person that he intends to do a thing gives no right of action to another who suffers loss because the former does not carry out his intentions. Such a declaration means only that an offer is to be made or invited in the future, and not that an offer is made now. A **letter of intent**, which contains no additional undertakings, does not oblige the writer to anything.

An auctioneer advertised in the newspapers that a sale of office furniture would be held at Bury St. Edmunds. A broker with a commission to buy office furniture came down from London to attend the sale, but all the furniture was withdrawn. The broker thereupon sued the auctioneer for his loss of time and expenses. *Held*, that a declaration of intention to do a thing did not create a binding contract with those who acted upon it, so that the broker could not recover: *Harris* v. *Nickerson* (1873) L.R. 8 Q.B. 286.

THE OFFER

How an offer is made

The offer may be express or implied from conduct. Examples (1) and (2) below are illustrations of express offers, and example (3) of an implied offer. The person making the offer is called the *offeror*, and the person to whom it is made is called the *offeree*. In examples (1) and (2) A is the offeror.

Examples—(1) A. offers to sell his motor cycle to B. at the price of £300. B. promises to pay £300 for the motor cycle.

(2) A. advertises in a newspaper offering £5 reward to anyone who returns his transistor radio. B. brings the radio to A.

(3) A bus goes along the street. This is an offer on the part of the transport enterprise to carry passengers at the published fares. The offer is accepted when a person gets on the bus with the intention of becoming a passenger. [Where, however, as on a modern bus, the customer pays the driver on entering the bus, it is probably the case that the customer makes the offer when he asks the driver for a ticket for a given price or to a given destination; the driver accepts the offer by issuing the ticket.]

An offer may be made to a definite person, to some definite class of persons, or to the world at large. An offer to a definite person can be accepted only by that person and by no one else. An offer to the world at large can be accepted by anyone. Examples (2) and (3) above are illustrations of this. An offer to some definite class can only be accepted by a member of that class.

Carbolic Smoke Ball Co. offered by way of reward £100 to anyone who contracted influenza after using their smoke ball as prescribed; the offer stated that they had lodged £1,000 with "the Alliance Bank, Regent Street, showing our sincerity in this matter." Mrs. Carlill used the smoke ball as prescribed but, notwithstanding, contracted influenza. She claimed £100.

Held, the company was bound to pay. The company raised four defences. (1) This was an offer made to the public; on this point Bowen L.J. said: "Why should not an offer made to all the world which is to ripen into a contract with anybody who comes forward and performs the condition?" (2) The promise of £100 was merely an advertising puff not intended to create legal relations; the court rejected this argument on the ground that the company had declared it had lodged £1,000 to meet its obligations. (3) Mrs. Carlill had not notified the company of her acceptance; the court rejected this contention on the ground that if the offeror expressly or impliedly intimated in his offer that it would be sufficient to act on his offer without communicating acceptance to him, performance of that condition was a sufficient acceptance without notification. (4) The promise to pay £100 was not supported by consideration; this argument failed because, in the judgment of the court, the inconvenience of applying the smoke ball to one's nostrils as prescribed was sufficient consideration: *Carlill* v. *Carbolic Smoke Ball Co.* [1893] 1 Q.B. 256.

All offers must be communicated

All offers must be communicated to the offeree before they can be accepted. The offeree cannot accept an offer unless he knows of its existence, because he cannot accept it without intending to do so, and he cannot intend to accept an offer of which he is ignorant. If A. offers by advertisement a reward of £5 to anyone who returns his transistor radio, and B., finding the radio, brings it to A. without having heard of the offer of the reward, he is not entitled to the £5.

An offer is made only when it actually reaches the offeree and not when it would have reached him in the ordinary course of post.

A., by letter dated September 2, offered goods to B. "receiving your answer in course of post." The letter was misdirected and did not reach B. until the 5th, when the offer was immediately accepted. The acceptance reached A. on the 9th, but on the 8th A. sold the goods to X. *Held*, there was a good contract between A. and B., because the offer was immediately accepted on its receipt by B.: *Adams* v. *Linsdell* (1818) 1 B. & Ald. 681.

However, if the date of the letter or other facts, *e.g.* the date of the postmark, had given the offeree warning that there was an unforeseen delay in transmission, the decision would probably have been different.

Lapse of offer

An offer lapses:

(a) On the death of either the offeror or the offeree before acceptance. Death after acceptance does not affect the obligations arising from a contract unless they are of a personal nature.

K. offered to redeem certain annuities payable to V. on payment of £6,000 and sent a draft deed of release to V.'s solicitors. V., who lived in Holland, executed the release on January 12 and died on January 17, but her death was not known to her solicitors in London until January 31. On January 24 V.'s solicitors told K. of V.'s acceptance of the offer and K. paid them £6,000. In an action to recover the money paid, *held*, (1) the offer lapsed by the death of V. before the communication of the acceptance on January 24; (2) V.'s death revoked the authority of her solicitors to notify her acceptance to K.: *Kennedy* v. *Thomassen* [1929] 1 Ch. 426.

(b) By non-acceptance within the time prescribed for acceptance by the offeror.

(c) When no time for acceptance is prescribed by non-acceptance within a reasonable time. What is a reasonable time depends on the nature of the contract and the circumstances of the case.

On June 8, M. offered to take shares in the R. Company. He heard nothing until November 23, when he received a letter of acceptance. M. refused to take the shares. *Held*, M. was entitled to refuse, as his offer had lapsed before November 23 and so could not be accepted: *Ramsgate Victoria Hotel Co.* v. *Montefiore* (1866) L.R. 1. Ex. 109.

The reason why the offer lapses is that the offeree is regarded as having refused it if he has not accepted it within a reasonable time. If the offeree indicates within a reasonable time that he accepts the offer but sends a formal letter of acceptance later, the offeror cannot claim that his offer has lapsed by effluxion of time.

A council offered school premises for sale by tender. On August 26, 1964 a company submitted a tender offering to buy the premises. On September 15, 1964 the council replied accepting the company's offer. Various formalities had to be complied with, and on January 7, 1965 the council posted a formal letter of acceptance but on the same day the company sent the council a letter withdrawing the offer. *Held*, the contract of sale was concluded on September 15, 1964. In the alternative, if it was not concluded on that date, it was still open to acceptance, and had been validly accepted, on January 7, 1965 *Manchester Diocesan Council for Education* v. *Commercial & General Investments Ltd.* [1970] 1 W.L.R. 241.

Revocation of offer

An offer may be revoked in accordance with the following rules:

1. An offer may be revoked at any time before acceptance.[1] As a general rule an offer is irrevocable after acceptance. There are, however, certain statutory exceptions to this rule which give the customer a cooling off period of a few days during which he is free to cancel the agreement after he has made it. These exceptions are designed to enable the customer to back out of a contract made during (or following) an unsolicited visit by a salesperson to the customer's home (see Cancellable Agreements at p. 29, *post*).

2. Revocation does not take effect until it is actually communicated to the offeree. Communication for this purpose means that the revocation must actually have reached the offeree.

A., of Cardiff, by letter of October 1 offered to sell goods to B. in New York, B. received the offer on the 11th and immediately telegraphed his acceptance. On the 8th, A. wrote revoking his offer, and this was received by B. on the 20th. *Held*, the revocation was of no effect until it reached B., and a contract was made when B. telegraphed: *Byrne* v. *Van Tienhoven* (1880) 5 C.P.D. 344.

The communication need not have been made by the offeror. It is enough that the offeree learns of the revocation from a source which he believes to be reliable.

X. agreed to sell property to Y. by a document which stated "this offer to be left over until Friday, 9 a.m." On the Thursday X. contracted to sell the property to Z. Y. heard of this from B., and on Friday at 7 a.m. he delivered to X. an acceptance of his offer. *Held*, Y. could not accept X.'s offer after he knew it had been revoked by the sale of the property to Z.: *Dickinson* v. *Dodds* (1876) 2 Ch.D. 463.

3. Apart from international sales to which the Uniform Laws on International Sales Act 1967 applies,[1] if the offeror agrees to keep his offer open for a specified time, he may nevertheless revoke it before the expiration of that time, unless:

[1] If the offer is made in an international sale to which the Uniform Law on the Formation of contracts for the International Sale of Goods applies, the offer is binding if:
(1) made for a fixed time, or
(2) otherwise indicating that it is firm or irrevocable:
Uniform Laws on International Sales Act 1967, Sched. 2, Art. 5(2); see p. 415, *post*.

(a) the offer has in the meantime been accepted before notice of revocation has reached the offeree, or
(b) there is consideration for keeping the offer open.

Rejection of offer

An offer is rejected:

(a) if the offeree communicates his rejection to the offeror, or
(b) if the assent of the offeree is qualified or is subject to conditions. In that case the assent constitutes the rejection of the original offer, combined with a counter-offer (see below, under "Acceptance must be absolute and unqualified.)"

THE ACCEPTANCE

Acceptance only possible if offer still in force

The acceptance must be made while the offer is still in force, and before the offer has lapsed, been revoked or rejected.

Once the acceptance is complete, the offer has become irrevocable.

Acceptance must be absolute and unqualified

Only an absolute and unqualified assent to all the terms of the offer constitutes an effective acceptance. If the offer requires the offeree to promise to do or pay something, the acceptance must conform exactly to the offer; if the offer requires an act to be done, the precise act and nothing else must be done. If the "acceptance" varies the terms of the offer it is a counter-offer, and not an acceptance of the original offer.[2]

M. offered land to N. at £280. N. replied accepting, and enclosing £80

[2] If the offer is made in an international sale to which the Uniform Law on the Formation of Contracts for the International Sale of Goods applies, an acceptance which contains additional or different terms that do not materially alter the offer constitutes a valid acceptance with the proposed modifications, unless promptly objected to by the offeror: Uniform Laws on International Sales Act 1967, Sched. 2, Art. 7(2); see p. 416, *post*.

with a promise to pay the balance by monthly instalments of £50 each. *Held*, no contract, as there was not an unqualified acceptance: *Neale* v. *Merrett* [1930] W.N. 189.

N., a Canadian company, negotiated with F., of North Wales, for the purchase of an amphibian aircraft. F. sent the following telegram: "Confirming sale to you Grummond Mallard aircraft. ... Please remit £5,000. ..." N. replied: "This is to confirm your cable and my purchase Grummond Mallard aircraft terms set out your cable. ... £5,000 sterling forwarded your bank to be held in trust for your account pending delivery. ... Please confirm delivery to be made thirty days within this date." *Held*, N.'s telegram was not an acceptance of F.'s offer because it introduced two new terms, one as to payment because F. had asked for £5,000 to be paid in advance and N. offered this sum to be released by the bank on delivery; and another as to the time of delivery which, according to F.'s offer, was a reasonable time but, according to N.'s purported acceptance, was within thirty days. N.'s telegram was a counter offer which had not been accepted by F.; hence there was no contract: *Northland Airliners Ltd.* v. *Dennis Ferranti Meters Ltd.*, *The Times*, October 23, 1970.

A conditional acceptance is not an acceptance.

Communication of acceptance

Here two cases have to be distinguished:

1. On principle, an unexpressed acceptance or an unmanifested assent to an offer does not result in a contract. The acceptance must be communicated in writing, by words or by conduct. What constitutes communication of an acceptance will be considered in the following sections; it will be seen that different rules apply to the communication of an acceptance in instantaneous contracts and in contracts by post.

F. offered by letter to buy his nephew's horse for £30, saying "If I hear no more about him, I shall consider the horse is mine at £30." The nephew did not reply, but he told the auctioneer who was selling his horses not to sell that particular horse because it was sold to his uncle. The auctioneer inadvertently sold the horse. *Held*, F. had no claim against the auctioneer because the horse had not been sold to him, his offer of £30 not having been accepted: *Felthouse* v. *Bindley* (1862) 11 C.B. (N.S.) 869.

If the offeror prescribes or indicates a particular method of acceptance and the acceptor accepts in that way, there will be a contract, even though the offeror does not know of the acceptance. If, for example, the offeror requires the offeree to accept by advertisement in a particular column of a certain newspaper, the acceptance will be communicated when the advertisement is published, whether or not the offeror reads it.

A request for an acceptance "by return of post" does not indicate a method of acceptance but merely a time requirement, so that the offer could be accepted by another method equally fast: *Tinn* v. *Hoffman* (1873) 29 L.T. 271. It seems that the same rule applies even if a particular method of communicating acceptance is stipulated; it is still open to the offeree to accept by any other method which is at least as quick as the stipulated method. If, however, some other method is used the postal rule will not apply and a letter of acceptance will take effect only upon arrival: *Manchester Diocesan Council* v. *Commercial & General Investment* [1970] 1 W.L.R. 241. Thus where an offer stated that acceptance should be sent by registered post or recorded delivery, it was held that the acceptance, which was sent by ordinary mail arriving just as quickly as registered post, was effective to make the contract: *Yates Building Company* v. *Pulleyn* (1975) 119 S.J. 370.

2. If the offer is one which is to be accepted by being acted upon, no communication of the intention to accept is necessary, unless communication is stipulated for in the offer itself. If an offer of reward is made for finding a lost dog, the offer is accepted by finding the dog, and it is unnecessary before beginning to search for the dog to give notice of acceptance of the offer.

Carlill v. *Carbolic Smoke Ball Co.* [1893] 1 Q.B. 256; on p. 13, *ante*.

The basic principle

The basic principle is that a statement addressed by one party to another is effective in law only if **communicated** to him. That principle applies to acceptances in the same manner as to offers, notices and other statements.

"Communication" means that the addressee must have been able to take notice of the statement in question. If it is in writing and has reached the addressee, the statement is duly communicated, even if for one reason or another he has not read it.

A distinction is drawn between an acceptance in an instantaneous contract and one in a contract by post.

Acceptance in instantaneous contracts

In the case of instantaneous communications, namely, communications between parties present, or communications by telephone, telex or facsimile transmission, the contract is complete only when the acceptance is received by the offeror and not merely when transmitted (*Entores Ltd.* v. *Miles Far East Corpn.* [1955] 2 Q.B. 327).

Brinkibon, an English company, negotiated with Stahag, an Austrian company, for the purchase of a quantity of steel. A contract was said to have been made by an acceptance by telex emanating from the English buyers and received by the Austrian sellers in Vienna. The contract was never performed. The buyers brought an action for damages for breach of contract in the English courts. They applied for leave to serve the writ on the sellers out of the jurisdiction. The court was authorised to grant leave if the contract was made within the jurisdiction. *Held*, an acceptance by telex from London to Vienna caused the contract to be made in Vienna: *Brinkibon Ltd.* v. *Stahag Stahl und Stahlwarenhandelsgesellschaft m.b.H.* [1983] 2 A.C. 34. [N.B. In this case the telex communications were between principals both present. Their lordships left open the issue of when an acceptance by telex would take effect if it were either communicated to an agent or reached the offeror's address out of office hours.]

Where, according to the terms of a charterparty the shipowner is entitled to withdraw from the contract if the charterer fails to make punctual payment, the notice of withdrawal, if given by telex, is effective when received by the party in default (*The Brimnes* [1975] Q.B. 929; for punctual payment of charter hire and notice of withdrawal, see p. 607, *post*).

Acceptance in contracts by post

Where contracts are made by letter, telegram or cable they are said to be made by post. In such a case it depends on the intention of the parties whether the general rules for the communication of a statement shall apply, *i.e.* whether the postal acceptance has to be communicated to the offeror, or whether the mere posting of such an acceptance, and not its arrival at the address of the offeror, shall be sufficient.[3] The general rule is that an acceptance must be communicated to the offeror to be effective. The postal rule is an exception to that. The postal rule is that where the post is reasonably to be expected as the means of communication, then the acceptance takes effect upon posting. This exceptional rule does not, however, apply to a revocation of an offer.

F. handed to H. a written option on some property at £750. The next day F. posted a withdrawal of the offer. This was posted between 12 and 1 and did not reach H. until after 5 p.m. In the meantime H. at 3.50 p.m. had posted an acceptance. *Held*, (1) although the offer was not made by post, yet the parties must have contemplated the post as a mode of communicating the acceptance; (2) F.'s revocation was of no effect until it actually reached H. and did not operate from the time of posting it; (3) a binding contract was made on the posting of H.'s acceptance: *Henthorn* v. *Fraser* [1892] 2 Ch. 27.

When the postal rule applies, acceptance is complete as soon as the letter of acceptance is posted, prepaid and properly addressed, whether it reaches the offeror or not; if the letter is lost or delayed in the post the contract is nevertheless made although the offeror may be quite ignorant of that fact.

G. applied for shares in a company. A letter of allotment was posted but never reached G. *Held*, G. was a shareholder in the company: *Household Fire Insurance Co.* v. *Grant* (1879) 4 Ex.D. 216.

But if the acceptance, instead of being properly posted, is handed to a postman to post, the contract is not complete until the acceptance is actually received by the offeror (*Re London and Northern Bank* [1900] 1 Ch. 220).

It is possible for the offeror, by the terms of his offer, to set aside the postal rule, *i.e.* to stipulate that the acceptance must reach him to be effective.

Dr. Hughes gave Holwell Securities an option on his house. The option

[3] If the acceptance by post is made in an international sale to which the Uniform Law on the Formation of Contracts for the International Sale of Goods applies, mere posting is not sufficient but the acceptance must be communicated to the offeror: Uniform Laws on International Sales Act 1967, Sched. 2 Art. 6(1); see pp. 415–416, *post*.

agreement stated that "the said option shall be exercisable by notice in writing to the intending vendor." Holwell Securities posted a letter to Dr. Hughes purporting to exercise the option but that letter never arrived. *Held*, the option was not duly exercised because the parties had not dispensed with the communication of the notice whereby it was exercised: *Holwell Securities Ltd.* v. *Hughes* [1974] 1 W.L.R. 155.

Acceptance subject to contract

An acceptance "subject to contract" normally means that the parties do not intend to be bound until a formal contract is prepared and signed by them.

C. and D. signed an agreement for the purchase of a house by D. "subject to a proper contract" to be prepared by C.'s solicitors. A contract was prepared by C.'s solicitors and approved by D.'s solicitors, but D. refused to sign it. *Held*, there was no contract as the agreement was only conditional: *Chillingworth* v. *Esche* [1924] 1 Ch. 97.

Unless there is an agreement to the contrary, the contract is made either when the formal contract is signed by both parties or, if each party is to sign a separate counterpart of the contract, when the separate counterparts so signed are exchanged. If the exchange is to be made by post, the contract is not concluded before the later of the two counterparts is posted.

B. sold a house to E. "subject to contract." The contract was agreed between the solicitors, and the parties were ready to exchange the counterparts, E. signed his part and posted it to B., but B. did not post his part. *Held*, there was no contract: *Eccles* v. *Bryant* [1948] Ch. 93.

The words "subject to" do not in all cases indicate that the parties do not intend to be bound until the event referred to has happened. While normally the phrase "subject to the purchaser obtaining a satisfactory mortgage" indicates that there is no binding contract because that term is too uncertain to give it a practical meaning (*Lee-Parker* v. *Izzet* (No. 2) [1972] W.L.R. 775), exceptionally a similar phrase has been interpreted by the court as meaning that the purchaser cannot withhold his satisfaction unreasonably and that there is already a binding contract (*Janmohamed* v. *Hassam*, *The Times*, June 11, 1976). Where the condition is "subject to survey," the purchaser must, at least, obtain the survey and consider it and must act bona fide (*Lim Ee* v. *Kaker* (1979) P. & C.R. 223).

An acceptance subject to an identified contract already in existence makes a contract.

A house was offered for sale by auction, but not sold. Later, X. wrote to Y. offering £350 and saying that if this offer was accepted he would "sign contract on auction particulars." Y. accepted the offer "subject to contract as agreed." *Held*, X. was bound by the auction particulars although he did not sign them: *Filby* v. *Hounsell* [1896] 2 Ch. 737.

An agreement subject to contract must be distinguished from an agreement between the offeror and the offeree which is only to become effective on the approval of a third party, as where X. agrees to sell and Y. to buy a piece of land subject to Z.'s approval. Here there is a binding contract from which neither X. nor Y. can withdraw until Z. approves or disapproves within the time stated in the contract or within a reasonable time.

Some Special Cases

Options

An option is a conditional contract to do something. For example, A., the owner of a piece of land, may, in consideration of £100, give B. an option to buy the land within six months at a certain price. An option is binding on the person giving it only if it is supported by consideration or expressed in a deed.

In the example just given, there are two contracts. The first is the option agreement whereby A. *allows B. to buy* the land within the time and upon the terms stated in that contract; if A. purports to revoke the option, B. can nevertheless exercise it and compel A. to sell the land to him. The second is the contract whereby B. actually *buys* the land from A.; that contract is conditional upon B. exercising the option granted him in the first contract.

An option has been described as a **unilateral contract** because it imposes only an obligation on the promisor but the promisee is not bound and will never be bound if he fails to exercise the option. If the promisee exercises it, a **synallagmatic contract**, *i.e.* a contract whereby each party undertakes obligations to the other, is constituted and both parties are bound. The option must be exercised within the time stated therein; if no time is stated, a condition is implied that it has to be exercised within a reasonable time (*United Dominions Trust* (*Commercial*) *Ltd.* v. *Eagle Aircraft Services Ltd.* [1968] 1 W.L.R. 74, see pp. 369–370, *post*).

The notice to exercise the option must be communicated to the person who granted the option (*Holwell Securities Ltd.* v. *Hughes* [1974] 1 W.L.R. 155, see pp. 21–22, *ante*).

Tenders

A tender is an offer. The acceptance of a tender has different legal results, depending on the terms of tender which are accepted. Examples of these different types of tender are as follows

1. The accepted tender may result in a contract by which the buyer undertakes to buy all the goods in the tender from the tenderer.

Example—A. requires 1,000 tons of coal. He invites tenders and B.'s tender is accepted. There is then a contract for the sale of 1,000 tons of coal from B. to A.

2. The accepted tender may result in a standing offer to supply goods as and when and if required by the buyer. When the buyer gives an order there is a contract.

A railway company invited tenders for such iron articles as they might require for a year. W. tendered and his tender was accepted. Orders were given and supplied for some time, but during the currency of the tender, W. refused to execute an order given. *Held*, as W.'s tender had been accepted he could not refuse to supply goods within the terms of the tender: *G.N. Ry.* v. *Whitham* (1873) L.R. 9 C.P. 16.

If the buyer gives no order or does not order the full quantity of goods set out in the tender, there is no breach of contract.

P. signed a tender addressed to the London County Council (L.C.C.) agreeing, on acceptance, to supply all the goods specified in the schedule to the extent ordered and in any quantity. Quantities were set out in the schedule and stated to be those estimated as the probable requirements for the period of the contract. P.'s tender was accepted, but the L.C.C. did not order the estimated amounts. P. claimed he was entitled to supply goods to the full amount in the schedule. *Held*, the L.C.C. were under no obligation to order any goods, but that P. was bound to deliver goods as and when they were ordered: *Percival Ltd.* v. *L.C.C.* (1918) 87 L.J.K.B. 677.

3. The buyer may not be bound to take any specified quantity, but bound to buy all the goods he needs. Such a contract is broken if the buyer does need some of the goods and does not take them from the tenderer.

X. invites tenders for his usual requirements of certain goods, and agrees to take his requirements from the person whose tender is accepted. If Y.'s tender is accepted, X. must order all goods of the stated kind he requires from Y., but if he requires none there is no breach of contract. X.'s "requirements" means what he needs in his own business, and Y. is not obliged to supply X. with goods for resale: *Kier* v. *Whitehead Iron Co.* [1938] 1 All E.R. 591.

Whichever type of tender is being referred to, the person inviting the tenders may undertake in his invitation that he will accept the tender which is the highest (if he is selling) or the lowest (if he is buying). If he does, then that is a binding commitment: *Harvela Investments Ltd.* v. *Royal Trust Company of Canada* [1986] A.C. 207. This is the same as when someone selling by auction undertakes that he will sell to the highest bidder, except of course in an auction each bidder knows what others have bid, whereas in competitive tendering, each competitor is usually unaware of the tenders of others.

Two people wished to buy shares in a company. The seller therefore decided to ask each of them to tender (in Canadian dollars) in a sealed bid for the shares. The terms of the invitation for the two tenders were that the seller undertook to accept the higher of the two and that the tenders were to be sent sealed to the seller's solicitor by the stated deadline and both would be opened at the same time. One of the two tenders was for $2,175,000. The other was for "$2,100,000 or $101,000 in excess of any other offer." *Held*, that the circumstances of an undertaking to accept the higher bid and an undertaking not before the deadline to disclose what the bids were, showed that the seller was creating a system of competitive fixed bids. Thus the second bidder had not been entitled to submit, and the seller had not been entitled to accept, the referential bid. The first bidder was therefore entitled to the shares for $2,175,000; *Harvela Investments Ltd.* v. *Royal Trust Company of Canada* [1986] A.C. 207.

Rewards

It has already been observed that the offer of a reward is accepted by acting upon the offer and that prior notice of acceptance is not required (see pp. 13–14, *ante*). The offer of a reward, like an option, is a unilateral contract.

On the other hand, where the act for which the reward is promised is done in ignorance of the promise of the reward, the reward cannot be claimed because there can be no acceptance without knowledge of the offer.

The Government of Western Australia offered a reward of £1,000 for information leading to the arrest and conviction of the murderers of two police officers. C. saw the offer but forgot it and later gave the necessary information. *Held*, C. was not entitled to the reward: *R.* v. *Clarke* (1927) 40 C.L.R. 277 (an Australian case).

The Agreement

When offer and acceptance correspond in every respect, the parties have reached agreement, or, as it is said, there is *consensus ad idem* (consent on the same [points]). A valid contract has come into existence, provided that the other requirements set out on p. 1, *ante*, are present.

The terms of the contract are, thus, settled by the parties themselves in their agreement, within the law. This is called the **doctrine of freedom of contract.**

Sometimes, however, it is not easy to determine whether negotiations between the parties resulted in an agreement.

Different terms in offer and acceptance

If the offer contains standard terms and conditions and the acceptance contains different standard terms and conditions, it may be difficult to determine whether the offeror's or acceptor's terms shall govern the contract. The result that there was no agreement between the parties should be avoided because it obviously does not correspond to the intention of the parties. " . . . in most cases, when there is a **battle of forms**, there is a contract as soon as the last of the forms is sent and received without objection being taken to it. . . . The difficulty is to decide which form, or which part of which form, is a term or condition of the contract. In some cases the battle is won by the man who fires the last shot. . . . In some cases the battle is won by the man who gets the blow in first." (*per* Lord Denning M.R. in *Butler Machine Tool Co. Ltd.* v. *Ex-Cell-O Corporation* (*England*) *Ltd.* [1979] 1 W.L.R. 401, 404–405). This is a matter of construction of the contract as a whole, in the light of the surrounding circumstances of the case.

Agreement to agree in future

If the parties have not agreed upon the terms of their contract but have made an agreement to agree in future, there may be no contract. There cannot be a contract to make a contract, if there is a material term of the future contract which is not agreed, expressly or by implication. The terms must be "definite or capable of being made definite without further agreement of the parties."

O. agreed to buy from S. a motor van giving another van in part exchange. The contract provided "This order is given on the understanding that the balance of the purchase price can be had on hire-purchase terms over a period of two years." *Held*, no contract, as the words "on hire-purchase terms" were too vague to be given a definite meaning: *Scammell* v. *Ouston* [1941] A.C. 251.

Tolaini, who wanted to develop a site in Hertfordshire, agreed with Courtney, a company of building contractors, that Courtney would introduce them to persons providing the necessary finance, upon the understanding that they would employ Courtney as their building contractors. Tolaini were to instruct their quantity surveyor "to negotiate fair and reasonable contract sums" with Courtney. Negotiations took place but broke down and Tolaini placed the contract with another firm of builders. *Held*, in a building contract the price was of such fundamental importance that there was no contract unless it was agreed by the parties or there was an agreed method of ascertaining it, independent of negotiations between the parties: *Courtney & Fairbairn Ltd.* v. *Tolaini Brothers* (*Hotels*) *Ltd.* [1975] 1 W.L.R. 297.

The contract may contain machinery for ascertaining the terms of the future contract, and then there is a binding contract. Such machinery may be provided either by allowing the court to fill the gap in the contract or by giving an arbitration tribunal power to do so (*Sweet & Maxwell Ltd.* v. *Universal News Service Ltd.* [1964] Q.B. 699).

F. sold land to a motor company for the purposes of their business. The sale was subject to an agreement that the company should buy all their petrol from F. at a price to be agreed by the parties from time to time, and that any dispute should be submitted to arbitration. The price was never agreed, and the company refused to buy from F. *Held*, there was a binding contract to buy petrol of reasonable quality at a reasonable price to be determined in case of dispute by arbitration: *Foley* v. *Classique Coaches Ltd.* [1934] 2 K.B. 1.

S. agreed to supply F. with broiler chicken for five years. The contract provided that S. should supply 30,000 to 80,000 chicken per week during the first year but failed to specify the number of chicken to be delivered in the second and subsequent years. The contract contained a clause according to which any difference between the parties as regards performance should be referred to an arbitrator. *Held*, as far as the supply of chicken for the second and subsequent years was concerned, the contract was binding because the number of chicken to be delivered could be ascertained by arbitration: *F. & G. Sykes (Wessex) Ltd.* v. *Fine Fare Ltd.* [1966] 2 Lloyd's Rep. 205.

Further, the modern tendency is for the courts to uphold a contract freely negotiated and intended to be binding, whenever they can give business efficacy to it, and not to hold it void for uncertainty. Thus a clause that there should be "suitable arbitration" is not void on the ground that it is too vague (*Hobbs Padgett & Co. (Reinsurance) Ltd.* v. *J. C. Kirkland* [1969] 2 Lloyd's Rep. 547, see p. 730, *post*). Also, an agreement by which a person was given the first option of purchasing certain land "at a figure to be agreed" has been held not to be void for uncertainty because the vendor, if desirous to sell the land, would have to offer it to the person to whom the option was given at a price at which he was bona fide willing to sell it (*Smith* v. *Morgan* [1971] 1 W.L.R. 803).

Meaningless terms

There is distinction between a term which has yet to be agreed and a term which has no meaning. A meaningless term can be disregarded.

N. ordered 3,000 tons of steel bars at £45 14s. 5d. a ton from S. S. accepted and wrote, "I assume that the usual conditions of acceptance will apply." There were no usual conditions of acceptance. *Held*, a binding contract: *Nicolene Ltd.* v. *Simmonds* [1953] 1 Q.B. 543.

If, however, upon the proper construction of the contract, it can be said that the parties have attributed a common meaning and intention to a clause which, on its face, is meaningless, the courts will give effect to the intention of the parties and uphold the clause. Thus, the insertion of the phrase "also Paramount Clause" into a charterparty is not meaningless but imports the Hague Rules relating to Bills of Lading into the charterparty (*Nea Agrex S.A.* v. *Baltic Shipping Co. Ltd.* [1976] Q.B. 933).

The parties attached to a charterparty a typed slip stating: "Paramount Clause. This bill of lading shall have effect subject to the Carriage of Goods by Sea Act of the United States ... 1936, which shall be incorporated herein." The Act provided in section 5 that it should not be applicable to charterparties. *Held*, that according to the common meaning and intention of the parties the words "bill of lading" on the slip meant "charterparty," and that the Act of 1936, so far as regulating the rights and liabilities of the parties, was incorporated into the charterparty, but that section 5 of the Act was to be disregarded as meaningless: *Adamastos Shipping Co. Ltd.* v. *Anglo-Saxon Petroleum Co. Ltd.* [1959] A.C. 133.

Cancellable Agreements

The rule at common law is that once the offer is accepted and the contract made, it is binding and neither side can withdraw without the consent of the other. In recent years, however, there have been moves to protect consumers against the high pressure techniques sometimes employed by salespeople who visit potential customers in their homes. Thus there are statutory provisions giving the consumer a cooling off period of a few days during which he is free to cancel a contract made during (or following) an unsolicited visit by a salesperson to the customer's home, *e.g.* in the case of certain insurance policies, personal pensions contracts (Insurance Companies Act 1982 and Financial Services Act 1986). For a long time the most notable of these provisions were the cancellation provisions relating to consumer credit and consumer hire agreements under the Consumer Credit Act which are explained fully in chapter 17 (page 396, *post*). Now, however, the concept of cancellation as an antidote to doorstep selling has been extended to contracts which involve no element of credit or hire. This was done by the *Consumer*

Protection (Contracts Concluded away from Business Premises) Regulations 1987.

These regulations give a seven day cooling-off period to a customer who enters a contract (to buy goods or services) during an unsolicited visit by the trader to the customer's home (or place of work or someone else's home). The Regulations are intended to protect ordinary consumers and therefore do not apply where the customer is a company or corporate body or is someone who makes the contract for his business purposes. The Regulations apply only if the trader's visit was unsolicited and not if, for example, the customer has expressly requested the visit by returning a reply paid card asking for the visit or by telephoning asking for it. If, however, the trader (without the customer having requested him to do so) has telephoned the customer indicating that he is willing to make a visit, the trader's subsequent visit **will** be unsolicited and the Regulations will apply.

Where the Regulations apply, they require the trader to give the customer a written notice of his right of cancellation and a detachable form must also be provided for the customer's use in case he decides to cancel. The customer is entitled to cancel by giving the trader written notice (whether or not on the detachable form) within the period of seven days following the making of the contract. That written notice takes effect upon posting.

By way of exception, the regulations do not apply to certain contracts:

1. where the price (including V.A.T.) is £35 or less,
2. to buy sell, dispose of, lease or mortgage land,
3. to finance, or provide bridging finance for, the purchase of land,
4. for the construction or extension of a building or other erection on land (N.B. contracts for repairs and improvements are *not* excepted unless they are secured by a land mortgage).
5. for the supply of food drink or other goods intended for current consumption by use in the household and supplied by regular roundsmen,
6. which provide credit of £35 or less
7. which are covered by certain other legislation: Insurance

Companies Act 1982, Financial Services Act 1986, Banking Act 1987,

8. which are made on the terms of certain mail order catalogues which expressly give their customers a similar right of cancellation.

CHAPTER 3

TERMS OF THE CONTRACT

THE undertakings and promises contained in the contract are known as the **terms of the contract.** They have to be distinguished from **representations** which are made before the contract is entered into and are not intended to form an integral part of it. (Liability for misrepresentation is considered in Chapter 6.)

The parties will usually state expressly in their contract the terms which they consider material and little difficulty exists in ascertaining these **express terms.** Sometimes, however, they consider a term as so obvious that they fail to express it in their contract and in these cases it becomes necessary to imply a term in order to give efficacy to their contractual intention; these **implied terms** and in particular the stringent legal requirements for admitting such an implication are considered later, see p. 38, *post.*

In simple contractual undertakings the terms of the contract are classified in **conditions** and **warranties.** However, these categories are not exhaustive; there exist also terms which can be evaluated only in the light of the events that have actually occurred; these terms produce in some events the effect of a broken condition and in others that of a broken warranty; they are usually referred to as **innominate terms.**

In modern commercial practice **standard contract forms** are often used. They are of two types. They may be **model contracts** aimed at the simplification and standardisation of contract terms; here the parties are free to alter the suggested terms of contract and to adapt them to their requirements; model contract forms are used particularly frequently in the commodity trade. The other type of standard contracts are **contracts of adhesion** which are imposed by the economically stronger party on the weaker party and place before him the choice to take it or leave it; these terms make a mockery of the principle of freedom of contracting because they are not open to negotiation.

The law relating to the terms of the contract is greatly modified by the **Unfair Contract Terms Act 1977**, p. 40, *post.* This enactment is one of the most important Acts affecting the law of contract. The Act deals in particular with the regulation of **exemption clauses.** They are clauses by which the party who proposes the contract, seeks to limit or to obtain exemption from some or all of his liabilities.

A clause, such as an exclusion clause, which is particularly onerous or unusual and unlikely to be known to the party adversely affected by it, will not be regarded as effectively part of the contract unless either it is incorporated by being in a contractual document signed by that party or else he was aware of it or reasonable steps had been taken to draw it to his attention before making the contract (*Interfoto Picture Library* v. *Stiletto Visual Programmes*, see below).

An advertising agency telephoned a transparency library with whom the agency had never previously dealt. The agency asked to hire some transparencies of the 1950s. Accordingly the library sent 47 transparencies with a delivery note clearly requiring that they be returned by March 19. The delivery note included nine conditions, printed in four columns, which the agency never read. Condition 2 stated that a charge for £5 plus V.A.T. per transparency was payable for each day they were late being returned. After the agency returned the transparencies 14 days late, the library claimed over £3,500 under this clause. *Held* the claim failed. The clause imposed an exorbitant charge and thus was particularly onerous and unusual and the library had not taken all reasonable steps to bring it to the attention of the agency. *Per* Bingham L.J. "... the more outlandish the clause, the greater the notice which the other party, if he is to be bound, must in all fairness be given.": *Interfoto Picture Library* v. *Stiletto Visual Programmes* [1988] 2 W.L.R. 615 (C.A.)

Conditions and warranties

A condition is a vital term of a contract, going to the root of the contract, a breach of which entitles the injured party, *either* to treat the contract as repudiated and terminate performance of the contract and claim damages for the termination *or* to affirm the contract and claim damages for the breach. It was defined by Fletcher Moulton L.J. in *Wallis* v. *Pratt* [1910] 2 K.B. 1003 at 1012 as an obligation "which goes so directly to the substance of the contract, or, in other words, is so essential to its very nature, that its non-performance may fairly be considered by the other party as a substantial failure to perform the contract at all."

Owners let their steamship *Mihalis Angelos* to charterers under a voyage charter for a voyage from Haiphong, North Vietnam, to Hamburg or another port in Europe. The cargo was to consist of the mineral apatite. The charterparty stated that the vessel was "now trading and expected ready to load under this charter about July 1, 1965," and that, should the vessel not be ready for loading on July 20, the charterers had the option of cancelling the contract of charterparty. In June and July 1965, the transport of apatite from the mines of Haiphong was prevented by bombings by the U.S.A. Air Force. On July 17, 1965, the charterers cancelled the charter-policy. The ship was delayed on her journey to Haiphong and could not have reached that port on or before July 20. The owners claimed damages from the charterers for repudiation of the charterparty. *Held*, (1) the clause that the ship was "ready to load" about July 1, 1965, was a condition and the charterers were entitled to cancel the contract on July 17 on the ground that that condition was broken; (2) even if the charterers had not been entitled to cancel on July 17 and by their repudiation of the charterparty had committed an anticipatory breach of contract, the owners would not have suffered a loss because the charterers would beyond doubt have cancelled on July 20: *Maredelanto Compania Naviera S.A.* v. *Bergbau-Handel GmbH*; *The Mihalis Angelos* [1971] 1 Q.B. 164.

A warranty is not a vital term in a contract, but one which is merely subsidiary, a breach of which gives no right to treat the contract as terminated, but only an action for damages for the loss arising from the breach. It may be made orally or in writing. It is described in the Sale of Goods Act 1979 as an agreement "collateral to the main purpose of" the contract, and by Fletcher Moulton L.J. in *Wallis* v. *Pratt* as an "obligation which, though it must be performed, is not so vital that a failure to perform it goes to the substance of the contract."

B. agreed to sing for G., the director of the Italian Opera in England, during certain dates and to arrive in London six days before the commencement of the engagement for rehearsals. He arrived only two days before, and G. thereupon refused to be bound by the contract. *Held*, the stipulation was not a condition, and the contract could not be rescinded on its breach: *Bettini* v. *Gye* (1876) 1 Q.B.D. 183.

Whether a term in a contract is a warranty or condition is a question of the intention of the parties to be deduced from the circumstances of the case. Thus in a commercial contract for the sale of goods the deadline for delivery of the goods is much more likely to be of vital importance to the parties than is a deadline for payment of the price. Therefore where the contract does not make clear the parties' wishes as to whether a term is intended to be a condition or a warranty, the courts will usually assume that they intended any term as the date of delivery to be a condition and any term as to the time of payment to be a warranty. It is, however, always open to the parties to make it clear in the contract what their intention is. This is traditionally and clearly done by the use in the contract of the expression that a term is "of the essence" of the contract. This denotes a clear intention to make it a condition.

An agreement for the hire of computers stated that prompt payment of all payments due under the agreement was "of the essence." When the hirer was late in payment of one instalment, *Held* that the owner was entitled to treat the contract as repudiated, retake possession of the computers and claim damages for repudiation of the contract: *Lombard North Central p.l.c.* v. *Butterworth* [1987] Q.B. 527.

Whilst the description "of the essence" clearly states the parties' intention that the term be a condition, the use of the word "warranty" or the word "condition" is not so clear. Thus, the term "condition" may be used as a lawyer's term of art (*i.e.* a condition) or in its common meaning as simply denoting a stipulation (*i.e.* whether a condition or a warranty), and when ascertaining what meaning the parties intended to give to that term, a reasonable meaning should be attributed to it (*Wickman Machine Tool Sales Ltd.* v. *L. Schuler A.G.* [1972] 1 W.L.R. 840). It is frankly an oddity that in the Marine Insurance Act 1906 the term "warranty" is used as meaning what is here described as a "condition."

Innominate terms

Innominate or intermediate terms combine the nature of a condition and a warranty in so far as in some events the breach of such undertaking may entitle the innocent party to rescind the contract and in other events the breach entitles him only to claim damages but does not entitle him to rescind the contract. These terms can only occur in synallagmatic contracts, *i.e.* contracts in which each party undertakes obligations to the other (*per* Diplock L.J. in *United Dominions Trust* (*Commercial*) *Ltd.* v. *Eagle Aircraft Services Ltd.* [1968] 1 W.L.R. 74, 82; see p. 24, *ante*).

An illustration of an innominate term is, *e.g.* the shipowner's undertaking in a charterparty to provide a seaworthy ship; "it can be broken by the presence of trivial defects easily and rapidly remediable as well as by defects which must inevitably result in total loss of the vessel": Diplock L.J. in *Hongkong Fir Shipping Co. Ltd.* v. *Kawasaki Kisen Kaisha Ltd.* [1962] 2 Q.B. 26. The unseaworthiness of the ship may, according to the nature of the defect, go to the root of the contract and then entitles the charterer to rescind the contract, or it may be of such trivial consequence that the charterer has to abide by the contract and can only claim damages if he has suffered a loss. Although the Sale of Goods Act 1979 distinguishes between conditions and warranties, the principle embodied in the *Hongkong Fir Shipping Co. Ltd.* case applies to contracts for the sale of goods just as to all other contracts; consequently, the term in a contract of sale that "shipment to be made in good condition" can be interpreted as not referring to a condition within the meaning of that Act, nor to a warranty strictly called, but may be indicative of one of those innominate stipulations which gives the buyer no right to reject the goods unless the breach goes to the root of the contract: *Cehave N.V.* v. *Bremer Handelsgesellschaft mbH*; *The Hansa Nord* [1976] Q.B. 44, (see p. 314, *post*).

Where an innominate term is broken, "while in many, possibly most, instances, breach of it can adequately be sanctioned by damages, cases may exist in which. in fairness to the buyer, it would be proper to treat the cancellation as not having effect. On the other hand, always so to treat it may often be unfair to the seller, and unnecessarily rigid" (*per* Lord Wilberforce in *Bremer Handelsgesellschaft mbH* v. *Vanden Avenne-Izegem P.V.B.A.* [1978] 2 Lloyd's Rep. 109, 113).

Collateral contracts of warranty

It happens sometimes that a party (X.) is induced by an undertaking of another (Y.) to enter into a contract with a third party (Z.). X., a customer, may decide to acquire on hire-purchase a second-hand car from Y., a car dealer, relying on Y.'s warranty that the car is in good working order. Y. will then sell the car outright to a finance company (Z.) which will enter into a hire-purchase contract with X. (p. 369, *post*). Here there are two contracts: the contract of hire-purchase between X. and Z., and a collateral contract of warranty between X. and Y.; if the car is not in good working order, X. can claim damages from Y. for breach of the collateral contract.

W., chrysanthemum growers, were assured by the defendants that B.W. sand supplied by them would conform to a certain analysis and, consequently, be suitable for propagation of chrysanthemum. W. then requested H., a firm dealing in builders' material to purchase B.W. sand from the defendants and to resell it to them. The sand was unsuitable for the propagation of chrysanthemum. *Held*, that W. were entitled to damages from the defendants for breach of the defendants' undertaking that the sand was suitable: *Wells (Merstham) Ltd.* v. *Buckland Sand & Silica Ltd.* [1965] 2 Q.B. 170 (similar: *Shanklin Pier Ltd.* v. *Detel Products Ltd.* [1951] 2 K.B. 854).

Esso Petroleum sought to find a tenant for a new petrol service station in Southport. The local manager of Esso, who had 40 years' experience in the petrol trade, induced Mr. Mardon to become tenant by representing that the estimated annual consumption would be 200,000 gallons. This estimate was erroneous because the planning authority had not allowed the pumps to face the main street, but it had never been revised. The actual throughput in the first 15 months was only 78,000 gallons. Mr. Mardon who had sunk all his capital in the business suffered heavy loss. *Held*, the statement as to the potential throughput was a collateral warranty whereby Mr. Mardon was induced to enter into the contract of becoming tenant of the petrol station. In addition, Esso were liable under the rule in *Hedley Byrne & Co. Ltd.* v. *Heller and Partners Ltd.* (see p. 94, *post*). Mr. Mardon recovered damages: *Esso Petroleum Co. Ltd.* v. *Mardon* [1976] Q.B. 801. (The Misrepresentation Act 1967 (see p. 94, *post*) was not in force at the relevant time).

B. negotiated with the defendants for the purchase of a second-hand car described by the defendants to be in perfect condition and good "for thousands of trouble-free miles." In reliance on this statement B. decided to buy the car on hire-purchase terms. The defendants sold it outright to a finance company which granted B. hire-purchase terms. The car was not in a satisfactory condition. *Held*, that B. had a claim in damages against the defendants for breach of the collateral contract of warranty: *Brown* v. *Sheen & Richmond Car Sales Ltd.* [1950] 1 All E.R. 1102 (similar: *Andrews* v. *Hopkinson* [1957] 1 Q.B. 299).

The correct measure of damages as between a hirer under a hire-purchase agreement and a dealer whose warranty has induced him to enter into the agreement with the finance company is the whole damage suffered by the hirer, including his liability under the contract with the finance company, and it not limited to the difference in value between the goods as warranted and as in fact they are: *Yeoman Credit Ltd.* v. *Odgers* [1962] 1 W.L.R. 215.

Implied terms

It may be presumed that the parties to a contract have expressed in it every material term and accordingly that there is no necessity to imply additional terms. A term will be implied, however, if it is necessary to carry out the presumed intention of the parties and is so obvious that the parties must have intended it to apply to the contract and therefore thought that it was unnecessary to express it. The term's implication must be *necessary* to give that efficacy to the contract which the parties intended (*The Moorcock*, below). "But there are varieties of implications which the courts think fit to make and they do not necessarily involve the same process. Where there is, on the face of it, a complete, bilateral contract, the courts are sometimes willing to add terms to it, as implied terms: this is very common in mercantile contracts where there is an established usage: in that case the courts are spelling out what both parties know and would, if asked, unhesitatingly agree to be part of the bargain. In other cases, where there is an apparently complete bargain, the courts are willing to add a term on the ground that without it the contract will not work—this is the case, if not of *The Moorcock* (1889) 14 P.D. 64 itself on its facts, at least of the doctrine of *The Moorcock* as usually applied," (*per* Lord Wilberforce in *Liverpool City Council* v. *Irwin*, below).

The owner of *The Moorcock* agreed with the defendant wharfingers that his vessel should be discharged and loaded at their wharf and for that purpose should be moored at a jetty which belonged to the wharfingers and extended into the river Thames. When the tide ebbed and the vessel took the ground, it struck a ridge of rock and was damage: *Held*, the contract contained an implied undertaking on the part of the wharfingers that it was reasonably safe for the vessel to be berthed at the jetty: *The Moorcock*, (1889) 14 P.D. 64.

Liverpool City Council were the landlords of a 15 storey tower block containing 70 dwelling units. The tenants rented one of these units, a maisonette on the 9th and 10th floor. The tenants withheld the payment of the rent as a protest against the conditions of the building and their maisonette. The landlords claimed possession and the tenants counterclaimed for damages. *Held*, as far as the common parts of the building were concerned, there was an implied obligation on the landlords that the tenants may use the staircase, the lifts and the rubbish chutes. The standard of this obligation was to take reasonable care to keep the means of access in reasonable repair and usability, with the recognition that the tenants themselves had their responsibilities according to what a reasonable set of tenants would do for themselves. In the present case it was not shown that the landlords were in breach of this implied obligation: *Liverpool City Council* v. *Irwin* [1977] A.C. 239.

A commercial contract which provides for the supply of goods at a fixed price but does not specify a period for termination is, on the construction of the contract, terminable by reasonable notice; this term has to be implied into the contract (*per* McNair J. in *Martin-Baker Aircraft Co. Ltd.* v. *Canadian Flight Equipment Ltd.* [1955] 2 Q.B. 556, 577; see p. 156, *post*).

A term will not be implied merely because it would be reasonable to imply it. The court refuses to make a contract for the parties; it leaves the contract-making to them. An implied term cannot override an express term.

Apart from those terms which are implied because they are obvious and necessary to make the contract work, there are also terms implied by virtue of various statutes. The commonest of these are the terms, implied by the Sale of Goods Act 1979, as to title, description, quality and sample, which are dealt with in chapter 15, *post.* In some instances, in the interest of consumer protection, statutory implied terms cannot be excluded by agreement of the parties. Provisions prohibiting or restricting the exclusion of statutory implied terms are contained in the Unfair Contract Terms Act 1977 and the Supply of Goods and Services Act 1982. This subject will be treated shortly.

Exemption Clauses

It follows from the doctrine of freedom of contract that the parties, in principle, may agree that in certain contingencies one of them shall be exempt from the liability imposed by the law. This rule is, however, subject to qualifications required by public policy or statute law. Thus, a term exempting a party from liability in the event of his committing a fraud against the other party to the contract is void because it infringes public policy. Further, the Unfair Contract Terms Act 1977 prohibits or restricts certain exemption clauses, particularly in consumer transactions. Also, a carrier by sea cannot contract out of the liability imposed by the Carriage of Goods by Sea Act 1971 because that statute prohibits it (*The Hollandia*, also called *The Morviken* [1983] 1 Lloyd's Rep. 1; see p. 614, *post*). The courts do not favour exemption clauses in contracts, although they have to respect the liberty of the parties to agree on their own contract terms.

The Unfair Contract Terms Act 1977

This Act, as amended by the Supply of Goods and Services Act 1982, has greatly affected the law relating to exemption clauses.

The Act is capable of applying to business liability under any contract, including the following types of contracts:

(a) contracts for the sale of goods (s.6(2)(a) of the 1977 Act and s.55(1) of the Sale of Goods Act 1979);
(b) contracts of hire-purchase (s.6(2)(b) of the 1977 Act);
(c) other contracts under which the possession or ownership of goods passes (s.7 of the 1977 Act); and
(d) contracts for the supply of goods or services to which the Supply of Goods and Services Act 1982 applies, *e.g.* the leasing or repair of goods (1982 Act, ss.11 and 16).

It does not apply to other types of contract, *e.g.* contracts of insurance. The prohibitions and qualifications which the Act provides apply only to **business liability**, *i.e.* liability arising in the course of a business (s.1(3)).

Liability in negligence

The 1977 Act provides a statutory definition of negligence which applies equally to breach of contract and torts. Negligence is defined as the breach:

(a) of any obligation, arising from the express or implied terms of a contract, to take reasonable care or exercise reasonable skill in the performance of the contract;
(b) of any common law duty to take reasonable care or exercise reasonable skill (but not a stricter duty);
(c) or of the common duty of care imposed by the Occupiers' Liability Act 1957 or the Occupiers' Liability Act (Northern Ireland) 1957.

Any contract clause excluding or restricting liability for death or personal injury resulting from negligence is absolutely void (s.2(1)).

In the case of other loss or damage arising from negligence, contract terms aimed at excluding or restricting liability are void, except if they satisfy the "requirement of reasonableness" (s.2(2)).

Standard terms of business and guarantees

Where one of the parties deals as a consumer or on the other's written **standard terms of business**, the other cannot by reference to any contract term:

(a) when himself in breach of contract, exclude or restrict any liability of his in respect of the breach; or
(b) claim to be entitled—
(i) to render a contractual performance substantially different from that which was reasonably expected of him, or
(ii) in respect of the whole or any part of his contractual obligations, to render no performance at all.

except in so far as the term in question satisfies the test of reasonableness (s.3).

In the case of goods of a type ordinarily supplied for private use or consumption, where loss or damage arises because the goods are defective in consumer use and the manufacturer or distributor was negligent, liability for the loss or damage cannot be excluded or restricted by reference to a term contained in a **guarantee of the goods** (s.5).

Implied terms

The Unfair Contract Terms Act 1977 (as amended by the Supply of Goods and Services Act 1982) prohibits the exclusion or restriction of terms implied by the law into the contracts listed earlier (see p. 40, *ante*) in certain circumstances. The Sale of Goods Act 1979 (*i.e.* taking that Act as a model) implies the following conditions:

(a) that the seller has title to sell the goods and the buyer shall enjoy quiet, *i.e.* undisturbed, possession (s.12);
(b) that, if the sale is by description, the goods correspond with it

and, if it is by sample and description, they correspond to both (s.13);

(c) that, if the seller sells in the course of business, the goods are of merchantable quality, *i.e.* that they are fit for the purposes for which goods of that kind are commonly bought (s.14); and

(d) that, if the sale is by sample, bulk will correspond with sample, the buyer is given a reasonable opportunity of comparing bulk with sample, and the goods are free from any defect, rendering them unmerchantable which was not apparent on reasonable inspection of the sample (s.15).

The terms implied by the Sale of Goods Act 1979 are treated in detail in Chapter 15, *post.*

With regard to a clause purporting to exclude (or limit) these implied terms, a distinction is drawn between the position where the buyer is "dealing as a consumer" and where he is not. In both cases, the liability under section 12 of the Sale of Goods Act cannot be excluded or restricted. Where the buyer is "dealing as a consumer," liability under sections 13–15 of the Sale of Goods Act 1979 cannot be excluded. If he is not "dealing as a consumer" such liability can be excluded, but only in so far as the exclusion clause satisfies the requirement of reasonableness (1977 Act, s.6).

A buyer is not "dealing as a consumer" if he buys at an auction or by competitive tender. Apart from those two situations, however, the buyer is "**dealing as a consumer**" if (i) the goods are of a type ordinarily supplied for private use or consumption; and (ii) the seller sells them in the course of his business to someone who is not buying or holding himself out as buying in the course of a business (1977 Act, s.12).

The seller, a boat builder, contracted to build a boat for a Mr. Atkinson. The contract of sale contained an exclusion clause claiming to exclude the seller's liability for breach of the implied terms as to merchantable quality and fitness for the purpose. Subsequently, before delivery, a limited company, Rasbora Ltd., was substituted as buyer in place of Mr. Atkinson. This was done by way of novation, *i.e.* an extinguishing of the original contract between the seller and Mr. Atkinson and the creation of a new one between the seller and Rasbora Ltd. Rasbora Ltd. was a company incorporated in Jersey. It was wholly owned by Mr. Atkinson and had been formed by him for the purpose of buying the boat and with the intention that the boat was to be used only by Mr. Atkinson and his friends; there was no intention to hire out the boat. Shortly after it was delivered, the boat caught fire and sank. *Held*, the seller was liable for breach of the implied term as to merchantable quality. The exclusion clause was totally ineffective (i) because the contract with Rasbora Ltd. (like the earlier one with Mr. Atkinson) was a consumer deal and, alternatively, (ii) because the exclusion clause, claiming to exclude the whole liability in respect of merchantable quality and fitness for the purpose, did not satisfy the requirement of reasonableness: *Rasbora Ltd.* v. *J.C.L. Marine Ltd.* [1977] 1 Lloyd's Rep. 645.

Someone who buys "in the course of business" is not "dealing as a consumer." What then is the position of someone who is in business and who makes a purchase which, though it is incidental to his business, is not something which is central to the operation of it. The answer, derived from a trade descriptions case on the meaning of "in the course of a business," is that such a purchase will be "in the course of a business" only if it is a type of transaction which the purchaser makes **regularly** (*Davies* v. *Sumner* [1984] 1 W.L.R. 1301).

A company whose business was shipping brokerage bought a car for the use its directors. This was only the second or third time in the five years of its existence that the company had bought a car. The contract of sale contained an exclusion clause purporting to exclude the seller's liability for the terms as to quality and fitness for purpose implied by the Sale of Goods Act. *Held* that there had not been a sufficient degree of regularity in the company's purchase of cars to make the purchase "in the course of a business." Therefore the company had "dealt as a consumer" in buying the car. Therefore the exclusion was ineffective, irrespective of whether it satisfied the requirement of reasonableness: *R. & B. Customs Brokers Co. Ltd.* v. *United Dominions Trust Ltd.* [1988] 1 W.L.R. 321 (C.A.).

The requirement of reasonableness

In the following situations an exemption or limitation of liability clause will not be effective except to the extent that it satisfies the requirement of reasonableness. Those situations are: (i) where the clause seeks to exclude or limit liability for loss or damage (other than death or personal injury) caused by negligence; (ii) where one of the parties deals as a consumer or on the other party's written standard terms of business; (iii) where the clause seeks to exclude or limit liability for certain statutory implied terms (as to description, quality and sample) where the customer is not dealing as a consumer; (iv) where the clause seeks to exclude or limit liability for misrepresentation.

The requirement is satisfied only if the exclusion or limitation term is:

> a fair and reasonable one to be included having regard to the circumstances which were, or ought reasonably to have been, known to or in the contemplation of the parties when the contract was made, (s.11(1)).

Guidelines for the application of the requirement of reasonableness are provided in Schedule 2 to the 1977 Act. The guidelines state that regard shall be had to any of the following:

(a) the relative strength of the bargaining positions of the parties, taking into account alternative means by which the customer's requirements could have been met;
(b) whether the customer received any inducement to agree to the exclusion clause or had an opportunity of entering a similar contract with other persons without having to agree to a similar clause;
(c) whether the customer knew, or ought reasonably to have known, of the clause;
(d) where the clause excludes or restricts a liability if some condition is not complied with, whether it was reasonable at the time of the contract to expect that compliance with that condition would be practicable; or
(e) whether the goods were manufactured, processed or adapted to the special order of the customer.

A contract on standard written terms provided for the sale of seed potatoes by potato merchants to farmers. One clause in the contract purported to exclude liability if the buyers had not given notice of any defects within three days of delivery. Another clause purported to restrict the seller's liability for any consequential loss, limiting that liability to the amount of the contract price. After the potatoes had been planted and had come up, they proved to have been infected with a virus. *Held*, the clauses excluding liability unless notice of the defect was notified within three days of delivery was unreasonable (see guideline (d) above). The other clause, however, had been in use for many years with the approval of the negotiating bodies representing potato merchants and farmers and its terms restricting the seller's liability to the contract price were reasonable: *R. W. Green Ltd.* v. *Cade Bros. Farmers* [1978] 1 Lloyd's Rep. 602.

The plaintiffs, farmers, ordered 30lb of cabbage seed from the sellers. The seed arrived together with invoices which included a clause excluding all liability for any loss or damage and limiting the sellers' liability to an obligation to replace the seed or repay the price. The price of the seed was £192. The farmers planted the seed which was not the seed contracted for and which produced a useless crop, causing the farmers a loss of over £61,000. In defence to a claim for that loss, the sellers sought to rely upon the exclusion clause. *Held*, the clause did not satisfy the requirement of reasonableness. Judgment was for the farmers: *George Mitchell (Chesterhall) Ltd.* v. *Finney Lock Seeds Ltd.* [1983] 3 W.L.R. 163. (Note that the statutory test applied in this case and in *Green* v. *Cade*, above, was the test laid down in the earlier Supply of Goods (Implied Terms) Act 1973 which was whether it was fair and reasonable to allow the defendants to rely on the exclusion clause. This has now been replaced by the test laid down in the Unfair Contract Terms Act 1977, *i.e.* was the clause a fair and reasonable one to be included in the contract).

Clauses merely *limiting* liability are, as far as the requirement of reasonableness is concerned, generally judged by less exacting standards than *exclusion* of liability or indemnity clauses (*Ailsa Craig Fishing Co. Ltd.* v. *Malvern Fishing Co. Ltd.* [1983] 1 W.L.R. 964, 970).

International supply contracts

The provisions of the 1977 Act prohibiting the exclusion or restriction of liability by means of contract terms do not extend to international supply contracts which are defined in a manner corresponding to the definition in the Uniform Laws of International Sales Act 1967, s.26 (see p. 415, *post*).

The common law relating to exemption clauses

Much of the common law relating to exemption clauses has become obsolete as the result of the introduction of the Unfair Contract Terms Act 1977 which has rendered ineffective many exemption clauses which might previously have been effective. The following points, which arise in the common law, still require attention.

An exclusion clause in an unsigned document is not incorporated into the contract (and therefore will have no effect) unless at the time of making the contract either the party adversely affected by the clause was aware of its existence or else reasonable steps had been taken to bring it to his attention (*Parker* v. *South East Railway* (1877) 2 C.P.D. 416).

Incorporating the terms in a business document given by one party and received by the other as the document containing the terms of the contract may constitute the taking of reasonable steps, unless the terms are printed in such a manner or are in such position as to mislead a reasonably careful business man. The harsher the clause, the greater is the effort needed to bring the clause to the attention of the party adversely affected.

R. ordered four lots of timber from N.'s traveller. The traveller left a sold note setting out the sale and containing a clause "Goods are sold subject to their being on hand and at liberty when the order reaches the head office." N. did not deliver the timber, and, on being sued by R., pleaded the clause set out above. R. did not know of the clause and had not read it. *Held*, R. was bound by the clause, unless it was so printed that from its position in the document and the size of the type an ordinary careful business man, reading the document with reasonable care, might miss it: *Roe* v. *R.A. Naylor Ltd.* [1971] 1 K.B. 712.

When the offeree has signified his acceptance by signing a document presented by the offeror, the offeree cannot plead ignorance of the terms of the offer, in the absence of fraud or misrepresentation, even if he is in fact ignorant of them.

The proprietress of a café bought an automatic cigarette vending machine from the defendants. She signed a document which contained a number of clauses in small print, amongst them a clause excluding "any express or implied condition statement or warranty, statutory or otherwise, not stated therein." She refused to pay the price on the ground that the machine did not work and contended *inter alia*, that she was not bound by the exclusion clause as she had not read it. *Held*, the clause was binding on her: *L'Estrange* v. *F. Graucob Ltd.* [1934] 2 K.B. 394.

If the contractual document is signed as a result of the offeree's oral misrepresentation of one of its terms, the offeree will not be able to rely on that term.

C. took a dress to D. to be cleaned and was asked to sign a receipt which contained, among other terms, a clause. "This article is accepted on condition that the company is not liable for any damage howsoever arising." C. asked why she had to sign and was told that D. would not accept liability for damage to beads or sequins. She then signed. The dress was returned stained. *Held*, D. could not rely on the clause, because C.'s signature was obtained by misrepresentation of the effect of the document: *Curtis* v. *Chemical Cleaning & Dyeing Co.* [1951] 1 K.B. 805.

Similarly, if at the time when the contract is made a person gives an oral promise which cannot be reconciled with a term in the printed contract, the oral promise takes priority over the printed clause.

M. left his car in N.'s garage. Contrary to the rules of the garage, the car attendant who took the car over told M. he must not lock the car. M. informed the attendant that there was valuable property in the car and the attendant promised to lock the car after he had moved it. By the terms of the ticket which the attendant gave M., N., excluded responsibility for the loss of contents of the car. A suitcase containing valuables was stolen from the car. *Held*, N. was liable. Though the attendant had no *actual* authority to promise to lock the car, he has *ostensible* authority to make a statement concerning the safety of the car and its contents. The printed exclusion clause was repugnant to the express oral promise and could not be relied upon by N.: *Mendelsohn* v. *Normand Ltd.* [1970] 1 Q.B. 177.

Where printed conditions in a contract are repugnant to a binding oral promise they do not provide exemption from liability for breach of that promise: *J. Evans & Son (Portsmouth) Ltd.* v. *Andrea Merzario Ltd.* [1976] 1 W.L.R. 1078 (see p. 51, *post*).

An exemption clause cannot be introduced into the contract unilaterally after it is made

Thus, a hotel proprietor who contracts at the reception desk to accommodate a guest cannot rely on an exemption clause displayed in a bedroom and stating that the proprietor shall not be responsible for articles stolen unless handed to him for safe custody.

The plaintiff and her husband took a room in a residential hotel owned by the defendants. At the reception desk they were asked to pay a week in advance. They did so and went to their bedroom in which a notice was displayed stating that the proprietors did not hold themselves responsible for the loss of theft of articles unless handed to the manageress for safe keeping. Owing to the negligence of the defendants' personnel, a stranger gained entrance into the hotel and stole articles from the plaintiff's room when she was absent. *Held*, the defendants were liable. The contract was concluded at the reception desk and the terms of the notice in the bedroom were not incorporated in it: *Olley* v. *Marlborough Court Ltd.* [1949] 1 K.B. 532.

Similarly, an attempt to introduce an exemption clause in a receipt given after the conclusion of the contract would not make it a term of the contract and is not binding on the person who receives it.

C. hired a chair from the council, paid for it and was given a ticket which he put in his pocket unread. The chair collapsed and C. was injured. The ticket held a clause that the council were not to be liable for accidents or damage. *Held*, this was not binding on C.: *Chapelton* v. *Barry U.D.C.* [1940] 1 K.B. 532.

Mr. Thornton wished to park his car in a multi-story automatic car park belonging to the defendants. A traffic light at the entrance of the car park showed red. A ticked was extruded from a machine. When Mr. Thornton took the ticket the light turned green and the car was taken up. When Mr. Thornton collected the car, an accident occurred and he was injured. The defendants pleaded that the ticket contained a notice in small print that it was issued "subject to the conditions of issue as displayed on the premises," and that these conditions, displayed inside the garage, contained a clause exempting the defendants from liability for personal injury. Mr. Thornton had not read the small print. *Held*, the exempting clause in the conditions did not protect the defendants. (1) Lord Denning M.R. held that the contract was concluded when Mr. Thornton positioned his car at the appointed place and the light turned green, and the ticket was only a receipt which could not alter the terms of the contract; (2) all three judges of the Court of Appeal agreed that the defendants had failed sufficiently to bring to the notice of Mr. Thornton the limitation of liability: *Thornton* v. *Shoe Lane Parking Ltd.* [1971] 2 Q.B. 163.

It should be noted that today, by virtue of Unfair Contract Terms Act 1977, s.2(1), the exemption clauses in the two cases above would be invalid because they attempt to exclude liability for personal injury arising from negligence.

Interpretation of exemption clauses

When interpreting exemption clauses, the courts "lean against" them, *i.e.* will allow a party to escape from his liability only if the words of the exemption clause are perfectly clear, effective and precise.

The doctrine of fundamental breach

Before the introduction of the statutory requirement of reasonableness and the other restrictive provisions of the Unfair Contract Terms Act 1977, the courts developed the **doctrine of fundamental breach of contract.** This was a rule of construction (*i.e.* interpretation) of a contractual term. The courts held that in common law an exemption clause had to be construed as not protecting a party if that party committed a breach which went to the foundation of the contract, unless the clause was sufficiently clear to indicate an intention of the parties that it should operate even in this event. This rule of construction was developed by the House of Lords in *Suisse Atlantique Société d'Armement Maritime S.A.* v. *N.W. Rotterdamsche Kolen Centrale* [1967] 1 A.C. 361. The doctrine of fundamental breach was, *e.g.*, applied to disallow a clause exempting a seller of a motor vehicle from liability if the vehicle was unroadworthy (see *Karsales (Harrow) Ltd.* v. *Wallis* [1956] 1 W.L.R. 936; *Farnworth Finance Facilities Ltd.* v. *Attryde* [1970] 1 W.L.R. 1053; see also *Alexander* v. *Railway Executive* [1951] 2 All E.R. 422 (see p. 510, *post*)).

The doctrine of fundamental breach, as enunciated in *Suisse Atlantique* in 1967 was, in the words of Lord Bridge in *George Mitchell (Chesterhall) Ltd.* v. *Finney Lock Seeds Ltd.* (see p. 45 *ante*) "forcibly evicted" from the common law by the decision of the House of Lords in *Photo Productions Ltd.* v. *Securicor Transport Ltd.* in 1980 (see below). The practical value of this doctrine was in any event greatly reduced by the Unfair Contract Terms Act 1977, s.3, which introduced the requirement of reasonableness for exemption clauses in written standard terms of business, if one of the parties is dealing as a consumer (see p. 41, *ante*).

Photo Productions Ltd., a company making Christmas cards, etc., contracted with Securicor Transport Ltd., a company providing security services, that Securicor should provide a night patrol service for Photo Productions' factory. The main perils which the parties had in mind were fire and theft. The contract was on Securicor's standard conditions, which provided, *inter alia*, that Securicor were under no circumstances to be responsible for any injurious act or default by any employee "unless such act or default could have been foreseen and avoided by the exercise of due diligence on the part of Securicor as his employer." On a Sunday night one of Securicor's employees entered the factory on duty patrol and then lit a fire which burned down the factory. The employee, who had satisfactory references and had been employed by Securicor for some three months, later said that he had only meant to start a small fire but that it had gone out of control. Photo Productions claimed damages from Securicor in the amount of £648,000. *Held*, the words of the exclusion clause were clear and on their true construction covered deliberate acts as well as negligence so as to relieve Securicor from responsibility from their implied duty to operate with due regard to the safety of the premises: *Photo Productions Ltd.* v. *Securicor Transport Ltd.* [1980] A.C. 827. [Note that this decision related to a contract made before the Unfair Contract Terms Act 1977 had come into force. If a similar clause had to be adjudicated upon today, it would not be effective unless it satisfied the requirement of reasonableness in the 1977 Act.]

A clause regulating the manner in which liability for breach of contract is to be established if the contractual performance has become impossible or has been given up, relates to a secondary obligation, which remains operative when the primary obligation (the performance of the contract) has come to an end. Such a secondary obligation is subject to the ordinary rules of construction (*Port Jackson Stevedoring Pty. Ltd.* v. *Salmond and Spraggon* (*Australia*) *Pty. Ltd. The New York Star* [1981] 1 W.L.R. 138.

Exemption clauses repugnant to main object of contract

If an exemption clause is **repugnant to the main object** and intent of the contract, it is invalid.

A clause in a bill of lading absolving a carrier from liability if he delivered the goods to a person unable to produce a bill of lading would be repugnant to the main object of the contract of carriage by sea: *Sze Hai Tong Bank Ltd.* v. *Rambler Cycle Co. Ltd.* [1959] A.C. 576.

The plaintiffs contracted with the defendants, road hauliers, that the latter should carry a load of copper wire from London to Glasgow. The transport manager of the defendants, without knowledge or consent of the plaintiffs, sub-contracted the carriage to a man who telephoned, giving the name of a non-existing firm. No adequate check was made of the man's credentials and he disappeared with the copper wire. *Held*, (1) the defendants were not entitled to sub-contract without consent of the plaintiffs, and (2) even if they were entitled to sub-contract, the manner of sub-contracting amounted to a deliberate interference, without justification, with the plaintiffs' rights and constituted a conversion of the goods: *Garn-*

ham, Harris & Elton Ltd. v. *Alfred W. Ellis* (*Transport*) *Ltd.* [1967] 1 W.L.R. 940.

Merzario, a freight forwarder, gave Evans, one of his customers, an oral promise that a container carrying an injection moulding machine would be shipped below deck on a voyage from Italy to England. Owing to an oversight, the container was shipped on deck and lost when the ship encountered a swell. Merzario contented that the printed terms and conditions exempted him from liability. *Held*, (1) the oral promise amounted to an enforceable contractual promise, and (2) the oral promise overrode the printed conditions: *J. Evans & Son* (*Portsmouth*) *Ltd.* v. *Andrea Merzario Ltd.* [1976] 1 W.L.R. 1078.

CHAPTER 4

FORM OF CONTRACT

CONTRACTS are of two kinds, namely **a contract in a deed** and **a simple contract**. A fundamental difference exists between these two types of contract: all simple contracts require **consideration** (see p. 55, *post*) but no consideration is required for a contract in a deed.

The expression "simple contracts" is a technical legal phrase denoting contracts requiring consideration. Simple contracts include **contracts which require a writing**, either for their validity or as evidence, and **oral contracts**, *i.e.* contracts which can be made by word of mouth.

Further, circumstances might exist in which a party has enriched himself unjustly at the expense of another and it appears to be appropriate to afford the latter a right to restitution. These cases cannot be classified under the category of contract because the element of consent is manifestly absent, nor do they fall under the heading of tort or trust. They are known as **quasi-contracts** and will also be considered in this chapter.

Consequently, the subject-matter of this chapter will be treated under four headings:

1. contract in a deed;
2. contracts which require a writing;
3. consideration; and
4. quasi-contracts.

CONTRACTS IN A DEED

A contract in a deed is a contract which is in writing and satisfies the requirements of s.1 of the Law of Property (Miscellaneous Provisions) Act 1989. Those requirements are:

1. The document must make it clear on its face that it is intended to be a deed by the person making it.
2. The person making it must sign it in the presence of someone who attests his signature. Alternatively it can be signed by

someone else at his direction and in his presence and in the presence of two witnesses who each attest the signature.
3. The document must be delivered by the person making it. This will usually be the handing over of the deed but could be any act by which he indicates that he regards the deed as binding upon himself.

A deed which is delivered, subject to a condition or lapse of a certain length of time, takes effect only on the fulfilment of that condition or the expiration of that time. It cannot be recalled by the person who executed it while the condition on which it depends has not been discharged (*Beesly* v. *Hallwood Estates Ltd.* [1961] Ch. 105), and he is bound when the condition is fulfilled (*Vincent* v. *Premo Enterprises* (*Voucher Sales*) *Ltd.* [1969] 2 Q.B. 609).

The following must be made in a deed:

1. Contracts made without consideration.
2. Conveyances of the legal estate in land or any interest in land, including leases of land for more than three years.
3. A transfer of a British ship, or any share therein.

A right of action under a contract in a deed is barred in 12 years, while a similar right under a simple contract is barred in six years; see p. 188, *post*.

Contracts which Require a Writing

In some cases the contract itself must be expressed in a writing and would be invalid if not contained in a written document.

In other cases the contract is perfectly valid if made orally but if a dispute arises and it is necessary to prove its existence or contents in court, on principle at least only written evidence of the contract and its terms is admitted.

Contracts required to be in writing

The following contracts are only valid if in writing:

1. Bills of exchange and promissory notes (Chaps. 22 and 23, *post*).
2. Contracts of marine insurance (Chap. 27, *post*).
3. Bills of sale (p. 518, *post*).

4. Acknowledgments of statute-barred debts (p. 191, *post*).
5. Consumer hire agreements and consumer credit agreements (including hire-purchase agreements) which are **regulated** by the Consumer Credit Act 1974 must be in writing embodying all the terms of the agreement other than implied terms (see p. 394, *post*).
6. A person is not liable to pay for an entry relating to him in a directory unless he, or his agent, has signed an order complying with the requirements of the Unsolicited Goods and Services Acts 1971 and 1975.
7. Contracts for the sale or other disposition of land or any interest in land, (other than contracts for leases of land of three years or less), must be in writing incorporating all the terms which the parties have agreed, Law of Property (Miscellaneous Provisions) Act 1989, s.2. Terms can be incorporated by means of reference to another document.

Contracts required to be evidenced by a note or memorandum in writing

Originally the Statute of Frauds 1677 required that certain classes of contract be evidenced in writing. Most of its provisions were repealed in 1954 and prior to the Law of Property (Miscellaneous Provisions) Act 1989, there were only two such categories of contract remaining which, though they were not required to be in writing, had to be evidenced in writing. However the 1989 Act removed one of those categories, namely contracts for the sale or disposition of an interest in land, and requires such contracts now to be in writing. Thus there remains just one class of contracts which are subject to the Statute of Frauds; these are contracts of guarantee and the requirements of the Statute of Frauds in relation to them are set out in the chapter on guarantees (see Chapter 25, *post*).

A **contract of employment** need not be in writing, nor need it be evidenced by a writing but the Employment Protection (Consolidation) Act 1978, s.1, provides that an employer must give his employees written particulars of the main terms of employment, if the contract is not in writing (see p. 236, *post*).

CONSIDERATION

Definition

Consideration is some benefit received by a party who gives a promise or performs an act, or some detriment suffered by a party who receives a promise. It may also be defined as "that which is actually given or accepted in return for a promise." It was defined by the court in *Currie* v. *Misa* (1875) L.R. 10 Ex. 153 as "some right, interest, profit or benefit accruing to one party, or some forbearance, detriment, loss, or responsibility given, suffered or undertaken by the other," but to this definition there should be added that the benefit accruing or the detriment sustained was in return for a promise given or received.

Examples: (1) A. receives £5 in return for which he promises to deliver goods to B. Here, the money A. receives is consideration for the promise he makes to deliver the goods.

2. C. promises to deliver goods to D., and D. promises to pay for the goods when they are delivered. Here, the benefit C. receives is D.'s promise to pay, and in return for it he promises to deliver the goods.

3. X. lends a book to Y. and Y. promises to return it. Here, the advantage is entirely on Y.'s side, but X. suffers a detriment in parting with his book, and this is consideration to support Y.'s promise to return it.

Executed and executory consideration

When the act constituting the consideration is completely performed, the consideration is said to be executed. In example (1) above, the payment by B. to A. is an executed consideration. When the consideration takes the form of a promise to be performed in the future, it is executory. In example (2), the consideration is executory. An executed consideration is therefore an *act* done by one party in exchange for a promise made or act done by the other; an executory consideration is a *promise* made by one party in exchange for a promise made or act done by the other.

General rules on consideration

Consideration required for all simple contracts

Consideration is necessary for the validity of every contract not in a deed. Even contracts in writing require it. "A promise without consideration is a gift; one made for consideration is a bargain."

Consideration must be of some value but need not be adequate

Consideration need not be adequate or equivalent to the promise, but it must be of some value. It is a matter for the parties themselves to determine what they consider is the proper value of their acts or promises. If the courts were to embark on an inquiry as to the adequacy of the consideration in all contracts which came before them, their task would be endless. If, for example, X. engages Y. as his clerk at a salary of £80 a week it would be a difficult, if not impossible, task in most cases for the courts to ascertain whether the salary was adequate to Y.'s work, or whether Y.'s services were worth the salary. In all cases, therefore, the courts concern themselves only with the presence of consideration, and assume that the parties themselves have attended to its value.

A. promised to pay certain bills if B. would hand over a guarantee to him. B. handed the guarantee over and it turned out to be unenforceable. *Held*, as A. had received what he asked for, there was consideration for his promise, although the guarantee was of smaller value than he had supposed: *Haigh* v. *Brooks* (1839) 10 A. & E. 309.

Inadequacy of consideration may be evidence of fraud.

A promise to perform an existing obligation is not sufficient consideration, but a promise to do something different is good consideration

Payment of a smaller sum of money is not a satisfaction of an agreement to pay a larger sum, even though the creditor agrees to take it in full discharge. If A. owes B. £100, and B. agrees to take £75, there is no consideration for the forgiveness of £25.

Mrs. Beer obtained a judgment against Dr. Foakes for £2,090. Dr.

Foakes asked for time to pay and the parties agreed that Mrs. Beer would not "take any proceedings whatsoever on the judgment" if Dr. Foakes paid that amount in stated instalments. After Dr. Foakes had paid off the debt, Mrs. Beer sued him on the judgment for interest. Dr. Foakes pleaded the agreement but Mrs. Beer replied that her promise to forgo interest was not supported by consideration. *Held*, she was entitled to recover interest: *Foakes* v. *Beer* (1889) 9 App.Cas. 605.

The practical effect of this remarkable rule is considerably reduced by the following:

(1) An agreement without consideration intended to create legal relations, which to the knowledge of the promisor has been acted on by the promisee, although it cannot be enforced, is binding on the promisor so that he will not be allowed to act inconsistently with it.

In 1937 C. let to H. a block of flats for 99 years at £2,500 a year. In 1940, owing to war, very few flats were let and C. agreed to reduce the rent to £1,250. In 1945, C. sued for arrears of rent at the rate of £2,500. *Held*, as the agreement for the reduction of rent had been acted upon C. could not claim the full rent, but that it was only operative during the conditions which had given rise to it. As the flats had been fully let in 1945 the full rent was payable from then: *Central London Property Trust* v. *High Trees House* [1947] K.B. 130.

On the other hand, in these circumstances, the creditor is not bound by his acceptance of the smaller sum if his agreement was obtained in an inequitable manner.

D., builders, had a claim for £482 against R. R.'s wife, knowing that D. were in financial difficulties, offered £300 in full settlement, adding that if D. would not take that sum, they would get nothing. D. accepted reluctantly. *Held*, that D. could recover £182 as the debtor's wife had "held the creditor to ransom": *D & C Builders Ltd.* v. *Rees* [1966] 2 Q.B. 617.

(2) An agreement by the creditor to take something different in kind, or a smaller sum paid before the larger becomes due, gives the debtor a good discharge. In this case the accord (agreement) is accompanied by satisfaction (consideration); on discharge of the contract by accord and satisfaction see p. 155, *post*.

Consequently, if X. owes B. £50, payable on June 1, his obligation will be legally discharged by an agreement on the part of B. to take £40 on May 10.

When a debtor makes an agreement with his creditors to compound his debts, although he is satisfying a debt for a larger sum by the payment of a smaller, the consideration is the agreement by the creditors with each other, and with the debtor, not to insist upon their full claims (*Good* v. *Cheesman* (1831) 2 B. & Ad. 328).

If a person makes a claim upon another in good faith whether or not the claim is likely to succeed, the withdrawal of his claim is valuable consideration so as to support a promise to pay him money (*Callisher* v. *Bischoffsheim* (1870) L.R. 5 Q.B. 449). Similarly, if an action has been commenced by one who honestly believes he has a claim upon another, a compromise of that claim is made for valuable consideration.

On the other hand there is an old rule (established in *Stilk* v. *Myrick* (1809) 2 Camp 317) that a promise to perform an existing obligation made to the person to whom the obligation is already owed will not constitute consideration. According to this rule, if C. owes D. £100 payable on December 1 and subsequently promises to pay it punctually if D. will give him a discount, there is no consideration for D.'s promise of a discount because C. was already bound to pay D. punctually. However a 1990 Court of Appeal decision has introduced a qualification to the rule in *Stilk* v. *Myrick.* Thus a promise by C. to D. that C. will do something which C. is already contracted to D. to do **can** be good consideration, *i.e.* provided that C. suffers some new detriment or D. gains some new benefit from the renewal of the promise. Thus where D. promises to pay C. a sum of money additional to that previously agreed as the contract price, in return for C.'s promise to perform his existing contractual obligations on time, and as a result of C.'s promise D. obtains a benefit (or obviates a disbenefit), that benefit is capable of being consideration for D.'s promise to pay the additional payment. In that case D.'s promise is legally binding unless it was obtained by economic duress: *Williams* v. *Roffey Bros. & Nicholls* (*Contractors*) *Ltd.* [1990] 2 W.L.R. 1153 (C.A.). (For economic duress see p. 112, *post.*)

The defendants were the main contractors for work refurbishing a block of flats. They engaged the plaintiffs as subcontractors to carry out carpentry work at an agreed price of £20,000. This proved to be too low a price and part way through the contract the plaintiffs got into financial difficulties. The defendants became worried that the plaintiffs might not finish the work on time or would stop work altogether. They had particular concern because there was a penalty clause in the main contract under which the defendants would be liable in the event of late completion of the work. The defendants agreed to pay the plaintiffs an additional sum of £10,300 if they completed on time. *Held*, the promise to pay the additional sum was binding because the defendants had obtained benefits from the plaintiffs' continuation with the contract. Those benefits were: seeking to ensure that the plaintiffs did not stop work; avoiding a penalty for delay; and avoiding the trouble and expense of engaging other people to complete the carpentry work: *Williams* v. *Roffey Bros.* [1990] 2 W.L.R. 1153.

A promise by C. to X. that C. will perform an obligation which C. already owes to D. under a contract between C. and D., is consideration for a promise by X. to C.

A. wrote to his nephew, B., promising to pay him an annuity of £150 in consideration of his marrying C. B. was already engaged to marry C. On his marriage with C., *held*, the fulfilment of B.'s contract with C. was consideration to support A.'s promise to pay the annuity: *Shadwell* v. *Shadwell* (1860) 9 C.B. (N.S.) 1591; see also *Pao On* v. *Lau Yiu Long* [1980] A.C. 614, p. 60 below.

Consideration must be legal

An illegal consideration makes the whole contract invalid.

Consideration must not be past

A past consideration is one which is wholly executed and finished before the promise is made. It must be distinguished from an executed consideration which is given at the time when the promise is made.

Examples: X. agrees to give and actually gives Y. £50 in return for Y. promising to go to Paris to transact some business for X. Here X. gives an executed consideration, since the promise to go to Paris is given at the time the £50 is handed over.

Y., without any arrangement with X., goes to Paris and transacts some business for X. On his return, X. promises to pay Y. £50 for his services in Paris. Here Y. has given a past consideration because Y.'s services have been rendered before X. has agreed to accept and pay for them.

A. sold a horse to B. and, after the sale was completed, promised that the horse was free from vice. It was in fact vicious. *Held*, the previous sale was no consideration for the promise, which was therefore unenforceable: *Roscorla* v. *Thomas* (1842) 3 Q.B. 234.

If services are rendered under circumstances which raise an implication of a promise to pay for them, the subsequent promise to pay is merely the fixing of the value of the services. (*Stewart* v. *Casey* [1892] 1 Ch. 104). Accordingly, if in circumstances in which he may expect a remuneration (*e.g.* because he is a solicitor) Y., at the request of X., goes to Paris on X.'s business, but without any prior promise of remuneration from X., and on his return X. promises to pay him £50, this will be regarded as the agreed value of Y.'s services which X. had impliedly promised to pay before Y. went to Paris.

The plaintiffs agreed to sell their shares in a private company to a company in which the defendants were majority shareholders in consideration of the issue to them of shares in the purchasing company (the main agreement). So as not to depress the market value of such shares the plaintiffs further agreed with the defendants that they would not sell 60 per cent. of the newly issued shares until April 1, 1974 and the defendants agreed, so that the plaintiffs might be protected against a fall in the value of the shares during such period, to purchase them at the end of the period at $2·50 each (the subsidiary agreement). Shortly afterwards the plaintiffs realised that the effect of the subsidiary agreement would be to deprive them of any increase in the value of the shares during that period. They therefore refused to complete the main agreement unless the defendants, in substitution for the subsidiary agreement, agreed to indemnify them against any reduction in value of the shares below the price of $2·50 each during the deferment period. The defendants, fearing the consequences of delay in completion of the main agreement, so agreed, the new indemnity agreement being expressed in consideration of the plaintiffs' obligations in the original main agreement. The main agreement was performed. Thereafter the value of the shares fell below $2·50 each. The plaintiffs claimed an indemnity under the new indemnity agreement: *Held*, an antecedent act could be valid consideration where it was done on the promisor's request, where the parties understood that such an act would be remunerated by the conferment of a benefit and where such benefit would have been enforceable if promised in advance. Further, a promise to perform a contractual obligation for the benefit of a third party was good consideration: *Pao On* v. *Lau Yiu Long* [1980] A.C. 614.

Consideration must move from the promisee

This means that the person to whom the promise is made must furnish the consideration.

At a time when the law did not restrict resale price maintenance, Dunlop who were wholesale tyre manufacturers sold tyres to X. under a contract whereby X. agreed not to sell the tyres below Dunlop's list prices and, as Dunlop's agent, to obtain from other traders an agreement similar to that which he had entered into. X. sold to Selfridge, who agreed with X. not to sell below list prices. They broke this contract and Dunlop sued for its breach. *Held*, assuming that X. was the agent of Dunlop when he obtained the price maintenance stipulation from Selfridge, Dunlop could not enforce the contract because no consideration moved from them: *Dunlop Pneumatic Tyre Co. Ltd.* v. *Selfridge & Co. Ltd.* [1915] A.C. 847.

This rule is based on the principle that a stranger to the contract cannot sue on it, a rule known as the doctrine of privity of contract (see p. 192, *post*). The rule in *Dunlop* v. *Selfridge* was reaffirmed by the House of Lords in *Scruttons Ltd.* v. *Midland Silicones Ltd.*, below.

In that case S., who were stevedores employed by a shipping company in the unloading of a cargo belonging to M. as consignees, damaged the cargo, causing a loss of £593. In an action by M. against S. for that sum, S., who had been employed by the shipping company as independent contractors and not as agents, sought to rely on a clause in the contract of carriage (and stated in the bill of lading) whereby the liability of the carriers was limited. *Held*, S. were strangers to the contract of carriage and could not rely on the clause limiting the liability: *Scruttons Ltd.* v. *Midland Silicones Ltd.* [1962] A.C. 446.

The rule was again asserted by the House of Lords in *Beswick* v. *Beswick*.

Peter, a coal merchant, entered into a written contract with his nephew John, whereby Peter sold his business to John. The contract provided that after the death of Peter the nephew should pay the widow (who was not a party to the agreement) an annuity of £5 a week. Peter died and the nephew refused to pay her. *Held*, the widow was entitled to the amount as the administratrix of Peter's estate, but she could not enforce the obligation in her personal capacity as she was not a party to the contract: *Beswick* v. *Beswick* [1968] A.C. 58.

Also *Snelling* v. *John G. Snelling Ltd.* [1973] 1 Q.B. 87, see pp. 5–6, *ante*.

Similarly,

When an employer takes out a personal accident group insurance covering his employees, the latter cannot sue the insurance company on the contract of insurance, since they are not a party to it: *Green* v. *Russell* [1959] 1 Q.B. 28.

The rule in *Dunlop* v. *Selfridge* is subject to a number of exceptions, some real and others apparent, in which an action by a stranger to the contract is admitted. The first two of the following are true exceptions, the others merely apparent exceptions.

(1) Under the Resale Prices Act 1976, s.26, where goods are sold by a supplier subject to a price maintenance condition, which is not unlawful under the Act (see p. 445, *post*), that condition may be enforced by the supplier against any trader who, though not a party to the sale, subsequently acquired the goods, as if he had been a party to the sale. The section does not give the supplier a right of action against a person who acquires goods for consumption and not for resale.

However, where section 26 applies, the third person who acquired the goods must have done so with notice of the condition and for the purpose of resale.

The notice requirement of the section must be strictly construed. Its effect is that no trader should be in a worse position than if he had been a party to the original contract. Express notice of the actual terms and conditions to be enforced is required (*Goodyear Tyre & Rubber Co.* (*Great Britain*) *Ltd.* v. *Lancashire Batteries Ltd.* [1958] 1 W.L.R. 857).

(2) The Third Parties (Rights Against Insurers) Act 1930 allows a third party to sue a bankrupt's insurer directly when the bankrupt is insured against a liability which the insured has incurred to the third party (see p. 558, *post*).

(3) In a contract made by an agent the principal (whether named or unnamed, see p. 265, *post*) can sue on the contract; he is in fact the contracting party who acted through the instrumentality of the agent.

(4) If a contract constitutes a trust relationship under which a trust fund is created in the hands of one of the contracting parties in favour of a third party, the latter can sue the trustee in case of breach of trust.

X. promised Y. out of moneys he owed him to pay £500 to Z., Y.'s brother, and informed Z. of this promise. Later X. refused to pay and Z.'s action against him was successful on the ground that X. held the £500 in a trust for Z. It was immaterial that the fund consisted merely of a monetary obligation and not of identifiable money: *Shamia* v. *Joory* [1958] 1 Q.B. 448.

The Married Women's Property Act 1882, s.11, provides that if a man insures his own life for the benefit of his wife or children, the policy shall create a trust in favour of the persons therein named; a similar provision applies to a wife who insures her life for the benefit of her husband or children.

(5) The assignee of a debt or chose in action may in certain circumstances sue the original debtor (see p. 194, *post*).

(6) The holder of a negotiable instrument may sue the acceptor and all parties to the bill who became parties prior to the giving of consideration by him (see pp. 471–473, *post*).

Quasi-Contracts

When one person has been enriched at the expense of another under such circumstances as to call for restitution the law imposes an obligation on him to make repayment. Such cases are called quasi-contracts, because, although there is no contract or agreement between the parties, they are put in the same position as if there were a contract between them. The following are the principal cases of quasi-contracts:

Where one person has paid money for the use of another

This occurs when A. pays money, which B. is liable to pay, at the implied request of B., as where a tenant pays his landlord's rent to prevent a distress by a superior landlord, or where one person's goods are taken in execution for another's debt. In such cases there is an obligation on the party benefited to repay the amount paid for his benefit.

G. imported skins from Russia and stored them in W.'s bonded warehouse. The skins were stolen without any negligence on W.'s part. After the theft, the customs demanded duty from W., which W. were bound to pay. W. paid and sued G. for what they had paid. *Held*, G. was liable as W. had been compelled by law to pay money for which G. was liable: *Brooks Wharf* v. *Goodman Bros.* [1937] 1 K.B. 534.

An account stated

This is an admission of indebtedness, from which the law may imply an undertaking to pay, *e.g.* an IOU. More correctly, it is where two parties in account with each other agree a balance. There is then a new contract by the party in debit to pay the balance, the consideration being the discharge of the items on each side of the account. An action can be brought on the account stated without going into all the transactions which led up to it.

Where money has been paid on a consideration which has wholly failed

If the consideration supporting a party's payment has totally failed, *i.e.* if he has received nothing at all for his money, he is entitled to recover his money. If, *e.g.* X. pays Y. £300 for a colour television set but Y. fails to supply the set, X. can recover the £300 which he paid. An illustration of a claim for repayment on the ground of total failure of consideration is *Comptior d'Achat* v. *Luis de Ridder* [1949] A.C. 293, see p. 413, *post.*

If the failure of consideration is not total but only partial, the quasi-contractual remedy is not available but the remedy is an action for damages for breach of contract.

Where money has been paid under a mistake of fact

Money paid under a mistake of fact can be recovered, provided that the payer did not intend the payee to have the money in any event, the money was not paid for good consideration, and the payee had not, in good faith changed his position.

L. was employed by the L.C.C. who agreed, on L.'s being called up for war service with the R.A.F., to pay him the difference between his service pay and his civil wages. L. agreed to inform the L.C.C. of any increase in his pay, but omitted to do so and in consequence was overpaid. *Held*, the overpayments could be recovered: *Larner* v. *L.C.C.* [1949] 2 K.B. 683.

A housing association drew a cheque for £24,000 on its account with Barclays Bank in favour of a building company. The housing association had sufficient funds in the bank to meet the cheque. The day after the cheque was drawn a receiver was appointed for the company (the payee) and the association stopped the cheque. By mistake the bank paid the cheque to the receiver of the company notwithstanding the association's stop. *Held*, the bank could recover the payment from the company: *Barclays Bank* v. *W.J. Simms, Son & Cooke* (*Southern*) *Ltd.* [1980] Q.B. 677.

Money paid under a mistake of law cannot be recovered.

M., an officer in the R.A.F., was entitled to a gratuity, the amount of which depended on the construction of certain regulations. H., an army agent and banker, mistook the meaning of the regulations, and credited M. with a larger gratuity than he was entitled to. M. did not know of the mistake and spent the money. *Held*, H. could not recover the excess paid, as his mistake was not a mistake of fact: *Holt* v. *Markham* [1923] 1 K.B. 504.

A mistake as to the existence of a private right, such as a right of property, is a mistake of fact, but a mistake as to the construction of a contract is a mistake of law.

If the mistake of fact is induced by the fraud of a third person, the payment can nevertheless be recovered.

B. owed W. & G. Ltd. £5,000 which he was unable to pay. He falsely represented to J. that he was the agent of a motor company and induced J. to pay him £5,000 as a deposit for the purchase of motor-cars. This payment was made by a cheque drawn by J. in favour of W. & G. Ltd. who were represented by B. as being interested in the motor company. B. handed the cheque to W. & G. Ltd. in payment of his debt, and they received it in good faith and in ignorance of B.'s fraud. *Held*, J. could recover the £5,000 from W. & G. Ltd. as money paid under a mistake of fact: *R.E. Jones Ltd.* v. *Waring & Gillow Ltd.* [1926] A.C. 670.

Where money has been had and received by one party to the use of another

This occurs when one person has wrongfully obtained money to which another is entitled or when a servant or an agent obtains money from another by the use of his master's or his principal's property. In such cases, the law compels the payment of the money so obtained.

R., a sergeant in the Army, received large sums of money from M. for sitting in uniform in the front of loaded lorries as they went through Cairo, so that the lorries were not inspected. *Held*, the Crown, as his employer, was entitled to the money, because R. had obtained it by the use of his uniform and the opportunities and facilities attached to it: *Reading* v. *Att.-Gen.* [1951] A.C. 507.

The agent of a housing society in Malaysia dishonestly agreed with one M. that M. should purchase 59 acres of land in Penang and sell it to the housing society at a much higher price. The agent agreed that he would neither tell the housing society that the land was for sale nor reveal the price which M. had paid for it. M. made a net profit of $443,000 on the deal and paid the agent $122,000 as a bribe. *Held*, the housing society could recover from the agent either the amount of the bribe as money had and received or, alternatively, compensation for the actual loss sustained through entry into the transaction in respect of which the bribe was given, as damages for fraud, but it was not entitled to double recovery: *T. Mahesan S/O Thambiah* v. *Malaysia Government Officers' Co-operative Housing Society Ltd.* [1979] A.C. 374.

It also occurs where a man's money is taken from him without his authority and is received by another, even in good faith and for value, who has notice of the want of authority.

P., B.'s sole executor, fraudulently drew cheques on the executor's banking account signed "P., executor of B., decd." L. cashed them for P., who used the money for his own purposes. *Held*, L. must have known of P.'s want of authority and must refund the amount of the cheques: *Nelson* v. *Larhold* [1948] 1 K.B. 339.

Quantum meruit claims

A claim on a *quantum meruit* is likewise of quasi-contractual nature, but it is convenient to consider claims falling under this heading later (see p. 184, *post*).

Where the equitable doctrine of specific restitution applies

Goods may be stolen and subsequently acquired by a purchaser acting in good faith, *i.e.* being unaware that he has acquired stolen property. If the purchaser, acting in good faith, improves the value of the goods by expending his money or labour and later the rightful owner asks for specific restitution of his property, equity requires that the owner shall recompense the purchaser for the improvement of the goods.

Mr. Bennett entrusted his Jaguar car which was worth £400 or £500 to Mr. Searle for repair which was to cost £85. Mr. Searle was a rogue who used the car for his own purposes and smashed it in a collision. Mr. Searle then sold the car in its damaged condition to Mr. Harper for £75 which was all it was worth in that state. Mr. Harper repaired the car and put it into good order, expending £226.47 for labour and material. Later Mr. Bennett claimed the car from Mr. Harper and the latter was prepared to return it to Mr. Bennett but claimed to be recompensed for the £226.47 spent on it. *Held*, Mr. Harper as innocent purchaser was entitled to recover the value of the improvements he had done to the car: *Greenwood* v. *Bennett* [1973] Q.B. 195.

Chapter 5

CAPACITY TO CONTRACT

Minors

A minor, as an infant is described in the Family Law Reform Act 1969, s.12, is a person who has not reached the age of majority. That age was reduced from 21 to 18 years by the Act of 1969, s.1. A person attains majority at the commencement of his eighteenth birthday (s.9(1) of the 1969 Act).

As a general rule a minor is not bound by any contract made during his minority. To this are three main exceptions: contracts for necessaries; contracts of an educational or employment or training nature; certain contracts which are voidable.

Necessaries

The term "necessaries" is not restricted to things which are required to maintain a bare existence, such as bread and clothes, but includes articles which are reasonably necessary to the minor having regard to his station in life. A watch, for example, and such things as a transistor radio or a motor cycle may well be considered to be necessaries, but not articles of mere adornment and luxury. An engagement ring may be a necessary, but not a diamond necklace bought for the minor's fiancée. Goods are not the only necessaries. The hire of a car may be a contract for necessaries.

The Sale of Goods Act 1979, s.3(3) gives the following definition of necessaries supplied to a minor or to a person who by reason of mental incapacity or drunkenness is incompetent to contract:

> . . . "necessaries" means goods suitable to the condition in life of the minor or other person concerned and to his actual requirements at the time of the sale and delivery.

When the necessaries are goods, the minor is liable only when the goods are:

(a) suitable to his condition in life;

(b) necessary to his requirements at the time of sale;
(c) necessary to his requirements at the time of delivery (Sale of Goods Act 1979, s.3(3)); and
(d) goods with which he was not sufficiently supplied at the time of sale and delivery.

A minor must pay a reasonable price for necessaries supplied to him. Although the goods supplied may be within the class of necessaries, they may not be necessary to the particular minor, because any of the four requirements set out above are not fulfilled.

I., a minor who was an undergraduate at Cambridge, bought eleven fancy waistcoats from N. He was at the time adequately provided with clothes. *Held*, the waistcoats were not necessaries, and I. was not liable to pay for any of them: *Nash* v. *Inman* [1908] 2 K.B. 1. [N.B. Under the terms of the Minors' Contracts Act 1987, the minor could now be ordered to return the waistcoats, see p. 71, *post*.]

Educational and employment contracts for the minor's benefit

Not every contract for the benefit of a minor is binding on him. But contracts for his education, service or apprenticeship, or for enabling him to earn his living (other than trading contracts) are binding unless they are detrimental to the interests of the minor.

D., a minor who was a professional boxer, held a licence from the British Boxing Board, under the terms of which his money was to be stopped if he was disqualified. In a boxing match he was disqualified and the Board withheld the money. D. sued to recover it. *Held*, the contract was for his benefit and was binding on him: *Doyle* v. *White City Stadium* [1935] 1 K.B. 110.

C., a minor aged 19, the son of a wealthy and world-famous comedian from whom he had become estranged, applied for National Assistance for himself, his wife and child. C. signed a contract with publishers for the publication of his autobiography, which contract he later sought to avoid. *Held*, the contract was binding on the minor, for it was similar to a contract of service in that it would enable him to earn his living and support his family, and it was a contract for his benefit: *Chaplin* v. *Leslie Frewin (Publishers) Ltd.* [1966] Ch. 71.

A contract relating to the minor's education which is not detrimental to his interests can be enforced although it is to be performed in the future, *e.g.* a contract by a minor billiards player to tour and play billiards matches with a well-known expert (*Roberts* v. *Gray* [1913] 1 K.B. 520).

In these cases, if the contract as a whole is for the benefit of the minor it will be binding on him, although particular parts of it, such as a restrictive covenant not to compete with his employer, may be against his interests. If, however, the clauses in the agreement which are adverse to the minor's benefit are clearly severable from the rest, the minor will not be bound by the adverse clauses.

Similarly, an arbitration clause in an apprenticeship deed has been held to be for the minor's benefit and to be binding on him (*Slade* v. *Metrodent Ltd.* [1953] 2 Q.B. 112, see p. 727, *post*).

A contract of apprenticeship is a contract of special character. If it is broken by the master, the apprentice can claim damages not only for his loss of earnings for the remainder of his training period, but also for the diminution of his future prospects (*Dunk* v. *George Waller & Son Ltd.* [1970] 2 Q.B. 163).

When a minor is engaged in trade, contracts entered into by him in the way of his trade, however much for his benefit they may be, are not binding on him. He is therefore not liable to pay for goods bought for trading purposes, or, if he is a haulage contractor, for a motor-lorry obtained under a hire-purchase agreement (*Mercantile Union Guarantee Corp. Ltd.* v. *Ball* [1937] 2 K.B. 498).

Voidable contracts

When a minor acquires an interest in a subject of a permanent nature, which imposes a continuous liability on him, the contract cannot be enforced against him during minority. But after he attains full age, it will be binding on him unless he avoids it within a reasonable time (*Edwards* v. *Carter* [1893] A.C. 360). Examples of these contracts are: leases, partnerships and the holding of shares in a company.

A fortnight before attaining his majority a minor took a lease of a flat. Three years later he was sued for current rent. *Held*, he was liable, as the lease was voidable, not void, and was binding on him unless repudiated within a reasonable time of attaining majority: *Davies* v. *Beynon-Harris* (1931) 47 T.L.R. 424.

A minor who was a partner in a partnership took no steps to avoid the partnership upon attaining his majority; he was held liable for the debts of the partnership incurred after he came of age: *Goode* v. *Harrison* (1821) 5 B. & Ald. 147.

Recovery by the minor

Money paid by a minor under a contract which is not binding on him, can be recovered by him only if there has been a complete failure of consideration.

S., a minor, agreed to take 500 £1 shares in a company and paid 10s. on each share. She received no dividend on the shares. While still a minor she repudiated the contract and brought an action (1) to recover the money she had paid, and (2) for a declaration that she was not liable for future calls. *Held*, (1) as the shares had some market value, S. could not recover money already paid, but (2) she was not liable for future calls: *Steinberg* v. *Scala* (*Leeds*) *Ltd.* [1923] 2 Ch. 452.

X., a minor, agreed with Y. to become the tenant of a house and to pay £102 for the furniture therein. He paid £68 on account, and after occupying the house and using the furniture for some months, sued to recover the money he had paid. *Held*, he could not recover money paid for something he had used: *Valentini* v. *Canali* (1889) 24 Q.B.D. 166.

Similarly if a minor has taken the benefit of a void contract for the sale of goods other than necessaries he cannot retain the goods and recover the money he has paid for them.

Again, if a minor delivers goods under a contract which is not binding on him, he cannot recover them back unless there is a total failure of consideration. Inadequacy of consideration is not enough (*Pearce* v. *Brain* [1929] 2 K.B. 310).

Recovery against the minor

In the case where a minor is not bound by a contract the Minors' Contracts Act 1987, s.3 gives the court power, if it considers it just and equitable to do so, to require the minor to return any property acquired by him under the contract, or any property representing it. Obviously the court would not make such an order where the minor has paid for the property. It is still the case, however, that the person who contracted with the minor can easily make a loss out of the whole transaction, *e.g.* if the minor has consumed or disposed of the property and has not obtained any replacement property. There is no power to order the minor to pay compensation and there is no power to make the minor liable in tort where this would be an indirect means of enforcing the contract.

S., a minor, by fraudulently representing himself to be of full age, induced L. to lend him £400. He refused to repay it and L. sued him for (a) fraudulent misrepresentation, or alternatively, (b) money had and received to S.'s use. *Held*, the contract was not binding upon S. and S. was not liable to repay the £400. The two claims by L. were indirect means of enforcing the contract and they failed: *R. Leslie Ltd.* v. *Sheill* [1914] 3 K.B. 607.

Where the performance, and not the conclusion, of the contract is in issue it is, however, sometimes possible to make a minor who cannot be made liable in contract liable in tort. The test is whether the act done by the minor was done in performance of the contract, though wrongfully, or whether it was something never contemplated by the contract at all.

A minor hired a mare and injured her through immoderate riding. *Held*, he was not liable: *Jennings* v. *Rundall* (1799) 8 T.R. 335.

A minor hired a radio set and in breach of contract parted with it to X. *Held*, he was liable, because his parting with the set was outside the contract altogether: *Ballet* v. *Mingay* [1943] 1 K.B. 281.

Recovery against a guarantor

As a general rule someone who guarantees someone else's debt is not liable on his guarantee unless the person whose debt is guaranteed is himself liable. Thus, for example, a bank which lent money to a minor and took from an adult a guarantee of that loan, would be unable to enforce either the loan or the guarantee. The Minors' Contracts Act 1987 s.2 altered that position, so that where the only reason a contract can not be enforced is that the party to be sued was a minor at the time the contract was made, any guarantee of the minor's liability is now enforceable.

Corporations

A corporation is an artificial person created by law. It is distinct from the individual persons who are members of the corporation, and has a legal existence separate and apart from them.

Salomon, a boot manufacturer, was the owner of a profitable business.

At a time when he and his business were perfectly solvent, he converted his business into a company limited by shares. He took 20,000 shares and his wife and five children took one each (at that time the minimum number of shareholders in all companies was seven). No other shares were issued. Salomon also received a debenture to the amount of £10,000. Later the company became insolvent. *Held*, Salomon could prove the debenture in the insolvency of the company. The "one man company" was a person different in law from the controlling shareholder: *Salomon* v. *Salomon & Co. Ltd.* [1897] A.C. 22.

A corporation may be (i) a body incorporated by royal charter; (ii) a company formed by special Act of Parliament; or (iii) a company registered under the provisions of the Companies Acts 1948 to 1989.

Lifting the veil

In company law, in exceptional cases the veil of corporateness is lifted and the separate personality of the company is disregarded. Examples of these exceptions are:

(a) In some cases the legislature has lifted the veil, *e.g.* in requiring holding and subsidiary companies to prepare group accounts;
(b) if the controlling shareholder uses the company as his agent; or
(c) if the corporate form is abused for an unlawful or improper purpose.

Mr. Lipman agreed to sell some property to Mr. and Mrs. Jones. Mr. Lipman did not want to perform the contract and sold and transferred the property to a private company that was wholly owned and controlled by him. The purpose of that transaction was to defeat the purchasers' claim for specific performance. *Held*, the private company was a sham to avoid enforcement of the equitable remedy of specific performance and an order for specific performance was granted against Mr. Lipman and the private company: *Jones* v. *Lipman* [1962] 1 W.L.R. 832.

Contractual capacity of a corporation

The contractual capacity of a corporation is limited:

1. by natural limits, *i.e.* by the fact that it is an artificial and not a natural person. A corporation can only contract through an agent, and therefore it cannot enter into any contract of a strictly personal

nature. For example, it cannot be the treasurer of a friendly society (*Re West of England and South Wales District Bank* (1879) 11 Ch.D. 768), and it cannot act as a solicitor, doctor or accountant.

2. by legal limits, *i.e.* by the restrictions imposed on the powers of a corporation on its formation. In the case of a body incorporated by royal charter, the charter sets out the powers of the corporation. If those powers are exceeded, the crown may forfeit the charter, or a member of the corporation may obtain an injunction restraining the corporation from doing an act which will be a ground for forfeiture (*Jenkin* v. *Pharmaceutical Society* [1921] 1 Ch. 392). But the *ultra vires* doctrine which, as we shall see presently, applies to companies incorporated by a special Act of Parliament or under the Companies Acts 1948 to 1989, does not apply to corporations created by royal charter.

The ultra vires doctrine

According to general principles of law, in the case of corporations formed by special Act of Parliament, their contractual capacity is limited by the statutes governing them. "Whenever a corporation is created by Act of Parliament . . . I am of opinion not only that the objects which the corporation may legitimately pursue must be ascertained from the Act itself, but that the powers which the corporation may lawfully use in furtherance of those objects must either be expressly conferred or derived by reasonable implication form its provisions" (*per* Watson L.J. in *Baroness Wenlock* v. *River Dee Co.* (1885) 10 App.Cas. 354). If the contractual capacity is exceeded, the contract is *ultra vires* and void, and cannot be made valid or ratified, even if all members of the corporation agree to the making of the contract.

A municipal council was authorised by certain Acts to establish baths, wash-houses and bathing places. It established a municipal laundry. A ratepayer objected and applied for an injunction. *Held*, the injunction had to be granted as the council had acted *ultra vires*: *Att.-Gen.* v. *Fulham Corporation* [1929] 1 Ch. 440.

The doctrine of *ultra vires*, however, "ought to be reasonably, and not unreasonably, understood and applied, and whatever may fairly be regarded as incidental to, or consequential upon, those things which the legislature has authorised, ought not (unless expressly prohibited) to be held, by judicial construction, to be *ultra vires*" (*per* Selborne L.J. in *Att.-Gen.* v. *G.E. Ry.* (1880) 5 App.Cas. 473).

In the case of companies created under the Companies Acts 1948 to 1989, or their predecessors, the *ultra vires* doctrine likewise applied. The company could contract only for the objects set out in the memorandum of the company. If these objects were exceeded, the company acted *ultra vires* and a contract purported to be made by it was void. Moreover, the company itself could plead that it had acted *ultra vires* and thus avoid the contract, though the party with which it had contracted was unaware that the contract was *ultra vires*.

Section 35(1) of the Companies Act 1985 (as amended by the Companies Act 1989 s.108) effectively abolished the *ultra vires* doctrine as far as concerns dealings with persons outside the company. It reads:

> "The validity of an act done by a company shall not be called into question on the ground of lack of capacity by reason of anything in the company's memorandum."

Thus, as regards third parties, a company now has full capacity.

Unincorporated Bodies

Associations of persons which are not incorporated, such as clubs or societies, contract through an agent. The committee or other persons authorising the agent to contract are liable, but the members are not liable, unless the rules provide that the agent is authorised by them.

Foreign Sovereigns

The State Immunity Act 1978 adopts the restrictive doctrine of immunity. Under that doctrine a foreign state is entitled to immunity only for acts of state (*acta jure imperii*) but not in commercial transactions (*acta jure gestionis*). In particular, a foreign state is not entitled to immunity:

(a) if it has submitted to the jurisdiction of the courts (s.2), or
(b) with respect to:
  (i) a commercial transaction entered into by the state; or

(ii) an obligation of the state which by virtue of a contract (whether a commercial transaction or not) falls to be performed wholly or partly in the United Kingdom.

A "commercial transaction" is defined thus:

(a) any contract for the supply of goods or services;
(b) any loan or other transaction for the provision of finance and any guarantee or indemnity in respect of any such transaction or any other financial obligation; and
(c) any other transaction or activity (whether of a commercial, industrial, financial, professional or other similar character) into which a state enters or in which it engages otherwise than in the exercise of sovereign authority (s.3).

In addition, there are other cases in which a foreign state is not entitled to immunity, *e.g.* with respect to certain contracts of employment, where the contract was made in the United Kingdom or the work is to be wholly or partly performed there (s.4), or where death or personal injury or damage to tangible property results from an act or omission in the United Kingdom (s.5), or where the state has agreed in writing to arbitration (s.9).

It is further provided that a separate entity is not immune from the jurisdiction of the courts in the United Kingdom except if:

(a) the proceedings relate to anything done by it in the exercise of sovereign authority; and
(b) the circumstances are such that a state would have been so immune (s.14(2)).

The property of a foreign state or state corporation is subject to enforcement proceedings, if used or intended to be used for commercial purposes (s.13). But the property of a state's central bank or other monetary authority shall not be regarded as in such use (s.14(4)).

The State Immunity Act 1978 accords with the European Convention on State Immunity signed by the United Kingdom on May 16, 1972.

Mentally Disordered and Drunken Persons

Contracts made by mentally disordered persons, referred to by the

Mental Health Act 1983 as "mental patients," are valid unless these persons are placed under the jurisdiction of the court (below); but if the other party knew that he was contracting with a person who, by reason of the unsoundness of his mind, could not understand the nature of the contract, the contract is voidable at the option of the patient.

L. sued S. on a promissory note. S. pleaded that he was insane at the time he made it. *Held*, for the defence to succeed S. must prove (1) that he was insane at the time, and (2) that L. knew of his insanity: *Imperial Loan Co.* v. *Stone* [1892] 1 Q.B. 599.

A person may suffer from delusions, and yet be capable of understanding the nature of the transaction into which he is entering. In such a case the contract is valid, although the other party may have known of the delusions (*Birkin* v. *Wing* (1890) 63 L.T. 80). A contract made during mental disability can be ratified in a lucid interval.

If a person is incapable by reason of mental disability to manage his property and affairs, he may execute an enduring power of attorney under the Enduring Powers of Attorney Act 1985 *or* the court may assume jurisdiction to manage them; this jurisdiction is exercised by certain judges of the Chancery Division and the Master of the Court of Protection (Mental Health Act 1983). If the property of the patient is under the control of the court, the patient cannot dispose of it by a contract; such a contract would not be binding on the court or the patient but the court has power to affirm it and in that case the other party is bound by it (see *Baldwyn* v. *Smith* [1900] 1 Ch. 588).

The Enduring Powers of Attorney Act 1985 provides an inexpensive method by which a person can confer power to manage his affairs on a person of his own choice (termed the attorney). If he confers an enduring power of attorney, that power will not be revoked by any subsequent mental incapacity of the donor. The donor of the power may already be incapable by reason of mental disorder of managing his own affairs. Nevertheless the enduring power of attorney will still be valid provided that, at the time it was executed, the donor understood its nature and effect (*In re K* [1988] 2 W.L.R. 781). As soon as practicable after the donor becomes incapable of managing his own affairs, the attorney must get the enduring power of attorney registered with the court. The attorney has power to make contracts on behalf of the donor.

Contracts made by persons who were so drunk at the time as not to understand what they were doing are voidable at the option of the person who was drunk, provided the other party knew of his condition (*Gore* v. *Gibson* (1845) 14 L.J. Ex. 151). The burden of proof in this, as in the case of mental patients, is on the party suffering from the incapacity to prove the knowledge of the other party. A contract made by a man when drunk can be ratified when he is sober.

B. agreed to buy some houses from M. At the time he was too drunk to know what he was doing, but he ratified the contract when he became sober. *Held*, the contract was binding: *Matthews* v. *Baxter* (1873) L.R. 8 Ex. 132.

Both mentally disordered and drunken persons are liable for necessaries supplied to them. In such a case they are bound to pay a reasonable price for the necessaries (Sale of Goods Act 1979, s.3).

CHAPTER 6

REALITY OF CONTRACT

UNENFORCEABLE, VOIDABLE, VOID AND ILLEGAL CONTRACTS

AN arrangement between two parties which, on first impression, appears to satisfy all requirements of a valid contract (see p. 3, *ante*) may, on closer examination, be found to lack reality because it is affected by a defect which renders the contract:

(a) unenforceable;
(b) voidable;
(c) void; or
(d) illegal.

An **unenforceable** contract is one which is valid but cannot be enforced by action because of some technical defect, such as, in the case of a contract of guarantee, the absence of a note or memorandum in writing required by the Statute of Frauds 1677 (see p. 522, *post*) or, in the case of an agreement regulated by the Consumer Credit Act, the absence of a signed agreement complying with the requirements of that Act. A claim under any contract could become statute barred by lapse of the time for bringing an action required by the Limitation Act 1980. Whether the defect is serious will depend upon the provisions of the particular statute in question. Thus lapse of time under the Limitation Act can be fatal to a claim (see page 188, *post*) whereas an infringement of the documentation requirements will usually leave the court with a discretion whether to enforce the contract (see page 396, *post*).

A **voidable** contract is one which one of the parties can put an end to at his option. His option can be exercised without reference to the other party, so that the contract is binding if he elects to treat it as binding, and not binding if he elects to set it aside. A contract might *e.g.* be voidable if one of the contracting parties has been induced by misrepresentation, or by duress or undue influence to enter into the contract.

Example—A., by innocent misrepresentation, induces B. to make a contract with A. The contract is binding on A., unless B. chooses to set it aside. B. may set aside the contract or not at his option, but A. has no option to set it aside.

A voidable contract must be distinguished from a contract terminable at the will of one of the parties. The latter kind of contract does not suffer from an inherent defect but is terminated in accordance with its terms, *e.g.* if A. is employed by B. subject to a week's notice on either side, and B. gives a week's notice, the contract comes to an end when the notice expires but it is not a voidable contract.

A **void** contract is one which is without legal effect. It is a complete nullity in law and confers no rights on either party. Examples of a void contract are a contract which is declared to be void by section 18 of the Gaming Act 1845 or a "contract" in which, owing to a genuine mistake, there is an absence of true agreement between the parties. Collateral contracts connected with a void contract are valid and enforceable in court.

Example—Two bookmakers form a partnership for the purpose of betting. Even if the betting contracts with the clients of the partnership are void, the partnership contract itself is valid and one of the partners may obtain a court order for an account against the other.

An **illegal** contract is affected by the most serious defect of all. Not only is the contract itself void but collateral contracts tainted by the illegality may likewise be void. That applies even to a collateral contract with a third party who knew of the illegal character of the main contract (*Pearce* v. *Brooks* (1866) L.R. 1 Ex. 213, on p. 124, *post*). Illegal contracts are considered in the following chapter (Chapter 7).

MISTAKE

Mistakes which do not affect the validity of the contract

The mere fact that one of the parties to a contract acted under a mistake does not, as a general rule, affect the validity of the contract. A contract is void on the ground of mistake only when the mistake is such that there was never any real agreement between the parties, or, if there was a real agreement, it was only entered into because the parties both made the same mistake on some vital matter, and would never have made the agreement at all if they had known that they both made that mistake. There is no mistake so as to avoid the contract in the following cases:

1. Mistake by one party of the expression of his intention.

Business premises were let to tenants who, with the permission of the landlords, sublet part of them. The sublease provided that the rent for the sublease should be increased to the current market value prevailing on December 12, 1982. The tenants wanted to surrender the head lease to the landlords, and it became necessary to assess the current market value of the subrent at the review date. Solicitors, acting for the landlords and the head tenants, wrote a letter to the subtenants inviting them to agree to a figure of £65,000 per annum as the appropriate rental value. The subtenants agreed by letter to this valuation. A few days later the solicitors acting for the landlords and head tenants informed the sub-tenants that their original letter contained a mistake and that the proposed review rent was £126,000 per annum, and not £65,000. The subtenants refused to agree to the suggested correction. *Held*, the landlords and head tenants were bound by their original offer of a review rent of £65,000. The subtenants were unware that a mistake had occurred and had given valid consideration when undertaking to perform their obligations under the agreement; *Centrovincial Estates plc* v. *Merchant Investors Assurance Ltd.* (1983) 127 S.J. 443.

2. Mistake as to the meaning of a trade description, when goods are sold under that trade description.

H. bought a quantity of kapok, described as "Sree" brand, from B., both parties thinking that goods of that brand were pure kapok. In fact, kapok of the "Sree" brand contained an admixture of cotton. Kapok of the "Sree" brand was delivered but proved to be unsuitable for H. *Held*, the mistake did not affect the validity of the contract: *Harrison & Jones Ltd.* v. *Bunten & Lancaster Ltd.* [1953] 1 Q.B. 646.

R. received an order from a customer abroad for "feveroles." He asked P. what that was and both parties thought it meant "horse beans." R. then bought a quantity of goods described in the contract as "horse beans" from P. and sent them to his customer who rightly rejected them as not being feveroles. *Held*, there was a binding contract for the sale of horse beans between R. and P.: *Frederick E. Rose (London) Ltd.* v. *William H. Pim Jnr. & Co. Ltd.* [1953] 2 Q.B. 450.

3. A mistake or error of judgment. If A. buys an article thinking

that it is worth £100, when it is only worth £50, the contract remains good and A has to bear the loss of his own ignorance of the true value of the article.

4. A mistake by one party of his ability to perform it. If X. agrees to build 10 houses by July 1, but finds it is impossible to complete them before September 1, he has mistaken his ability to perform the contract, but nevertheless cannot escape from the contractual obligation he has undertaken.

Mistakes which render the "contract" void

A void contract is a contradiction in terms, because it is not a contract at all. Mistake will render a contract void in the following cases:

Mistake as to the nature of the contract itself

If a person signs a contract in the mistaken belief that he is signing a document of a fundamentally different character, there will be mistake which, provided the signer was not careless in signing, renders the contract void. The mistaken party can successfully plead *non est factum* (it is not my deed[1]). The essential point is that the consent, a necessary requirement of contract, is missing.

M., an old man of feeble sight, indorsed a bill of exchange for £3,000 thinking it was a guarantee. *Held*, as he was not negligent in indorsing the bill he was not liable: *Foster* v. *Mackinnon* (1869) L.R. 4 C.P. 704.

K. was to be released from his hire-purchase agreement with a finance company on the understanding that the dealer found a purchaser for the car. The dealer sold the car to H. on hire-purchase terms and asked K. to sign a document which he described as a release note. The document was in fact an indemnity obliging K. to pay if H. defaulted. When K. signed, the document, apart from its lower portion, was covered by other papers on the dealer's desk. *Held*, K. was not bound by his signature: *Muskham Finance Ltd.* v. *Howard* [1963] 1 Q.B. 904.

The principle on which the plea of *non est factum* is founded is this: A person of full age and understanding who signs a document evidently intended to have legal effect is bound by his signature and

[1] The expression "deed" is not used here in a technical sense but denotes every written document signed by the person raising this plea.

cannot avoid it by claiming that he did not read the document, or did not inform himself of its purport or effect, or that he relied on the word of another who read it over to him or explained it. The strictness of this rule is mitigated by the plea of *non est factum* which is admissible only if the signer can prove that the document which he signed is fundamentally different, as regards character or effect, from that which he intended to sign; in that case the signer can avoid the contract. The plea of *non est factum* is thus available only within narrow limits and the onus is on the person who wishes to rely on it. These are the rules which apply to persons of full age and understanding; if the signer of the document was illiterate, blind or lacking in understanding, the law is more easily prepared to give relief, if consent is truly lacking and the signer acted carefully. The plea of *non est factum* is not admissible if the signer acted carelessly because "a person who signs a document, and parts with it so that it may come into other hands, has a responsibility, that of the normal man of prudence, to take care what he signs, which, if neglected, prevents him from denying his liability under the document according to its tenor" (*per* Lord Wilberforce in *Saunders* v. *Anglia Building Society*, *post*). (This case is more generally known by its name in the Court of Appeal, *Gallie* v. *Lee*).

G. intended to give her nephew her house on condition that he would allow her to live there for life. She knew that her nephew wanted to raise money on the house and that Lee, her nephew's business associate, was to help him in that respect. Her underlying purpose in wanting to convey the house was to provide her nephew and Lee with an asset they could use as security for a loan they needed for their business. Lee and her nephew asked her to sign a document. She had broken her spectacles and asked what it was and was told that it was a deed of gift of the house to her nephew. She executed the document in that belief. The document was, in fact, an assignment of the house (which was leasehold property) by G. to Lee for £3,000 which was never paid nor intended to be paid. Lee mortgaged the house for £2,000 to the defendant building society. *Held*, G. could not plead *non est factum* and could not recover the title deeds of the house. Although G. had not been careless in signing, her mistake had not been sufficiently radical to allow the plea of *non est factum*, since her underlying purpose had still been possible: *Saunders* v. *Anglia Building Society* [1971] A.C. 1004.

A successful plea of *non est factum*, because it renders a contract void can affect not just the parties to the void contract but also innocent third parties. It is for this reason that the courts view the plea as very much an exception to the general rule that a person is bound by his signature on a document intended to have legal effect. If the plea had been successful in *Saunders* v. *Anglia Building Society*, the conveyance to the nephew's partner would have been void; thus the partner would have had no title to the house and thus the security (mortgage) subsequently granted by the partner to the building society would also have been void. This would have left the building society, an innocent third party, with no security for the loan it had made. The courts therefore insist on two requirements for a successful plea of *non est factum*: (1) a radical mistake, and (2) an absence of carelessness in signing. Otherwise, the normal rule applies and the signer is bound (at least he is as regards any innocent party) by his signature on a document intended to have legal effect. This latter rule applies not only to signature on a completed document but also to signature in blank on a document with authority for another to complete it later (*United Dominions Trust Ltd.* v. *Western*, *post*).

Mr. Western bought a second-hand Ford Corsair from a dealer. He agreed with him that the price should be £550 and the deposit £34 which Mr. Western paid. The parties further agreed that Mr. Western should have the car on hire-purchase terms and Mr. Western signed the documents offered him by the dealer in blank. The dealer completed the documents, showing the purchase price as £730, and not £550, and the deposit as £185, and not £34; further, the document evidenced a loan agreement and not a hire-purchase contract. The plaintiff finance company accepted the documents as sent in by the dealer. Mr. Western, when receiving copies, noticed the difference but did not complain because on the figures he was not substantially worse off than agreed with the dealer. *Held*, when sued by the finance company, Mr. Western could not plead *non est factum*: *United Dominions Trust Ltd.* v. *Western* [1976] Q.B. 513. (But the position is different in cases to which the Consumer Credit Act 1974, s.56, applies; see p. 375, *post*).

Non est factum cannot be successfully pleaded if dissimilar documents produce a similar legal effect and "the object of the exercise" is achieved, albeit by legal means different from those which the signer had in mind. This point was mentioned by the court incidentally, but not as its main reason, in *United Dominions Trust Ltd.* v. *Western*, *ante*.

H. contemplated raising money on the security of her car. She signed certain documents in blank and without reading them and left them with her car dealer whom she instructed not to pass them to the finance company without getting her prior approval. Nevertheless the car dealer passed them to the finance company. The documents did not, as H. supposed, propose a loan on the security of her car, but they resulted in a so-called refinancing agreement, whereby H. purported to sell her car to a dealer who resold it to the plaintiff finance company which, in turn, let H. have her car (which never left her possession) on hire-purchase terms. H. claimed to repudiate the arrangement. *Held*, she could not succeed on *non est factum*, but she succeeded on other grounds, namely that the car dealer had acted without H.'s authority in forwarding the forms to the finance company: *Mercantile Credit Co. Ltd.* v. *Hamblin* [1965] 2 Q.B. 242.

B. was induced by C.'s fraud to execute a deed. This deed mortgaged some land to C. and contained a covenant by B. to pay £1,000. B. knew that the deed disposed in some manner of the land, but he did not know that it was a mortgage and he did not read it. *Held*, B. could not rely on a plea of *non est factum* and thus in the hands of an innocent assignee for value the deed was enforceable against B.: *Howatson* v. *Webb* [1907] 1 Ch. 537.

Mistake as to the identity of the person contracted with

If A. intends to contract with B., but finds he has contracted with C., there is no contract if the identity of B. was a material element of the contract and C. knows it. A.'s offer is addressed to B. but accepted by C. who knows that he cannot accept it; there is no agreement.

Blenkarn, by imitating the signature of a reputable firm called Blenkiron, induced X. to supply him with goods on credit. *Held*, as X. never intended to contract with Blenkarn there was no contract between them. Thus Blenkarn never obtained title to the goods and it followed that an innocent purchaser of the goods from Blenkarn did not get a good title: *Cundy* v. *Lindsay* (1878) L.R. 3 App.Cas. 459.

In *Cundy* v. *Lindsay* the deception was effected by letter but the situation will usually be different if the deceived person deals with the fraudster face to face: *Phillips* v. *Brooks Ltd.*, *post*.

This principle holds good, however, only when the personality of the contracting party is of importance. If, in the illustration given earlier, A. intends to contract with B., but would have been content with C. as long as he got performance of the contract, a contract with C. in mistake for B. is binding. But if C. knows that A. does not intend to contract with him, the contract is void.

B., the managing director of a theatre, gave instructions that a ticket was not to be sold to S. S. knew this, and asked a friend to buy a ticket for him. With this ticket S. went to the theatre, but B. refused to allow him to enter. *Held*, no contract, as the theatre company never intended to contract with S.: *Said* v. *Butt* [1920] 3 K.B. 497.

If A. is prepared to sell to anyone who will pay his price and C. pretending to be B., comes into his shop and buys, there is a contract between A. and C.

N. went into a jeweller's shop and represented himself to be Sir G.B., a person of credit and stability. The jeweller sold him a ring for which N. gave a cheque purporting to be signed by Sir G.B. The cheque was a forgery and the ring was subsequently pawned. *Held*, the pawnbroker had a good title to the ring, because the contract between the jeweller and N. was good until the jeweller disaffirmed it: *Phillips* v. *Brooks Ltd.* [1919] 2 K.B. 243.

Here the jeweller intended to contract with the person he saw in the shop, N., the representation by N. that he was Sir G.B. only affecting the question of payment. Had N. paid cash there would undoubtedly have been a sale, and there was equally a sale, though a voidable one, when he paid by forged cheque. If a person is deceived by another actually present before him, the contract is normally only voidable (*Lewis* v. *Averay* [1972] 1 Q.B. 198) but exceptionally even in this situation the contract may be void.

I. and her two sisters were joint owners of a car which they advertised for sale. X. bought it and began to write out a cheque for the price. I. told X. that the sale was for cash, that the owners were not prepared to accept a cheque and that the sale was cancelled. X. replied that he was H., a reputable business man, giving an address which was checked by one of I.'s sisters. I. believed X. to be H. and let him have the car in exchange for his cheque. X. had nothing to do with H. and the cheque was dishonoured. The car was acquired by L. in good faith for value. *Held*, the owners intended to sell their car only to H. and their offer was only addressed to him; X. was incapable of accepting the offer and the owners could recover the car from L.: *Ingram* v. *Little* [1961] 1 Q.B. 31.

Mutual[2] *mistake as to the identity of the thing contracted for*

If A. makes an offer to B. about one thing, and B. accepts, thinking that A. is referring to another thing of the same name, the contract is void because there is no *consensus ad idem*.

E. agreed to buy from F. a cargo of cotton to arrive "ex *Peerless* from Bombay." There were two ships called *Peerless* sailing from Bombay, one sailing in October and the other in December. E. meant the earlier one and F. the later. *Held*, there was no contract: *Raffles* v. *Wichelhaus* (1864) 2 H. & C. 906.

The result is the same even if the mistake was caused by the negligence of a third party.

X. by telegram ordered three rifles. Owing to the telegraph clerk's mistake, the message was transmitted as "the" rifles. From previous negotiations this was understood to mean fifty rifles, and that number was dispatched. *Held*, there was no contract between the parties: *Henkel* v. *Pape* [1870] L.R. 6 Ex. 7.

If a code message is understood in one sense by the sender and in another by the recipient, there is no contract. If the message is ambiguous it is for the party relying on it to show that it is so clear that the other party cannot be heard to say that he misunderstood it: *Falck* v. *Williams* [1900] A.C. 176.

Common mistake as to the existence of the thing contracted for

If both parties believe the subject-matter of the contract to be in existence, but in fact at the time when the contract is made it is non-existent, there is no contract.

In a contract for the sale of specific goods if the goods, unknown to the seller have perished before the contract, the contract is void: Sale of Goods Act 1979, s.6.

G. agreed to assign to H. a policy of assurance upon the life of L.

[2] *Mutual* mistake occurs where the two contracting parties mean different things; *common* mistake occurs where they mean the same thing which, however, is different from reality. Mutual mistake: A. means a black car and B. a white one. Common mistake: A. and B. mean a black car but the car, is in fact, white.

L. had died before the agreement was made. *Held*, no contract: *Scott* v. *Coulson* [1903] 2 Ch. 249.

Common mistake as to the fundamental subject-matter of the contract

If the parties have made a contract on the mistaken assumption that there exists a state of affairs which is of such fundamental importance to them that they would not have made the contract had it not existed, the contract is void.

It should be noted that not every common mistake produces that effect, even if it concerns a matter of importance to the parties. The doctrine of common mistake relating to the foundation of the contract is interpreted restrictively and applies only if, in the words of Lord Atkin in *Bell* v. *Lever* [1932] A.C. 161 (below), the state of affairs which exists in reality "makes the contract something different in kind from the contract in the . . . state of facts" that the parties erroneously assumed to exist.

If, *e.g.* there was no mistake when the contract was made but facts subsequently come to light which, though important, do not destroy the identity of the subject-matter as it was when the contract was made, the contract is not void.

B. and S. were employed by L. under agreements for a fixed time. Later, L. paid B. and S. £50,000 to be discharged from these agreements. B. and S. had been making secret profits, which would have entitled L. to dismiss them without notice, but this was unknown to L. at the time the £50,000 was paid. The jury negatived fraud on the part of B. and S. *Held*, L. could not recover the £50,000. There was no mistake on either side as to the contracts which were being released. The fact that L. could have obtained a release on much cheaper terms did not, in the absence of fraud or breach of warranty, render the contract void: *Bell* v. *Lever Bros. Ltd.* [1932] A.C. 161.

Further illustrations of common mistake which, though affecting an important aspect of the contract, were not regarded to be fundamental, are *Harrison & Jones Ltd.* v. *Bunten & Lancaster Ltd.* and *Frederick E. Rose* (*London*) *Ltd.* v. *William H. Pim Jnr. & Co. Ltd.*, both on p. 81, *ante*, and further *Leaf* v. *International Galleries*, on p. 351, *post*.

Since the effect of the doctrine of common mistake relating to the foundation of the contract is restricted in common law, equity has intervened and granted discretionary relief and set the contract aside where the mistake is not sufficiently fundamental in the eyes of the common law but is, nevertheless, serious; in these cases, however, the contract is not void (as in cases in which the common law doctrine applies) but it is voidable. The correct approach was laid down by Steyn J. in *Associated Japanese Bank (International) Ltd.* v. *Crédit du Nord* [1989] 1 W.L.R. 255 as follows. When mistake has been pleaded, the court must first decide whether the contract is void at common law. If it is void, then no question of mistake in equity arises. If however it is valid at common law, the court must consider whether the contract can be set aside in equity.

B. granted S. the lease of a flat at a yearly rental of £250. Both parties believed erroneously that, as the result of structural alterations, the flat was not subject to rent control. The tenant claimed a declaration that the lease was under rent control, and the landlord counter-claimed for rescission of the lease on the ground of common fundamental mistake. *Held*, the lease was subject to rent control: the common mistake of the parties was one of fact and not of law; the lease was voidable and could be set aside at the instance of the landlord: *Solle* v. *Butcher* [1950] 1 K.B. 671.

G. bought a house from B. for £850. Both parties believed that a tenant who was in occupation of the house was a statutory tenant, whereas he was not protected and could have been compelled to quit on notice. The value of the house, with vacant possession was £2,250. *Held*, the parties were under a common mistake of fundamental nature. While at common law the contract was not void, equity would grant relief and treat the contract as voidable. The seller was entitled to rescind the contract: *Grist* v. *Bailey* [1967] Ch. 532.

M., who could not drive and had no licence, took out a car insurance with the defendant company. He stated in the proposal, contrary to the truth, that he had a provisional licence and that the car would be driven by himself and his two sons both of whom had licences. The car was involved in an accident when driven by the younger son. The insurance company agreed to pay £385 for the damage to the car but later sought to avoid the compromise on the ground that M.'s statements in the proposal form were untrue. *Held*, that, when concluding the compromise agreement, both parties were under the common fundamental mistake that M. had a valid claim under the insurance policy and that in the circumstances the agreement was voidable and could be set aside by the company: *Magee* v. *Pennine Insurance Co. Ltd.* [1969] 2 Q.B. 507.

A landlord let two floors of premises to tenants. Both parties assumed that planning permission had been granted for the whole of both floors for office use. In fact permission had been limited to the ground floor and to part only of the first floor. Later permission was granted for the whole of both floors but was limited to two years on account of the local authority's future road plans on the site. *Held*, there had been a serious common mistake rendering the contract voidable and the tenants were entitled to rescind the contract: *Laurence* v. *Lexcourt Holdings Ltd.* [1978] 1 W.L.R. 1028.

Mistake as to the promise of one party known to the other

The general rule is that if a person makes a mistake as to the offer of the other party to the contract, the contract is nevertheless binding upon him. "If, whatever a man's real intentions may be, he so conducts himself that a reasonable man would believe that he was assenting to the terms proposed by the other party, and that other party upon that belief enters into the contract with him, the man thus conducting himself would be equally bound as if he had intended to agree to the other party's terms" (*per* Blackburn J. in *Smith* v. *Hughes* (1871) L.R. 6 Q.B. at p. 607 (below)).

S. sold H. a quantity of oats, a sample of which S. had shown H. The oats were new oats but H. who had inspected the sample erroneously thought that he was buying old ones. The price was high for new oats but oats were very scarce at that season. *Held*, H.'s mistake was irrelevant unless S. positively knew that H. wanted to buy old oats only: *Smith* v. *Hughes* (1871) L.R. 6 Q.B. 597.

If, however, in the last case, S. had *known* that H. had made a mistake in accepting his offer, there would have been no contract.

M., after declining an offer from P. to buy certain property for £2,000, wrote to P. offering to sell it for £1,250. This was a mistake for £2,250. P., immediately on receipt of the offer, wrote accepting it. *Held*, the contract would not be specifically enforced as P. had snapped at an offer he perfectly well knew to be made by mistake: *Webster* v. *Cecil* (1861) 30 Beav. 62.

Rectification

If the parties were in agreement on all important terms but by mistake wrote them down wrongly, rectification of the written document may be ordered. To obtain rectification it must be proved:

(a) there was complete agreement between the parties at all important terms;
(b) the agreement continued unchanged until it was reduced into writing; and
(c) the writing did not express what the parties had already agreed.

U. owned two adjoining pieces of land, plots 1 and 2. Behind plot 1, but forming part of it, was a yard used with plot 2. P. bought plot 1, excluding the yard, and Q. bought plot 2, with the yard. By mistake plot 1 was conveyed to P. without the yard being excluded, and plot 2 was conveyed to Q. without any mention of the yard. *Held*, the deeds could be rectified, so that the yard was conveyed to Q. and not to P.: *Craddock Bros.* v. *Hunt* [1923] 2 Ch. 136.

The object of rectification is "to bring the written document executed in pursuance of an antecedent agreement into conformity with that agreement" (*per* Warrington L.J. in *Craddock Bros.* v. *Hunt*, *ante*). It is sufficient to show a continuing common intention in regard to a particular provision or aspect of the antecedent agreement, although, until the written instrument is executed, a binding contract cannot be said to exist between the parties. But strong and convincing proof is required that the concluded instrument does not represent the common accord of the parties, and that is particularly the case if rectification is claimed merely on the strength of a continuing common intention and not on that of a complete contract.

A father agreed with his daughter to transfer his house and car hire business to her in consideration of her paying him a small weekly pension and defraying certain of his household expenses, including gas, electricity and coal bills and the cost of a home help for the invalid mother. The written agreement provided that the daughter should "discharge all expenses" in connection with the house in which she and the parents lived in separate households in self-contained flats. The daughter met the expenses for the father's gas, electricity and coal and for the home help for some time but refused to continue paying them after differences had broken out; she relied on the wording of the written agreement. *Held*, there was a common continuing intention that the expenses in dispute should be paid by the daughter and the written agreement had to be rectified by writing a clause to that effect into it: *Joscelyne* v. *Nissen* [1970] 2 Q.B. 86.

Exceptionally, rectification may be ordered if a party provides convincing proof of a unilateral mistake, *i.e.* that he believed a particular term to be included in the contract but that the other party, without informing him, omitted or varied that term, well knowing that he still believed the term to be included (*A. Roberts & Co. Ltd.* v. *Leicestershire County Council* [1961] Ch. 555). Rectification cannot be granted in respect of a *unilateral* mistake by one party unless the other party had actual knowledge of the existence of the former's mistake when the contract was signed: *Agip SpA* v. *Navigione Alta Italia SpA* (below).

During negotiations for a charterparty, the two parties agreed on the inclusion of an escalation clause (providing for a refund by the charterers to the owners for increased costs of maintenance and repairs) expressed in Italian currency. In the written contract which the two parties subsequently both signed, the clause was expressed in American dollars, thereby increasing the liability of the charterers. The charterers had failed to spot this when reading the contract before signing it and mistakenly assumed that the contract reflected their earlier understanding. *Held*, since the owners were unaware of the charterers' mistake, rectification would not be granted: *Agip SpA* v. *Navigione Alta Italia SpA* [1984] 1 Lloyd's Rep. 353.

Recovery of money paid under a mistake

Money paid under a *mistake of fact* can be recovered, provided that the payer did not intend the payee to have the money in any event, the money was not paid for good consideration and the payee had not in good faith changed his position (*Barclays Bank Ltd.* v. *W. J. Simms Son & Cooke (Southern) Ltd.* (see below). Money paid under a *mistake of law* is usually unrecoverable. In the former case the action is founded on quasi-contract (see p. 64, *ante*). If a bank mistakenly credits money to a customer's account this will normally entitle the bank to recover the money, unless the customer has relied upon the accuracy of the stated account and spent the money, thereby altering his mode of living in a way which he would not have done but for his mistaken belief that he was richer than he was (*United Overseas Bank* v. *Jiwani* [1976] 1 W.L.R. 964). If an employer mistakingly overpays an employee, this may amount to a mistake of fact entitling the employer to recover the overpayment. But if, in reliance on the overpayment, the employee has altered his financial position, *e.g.* by spending the overpayment, the employer may be estopped from recovering it: *Avon County Council* v. *Howlett* [1983] 1 W.L.R. 605.

Barclays Bank paid by mistake a cheque which had been stopped. *Held*, the bank could recover the amount paid from the payee: *Barclays Bank Ltd.* v. *W. J. Simms Son & Cooke (Southern) Ltd.* [1980] Q.B. 677.

MISREPRESENTATION

Representations distinguished from terms of contract

It happens often that the actual conclusion of the contract is preceded by negotiations between the interested parties. These negotiations might not be smooth: one party might be eager to contract while the other might be reluctant. A statement of fact which one party makes in the course of the negotiations with a view to inducing the other to enter into the contract and to conclude it is known as a representation; if such statement is false, it is a **misrepresentation**.

It is characteristic of a misrepresentation that it is made **before** the parties conclude the contract, and made just for the purpose of inducing one of them to accept contractual obligations. Such statement must be distinguished from a statement actually embodied in the contract which forms part of the **terms** of the contract (see p. 28, *ante*).

From the point of view of the person to whom the statement is made, the distinction is between merely relying on what was said in the negotiations or contracting that the statement is true.

H., rubber merchants, in reply to B.'s question, told B. that they were bringing out a rubber company. B. asked if it was all right, and H. said they were bringing it out. B. therefore said that was good enough for him and bought 5,000 shares from H. at a premium. The shares depreciated and B. claimed damages. The jury found the company was not a rubber company but negatived fraud. *Held*, the statement that the company was a rubber company was not a term of the contract of sale of the shares, nor was there a contractual collateral warranty that the company was a rubber company: *Heilbut, Symons & Co.* v. *Buckleton* [1913] A.C. 30.

W. sold a Morris car to O. C. Ltd. Before the sale W. told the representative of O. C. Ltd. that the car was a 1948 Morris and produced the registration book that showed 1948 as the year of first registration. W.'s mother had bought the car second-hand as a 1948 model. The car was, in fact, a 1938 model and the registration book was forged, unknown to all parties concerned. *Held*, W.'s statement was a representation and not a term of the contract; as the misrepresentation was innocent, the buyer could not recover damages: *Oscar Chess Ltd.* v. *Williams* [1957] 1 W.L.R. 370.

A statement could, however, be **both** a representation **and** a term of the contract. The circumstances may show that a statement of fact which first was merely a representation was then embodied by the parties into the contract as a term of it (*Couchman* v. *Hill* [1947] K.B. 554; see pp. 322–323, *post*). Even if the misrepresentation has become a term of the contract, such as a condition or a warranty, the remedy of rescission for innocent misrepresentation is available to the misled party (Misrepresentation Act 1967, s.1(*a*)); he can, of course, always rescind if the misrepresentation was fraudulent. The remedies for breach of conditions and warranties have been discussed earlier (p. 33, *ante*).

The basis of the law of misrepresentation

The rules of the common law and equity on misrepresentation have been considerably affected by two events: the **Misrepresentation Act 1967** and the decision of the House of Lords in *Hedley Byrne & Co. Ltd.* v. *Heller and Partners Ltd.* [1964] A.C. 465, which has been applied in many subsequent decisions.

The Misrepresentation Act 1967 altered these rules, as far as the law of contract was concerned. The main feature of the Act is that whilst it leaves the category of fraudulent misrepresentations, it divides other misrepresentations into those which are negligent and those which are not. The Act equates negligent misrepresentation to fraudulent misrepresentation in many respects. Another provision of the Act states that, if a misrepresentation has occurred, it is presumed that it was made negligently, so that the burden of proving that it was not negligent rests on the defendant.

Hedley Byrne & Co. Ltd. v. *Heller and Partners Ltd.* is a decision in the law of torts. The House of Lords extended the rule in *Donoghue* v. *Stevenson* [1932] A.C. 562, by holding that a person who made a negligent statement might be liable for financial loss suffered by the person to whom the statement was made. He would be, if he possessed special skill and competence and owed the person who suffered the loss a duty to apply these qualities when making the statement; he may, however, be able to exclude his liability in these circumstances. Unlike the situation under the Misrepresentation Act 1967, however, the burden of proving negligence falls on the plaintiff.

Hedley Byrne, advertising agents, were instructed by Easipower Ltd., one of their clients, to conclude advertising contracts which would involve Hedley Byrne in personal liability to the advertisers. They made inquiries about the creditworthiness of Easipower with Heller, who were merchant bankers. Heller gave a favourable reply but stipulated that it was "without responsibility." In reliance on that statement Hedley Byrne placed the advertising contracts on behalf of Easipower and, when the latter went into liquidation, became personally liable for £17,000. Hedley Byrne contended that Heller had acted negligently. The House of Lords, without deciding on Heller's alleged negligence, held that a negligent though honest misrepresentation could give rise to an action in tort for negligence, where no contractual or fiduciary relationship existed between the parties, but only if the person making the statement owed a duty of care to the person to whom the statement was made; such duty was owed if the person making the statement possessed special skill and judgment and he knew or ought to have known that the other party relied on these qualities. In the result, the House of Lords held that there was no liability on Heller as there was an express disclaimer of liability: *Hedley Byrne & Co. Ltd.* v. *Heller and Partners Ltd.* [1964] A.C. 465.

The rule established in *Hedley Byrne* covers the following proposition: "If a man, who has or professes to have special knowledge or skill, makes a representation by virtue thereof to another—be it advice, information or opinion—with the intention of inducing him to enter into a contract with him, he is under a duty to use reasonable care to see that the representation is correct, and that the advice, information or opinion is reliable. If he negligently gives unsound advice or misleading information or expresses an erroneous opinion, and thereby induces the other side to enter into a contract with him, he is liable" (*per* Lord Denning M.R. in *Esso Petroleum Co. Ltd.* v. *Mardon* [1976] Q.B. 801). The same principles must apply if the person who has or professes to have special knowledge or skill by his advice negligently induces the other side to enter into a contract with a third party. The rule in *Hedley Byrne* applies not only to professional advisers but also to other persons, *e.g.* those who are in a special relationship to the adviser or those who have a financial interest in the transaction on which they advise. It also covers pre-contractual negotiations (*Esso Petroleum Co. Ltd.* v. *Mardon*, see p. 37, *ante*), but here it is more easy for the advised to recover damages under the Misrepresentation Act 1967 (see *post*). The rule never applies to advice given only casually or in a social context (*Mutual Life and Citizens' Assurance Co. Ltd.* v. *Evatt* [1971] A.C. 793). A bank manager may find himself in a difficult position: a conflict may arise between the interests of the bank, which employs him, and those of a customer, to whom the bank stands in a relationship of confidence; in such a case the manager should advise the customer to obtain independent advice (*Lloyds Bank* v. *Bundy* [1975] Q.B. 326, see p. 115, *post*; *National Westminster Bank Ltd.* v. *Morgan* [1985] A.C. 686.

Because someone claiming damages for an actionable **contractual** misrepresentation under the Misrepresentation Act does not have to prove negligence (the burden of proof being on the defendant to show absence of negligence), the real significance of the decision in *Hedley Byrne* v. *Heller* is in relation to claims by a plaintiff against someone with whom he made no contract. In relation to such claims, later cases have clarified the extent of possible liability under the *Hedley Byrne* v. *Heller* principle. The principle does not impose liability for negligence upon a professional person (*e.g.* a surveyor or accountant) just because it is foreseeable that his report or statement might be relied upon by a variety of strangers for any one of a variety of different purposes; there is no special relationship of proximity between the professional person and any of such strangers. The position is different, however, where the professional person knows that his report or statement will be communicated to someone specifically in connection with a particular transaction (or a transaction of a particular kind) **and** he knows that that person would be very likely to rely on it. For example, a valuer who values a house for the purpose of a mortgage, knowing that the house buyer (the mortgagor) as well as the building society (the mortgagee) will probably rely on the valuation, and knowing that the purchaser has in effect paid for the valuation, is under a duty to exercise reasonable care and skill; that duty is owed to the purchaser as well as the building society even though it was not the purchaser who made the contract with the valuer (*Smith* v. *Eric S. Bush* [1989] 2 W.L.R. 790). (In that case a disclaimer was held to be ineffective to protect the valuer from liability, because the disclaimer failed the reasonableness test of the Unfair Contract Terms Act 1977, see p. 43, *ante*). An auditor of a company's accounts, on the other hand, owes no duty of care to members of the public at large who may rely on the accuracy of the accounts in deciding to buy shares in the company, or to others who may decide to advance credit to the company. Equally the auditor owes no duty to shareholders who may rely on the accounts in deciding either to reduce or to increase their shareholdings. This is because the accounts are not prepared and audited for communication to these persons in connection with any particular, or any particular type of, transaction, *Caparo Industries* v. *Dickman* [1990] 1 All E.R. 568.

We will now turn our attention to contractual misrepresentations, *i.e.* those made by one party to the other party before a contract is made between them.

Innocent and fraudulent misrepresentation

Requirements of misrepresentation

A misrepresentation is actionable (*i.e.* can give rise to a valid claim) if it satisfies the following requirements: it must—

(a) be a representation of a material fact,
(b) be made before the conclusion of the contract with a view to inducing a party to enter into the contract,
(c) be made with the intention that it should be acted upon by the party to whom it is addressed, and
(d) actually have been acted upon and must have induced the contract.

If the person who made the statement honestly believed it to be true, the **misrepresentation** was **innocent**. There are two types of innocent misrepresentation: *innocent but negligent misrepresentation* which occurs if the person making the statement had no reasonable ground to believe it to be true, and *innocent and not negligent* misrepresentation which occurs if he had reasonable grounds to believe it to be true.

If the person making the statement did not honestly believe it to be true, the **misrepresentation** was **fraudulent**.

In the following, the requirements of an actionable misrepresentation will be considered more closely.

1. The representation must be one of fact, and not of general opinion or of intention. Mere puffing or commendatory statements by traders as to their wares are not representations of fact. For example:

(a) A statement that a second-hand car is good value is a statement of opinion.
(b) A statement that the car has only run 6,000 miles is a statement of fact.
(c) A statement that the car is the best model ever produced by the makers is puffing.

If statement (b) is untrue and the person making it knows it to be untrue, the remedies for fraudulent misrepresentation are available, p. 102, *post*). Whether the statements (a) and (c) are true or not has no effect on the contract, subject to the rule in *Hedley Byrne* (see p. 94, *ante*).

Although, as a general rule, a statement of opinion or intention is not a statement of fact, yet if it can be proved that no such opinion or intention was held, the remedies for fraudulent misrepresentation are available, because "the state of a man's mind is as much a fact as the state of his digestion" (*per* Bowen L.J. in *Edgington* v. *Fitzmaurice* (1885) 29 Ch.D. 483). The difficulty in such cases is chiefly one of proof. Moreover, if the facts are not equally known to both parties, a statement of opinion by the one who knows the facts better may be a statement of a material fact, for it may be implied that he knows facts which justify his opinion (*Brown* v. *Raphael* [1958] Ch. 636).

Misrepresentation of a general rule of law is irrelevant, but misrepresentation of particular rights, such as the existence and contents of a private Act of Parliament, is a misrepresentation of fact (*West London Commercial Bank* v. *Kitson* (1884) 13 Q.B.D. 363).

2. The representation must have been made before the making of the contract with a view to inducing the other party to enter into the contract. This requirement has already been explained when the distinction between representations and terms of the contract was discussed (p. 93, *ante*).

A representation which is true when made but, to the knowledge of the party making it, becomes untrue before the contract is entered into must be corrected. If it is not, it is an actionable misrepresentation.

In negotiating a sale of a medical practice in January, X. represented the takings to be at the rate of £2,000 a year. In May, when the contract was signed, the takings had, owing to X.'s illness, fallen to £5 a week. *Held*, the contract could be rescinded owing to X.'s failure to disclose the fall in the takings: *With* v. *O'Flanagan* [1936] 1 Ch. 575.

3. The representation must be made with the intention that it should be acted upon by the person to whom it is addressed.

Z., on the faith of statements appearing in the prospectus of a company, bought some shares in a company from a holder of them. Some of the statements were false, and Z. thereupon sued the directors. *Held*, the statements were only intended to mislead the public into being original subscribers of the shares from the company. As Z. was not an original subscriber, but had purchased the shares later from a subscriber, he was not within the class intended to be misled, and therefore could not maintain the action: *Peek* v. *Gurney* (1873) L.R. 6 H.L. 377.

If, however, it can be shown that the statements in the prospectus were intended to induce persons to buy in the market, those persons can sue for the damage they have suffered (*Andrews* v. *Mockford* [1896] 1 Q.B. 372).

While it is doubtful whether, in view of modern developments, particularly the provisions of the Misrepresentation Act 1967 and the rule in *Hedley Byrne* v. *Heller*, *Peek* v. *Gurney* would be decided in the same way today as it was a hundred years ago, the principle is undoubtedly correct that if A. induces B. by fraudulent misrepresentation to buy land or chattels and B. resells them to C., C. has no right to claim the remedies for fraudulent misrepresentation directly against A. because the original misrepresentation spent itself when B. sold the land or chattels to C.

Gross asked Grace Rymer Investments Ltd. to find a suitable shop for her to purchase as an investment. Grace Rymer were induced by misrepresentation to purchase a shop themselves from certain sellers and then resold the shop to Gross. The shop was conveyed directly from the sellers to Gross, who suffered loss as the result of the original misrepresentation. *Held*, even if the misrepresentation was fraudulent (which, according to the finding of the judge of first instance was not the case), Gross could not rescind the conveyance of the shop on the ground of the sellers' misrepresentation because the right to rescind was not an equity which ran with the land and the effect of the misrepresentation had spent itself when Grace Rymer sold the shop to Gross: *Gross* v. *Lewis Hillman Ltd.* [1970] Ch. 445.

4. The representation must actually have been acted upon and must have induced the contract.

If the party to whom the misrepresentations are made does not rely upon them, but relies instead upon his own skill and judgment, or upon his own inquiries and investigations, he cannot bring an action. For example, if C. offers a business to D. for sale, representing the takings to be £5,000 a week (knowing that this statement is untrue), and D., after investigating the books, decides as a result of that investigation to buy the business, D. will not be able to sue C. upon his fraudulent representation as to the takings. But if D. relies even partly on C.'s representation, C. will be liable for fraud. A seller of goods is not obliged, unasked, to draw the attention of the buyer to any defects of the goods but he must not make a false statement relating to them (see p. 109, *post*).

The fact that the party misled had the means, of which he did not avail himself, of discovering the falseness of the representation is immaterial because he was entitled to rely on the representation made to him by the other party.

In the negotiations for the sale of X.'s business to Y., X. represented that his takings were £300 a year and produced papers to Y. which, he said, bore out his statement. Y. bought the business without examining the papers. If he had examined them, he would have discovered that X.'s statements were false. *Held*, as Y. had relied on X.'s statements he could rescind the contract and it was no defence to say that he had the means of discovering their untruth: *Redgrave* v. *Hurd* (1881) 20 Ch.D. 1.

Innocent misrepresentation

Innocent misrepresentation occurs where the false statement has been made honestly, whether made negligently or not, but, as will be seen later, the remedies for negligent misrepresentation differ from those for non-negligent misrepresentation.

An innocent misrepresentation is presumed to have been made negligently. The onus is on the person making the statement to prove "that he had reasonable ground to believe and did believe up to the time the contract was made that the facts represented were true" (Misrepresentation Act 1967, s.2(1)). The test of negligence is thus—as always—the objective one of reasonableness. A person of unusual simplicity of mind who makes a statement which he believes to be true but which any reasonable man would not make without further investigation of the facts, is liable for negligent misrepresentation; it will be seen that the remedies for that type of misrepresentation are the same as those for fraudulent misrepresentation.

Howard Marine and Dredging Co. Ltd. were the owners of two barges, *Howard II* and *Howard III*. The marine manager of Howards negotiated with A. Ogden & Sons (Excavators) Ltd. who were interested in chartering the two barges. In negotiations before the conclusion of the contract the marine manager told Ogdens that the barges could carry approximately 1,600 tonnes of clay. The marine manager had taken this information from Lloyd's Register which gave the capacity of the barges as 1,800 tonnes. The entry in the Register was incorrect; the correct deadweight capacity of the barges was only 1,055 tonnes. This could have been ascertained from the ship's documents in the owners' possession. Ogdens chartered the barges, relying on the marine manager's statement on the capacity of the barges. *Held*, (1) Howards, acting through their marine manager, had committed an innocent misrepresentation as to the capacity of the barges; (2) they had failed to prove that their marine manager had reasonable grounds for disregarding the figures in the ships' documents; (3) Howards were liable in damages under section 2(1) of the Misrepresentation Act 1967: *Howard Marine and Dredging Co. Ltd.* v. *A. Ogden & Sons (Excavators) Ltd.* [1978] Q.B. 574.

Where the misrepresentation was made by an agent acting within his actual or ostensible authority, the remedies under section 2(1) of the Misrepresentation Act 1967 are available against the principal, and not against the agent, but the agent may be liable under the rule in *Hedley Byrne* v. *Heller* (*Resolute Maritime Inc.* v. *Nippon Kaiji Kyokai. The Skopas* [1983] 1 W.L.R. 857).

Fraudulent misrepresentation

"Fraud is proved" said Lord Herschell in *Derry* v. *Peek* (1889) 14 App.Cas. 337, 374, "when it is shown that a false representation has been made:

(a) knowingly; or
(b) without belief in its truth; or

(c) recklessly, careless whether it be true or false."

A misrepresentation is not fraudulent if the person who made it honestly believes it to be true.

A tram company had statutory powers to run trams by animal power, and, with the consent of the Board of Trade, by steam power. A prospectus was issued inviting the public to apply for shares and stating that the company had the right to use steam power. The Board of Trade refused its consent to the use of steam power and the company was wound up. *Held*, as the directors honestly believed the statement in the prospectus they were not guilty of fraud: *Derry* v. *Peek* (1889) 14 App.Cas. 337. (As a result of this case the law relating to the liability of directors for false statements in the prospectus was altered; see now Companies Act 1985 ss.66–69.)

For the ascertainment of fraud, the test of honest belief is purely subjective; the question is not whether the belief that the statement was true could be reasonably entertained on an objective consideration of its truth or falsity, but the test is whether the person who made the statement believed it to be true in the sense in which he understood it albeit erroneously when it was made.

The defendants induced the plaintiffs by a false statement to subscribe to a company in Kenya. The company was a failure and the plaintiffs who had lost their money claimed damages for fraudulent misrepresentation. *Held*, there was no fraudulent misrepresentation as the defendants honestly believed the statements to be true in the sense in which they made them: *Akerhielm* v. *De Mare* [1959] A.C. 789.

Absence of reasonable grounds for belief in the truth of a fact may, however, tend to show that in fact the belief was not held.

If the representation be made knowing it to be false the fact that it was made from an honest motive will not prevent it from being a fraud. Where, therefore, X. accepted without authority a bill of exchange drawn on Y., honestly believing that Y. would confirm his act, he was held liable for fraud (*Polhill* v. *Walter* (1832) 3 B. & Ald. 114).

Remedies for fraudulent and innocent misrepresentation

Remedies for fraudulent misrepresentation

They are:

(a) a claim for damages by the misled party, if he has suffered a loss. This claim is founded on the common law tort of deceit and may be combined with any of the two following:
(b) rescission of the contract by the misled party.
(c) refusal of the misled party to perform the contract.
(d) although this is not a remedy for fraudulent misrepresentation, it should be added that the misled party has always the right to affirm the contract, if he so wishes.

Remedies for innocent but negligent misrepresentation

The remedies are the same as in the case of fraudulent misrepresentation but:

1. The right to claim damages is not founded on the common law but is statutory; it arises under the Misrepresentation Act 1967, s.2(1). The measure of damages is the same as in a claim founded on the tort of deceit, *Royscot Trust Ltd.* v. *Rogerson*, below.

Mr. and Mrs. Spence were the joint owners of a house in London. Without authority from his wife and without her consent, Mr. Spence sold the house to Mr. Watts. Mrs. Spence refused to agree to the sale. *Held*, Mr. Spence was liable to Mr. Watts under the Misrepresentation Act 1967, s.2(1) because at the time of the sale he was well aware that his wife had not consented and he falsely represented to Mr. Watts that he was entitled to sell the house: *Watts* v. *Spence* [1976] Ch. 165.

A finance company had a policy of not accepting any proposal for hire-purchase of a motor vehicle unless the deposit paid represented at least 20 per cent. of the cash price of the vehicle. The defendants, a car dealer and his customer, proposed a hire-purchase transaction to the finance company by sending forms to the company which showed the cash price of the vehicle as £8,000 and the deposit as £1,600, leaving a balance of £6,400. In fact these were misrepresentations. The actual purchase price was £7,600 and the actual deposit paid was £1,200. Without these misrepresentations the finance company would not have accepted the transaction. A few months later the customer wrongfully sold the car to a private purchaser (who obtained good title by virtue of the Hire Purchase Act 1964, Part III, see p. 385, *post*). The finance company brought a claim for misrepresentation, but without alleging any deceit, against both the car dealer and the customer. The claim succeeded but the finance company appealed against the amount of damages awarded against the dealer. *Held*, the measure of damages for a negligent misrepresentation under the Misrepresentation Act 1967 s.2(1) was the same as in an action for deceit; the finance company was therefore awarded £3,625, *i.e.* the difference between the cash price paid by the company to the car dealer (£6,400) and the amount of payments received by the finance company from the customer (£2,775). The wrongful sale of the car by the customer, which prevented the finance company recovering possession of the car, was not unforeseeable and therefore was not a *novus actus interveniens* breaking the chain of causation: *Royscot Trust Ltd.* v. *Rogerson* [1991] 135 S.J. 444.

2. Further, although the misled party would be entitled to rescind the contract, the judge (or arbitrator) had a discretionary power to declare the contract as subsisting and to award damages in lieu of rescission (section 2(2)), but these damages have to be taken into account when the damages to which the misled party is entitled under section 2(1) are calculated (section 2(3)).

Remedies for innocent and not negligent misrepresentation

They are:

(a) rescission of the contract by the misled party, but the judge (or arbitrator) has a discretionary power to declare the contract as subsisting and to award damages in lieu of rescission (section 2(2)).
(b) refusal of the misled party to perform the contract.
(c) affirmation of the contract.
(d) it should be noted that the misled party has no *right* in common law or under the statute to claim damages; all he can do is invoke the *discretionary power* of the judge to award damages in lieu of rescission.

The right to damages

Damages can be demanded, as stated earlier, in the case of fraudulent and negligent misrepresentation. The measure of damages is the same in both cases although the former is founded on the common law and the latter on the statute (see *Royscot Trust Ltd.* v. *Rogerson*, above).

The discretionary power to award damages in lieu of rescission

The judge (or arbitrator) has this power in the case of negligent or innocent misrepresentation but not in the case of fraudulent misrepresentation. He should exercise it "if of opinion that it would be equitable to do so, having regard to the nature of the misrepresentation and the loss that would be caused by it if the contract were upheld, as well as to the loss that rescission would cause to the other party" (section 2(2)).

Rescission of the contract

A contract induced by innocent or fraudulent misrepresentation is voidable at the option of the party misled. The guilty party cannot set up his own wrong as a ground for repudiating the contract.

The party who has been misled may rescind the contract either by his own act or by bringing an action for rescission. The general rule is that the party wishing to rescind must communicate his intention to the other party. An exception is admitted where a contract has been induced by fraudulent misrepresentation and the party guilty of the fraud has absconded with the intention of avoiding communication; in such a case the innocent party may rescind the contract by overt means falling short of communication or repossession, *e.g.* by informing the police (*Car and Universal Finance Co. Ltd.* v. *Caldwell* [1965] 1 Q.B. 525, see p. 340, *post*).

The mere fact that the contract has been performed does not deprive the misled party of his right to rescind (Misrepresentation Act 1967, s.1(b)). The injured party does, however, lose the right of rescission in the following circumstances:

1. If, in the exercise of his discretionary power, the judge (or arbitrator) declares the contract as subsisting and awards damages in lieu of rescission (section 2(2)).

2. If, with knowledge of the misrepresentation, he takes a benefit under the contract or in some other way affirms it.

3. If the parties cannot be restored to their original positions.

The L. Syndicate sold nitrate works to the L. Company under a contract which contained misleading particulars. The company sued for rescission of the contract. *Held*, owing to the alteration of the property consequent on its being worked by the company, the position of the parties had been so changed that they could not be restored to their original positions, and therefore the contract could not be rescinded: *Lagunas Nitrate Co.* v. *Lagunas Syndicate* [1899] 2 Ch. 392.

The same result obtains where a person is induced by false statements in the prospectus to take shares in a company, and before he rescinds the contract the company goes into liquidation. In such a case it is too late to rescind the contract. If the shares have merely fallen in value, rescission can be obtained.

A broker employed to buy shares on behalf of a client fraudulently pretended to do so, while in fact selling shares of his own to the client. On discovering this, the client brought an action for rescission. At the time of the purchase the shares were worth nearly £3 each, but at the date of the commencement of the action they had fallen to 5s. *Held*, the contract could be rescinded because the same shares could be handed back, the deterioration in value being immaterial: *Armstrong* v. *Jackson* [1917] 2 K.B. 822.

In the case of fraud, lapse of time alone does not prevent the contract from being rescinded as long as the action is brought within six years of the time when the fraud was or with reasonable diligence could have been discovered: Limitation Act 1980, s.32.

4. If a third party has acquired for value rights under the contract.

If A. obtains goods from B. by fraud and pawns them with C., B. cannot normally rescind the contract on learning of the fraud so as to be able to recover the goods from C. (*Phillips* v. *Brooks* [1919] 2 K.B. 243; see p. 86, *ante*).

Refusal of the injured party to perform the contract

The misled party can either refuse to perform his part or he can resist a suit for specific performance or an action for damages brought against him on account of it.

Misrepresentation and exemption clauses

A term of a contract which excludes or restricts

(a) the liability of a party for misrepresentation, or
(b) any remedy of a party for misrepresentation

is null and void, except in so far as it satisfies the requirement of reasonableness under the Unfair Contract Terms Act 1977 (Misrepresentation Act 1967, s.3, as substituted by the Unfair Contract Terms Act 1977, s.8).

This section also applies to the conditions of sale of land by auction (*Southwestern General Property Co. Ltd.* v. *Marton* (1982) 263 E.G. 1090). But it only limits clauses excluding or restricting liability for misrepresentations made by a party or his agent; it does not qualify the right of a principal publicly to limit the otherwise ostensible authority of his agent (*Overbrooke Estates Ltd.* v. *Glencombe Properties Ltd.* [1974] 1 W.L.R. 1335).

Estoppel by conduct

An innocent misrepresentation may give rise to an action for damages through the **doctrine of estoppel**. Estoppel means that a person is prevented (or estopped) from denying the truth of a statement which he has made.

The basis of estoppel is, in the words of Lord Denning M.R. (in *Panchaud Frères S.A.* v. *Etablissements General Grain Co.* [1970] 1 Lloyd's Rep. 53, 57, see p. 411, *post*) "that a man has so conducted himself that it would be unfair or unjust to allow him to depart from a particular state of affairs which another has taken to be settled or correct."

To set up an estoppel there must be:

(a) *either* representation of fact intended to be acted on by the person to whom it was made, *or* a representation of fact made negligently to someone;
(b) action taken upon it by that person;
(c) detriment to that person by acting on it.

Two parcels of cans of frozen eggs were shipped on O.'s ship under a bill of lading, signed by the master, stating that they were shipped "in apparent good order and condition." They were delivered damaged. *Held*, as against the consignees of the eggs, O. was estopped from proving that the parcels were already damaged when they were shipped, and consequently O. was liable for the damage: *Silver* v. *Ocean Steamship Co.* [1930] 1 K.B. 416.

Here, the cause of action was that O. had damaged the eggs during transit, but the statement that they were in good order on shipment was an essential fact to be proved. Had there been no such statement in the bill of lading, the consignee would not have paid for the eggs. It was because the statement (which may have been false) was made that damages were payable.

The plaintiff, Peter Cremer, an importer in West Germany, bought a quantity of tapioca roots from a seller in Bangkok for shipment from Thailand to Bremen on c.i.f. terms. When the goods were loaded in the

Dona Mari, a vessel owned by the defendants, the chief officer noticed a bitter smell which indicated that the tapioca was mouldy, and he claused the mate's receipts "not quite dry." The clausings were not transferred to the bills of lading which were issued clean. The plaintiff and a buyer who had acquired part of the consignment paid against the clean bills of lading. When on arrival it was discovered that the tapioca was mouldy, they claimed damages from the defendant shipowners. *Held*, the shipowners were estopped by the issue of clean bills of lading from relying on the pre-shipment condition of the goods: *Cremer and Others* v. *General Carriers S.A.* [1976] 1 W.L.R. 341.

For an estoppel to be raised successfully, there has to have been a representation of fact which was intentionally made or negligently made. There is no negligence unless there is a breach of a legal duty.

As owners, Moorgate Mercantile Co. Ltd., a finance company, let a car to Mr. McLorg on hire-purchase terms. Owing to some oversight, they failed to register the agreement with Hire Purchase Information Ltd. (H.P.I.) with which the great majority of hire-purchase agreements were registered. Later Mr. Twitchings who contemplated buying the car from Mr. McLorg inquired from H.P.I. whether there was any hire-purchase agreement registered against the car and Mr. Twitchings received a negative reply from H.P.I. He then purchased the car and resold it. The finance company sued Mr. Twitchings for damages for conversion. *Held*, that the finance company was not under a legal duty to join H.P.I. and therefore having joined was not under a legal duty to register its hire-purchase agreements. Thus, in the absence of negligence, the finance was not estopped by the negative reply of H.P.I. H.P.I. were not their agents and, even if they had been agents, the terms of the reply of H.P.I. excluded an estoppel: *Moorgate Mercantile Co. Ltd.* v. *Twitchings* [1976] Q.B. 225.

Over some 3½ years a bank paid out on a number of cheques drawn on a company's account but which were forgeries, forged by an accounts clerk working at the company. The cheques were debited from the company's account. When the fraud was eventually discovered, the company sought a declaration that the bank was not entitled to debit the company's account with the amount of the forged cheques. The bank claimed that the company was estopped from denying that the cheques were fully valid, because the statements of its account sent to the company had revealed the debits over the previous three years and thus the company in not bringing the forgeries to light earlier had thereby represented that the cheques were valid. *Held*, the declaration would be granted and the estoppel refused, because the company had not been in breach of any duty to the bank. In the absence of any express agreement between the bank and its customer, the only duty of care owed by the customer to the bank was the duty to exercise due care in drawing cheques so as not to facilitate fraud or forgery, and a duty to notify the bank immediately of any unauthorised cheques of which the customer becomes aware. The customer is not under a duty to monitor his bank statements in order to detect unauthorised debits: *Tai Hing Cotton Mill Ltd.* v. *Liu Chong Hing Bank Ltd.* [1986] A.C. 80.

Disclosure of Material Facts

Silence not a misrepresentation

The general rule of the common law is that mere silence is not a misrepresentation. In general, a contracting party is not bound to disclose to the other material facts which he knows will influence him in coming to a decision about the contract; even if he knows that the other party is ignorant of an important fact or if he thinks that the other party is under some misapprehension, he is under no obligation to enlighten him (*Smith* v. *Hughes*). This rule has not been affected by the Misrepresentation Act 1967.

In contracts of sale of goods, this rule is summed up in the maxim "*caveat emptor*," but its harshness is greatly modified by the Sale of Goods Act 1979 which implies certain conditions into every contract of sale (ss.12–15) (see pp. 314–322, *post*), the Unfair Contract Terms Act 1977, s.6 and the Supply of Goods and Services Act 1982, ss.2–16 (see p. 40, *ante*).

Duty to disclose

Exceptionally, however, in the following cases, a party is under a duty unasked to disclose all material facts.

1. When in the course of the negotiations a party makes a representation of fact which is true when made but which, before the contract is concluded, becomes untrue to the knowledge of the party who made it, that party is bound, without being asked, to correct his former representation to the other party (see pp. 98–99, *ante*).

2. If part only of a state of facts is disclosed, and the undisclosed part so modifies the part disclosed as to render it, by itself, substantially untrue, there is a duty to disclose the full facts. For example, if an accountant reporting on accounts says that the accounts are correct, subject to some observations which he makes, there is a duty on the person disclosing the report not only to quote that part which says that the accounts are correct, but also to reveal that the correctness is subject to qualifications. In such a case, the

statement of part of the report represents by implication that the part is complete, and that there is nothing more to disclose.

A prospectus contained statements, which were true, that the company had paid dividends every year between 1921 and 1927. In fact, during each of those years the company had incurred substantial trading losses, and was only able to pay the specified dividends by the introduction into the accounts of non-recurring items such as repayments of excess profits duty, adjustment of income tax, reserves and the like. No disclosure was made of these trading losses. *Held*, the prospectus was false, because it put before intending investors figures which apparently disclosed the existing position of the company, but in fact hid it, and K., a director, who knew that it was false, was guilty of fraud: *R.* v. *Kylsant* [1932] 1 K.B. 442.

3. Contracts *uberrimae fidei*. They require further explanation.

Contracts of utmost good faith

Contracts of utmost good faith (*uberrimae fidei*) constitute the most important exception to the general rule that silence does not amount to misrepresentation. These are contracts in which one party alone has full knowledge of the material facts and therefore the law imposes on him a duty to disclose these facts to the other party.

Contracts of utmost good faith are:

(a) contracts of insurance;
(b) contracts for the allotment of shares in companies;
(c) contracts of family arrangement;
(d) certain contracts for the sale of land; and
(e) contracts of suretyship and partnership, in some respects.

1. In insurance contracts there is an obligation on the assured to disclose to the insurer all material facts. These are facts which would influence the judgment of a prudent insurer in fixing the premium or determining whether he will take the risk. Failure to fulfil this obligation renders the contract voidable at the option of the insurer. It is irrelevant that the assured did not appreciate the materiality of the fact which he failed to disclose. (See Chaps. 26 and 27, *post*).

2. When the public is invited to subscribe for shares or debentures in a company, a prospectus must be issued. The prospectus must disclose the various matters set out in the Companies Act 1985, ss.56 and 65. The omission to disclose any of these matters may

render those responsible for the prospectus liable in damages (*Re South of England Natural Gas Co.* [1911] 1 Ch. 573).

3. When members of a family make arrangements for the settlement of the family property, each member of the family must make full disclosure of every material fact within his knowledge (*Gordon* v. *Gordon* (1816) 3 Swanst. 400).

4. In contracts for the sale of land, there is normally no duty to make disclosure, except that the vendor is under the obligation of disclosing every defect in his title, such as the existence of restrictive covenants affecting the user of the land. This, however, is in reality not a case of a duty to disclose but one of inability to perform because, if the vendor has undertaken to convey an unencumbered title to the purchaser and cannot do so, he has failed to perform his contract.

5. Suretyship and partnership, though often described as contracts of utmost good faith, are not properly so described. In both cases, *after* the contract has been made there is a duty to disclose every material circumstance affecting the relationship between the parties, but there is no such duty *before* the contract is entered into.

Duress and Undue Influence

A contract entered into under duress or undue influence is voidable at the option of the party coerced or influenced, because his consent to the making of the contract is not freely given.

Duress

Duress at common law had a much narrower meaning than undue influence in equity. They are now merged in one another, and prevent a contract from being made when it is entered into under compulsion, physical or moral, or under some persuasion which the law regards as unfair. A contract can be voidable under this head when there is:

1. Actual or threatened physical violence or imprisonment.

A. and B. each had a large shareholding in the same company. Some hostility broke out between the two and A. issued threats against B. including threats to kill him. Subsequently B. executed a deed buying out A.'s interest in the company on terms which were very favourable indeed to A. *Held*, the deed would be set aside on the grounds of duress. It was not necessary for the duress to have been the only factor leading B. to execute the deed, so long as it was one of the reasons. It was not even necessary for B. to show that but for the threats he would not have executed the deed: *Barton* v. *Armstrong* [1976] A.C. 104.

2. Threatened criminal proceedings.

The person threatened need not be the actual contracting party, but may be the husband or wife or near relative of the party.

K. sued G. on a contract made in France, which K. had coerced G. into making by threats of prosecuting G.'s husband for a criminal offence which he had committed. *Held*, G. was not liable, as her consent was obtained through duress: *Kaufman* v. *Gerson* [1904] 1 K.B. 491.

3. Wrongful detention or threatened seizure of property.

H. owned a market and claimed tolls from M., a produce dealer. M. refused to pay, and H. seized his goods, whereupon M. paid and continued to pay yearly under protest. H.'s right to tolls was subsequently declared illegal. *Held*, M. could recover the payments made: *Maskell* v. *Horner* [1915] 3 K.B. 106.

Economic duress

The common law recognises that a form of economic or commercial pressure may constitute duress. Economic duress has two ingredients: first, there must be a coercion or compulsion overbearing the will of the victim and thus vitiating the accord between the parties, and secondly the pressure must be illegitimate or even unlawful. Where these two requirements are satisfied, economic duress is established. In this case the contract is voidable, if the victim so desires, and, if the pressure was unlawful, economic duress may even constitute the tort of intimidation, entitling the victim to claim damages. An unlawful pressure would, *e.g.* be the threat of physical violence or even in certain circumstances the threat to break a contract (*Rookes* v. *Barnard* [1964] A.C. 1129), or the threat of a debtor to pay nothing at all if the creditor does not accept in full settlement a smaller sum than is due to him (*D. & C. Builders Ltd.* v. *Rees* [1966] 2 Q.B. 617).

Economic pressure which does not *coerce* the person exposed to it into entering into a disadvantageous contract or otherwise affecting his legal position, does not amount to economic duress (*Pao On* v. *Lau Yiu Long* [1980] A.C. 614).

A Liberian company was the owner of the *Universe Sentinel*, a ship flying the Liberian flag. The owners of all the shares in the company lived in the United States of America. In 1978 the vessel was on time charter to Texaco and arrived at the British port of Milford Haven. The crew of the ship consisted mainly of Asians who received wages considered by the International Transport Workers Federation (I.T.F.) as too low. The I.T.F. blacked the vessel so as to prevent her from leaving port. The I.T.F. demanded from the owners the payment of $80,000, which, *inter alia*, consisted in a contribution to the Seafarers' International Welfare Fund. The owners made the payment and the vessel sailed away. The owners then claimed to recover the amount paid to the Welfare Fund. *Held*, payment was made under economic duress, the industrial legislation did not sanction the payment and consequently the payment to the Welfare Fund could be recovered by the owners (*Universe Tankships Inc. of Monrovia* v. *International Transport Workers Federation* [1983] 1 A.C. 366).

Duress renders the contract voidable at the option of the innocent party. If, however, he affirms the contract, the innocent party loses his right to set aside the contract (*North Ocean Shipping Co.* v. *Hyundai Construction Co.*, below).

The sellers were contracted to build and supply a ship to the buyers for an agreed price payable in instalments in US dollars. Subsequently the US dollar was devalued. The sellers demanded that the price be increased by 10 per cent. The buyers protested and at first refused but they had by now made an advantageous contract to charter the ship after delivery. The buyers offered to go to arbitration over the claim for extra payment. The sellers then demanded (in June 1973) an immediate answer to their request for an increase in price or else they would terminate the contract. The buyers agreed and instructed their bank to pay instalments of the price at the increased rate. The buyers took delivery of the ship in November 1974 without protest until in July 1975 they claimed the return of the extra 10 per cent. *Held*, the buyers had been the victims of economic duress but since they had paid the extra 10 per cent. and had taken delivery of the ship without protest until eight months later, they had affirmed the agreement for the extra 10 per cent. and thereby lost the right to set the agreement aside and recover the extra 10 per cent.: *North Ocean Shipping Co.* v. *Hyundai Construction Co.* [1978] 3 All E.R. 1170.

Undue influence

The same doctrine of undue influence applies to contracts as to gifts. Before a contract can be set aside on grounds of undue influence, two basic requirements must be fulfilled; there must be:

1. a contract so one-sided (or gift so substantial) that it cannot be explained by the ordinary motives from which men act.
2. a relationship of confidence or trust such as to place the advantaged party in a position to exercise undue influence.

The first of these requires that the transaction was wrongful, in that it constituted a clear and unfair disadvantage to the party seeking to have the contract set aside (*National Westminster Bank* v. *Morgan* [1975] A.C. 686).

In order to see if the second requirement is fulfilled, it must first be determined which of the following groups the case falls in, *i.e.* a case where undue influence is presumed or a case where actual undue influence must be established.

Presumed undue influence

This group includes:

(a) those well-established categories of relationship which raise a presumption of undue influence, *e.g.* solicitor and client, doctor and patient, religious adviser and disciple.
(b) relationships which do not fall within the first category but which are such as to enable the court to apply the same presumption.

These are cases where the one party stands in such a fiduciary relation to the other that a presumption of undue influence arises. The burden then rests upon the party seeking to uphold the contract to show that undue influence was not exercised.

Two months after the death of his wife, an elderly widower employed a young woman as his secretary and companion. Over the following six years he made gifts to her worth £28,000. *Held*, there was such a relationship of confidence between them as to create the presumption of undue influence and she had failed to rebut that presumption. Therefore the gifts would be set aside: *Re Craig* [1971] Ch. 95.

The usual way of rebutting the presumption of undue influence is showing that the other had independent professional advice.

Actual undue influence

These are cases where there has been some unfair or improper conduct. The undue influence must be proved by the person alleging it.

Cases of undue influence "tend to arise where someone relies on the guidance or advice of another, where the other is aware of that reliance and where the person upon whom reliance is placed obtains, or may well obtain, a benefit from the transaction or has some other interest in it being concluded. In addition, there must, of course, be shown to exist a vital element which in this judgment will for convenience be referred to as confidentiality" (*per* Sir Eric Sachs in *Lloyds Bank Ltd.* v. *Bundy* [1975] Q.B. 326, 341).

The defendant, Mr. Herbert Bundy, an elderly farmer, and his only son had been customers of the local country branch of the plaintiffs, Lloyds Bank, for many years. Mr. Bundy wished to assist his son in the promotion of the son's company called M. J. B. Plant Hire Ltd. The company was indebted to Lloyds Bank and the defendant had guaranteed the company's overdraft and secured it by a charge on his house. Subsequently the manager of the local branch made the continuance of the overdraft dependent on the defendant giving the bank a further charge to the full value of his house. The defendant who trusted the bank manager implicitly agreed to his proposal. The bank manager had failed to advise the defendant to seek independent legal advice. The plaintiff bank tried to sell the defendant's house and claimed possession. *Held*, the bank, in the circumstances of the case, was under a duty of confidentiality to the defendant and exercised undue influence. The defendant could avoid the guarantee and the charge: *Lloyds Bank* v. *Bundy* [1975] Q.B. 326.

It should not be inferred from this case that the relationship between bank and customer is invariably of a fiduciary character. That is not so; all that *Lloyds Bank* v. *Bundy* establishes is that in exceptional circumstances that relationship may be of that character.

A Malay woman of great age and wholly illiterate made a deed of gift of valuable property in Singapore to her nephew, who managed her affairs. She was advised by her lawyer, who did not know that the gift constituted practically the whole of her property and did not tell her that she could equally benefit her nephew by will. *Held*, the gift should be set aside on the ground of undue influence: *Inche Noriah* v. *Shaik Allie Bin Omar* [1929] A.C. 127.

A third party contracting with notice of the exercise of undue influence by another is in no better position than if he had exercised undue influence himself.

B., a married woman, under the undue influence of her mother, entered into improvident moneylending contracts for her mother's benefit. The moneylenders knew all the circumstances between B. and her mother. *Held*, the moneylenders were in no better position than the mother, and the contracts were voidable: *Lancashire Loans Ltd.* v. *Black* [1934] 1 K.B. 380.

The rights of a party who is unaware that undue influence has been exercised will not be affected by the undue influence unless an agent of that party exercised the undue influence, (*Coldunell* v. *Gallon*, below).

An elderly couple were persuaded by their son to obtain a loan on the security of their bungalow in order to provide funds for the son's business ventures. The lending company prepared all the documents for the parents to sign and put them in envelopes together with a covering letter advising them to get independent legal advice. Somehow the letters came into the possession of the son who got his parents to sign, using undue influence. *Held*, the son had not been constituted the agent of the lender and therefore the lender, not being tainted with the undue influence was entitled to enforce the agreements against the parents: *Coldunell* v. *Gallon* [1986] Q.B. 1184.

Mr. K. ran up a bank overdraft. The bank manager asked him to grant a charge over his matrimonial home as security for the continuing overdraft. They arranged that Mr. K.'s wife would also execute the charge and that Mr. K. would secure her attendance at the bank for this purpose the following Monday. Mrs. K. came after having been spoken to by Mr. K. and she executed the charge in the presence of a clerk who explained it to her. At no time was she advised to take independent legal advice and her attendance was a formality in order to sign. She claimed that she had signed after undue influence had been exercised on her by her husband. *Held*, since it was in the bank's interest to have Mrs. K. sign, and the bank had been content to leave it to Mr. K. to persuade Mrs. K. to come to the bank and sign, Mr. K. was accordingly the bank's agent. The bank was therefore tainted with any undue influence exercised by Mr. K.: *Barclays Bank* v. *Kennedy* [1989] CCLR 31.

Extortionate Credit Bargains

The Consumer Credit Act 1974, s.137(1) empowers the court to reopen an extortionate credit bargain, so as to do justice between the parties. Section 138(1) of the 1974 Act provides that a credit bargain is extortionate if it:

(a) requires the debtor or a relative of his to make payments (whether unconditionally, or on certain contingencies) which are grossly exorbitant,

or

(b) otherwise grossly contravenes ordinary principles of fair dealing.

Among the facts which are taken into consideration when determining whether the credit bargain is extortionate, are the rate of interest payable by the borrower, his age, and whether he was under financial pressure (see generally p. 402, *post*).

CHAPTER 7

ILLEGAL CONTRACTS

A CONTRACT which is illegal is normally unenforceable. The illegality may be present:

(a) in the formation of the contract, if a contract made in England contravenes English public policy;
(b) in the performance of the contract, *e.g.* a contract to commit a crime;
(c) in the consideration for the contract; or
(d) in the purpose for which the contract is made, *e.g.* if a motor boat is hired for the purpose of smuggling drugs into the country.

Contracts are illegal because they are forbidden by statute or because they are contrary to public policy, which is a common law concept. A contract is contrary to public policy when it is in the public interest that it should not be enforced.

Illegality is a matter of degree, varying according to the gravity of the legal prohibition. Two general categories of illegal contracts can be distinguished: some illegal contracts contain an element of obvious moral turpitude, *e.g.* an agreement to commit a crime; in others such taint is absent, *e.g.* in a contract in restraint of trade. The courts treat contracts of the latter category more leniently than contracts of the former class; in particular, collateral agreements not tainted by illegality of moral turpitude are not void.

In addition, an act rendered illegal by statute might be committed in performance of an otherwise perfectly legal contract. Here a question of interpretation of the statute arises: Was it the intention of Parliament to preclude a party from enforcing the contract or was it only intended that other consequences should ensue, *e.g.* the imposition of a penalty? In the latter case the contract would remain enforceable. Later, when the effect of illegality will be considered, this type of illegality will require attention (see p. 139, *post*).

The following contracts are illegal—

Contracts tending to injure the public service

These include agreements for the sale of public offices or for the assignment of salaries of public officials or of pensions granted for public services. A contract to procure a title of honour for reward is also void.

The secretary of the College of Ambulance promised Col. Parkinson that if he made a large donation to the college, which was a charitable institution, he would receive a knighthood. The Colonel made a large donation, and, not receiving his knighthood, sued for the return of his money. *Held*, the action failed because the contract was against public policy and illegal: *Parkinson* v. *College of Ambulance Ltd.* [1925] 2 K.B. 1.

A contract by a person to use his position and influence with the Government to procure a benefit for another is void as being against public policy (*Montefiore* v. *Menday Motor Components Ltd.* [1918] 2 K.B. 241), as is also a contract to restrain a person from serving in the naval or military forces of the country (*Re Beard* [1908] 1 Ch. 383).

Contracts tending to impede the administration of justice

Contracts relating to criminal prosecution and bankruptcy

An agreement to stifle a prosecution for a criminal offence is void, because the public has an interest in the proper administration of justice. On the other hand an agreement to compromise, and settle out of court, a civil claim is valid. That is so even if the claim is in respect of conduct which amounts to a criminal offence. An agreement between a prisoner and a person who has gone bail for him to indemnify him against the bail is void, as tending to defeat the object for which bail was granted (*R.* v. *Porter* [1910] 1 K.B. 369).

A contract tending to defeat the bankruptcy law is void.

M. owed J. £852 and promised that if J. would tell M.'s trustee in bankruptcy that the money was a present, M. would, notwithstanding, still be J.'s debtor. *Held*, the agreement was void: *John* v. *Mendoza* [1939] 1 K.B. 141.

Contract of maintenance and champerty

Maintenance has been defined as "improperly stirring up litigation and strife by giving aid to one party to bring or defend a claim without just cause or excuse" (*per* Lord Denning M.R. in *Re Trepca Mines Ltd.* (*No. 2*) [1963] Ch. 199, 219). Champerty[1] is an arrangement whereby a person obtains a promise of a share in the proceeds of an action in return for providing evidence or financial assistance to the person who conducts the litigation. Contracts having maintenance or champerty as their object tend to pervert the course of justice and are illegal.

It is not maintenance, however, when the person giving assistance is a new relation, or acts from motives of charity, or has a common interest with the person assisted. In modern law, "common interest" is interpreted widely; a person who has "a legitimate and genuine business interest in the result of an action" must be taken to have such interest (*Martell* v. *Consett Iron Co. Ltd.* [1955] Ch. 363). "Trafficking in litigation," *i.e.* the assignment of a bare English cause of action, is champerty, unless the assignee has a genuine and substantial interest in the litigation.

Trendex, a Swiss corporation, supplied cement to an English company for shipment to Nigeria. Payment of the purchase price and demurrage was to be made by the Central Bank of Nigeria (C.B.N.) under a letter of credit. The C.B.N. failed to pay and Trendex made a claim against it for US $ 14,000,000. The C.B.N. raised the plea of sovereign immunity but this plea was rejected by the Court of Appeal in January 1977 (*Trendex Trading Corporation* v. *Central Bank of Nigeria* [1977] Q.B. 529). The C.B.N. was given leave to appeal to the House of Lords. Credit Suisse, which was a substantial (though not the only) creditor of Trendex, had guaranteed the legal costs incurred by Trendex in the English proceedings against C.B.N. In 1976 Trendex assigned to Credit Suisse all its claims arising out of the cement contracts. On January 4, 1978 an agreement was made between Credit Suisse and Trendex whereby Trendex agreed not to oppose the sale to a third party by Credit Suisse of all Trendex's claims against C.B.N. This agreement contained an exclusive jurisdiction clause in favour of the court of Geneva. Credit Suisse then sold Trendex's cause of action against the

[1] The word "champerty" is derived from the latin *campi partitio*, *i.e.* division of the spoils of litigation.

C.B.N. to an anonymous third party for US $1,000,000 and assigned Trendex's cause of action to him. The third party settled the C.B.N. case for a payment of US $8,000,000. Trendex claimed that the agreement of January 4, 1978 was void as being champertous. *Held*, (1) the first assignment (from Trendex to Credit Suisse) was not champertous because Credit Suisse had guaranteed Trendex's legal costs in the English proceedings and thus had a genuine and substantial interest in them. (2) The second assignment (from Credit Suisse to the third party) "savoured of champerty" and was illegal and void. (3) This illegality did not affect the exclusive jurisdiction clause in favour of the court of Geneva and the English proceedings should be stayed, so that the dispute could be decided by the court of Geneva: *Trendex Trading Corporation* v. *Credit Suisse* [1982] A.C. 679.

Maintenance and champerty are no longer criminal offences or torts, but the abolition of criminal and civil liability has not affected the rule that contracts aimed at these activities are illegal. (Criminal Law Act 1967, ss.13(1)(*a*) and 14).

Witness's contract not to give evidence

A contract by which a witness binds himself not to give evidence before the court on a matter on which the judge says he should give evidence, is contrary to public policy and is not enforced by the court (*Harmony Shipping Co. S.A.* v. *Saudi Europe Line Ltd.* [1979] 1 W.L.R. 1380, 1386).

Contracts of trading with the enemy

At common law, and also by virtue of the Trading with the Enemy Act 1939, all contracts made with a person voluntarily residing in enemy territory in time of war are illegal unless made with the licence of the Crown. "Contracts made directly with enemies as contracting parties are declared illegal on the ground of public policy based upon one of two reasons, either that the further performance of the contract would involve intercourse with the enemy, or that the continued existence of the contract would confer upon the enemy an immediate or future benefit" (*per* Russell J. in *Re Badische Co. Ltd.* [1921] 2 Ch. 331).

But war does not expropriate; accrued rights of an enemy are preserved and kept in suspense until the war is over; often their administration is entrusted to an administrator of enemy property during the war (*Arab Bank Ltd.* v. *Barclays Bank* [1954] A.C. 495).

Contracts to commit a criminal offence or a civil wrong

An agreement to defraud the inland revenue by tax evasion is illegal and cannot be relied upon in a court of law (*Napier* v. *National Business Agency Ltd.* [1951] 2 All E.R. 263; see p. 143, *post*). The same principle applies to an agreement to defraud a local rating authority.

A. let a flat to R. at a rent of £1,200 a year. With the object of getting a low rateable value for the flat, two written agreements were entered into, one purporting to let the flat for £450 a year, the other being an agreement by R. to pay £750 a year for services in connection with the flat. A. sued R. for an instalment of £750. *Held*, the agreement, being made to defraud the rating authority, was void, and A. failed: *Alexander* v. *Rayson* [1936] 1 K.B. 169

An agreement to take shares in a company in order fraudulently to induce the public to believe that there is a market for the shares is an indictable conspiracy and is illegal (*Scott* v. *Brown* [1892] 2 Q.B. 724). Similarly, an agreement by the proprietors of a newspaper to indemnify the printers against claims arising out of libels published in the newspaper is void (*W. H. Smith & Son* v. *Clinton* (1908) 25 T.L.R. 34). Further, an insurance policy indemnifying the assured against legal liability for deliberate and unlawful acts caused by him cannot be enforced (*Gray* v. *Barr*, *below*).

Gray had an affair with Barr's wife. Barr, armed with a loaded shotgun, went to Gray's farm to search for his wife. In a struggle with Gray, Barr fell down the stairs, the gun was involuntarily discharged, and the shot killed Gray. Barr was acquitted of murder and manslaughter. The administrators of Gray's estate sued Barr for damages under the Fatal Accidents Act and Barr, by way of third party proceedings, claimed to be indemnified by the Prudential Assurance under an accident liability policy. *Held*, (i) Barr was liable for having caused Gray's death by gross negligence; (ii) the killing was not an "accident" within the meaning of the insurance policy; (iii) even if the killing was an "accident," it was caused by the deliberate and unlawful act of the assured, and it was therefore against public policy to admit a claim for indemnity against the insurance company: *Gray* v. *Barr* [1971] 2 Q.B. 554 (C.A.).

The suicide of the assured, if sane at the time, rendered the sum assured irrecoverable at a time when suicide was a crime.[2]

B. insured his life under a policy which provided that the policy should be void if the assured committed suicide whether sane or insane within a year of the policy. Nine years after, while he was sane, B. committed suicide. *Held*, the sums assured could not be recovered because, suicide then being a crime, it was against public policy that a man or his estate should benefit from his own crime: *Beresford* v. *Royal Insurance Co.* [1938] A.C. 586.

The "forfeiture rule" of public policy would also apply to prevent someone who committed murder or manslaughter from benefiting from the victim's death, *e.g.* under the will. However, the court now has a discretion "where justice of the case requires" to modify the effect of this rule in any particular case (the Forfeiture Act 1982).

An agreement to perform in a foreign and friendly country an act which is illegal in that country, is void in English law as a matter of public policy based on international comity.

In 1927, when the United States was subject to Prohibition and the sale and importation of alcoholic liquors were illegal, a partnership was formed in England for the purpose of smuggling whisky into the States, in contravention of the American Prohibition legislation. In proceedings between the partners in the English courts, *held*, the partnership agreement was illegal in English law: *Foster* v. *Driscoll* [1921] 1 K.B. 470.

S. agreed to sell and deliver jute bags to R., both parties contemplating and intending that the goods would be shipped from India and be made available in Genoa so that R. might import them into South Africa. Both parties knew that the law of India prohibited the direct or indirect export of goods from India to South Africa. The proper law of the contract was English law. S. repudiated the contract. *Held*, the contract was likewise illegal in English law: *Regazzoni* v. *K. C. Sethia (1944) Ltd.* [1958] A.C. 301.

Immoral contracts

Contracts relating to sexual immorality, such as agreements for future illicit cohabitation, are void. Contracts in consideration of

[2] Suicide ceased to be a crime by virtue of the Suicide Act 1961, s.1.

past illicit cohabitation are made for no consideration, but are not illegal. Moreover, collateral contracts good in themselves will become void if they are knowingly made to further an immoral purpose.

A. let a cab on hire to B., a prostitute, knowing that it was to be used for immoral purposes. *Held*, A. could not recover the hire: *Pearce* v. *Brookes* (1866) L.R. 1 Ex. 213.

Agreements between husband and wife for future separation, and between a married man, with a woman who knows him to be married, for marriage after his wife's death have been held to be void (*Wilson* v. *Carnley* [1908] 1 K.B. 729). A contract, made between decree nisi and decree absolute, for marriage after the dissolution of the existing marriage used to be valid (*Fender* v. *Mildmay* [1938] A.C. 1). However statute now provides that it is no longer possible to maintain an action for breach of promise to marry (Law Reform (Miscellaneous Provisions) Act 1970).

Contracts affecting the freedom of marriage

Contracts in general restraint of marriage are void, as also are contracts unreasonably affecting freedom of choice in marriage. But contracts restraining marriage with a particular person, or otherwise only partially restraining marriage, are valid.

Marriage brokerage contracts, that is, contracts to introduce men and women to each other with a view to their subsequent marriage, are void.

Miscellaneous contracts contrary to public policy

A contract by a newspaper proprietor not to comment on the conduct of a particular person is void. "For a newspaper to stipulate for a consideration that it will refrain from exercising its right of commenting upon fraudulent schemes, when it is the ordinary business of the company to comment upon fraudulent schemes, is in itself a stipulation which is quite contrary to public policy, and which cannot be enforced in a court of law" (*per* Atkin J. in *Neville* v. *Dominion of Canada News Co. Ltd.* [1915] 3 K.B. 556).

A contract unduly fettering the liberty of the individual is void. Where, therefore, a man agreed with a moneylender not to change his residence, or his employment, or to consent to a reduction of his salary, or to part with any of his property, or to incur any obligations on credit, or any obligations, legal or moral, without the consent of the moneylender, it was held that the contract was void (*Horwood* v. *Millar's Timber Co.* [1917] 1 K.B. 305). But where a father, whose son was of dissolute habits, agreed to pay his son's debts, and the son, in consideration thereof, agreed not go to within 80 miles of London, it was held that the contract was binding, because the object of the restriction was to reform the son (*Denny's Trustee* v. *Denny* [1919] 1 K.B. 583).

Contracts in restraint of trade

A contract in restraint of trade is one which restricts a person wholly or partially, in the carrying on of his trade or business. All such contracts are prima facie void and will only be enforced if they are reasonable

A contract in restraint of trade may be enforceable if it is intended to protect a legitimate interest. For example, the purchaser of the goodwill of a business has a legitimate interest in protecting that goodwill by getting the seller to agree not to set up immediately next door in the same line of business. An employer also has a legitimate interest to prevent an employee from revealing trade secrets or, after he has left the employment, using his influence with customers to syphon them off to a competitor of the employer. A contract provision which is in restraint of trade and which is intended to protect a legitimate interest will be enforced if it is:

(a) no wider than necessary to protect the legitimate interest of the party in whose favour it is made; and
(b) reasonable in the public interest.

Public interest

The concept of "reasonable in the public interest" appears to refer to a *legal* principle or proposition, rather than to *economic* theories ". . . reasonableness in the interest of the public refers to the interest of the public as recognised in a principle or proposition of law and not to the interests of the public at large. . . . For my part, I prefer to decide that the restraints relied on in our case are reasonable in the interests of the public, not on balance of existing or possible economic advantages and disadvantages to the public but because there is, in conditions as they are, no unreasonable limitation of liberty to trade" (*per* Ungoed-Thomas, J. in *Texaco Ltd.* v. *Mulberry Filling Station Ltd.* [1972] 1 W.L.R. 814, 828).

The categories of restraint of trade are not closed. The doctrine is not limited to contracts between employer and employee, vendor and purchaser of a business, and combinations to restrict trading activities. It extends to unnecessarily wide solus agreements and to other contracts which unreasonably restrict a party's ability to engage in commerce or exploit his own talents. The doctrine may apply to restrictions intended to promote trade, to restrictions on part only of a multiple business.

Width of the Restraint

A provision which is wider than is necessary to protect a legitimate interest is unenforceable.

"Such a restraint has . . . never been upheld, if directed only to the prevention of competition or against the use of the personal skill and knowledge acquired by the employee in his employer's business": *per* Lord Parker in *Morris* v. *Saxelby* [1916] 1 A.C. 668. 710.

If the restraint, although against competition, is necessary to protect the employer against any improper use by the employee of the knowledge he has acquired in the service of his employer, *e.g.* trade connections, trade secrets, or confidential information, it will be enforced provided that it is no wider than is reasonably necessary to effect that purpose.

A., a tailor, employed B. as his assistant under a contract by which B. agreed on the termination of his employment not to carry on business as a tailor within 10 miles of A. *Held*, the agreement was merely to prevent B. from using such skill as he possessed in competition with A. and was therefore void. "An employer may not, after his servant has left his employment, prevent that servant from using his own skill and knowledge in his trade or profession, even if acquired when in the employer's service": *per* Younger L.J. in *Attwood* v. *Lamont* [1920] 3 K.B. 571.

X. was a solicitor at Tamworth and Y. was successively his junior clerk, articled clerk and managing clerk. In his contract of service Y. agreed, on leaving X.'s employment, not to practise as a solicitor within seven miles of Tamworth. *Held*, the agreement was good, because Y. during his service with X., had become acquainted with the details of the business of X.'s clients, and therefore he could be restrained from using that knowledge to the detriment of X.: *Fitch* v. *Dewes* [1921] 2 A.C. 158.

The extent of the protection depends on (a) the nature of the employer's business, and (b) the business position of the employee. A wider protection will be upheld, for instance, in the case of a manager of a business than in the case of a subordinate. Thus, a wider protection will be upheld where the employee has had personal contact with customers in cash transactions, and the business was not primarily conducted over the telephone on a credit basis (*S. W. Strange Ltd.* v. *Mann* [1965] 1 W.L.R. 629).

If the employee, in an attempt to evade a contract in restraint of trade, forms a company to carry on business as a cloak or sham to enable him to break the contract, an injunction will be granted to restrain the company as well as the employee from breaking the contract (*Gilford Motor Co.* v. *Horne* [1933] Ch. 935).

There is no confidential relationship in respect of which the master is entitled to protection between a reporter and a newspaper proprietor (*Leng* v. *Andrews* [1909] 1 Ch. 763); a canvasser and a clothing company (*Mason* v. *Provident Clothing Co.* [1913] A.C. 724); a motor salesman and a firm of motor-car dealers (*Vincents of Reading* v. *Fogden* (1932) 48 T.L.R. 613).

It is, in practice, extremely difficult to frame restrictions which will adequately protect a trade connection and which will not at the same time cover some cases where the breach will not injure it; an employee cannot claim that a restraint is too wide by referring to situations which were clearly outside the contemplation of the parties when entering into the contract, although, on a literal interpretation, they might fall under the restraint clause.

A dairy agreed with a roundsman that after termination of his contract he should not serve for one year any person who was a customer of the dairy with "milk or dairy produce." The roundsman left the employment of the dairy and immediately started to operate a milk round covering the same area for a competitor. The dairy applied for an injunction, and the roundsman contended that the restraint was too wide as it would have prevented him from serving dairy produce, such as butter and cheese, in a grocery shop. *Held*, the restraint was valid because it had to be construed as relating only to the future activities of the defendant as a milk roundsman: *Home Counties Dairies Ltd.* v. *Skilton* [1970] 1 W.L.R. 526.

It follows that such a restraint must be read in the context of the business in relation to which it was entered and must not be given an artificial and extended meaning.

Ann Francis worked as a ladies' hairdresser in the establishment of Marion White Ltd. She signed an agreement which provided that after termination of her employment she would not accept employment with a competitive enterprise within half a mile of the place where she was last employed for three months, the restraint to be valid for 12 months. Ann Francis was dismissed for a valid reason and a week later entered employment with a rival hairdresser within the prohibited area. It was argued on her behalf that the restraint was too wide because it would have prevented her from working for a rival as receptionist or bookkeeper. *Held*, the restraint was not too wide. The covenant aimed only at her active participation in the hairdressing aspects, if read in the business context of her employment: *Marion White Ltd.* v. *Francis* [1972] 1 W.L.R. 1423.

If a restraint is wider than is reasonably necessary to protect the legitimate interest in question, the courts will refuse to alter it to what would have been a proper limit. But if an agreement has several clauses, some valid and others void, the court will, if the valid clauses can be **severed** from the void, enforce those clauses which are valid if the severance does not affect the meaning of the remaining part of the contract.

S. carried on business as an estate agent in Dartmouth and in Kingsbridge. He employed S.J. as clerk and negotiator at the Kingsbridge office. S.J. signed a covenant whereby he undertook for three years not to set up in business within a radius of the Dartmouth or of the Kingsbridge offices of S. After termination of the contract of employment S.J. forthwith opened an office of his own within the five-mile radius of Kingsbridge. *Held*, the restraint, as agreed was too wide, as S.J. had never worked at the Dartmouth office. However, the Dartmouth restraint was severable from the Kingsbridge restraint, which was not too wide, While the former was invalid, the latter had to be upheld: *Scorer* v. *Seymour Jones* [1966] 1 W.L.R. 1419.

The plaintiff company, T. Lucas & Co. Ltd., manufactured a binder and filler used in the production of processed meat products. They employed the defendant, Mr. Mitchell, as a sales representative in Greater Manchester. The service contract provided that Mr. Mitchell should not "deal" in similar goods, or "solicit" orders for them, or "supply" them within the allocated area for 12 months after termination of his employment. Mr. Mitchell terminated his employment with Lucas and at once began to canvass on behalf of a rival firm a considerable number of customers of Lucas in the Greater Manchester area. *Held*, the restraint relating to "dealing" was wider than was necessary to protect the legitimate interests of Lucas and was therefore invalid, but it could be severed from the restraint relating to "soliciting" and "supplying." An injunction was granted to Lucas against the solicitation and supply by Mitchell: *T. Lucas & Co. Ltd.* v. *Mitchell* [1974] Ch. 129.

A servant who copies the names and addresses of his employer's customers for use after he has left his employment can be restrained from using the list, apart from any express restriction in his contract of service (*Robb* v. *Green* [1895] 2 Q.B. 315). Similarly, if he retains a secret process in his memory he can be restrained from disclosing it (*Amber Size and Chemical Co.* v. *Menzel* [1913] 2 Ch. 239). A skilled man with access to his employer's secrets must not work for a rival firm on similar work in his spare time.

H. employed D. on highly skilled work with access to their manufacturing data. In his spare time D. worked for P. on similar work in competition with H. *Held*, D. was in breach of his duty to be faithful to H. and could be restrained from working for P.: *Hivac Ltd.* v. *Park Royal Scientific Instruments Ltd.* [1946] Ch. 169.

If an employee is wrongfully dismissed from his employment, the employer, having broken the contract, cannot rely on it so as to enforce a restrictive agreement against the servant (*General Billposting Co.* v. *Atkinson* [1909] A.C. 118). The court will refuse the contract-breaker an interlocutory injunction on the equitable ground that "he who comes to equity must do equity and come with clean hands" (*Consolidated Agricultural Suppliers Ltd.* v. *Rushmere*, (1976) 120 S.J. 523).

The principles applying to a restraint on an employee imposed for the benefit of an employer apply also if the restraint is contained in a contract between two employers with respect to their employees.

Two companies manufacturing similar products agreed that neither would, without the written consent of the other, employ any person who had been a servant of the other during the previous five years. *Held*, the restraint was too wide and, consequently, void: *Kores Manufacturing Co. Ltd.* v. *Kolok Manufacturing Co. Ltd.* [1959] Ch. 108.

Solus Agreements

A solus agreement—one where a trader agrees to restrict his business (or one aspect of it) to a sole supplier or sole outlet—is subject to the scrutiny of the courts to see if the restraint on the trader is reasonable.

A solus agreement whereby a garage proprietor binds himself to buy all his petrol from an oil company, though it is in restraint of trade, is not necessarily unenforceable, for in view of existing arrangements for the distribution of petrol, the widespread incidence of solus agreements and the necessity for oil companies to protect their trade outlets, such an agreement might be reasonable. It depends on the nature and duration of the restrictions imposed on future liberty to trade.

M., who was negotiating to buy a garage, signed as a condition of the sale a solus agreement with P., an oil company. The agreement provided, *inter alia*, that M. would obtain all petrol from P. and sell no other brand of petrol, that M. would advertise only P.'s lubricating oil and use only that oil in the lubricating bay, that M. would not sell or otherwise dispose of the garage without first giving P. first refusal and then only to a person willing to enter into a solus agreement in similar terms, and that the agreement was to continue for 12 years although it could be determined before on three months' notice once 600,000 gallons of P.'s petrol had been sold. *Held*, (i) as the agreement operated as a restriction on the way in which M. could carry on his trade on his own land—P. having no interest by way of mortgage, lease or sale in respect of that land—the doctrine of restraint of trade applied; (ii) the restriction of M.'s power to dispose of his property, the period of restriction and the restriction of the lubricating oils were all unreasonable restrictions; (iii) as these provisions were not severable, the agreement as a whole was in unreasonable restraint of trade and unenforceable: *Petrofina* (*Great Britain*) *Ltd.* v. *Martin* [1966] Ch. 146.

A solus agreement is often combined with a property transaction. The oil company which imposes the tie may own the property on which the service station is situate and grants the manager of the station a lease; or, if the property is owned by the manager of the service station, the oil company may grant him a mortgage on the premises in question; or the premises are leased to the oil company and leased back to the manager of the service station. Where the solus agreement is combined with a property transaction, two questions arise: is the solus agreement and the property transaction a single commercial transaction, and, if so, is the restraint of trade clause in the solus agreement, if unreasonable and therefore void, severable from the property transaction? The answer to these two questions depends on the interpretation of the clauses in question and the factual matrix of the case. Consequently, where there is a mortgage of the premises in question in favour of the oil company, the court may regard the solus and loan agreements and the mortgage as constituting one transaction and the decision will turn on whether or not the restrictions, including any prohibition or restriction on redemption of the mortgage, are reasonable; a restriction of four years and five months was held to be reasonable to afford adequate protection to the oil company in maintaining a stable system of distribution, but a tie of 21 years was held to be excessive and void (*Esso Petroleum Co. Ltd.* v. *Harper's Garage* (*Stourport*) *Ltd.* [1968] A.C. 268). Further, in the case in which the oil company was granted a lease of the site of the service station for 51 years and arranged a lease-back for 21 years, combining the lease-back with a solus agreement containing a tie of the same length as the underlease, it was held that the property transaction and the solus agreement constituted a single transaction, that the tie of 21 years was an unreasonable restraint of trade, but that the offending clauses were severable from those of the underlease which remained effective (*Alec Lobb* (*Garages*) *Ltd.* v. *Total Oil Great Britain Ltd.* [1983] 1 W.L.R. 87).

Amoco Australia was an oil company operating in Australia. Amoco contracted with Rocca that the latter should build a service station on their land and lease it to Amoco who would underlease it to Rocca. The underlease contained tying covenants with respect to the supply of petrol and oil by Amoco, which constituted an unreasonable restraint. The headlease contained a provision that it should be independent of any other agreement. *Held* by the Privy Council (on appeal from the Supreme Court of South Australia), (1) covenants in restraint of trade in a lease had to be treated on the same principles as such terms in contracts; (2) the restraint in the underlease was not severable from the other covenants in the underlease; (3) the headlease and the underlease were parts of a single commercial transaction and the statement in the headlease that it should be independent was not true; (4) consequently, the invalidity of the underlease rendered the headlease also invalid as it could not be severed from the underlease: *Amoco Australia Pty Ltd.* v. *Rocca Bros. Motor Engineering Co. Pty. Ltd.* [1975] A.C. 561.

Other Restraints of Trade

A contract is in restraint of trade if a person, by making use of his superior bargaining power, imposes unfair restrictions on another person's ability to exploit his earning power. This principle, in essence, underlies the whole doctrine of restraint of trade.

Mr. Macaulay (formerly Mr. Instone), a song writer, entered into an agreement with Schroeder Music Publishing Co. Ltd., a powerful firm of publishers of music, whereby he gave Schroeder the exclusive right to publish his songs for five years, with an automatic extension to 10 years if his songs were successful. The publishers did not undertake to publish the song writer's songs but promised him a royalty if they published and sold them. The agreement, which was on a standard form prepared by the publishers, further provided that the publishers could terminate it but no corresponding right was given to the song writer. *Held*, the agreement constituted an unreasonable restraint of trade and was contrary to public policy. It was an unfair restriction on the earning power of the song writer, obtained by the publishers who had made use of their superior bargaining power: *A Schroeder Music Publishing Co. Ltd.* v. *Macaulay* (formerly Instone) (known as *Instone* v. *A. Schroeder Music Publishing Co. Ltd.* [1974] 1 W.L.R. 1308).

In a similar case the Court of Appeal refused to grant publishers of music an interlocutory injunction against the song writer (*Clifford Davis Management Ltd.* v. *W.E.A. Records Ltd.* [1975] 1 W.L.R. 61).

The decision of a trade association to restrict the trading activities of its members is subject to the rules governing a restraint of trade.

The Pharmaceutical Society of Great Britain decided that existing pharmacies should not extend their trading activity to non-traditional goods. Boots objected. *Held*, that the Society's decision was a restraint of trade and contrary to public policy, and the objection of Dickson (who was the retail director of Boots) had to be upheld, since no attempt had been made to justify the restraint: *Dickson* v. *Pharmaceutical Society of Great Britain* [1966] 1 W.L.R. 1539.

The principles relating to restraint of trade are also applicable to restrictions in a partnership agreement purporting to apply after dissolution of the partnership or expulsion of a partner from it. In the case of a partnership of **general medical practitioners** section

35(1) of the National Health Services Act 1946 prohibits the sale of goodwill of a general medical practice or any part of it; nevertheless the tendency of patients whom partners had treated to resort to the practice for further treatment is a partnership asset (though an unsaleable one) which it is legitimate to protect. Thus a promise by a doctor partner not to set up as a general practitioner within a radius of two miles of the practice after leaving it has been upheld (*Kerr* v. *Morris* [1987] Ch. 90). Where medical practitioners are in general medical practice as partners, a covenant purporting to prohibit a partner after retirement from engaging in practice as a "medical practitioner" would be too wide, as it would prevent him from practising as a medical consultant (*Lyne-Pirkis* v. *Jones* [1969] 1 W.L.R. 1293; *Peyton* v. *Mindham* [1972] 1 W.L.R. 8).

Normally the question whether a term of a contract constitutes an unreasonable restraint of trade has to be decided by reference to the wording of the term, construed in the context of the business which it is designed to protect. But a clause which, on its face, is innocent may, in connection with other clauses of the agreement, produce a restrictive effect and then has to be treated as an unreasonable restraint (*Stenhouse Australia Ltd.* v. *Phillips* [1974] A.C. 391 (P.C.)). Moreover, a restraint clause which, at its inception, is not unreasonable cannot be enforced so long as the person in whose favour it is stipulated carries out his own obligations under the contract in a discriminatory manner which causes hardship to the person restrained.

Shell U.K. Ltd. had a reasonable and, on principle, enforceable solus agreement with Lostock Garage Ltd., a small garage in Cheshire. Under the agreement Shell were obliged to supply the garage with petrol. In December 1975 there was a price war in petrol. Shell operated a support scheme enabling garages which had suffered a drop in sales of 40,000 gallons in 1975 to sell petrol at a cut price. Lostock did not profit from that scheme because, being a small garage, its drop was only 13,000 gallons. Lostock was thus faced with a situation in which all garages in the neighbourhood, including those supplied by Shell, sold petrol at a cut price but Lostock was bound by the solus agreement to sell at a higher price. Lostock then began to buy petrol from a cheaper source. *Held*, so long as Shell discriminated against Lostock, the restraint was not enforceable: *Shell U.K. Ltd.* v. *Lostock Garage Ltd.* [1976] 1 W.L.R. 1187.

Restrictive trade practices and resale prices

This subject is treated in Chap. 20, *post.*

Gaming contracts

By section 18 of the Gaming Act 1845:

(a) contracts by way of gaming or wagering are null and void and
(b) no action can be brought to recover money won upon any wager.

By the Gaming Act 1892 any promise, express or implied:

(a) to pay any person any sum of money paid by him in respect of any contract rendered null and void by the Gaming Act 1845; or
(b) to pay any sum of money by way of commission, fee, reward, or otherwise in respect of any such contract, or of any services in connection therewith;

is null and void and no action can be brought to recover any such sum of money.

A wagering contract is not illegal, but the law gives no assistance in enforcing it, and it is therefore a void contract.

A wager is an agreement between two parties that upon the happening or ascertainment of some uncertain event, one party shall pay a sum of money to the other, which party is to pay depending on the issue of the event. Neither party must have any other interest in the contract than the sum he shall win or lose. If either of the parties may win but cannot lose, or may lose but cannot win, it is not a wagering contract.

In contracts on the Stock Exchange and other commercial exchanges, if the parties intend that no stock or goods shall be delivered, but that "differences" only shall be accounted for, then the contracts are void as being wagers. The fact that it is provided that either party may require completion of the purchase does not prevent this result (*Universal Stock Exchange* v. *Strachan* [1896] A.C. 166). If, however, the contracts genuinely contemplate the transfer of stock or goods, but the parties, instead of carrying out the actual bargain, agree that the difference between prices shall be paid instead, the contracts will be enforceable.

B., a metal broker, acted for S. in speculative transactions on the London Metal Exchange. The contracts were legally enforceable, but neigher party expected to have to take or give delivery. A balance was struck when the account was closed and the difference paid by B., who sued S. to recover the amount. *Held*, the transactions, though speculative, were not gaming contracts and B. could recover from S.: *Barnett* v. *Sanker* (1925) 41 T.L.R. 660.

A contract of gaming is a wager upon any game, such as a horse-race or a football-match. Gaming is largely regulated by the Gaming Act 1968 but the Act does not apply where:

(a) the game involves playing or staking against a bank, whether the bank is held by one of the players or not;
(b) the nature of the game is such that the chances in the game are not equally favourable to all the players; or
(c) the nature of the game is such that the chances in it lie wholly or partly between the players and some other person, and those chances are not as favourable to the players as they are to the other person (Gaming Act 1968, s.2).

The prohibition of gaming does not apply where:

(i) the gaming takes place on a domestic occasion in a private dwelling or in a hostel, hall of residence or similar establishment which is not carried on by way of trade or business and the players consist exclusively or mainly of residents or inmates of that establishment (section 2(2) of the Act of 1968);
(ii) the gaming takes place in licensed premises or at a club or a miner's welfare institute which is duly registered (section 1(1)). These licensed or registered premises are strictly controlled;
(iii) special provisions apply to gaming machines, gaming at entertainments not held for private gain, and gaming which constitutes the provision of amusements with prizes (section 1(2));
(iv) certain types of gaming, such as dominoes and cribbage, are exempted from the prohibition of gaming in public places, *e.g.* in public houses (section 6).

The Gaming Act 1968 draws a distinction between "hard gaming" and bingo and contains relaxations in favour of bingo club premises (section 20).

A competition which has no element of skill, and does not satisfy the statutory requirements, is an unlawful lottery. In deciding whether a competition is a lottery or not, a realistic view must be taken and regard must be had to the way in which the competition is conducted (*Singette Ltd.* v. *Martin* [1971] A.C. 407).

A wagering contract is more comprehensive than a gaming contract, and includes all kinds of wagers. A contract of insurance is not a wagering contract, because the insured must have an insurable interest in the subject-matter insured before the contract is made. The effect of this is that he stands to lose on the happening of the event insured against, quite apart from the contract of insurance.

The following points should be noted:

1. An agent employed to make wagering contracts must hand over to his principal any winnings he has received (*De Mattos* v. *Benjamin* (1894) 63 L.J.Q.B. 248), but he cannot compel his principal to reimburse him losses he has paid away on his behalf: Gaming Act 1892.

The plaintiffs, A. R. Dennis & Co. Ltd., operated a betting shop. The defendant, Mr. Campbell, was the manager of the shop. Mr. Campbell allowed a customer to place a bet with his employers for £1,000 on credit terms. It was not the custom of betting shops to allow credit facilities for gaming, and, if such facilities were granted, the owners of the betting shop could not recover the amount from the customer because the contract was void as a wagering contract. Thereupon Dennis as principals sued Mr. Campbell as their employee, alleging that he had made a bet which he was not employed to make. *Held*, the principals could not recover from the employee because the Gaming Act 1845, s.18, provided that no suit could be brought for the recovery of any sum alleged to be won upon a wager: *A. R. Dennis & Co. Ltd.* v. *Campbell* [1978] Q.B. 365.

2. Money paid to a stakeholder to abide by the result of a wager can be recovered from him at any time before it has been paid away (*Burge* v. *Ashley and Smith Ltd.* [1900] 1 Q.B. 744). This is so even if the person demanding the return of the money has lost the wager, provided that the demand is made before the money has been paid over.

3. Money knowingly lent for the purpose of gaming in England

cannot be recovered (*Carlton Hall Club* v. *Laurence* [1929] 2 K.B. 153); but if it is lent to make bets in a country where betting is lawful it can be recovered (*Saxby* v. *Fulton* [1909] 2 K.B. 208). Money lent to pay bets already lost cannot be recovered (*Macdonald* v. *Green* [1951] 1 K.B. 594), but if it is lent to enable the loser to pay such bets, though not so as to bind him to do so, it can be recovered (*Re O'Shea* [1911] 2 K.B. 981). Where chips are issued to members of a club, a member's promise to repay any gaming losses through a weekly account is void (*C.H.T. Ltd.* v. *Ward* [1965] 2 Q.B. 63). Licensed clubs are prohibited from allowing any form of credit for gaming (except the cashing of cheques before the issue of chips) by section 16 of the Gaming Act 1968 (*Ladup Ltd.* v. *Siu*, *The Times*, November 24, 1983).

4. A new contract to pay money lost by a wager cannot be enforced, whether there is fresh consideration or not, if the intention of the parties in making it is to enable the money so lost to be recovered.

H. owed £3,635 to W. for lost bets. An order was made by Tattersalls that H. should pay £635 within fourteen days and the remainder by monthly instalments of £100. H. failed to comply with the order, but gave W. a cheque for £635 and a promise to pay the instalments in consideration of W. not enforcing the order. The instalments were not paid. *Held*, H. was not liable to pay, in spite of the fresh consideration, as W.'s action was to recover money won upon a wager which was prohibited by the Gaming Act 1845, s.18: *Hill* v. *William Hill* (*Park Lane*) *Ltd.* [1949] A.C. 530.

5. **Securities given for gaming contracts** are deemed to be given for an illegal consideration. They are therefore void as between the parties, but holders in due course who are not aware of their origin can sue upon them: Gaming Act 1835. Securities given for other wagering contracts are given for no consideration, and, therefore, although they are void as between the parties, they can be sued upon by third parties to whom they have been assigned without their having to prove ignorance of their origin.

6. Numerous enactments not mentioned here, notably the Betting and Gaming Act 1960 and the Gaming Act 1968, contain detailed provisions for the use of premises as licensed betting offices, the licensing and registration of bookmakers and their agents, the provision of amusements with prices, amusement machines and other matters.

7. **Lotteries** are subject to special regulation, mainly contained in the Lotteries and Amusements Act 1976. Lotteries which do not constitute gambling are unlawful, except as provided by that Act (section 1). The Act admits, subject to specified conditions, exceptions in the case of small lotteries incidental to entertainments such as a bazaar, sale of work, fete, dinner, dance, sporting or athletic event or other entertainment of a similar character (section 3); private lotteries (section 4); lotteries arranged by charitable or similar societies (section 5); or local authorities (section 60).

Other enactments

The Race Relations Act 1976 makes it unlawful to discriminate against a person on the ground of colour, race or ethnic or national origins in a number of specified situations. These situations are in the employment field (see p. 254, *post*); education; the provision of goods, facilities or services; or in the disposal or management of premises. It is also unlawful to publish or cause to be published discriminatory advertisements (section 29). The Act admits, however, important exceptions in which such discrimination is not unlawful.

The Act further provides that a term of contract shall be void if it provides for anything unlawful by the Act; where it provides for discrimination which is not unlawful but not authorised by the Act, it is unenforceable against the person against whom it is directed, but this provision is subject to certain exceptions (section 72). In the employment field, the industrial tribunals have jurisdiction to administer remedies, including the award of compensation (sections 54–56). In other situations jurisdiction is vested in the courts and the Commission for Racial Equality may apply to the County Court for an injunction against persistent offenders (section 62).

The Sex Discrimination Act 1975 renders unlawful certain kinds of sex discrimination and discrimination on the ground of marriage and establishes the Equal Opportunities Commission with the Function of working towards the elimination of such discrimination.

The Trade Description Act 1968 which provides criminal sanctions in the case of false trade descriptions (see p. 355, *post*), provides that a contract for the supply of goods shall not be void or unenforceable by reason only of a contravention of the Act of 1968 (section 35). If such a contravention constitutes a misrepresentation, the normal civil remedies for misrepresentation (see p. 93, *ante*) are available.

Effect of illegality

Contracts tainted by illegality are normally unenforceable

The effect of illegality on a contract is to render it unenforceable, the maxim being *ex turpi causa non oritur actio*. The law gives no assistance of any kind to the guilty party in such a case, and consequently he cannot recover any money paid or goods supplied under such a contract, nor can he sue for damages or the price of goods if, in order to be successful, he has to rely on his own illegality (*Yin* v. *Sam* [1962] A.C. 304).

B. a tobacconist, was put on the stop-list by a tobacco association for breach of its rules. Concealing his identity and by means of an agent, he induced S. to sell him cigarettes, and paid £72. 19s. for them. Later S. suspected the fraud and refused to deliver the cigarettes. *Held*, B. could not recover the £72. 19s. paid, because it was paid for an illegal purpose, namely, to obtain goods from S. by false pretences: *Berg* v. *Sadler* [1937] 2 K.B. 158.

When an action is admitted although unlawfulness or illegality has occurred

The rule that the courts will not entertain an action founded on, or brought in connection with, an illegal contract is subject to the following exceptions:

1. Where the parties are not *in pari delicto* the innocent party may recover anything he has paid under the contract. For example, when a person was induced by fraud to take over some insurance policies on a life in which he had no insurable interest (such a contract being illegal), he was entitled to recover the premiums he had paid under the illegal contract (*Hughes* v. *Liverpool Victoria Friendly Society* [1916] 2 K.B. 482).

2. Where the illegal purpose has not been carried out, one party to the contract may repent his illegal purpose and if he does so before performance takes place the law will assist him. If, however,

non-performance is due, not to his repentance but to other causes, the law will not assist him.

X. wanted to send his wife to Italy for her health. He agreed with Y. that Y. should provide her in Italy with Italian currency to the value of £150, contrary to the Exchange Control Act 1947 then in force, and deposited shares with Y. as security for repayment. X.'s wife went to Italy, but Y. failed to supply the currency. *Held*, as the contract was illegal and the failure of the contract was Y.'s conduct and not X.'s repentance, the action failed: *Bigos* v. *Bousted* [1951] 1 All E.R. 92.

3. A contract can be enforced to the extent allowed where statute provides specifically for it to be enforceable despite being illegal. A statute may, for example, provide that the validity of contracts shall be unaffected by the illegality (see, *e.g.* the Trade Descriptions Act, p. 138 above). Statute may take a slightly different approach as where an insurer makes an insurance contract of a kind which he was not authorised by the Insurance Companies Act 1982 to make; the consequences of this are spelt out by the Financial Services Act 1986, s.132. Those are that, although the contract is not enforceable by the insurer, the insured has an option either to undo the contract and recover his premiums or to enforce the contract. This section puts an end to a series of earlier conflicting cases some of which decided that the insured could only recover his premiums and others of which held that the insured could enforce the contract by making a claim in the usual way. Now, by statute the insured can elect to do either.

Illegal act committed in the course of performance of a legal contract

It happens sometimes that in the course of performance of a perfectly legal contract an act is committed which is made illegal by statute but which is not directly connected with the object of the contract. Here a question of interpretation of the statute in question arises. If it is the intention of the legislature that the illegality in performance shall result in the prohibition of the whole contract, no action can be brought on it. That is, in particular, the case if both parties know that the chosen mode of performance contravenes the statutory prohibition.

The plaintiffs were manufacturers of heavy engineering equipment known as tube banks. They arranged with the defendant, a small company of road hauliers, for the carriage of two tube banks from Stockton-on-Tees to Hull for shipment to Poland. Contrary to the regulations made under the Road Traffic Act 1960 each of the tube banks, which weighed 25 tons, was loaded on a vehicle which had an unladen weight of 10 tons. According to the regulations, the maximum total weight allowed was 30 tons and that limit was, to the knowledge of both parties, exceeded by five tons. In addition, the load was top-heavy and unsuited to be carried in the vehicles in question. On the road, one of the vehicles toppled over and the load was damaged. In an action for damages, *held*, that, although the contract was lawful in its inception, its performance was illegal to the knowledge of both parties and consequently the plaintiffs could not recover damages from the defendants: *Ashmore, Benson, Pease & Co. Ltd.* v. *A. V. Dawson Ltd.* [1973] 1 W.L.R. 828.

On the other hand, if Parliament intended that the illegality should only have other consequences, *e.g.* the guilty person should be liable to a penalty, the contract is not tainted by the illegality and remains enforceable in a court of law.

The *St. John*, which was registered in Panama, carried a consignment of grain from the United States to England. When the ship arrived in Birkenhead it was found that she was overloaded and that her loadline was submerged. This was an offence under the Merchant Shipping (Safety and Loadlines Conventions) Act 1932. The defendants who were holders of a bill of lading refused to pay the freight on the overloaded portion of the cargo. *Held*, on the true construction of the Act of 1932, contracts for the carriage of goods were not within its ambit and the defendants were liable to pay the retained part of the freight: *St. John Shipping Corporation* v. *Joseph Rank Ltd.* [1957] 1 Q.B. 267.

A. arranged with S. to carry a consignment of whisky from Leeds to London docks. The goods were stolen in transit owing to the negligence of S. In an action for damages by A., S. pleaded that the contract of carriage was illegal because S.'s van was not licensed to carry the goods. *Held*, the defence failed; the contract was not *ex facie* illegal and public policy did not require the court to refuse aid to A. who did not know that the contract would be performed illegally: *Archbolds (Freightage) Ltd.* v. *S. Spanglett Ltd.* [1961] 1 Q.B. 374.

A landlady let an unfurnished room in her house to a tenant. She gave her a rent book which did not contain all the information required by the Landlord and Tenant Act 1962 and the Rent Book (Forms of Notice) Regulations 1965, and thereby she committed an offence. She sued the tenant for arrears of rent, but the tenant contended that she was precluded from recovering the rent owing to the insufficiency of the rent book. *Held*, the landlady could recover the rent. She had not to rely on the rent book as an essential ingredient of her cause of action and the rent book was only a statutory requirement collateral to the contract. It was not the intention of Parliament, when requiring a rent book in a specified form, that a landlord who failed to comply with this requirement should be precluded from recovering the rent: *Shaw* v. *Groom* [1970] 2 Q.B. 504.

Certain land situated in Richmond, Surrey, was owned by Curragh Investments Ltd., a company incorporated in the Isle of Man, which in England was treated as an overseas company but had failed to register the documents required to be registered under sections 407 and 416 of the Companies Act 1948. The company sold the land to the defendant. The latter, having discovered the company's failure to register the documents, refused to perform the contract of sale. *Held*, (1) no question of illegality of the contract arose because there was no nexus or link between the contract and the statutory requirements which were infringed; and (2) even if the vendor was in breach of sections 407 and 416, there was no justification for the purchaser to refuse the performance of the contract: *Curragh Investments Ltd.* v. *Cook* [1974] 1 W.L.R. 1559.

Severance of illegal parts

If only part of a contract is illegal, the whole contract will not be void if the illegal part can be severed from the rest of the contract. The question of severability of the illegal part of the contract has already been considered in connection with employment contracts and solus agreements (see pp. 126–131, *ante*).

Mr. Ailion, the lessee of a flat which he occupied as a protected tenant, agreed to assign the remainder of his lease to Mr. Spiekermann and his wife. The rent was £850 per annum and the purchasers agreed to pay £3,750 for certain furniture which was worth much less; the purchase price for the furniture thus contained a premium prohibited by the Rent Act 1968. *Held*, the illegal element, *i.e.* the premium, was severable. Consequently, the lease was valid and the Spiekermanns were entitled to specific performance, but without payment of the illegal premium represented by the excess purchase price of the furniture: *Ailion* v. *Spiekermann* [1976] Ch. 158.

If, however, the whole purpose of the contract is an illegal one, the court will not make a new contract for the parties by attempting to cut out those portions which are illegal and enforce the rest.

N. was employed as secretary and accountant at a salary of £13 a week with £6 a week expenses. Both parties knew his expenses were less than £1 a week. *Held*, the contract was to evade tax and was illegal. It was impossible to sever the part dealing with salary from the part dealing with expenses, so that the whole was unenforceable: *Napier* v. *National Business Agency Ltd.* [1951] 2 All E.R. 264.

Generally where parties enter into a lawful contract and there is an ancillary provision which is illegal but exists for the exclusive benefit of the plaintiff, the court usually will, if the justice of the case so requires and there is no public policy objection, permit the plaintiff if he so wishes to enforce the contract, but without the illegal ancillary provision.

The defendant agreed to buy from the seller the latter's shares in A. Ltd. The purchase price was secured by mortgages given by N. Ltd. (of which the defendant was a director) over its property. Because N. Ltd. was a subsidiary of A. Ltd., N. Ltd. was thus granting security to guarantee the purchase of shares in its holding company. For this reason the mortgages were illegal as contravening the Companies Act. *Held* by the Privy Council (on appeal from Australia) that the mortgages, being ancillary to the main transaction of the defendant's purchase of the shares, could be severed: *Carney* v. *Herbert* [1984] 3 W.L.R. 1303.

Passing of title under a fully executed illegal contract

If a contract of sale or a similar transaction is illegal, the buyer cannot claim the goods from the seller because to do so he would have to rely on the illegal contract and the court will not assist him in its enforcement.

The position is, however, different if the illegal contract has been fully executed and the seller has transferred the title to the goods to the buyer. Title can pass under an illegal contract and when it has passed the buyer has the normal remedies of an owner; he can, in particular, sue in trespass or detinue (*Singh* v. *Ali* [1960] A.C. 167) or in conversion (*Belvoir Finance Co. Ltd.* v. *Stapleton*, below).

The plaintiffs, a finance company, bought cars and hired them out to a car hire company on hire-purchase terms which were illegal to the knowledge of both parties because the deposit paid by the car hire company was much smaller than prescribed by the hire-purchase regulations then in force. The car hire company, of which the defendant was assistant manager, sold the cars (which had never been delivered into the possession of the plaintiffs) without authority of the plaintiffs. *Held*, although the hire-purchase contracts were illegal, they were fully executed and a valid title to the cars had passed under them to the plaintiffs. Their claim for damages for conversion against the defendant was successful: *Belvoir Finance Co. Ltd.* v. *Stapleton* [1971] 1 Q.B. 210.

CHAPTER 8

DISCHARGE OF CONTRACT

A CONTRACT may be discharged by:

(a) performance,
(b) agreement,
(c) termination by notice,
(d) acceptance of breach, or
(e) frustration.

PERFORMANCE

If both parties have performed what they agree to do under the contract, the contract is discharged. Performance must be strictly in accordance with the terms of the contract to be a discharge.

Time

Time for performance may be fixed in the contract. In that case, the contract must be performed within that time when time is of the essence of the contract. Time is of the essence of the contract when the parties have expressly said so in the contract or when the circumstances of the contract show that they intended it to be so. In mercantile contracts which provide for *performance* in a specified time the general rule is that the contract must be performed in that time, otherwise it is broken. Stipulations as to time of *payment*, however, are not as a rule of the essence of the contract in the absence of a contrary intention. The Sale of Goods Act, 1979, s.10, applies this rule to contract of sale of goods.

If no time for performance is agreed, performance is to be made within a reasonable time.

The requirement that performance at the agreed or a reasonable time shall be of the essence of the contract can be waived by showing indulgence, but normally the strictness of the contract can be restored by notice or, if the circumstances indicate such an intention, even without a notice (see p. 153, *post*).

Tender

Tender is an offer of performance in accordance with the terms of the contract. If such a tender is made but the other party refuses to accept it, the party tendering is free from liability under the contract if the tender was made under such circumstances that the party to whom the tender was made had a reasonable opportunity of examining the goods or money tendered. The object of tender is to show that the party tendering was ready and willing to perform his obligations under the contract and was only prevented from doing so by the act of the other party. Accordingly, if goods are tendered by the seller and refused by the buyer, the seller if free from liability. A tender of money, on the other hand, only discharges the tenderer if it is followed by payment of the sum tendered into court on action being brought.

In tender of money the exact amount owed must be tendered without any request for change. Legal tender are Bank of England notes for any amount (Currency and Bank Notes Act 1954, s.1); gold coins for any amount; coins of cupro-nickel or silver exceeding 10 pence in value up to 10 pounds, coins of cupro-nickel or silver of not more than 10 pence in value up to five pounds only, coins of bronze up to 20 pence only (Coinage Act 1971, s.2 as amended by Currency Act 1983).

Tender by cheque or other negotiable instrument is not good tender, unless the creditor does not object to this form of payment, but only to the amount tendered. Tender must be unconditional and must comply with the conditions of the contract as to time, place and mode of performance. It may be made "under protest" so as to reserve the right of the payer to dispute the amount.

Payment

Payment of the amount due under a contract is a discharge. Payment of a smaller amount is not a discharge, unless it is accepted by the creditor as being full satisfaction **and** either an estoppel can be raised or else the payment of the smaller amount is made at an earlier date or in different manner from that prescribed by the contract, *e.g.* at the debtor's instead of the creditor's place (for estoppel, see waiver p. 152 below). The following points should be noted—

1. Payment to an agent is a good discharge if the agent is authorised or held out as having authority to receive payment.

2. Payment to one of several joint creditors discharges the debt.

3. Payment by a third party is not a discharge, unless it was made by the third party as agent for the debtor, or has been ratified by, the debtor. The agency or the ratification may be implied.

S. was R.'s tenant and C. was R.'s agent to collect the rent. S. owed £260 arrears, but C., knowing that R. was old and poor, accounted to R. as if the rent had been paid. C. distrained and it was argued that the distress was wrongful because R. had been paid. *Held*, C.'s payments to R. were not made as agent for S., S. was a debtor and the distress was lawful: *Smith* v. *Cox* [1940] 2 K.B. 558.

4. A receipt is evidence, but not conclusive evidence of payment. It is therefore always open to the person who has given the receipt to show either that he has not in fact received payment or that the receipt was given by mistake or obtained by fraud. Again, payment may be proved by parol evidence although no receipt was taken, or, if taken, has been subsequently lost.

The practice of not giving receipts unless asked for, is common today because it is provided by the Cheques Act 1957, s.3, that an unindorsed cheque which appears to have been paid by the banker on whom it is drawn shall be evidence of the receipt of the money by the payee.

5. Payment by cheque or any other negotiable instrument is, in the absence of any agreement to the contrary, a conditional payment only; that is, the creditor, on the dishonour of the negotiable instrument, may sue either on the original contract or on the negotiable instrument. Pending payment or dishonour of the instrument, the creditor's right of action is suspended. A creditor is not bound to take a negotiable instrument in payment of a debt, but may insist on payment in cash.

6. Payment by post is not a good payment in the event of the letter being lost in the post, unless the creditor requested the debtor to pay by post.

C. had bought goods from P. for many years and had always paid him by cheque through the post, without any objection being made by P. One of C.'s cheques was lost in the post. *Held*, there was no payment, because there was nothing from which a request by P. for payment by cheque could be inferred so as to make the loss during transmission by post fall upon him: *Pennington* v. *Crossley & Son* (1897) 77 L.T. 43.

Even a request to pay through the post does not absolve the debtor from paying in a reasonable manner and in accordance with business practice.

An insurance company sent to M. a written notice for payment of £48 and asking him "when remitting" to return the notice. M. sent £48 in Treasury notes by registered post and the letter was stolen. *Held*, that there was no payment. Although the words "when remitting" authorised M. to pay by post, they did not authorise him to depart from usual business methods and send so large a sum as £48 in notes: *Mitchell-Henry* v. *Norwich Life Insurance Society* [1918] 2 K.B. 67.

Where there is a request by the creditor or an agreement between the parties that payment should be made by post, payment is established by posting even though the letter be lost in the post. (*Thairlwell* v. *G.N. Ry.* [1910] 2 K.B. 509).

N., a milliner, wrote to R., a customer, saying "the favour of a cheque within a week will oblige." R. sent a cheque by post, but it was stolen in transit and cashed by the thief. In an action by N., *held*, N.'s letter to R. was a request to pay by post, and the posting of the letter with the cheque was a good payment: *Norman* v. *Ricketts* (1886) 3 T.L.R. 182.

When periodical payments have to be made under a contract, evidence is admissible to prove the method of payment accepted by the parties. If the method is by post, delay in the post excuses late payment.

Hire under a charterparty was payable in London on the 27th of each month, the owners having a right to cancel in default of prompt payment. The practice was to pay by cheque posted to a London bank. The cheque was sent in time to arrive on September 27, but was late owing to postal delay caused by war. The owners cancelled the charterpolicy. *Held*, payment was made in time: *Tankexpress* v. *Compagnie Financière Belge des Petroles* [1949] A.C. 76.

7. A settled account is an arrangement whereby two persons, with

mutual debits and credits, strike a balance which they agree represents the financial results of their transactions. On payment of a settled account the transactions cannot be reopened. There is no settled account when one party only renders an account which is accepted and paid by the other.

A. appointed R. their sole licensees for the manufacture and sale of their road-making specialities, payment to be made by R. of royalties on the materials they manufactured under the licence. A. were given power to inspect accounts. For many years R. submitted statements showing the materials manufactured and made payments accordingly which A. accepted. A. applied for inspection of R.'s books over the period of the licence. *Held*, the principle of settled account did not apply where the whole account was to be rendered by one party to the other, and A. could inspect R.'s books for the six years before action: *Anglo-American Asphalt Co.* v. *Russell & Co.* [1945] 2 All E.R. 324.

A bank is entitled to combine several accounts of a customer, even if kept at different branches (*Barclays Bank Ltd.* v. *Okenarhe* [1966] 2 Lloyd's Rep. 87), and to set off credits in one against debits in another. This right of combination is analogous to the general lien of the banker (see p. 515, *post*). But this right of combination may be excluded by an agreement, express or implied, to keep the accounts separate.

H. had a loan account with W. bank. This account was overdrawn by £11,339. H. also had a trading account with the L. Bank which was operated on a credit basis and out of which the wages for H.'s employees were paid. In April 1968 H. agreed with W. that H. should transfer the trading account from L. to W. and that the accounts should then be operated on the following basis: the loan account should become No. 1 account and should be frozen, and the trading account should become No. 2 account which had to be constantly kept in credit and to which the interest for the loan on No. 1 account should be debited; W. agreed to adhere to this arrangement for four months, in the absence of materially changed circumstances. On the morning of June 12, 1968 H. paid a cheque drawn in its favour of £8,611 into No. 2 account. In the afternoon of the same day H. went into voluntary winding up and a liquidator was appointed. W. claimed to combine No. 1 and No. 2 accounts and to set off the credit of £8,611 on No. 2 account against H.'s debit of £11,339 on No. 1 account, but the liquidator contended that W. was not entitled to combine the accounts, that the £8,611 had to be used for the benefit of the general creditors, and that W. had to prove for the £11,339 as an unsecured creditor. W. argued that the debit on the No. 1 account could be set off against the credit on the No. 2 account because the two items amounted to "mutual dealings" within section 31 of the Bankruptcy Act 1914, which was applicable by virtue of section 317 of the Companies Act 1948. H. argued that W. had contracted that the two accounts should not be combined. *Held*, (1) there were "mutual dealings" within section 31 and that section was mandatory and could not be contracted out; and (2) even if it was possible to contract out of section 31, the agreement between W. and H., on its true construction, had only been intended to be operative while H. was a going concern and consequently had come to an end: *National Westminster Bank Ltd.* v. *Halesowen Presswork & Assemblies Ltd.* (known as *Halesowen Presswork & Assemblies Ltd.* v. *National Westminster Bank Ltd.* [1972] A.C. 785.

If a bank receives a cheque payable to a company which is its customer on condition that the cheque shall only be used for the payment of dividend declared by the company and it places the proceeds of the cheque into a special dividend account, it has received the cheque in pursuance of a fiduciary relationship or trust and cannot combine the dividend account with the other accounts of the customer; if the customer is wound up before the dividend is paid, there is a resulting test for the benefit of the drawer of the cheque and the bank must repay the money to him (*Quistclose Investments Ltd.* v. *Rolls Razor Ltd.* [1970] A.C. 567).

Appropriation of payments

When a debtor owes several debts to the same creditor and a payment is made, it is a question to which debt the payment should be appropriated. The rules are:

1. The debtor can appropriate, expressly or by implication, provided he does so at the time of payment. For example, if the debtor owes £100 and £57, and sends a cheque for £57, it will be an implied appropriation, in the absence of anything to the contrary, to the second debt. A cheque for £50 would be unappropriated by the debtor and would bring into operation the next rule.

2. In the absence of an appropriation by the debtor, the creditor can appropriate at any time. A creditor can appropriate the debtor's payment to a debt which the creditor cannot enforce by action because it is statute-barred, or if it is a guarantee, which he cannot prove in the form required by the Statute of Frauds 1677, but the creditor cannot appropriate the debtor's payment to a debt which is illegal.

S. was an unregistered dentist who could not recover any fee for performing a dental operation, but could sue for the price of materials supplied. S.'s bill against P. was £45, £20 for services and £25 for materials supplied. P. paid £20 without appropriating it. In an action by S. *held*, (i) S. could appropriate the £20 to the payment of his professional fees; (ii) the appropriation could be made by S. for the first time in the witness box: *Seymour* v. *Pickett* [1905] 1 K.B. 715.

3. In the case of a current account there is "no room for any other appropriation than that which arises from the order in which the receipts and payments take place and are carried into the account. Presumably, it is the sum first paid in that is first drawn out. It is the first item in the debit side of the account that is discharged or reduced by the first item on the credit side; the appropriation is made by the very act of setting the two items against each other": *per* Sir William Grant in *Clayton's* case (1816) 1 Mer. 572.

Example—X. guarantees Y.'s account with the bank. When Y. is overdrawn up to £1,000, X. revokes his guarantee as to future transactions. The bank keeps the old account going and Y. pays in various sums amounting to £1,000, but drawn out sums equal to that amount. As soon as Y. had paid in £1,000, the liability of X. to the bank will be extinguished, because these payments in will be appropriated by the rule in *Clayton's* case to the satisfaction of the overdraft existing when they were paid in. See *Deeley* v. *Lloyd's Bank Ltd.* [1912] A.C. 756.

This rule only applies to current accounts, but it is not confined to banking accounts. It includes "current accounts for goods supplied and work done rendered periodically with a balance carried forward" (*per* Scrutton L.J. in *Albermale Supply Co. Ltd.* v. *Hind & Co.* [1928] 1 K.B. 307, 319). It does not mean that when an account containing several items is rendered by the creditor, a payment by the debtor "on account" is appropriated to the first item on the account. In such a case the creditor can appropriate as stated in the second rule (*The Mecca* [1897] A.C. 286).

In spite of the rule in *Clayton's* case, the balance owed on current account is a single and undivided debt and for that reason payment constitutes part payment of that debt within the meaning of the Limitation Act 1980 and revives the whole outstanding balance (*Re Footman, Bower & Co. Ltd.* [1961] Ch. 443).

Waiver

It is a common experience in commercial practice that a party does not insist on its strict contractual rights but, when requested by the other party, shows some indulgence. Thus, a contract of sale may provide for delivery on February 1 but the buyer may ask the seller to defer delivery until March 1. Or a building contract may provide for payment within one month after completion of the work and, the work being completed on April 1, the owner may ask the builder to agree to payment on May 15.

If in these cases the party who agrees to the relaxation of the strict terms of contract receives consideration, a **variation** of the contract takes place and the new agreement is binding on both parties.

More difficult, from the legal point of view, but more frequent in practice is the case where an indulgence shown by a party is not supported by consideration. Here the doctrine of **waiver** applies. The courts have evolved the following rules.

1. The party in whose favour the indulgence has been exercised cannot later claim that the other party has not performed his obligations in time. If, *e.g.* the contract of sale provides for delivery on February 1 but, by request of the buyer, the seller postpones delivery until March 1 and then tenders the goods, the buyer cannot refuse acceptance on the ground that the goods ought to have been tendered on February 1 (*Levey* v. *Goldberg* [1922] 1 K.B. 688).

2. The party who grants indulgence is also bound by his undertaking. "If one party, by his conduct, leads another to believe that the strict rights arising under the contract will not be insisted upon, intending that the other should act on that belief, and he does act on it, then the first party will not afterwards be allowed to insist on the strict rights when it would be inequitable for him to do so" (*per* Denning L.J. in *Plasticmoda S.p.A.* v. *Davidsons* (*Manchester*) *Ltd.* [1952] 1 Lloyd's Rep. 527). The rule, which is an extension of the rule in *Central London Property Trust Ltd.* v. *High Trees House Ltd.* ([1947] 1 K.B. 130, see p. 57 *ante*), has been developed from the equitable principle of estoppel by conduct.

A contract for the sale of flour to a buyer in Greece provided for payment under a banker's confirmed documentary credit, each shipment to be a separate contract. The buyer opened an unconfirmed credit. The sellers did not at first reject that credit but made some shipments and received payment under it. Later they cancelled the contract on the ground that the credit was not confirmed. *Held*, (i) by accepting payment under the unconfirmed credit the sellers had waived the right to insist on a confirmed credit; (ii) in spite of their acceptance of the unconfirmed credit, they could still have given the buyer reasonable notice of their insistence that the credit must be confirmed for future shipments; (iii) they could not cancel the contract without such notice: *Panoutsos* v. *Raymond Hadley Corporation of New York* [1917] 2 K.B. 473.

3. If no time limit is provided for the forbearance, the party who has agreed to relax the strict terms of the contract can unilaterally restore them. This is normally done by giving the other party notice of reasonable length that the indulgence is over.

C. agreed to sell to O. a Rolls-Royce chassis with a body built on it, delivery to be made by March 20. It was not delivered then. O. pressed for delivery and finally said in June that he would not accept delivery after July 25. Delivery was not made then and O. bought another car. Delivery was offered in October but O. refused it. C. sued for the price. *Held*, the action failed. O. had waived the original time for delivery but was entitled, on giving reasonable notice, again to make time of the essence of the contract: *Charles Rickards Ltd.* v. *Oppenhaim* [1950] 1 K.B. 616.

But such notice is not essential. It is not required if it is clear from the circumstances that the time of relaxation is over and the strictness of the contract is restored (*Tool Metal Manufacturing Co. Ltd.* v. *Tungsten Electric Co. Ltd.* [1955] 1 W.L.R. 761).

Agreement

A contract may be discharged by agreement in any one of the following ways: (a) release, (b) new agreement, (c) accord and satisfaction, (d) provision for discharge contained in the contract itself.

Release

At any time before the performance of a contract is due, or after a breach of the contract has taken place, a release of the obligations under the contract may be granted by deed. Such a deed dissolves the contract and is binding, whether or not it is based on consideration.

New agreement

A contract may be rescinded by a new agreement between the parties at any time before it is discharged by performance or in some other way. Discharge by mutual agreement can only take place as long as there is something to be done by each party to the contract; if one party has completely performed all his obligations under the contract, discharge must be either by release by deed or by accord and satisfaction (*per* Parke B., *Foster* v. *Dawber* (1851) 6 Ex. at p. 851). An exception to this is a bill of exchange, which can be discharged in writing or by delivering the bill to the acceptor (Bills of Exchange Act 1882, s.62). In the case of a contract completely executed by one party, there is no consideration for his discharging the other party from his obligations under the contract.

The agreement for rescission may be either express or implied. Non-performance for a long period may lead to an inference of **abandonment**.

In September 1913, X. agreed to sell to Y. 50 dozen skins "delivery as required." By September 1914, Y. had from time to time requested delivery of 20 dozen which had been duly delivered, but no more deliveries were asked for until July 1917. *Held*, an inordinate delay having taken place, the parties must be taken to have abandoned the contract: *Pearl Mill Co.* v. *Ivy Tannery Co.* [1919] 1 K.B. 78.

But abandonment by conduct should not be assumed lightly. It occurs only in two cases which are described by Lord Brandon in *Paal Wilson & Co. A/S.* v. *Partenreederei Hannah Blumenthal. The Hannah Blumenthal* [1983] 1 Lloyd's Rep. 103, 114, as follows: "Where A. seeks to prove that he and B. have abandoned a contract in this way, there are two ways in which A. can put his case. The first way is by showing that the conduct of each party, as evinced to the other party and acted on by him, leads necessarily to the inference of an implied agreement between them to abandon the contract. The second method is by showing that the conduct of B., as evinced towards A., has been such as to lead A. reasonably to believe that B. has abandoned the contract, even though it has not in fact been B.'s intention to do so, and that A. has significantly altered his position in reliance on that belief. The first method involves an actual abandonment by both A. and B. The second method involves the creation by B. of a situation in which he is estopped from asserting, as against A., that he, B., has not abandoned the contract."

A contract in writing may be rescinded or varied by an oral agreement. Similarly, a contract in a deed may be rescinded or varied by a simple contract (*Berry* v. *Berry* [1929] 2 K.B. 316). But a contract which is required by statute to be in writing, can be rescinded (*Morris* v. *Baron* [1918] A.C. 1), but cannot be varied, by an oral agreement; *Goss* v. *Nugent* (1833) 5 B. & Ad. 58.

Accord and satisfaction

Accord and satisfaction occurs when after a contract is concluded a party obtains the release from his contractual obligation by giving or promising a consideration other than that which the other party is bound to accept under the contract. The agreement is known as accord and the consideration as satisfaction.

Accord without satisfaction is no discharge of a contract or of a right of action arising from the contract. The satisfaction may, however, consist of a promise which, as has been seen (p. 51, *ante*) is good consideration, and an accord supported by such consideration amounts to an enforceable agreement.

> "It is still the law that a mere accord without satisfaction does not put an end to an existing liability after breach, but I think it amounts to an agreement which can be enforced by a claim for damages if it is broken by one of the parties when the other has shown his readiness to perform the terms of the agreement": Greer L.J. in *British Russian Gazette* v. *Associated Newspapers* [1933] 2 K.B. 616, 650.

The agreement of a creditor to accept a smaller sum than is due to him is accord without satisfaction (*Foakes* v. *Beer* [1889] 9 App.Cas. 605; see pp. 56–57, *ante*), but the agreement of a creditor to accept a smaller sum than is due to him in consideration of something to which he was not entitled under the original contract is a valid accord and satisfaction and, as such, is binding on both parties.

Provision for discharge in the contract

The contract may contain a term providing for its termination on the non-fulfilment of a condition, the happening of an event, or on the exercise by one or either of the parties of a power to terminate it.

The non-fulfilment of a **condition precedent** gives a right to the party in whose interest the condition was imposed to terminate the contract.

T. sold a horse to H. warranting that it had hunted with the B. hounds and giving H. the right to return it by a certain date if it did not comply with the warranty. The horse had not hunted with the B. hounds and H. returned it in time, but in the meantime it had been injured through no fault of H. *Held*, H. was given a right to terminate the contract and T. had to accept the injured horse: *Head* v. *Tattersall* (1871) L.R. Ex. 7.

The contract may contain a term releasing the parties from liability on the happening of a certain event. Such a term is a **condition subsequent**.

G. chartered a vessel from S. by a charterparty under which S. agreed to go to Hamburg and load coal, with an exception in the case of "restraints of princes and rulers." War broke out between France and Germany, and Hamburg was blockaded, so that S. refused to load a cargo. *Held*, S. was released by the exception in the charterparty: *Geipel* v. *Smith* (1872) L.R. 7 O.B. 404.

Termination by Notice

The contract may contain a term giving either party a power to terminate it by notice. Examples are a lease that can be terminated by notice to quit or a contract of agency with power to either party on giving notice to end the contract. Similar provisions are also found in contracts of employment but these contracts are subject to special regulations which will be considered later (see Chap. 12, *post*).

More difficult is the position in a long-term contract which is unlimited in time and does not contain a term providing for termination by notice of a specified length. It cannot be assumed that the parties to a commercial contract intend to bind themselves in eternity, particularly as changing economic circumstances, such as the progressive inflation and increase in the costs of raw material and labour, may affect the original agreement of the parties and lead to a fundamentally different situation. In these cases a term has to be implied into the contract, by necessary implication, entitling each party to terminate the contract unilaterally by giving notice of reasonable length. What is reasonable depends on the circumstances, but no case is recorded in which the length of reasonable notice has been held to exceed twelve months.

In July 1929 the South Staffordshire Waterworks Company agreed with the county council (now the Staffordshire Area Health Authority) by a contract under seal "at all times herefter" to supply a hospital with 5,000 gallons of water per day free of cost. The agreement continued until September 1975, when the water company, in view of the great increase in water rates, gave the Area Health Authority six months' notice to terminate the agreement. *Held*, the contract was terminable by reasonable notice: *Staffordshire Area Health Authority* v. *South Staffordshire Waterworks Co.* [1978] 1 W.L.R. 1387.

By letters of December 1969 and January 1971 the British Gas Corporation agreed to supply Tower Hamlets London Borough Council with gas at fixed prices for two housing estates. The agreement was of unspecified length and contained no terms for terminating it by notice. By a letter of December 29, 1977, British Gas purported to terminate the agreement on December 31, 1978 because owing to the enormous increase in the costs of gas the circumstances were fundamentally different from those obtained when the agreement was entered into. The Council claimed that there was an inference in the contract that gas was to be supplied for 20 years, being the life of the gas boilers which British Gas had installed. *Held*, the contract was terminable by reasonable notice. A notice of 12 months was reasonable in the circumstances: *Tower Hamlets London Borough Council* v. *British Gas Corporation*, *The Times*, March 23, 1982.

Acceptance of Breach

A party to a contract may commit a breach of that contract

(a) by repudiating his liability under the contract before the time for performance is due;
(b) by his own act disabling himself from performing the contract; or
(c) by failing to fulfil his obligations when purporting to perform the contract.

Breach always entitles the injured party to bring an action for damages. It may also entitle him to treat the contract as discharged, but he can only treat it as discharged on proving that the breach: is of the entire contract or; is of some term which is so vital that it goes to the root of the contract or; has the effect of depriving the innocent party of substantially the whole benefit of the contract.

The breach must be such as to show that the party in default has repudiated his obligations under the contract.

Repudiation before time for performance

Before the time for performance arrives a party to the contract may declare his intention of not performing the contract. This is called a repudiation of contract or an **anticipatory breach**. In such a case the other party is not bound to wait until the actual time for performance has arrived, but may immediately accept the repudiation and treat the contract as discharged and sue for damages.

B. engaged C. as a courier, his services to start on June 1. On May 11 B. told C. he would not require his services. C. before June 1 arrived, brought an action against B., *Held*, he was entitled to do so: *Hochster* v. *De La Tour* (1853) 2 E. & B. 678.

K. promised to marry F. on the death of his, K.'s father. The father still living, K. informed F. that he would not marry her on his father's death. F. sued him at once for breach of promise (which was then actionable as breach of contract). *Held*, F. was entitled to accept K.'s repudiation of the contract to marry her and to bring her action for breach of promise at once: *Frost* v. *Knight* (1872) L.R. Exch. 111.

The doctrine of anticipatory breach does not apply in the case of a time charterparty which contains a clause obliging the charterer to pay the charter hire to a named bank semi-monthly in advance and giving the owner the right to withdraw the vessel from the charter "failing the punctual and regular payment of the hire"; under this clause the charterer has the whole day when the payment falls due until midnight and the owners must wait until this time has expired and cannot treat earlier failure to pay as an anticipatory repudiation of the contract on the part of the charterer; a notice under an anti-technicality clause (see p. 607, *post*) served by the owner on the charterer is ineffective if given before the date of payment of the hire has expired (*Afovos Shipping Co. S.A.* v. *Romano Pagnan and Pietro Pagnan* [1983] 1 W.L.R. 195).

Acceptance of repudiation

A minor breach of contract, such as a short delay in payments likely to be made later does not amount to repudiation, but "the case would be quite different if the defendants' breaches had been such as reasonably to shatter the plaintiffs' confidence in the defendants' ability to pay for the goods" (*per* Salmon L.J., in *Decro-Wall International S.A.* v. *Practitioners in Marketing Ltd.* [1971] 1 W.L.R. 361).

Repudiation by one party does not of itself discharge the contract. The contract is only discharged if the repudiation is accepted by the other (*i.e.* innocent) party (*Heyman* v. *Darwins Ltd.* [1942] A.C. 356). The innocent party has a choice. He can either accept the repudiation as putting an end to the contract or affirm the contract as still in force. If he affirms it (*e.g.* by indicating that performance was still expected), he has lost the chance of accepting the contract as being repudiated (unless, of course, the other party makes a further repudiation), *Fercometal* v. *Mediterranean Shipping* 1988 3 W.L.R. 200 (H.L.). Thus if the repudiation is not accepted, the contract remains in existence. The party in default may then change his mind and proceed with performance, unless, of course, a supervening event occurs which relieves him from further performance.

Under a charterparty X. agreed to load a cargo of wheat on Y.'s ship at Odessa within a certain number of days. On the arrival of the ship, X. refused to load a cargo. Y. would not accept this refusal and continued to demand a cargo. Before the last day for loading had expired, the Crimean War broke out, rendering performance of the contract illegal. *Held*, Y. had no cause of action against X., because he had refused to accept X.'s breach of contract as a discharge, and the contract had, in the meantime, become discharged by something beyond the control of either party: *Avery* v. *Bowden* (1856) 6 E. & B. 953.

When a repudiation is not accepted by the innocent party, the latter may be able to continue to perform his part of the contract and to claim the contractual payment of it.

A. was a garage company and B. an advertising agency. B. supplied litter bins to the local council and had the right to put advertisements on the bins. A. and B. contracted that B. would put A.'s advertisements on the bins for a period of two years at a rental; if the rental became in arrears by four weeks or more the whole rental for the two years would become payable. Later the same day as the contract was made, A. told B. that A. was cancelling the contract. B. refused to accept this and went ahead and performed A.'s part of the bargain. After four weeks B. claimed the full two years' rental. *Held*, B.'s claim succeeded. B. was entitled not to accept A.'s repudiation, to perform B.'s part of the contract and to claim B.'s contractual rights: *White & Carter* v. *Macgregor* [1962] A.C. 413.

Even if the innocent party does not accept the repudiation, he may not be entitled to claim the contractual payment, if he had no legitimate interest (financial or otherwise) in performing the contract after the repudiation rather than simply claiming damages.

In December 1979 A. chartered a vessel to B. for two years. In October 1979 the vessel's engine suffered a serious breakdown. The repairs were to take some months. At this stage B. indicated that B. no longer needed the vessel. A. nevertheless carried out the repairs and on completion of the repairs in April 1981 informed B. that it was ready. B. wrongly made no use of the vessel and this amounted to a wrongful repudiation which A. could have accepted. Instead, however, A. maintained the ship at anchorage with a full crew until the end of the two years of the charter. A. had already received the full hire charge and claimed to be entitled to keep it. B. claimed that B.'s repudiation should have been accepted and that A. should have claimed only damages. The arbitrator upheld B.'s claim. On appeal to the High Court, *Held*, confirming the arbitrator's decision, that the innocent party was denied, on equitable grounds, the ability to enforce his full contractual rights, since the arbitrator had decided that A. had no legitimate interest in claiming the hire fee: *Clea Shipping Corporation* v. *Bulk Oil International Ltd.*, *The Alaskan Trader* [1984] 1 All E.R. 129.

Where a repudiation is accepted by the innocent party, he is entitled to the same damages as he could have claimed if the contract had been broken on due date. But if the injured party would not have been able to perform himself on due date and consequently would then have been in breach himself, he cannot claim any damages for the anticipatory breach of contract by the other party.

Maredelanto Compania Naviera S.A. v. *Bergbau-Handel GmbH*; *The Mihalis Angelos* [1971] 1 Q.B. 164, see p. 34, *ante*.

In the case of the repudiation of part of the contract, it is a question of construction whether the part repudiated is so vital as to entitle the other party to treat the whole contract as discharged.

Disability

If a party to a contract by his own act disables himself from performing the contract, the other party can treat the contract as discharged. For example, in *Synge* v. *Synge* [1894] 1 Q.B. 466, a man agreed before marriage to settle a house on his wife after marriage. He subsequently conveyed the house to a third person, and it was held that his wife could bring an action for breach of contract, although it was not beyond the bounds of possibility that he might have repurchased the house and then settled it upon her.

X. chartered from Y. a steamer which was being built. After the ship was built Y. sold it to Z. free from the charterparty. *Held*, Y. by selling the steamer had repudiated the charterparty and was liable in damages: *Omnium d'Enterprises* v. *Sutherland* [1919] 1 K.B. 618.

Breach in performance

During the performance of a contract one party may either fail or refuse to perform his duties still outstanding under the contract. In such a case, if the failure or refusal amounts to a repudiation of the whole contract, the other party may treat the contract as discharged by breach.

C. agreed to supply the railway company with 3,900 tons of railway chairs. After 1,787 tons had been delivered the company told C. that no more were required. *Held*, C. could bring an action at once without showing an actual delivery: *Cort* v. *Ambergate Ry.* (1851) 17 Q.B. 127.

In contracts of sale of goods the breach of any of the implied conditions set out in the Sale of Goods Act 1979, ss.12–15, entitles the buyer to rescind the contract.

Frustration

The principle

When the common object of the contract can no longer be achieved because, in the light of the circumstances, a situation fundamentally different from that contemplated when the parties entered into the contract has unexpectedly emerged, the contract is at an end, for otherwise the parties would be bound to perform a contract which they did not make.

An unexpected turn of events which does not create a fundamentally different situation does not enable a party to refuse the performance of the contract on the ground that the contract is frustrated. In particular, frustration cannot be pleaded merely because the performance of the contract has become more difficult or more costly than expected, or will result in a loss rather than the anticipated profit, or even has become impossible.

It should be noted that impossibility, as a general rule, does not excuse from performance. "Frustration is a doctrine . . . very rarely relied upon with success. It is, in fact, a kind of last ditch, and . . . it is a conclusion which should be reached rarely and with reluctance" (*per* Harman L.J. in *Gaon (Albert D.) & Co.* v. *Société Interprofessionelle des Oléagineux Fluides Alimentaires* [1960] 2 Q.B. 318, 370). In short, the discharge of a contract by frustration is the exception, and not the rule.

Circumstances in which the contract is not frustrated

Where a party gives an absolute undertaking

A contract to perform something that is obviously impossible, *e.g.* to build a castle in the air, is void because there is no real consideration for the contract, but an absolute undertaking is binding though it might be difficult or even impossible to perform.

Finnish exporters sold a quantity of ant eggs to English buyers, "delivery: prompt, as soon as export licence granted." The sellers were unable to obtain the export licence and failed to ship the goods. *Held*, the sellers were liable for breach of contract; they had undertaken absolutely that they would obtain the export licence: *Cassidy (Peter) Seed Co. Ltd.* v. *Osuustukkauppa I.L.* [1957] 1 W.L.R. 273.

A. sold to B. 70 standards of Finnish birch timbers to be delivered at Hull from July to September 1914. No deliveries were made before August when the war broke out and disorganised transport, so that A. could not get any timber from Finland. *Held*, B. was not concerned with the way in which A. was going to get the timber to fulfil his contract, and the impossibility of getting timber from Finland did not discharge A.: *Blackburn Bobbin Co.* v. *Allen & Sons* [1918] 2 K.B. 467.

Where the change is not fundamental

Builders contracted with Fareham Council to build 78 houses for a fixed sum within a period of eight months. Owing to lack of adequate supplies of labour it took the builders 22 months to complete the work. The costs of building having risen, the builders claimed that their contract with the council was frustrated and that they were entitled to a higher sum than the agreed sum on a *quantum meruit*. *Held*, what had taken place was an unexpected turn of events which made the contract more onerous than had been contemplated, but this did not operate to frustrate the contract: *Davis Contractors* v. *Fareham U.D.C.* [1956] A.C. 696.

Before the closure of the Suez Canal on November 2, 1956, sellers in the Sudan sold a quantity of groundnuts to a German company; the terms were shipment c.i.f. Hamburg, November/December 1956. The normal shipment which was via the Suez Canal became impossible because the canal was closed but shipment via the Cape of Good Hope was still possible. The sellers failed to ship the goods. *Held*, the sellers were liable for breach of contract; the change in circumstances was not fundamental and did not amount to frustration, inasmuch as the contract provided only for a time of shipment but not of arrival: *Tsakiroglou & Co. Ltd.* v. *Noblee Thorl GmbH* [1962] A.C. 93.

In April 1967 the charterers chartered *The Captain George K* for a voyage from Mexico to India. The charterparty provided in Clause 21 that the master should give estimated dates of arrival 96 hours before due to arrive off Suez and 96 hours after passing Suez. On June 13, when the ship approached Suez, she was informed that the Canal was closed (owing to the Six Days War between Egypt and Israel). The ship then proceeded via the Cape of Good Hope. If she had passed through the Canal, she would have covered 9,700 miles but in fact she covered 18,400 miles. The owners claimed additional freight for the extended voyage as a *quantum meruit*, contending that the contemplated voyage was frustrated. *Held*, the difference between the contemplated voyage via Suez and the actual voyage via the Cape amounted only to the difference in expense and for that reason was insufficient to produce frustration: *Palmco Shipping Inc.* v. *Continental Ore Corporation*; *The Captain George K.* [1970] 2 Lloyd's Rep. 21.

Strikes and outbreak of hostilities

A war, in which the United Kingdom is involved, frustrates a contract with a person or company in the hostile country at once. A strike or outbreak of hostilities between foreign nations, in which the United Kingdom is not involved, may affect the performance of the contract but these events do not automatically operate as frustration. The strike may be over soon and the hostilities may not affect the performance of the contract. But if, usually after some time, it becomes obvious that these disturbances will be of lengthy duration and the nature of the outstanding rights and obligations of the parties to the contract are so significantly changed by these events that the performance becomes different from that which the parties reasonably contemplated when they entered into the contract, it would be unjust to hold them to its performance and frustration occurs at this—later—date (*National Carriers Ltd.* v. *Panalpina Ltd.* [1981] A.C. 675).

The vessel *Wenjiang* was hired out by its owners to charterers. On September 21, 1980 she was in the Shatt Al Arab, which separates Iran from Iraq, when heavy fighting broke out between these two countries. The *Wenjiang*, in common with many other ships, could not leave the Shatt. First it was thought that the war would be of short duration or that international attempts to allow the trapped vessels a free passage out of the war zone would be successful but these hopes were disappointed. On March 2, 1981, when an arbitration award was made in this matter, the vessel was still trapped in the Shatt Al Arab. *Held*, the charterparty was frustrated on November 24, 1980: *International Sea Tankers Inc.* v. *Hemisphere Shipping Co. Ltd. The Wenjiang* (*No.* 2) [1983] 1 Lloyd's Rep. 400.

Circumstances in which the contract is frustrated

Statutory interference

A contract which is contrary to law at the time of its formation is normally void or unenforceable. But if, after the making of the contract, owing to an alteration of the law or the act of some person armed with statutory authority, the performance of the contract becomes impossible, the contract is discharged.

D. leased some land to B. and covenanted that he would not erect any but ornamental buildings upon the adjoining land. A railway company, under statutory powers, took this adjoining land and built a railway station on it. *Held*, D. was excused from performance of his covenant, because the railway company's statutory powers had rendered it impossible: *Baily* v. *De Crespigny* (1869) L.R. 4 Q.B. 180.

X. sold to Y. a specific parcel of wheat in a warehouse in Liverpool. Before delivery and before the property in the wheat passed to Y., the wheat was requisitioned by the Government under statutory powers. *Held*, as delivery was being rendered impossible by the lawful requisition of the wheat by the Government, X. was excused from performance of the contract: *Re Shipton, Anderson & Co. and Harrison Bros. & Co.'s Arbitration* [1915] 3 K.B. 676.

On the other hand, if at the time of the making of the contract compulsory powers are in existence, the exercise of which may affect the contract, a party knowing of those powers cannot rely on the fact that they are subsequently exercised, as a defence to his breach of contract. The exercise of the compulsory powers was an event which might have been anticipated and guarded against in the contract (*Walton Harvey Ltd.* v. *Walker and Homfrays Ltd.* [1931] 1 Ch. 274).

If a contract to be performed in a foreign country becomes illegal owing to a change in the law of that country, the contract is discharged (*Ralli* v. *Compania Naviera* [1920] 2 K.B. 287).

The Polish State trading corporation Rolimpex sold C. Czarnikow Ltd., London sugar merchants, a quantity of Polish beet sugar. The contracts were made in May and July 1974 and provided for delivery of the sugar in November/December of that year. The contracts were made subject to the standard rules of the Refined Sugar Association which contained a force majeure clause allowing cancellation of the contracts in case of "government intervention." Owing to heavy rains in August, the sugar crop failed in Poland and on November 5 the Polish Minister of Foreign Trade signed a decree making the export of sugar illegal by Polish law. Rolimpex failed to deliver the sugar. *Held*, the Polish decree was "government intervention" within the force majeure clause and the contract was frustrated: *C. Czarnikow Ltd.* v. *Rolimpex* [1978] Q.B. 176.

The destruction of a specific object necessary for the performance of the contract

The contract may contemplate the continued existence of a particular thing as essential to the contract, so that if it ceases to exist the contract cannot be performed.

Caldwell let a music-hall to Taylor for a series of concerts on certain days. The music-hall was burnt down before any of the days arrived. *Held*, Caldwell was excused from performance. "In contracts in which the performance depends on the continued existence of a given person or thing, a condition is implied that the impossibility of performance arising from the perishing of the person or thing shall excuse the performance": *per* Blackburn J. in *Taylor* v. *Caldwell* (1862) 3 B. & S. 826.

The destruction of the essential object need not be total, as long as it is sufficient to prevent the contract from being carried out.

A. sold to N. a cargo of cotton seed to be shipped by a specific ship in a named month. Before the time for shipping arrived, the ship was so damaged by stranding as to be unable to load by the agreed time. *Held*, the contract was discharged: *Nickoll and Knight* v. *Ashton, Eldridge & Co.* [1901] 2 K.B. 126.

If A., in the case just quoted, had not named the ship on which the cargo was to be loaded in his contract, he would not have been excused from performance by the destruction of the ship on which he had intended, in his own mind, to load the cargo.

When specific goods are sold and, before the property passes to the buyer, they perish without the fault of either party, the contract is avoided (Sale of Goods Act 1979, s.7).

Fundamental change in circumstances

It has already been seen that only events which are of such gravity that they result in a fundamentally different situation from that contemplated by the parties when they entered into the contract can be regarded as frustrating events; a mere unexpected turn of events is insufficient.

Frustration occurs if the following three requirements are satisfied:

1. An event occurs which was outside the contemplation of the parties;

The *Kingswood* was chartered to go to Port Pirie and load a cargo for Europe. Before she arrived, there was a violent explosion in one of her boilers, and she was unable to perform the charter. The cause of the explosion was unknown. *Held*, the explosion "frustrated" the contract; the shipowners did not have to negative negligence, the charterers had to prove it: *Joseph Constantine Line* v. *Imperial Smelting Corpn.* [1942] A.C. 154.

A ship was chartered to go with all possible dispatch from Liverpool to Newport and there load a cargo for San Francisco. The vessel was stranded on the way to Newport and could not be repaired for some months. *Held*, the delay put an end, in a commercial sense, to the commercial venture entered upon and the contract was discharged: *Jackson* v. *Union Marine Insurance Co.* (1893) L.R. 10 C.P. 125.

2. The contract, if performed, would thereby be made a different contract from that entered into. This is really the decisive requirement: if a fictitious person, "the officious bystander," had told the parties what would happen, and both parties had replied: "of course, if that event happens the contract is off," only then this requirement is satisfied. Lord Radcliffe in *Davis Contractors Ltd.* v. *Fareham Urban Council* [1956] A.C. 696, 729 (see above) expressed this principle in what has become the classic statement on the doctrine of frustration: ". . . frustration occurs whenever the law recognises that without default of either party a contractual obligation has become incapable of being performed because the circumstances in which performance is called for would render it a thing radically different from that which was undertaken by the contract. *Non haec in foedera veni.* It was not this that I promised to do."

D. contracted with M. to construct a reservoir within six years, with power for M.'s engineers to grant an extension of time. After two years the Government, acting under statutory powers, required D. to cease work on the contract. D. did so and claimed that this put an end to the contract. *Held*, the interruption created by the Government's action was of such a character and duration as to make the contract, when resumed, different from the contract when broken off, and discharged it: *Metropolitan Water Board* v. *Dick, Kerr & Co. Ltd.* [1918] A.C. 119.

3. The event is one for which neither party was responsible.

N chartered O's trawler to use it for trawling. A licence was necessary, but N could not get one, as they already had three licences, which was their full allowance. *Held*, N's failure to get a licence did not excuse them from performance because it was their own act in appropriating the licences to their other trawlers which frustrated the contract: *Maritime National Fish Ltd.* v. *Ocean Trawlers Ltd.* [1935] A.C. 524.

The defendants contracted to use one of their two barges to transport the plaintiffs' oil rig. They allocated one of their two barges to the plaintiffs' contract and the other to different contracts. Unfortunately, after the contract was made but before the time for performance, the barge allocated to the plaintiffs' contract sank. The other barge, having been allocated elsewhere, could not be used. The plaintiffs alleged that the defendants were in breach of contract. The defendants claimed that the sinking had frustrated the contract. *Held*, the contract was not frustrated because the defendants had a choice of which barge to allocate to which contract; thus the frustration was self-induced; *J. Lauritzen A/S* v. *Wijsmuller BV*, *The Super Servant Two*, *The Times*, October 18, 1979 C.A.

Frustration, when it occurs, automatically brings the contract to an end. No notice or other action by either party is required to terminate it.

The doctrine of frustration applies to leases, but only in rare circumstances (*National Carriers Ltd.* v. *Panalpina Ltd.* [1981] A.C. 675).

Personal incapacity in contracts where the personal qualifications of one of the parties are important

C. who was 16 years old was employed as the drummer by the Barron Knights band under a contract for a term of five years. His duties were, when the band had work, to play on seven nights a week. C. fell ill and the doctor ordered that he was only fit to play on four nights a week. Thereupon the band terminated his contract. *Held*, that in the business sense it was made impossible for C. to continue his contract and that the contract was properly terminated: *Condor* v. *The Barron Knights Ltd.* [1966] 1 W.L.R. 87.

In the case of the employment of a servant for a fixed period, the temporary illness of the servant will not discharge the contract.

Mr. Marshall was employed as a shipyard fitter by Harland & Wolff. He was absent from work for 18 months owing to illness and received no wages during that time. It was not the policy of the employers to terminate employment on grounds of illness. The employers decided to close down the shipyard and gave Mr. Marshall four weeks' notice of dismissal. They argued that he was not entitled to redundancy payment because the contract of employment was terminated by frustration caused by his inability to work. *Held*, since it was the policy of the employers not to terminate employment during illness of the employee and the latter might recover and resume work, the contract was not frustrated. Mr. Marshall was entitled to redundancy payment: *Marshall* v. *Harland & Wolff Ltd.* [1972] 1 W.L.R. 899.

If, however, such illness goes to the root of the whole contract, it will discharge the contract (*Poussard* v. *Spiers* (1876) 1 Q.B.D. 410).

Apart from the payment of social benefit in the case of sickness, whether wages are payable during sickness depends on the terms of the contract of employment. In the absence of an express term, wages will only be payable if there is an implied term to pay based on what the parties intended (*Petrie* v. *MacFisheries Ltd.* [1940] 1 K.B. 258).

Partial frustration

Partial frustration occurs if a person is under two contractual obligations but, owing to a frustrating event, cannot fulfil both. Thus, if a seller sells 1,000 tons of sugar to A. and another 1,000 tons to B., but by a government order made unexpectedly after he entered into these two contracts is restricted to ship only 1,000 tons in all, what is he to do? Shall he divide the permitted quantity *pro rata* between A. and B. and ship 500 tons to each, or shall he follow the chronological order of the contracts and perform the first one fully and fail on the second one? It has been held in *Intertradax S.A.* v. *Lesieur-Tourteaux S.A.R.L.* [1978] 2 Lloyd's Rep. 509 that in such a quandary the seller may appropriate the goods in any way which the trade considers to be proper and reasonable, whether the basis of appropriation is *pro rata*, chronological order of contracts or some other basis. But where a legal commitment to one customer conflicts with a moral commitment to another, the supplier must honour the legal commitment fully and disregard the non-legal commitment (*Pancommerce S.A.* v. *Veechema B.V.* [1983] 2 Lloyd's Rep. 304).

Effect of discharge by frustration

This is governed by the Law Reform (Frustrated Contracts) Act 1943 as follows:

1. All sums paid to any party in pursuance of the contract before it is discharged are, in principle, recoverable. Sums payable cease to be payable (s.1(2)).

English sellers agreed to sell machinery to Polish buyers for £4,800, one-third of which was to be paid with order. The buyers paid £1,000 only. Before delivery was due, Germany occupied Poland. *Held*, the contract was discharged by frustration. The buyers could recover the £1,000 paid and were not liable to pay the balance of £600: *Fibrosa etc.* v. *Fairburn etc.* [1943] A.C. 32 (which was decided before the 1943 Act came into operation).

If the payee has incurred expenses, before the time of discharge, in performing or for the purpose of performing the contract, the court may allow him to retain or recover from the payer the whole or part of these expenses where it considers it just (s.1(2) proviso).

Example—A ship repairer repairs a ship, but before completion of the repairs the ship is destroyed by fire. He may be allowed to retain his expenses, including his overhead expenses.

2. Where one party has, by reason of anything done by the other party to the contract, obtained a valuable benefit (other than the payment of money), that other party may recover from him such sum as the court considers just (s.1(3)).

In December 1957 the Libyan government granted Mr. Hunt, a Texan financier, an oil concession. As he did not have the experience and equipment to explore and develop the concession himself, he entered in June 1960 into a "farm-in" agreement with B.P. Exploration, under which B.P. was entitled to a half-share in the concession. The farm-in agreement was governed by English law. The exploration was highly successful. In December 1971, the Libyan government, which was of a different political complexion as the result of a revolution in Libya, expropriated B.P.'s half-share of the concession and in June 1973 it expropriated Mr. Hunt's half-share. Both received from the Libyan government compensation which was unrealistically inadequate. B.P. which had not been fully reimbursed for its endeavours for Mr. Hunt began proceedings against him. B.P. claimed that the farm-in agreement was frustrated and that they were entitled to a just sum under section 1(3) of the Law Reform (Frustrated Contracts) Act 1943. *Held*, (1) the farm-in contract was frustrated in December 1971, when B.P.'s half-share in the concession was expropriated; (2) as the farm-in agreement was governed by English law, the effect of the frustration was regulated by the Act of 1943; (3) the farm-in agreement did not contain a clause dealing with the political risk, such as the expropriation of the concession by the Libyan government; (4) B.P. was entitled to a just sum by virtue of section 1(3) of the 1943 Act; this sum was awarded in US Dollars, under the *Miliangos* principle (see p. 210, *post*): *B.P. Exploration Co. (Libya) Ltd.* v. *Hunt* (*No. 2*) [1982] 2 W.L.R. 253.

Payments under contracts of insurance are to be disregarded in considering the sum to be retained or recovered under 1 or 2 above (s.1(5)).

3. The Act does not apply to:

(a) Contracts containing a provision to meet the case of frustration (s.2(3)).
But a clause providing for a reasonable extension of time in case performance is hindered or delayed does not prevent frustration by reason of war, because war involves indefinite delay and in that case the Act applies.
(b) Contracts which are not governed by English law (s.1(1)).
(c) Charterparties (except time charterparties or charterparties by way of demise) (s.1(5)(*a*)).
(d) Contracts for the carriage of goods by sea (s.2(5)(*a*)).
(e) Contracts of insurance (s.2(5)(*b*)).
(f) Contracts for the sale of specific goods which have perished before the risk has passed to the buyer (Sale of Goods Act 1979, s.7), and any other contracts of sale where the contract is frustrated by reason of the fact that the goods have perished. The second category, unlike the first, extends to cases in which the risk has already passed to the buyer (s.2(5)(*c*)).

CHAPTER 9

REMEDIES FOR BREACH OF CONTRACT

WHEN a contract is broken, the injured party may have several courses of action open to him. These are:

(a) to refuse further performance of the contract;
(b) to bring an action for damages;
(c) to sue on a *quantum meruit*;
(d) to sue for specific performance;
(e) to sue for an injunction.

REFUSAL OF FURTHER PERFORMANCE

If one party has broken his contract, the other party may treat the contract as rescinded and refuse further performance. By treating the contract as rescinded he makes himself liable to restore any benefits he has received, *e.g.* if he has agreed to sell goods and has received all or part of the price, he must return it, unless it is a term of the contract that he need not do so (*Dies* v. *British and International Mining Corpn.* [1939] 1 K.B. 724); if the injured party claims damages from the party who has broken the contract, he must give credit in his calculation of damages for the purchase price (or any other benefit) received by him. A deposit paid by the purchaser need not be repaid if the sale goes off by the purchaser's default, but a sum given in part payment of the price is returnable (*Howe* v. *Smith* (1884) 27 Ch.D. 89). If the breach has only been a breach of warranty, the injured party must perform his part, although he has a right of action for damages.

DAMAGES

Whenever there is a breach of contract by one party, the other is entitled to bring an action for damages. If in fact he has sustained no loss from the breach he will not be entitled to substantial damages but can only claim nominal damages, *i.e.* damages which recognise that he has had a legal right infringed.

By a c.i.f. contract the buyers, an Italian firm, bought a quantity of Brazilian yellow maize from the sellers, a Brazilian company. The price was $64 per 1,000 kilos delivered weight. When the goods arrived in Trieste, part of them were found to be damaged and the buyers rejected them. Negotiations ensued and eventually the buyers bought the goods which were stored in Trieste at $51.40 per 1,000 kilos. The buyers claimed damages for breach of contract on the ground that the goods were damaged on arrival. *Held*, the purchase of the consignment at $51.40 formed part of a continuous course of dealing between the same parties in respect of the same goods and the profit which the buyers had made by their eventual purchase extinguished their alleged loss which was purely fictitious: *Pagnan & Fratelli* v. *Corbisa Industrial Agropacuaria Ltda.* [1970] 1 W.L.R. 1306.

On February 19, 1974 Lazenby Garages sold a second-hand BMW 2002 car to Mr. Wright for £1,670. On the following day Mr. Wright cancelled the purchase. Lazenby continued to offer the car for sale and sold it on April 23, 1974 for £1,770. Lazenby claimed £345 from Wright as the difference between their buying price and the price which Mr. Wright was obliged to pay, on the ground that they had lost a sale. *Held*, a second-hand car, unlike new cars, was a unique article which had no "available market" within section 50 of the Sale of Goods Act 1979. In the circumstances the cases relating to new cars, such as *Thompson Ltd.* v. *Robinson* (*Gunmakers*) *Ltd.* [1955] Ch. 177 (see p. 349, *post*), did not apply. Lazenby had suffered no loss and could not recover damages: *Lazenby Garages Ltd.* v. *Wright* [1976] 1 W.L.R. 459.

Calculation of damages

If the aggrieved party has sustained loss, he is entitled to substantial damages, which are calculated in accordance with the following rules—

1. The injured party is to be placed in the same financial position as if the contract had been performed.

C. agreed to carry S.'s machine to Guernsey, but owing to their delay, the machine arrived a week late. S. proved no loss of profit. *Held*, S.'s damages were (1) £20, one week's depreciation of the machine; (2) £10, interest on the capital cost, maintenance and wages: *Sunley Ltd.* v. *Cunard White Star Ltd.* [1940] 1 K.B. 740.

The measure of damages is the value of performance to the plaintiff, not the cost of performance to the defendant. In a contract of sale of goods the measure of damages when there is an available market for the goods is the difference between the market price at the date of the breach and the contract price. If, therefore, the market price is equal to or below the contract price the plaintiff will be in the same financial position as if the contract had been performed, and so will only be entitled to nominal damages (see p. 349, *post*).

A sale to a merchant who has bought for resale makes no difference to the measure of damages where there is a market. If goods of special manufacture are sold and it is known they are to be resold and cannot be bought in the market, loss of profit is the measure of damages. In string contracts, where the seller knows the merchant is not buying for resale generally but for resale of those specific goods and no others, loss of profit is the right measure (*Kwei Tek Chao* v. *British Traders & Shippers Ltd.* [1954] 2 Q.B. 459).

In accordance with these principles, in calculating damages the tax liability of the person who suffers a breach of contract may have to be taken into account. In an action in tort for injuries from negligence or in contract for wrongful dismissal where the loss of the plaintiff consists wholly or in part in a loss of earnings, which would attract income tax, the amount of that tax must be deducted from his damages because otherwise he would obtain more than restitution (*British Transport Commission* v. *Gourley* (below); and *Parsons* v. *B.N.M. Laboratories Ltd.* [1964] 1 Q.B. 95).

G., a civil engineer, was injured in a railway accident for which the British Transport Commission accepted liability. The damages for earnings, actual and prospective, were agreed to be £37,720 but, if income tax and surtax, to which G. was liable, were taken into account they would be reduced to £6,695. *Held*, it would be unrealistic to ignore the tax element; if the tax liability were not taken into account G. would receive more than he had lost. Consequently, the B.T.C. had only to pay the lower amount: *British Transport Commission* v. *Gourley* [1956] A.C. 185.

If there is an anticipatory breach of contract (see p. 158, *ante*) the injured party can claim the same amount of damages as he could have claimed if the contract were broken on due date, but if the injured party himself would have been in breach on due date, so that the other party could have treated the contract as repudiated, he can recover nothing (*Maredelanto Compania Naviera S.A.* v. *Bergbau-Handel GmbH; The Mihalis Angelos* [1971] 1 Q.B. 164, see p. 34, *ante*).

2. Subject to the preceding rule, the damages must be such as were reasonably foreseeable, when the contract was made, as liable to result from the breach of the contract. This principle was laid down in *Hadley* v. *Baxendale* (below). The purpose of the rule in that case is to establish that damages can only be recovered if they are caused by a proximate cause but not if they are caused by an event that is too remote.

A mill belonging to X. had a broken shaft, and X. delivered the shaft to Y., a carrier, to take to a manufacturer to copy it and make a new one. Y. delayed delivery of the shaft beyond a reasonable time, as a result of which the mill was idle for a longer period than would have been necessary. X. did not make known to Y. that delay would result in a loss of profits. *Held*, Y. was not liable for loss of profits during the period of delay: *Hadley* v. *Baxendale* (1854) 9 Ex. 341.

Loss of profits for non-delivery or delayed delivery may be recovered when the party in breach could reasonably have contemplated that it was not unlikely or that there was a serious possibility that such loss will be incurred.

V. bought from N. a boiler for use in his laundry. Delivery was to be made on June 5 but was not made until November 8. V. claimed (1) loss of the profit the laundry would have made had the boiler been delivered in time; (2) loss of profit from some highly profitable dyeing contracts. *Held*, (1) the laundry profits lost were recoverable, as N. must have contemplated their loss if there was delay, but (2) the loss on the dyeing contracts, which could not have been contemplated, could not be recovered: *Victoria Laundry* v. *Newman Industries* [1949] 2 K.B. 528.

Charterers chartered the *Heron II* to carry a cargo of white sugar from Constanza to Basrah. The normal length of the voyage was 20 days. The shipowner deviated in his own interest and thereby prolonged the voyage by nine days. At Basrah there was, as the shipowner knew, a market for white sugar. During the nine days, the market fell and the charterers suffered a loss of more than £4,000. *Held*, the charterers could recover that sum from the shipowners by way of damages for breach of the contract of carriage by sea. The very existence of a "market" for a commodity implied that prices fluctuated and the likelihood that the market price may fall was reasonably foreseeable by the shipowner: *C. Czarnikow Ltd.* v. *Koufos* [1969] 1 A.C. 350.

3. Although not arising naturally from the breach, if the damages may reasonably be supposed to have been in the contemplation of

both parties at the time when they made the contract as the probable result of the breach of it, they may be recovered.

P. bought from L. some copra cake. P. resold the copra cake to B., who resold it to dealers, and they in turn resold it to farmers, who used it for feeding cattle. The copra cake was poisonous and cattle fed on it died. Claims were made by the various buyers against their sellers, and P. claimed against L. the damages and costs he had had to pay to his purchaser. *Held*, as it was within the contemplation of the parties that the copra cake was to be used for feeding cattle, P. was entitled to succeed in his claim: *Pinnock Bros.* v. *Lewis & Peat Ltd.* [1923] 1 K.B. 690.

If unusual damages are likely to be sustained as the result of a breach of contract, their nature should be communicated to the other party before the contract is made, so that he contracts subject to the prospective liability.

H. contracted to deliver boots for the French Army at a price above the market price. He delivered them to the railway company to be carried, and owing to their delay the purchasers rejected them. *Held*, although H. was entitled to ordinary damages for delay, he could not recover the loss he had sustained through the loss of a price above market price unless he could show that the railway company had undertaken to be liable for such loss: *Horne* v. *Midland Ry.* (1873) L.R. 8 C.P. 131.

4. The damages must be caused by the proximate cause and must not be too remote. Such proximity must exist between the breach of contract and the loss or damage caused. If the loss or damage is caused by another event, *e.g.* the claimant's own negligence, the chain of causation is broken.

A farmer bought from a dealer a towing hitch which was dual purpose in that it could be coupled to either a cup or ring attachment. The coupling was advertised by the manufacturers as foolproof and not requiring maintenance. The farmer used the towing hitch to attach the cup attachment of a trailer to his Land Rover. A brass spindle and handle became detached from the towing hitch and only dirt was holding the towing pin in position. The farmer was aware that the mechanism of the towing hitch was broken but took no steps to have it mended or to ascertain whether it was safe to use on the road. When an employee of the farmer drove the Land Rover with the trailer attached, the trailer broke loose and careered across the road into the path of a car. The driver of the car and his son were killed and the driver's wife and daughter were injured. The court held that the manufacturer of the towing hitch was liable to 75 per cent. because the design was defective, and that the farmer was liable to 25 per cent. because he failed to ascertain whether the coupling was still safe to use. The farmer then claimed an indemnity from the dealer for breach of the contract of sale, on the ground that the implied condition of fitness had been broken. *Held*, the farmer's claim against the dealer failed because his (the farmer's) liability resulted directly from his own negligence and not from the alleged breach of the condition of fitness: *Lambert* v. *Lewis* [1982] A.C. 225.

In the law of contract, it has never been doubted that the aggrieved party can recover damages for **economic loss**, *e.g.* loss of profit, as long as the loss was reasonably foreseeable under the rule in *Hadley* v. *Baxendale* (above) and was not too remote. In the law of torts, as far as a claim for negligent misstatements is concerned, the recovery of economic loss was only admitted, in limited circumstances, by *Hedley Byrne & Co. Ltd.* v. *Heller & Partners Ltd.* [1964] A.C. 465 (for a discussion of this and later cases on negligent misstatements, see pp. 95–97 above.)

5. The fact that damages are difficult to assess does not prevent the injured party from recovering them.

H. advertised a beauty competition, by which readers of certain newspapers were to select 50 ladies, from whom H. himself would select 12 and for whom he would provide theatrical engagements. C. was one of the 50, and, by H.'s breach of contract, she was not present when the final selection was made. *Held*, although it was problematic whether she would have been one of the selected 12, and although it was difficult to assess damages, C. was entitled to have the damages assessed: *Chaplin* v. *Hicks* [1911] 2 K.B. 786.

The difficulty in assessing damages is enhanced if the damages are for disappointment or mental distress but even in these cases the court has to express them in monetary values.

Mr. Jarvis booked a 15 day Christmas Winter sports holiday in Switzerland with Swan's Tours. Contrary to the promises of the travel agency, there was no houseparty at the hotel, the skiing facilities were inadequate and there were other disappointments. *Held*, Mr. Jarvis was entitled to damages compensating him for loss of entertainment and enjoyment. The damages were fixed at £125: *Jarvis* v. *Swan's Tours Ltd.* [1973] Q.B. 233.

Mr. Cox, an industrial metallurgical engineer, had differences with his employers, Philips Industries Ltd. He was removed without notice to a position of less responsibility but at the same salary. He became depressed, anxious, frustrated and ill. *Held*, the relegation of Mr. Cox to a position of lesser responsibility was a breach of contract and he could recover damages for the vexation, frustration and distress suffered by him. The damages were assessed in £500: *Cox* v. *Philips Industries Ltd.* [1976] 1 W.L.R. 638.

A husband and wife contracted with a surgeon that he would perform a vasectomy operation on the husband. The surgeon stressed that if the operation was successful it was irreversible by surgery. He failed to explain, however, that there was a small risk that the husband would by natural process recanalise and thus become fertile again. Subsequently that risk materialised and the wife conceived and produced a healthy child. The parents brought proceedings claiming damages for breach of contract and negligence. *Held*, the defendant was liable in both tort and contract because the arrival of a child was a foreseeable risk of his negligence in failing to warn of the slight risk that the husband might become fertile again. No damages were awarded for the future trouble and care in the child's upbringing which were offset by the joy of having a child; damages would, however, be awarded for the normal ante natal pain and suffering: *Thake* v. *Maurice* [1986] 2 W.L.R. 337.

6. Instead of claiming damages calculated on the usual basis of loss of bargain *i.e.* securing compensation for the consequences of the contract not being carried out, the plaintiff may elect to have damages assessed and awarded for wasted expenditure.

A television company spent money on preparing a television play. Then they entered a contract with Mr. Reed for him to play the leading role. Reed later repudiated the contract. The company took all reasonable steps to find a substitute actor but failed and thus had to abandon the play. *Held*, the television company was entitled to recover the whole of the expenditure which had thereby been written off (*i.e.* wasted), *i.e.* irrespective of whether that expenditure had been incurred before or after the contract with Mr. Reed had been made: *Anglia T.V.* v. *Reed* [1972] 1 Q.B. 60.

A defendant who is sued for wasted expenditure can reduce his liability to the extent that he can show that the wasted expenditure would not have been recovered by the plaintiff if the contract had been performed (*CCC Films* (*London*) *Ltd.* v. *Impact Quadrant Films Ltd.* [1985] Q.B. 16).

7. Vindictive or exemplary damages, that is, damages awarded by way of punishment, cannot be awarded for breach of contract, and even in an action founded on tort an award of exemplary damages is anomalous (*Cassell & Co. Ltd.* v. *Broom*, known as *Broome* v. *Cassell & Co. Ltd.* [1972] A.C. 1027).

A. was wrongfully dismissed by G. from his employment and he claimed (1) damages for his injured feelings for having been dismissed from his employment, and (2) damages for the manner of his dismissal. *Held*, they were not recoverable: *Addis* v. *Gramophone Co.* [1909] A.C. 488. (The difference between this case and *Cox* v. *Philips Industries Ltd.* (*ante*) is that Mr. Cox could not claim damages for wrongful dismissal as he had been paid the appropriate compensation.)

8. It is the duty of the injured person to take reasonable steps to minimise the damages. "The fundamental basis is compensation for pecuniary loss naturally flowing from the breach; but this first principle is qualified by a second, which imposes on a plaintiff the duty of taking all reasonable steps to mitigate the loss consequent on the breach and debars him from claiming any part of the damage which is due to his neglect to take such steps" (*per* Lord Haldane *British Westinghouse Electric and Manufacturing Co.* v. *Underground Electric Ry.* [1912] A.C. 673, 689). The reason for this rule is that the injured party "can recover no more that he would have suffered if he had acted reasonably, because any further damages do not reasonably follow from the defendant's breach" (*per* Scrutton L.J. *Payzu Ltd.* v. *Saunders* [1919] 2 K.B. 581, 589). He is not bound to spend money on a risky venture or to risk his commercial reputation in order to minimise the loss.

B. was employed by a partnership consisting of four members for a period of two years certain. After six months the partnership was dissolved through the retirement of two of the partners, the business being carried on by the other two. The continuing partners were willing to continue B.'s employment on the same terms, but B. declined. *Held*, although the dissolution of the partnership operated as a wrongful dismissal of B. he was only entitled to nominal damages as he had suffered no loss: *Brace* v. *Calder* [1895] 2 Q.B. 253.

A person who is wrongfully dismissed, cannot "sit in the sun" but must reasonably attempt to obtain alternative equivalent employment (*Denmark Productions Ltd.* v. *Boscobel Productions Ltd.* [1969] 1 Q.B. 699).

A person who has suffered damage has not performed his obligation reasonably to minimise damages if, instead of replacing a damaged chattel at the market price, he has it repaired at a cost exceeding its market value; he cannot recover such excess by way of damages (*Darbishire* v. *Warren* [1963] 1 W.L.R. 1067).

The duty reasonably to mitigate the damages may extend to a duty on the part of the aggrieved party to negotiate a new contract with the contract breaker.

Norwegian sellers sold the vessel *Solholt* to Greek buyers for U.S. $5,000,000. The sellers tendered the vessel for delivery too late and were consequently in breach of contract. The parties agreed that the value of the vessel was $5,500,000. The buyers offered to buy the vessel from the sellers for $4,750,000 but this offer was refused. The buyers claimed damages from the seller in the amount of $500,000. *Held*, the buyers had failed reasonably to mitigate their damages. They should have offered to buy the vessel at the original price of $5,000,000: *Sotiros Shipping Inc.* v. *Sameiet Solholt. The Solholt* [1983] 1 Lloyd's Rep. 605.

Where one party to the contract commits an anticipatory repudiation of the contract, the rules relating to mitigation are different according to whether the innocent party accepts the repudiation thereby putting the contract to an end immediately or he affirms the contract thereby keeping it alive. In the latter case, he is not under an obligation to mitigate his loss until there is an actual breach, *i.e.* a failure to perform the contract on the date due for performance. Where, however the innocent party accepts the repudiation, he becomes under a duty to take reasonable steps immediately to mitigate his loss, for example by trying straight away to arrange to meet from elsewhere his requirements which were to have been supplied via the repudiated contract. It could, however, happen that reasonable steps taken in an attempt to minimise the loss will turn out to have increased it. In that case the injured party can claim the whole loss, including the amount by which his reasonable attempt to minimise it have actually increased it (*Hoffberger* v. *International Bloodstock Bureau* (1976) 120 S.J. 130 C.A.) This rule can be seen worked out in a sale of goods case where the buyer makes an anticipatory repudiation which the seller accepts. The usual rule on the measure of damages is that it is to be the difference between the contract price for the goods and the (lower) market price on the date when performance was due to take place. If before then, however, the seller sees the market falling and goes into the market and sells, only to discover that subsequently, say just before the original contractual date for the sale to take place, the market recovers, he can claim the increased loss occasioned by his reasonable decison to go into the market to sell (*Johnson* v. *Agnew* [1970] A.C. 367; *Gebruder Metelman GmbH* v. *N.B.R.* (*London*) *Ltd.* [1984] 1 Lloyd's Rep 614.)

9. The parties may agree in their contract that in case of breach the damages shall be a fixed sum or be calculated in a specified manner; such damages are *liquidated* damages. Damages are *unliquidated* when they are not assessed by agreement of the parties and a party seeks to recover such an amount as the court may hold is the proper measure of damages; in this case the amount of damages recoverable is at large and uncertain until the court has given its ruling.

In the case of liquidated damages, no more and no less can be claimed than the agreed sum and the injured party is entitled to recover that amount without proving actual loss.

W. agreed to erect a plant for C. by a certain date, and also agreed to pay £20 for every week they took beyond that date. They were 30 weeks late, and C. claimed £5,850, their actual loss from the delay. *Held*, W. had only agreed to pay £20 a week for delay and were not liable for more: *Cellulose Acetate Silk Co.* v. *Widnes Foundry* [1933] A.C. 20.

Liquidated damages and penalties

When a contract provides that, on a breach, a fixed sum shall be payable by the party responsible, it is a question of construction whether this sum is a penalty or liquidated damages. The distinction is important, because if it is a penalty only the actual damage suffered can be claimed, while if it is liquidated damages the sum fixed can be recovered.

The rules for distinguishing a penalty from liquidated damages are:

1. The use of the words "penalty" or "liquidated damages" in the contract is not conclusive. The court will ascertain whether a sum is in truth a penalty or liquidated damages.

A professional footballer received an injury during a match. He was insured against this risk and the underwriters paid him £500 for total disablement, having first obtained from him an undertaking that he would repay this sum by way of "a penalty" if he took part in a professional football match thereafter. The footballer infringed this undertaking. *Held*, the sum was not a penalty and the footballer had to return it: *Alder* v. *Moore* [1961] 2 Q.B. 57.

2. The essence of a penalty is the payment of money stipulated as *in terrorem* of the offending party; that is to say, its intention is to compel the performance of the contract by providing something by way of punishment if the contract is not performed. The essence of liquidated damages is a genuine pre-estimate of damage.

3. It is a penalty if the sum is extravagant and unconscionable compared with the greatest loss that could conceivably be proved to have followed from the breach.

Under a hire-purchase agreement in respect of a motor car the purchase price was £558, H. paid a deposit and four instalments amounting to £302, but failed to pay the fifth instalment. L. terminated the agreement, retook possession of the car and sold it for £270. L. claimed £122 under a clause making H. liable to pay in respect of "depreciation" a sum sufficient to bring his total payments up to £425 which was approximately three-quarters of the purchase price. *Held*, the sum of £425 was not a genuine pre-estimate of damage but was an extravagant and extortionate sum held *in terrorem* over the head of the hirer. It was a penalty and as such not recoverable: *Lamdon Trust Ltd.* v. *Hurrell* [1955] 1 W.L.R. 391.

A term of a contract of hire by which the hirer agrees to pay to the owners of the goods a percentage of the balance of the outstanding rentals in the event of his breach of the contract is not a penalty if such percentage is not extravagant and unconscionable (*Robophone Facilities Ltd.* v. *Blank* [1966] 1 W.L.R. 1428).

4. It is a penalty if the breach consists of not paying a sum of money by a certain time, and the sum fixed is greater than the sum to be paid.

Example—B. agrees to pay C. £100 on June 1, and, if he fails to make the payment at the stipulated time, to pay £150 as liquidated damages. The extra £50 will be a penalty and irrecoverable.

5. When a single sum is made payable on the occurrence of one or more of several events, some of which may occasion serious and others trifling damage, there is a presumption (but no more) that the sum is a penalty.

F. agreed to act at K.'s theatre and to conform to all the regulations of the theatre. Each party agreed on breach by either of them of the agreement to pay £1,000 as liquidated damages. F. broke the contract, and the jury assessed the damages at £750. *Held*, the £1,000 was a penalty because it was payable even if F. had broken any of the smallest regulations of the theatre, and K. could only recover £750: *Kemble* v. *Farren* (1829) 6 Bing. 141.

6. The fact that the possible consequences of the breach make an accurate pre-estimation of the damages almost impossible does not prevent the sum from being liquidated damages.

Before the passing of the Resale Prices Act 1964[1] N. agreed with D. not to sell motor tyres at less than D.'s list prices, and to pay £5 by way of liquidated damages for every tyre sold in breach of the agreement. *Held*, the £5 was liquidated damages and the whole of it was recoverable: *Dunlop Pneumatic Tyre Co. Ltd.* v. *New Garage Ltd.* [1914] A.C. 79.

In a case like this, the contrast is not between the price of the article and the sum fixed as damages, but between the sum fixed and the probable amount of the damages.

7. A clause providing that in case of actual loss suffered by a party another party shall indemnify the first-named party for the loss is not a penalty clause (*Export Credits Guarantee Department* v. *Universal Oil Products Co.* [1983] 1 W.L.R. 399).

Interest

Interest is recoverable in the following cases—

1. Where there is an express agreement to pay it.

2. Where there is an implied agreement to pay it, resulting from the course of dealing between the parties or from trade usage (*Re Anglesey* [1901] 2 Ch. 548).

3. Upon overdue bills of exchange and promissory notes.

4. By the Administration of Justice Act 1982, section 15 the court may allow simple interest at such rate as it thinks fit on all claims for debt or damages from the date when the claim arose to judgment. The court can also award interest on any sums paid by the debtor after their due date but before judgment.

The measures of damages for failure to pay money by a due date is, as a general rule, interest at the market rate.

[1] Which preceded the Resale Prices Act 1976 now in force (see p. 445, *post*).

Quantum Meruit

Where there is a breach of contract, the injured party, instead of suing for damages, may claim payment for what he has done under the contract. His right to payment does not arise out of the original contract, but is based on an implied promise by the other party arising from the acceptance of an executed consideration. This is termed a *quantum meruit*. Cases of *quantum meruit* fall under the category of quasi-contracts (see p. 66, *ante*).

The claim on a *quantum meruit* arises—

1. When one party abandons or refuses to perform the contract.

P. was engaged by C. to write a book to be published by instalments in a weekly magazine. After a few numbers had appeared the magazine was abandoned. *Held*, P. could recover on a *quantum meruit* for the work he had done under the contract: *Planché* v. *Colburn* (1831) 8 Bing. 14.

2. When work has been done and accepted under a void contract.

C. was employed as managing director by a company under a written contract. The contract was not binding, because the directors who made it were not authorised to enter into it. C. rendered the services and sued for remuneration. *Held*, he could recover on a *quantum meruit*: *Craven-Ellis* v. *Canons Ltd.* [1936] 2 K.B. 403.

The reason why the law admits a claim for a *quantum meruit* is that otherwise the recipient of the benefit would be unjustly enriched at the expense of the supplier of goods or services. But English law has not yet developed a general doctrine of unjust enrichment.

Lump sum contracts

A lump sum contract is one where the intention of the parties is that complete performance must take place before payment can be demanded. Failure to make complete performance prevents any payment being recovered either under the contract or on a *quantum meruit*.

S. agreed with H. to erect buildings for £565. He did work to the value of £333 and then abandoned the contract. H. thereupon completed the contract. *Held*, (i) S. could not recover anything under the original contract because he was only entitled to payment on completion of the work; (ii) S. could not recover on a *quantum meruit* based on H.'s acceptance of his work, because H. had no option but to accept the work, and no fresh contract to pay could be implied from his acceptance: *Sumpter* v. *Hedges* [1898] 1 Q.B. 673.

But where there is a lump sum contract which is completely performed, though insufficiently and badly, the person who has performed the work can recover the lump sum, less a deduction for his bad work (*Dakin & Co. Ltd.* v. *Lee* [1916] 1 K.B. 566).

X. agreed to decorate Y.'s flat and to fit a wardrobe and a bookcase for the lump sum of £750. The work was done, but Y. complained of faulty workmanship, the cost of remedying it being £294. *Held*, X. could recover from Y. £750 less £294: *Hoenig* v. *Isaacs* [1952] 1 All E.R. 176.

Specific Performance

Instead of, or in addition to, awarding damages to the injured party, a decree for specific performance may be granted. Specific performance means the actual carrying out by the parties of their contract, and in a proper case the court will insist on the parties carrying out their agreement (*Beswick* v. *Beswick* (see p. 61, *ante*)).

This remedy, however, is discretionary, and will not be granted in any of the following cases:

(a) Where damages are an adequate remedy.
(b) Where the court cannot supervise the execution of the contract, *e.g.* a building contract.
(c) Where the contract is for personal services (see Trade Union and Labour Relations Act 1974, s.16; p. 246, *post*).
(d) Where one of the parties is a minor.
(e) In contracts to lend money.

Specific performance is usually granted in contracts connected with land or to take shares or debentures in a company. In the case of the sale of goods, it can only be granted in the case of specific goods and is not ordered as a rule unless the goods are unique and cannot easily be purchased in the market.

Although the court will not order specific performance of a contract for personal services, it may order that such a contract be entered into (*C.H. Giles & Co. Ltd.* v. *Morris* [1972] 1 W.L.R. 307).

INJUNCTION

An injunction is an order of the court restraining a person from doing some act. It will be granted to enforce a negative stipulation in a contract where damages would not be an adequate remedy. Even if there is no express negative stipulation, one may be inferred.

G. agreed to take the whole of the electric energy required by his premises from the plaintiffs. *Held*, this was in substance an agreement not to take energy from any other person and it could be enforced by injunction: *Metropolitan Electric Supply Co.* v. *Ginder* [1901] 2 Ch. 799.

In a contract for personal services a clear negative stipulation will be enforced by injunction in a suitable case.

W. agreed to sing at L.'s theatre and nowhere else. *Held*, she could be restrained by injunction from singing for Z.: *Lumley* v. *Wagner* (1852) 5 De G.M. & G. 604.

N., a film actress, agreed to act exclusively for W. for a year and for no one else. During the year she contracted to act for X. *Held*, she could be restrained by injunction: *Warner Bros.* v. *Nelson* [1937] 1 K.B. 209.

Like specific performance, injunction is an equitable remedy, and is only granted if, in all the circumstances, it is just and equitable to do so.

The Mareva injunction

If the English courts have jurisdiction over a dispute, it is possible to obtain an injunction against the defendant ordering him not to remove specified assets from the jurisdiction. The purpose of this injunction is to prevent the defendant from nullifying the effect of a judgment which the plaintiff is likely to obtain against him.

This type of injunction is known as the *Mareva* injunction because it was granted in *Mareva Compania Naviera S.A.* v. *International Bulkcarriers S.A.*; *The Mareva* [1975] 2 Lloyd's Rep. 509. It is now granted by virtue of the Supreme Court Act 1981, s.37(3).

The *Mareva* injunction is an interlocutory injunction, *i.e.* a temporary injunction granted while the case is pending in court and before final judgment is given. It is only ancillary to other proceedings, which must have been commenced when it is granted (*Siskina* (*Cargo Owners*) v. *Distos Compania Naviera S.A.* [1979] A.C. 210). The grant of the injunction is discretionary and depends on the balance of convenience. A *Mareva* injunction will be granted only if (1) the plaintiff is likely to recover judgment, and (2) there are reasons to believe that the defendant has assets in the jurisdiction to meet the judgment but may well take steps designed to ensure that they are no longer available when judgment is given against him. The plaintiff will normally apply for this type of injunction *ex parte*, *i.e.* without the defendant being heard. If the injunction is granted, the plaintiff will usually be asked to give an indemnity, in case he loses his action and the injunction was, in retrospect, unjustified. The plaintiff should specify the assets which he wishes to "freeze" by way of a *Mareva* injunction. A general "trawl" through all branches of a bank, in order to discover such assets, is discouraged (*Z Ltd.* v. *A-Z and AA-LL* [1982] 2 W.L.R. 288, 308).

The Anton Piller injunction

This is an *ex parte* injunction which authorises the inspection, photographing, custody or taking away of documents or other property held by a person other than the applicant. It will be granted only in very exceptional circumstances.

Such an injunction was granted in *Anton Piller K.G.* v. *Manufacturing Processes Ltd.* [1976] Ch. 55. In this case a German manufacturer of frequency converters for computers feared that his English agent would pass on confidential information of a new range of machinery to a competitor; the German principal obtained an injunction against the English agent authorising the principal's solicitor to enter the agent's premises, to inspect the relevant documents, and to remove them into his (the solicitor's) custody. This type of injunction is now granted by virtue of the Supreme Court Act 1981, s.33.

If such an injunction is granted, it is usually carried out by the applicant's solicitor who, if necessary, is accompanied by a police officer.

Limitation of Actions

Time for bringing actions

An action will be barred unless it is brought within the period laid down in the Limitation Act 1980. The Act does not extinguish the right; it has no substantive effect but bars only the procedural remedy. The defence of limitation is relevant only when it is pleaded by the party entitled thereto. The court will not reject a claim *ex officio* on the ground that it is statute-barred.

Periods of limitation

The periods of limitation are:

1. Actions founded on simple contract, six years after the cause of action accrued (section 25(1)).
2. Actions upon a deed, 12 years after the cause of action accrued (section 8(1)).
3. Actions brought to recover land, 12 years after the cause of action accrued, except in the case of the Crown, when the time is 30 years (section 15, and Sched. 1, Pt. II, para. 10).
4. Special provisions apply to an action for damages for personal injuries, whether founded on tort or the breach of a contractual or statutory duty. In such a case the period of limitation is, in principle, three years from the date of the accrual of the action or the date of knowledge (if later) of the person injured (section 11(4)), but the court has power to override the time limit (section 33).
5. Special provisions apply in the case of claims (whether in contract or tort) for **latent** damage caused by negligence. These provisions are the result of amendments to the Limitation Act 1980 by the Latent Damage Act 1986. The rules are that such a claim can be brought *either* within six years of the date of the accrual of the cause of action *or* within three years of when the plaintiff had (or ought to have had) knowledge of the actionable damage. Thus if the damage is latent and does not manifest itself for a number of years, the plaintiff will have a further three years after that in which to commence proceedings. This concession is, however, subject to a long-stop rule which is that in no circumstances can the period for

commencing proceedings be extended beyond 15 years from the date when the alleged act of negligence occurred.

6. Special provisions apply to claims for **product liability** under the Consumer Protection Act 1987 (see p. 363, *post*). Such a claim (whether it is for personal injury or for other loss or damage) must be brought *either* within three years of when the injury or damage occurred *or*, if it was latent, within three years of when the plaintiff discovered (or ought to have discovered) the injury or damage. Here also there is a long-stop rule, this time that no proceedings may be commenced more than 10 years after the defendant supplied the defective product in question.

In actions concerning the payment of money, time begins to run from the moment the right of action arose, *e.g.* breach or non-payment. When money is lent and no time for payment is specified, time runs from the date of the loan. If a date for payment is specified, time runs from that date. In a bill or a note payable on demand, time runs from the date of the making of the bill or note and not of the demand. Where a customer has paid money into a current account with a bank, time begins to run when a demand for payment has been made (*Joachimson* v. *Swiss Bank Corporation* [1921] 3 K.B. 111); in the case of a deposit account, where the customer has to give notice of his intention to withdraw, the period of limitation begins to run from the expiration of the notice.

If the plaintiff is a minor or a mentally disordered person when the cause of action accrued, time does not begin to run until the disability has ceased to operate. Once time has begun to run, no subsequent disability on the part of the person entitled to the cause of action prevents it from continuing to run (section 28).

The fact that the court offices are closed on a particular day does not lead to an extension of the period of limitation; that period expires on the earlier date on which the court offices were open (*Pritam Kaur* v. *S. Russell & Sons Ltd.* [1973] Q.B. 336).

Effect of fraud, concealment and mistake (*section 32*)

When:

1. the action is based on the fraud of the defendant or his agent; or

2. the right of action is concealed by the fraud of the defendant or his agent; or

3. the action is for relief from the consequences of a mistake; time does not begin to run until the plaintiff either has or with reasonable diligence could have discovered the fraud or mistake. "Fraud" in section 32 is not limited to common law fraud or matters of dishonesty or moral turpitude. It includes "equitable fraud," *i.e.* conduct which is unconscionable, having regard to the special relationship of the parties but it does not cover mere negligence (*Kitchen* v. *Royal Air Force Association* [1958] 1 W.L.R. 563, 572).[2]

In 1921 L. bought plum trees from B. warranted as "Purple Pershore." In 1928 L. discovered that they were not "Purple Pershore," and sued for damages for breach of warranty. B. pleaded the Statutes of Limitation (the forerunner of the Limitation Act 1939). *Held*, fraudulent misrepresentation and fraudulent concealment of the breach of warranty on the part of B. were good defences to this plea: *Lynn* v. *Bamber* [1930] 2 K.B. 72.

In 1961 Mr. King agreed to have a house built by Victor Parsons & Co. To the knowledge of the builders, but not of Mr. King, the foundations of the house were built on a disused chalk pit and were not underpinned sufficiently. In 1968 cracks appeared and the house was found to be unsafe for human habitation. In 1969 Mr. King commenced proceedings against the builders. *Held*, the defence of limitation failed because there had been unconscionable concealment constituting fraud within what is now section 32 of the 1980 Act: *King* v. *Victor Parsons & Co.* [1973] 1 W.L.R. 29.

The limitation period is only postponed by virtue of section 32(1) until the plaintiff has either discovered the fraud, concealment or mistake or "could with reasonable diligence have discovered it." The latter requirement obliges the plaintiff to act as a reasonable and prudent person would have acted in his position, but it does not oblige him to do everything possible to discover the true facts (*Peco Arts Inc.* v. *Hazlitt Gallery Ltd.* [1983] 1 W.L.R. 1315).

If property obtained by fraud or mistake is subsequently bought for valuable consideration by a person who neither knew nor had reason to believe that a fraud or mistake had occurred, it cannot be recovered nor can its value be claimed from the purchaser in good faith (section 32(3)) (*Eddis* v. *Chichester Constable* [1969] 2 Ch. 345).

[2] Some of the cases referred to in this section were decided under the Limitation Acts 1939 to 1976, which were repealed by the Limitation Act 1980.

Extension or exclusion of ordinary time limits

The ordinary time limits are sometimes extended. The extension in favour of a minor or a mentally disordered person has already been noted (above). Further, the right of action to recover a debt or other liquidated pecuniary claim (whether on simple contract or upon a deed) has a **fresh accrual** when there is:

1. An acknowledgment in writing signed by the person liable or his agent, and made to the person whose claim is being acknowledged. The acknowledgment need not contain or imply a promise to pay, or,

2. Payment in respect of the debt or claim made by the person liable or his agent to the creditor or his agent. The payment may be a payment of interest or a part payment of principal or interest (section 29(5)).

When there is an acknowledgment or a payment, time runs from the date of the acknowledgment or the last payment.

There is no fresh accrual of a right of action by acknowledgment or part payment unless the claim is for an amount which can be quantified in figures or is liquidated in the sense that it can be ascertained without further agreement of the parties (*Good* v. *Parry* [1963] 2 Q.B. 418); thus there is no fresh accrual of a right of action for unliquidated damages. Where the claim is for a debt, *i.e.* it is a liquidated claim, an acknowledgment under the Act need not identify the amount of the debt but may acknowledge a general indebtedness, provided that the amount of the debt can be ascertained by extraneous evidence (*Dungate* v. *Dungate* [1965] 1 W.L.R. 1471).

Part payment of the balance of a current account cannot be set off against the oldest debts in the account under the rule in *Clayton's* case, but is an acknowledgment of the whole amount of the outstanding balance (see *Re Footman, Bower & Co. Ltd.* [1961] Ch. 443, on p. 151, *ante*).

CHAPTER 10

OPERATION, ASSIGNMENT AND INTERPRETATION OF CONTRACT

PRIVITY OF CONTRACT

IN common law there must be privity of contract between the parties. Consequently a contract cannot impose liabilities upon one who is not a party to the contract.

X. sold to Y. some rubber heels packed in a box, in the lid of which was a notice that the heels were sold on the express agreement that they were not to be resold below certain prices. Z. bought the heels from Y. with notice of the agreement, but resold them below the prices. *Held*, as there was no contract between X. and Z., X. could not enforce the agreement: *McGruther* v. *Pitcher* [1904] 2 Ch. 306. But now see the Resale Prices Act 1976, p. 445, *post*.

The requirement of privity of contract further means that, except as stated earlier (pp. 62–63, *ante*), a contract cannot confer rights upon one who is not a party to it. Consequently, in English law—different from Scots law and many other legal systems—a contract for the benefit of a third party, giving the latter an actionable right to sue the promiser, is not admitted. If A. validly contracts with B. to pay C. £100, B.'s obligation can only be enforced by A., but it cannot be enforced by C. The technical reason for this antiquated rule is that no consideration has moved from C. to B.

G. married H., and their fathers, L. and M., agreed each to pay a sum of money to G. on a particular date, and that G. should have power to sue for the sums. G. sued L.'s executors for the sum. *Held*, he could not do so, as he was a stranger to the contract: *Tweddle* v. *Atkinson* (1861) 1 B. & S. 393.

See also *Scruttons Ltd.* v. *Midland Silicones Ltd.* [1962] A.C. 446 and *Beswick* v. *Beswick* [1968] A.C. 58 (p. 61, *ante*).

Although no rights are conferred, benefits obtained by one who is not a party to the contract can be retained.

S. was employed by a company. On the termination of his employment it was agreed between S. and the company that the company should make certain payments to S. during his life and after his death other payments to his wife and daughter. S. became bankrupt and died, and his trustee in bankruptcy claimed from his widow all sums paid to her by the company. *Held*, the claim failed, as the company fulfilled its contractual obligations in paying the widow, although she could not compel payment: *Re Schebsman* [1944] Ch. 83.

A contract imposes a duty on third parties not to induce any of the contracting parties to commit a breach of contract.

L. engaged W., an opera singer, to sing in his theatre for a season, and G., knowing of his contract, induced W. to break it and to sing for him. *Held*, L. could recover damages from G.: *Lumley* v. *Gye* [1853] 2 E. & B. 216.

If a third party induces another to terminate a contract in a lawful manner, *e.g.* by giving notice, he will not be liable to an action. It is not actionable to induce a person by peaceful means not to enter into a contract with another, but if physical violence or threats are used, the person using them may be sued.

Special provisions apply to **trade disputes.** The Trade Union and Labour Relations Act 1974, as amended,[1] affords trade unions and employers' associations and their officers and members immunity from actions in tort but, speaking generally, this immunity is not available in disputes in which they are not directly involved. Section 13 of the Act, as amended by the Employment Act 1980, provides that an act done by a person in contemplation or furtherance of a trade dispute shall not, in principle, be actionable in tort; but this protection is not available in the case of so-called *secondary action*, unless the 1980 Act admits such action (s.17(3) and (4)). The main purpose of secondary action is to prevent or disrupt the supply of goods or services to an employer who has a trade dispute with his employees; the employees of the supplier, who is under contract to deliver goods or to perform services to the "blacked" employer, are called out on strike. Secondary action may, in appropriate cases,

[1] By the Trade Union and Labour Relations (Amendment) Act 1976 and the Employment Acts 1980 and 1982.

give rise to a civil action for damages by the "blacked" employer against the trade union engaged in this practice, its officers or its members, if such action constitutes the tort of intimidation, or the tort of inducing a breach of contract is committed (*Merkur Island Shipping Corp.* v. *Laughton* [1983] 2 W.L.R. 778). Peaceful picketing at or near one's own place of work is protected but, *secondary picketing*, *i.e.* picketing of other persons' place of business, is, in principle, not protected and if a tort is committed in the course of secondary picketing, the tortfeasor may be liable in damages (section 15, as substituted by the Employment Act 1980, s.16). It is further provided that the courts shall not compel an employee to do any work or attend at any place of employment, by ordering specific performance of a contract of employment or by issuing an injunction restraining a breach or threatened breach of such a contract (section 16).

Assignment of Contract

Liabilities under a contract cannot be assigned without the consent of the other party to the contract. They can only be assigned by novation which, as will be seen, requires the consent of the other party.

Rights under a contract can normally be assigned, provided they are of proprietary character. This would normally include the assignment of a claim of damages for breach of contract and may even include the assignment of a "bare" right to litigate, unless such assignment offends against the law of maintenance and champerty, by involving "trafficking in litigation" (*Trendex Trading Corporation* v. *Credit Suisse* [1982] A.C. 679; see pp. 116–117, *ante*). On the other hand, highly personal rights, *e.g.* those arising from a contract of service, cannot be assigned, except by consent of the other party to the contract.

On the amalgamation of companies the court had power to order "the transfer to the transferee company of the whole or any part of the undertaking and of the property or liabilities of any transferor company" (Companies Act 1948, s.208(1)(*a*)). *Held*, such order did not include an assignment of a contract of service because an employee was free to choose his employer and the right to the employee's services could not be transferred without his consent: *Nokes* v. *Doncaster Amalgamated Collieries Ltd.* [1940] A.C. 1014.

The assignment of rights under a contract is carried out by:

1. Novation.
2. Legal assignment.
3. Equitable assignment.
4. Assignment by operation of law.

Novation

This is a transaction whereby, with the agreement of all parties concerned, a new debtor is substituted for the old one. The creditor, at the request of the debtor, agrees to take another person as his debtor in the place of the original debtor. The effect of novation is to release the original debtor from his obligations under the contract and to impose those obligations on the new debtor. Novation frequently arises in partnerships on a change in the membership of the firm when the creditors, expressly or by implication, agree to accept the liability of the new firm and to discharge the old firm.

M. insured his life with the B. N. Association. The Association became amalgamated with the E. Society and ceased to carry on business, and a memorandum was indorsed on M.'s policy that the E. Society would be liable for the policy money. Subsequent premiums were paid to the E. Society. *Held*, there was a complete novation, and, on the winding up of the two companies, M. had no right of proof against the B. N. Association: *Re European Assurance Society* (1876) 3 Ch.D. 391.

Legal assignment

By the Law of Property Act 1925, s.136, all debts and other legal things in action—*choses in action*—may be assigned, but the assignment must be:

(a) in writing, signed by the assignor;
(b) absolute and not purporting to be by way of charge only;
(c) followed by express notice in writing given to the debtor, trustee, or other person from whom the assignor would have been entitled to claim such a debt or thing in action.

A *chose in action* is a right of property which can only be enforced by action and not by taking physical possession, as can be done with *choses in possession.* Choses in action include rights arising under a contract.

An assignment, to be absolute, must be of the whole interest of the assignor and not of a portion of it, so that the debtor will not be inconvenienced by having to seek out two creditors. It is absolute although it is by way of mortgage or by way of trust. Conditional assignments and assignments of part of a debt are not absolute.

A schoolmaster assigned to a moneylender so much of his salary as should be necessary to repay the sums borrowed from the moneylender. *Held*, this was not an absolute assignment but it was an assignment purporting to be by way of charge only; *Jones* v. *Humphreys* [1902] 1 K.B. 10.

The notice informing the debtor of the assignment need not state the date of the assignment (*Van Lynn Developments Ltd.* v. *Pelias Construction Co. Ltd.* [1969] 1 Q.B. 607). An assignment of which no notice has been given, does not operate as a legal assignment under section 136 of the Law of Property Act, but operates only as an equitable assignment (*Warner Bros. Records Inc.* v. *Rollgreen Ltd.* [1976] Q.B. 430).

The assignment takes effect subject to any defences or claims open to the debtor against the assignor existing at the time of his receipt of the notice of assignment. This is expressed by saying that the assignee takes "subject to equities." The defences or claims, however, must arise out of the contract itself to which the assignment relates. Further, a set-off founded on damages for fraud inducing the debtor to enter into the contract cannot be made against an innocent assignee (*Stoddart* v. *Union Trust Ltd.* [1912] 1 K.B. 181).

The effect of the assignment is to transfer to the assignee—

(a) the legal right to the debt or chose in action;
(b) the right to sue the debtor and all other remedies against him;
(c) the power to give a good discharge without the concurrence of the assignor.

The assignment of a legal chose in action does not require consideration (*Re Westerton* [1919] 2 Ch. 104).

Equitable assignment

An assignment which does not comply with the requirements of a legal assignment may still be valid as an equitable assignment, as long as the intention to assign is clear. If the intention is clear, no particular formalities are necessary and the assignment need not be in writing. Notice to the debtor need not be given to perfect the assignee's title, but it should be given:

1. Because the debtor can set up any defences against the assignee which he had against the assignor up to the date of his receipt of the notice. If, therefore, he makes a payment to the assignor before he receives notice of assignment, this payment is good as against the assignee.

2. To gain priority over any subsequent assignee without notice of his assignment.

It is no objection to an equitable assignment that part only of a debt is assigned or that it includes future debts.

K. agreed with B., who financed him, that the purchase price of all goods sold by K. should be paid direct to B. K. sold goods to D., B. gave notice to D. to pay the price to B., but D. disregarded the notice and paid K. *Held*, there was an equitable assignment of the price, and D. was liable to pay B. notwithstanding that they had already paid K.: *Brandt* v. *Dunlop Rubber Co.* [1905] A.C. 454.

An equitable assignee cannot enforce the right assigned by action without joining the legal owner (*Performing Right Society* v. *London Theatre of Varieties Ltd.* [1924] A.C. 1).

An equitable assignment which is complete does not require consideration, but an incomplete equitable assignment made without consideration is ineffective (*Re McArdle* [1951] Ch. 669).

An equitable assignment of a legal chose in action must be distinguished from the assignment of an equitable chose in action. Examples of the latter are: a claim by a beneficiary against his trustee, and a claim by a legatee against an executor.

Contracts involving the personal credit, ability or other personal qualifications of a party cannot be assigned, either legally or equitably. Examples are: a contract to paint a picture, or a contract of service. Even a contract for the sale of goods may be incapable of being assigned on this ground.

B. agreed to supply K., a cake manufacturer, with all the eggs he required for a year. K. transferred his business to a company to which he assigned the benefit of his contract with B. B. refused to supply the company. *Held*, he was entitled to refuse, as the contract was a personal one, referring to the number of eggs K. would require personally, and so could not be assigned without B.'s consent: *Kemp* v. *Baerselman* [1906] 2 K.B. 604.

The following are transferred at law in accordance with the statute relating to them and not in the manner laid down in the Law of Property Act 1925, s.136:

(a) Bill of exchange and promissory notes according to the Bills of Exchange Act 1882.
(b) Shares in companies registered under the Companies Acts 1948 to 1985, according to those Acts.
(c) Bills of lading according to the Bills of Lading Act 1855.
(d) Policies of marine insurance according to the Marine Insurance Act 1906.
(e) Policies of life assurance according to the Policies of Assurance Act 1867.

Assignment by operation of law

Contracts are assigned by operation of law on—

(a) death, and
(b) bankruptcy.

Death of a party passes all his rights and liabilities under a contract to his personal representatives. The only exceptions to this are contracts of personal service and contracts involving personal skill.

Bankruptcy passes all rights and liabilities to the bankrupt's trustee in bankruptcy (see p. 698, *post*).

Interpretation of Contract

The provisions of the Interpretation Act 1978 apply to contracts in the same manner as to other legal transactions. The general principle on interpretation of contracts was, in the older view, to ascertain the actual intention of the parties to the contract. The modern view is to ascertain "what each [party] was reasonably entitled to conclude from the attitude of the other" (*per* Lord Reid in *McCutcheon* v. *David Macbrayne Ltd.* [1964] 1 W.L.R. 125, 128). An objective standard is thus substituted for a subjective one.

Parol evidence

If a contract is reduced by the parties into writing, the general rule is that it cannot be varied by parol evidence. The exceptions to this rule are:

1. Parol evidence may be given to show that the written contract was made subject to a condition.

P. agreed to sell a share in an invention to C. A written agreement was drawn up setting out the agreement, but it was verbally agreed that it should not be binding unless X. approved the invention. X. did not approve. *Held*, parol evidence of X.'s non-approval could be given: *Pym* v. *Campbell* (1856) 6 E. & B.370.

2. If the whole contract was not intended to be put into writing, parol evidence can be given of the additional terms. If the whole contract is required by statute to be in writing, this exception does not apply, and no parol evidence incorporating terms can be given.

A. granted to B. the lease of a house for three years. The terms were arranged, but B. refused to hand over the counterpart which he had signed unless he was assured that the drains were in order. A. gave this assurance. The lease did not refer to the drains, which were bad. *Held*, B. could give parol evidence of the warranty as to the drains, because it was collateral to the lease and did not contradict it: *De Lassalle* v. *Guildford* [1901] 2 K.B. 215.

3. Parol evidence can be given to prove the rescission of a written contract. This applies even to contracts required by statute to be in writing (*Morris* v. *Baron & Co.* [1918] A.C. 1).

4. Parol evidence can be given to explain a latent but not patent ambiguity.

A patent ambiguity is an ambiguity which is apparent on the face of the document. If in a cheque the amount is stated to be "one hundred pounds" in words and "£150" in figures, the ambiguity is patent. In such a case no evidence can be given to show which is correct, the law conclusively presuming in favour of the words as against the figures.

A latent ambiguity is one which is not apparent. For example, if two men have the same name or if a man agrees to buy "your wool," parol evidence can be given to identify the man in the one case and to show the quantity and the quality of the wool in the other.

5. Parol evidence can be given to prove a trade usage or a local custom.

Thus, where in a charterparty the charterer agrees to take the cargo from alongside the ship at his own expense, parol evidence is admissible to show where "alongside" is according to the custom of a particular port.

Chapter 11

CONFLICT OF LAWS

Conflict of laws is the branch of English law which deals with cases having a foreign element. Such foreign elements are very common in commercial law, as so many business transactions are of an international kind. This chapter is primarily concerned with the three main ways (in Business law at least) in which such issues can arise.

The first of these is "which country's law is to govern the contract?" In the field of business law there is very often a foreign element. For instance, if a Greek company contracts with an Iranian company for the shipment of oil from Bahrain to South Africa, payment to be in Swiss francs, the question arises of which law is to govern the contract. Sometimes the parties may have thought about this matter and inserted a choice of law clause into their contract, specifying which law will govern. Very often, however, they have not thought about it, and it is only when a dispute arises between the parties that the choice of law governing their contract becomes a major issue. If they decide to litigate their dispute, the courts will be concerned to determine the applicable law governing the contract (although if neither party pleads that a foreign law applies, the English courts will automatically apply English law). Complex rules known as the "choice of law" rules are applied by the courts to determine this.

Secondly, should a dispute between parties arise, there may be problems determining the appropriate forum (country) for litigation. This is a matter of deciding which courts have jurisdiction to deal with the case. The parties are not free to litigate in whatever courts they please. There may be specific advantages to be gained from litigating in one forum rather than another (*e.g.* awards of damages tend to be higher in the U.S. courts than in many others, which is why the victims of the Union Carbide disaster at Bhopal tried to sue in the U.S.; or the rules on admissibility of evidence may be more favourable to one party in some jurisdictions). There may, therefore, be good reasons why a litigant would wish to proceed in one forum rather than another, but it must be determined first, whether according to the chosen forum's conflicts rules, the courts in the country chosen have jurisdiction. The rules are very complex.

Thirdly, a litigant may be faced with another sort of problem. His case may have proceeded to judgment in the courts of one country, only for him to discover that the defendant has no assets there. If, however, the defendant has any property elsewhere, it may be possible to enforce the judgment against him in the courts of another jurisdiction. English law has developed rules as to the types of foreign judgments that will be recognised and enforced here.

It is notable that these issues arise mainly in the course of litigation. Indeed, conflicts problems frequently arise in commercial litigation. It is a fast developing area of the law, and one where statute law has recently made major inroads.

Determining the Applicable Law to Govern the Contract

As indicated earlier, the choice of law governing a contract may be problematic. Even if the parties have expressly chosen a law to govern the contract, this choice may not be upheld by the courts if they feel that this choice was undesirable (because, *e.g.* the parties have chosen a law totally unconnected with their contract in order to avoid particular mandatory rules, such as those concerning exclusion clauses, that would normally apply).

The Contracts (Applicable Law) Act 1990 will now (mostly) govern the application of choice of law rules in contract. This Act brings into force the Rome Convention on the Law Applicable to Contractual Obligations of 1980, which is scheduled to it. The Convention came into force on April 1, 1991. It applies to all contracts **concluded** after that date (Article 17). The Rome Convention is not strictly an EC creation (it does not fall within the ambit of Article 220 of the Treaty of Rome) but it does bear a strong EC stamp. The signatories so far are all members of the EC. Its purpose is to harmonise the choice of law rules in contract and so prevent forum shopping (a somewhat similar objective to the 1968 Brussels Convention on Jurisdiction and Judgments, see below).

The Convention covers contractual obligations involving a foreign element (*i.e.* international contracts). However, it does not cover all types of contractual obligation—those relating to trusts and succession, matrimonial property rights, maintenance obligations and family relationships are excluded (Article 1). Bills of exchange, cheques and promissory notes are also excluded (Article 1(2)(*c*)). Nor does the Convention apply to arbitration agreements and agreements on the choice of court. Questions concerning the creation, capacity and internal organisation of companies and other incorporated bodies and unincorporated bodies, their winding up, mergers and liability and that of officers do not fall within its scope (Article 1(2)(*e*)). Contracts of insurance covering risks situated in the EC are not covered by the Convention (these are already covered by EEC Directives 73/239 and 88/357). Other types of insurance as well as reinsuance contracts fall within the Convention (Article 1(3) and 1(4)).

Apart from this, the Convention affects all types of contracts, not just those which have an EC connection (Article 2). Unlike the Brussels Convention on Jurisdiction and Judgments, the domicile of the defendant is irrelevant. So, even if the contracting parties are American and Australian, the Convention will apply, provided their dispute is to be settled by the courts of a contracting state.

The applicable law

The basic rules of the Convention are not so different from those existing prior to its application, as will be seen. The Convention uses the term "applicable law" rather than the term "proper law" previously used by the English courts, but these terms signify the same concept. The two principal provisions for determining the law to govern a particular contract are contained in Articles 3(1) and 4(1). Article 3(1) states:

> "A contract shall be governed by the law chosen by the parties. The choice must be express or demonstrated with reasonable certainty by the terms of the contract or the circumstances of the case. By their choice the parties can select the law applicable to the whole or a part only of the contract."

The law chosen by the parties may be one with which they have no connection and need not be the law of a contracting state (Article 2). In the absence of an express choice of law an arbitration clause (locating the aribitration in a particular country) or previous course of dealing would probably be sufficient demonstration of the parties' choice. If the choice of law is neither express, nor able to be demonstrated with reasonable certainty, then resort is to be had to the provisions of Article 4, *i.e.* the law with which the contract is most closely connected.

Article 4(1) provides:

> "To the extent that the law applicable to a contract has not been chosen in accordance with Article 3, the contract shall be governed by the law of the country with which it is most closely connected . . . "

This is very similar to the test employed up to now by the English courts. However, the Convention provides (Article 4(2), 4(3) and 4(4)) that certain rebuttable presumptions will assist in determining the country with the closest connection. The most important of these is the presumption that the law of the party who has to effect "the performance which is characteristic of the contract" will apply (Article 4(2)). This will usually be the law of the habitual residence of that party or of that party's place of business (Article 4(2)). The concept of characteristic performance is taken from Swiss law and the most novel feature of the Convention.

Article 4(5) provides that the presumptions shall not apply when "it appears from the circumstances as a whole that the contract is more closely connected with another country."

Consumer and employment contracts

These are subject to special rules (Articles 5 and 6). These provisions are a concession to the view that consumers and employees are weaker parties open to exploitation by their supplier/employer. The applicable law of these contracts in the absence of express choice is that of the consumer's habitual residence (Article 5(2)) or where the employee habitually carries out his duties (Article 6).

Mandatory rules

The Convention also makes use of the somewhat novel concept (to English lawyers at least) of "mandatory rules." These are rules which cannot be derogated from by the contract (Article 3(3)), *i.e.* the parties cannot avoid them by expressly choosing another system of law to govern their contract. Examples of such rules common to English law are the Unfair Contract Terms Act 1977, the Carriage of Goods by Sea Act 1971 and Article X of the Hague-Visby Rules. Article 7(1) of the Convention states that "effect may be given to the mandatory rules of the law of another country with which the situation has a close connection." However, Article 22 of the Convention allows Contracting States to reserve the right not to apply this provision, and the U.K. has adopted this reservation, fearing the commercial and legal uncertainty caused by the provision. Section 2(2) of the Contracts (Applicable Law) Act confirms that Article 7(1) does not have the force of law in the U.K.

However, by Article 7(2), which does have the force of law in the U.K., the courts may apply the mandatory rules of the **forum** in which the issue is litigated. This provision reflects traditional practice. For instance in *The Hollandia* [1983] 1 Lloyd's Rep. 1, it was held that a clause in a bill of lading which provided for a lower maximum limitation of liability of the carrier than that contained in the Hague-Visby Rules was invalid when litigated in England, in a case to which the Hague-Visby rules applied. Article 7(2) was introduced with a view to safeguarding the rules of laws of the **forum**, especially the rules on cartels, competition and restrictive practices.

Familiar too, to English lawyers, is the provision which allows the court to refuse to apply the rules of any applicable law where to do so would be "manifestly incompatible" with the public policy of the forum (Article 16). For example, the court may refuse to enforce a contract which involves trading with the enemy (see *Dynamit A/G* v. *Rio Tinto Co.* [1918] A.C. 292 H.L.).

It is not certain whether the Convention makes any great changes to the traditional (and often confusing) English choice of law rules on illegality (see below under the common law). It would seem that many of the cases decided at common law could be decided the same way under the Convention. The courts may find a contract illegal because it would be "manifestly incompatible" with some public policy of the forum. Alternatively, illegality under the law of the place of performance would have an effect if that law were the applicable law.

These basic rules outlined above will cover most of the questions arising out of the contract. Article 10 provides a non-exhaustive list of the types of situation where the applicable law will apply. It will govern questions of interpretation, performance, consequences of breach, and discharge of obligations. Article 10(1)(*c*) states that the assessment of damages is a matter for the applicable law except in so far as this is to be considered procedural. Under English law the assessment of damages is considered to be a procedural matter (for the consequences of classifying a matter as substantive or procedural, see below).

However, the applicable law will not govern certain specific issues, such as material and formal validity and incapacity (Articles 8–13).

For instance, the existence and validity of the contract will be governed by what English lawyers call the "putative proper law" (Article 8), *i.e.* the court pretends that the contract is valid, finds the applicable law, and then determines whether, according to that law, the contract actually is valid. This approach follows the practice already established at common law (*Albeko Schumaschinen* v. *Kamborian Shoe Machine Co. Ltd.* [1961] 111 L.J. 519.

The Convention does not apply to questions of capacity, except that it provides that those who contract in good faith with someone who is incapable under another law are protected from that incapacity unless they were aware (or should have been aware) of it (Article 11).

Article 15 expressly excludes the operation of the doctrine of renvoi (*i.e.* the Convention is concerned only with the **internal** law, not the conflicts rules of the relevant country. This has been the position at common law for some while).

As with the 1968 Brussels Convention, the European Court of Justice will have jurisdiction to give rulings on matters of its interpretation (by virtue of the Brussels Protocol, Schedule 3 to the Contracts (Applicable Law) Act 1990). However, unlike the position with regard to the Brussels Convention, the House of Lords **may** (as is the case with other states' final appeal courts), but is not bound to, request a preliminary ruling from the European Court of Justice on the interpretation of the Convention. Section 3 of the Contracts (Applicable Law) Act provides that if the matter is not so referred it shall be determined in accordance with principles laid down by the European Court.

The Common Law

The traditional choice of law rules will continue to apply to contracts made prior to the coming into force of the Act, and to those types of contractual obligation that do not fall within its scope.

To determine the law which applies, the English courts look for the "proper law" of the contract. Provided the parties' intention is bona fide, they are free to choose as the proper law any law they like, even the law of a country with which the contract has no connection: *Vita Food Products Inc.* v. *Unus Shipping Co. Ltd.* [1939] A.C. 277. Where the parties have not made an express choice, the courts look for a law that can be inferred from the parties' conduct, *e.g.* a choice of forum clause, which will usually be decisive in this respect (although the position will be different if the parties have chosen an arbitration tribunal which does not have a permanent location: *Compagnie Tunisienne de Navigation S.A.* v. *Compagnie d'Armement Maritime S.A.* (1971) A.C. 572, where a clause in the contract providing for arbitration in London was held not to be conclusive).

If the court is unable to find an inferred choice of law it determines "the system of law . . . with which the transaction has its closest and most real connection" (*Bonython* v. *Commonwealth of Australia* [1951] A.C. 201 at 219). This is the law which, in the judgment of the court, "ordinary, reasonable and sensible businessmen would have been likely to have (intended) if their minds had been directed to the question" (*per* Singleton L.J. in *The Assunzione* [1954] P. 150, 176). Matters to be considered are: the law of the place where the contract was made, the law of the place where it is to be performed, the currency in which payment is to be made, the form of the contract and the language in which it is written, etc. Thus in *The Assunzione*:

The court had to determine whether a charter party was governed by French or Italian law. An Italian ship had been chartered by French shippers to carry grain from Dunkirk to Venice. The charter party was concluded in Paris, but written in English, although with a supplement in French. The bills of lading were in the French standard form. The ship flew the Italian flag, freight and demurrage were payable in Naples in Italian currency. Italy was the place of performance. Although no factor seemed to be of decisive significance, the Court of Appeal, weighing up all the factors in the balance, held that the proper law was Italian law—the crucial factor seemed to be the obligation to pay freight and demurrage at Naples.

Normally, the proper law of an insurance contract will be the law of the insurer's place of business (*Rossano* v. *Manufacturer's Life Insurance Co.* [1963] 2 Q.B. 352, although this law was displaced in *Amin Rasheed Shipping Corp.* v. *Kuwait Insurance Co.* [1984] A.C. 50). Reinsurance contracts are generally governed by the law of the country where the market (*e.g.* Lloyd's) is situated.

A bank account will generally be governed by the law of the place where the branch at which the account is kept is situated, not where the bank has its head office (*X A.G. and Others* v. *A Bank* [1983] 2 All E.R. 464) but this presumption is rebuttable—*Libyan Arab Foreign Bank* v. *Manufacturer's Hanover Trust* [1989] 3 W.L.R. 314. Commodity agreements, *e.g.* for the sale of coffee, will normally be governed by the law of the country in which the market is situated (*Tamaro and Tamari* v. *Bernhard Rofhos* [1980] 2 Lloyd's Rep. 55).

Arbitration clauses

As these are specifically excluded by Article 1(2)(*d*) of the Rome Convention, the common law determines the law to be applied to such agreements. The proper law of the arbitration agreement will be determined in the same way as that of any contract. The law of the place at which the arbitration is to be held is likely to be the proper law, although this is not conclusive (see *Compagnie Tunisienne, supra*).

The substantive provisions of the proper law determine many issues raised by the contract. However, some important issues are not governed by the proper law—notably the form of the contract (usually determined by the law of the place of contracting) and the effect of illegality.

Illegality

The rules determining the effect of illegality are not straightforward. It is, however, clear that if a contract, or its performance, is illegal by its proper law then it will not be enforced in England (*Kahler* v. *Midland Bank* [1950] A.C. 24). The English courts will also refuse to enforce any contract which they regard as contrary to

English public policy, *e.g.* a contract for sexual immorality, even if the contract is governed by a foreign law under which it is lawful (*Kaufman* v. *Gerson* [1904] 1 K.B. 591). In particular, they will not enforce any contract whose performance requires the doing of an act in a foreign friendly country which is an offence by its law—as in *Foster* v. *Driscoll* [1929] 1 K.B. 470, where the parties had entered into an agreement to import whisky into the U.S., contrary to its prohibition laws. The Court of Appeal held that it would be contrary to public policy to enforce the contract. In *Ralli Bros.* v. *Compania Naviera Sota y Aznar* [1920] 2 K.B. 287, the English courts held that an action for the balance of freight payable on a cargo of jute could not be recovered, as such payment was illegal in Spain, where payment ought to have been made (due to a Spanish law that freight must not exceed £10 per ton). However, it is submitted that the *Ralli* case is not necessarily authority for the proposition that illegality by the law of the place of performance renders a contract unenforceable, since, in *Ralli*, English law was the proper law, and by English law the contract was frustrated.

A contract will not be enforced in England if it is contrary to mandatory provisions of English law, such as those contained in the Unfair Contract Terms Act 1977.

It would seem that many of the cases on illegality, discussed above could still be decided the same way under the provisions of the Rome Convention on Contractual Obligations (see above).

Exchange contracts

The English courts will not enforce an exchange contract which its contrary to the Bretton Woods Agreement Act 1945. An exchange contract is a contract concerning the exchange of the currency of one country for that of another and it will be contrary to the Bretton Woods Agreement if it contravenes the exchange control regulations of a foreign country which is a member of the Agreement. A contract which is not a monetary transaction and is, in essence, a commercial contract for the sale or purchase of merchandise or commodities is not an exchange contract within the meaning of the Bretton Woods Agreement even if the price is expressed in foreign currency (*Wilson, Smithett & Cope Ltd.* v. *Terruzzi* [1976] Q.B. 683). Where, however, a sales transaction is used as a disguise for a contract, which, according to its true nature, is an exchange contract under the Bretton Woods Agreement, the contract is unenforceable in English law when it contravenes this agreement (*United City Merchants* v. *Royal Bank of Canada* [1983] A.C. 168).

Substance and Procedure

If a matter is classified as procedural, it is governed by English law whatever the proper law, or applicable law, of the contract might be. Remedies are classified as procedural and so a matter to be determined by the *lex fori* (the law of the country where the litigation occurs). However, sometimes it may be very difficult to determine whether a rule of law is procedural or substantive. In *Chaplin* v. *Boys* [1971] A.C. 356, the House of Lords had to determine whether the recovery of damages for pain and suffering should be classified as a question of remoteness of damage (a question of substance) or as a question of quantification of damages (a question of procedure). The majority classified it as a question of remoteness.

Judgments in foreign currency

The English courts normally award damages only in English currency. However, in *Miliangos* v. *George Frank* [1976] A.C. 443, the House of Lords held that in certain cases the English courts could give judgment in a foreign currency. In this case, Miliangos, who carried on business in Switzerland, sold a quantity of polyester yarn to a company in England. The purchase price was fixed in Swiss francs. The buyer failed to pay. The House of Lords held that the court had jurisdiction to order payment of the price in Swiss francs.

Jurisdiction of the English Courts

If the English courts do not have jurisdiction, they cannot try the case. The English courts apply different sets of rules depending on the situation of the parties. Roughly speaking, the question of jurisdiction will depend on either the domicile of the defendant, the parties' choice of forum or sometimes on the subject matter of the case.

As a general guideline:

1. Where the defendant is domiciled in the European Community, the Brussels Convention on Jurisdiction and Enforcement of Judgments in Civil and Commercial Matters 1968 will apply. This Convention was given the force of law in the U.K. by the Civil Jurisdiction and Judgments Act 1982 (since amended by the Civil Jurisdiction and Judgments Act (Amendment) Order 1990). An amended form of this Convention applies to intra-U.K. jurisdiction.
2. Where the defendant is domiciled in an E.F.T.A. country (*i.e.* Austria, Finland, Iceland, Norway, Switzerland, Sweden) which has ratified the Lugano Convention on Jurisdiction and Judgments in Civil and Commercial Matters 1988, then the provisions of this Convention (as implemented in the U.K. by the Civil Jurisdiction and Judgments Act 1991) will apply.
3. Where the defendant is domiciled elsewhere, or the case does not fall within the scope of either Convention, the English courts will apply their traditional rules.

1. Jurisdiction under the Brussels Convention

A principal aim of the 1968 Brussels Convention was to provide for the free circulation of judgments within the EEC. This, it was decided, could be brought about only by harmonisation of the laws on jurisdiction, and the Convention sets out complex rules in this area.

The provisions of the Brussels Convention have now been amended (although not greatly) by the San Sebastiano Convention which was concluded on the Accession of Spain and Portugal to the Brussels Convention in 1989). In the U.K. these amendments take the form of the C.J.J.A. 1982 (Amendments) Order 1990 (S.I. 1990 No. 2591). This order amends Schedule I to the 1982 Act, which contains the text of the Brussels Convention, to incorporate all changes made by the San Sebastiano Convention, although it does not amend the intra-U.K. rules in Schedule 4 to the Act. This order will come into force when the U.K. ratifies the San Sebastiano Convention (probably before the end of 1991). The Convention, in its amended form, will apply only to "legal proceedings instituted and to authentic instruments formally drawn up or registered after entry into force of this Convention" (Title VI Accession Convention). So, for some time, the provisions of the Brussels Convention in both its original and amended forms will have to be considered. Substantial amendments are considered in the text below.

Scope

The Convention is concerned only with the international jurisdiction of the contracting states and does not apply where the dispute contains no foreign element.

The Convention applies only to civil and commercial matters (Article 1). Unfortunately, no definition is given of "civil and commercial matters" although Article 1 states that it does not include "revenue, customs or administrative matters." Thus public law matters are excluded from the scope of the Convention (see, for guidance on this the case of *L.T.U.* v. *Eurocontrol* [1977] 2 E.L.R. 61, where it was held that the Convention did not apply to the situation where a public authority was acting in the exercise of its powers).

Certain matters are specifically excluded from the scope of the Convention by Article 1, namely:

(i) The status or legal capacity of natural persons, rights in property arising out of a matrimonial relationship, wills and succession.
(ii) Bankruptcy, proceedings relating to the winding up of insolvent companies or other legal persons, judicial arrangements, compositions and analogous proceedings.
(iii) Social Security.
(iv) Arbitration.

What types of cases then fall within the scope of the Convention? Basically, when the defendant is domiciled in a contracting state, and the case concerns a civil and commercial matter of a type not excluded by Article 1, the bases of jurisdiction under the Convention will apply. Generally, if the defendant is not domiciled in a contracting state then the Convention will not apply, and the courts will apply their traditional (pre-Convention) bases of Jurisdiction instead. However, there are some exceptions to this general principle, and some provisions of the Convention (*e.g.* Articles 16 and 17) will operate to determine which courts have jurisdiction, even in cases where the defendant is not domiciled in a contracting state.

General jurisdiction

Article 2 of the Convention provides that "persons domiciled in a Contracting State shall, whatever their nationality, be sued in the Courts of that State." This provision operates as a general rule, to which there are a few exceptions. The domicile of the plaintiff is usually irrelevant. So it will not be possible for the plaintiff to sue in the courts of his own domicile, because it suits his own personal convenience (contrast this with the traditional rules on jurisdiction). If he tries to do so, those courts will have to decline jurisdiction. To determine the actual domicile of the defendant, reference must be made to sections 41 and 42 of the Civil Jurisdiction and Judgments Act and Article 52 of the Convention. Roughly speaking, a person's domicile must be determined according to the laws of the member state where he is allegedly domiciled.

For the purposes of the Convention a natural person will be domiciled in the **U.K.** if he resides there and has a substantial connection with the U.K., or a particular part of it—section 41 of the Civil Jurisdiction and Judgments Act. A corporation will be domiciled in the U.K. if it has its seat there. Section 42 of the Act provides that a corporation's seat will be in the U.K. if either (a) it was incorporated or formed under the law of part thereof and has its registered office or some other office address therein, or (b) its central management or control is exercised there.

Separate provision is made for the domicile of insurers and suppliers of goods, services or credit to customers (section 44). A trust is domiciled in that part of the U.K. with whose law it has the closest and most real connection (section 45(3)).

Mere physical presence is not sufficient for the provisions of Article 2 to operate. The defendant must actually be domiciled in that state.

Special Jurisdiction

In some cases a defendant domiciled in a member state may **also** be sued in the courts of another contracting state. This is known as the Special Jurisdiction of the Convention. The relevant provisions are in Section 2 (Articles 5 and 6) of the Convention. Only the most important provisions will be considered here.

The relevant situations where the defendant can be sued in a contracting state other than that of his domicile are these:

Article 5(1) in matters relating to a contract, in the courts for the place of the performance of the obligation in question

Since the laws of the different states which are parties to the Convention have different concepts of contract, the European Court has interpreted "contract" as an autonomous Community concept for the purposes of Article 5(1) (see *Peters* v. *ZNAV* (1983) E.C.R. 987).

What is the "obligation in question" to which Article 5(1) refers? In *De Bloos* v. *Bouyer* (1976) E.C.R. 1497 the European Court of Justice held that Article 5(1) refers to the contractual obligation which forms the basis of the legal proceedings. Thus, where the plaintiff sues the defendant for breach of contract, he will be able to sue in the courts of the state where that performance of the obligation should have occurred, as well as in the courts of the defendant's domicile. However what is the position where the plaintiff sues in respect of several different contractual obligations and places of performance? In *Ivenel* v. *Schwab* [1982] E.C.R. 1891, the European Court held that, in such a case, the relevant obligation is that which characterises the contract as a whole (borrowing the doctrine of "characteristic performance" from the European Contract Convention). However, in the later case of *Shenavai* v. *Kreischer*, [1987] E.C.R. 239, the European Court decided that *Ivenel* was to be confined to contracts of employment and the *De Bloos* approach to be applied in all other cases. In cases where the plaintiff claims performance of several different obligations, the Court held that the judge must determine the principal obligation on which the action is based, and jurisdiction should be determined accordingly. This approach was confirmed by the English courts in *Medway Packaging* v. *Meurer Maschinen Gmbh* [1989] F.T.L.R. October 20 (Hobhouse J.).

Article 5(1) is amended by the San Sebastiano Convention to include a new provision relating to contracts of employment. In such cases, the place of performance of the obligation in question will be "that where the employee habitually carries out his work, or if the employee does not habitually carry out his work in any one country, the employer may also be sued in the courts for the place where the business which engaged the employee was or is now situated."

This provision is intended to protect employees.

Article 5(3) in matters relating to tort, delict or quasi-delict, in the courts for the place where the harmful event occurred

What is meant in this context by a tort or a delict? In *Kalfelis* v. *Schroder, Munchmeyer, Hengst* [1988] E.C.R. 5565 the European Court held (rather unhelpfully) that "matters relating to tort delict or quasi-delict" included any action which sought to call in question the liability of a defendant and which was not connected with matters related to a contract under Article 5(1).

In *Bier* v. *Mines de Potasse d'Alsace* [1976] E.C.R. 1735, the European Court held that the place where the harmful event occurred is both the place where the wrongful event occurred and that where the plaintiff sustained damage or harm. In that case a French defendant was alleged to have polluted the waters of the Rhine in France. The Rhine flowed into Holland, where damage was caused to the Dutch plaintiff's horticultural property. It was held that both the French and Dutch courts had jurisdiction. This ruling was justified on the basis that Article 5(3) is designed to give the plaintiff the option of suing elsewhere than in the Contracting state where the defendant is domiciled. Applying a place of acting rule would not normally allow this.

Article 5(5) as regards a dispute arising out of the operations of a branch, agency or other establishment, the courts for the place where the branch, agency or other establishment is situated

In *Somafer* v. *Ferngas* [1978] E.C.R. 2183 the European Court held that a Community interpretation should be given to the words "branch, agency or other establishment" in the interests of legal certainty. The applicable test was whether the branch or agency was subject to the parent's direction or control. In *De Bloos* v. *Bouyer* [1976] E.C.R. 1497, it was held that the holder of an exclusive sales concession was not a branch, agency or other establishment of the defendant suppliers as it was not subject to the direction or control of the parent.

Additionally, under Article 5(5), the dispute must also arise out of the operations of the branch, such as a contract entered into by it *Somafer* v. *Ferngas*).

Insurance and Consumer contracts

These are covered by Sections 3 and 4 of the Convention.

In the case of insurance contracts, under Article 8(2), the insured may alternatively start proceedings at the place of his domicile (although this policy of favouring the insured has been criticised by English lawyers on the basis that the insured is not always the weaker party). Section 3 does not apply to cases of reinsurance.

The rules for consumer contracts are also designed to give extra protection to consumers. A consumer is defined as a person who concludes a contract for a purpose outside his trade or profession (Article 13). The consumer may sue in the courts of his own place of domicile.

Exclusive jurisdiction

Article 16 provides that in certain types of dispute, some courts will have exclusive jurisdiction. This applies regardless of domicile and is an exception to the rule that the Convention will apply only when the defendant is domiciled in a contracting state. Roughly speaking, Article 16 applies to proceedings involving immovable property; certain company law matters; validity of entries in public registers; certain matters involving intellectual property; enforcement of judgments.

Certain courts, in these types of cases, have exclusive jurisdiction because they are thought to be uniquely well placed to deal with the subject matter. Few cases have been reported under Article 16. Generally speaking, the European Court has tended to give a community meaning to these terms, interpreting these heads of jurisdiction in the light of their purpose and within the scheme of the Convention.

The San Sebastiano Convention introduces a new Article 16 (1)(b):

"however, in proceedings which have as their object tenancies of immovable property concluded for temporary private use for a maximum period of six consecutive months, the courts of the Contracting State in which the defendant is domiciled shall also have jurisdiction, provided that the landlord and tenant are natural persons and are domiciled in the same Contracting State."

This is to reverse the decision in *Rosler* v. *Rottwinkel* [1985] E.C.R. 99, where it was held that the Italian courts had exclusive jurisdiction over a claim for recovery of rent and other charges in relation to a short term lease of a holiday home in Italy by one German domicile to another.

Submission

(a) Submission by agreement

The Convention allows the parties to a contract to nominate a court in a contracting state, which shall have exclusive jurisdiction to settle any disputes which may arise. This is called a choice of jurisdiction clause (not to be confused with a choice of law clause—see above). Article 17 provides, in effect, that:

If the parties, one or more of whom is domiciled in a contracting state, have by agreement in writing or by an agreement evidenced in writing or, in international trade or commerce in a form which accords with practice in that trade or commerce of which the parties are, or ought to have been, aware agreed that a court or the courts are to have jurisdiction to settle any disputes arising in connection with a legal relationship, that court or those courts have exclusive jurisdiction.

The San Sebastiano Convention changes the wording of Article 17, adding a new Article 17(1)(b) so that the agreement may be "in a form which accords with practices which the parties have established between themselves." If the agreement is one of international trade or commerce, Article 17(1)(c) adds the requirement to the existing wording that the form of the agreement be one that is "widely known to, and regularly observed by, parties to contracts of the type involved in the particular trade or commerce concerned."

In *Partenreederei M.S. "Tilly Russ"* v. *Nova N.V.* [1984] 1 C.M.L.R. 49 it was held that where the choice of jurisdiction clause is in writing (in this case the conditions printed on a bill of lading) this can be regarded as written confirmation of an earlier communicated oral agreement between the parties.

Article 17 further provides that where neither party is domiciled in a Contracting State "the courts of other Contracting States shall have no jurisdiction over their disputes unless the court or courts chosen have declined jurisdiction." So in these circumstances, the court chosen will simply apply its own traditional rules of jurisdiction.

A jurisdiction clause under Article 17 cannot displace another court's exclusive jurisdiction under Article 16.

(b) Submission by appearance

Article 18 provides that " . . . the courts of a Contracting State before whom a defendant enters an appearance shall have jurisdiction." However, for Article 18 to apply, the defendant must be domiciled in a Contracting State. Nor will it apply if another state's courts have exclusive jurisdiction under Article 16. If a defendant enters an appearance solely to contest jurisdiction he will not be taken to have submitted.

Lis Pendens

Article 21 provides that "where proceedings involving the same cause of action and between the same parties are brought in the courts of different Contracting States, any court other than the court first seised shall of its own motion decline jurisdiction in favour of that court." It should be noted that neither court has any discretion in the matter (contrast this with the position at common law). In *S. & W. Berisford Plc.* v. *New Hampshire Insurance* [1990] 3 W.L.R. 688, Hobhouse J. confirmed that there is no discretion to stay proceedings on the basis of *forum non conveniens* where the case falls within the provisions of the Brussels Convention. This decision was followed by Potter J. in *Arkwright Mutual Insurance Co.* v. *Bryanston Insurance* [1990] 3 W.L.R. 705. However, in *Re Harrods (Buenos Aires) Ltd., The Times*, January 11, 1991, the Court of Appeal held that proceedings might be stayed where there was a conflict of jurisdiction in proceedings between a defendant domiciled in England and a plaintiff domiciled in a non-contracting state.

If related actions are brought in different courts, the courts other than that first seised may (rather than must) stay the actions before them pending the outcome of the first action (Article 22, which also defines "related actions").

Provisional and Protective Measures (Article 24)

An application may be made to the courts of a contracting state for such provisional measures as may be available, even if, under the Convention, the courts of another state have jurisdiction over the substance of the matter. An example of such a measure would be an interim injunction, such as a Mareva Injunction or the Continental saisie conservatoire.

Section 25 of the Civil Jurisdiction and Judgments Act provides the High Court with the power to grant such interim relief.

It was decided in *Republic of Haiti* v. *Duvalier* [1989] 2 W.L.R. 261 that the English courts had jurisdiction, by virtue of section 25, to make a Mareva order, freezing the defendant's assets worldwide, where substantive proceedings were pending in the French courts. Such a jurisdiction would, however, be exercised only in exceptional circumstances.

Jurisdiction within the U.K.

The Brussels Convention does not make provision for the division of jurisdiction within the U.K. However, the Civil Jurisdiction and Judgments Act contains such provisions. These are a modified version of the Convention's jurisdictional rules (see sections 16 and 17 and Schedule 4).

2. Jurisdiction under the Civil Jurisdiction and Judgments Act 1991

This Act gives effect to the Lugano Convention on Jurisdiction and the Enforcement of Judgments in Civil and Commercial Matters in the U.K. This Convention (often called the Parallel Convention, because it is so closely modelled on the 1968 Brussels Convention) basically extends the same jurisdictional rules as those of the 1968 Convention, to those E.F.T.A. States which ratify it (and, possibly, in the future, to other non-E.F.T.A. countries). The U.K. had not ratified the Convention at the time of writing. Although the Lugano Convention is very closely modelled on the Brussels Convention, there are some changes of substance. These are mentioned below.

The provisions of the Lugano Convention will apply where the defendant is domiciled in an E.F.T.A. state which has ratified the Convention. It will also apply where jurisdiction has been conferred on an E.F.T.A state by agreement or where an E.F.T.A state has exclusive jurisdiction by virtue of the Convention.

Article 5(1)(b) of the Convention creates a special new rule for individual contracts of employment. The place of performance of the obligation in question in individual employment contracts is the place where the employee habitually carries out his work. Where the employee does not habitually carry out work in one country the place of performance is the place of business through which the employee was engaged. This differs somewhat from the Brussels Convention in its amended form (see above).

Article 6(4) allows an action *in personam* in contract to be combined with an action against the same defendant in matters relating to rights *in rem* in immovable property in the court of the *situs* (*i.e.* the country where the property is located).

Article 16(1)(b) of the Lugano Convention, like that of the amended Brussels Convention, removes the exclusive jurisdiction of the courts of the *situs* in relation to short term tenancies of immovable property. However, the wording differs slightly from that of the Brussels Convention in its amended form (see above). Only the tenant need be a natural person, and the parties need not be domiciled in the same Contracting State, providing "neither party is domiciled in the Contracting State in which the property is situated."

Article 17(1) of the Lugano Convention changed the wording of the Brussels Convention. This new wording was adopted by the San Sebastiano Convention (see above). The changes take account of the interpretation of Article 17 by the European Court.

Cases may not be referred to the European Court under the Parallel Convention. However, Protocol 2 to the Parallel Convention sets up a system of consultation and exchange of information to make it easier for national judges to determine cases concerning the Convention.

3. Jurisdiction where neither the Brussels nor Lugano Conventions apply

An English court has jurisdiction:

(a) If the defendant is **present** in England when he is served with the writ, even if he is only on a brief visit (*Maharanee of Baroda* v. *Wildenstein* [1972] 2 Q.B. 283). A company is regarded as present in the jurisdiction and may be served with process here if either (a) it has filed with the registrar of companies the name and address of a person authorised to accept service on its behalf (Companies Act, section 691), or (b) it has a place of business here (Companies Act, section 695)—for what amounts to establishing a place of business here see *South India Shipping Corp. Ltd.* v. *Export-Import Bank of Korea* [1985] 1 W.L.R. 585.

(b) If the defendant **submits** to the jurisdiction, *e.g.* by accepting service of process.

(c) If the case falls within R.S.C., Ord. 11, r. 1(1) and the court gives leave for service of the writ outside England. Order 11 is an extremely important basis of jurisdiction. Many other countries have similar provisions (or "long arm" statutes as they are called in the U.S.) which allow for service of process on a defendant resident abroad. The grant of leave is discretionary, and the court will be exceptionally careful in deciding whether to grant leave. Two conditions must be satisfied:

(i) The case must fall under at least one of the heads of Order 11. These include, *inter alia*:

Order 11, rule 1(1)(*d*). This subrule deals with cases of contract and provides that service of process on a defendant abroad can be allowed if the claim is brought to enforce, rescind, dissolve, annul or otherwise affect a contract, or to recover damages or to obtain other relief in respect of the breach of a contract, being (in either case):

(i) a contract which "was made within the jurisdiction";

(ii) a contract which "was made by or through an agent trading or residing within the jurisdiction on behalf of a principal trading or residing out of the jurisdiction."
In this case the contract need not be concluded here, nor need the agent have the authority to conclude the contract

here. The agent must, however, be acting on behalf of the defendant principal (see *National Mortgage and Agency Co. of New Zealand Ltd.* v. *Gosselin* [1922] 38 T.L.R. 832);

(iii) a contract which "is by its terms, or by implication, governed by English law"
(For determining which law governs the contract, see above);

(iv) a contract which "contains a term that the High Court shall have jurisdiction to hear and determine any action in respect of the contract."

It is probably easier to get leave under this head than most of the others under Order 11, rule 1(1). The courts are also unlikely to grant a stay of proceedings on the basis of forum non conveniens where there is such a jurisdiction clause.

Order 11, rule 1(1)(*e*). This deals with cases where "the claim is brought in respect of a breach committed within the jurisdiction of a contract made within or out of the jurisdiction, and irrespective of the fact, if such be the case, that the breach was preceded or accompanied by a breach committed out of the jurisdiction that rendered impossible the performance of so much of the contract as ought to have been performed within the jurisdiction."

If the breach complained of is a failure to perform, it must be shown that performance was due in England.

Order 11, rule 1(1)(*f*). This subrule deals with cases "where the claim is founded on a tort and the damage was sustained, or resulted from an act committed, within the jurisdiction." The English courts have jurisdiction under this subrule to hear a case in which damage results from a negligent statement made abroad if the harmful event occurred in the U.K.—*Minster Investments* v. *Hyundai Precision Industry Co.*, *The Times*, January 26, 1988. It will be noted that this rule provides a similar basis of jurisdiction to that of Article 5(3) of the Brussels Convention (*supra*).

(ii) Under Order 11, rule 4(2) the court will not grant leave unless the case is a proper one for service out of the jurisdiction. In deciding this, the court will take into account the following factors:

(a) England must be the **forum conveniens**—*i.e.* "clearly the most appropriate forum for the case to be tried for the interests of all the parties and the ends of justice," *per* Lord Goff in *Spiliada Maritime Corp.* v. *Cansulex Ltd.* [1986] 3 W.L.R. 972. Whether England is the most appropriate forum will involve considerations such as, for example, where the witnesses are located; nationality and residence of the parties; the law governing the matter.

(b) The plaintiff must make out a prima facie case before leave will be granted.

Other matters relating to jurisdiction under the traditional rules

Stays of Action

An English court may be asked to stay the action before it because there is a more appropriate forum to hear the case. In cases such as these, the courts already have jurisdiction under the traditional rules, but it seems that, for certain reasons, the action would be better tried elsewhere. The courts have an inherent jurisdiction to stay proceedings already before them under section 49(3) of the Supreme Court Act 1981. In the past the courts were sparing in the exercise of this jurisdiction and a defendant could only obtain a stay of action if he could show that continuing the action in England caused vexation or oppression to him or was an abuse of the process of the court (*per* Scott L.J. in *St. Pierre* v. *South American Stores* (1936) 1 K.B. 362).

This test has been gradually relaxed in a string of cases and the doctrine of **forum non conveniens** is now applied. The present test was laid down by Lord Goff in *Spiliada Maritime Corp.* v. *Cansulex* [1986] 3 W.L.R. 972 (*supra*) who said (at 987):

> "if there is some other available forum which prima facie is clearly more appropriate for the trial of the action, it (the court) will ordinarily grant a stay unless there are circumstances by reason of which justice requires that a stay should nevertheless not be granted."

Lord Goff also stressed that the test was the same whether the court was dealing with an Order 11 case or a stay of action. In *The Vishra Ajay* [1989] 2 Lloyd's Rep. 558 the court held that justice would require a stay not to be granted where the successful litigant in the other forum (India) would have to bear a large proportion of his own costs, and trial there would be delayed for many years, making the witness evidence unreliable.

Enjoining foreign proceedings

Just as the English courts may stay proceedings before them, so they may, on application, restrain a party from proceeding in a **foreign** jurisdiction. This rather draconian power is not readily exercised, and a different, much stricter test is employed than the **forum non conveniens** test laid out in *The Spiliada* for staying actions here—see *Societe Nationale Aerospatiale* v. *Lee Kui Jak* (1987) 3 All E.R. 510, *per* Lord Goff. Basically, the party seeking restraint of the proceedings abroad must show that it is vexatious and oppressive to him for those proceedings to continue. In *Du Pont de Nemours (E.I.) & Cov Agnew (I.C.)* (No. 2) (1988) 2 F.T.L.R. 39 the Court of Appeal refused to restrain a defendant from proceeding in a foreign jurisdiction where both the English court and the foreign court claimed to be the natural forum for trial.

Foreign jurisdiction clauses

Where the parties have agreed that their disputes shall be referred to a foreign tribunal the English court may, and usually will, in its discretion stay the action (*The Eleftheria* [1970] P. 99; *The Fehmarn* [1958] 1 W.L.R. 159). The burden of proof is on the plaintiff to show that it is just and proper to allow the English proceedings to continue.

Actions in rem

The only action *in rem* known to English law is an Admiralty action brought against a ship or its cargo. The Supreme Court Act 1981, section 21, lists the circumstances under which an action *in rem* may be brought. In these cases, the English courts assume jurisdiction on the basis of the presence of the ship within the jurisdiction, rather than on any of the other bases outlined above. Even if the defendant is domiciled in a contracting state to the Brussels Convention and the matter in question is a civil and commercial one, the English courts may be able to take jurisdiction under the provisions of the Supreme Court Act. This is because

Article 57 of the Brussels Convention preserves other conventions concerning jurisdiction previously entered into by the U.K., such as the 1952 Arrest Convention, which concerns Admiralty jurisdiction *in rem*. If, in such a case, the Arrest Convention does not apply, then jurisdiction will have to be taken under the Brussels Convention—see Article 5(7) of the Brussels Convention.

Recognition and Enforcement of Foreign Judgments

Some judgments (*i.e.* foreign divorce decrees) require only recognition. Others require enforcement, *i.e.* those where the defendant has assets here. The procedure for enforcement depends on where the foreign judgment was obtained.

Foreign judgments obtained outside the EEC

The method of and provisions for enforcement of non-EEC judgments will vary depending on where the foreign judgment was obtained—*i.e.* on whether it has to be enforced under Part II of the Administration of Justice Act (A.J.A.) 1920 (which covers judgments obtained in some commonwealth countries; for a list see Reciprocal Enforcement of Judgments (A.J.A. 1920 Part II) Consolidation Order 1984 (S.I. 1984 No. 129)); or under the Foreign Judgments (Reciprocal Enforcement) Act (F.J.(R.E.)A.) 1933 (this covers judgments obtained in Austria, Israel, Norway, Surinam, Pakistan, Australian Capital Territory, Guernsey, Jersey, Isle of Man, India, Tonga); or otherwise at common law. Although this in effect means that there are three different sets of rules and procedures for enforcement of such foreign judgments, in practice they are all fairly similar. The text below is a broad summary of the principles that apply to all three.

Jurisdiction of the foreign court—general

The English court will enforce a foreign judgment provided the foreign court had jurisdiction to render it, but:

(a) The foreign court must have had jurisdiction in the eyes of English law—it is not relevant that the foreign court had jurisdiction under its own rules (see *Buchanan* v. *Rucker* (1809) 9 East 192).

(b) The English courts do not recognise the foreign court's competence or jurisdiction merely because the English courts would have had jurisdiction in similar circumstances. They will not, for example, recognise jurisdiction analogous to that of R.S.C. Order 11, rule 1(1) (see *Schibsby* v. *Westenholz* (1870) L.R. 6 Q.B.).

What are the accepted bases of Jurisdiction?

(a) Residence of the defendant in the foreign jurisdiction (see *Schibsby* v. *Westenholz* (*supra*) and *Adams* v. *Cape Industries* [1990] 2 W.L.R. 657).
(b) Submission by the defendant to the foreign jurisdiction.

Additionally, the foreign judgment must be final and conclusive. A foreign judgment reached by a process of reasoning irreconcilable with an earlier English judgment will not be recognised as final by an English court—*E. D. & F. Man* (*Sugar*) v. *Haryanto* [1990] FTLR June 6. The judgment must also be for a fixed sum of money and not brought for the recovery of a tax or penalty, or to enforce a foreign penal law (*U.S.* v. *Inkley* [1988] 3 W.L.R. 304).

In addition, the defendant may be able to raise certain defences against enforcing the judgment in this country, for example:

(a) That it was obtained by fraud. The foreign court's view of the fraud is not conclusive—*Jet Holdings* v. *Patel* [1988] 3 W.L.R. 295. However, where the issue of fraud was determined in a separate action in the foreign jurisdiction, the judgment will be enforceable (*House of Spring Garden* v. *Waite* [1990] 3 W.L.R. 347).
(b) That it is contrary to natural justice or public policy.
(c) That it is contrary to section 5 of the Protection of Trading Interests Act 1980. (The foreign judgments most likely to be affected by this provision are judgments of the courts of the U.S., which sometimes impose multiple damages in anti-trust suits).

(See additionally, F.J.(R.E.)A. sections 1 and 4, A.J.A. sections 9 and 12).

The Lugano Convention

When the U.K. has ratified this Convention a system for recognition and enforcement of foreign judgments modelled on that of the 1968 Brussels Convention will apply to those E.F.T.A. countries which have also ratified the Convention. The Lugano Convention has made only a few minor amendments to the 1968 Convention (see *e.g.*, Article 28 of the Lugano Convention which adds a few more grounds for non recognition of a judgment relating to Articles 54B and 57(4) of that Convention).

Foreign judgments obtained within the EEC

These are dealt with in Title III of the Brussels Convention 1968. This covers **all** types of judgment, *i.e.* decrees, declarations (Article 25) and the domicile of the defendant is irrelevant. However, the subject matter must fall within the scope of the Convention, *i.e.* it must be a civil or commercial matter (see Article 1). Jurisdiction of the court of the state in which judgment was given may not be reviewed (Article 28(3)).

Recognition

Article 26 states that a judgment given in a contracting state shall be recognised in the other contracting state without any special procedure being required. The judgment need not be final or conclusive.

A judgment obtained by virtue of the foreign court exercising its jurisdiction on an "exorbitant" basis (*i.e.* French Civil Code Article 14) against a defendant not domiciled in the EEC will be recognised (but see the provision in Article 59 for contracting states to enter conventions with non-contracting states not to recognise or enforce such judgments).

Enforcement

The procedure is by registration in the High Court (Articles 31–32). Application is made *ex parte*.

Grounds on which recognition or enforcement may be refused Articles 27, 28 and 34:

(a) where the judgment is contrary to public policy in the state in which recognition is sought;
(b) if the judgment was in default and the defendant was not duly served in sufficient time to prepare his defence;

(c) the judgment is irreconcilable with a judgment given by the English court between the parties;
(d) the judgment conflicts with an earlier judgment in a non-member state, provided that judgment is also entitled to recognition or enforcement;
(e) if the court that gave the judgment decided a preliminary question concerning the status or legal capacity of natural persons, rights in property arising out of a matrimonial relationship, will or succession, in a way that conflicts with a rule of English private international law unless the same result would flow from the application of that rule.

Judgments obtained in EEC contracting states may not be reviewed as to substance (Articles 29 and 34).

The San Sebastiano Convention

This Convention has made only a few minor amendments to those provisions of the Brussels Convention which concern the recognition and enforcement of judgments.

Arbitration awards

The enforcement of foreign arbitral awards is governed by international conventions. The Arbitration Act 1950 gives effect to the Geneva Protocol on Arbitration Awards 1923 (Schedule 1 of the Act) and the Geneva Convention on the Execution of Foreign Arbitral Awards of 1927 (Schedule 2). The Arbitration Act 1975 aims at giving effect to the New York Convention on the Recognition and Enforcement of Foreign Arbitral Awards 1958.

PART 2: CONTRACT OF EMPLOYMENT, AGENCY AND PARTNERSHIP

CHAPTER 12

CONTRACT OF EMPLOYMENT

Nature of the contract of employment

THE contract of employment is a contract of service and not for services. Under a contract of service a person places his or her labour at the disposal of another and thus the relationship is constituted of employer and employee. On the other hand, if a person is "in business on their own account" the relationship is that of employer and independent contractor. A chauffeur is an employee whereas a taxi-driver is an independent contractor.

The distinction is important, not only to determine general vicarious liability for torts committed by employees in the course of their employment, but also to establish eligibility for bringing cases of unfair dismissal or discrimination. Trade Union membership, Social Security rights and tax liabilities are also determined by employment status, as also is protection under health and safety legislation.

The Employment Protection (Consolidation) Act 1978 (E.P.(C.)A. 1978), s.153(1) defines an 'employee' as 'an individual who has entered into or works under a contract of employment.' The test to determine a person's employment status has altered over the years from the original one of control and supervision of the worker to whether or not a person was an integral part of the employer's business. In *Young & Woods Ltd.* v. *West* [1980] I.R.L.R. 201 Stephenson L.J. stated that the decision is one of law and that reliance must not be placed upon the self-description of the parties. In practice, however, the appellate bodies are reluctant to overturn a finding of fact unless the trial court "took a view of the facts which could not reasonably be entertained" (*per* Cooke J. in *Market Investigations* v. *Ministry of Social Security* [1969] 2 Q.B. 173).

In *Addison* v. *London Philharmonic Orchestra Ltd.* [1981] I.C.R. 261 (E.A.T.) it was suggested that the factors that the court must have regard to are: (i) the degree of control exercised by the employer; (ii) whether the employee had a prospect of profit or risk of loss in the performance of the work; (iii) whether the employee was properly to be regarded as part of the employer's organisation; (iv) whether the employee was carrying on business on his own account or carrying on the employer's business; (v) the source of any equipment used in the work; (vi) the incidence of tax and national insurance contributions; (vii) the parties' own view of the relationship; and (viii) the traditional structure of the employee's occupation and the arrangements within it.

However, McNeill J. in *Warner Holidays Ltd.* v. *Secretary of State for Social Security* [1983] I.C.R. 440 counselled that an aggregate view be taken to determine the intention of the parties in the absence of an unambiguous written agreement.

The next development was to apply an economic reality or "mixed or multiple" test which had its origins in the case of *Ready Mixed Concrete* (*South East*) *Ltd.* v. *Minister of Pensions and National Insurance* [1968] 2 Q.B. 497 in which a 30 page written contract had purported to establish a relationship of independent contractor for the firm's lorry drivers. A driver purchased his lorry from the company and was obliged to maintain it and his payment depended upon the driving undertaken, which factors would indicate self-employment. However, the worker was also required to paint the lorry in the company colours and use it exclusively for company business. The contract further required him to obey reasonable orders all of which pointed to employee status. McKenna J. stated that a contract of service will exist if an individual agrees to provide his own work and submit to the employer's control and if the majority of the contractual provisions are consistent with a contract of service. In the *Ready Mixed Concrete* case the decisive point in favour of self employment was the power of delegation which the driver could exercise if he was not personally willing to perform the work on a particular occasion.

Recent decisions confirm that no single factor is conclusive. However, an "entrepreneurial" test involving the question "is the person who has engaged himself to perform these services performing them as a person in business on his own account?" has recently found favour in the courts. This test, originally posed by Cooke J. in the *Market Investigations* case, was recently approved in a decision of the Privy Council where a stonemason being paid at a daily rate, working for several contractors but relinquishing this other work when the respondent required him, was held to be an employee (*Lee* v. *1. Chung and 2. Shun Sing Constructions and Engineering Co. Ltd.* [1990] I.R.L.R. 236. It was noted that he was not undertaking any risk save that which may befall all employees of unemployment.

Other classes of workers

The common law of the contract of employment applies uniformly to nearly all classes of employee, although Crown employees and perhaps certain other public employees may be under special disabilities. Office holders such as trustees, trade union officials, police officers, prison officers and clergymen are independent of any contract. A director is an officer of the company but a contract of service will commonly have been negotiated, whereas partners are not employees.

It is unclear whether Crown Servants have a contract of employment, notwithstanding that the Crown has the necessary capacity and most are expressly included in the employment protection legislation by virtue of s.138 of the E.P.(C.)A., 1978.

Legal machinery for resolving disputes about the contract of employment

Questions concerning the common law of the contract of employment have traditionally been settled by the ordinary civil courts, in the first instance by the county court or the High Court. From the mid 1960s, however, disputes under statutory rules have been referred in the first instance to **industrial tribunals.**

Industrial tribunals are chaired by a lawyer, but also have two lay "wing persons" who each have an equal voice with the chair, even on points of law. The two wing persons are chosen for their industrial experience on the employees' side and on the employers' side respectively. The tribunals were designed to be informal, speedy and cheap but there is justified criticism about excessive legalism and delay. They are the final arbiters of fact and might aptly be described as an "industrial jury."

The tribunals are not bound by strict rules of procedure or of evidence. Legal aid is not available for representation before tribunals, although clients may receive "Green Form" advice and assistance from a solicitor, subject to means testing. In addition to the applicant, Trades Union and employers' association officials, personnel managers, and indeed anyone who can be described as a "friend" may usually appear and present a case. Travel and modest subsistence payments are made to witnesses and representatives other than lawyers.

Costs are normally to be awarded against a losing party only if s/he has acted frivolously and vexatiously. However, either party may apply for a pre-hearing assessment which requires the Tribunal to look at the strength of the claim and the merit, if any, of the defence. If an opinion is reached that the claim is weak, an insistence upon continuing the matter would probably result in a costs sanction. The Secretary of State for Employment under s.20 of the Employment Act 1989 has power to require payment of a deposit of £150 if it is deemed that there is no reasonable prospect of success.

Appeal from an industrial tribunal lies on a point of law only to the Employment Appeal Tribunal (E.A.T.) in London. This body also is of tripartite composition, the chair being a High Court judge. From the E.A.T. appeals lie in the ordinary way to the Court of Appeal and the House of Lords. Increasingly, the European Court of Justice has had strong influence on the development of employment law, notably in the case of *Barber* v. *Guardian Royal Exchange Assurance Group* [1990] I.R.L.R. 240 concerning the direct enforceability of Article 119 of the Treaty of Rome 1957 in the national courts of member states. As a result of this decision the retirement ages of men and women in occupational pension schemes must be identical.

The Advisory, Conciliation and Arbitration Service (ACAS) has considerably extended its crucial functions of pre-hearing conciliation and arbitration, as well as in advising generally and developing codes of practice in both the individual and collective areas of the law.

The industrial tribunals handle a wide variety of claims that an employee may wish to make against the employer including unfair dismissal, redundancy, sex, race and marital discrimination, equal pay, trade union rights and balloting.

Section 131 of the E.P.(C)A 1978 provides that jurisdiction over a limited category of claims arising out of the common law of the contract of employment may also be conferred upon the industrial tribunals. This has not yet been done, despite an urgent need in order to resolve, *inter alia*, matters arising under the Wages Act 1986. (see *post*).

From April 1, 1990 interest is available following an order for payment under the Industrial Tribunals (Interest) Order S.I. 1990 No. 479.

Formation of the contract of employment

The contract of employment may be embodied in a written document, may be wholly oral, may need to be deduced from the parties' conduct, or may be partly in one of the forms and partly in another. Although it is not usually problematic whether or not there is a contract, where the contract is not written it is often difficult to be sure of its precise terms. This is not merely because proof of an oral agreement is more difficult, but, more important, because in an oral hiring very little may have been expressly agreed between the parties. In *Ferguson* v. *John Dawson & Partners (Contractors) Ltd.* [1976] 1 W.L.R. 1213), "the plaintiff came with four other Irishmen already working for the defendants, and he asked, or perhaps one of his friends asked, if he could 'come along.' Mr. Murray's evidence [the site agent] is: 'I said he could start on Monday and that was it. But I did inform him . . . we were working as a lump labour force.' "

To supplement what has been expressly agreed between the parties the law may treat rules derived from various other sources as part of the contract of employment. Such sources include the employer's works rules, relevant collective agreements, custom and practice, and terms implied by common law or by statute. But whether any terms from these sources have in fact been incorporated into a particular contract of employment may be very uncertain. With regard to the first three sources the basic question is whether the parties have implicitly agreed to incorporation, a question that may be very difficult to answer when the employee is first hired, but which may become clearer later "as particular questions of the rights and obligations of the parties arose during the progress of the work" (*per* Megaw L.J. in *Ferguson* v. *John Dawson Ltd.*, above).

Written particulars of the contract of employment

Since even lapse of time may not make the contents of the contract clear, Parliament in 1963 attempted a modest degree of formalisation of the contract of employment. By what is now Part I of the Employment Protection (Consolidation) Act 1978, except in the case of certain written contracts, an employer must provide his employees with a written statement of the particulars of certain terms of the contract within 13 weeks of the commencement of the employment. The terms in question relate to the parties to the contract, the date employment began, pay and whether there is any continuous service with a previous employer, hours of work, holidays, incapacity for work, pensions, notice required by the employee to terminate the contract, and the employee's job title. If the contract in question contains no such provisions on any of these matters, the particulars must so state. Within four weeks of any change in the written particulars the employee must be informed in writing. In addition, the written particulars must be accompanied by a note specifying the disciplinary rules applicable to the employee, the person to whom application for redress of grievances may be made, and the grievance procedure (if any) available to the employee.

The written particulars do not constitute the contract of employment nor ought they to be treated as conclusive evidence of its terms. Thus the employee may apply to an industrial tribunal under section 11 of the Act seeking to have the written particulars issued to him by his employer amended so as to correspond with the terms of his contract (*System Floors (U.K.) Ltd.* v. *Daniel* [1982] I.C.R. 54 (E.A.T.); *Mears* v. *Safecar Security Ltd.* [1983] Q.B. 54 (C.A.)).

The main impact of the written particulars, however, has been as a method whereby terms from the other sources mentioned above may be incorporated into the contract of employment. Section 2(3) provides that the particulars themselves need not contain the details of the terms, but may instead "refer the employee to some document which the employee has reasonable opportunities of reading in the course of his employment or which is made reasonably accessible to him in some other way." Thus, the particulars may refer to a collective agreement or the works rules, so making it clear that parts of these documents have been incorporated into the contract of employment. Indeed, if the written particulars refer generally to, say, a collective agreement, the effect may be to incorporate into the contract of employment parts of the collective agreement which deal with matters beyond those which must be covered in the written particulars.

The employee's statement under the Contracts of Employment Act said that his terms and conditions of employment were those set out in the memorandum of agreement for the steel erecting industry concluded between the Engineering Employers' Federation and the Constructional Engineering Union. The court's interpretation of the memorandum was that steel erectors could be required to work anywhere in the country. Because the statement incorporated the memorandum in the contract of employment, the employer could require the employee to move to another site when work finished at the current site, even though geographical mobility is not one of the terms of employment of which the Act requires employees to be informed: *Stevenson* v. *Teesside Bridge and Engineering Ltd.* [1971] 1 All E.R. 296.

Of course, not all the terms of the collective agreement will be appropriate for incorporation into the individual contract of employment, *e.g.* those intended to affect only the relations between the parties to the collective agreement. Section 18(4) of the Trade Union and Labour Relations Act 1974 restricts terms from the collective agreement which prohibit or restrict the employee's freedom to engage in industrial action. Incorporation of these terms will only be permitted if there is a written collective agreement which provides for express incorporation, reasonably accessible at the workplace during working hours and where the worker's contract expressly or impliedly incorporated such a term.

Terms implied by common law

With the transformation since 1963 of the contract of employment into a contract by incorporation (via the written particulars), customary practices, on the one hand, and terms implied by common law, on the other, have been afforded a more restricted scope as sources of the contract of employment. Nevertheless, certain categories of implied term were strongly established by judicial decision in the nineteenth and first half of the twentieth centuries and will normally be treated as part of the contract unless contradicted by something expressly agreed or incorporated. Despite an apparently strict adherence to the "business efficacy" test whereby courts only imply terms to give effect to the presumed intention of the parties, Slade L.J. sitting in the Court of Appeal in *Courtaulds Northern Spinning Ltd.* v. *Sibson and T.G.W.U.* [1988] I.C.R. 451 said that

> "in cases . . . where it is essential to imply some term into the contract of employment as to place of work, the court does not have to be satisfied that the parties, if asked, would in fact have agreed the term before entering the contract. The court merely has to be satisfied that the implied term is one which the parties would probably have agreed if they were being reasonable."

The most important of these implied terms are briefly noted below. Moreover, the potential creativity of the implied term has not been destroyed, and in the context of "constructive" dismissal the common law has implied terms to limit managerial prerogatives.

1. *Co-operation*

It is an implied term that both parties to the contract should facilitate the performance of their mutual obligations under it. This principle is useful as an aid to the interpretation of particular contractual obligations, but there is a risk that the contract will become removed from the reality of the situation if the principle is used to import obligations into the contract.

The railway unions called their members out on a "work-to-rule," *i.e.* the employees, contrary to their usual practices, meticulously observed the requirements of their employer's rule book, with the result that the working of the railways was extensively disrupted. The employees were held to be in breach of their contracts of employment. The judges gave slightly varying reasons for their conclusions, but the view was expressed that the deliberate non co-operation involved in the work-to-rule was at the basis of the decision: *Secretary of State for Employment* v. *ASLEF* (*No.* 2) [1972] 2 Q.B. 455.

There is an implied term of the contract that the employer treat the employee with respect, and not break the mutual relationship of trust, confidence and faith. Should this occur, the employee may resign and claim constructive dismissal. A unilateral variation of contract imposing a lower wage on employees will therefore be regarded as a repudiatory breach requiring full reimbursement from the date of the reduction (*Rigby* v. *Ferodo Ltd.* [1988] I.C.R. 29 H.L).

However, where the employee puts him/herself in breach by taking industrial action, the employer need not, *inter alia* continue to comply with the duty to pay wages. Thus in *Miles* v. *Wakefield Metropolitan District Council* [1987] A.C. 539 the House of Lords supported the principle that an employer was not obliged to accept part performance of a contract. A registrar who refused, pursuant to industrial action, to conduct marriages on a Saturday morning, although fulfilling his other duties suffered a loss representing a proportion for the whole morning. Note that provisions of the Wages Act 1986 (see *post*) regarding unlawful deductions from pay do not apply because there is an exemption which covers industrial action.

The employer is not generally under an obligation to provide work except in limited circumstances, one of which is where there is an implied term in the contract. In that event payment is required for an employee ready and willing to work, in the absence of an express term reserving the right to reduce pay or move to short-time working.

Included within the implied duty of co-operation would be the requirement for an employee to relocate, notwithstanding the personal inconvenience caused (*Little* v. *Charterhouse Magna Assurance Co. Ltd.* [1980] I.R.L.R. 19 E.A.T.). However, in *United Bank Ltd.* v. *Akhtar* [1989] I.R.L.R. 507, an unsuccessful case for the employer involving an express mobility clause, part of the decision concerned an implied term that the employers would not, without reasonable and proper cause conduct themselves in a manner likely to destroy or seriously damage the relationship of mutual trust and confidence.

The employee's duty to obey all lawful and reasonable orders of the employer may also be viewed under this heading.

Pepper was employed as head gardener by Major Webb. Pepper worked satisfactorily for three months, but then his work and his manners towards his employer deteriorated. One day the employer asked Pepper about the arrangements for the greenhouse in his absence over the weekend and Pepper replied: "I couldn't care less about your bloody greenhouse or your sodding garden," and walked off. He was dismissed summarily. *Held*, the dismissal was justified. The plaintiff's remark and conduct, taken against the background of his previous disobedience and insolence, clearly indicated an intention to repudiate the contract of employment: *Pepper* v. *Webb* [1969] 1 W.L.R. 514.

But compare *Wilson* v. *Racher* [1974] I.C.R. 428, where an isolated instance of obscene language by a gardener who was provoked by his employer was held not to justify summary dismissal.

2. *The duty of fidelity*

The duty of good faith and mutual respect includes an obligation on the employee to respect confidences, obey reasonable instructions, take care of the employer's property and not disrupt the employer's business. Both *Miles* v. *Wakefield* and *Rigby* v. *Ferodo* further illustrate these points.

Breaches by the employers have included the use of foul language, a groundless accusation of theft, and a failure to show proper respect for a senior employee. In *Cresswell & Ors.* v. *Board of Inland Revenue* [1984] I.R.L.R. 190, employees who refused to use new computerised equipment were not allowed to attend work or be paid and it was held that pay could properly be withheld. There was no breach of contract by the employer, employees were impliedly required to adapt to new methods of working.

Duties to obey all lawful and reasonable orders and of confidentiality exist but are specifically referred to under Unfair Dismissal at page 246 and in Chapter 7 under Restraint of Trade clauses.

3. *Duty of care*

Both parties are under a duty to take care in the performance of the contract. The employer must take reasonable care for the safety of his employees in the course of their employment and in particular must provide safe tools, a safe place of work, a safe system of working and select properly skilled fellow employees. Thus an employer's failure in *British Aircraft Corporation Ltd.* v. *Austin* [1978] I.R.L.R. 332 to investigate a complaint relating to protective glasses was held to be a repudiatory breach of the contract, leading to constructive dismissal. In *Reid* v. *Rush & Tompkins Group plc* [1989] I.R.L.R. 134 there was no duty on the employer to take reasonable care to protect an employee from economic loss arising from physical injury because of a lack of adequate insurance cover. However the Court of Session on July 12, 1990 in *Rutherford* v. *Radio Rentals Ltd.* held that insurance cover under the terms of a contract of employment gave rise to an implied term that the employer would pay up on any qualifying claim even though the insurance company refused to pay the employer. The employer had argued that its obligation stopped at making the appropriate claim under the insurance policy.

The duty of care may be regarded as arising in tort or as an implied term of the contract of employment. The employer is not only liable for his own failure to use due care and diligence. The employer must be covered by an insurance policy pursuant to the Employers' Liability (Compulsory Insurance) Act 1969 and the Employers' Liability (Defective Equipment) Act 1969 also provides that an employer shall be liable in negligence if an employee in the course of employment is injured in consequence of defective equipment being used for the purposes of the employer's business and the defect is attributable wholly or partly to the negligence of a third party, such as the maker of the equipment, whether the third party is identified or not. However, the employer's liability is without prejudice to the law of contributory negligence and to any remedy by way of contribution or in contract or otherwise which is available to the employer in respect of the injury. An agreement between employer and employee to exclude or limit the employer's liability under the Act would be void.

The employee must exercise reasonable skill and care in the performance of his duties. From this the law has deduced an implied duty upon the employee to indemnify the employer in respect of the consequences of his negligent conduct.

Lister was employed by a company as a lorry driver. He was accompanied by his father, a co-employee. When Lister backed his lorry into a yard, he knocked down his father who had previously alighted from the lorry and injured him. The company was held to be vicariously liable to the father in damages and by the present action claimed to recover damages from Lister for breach of the implied term of his contract of employment that he would use reasonable skill and care in driving. *Held*, the company was entitled to succeed: *Lister* v. *Romford Ice and Cold Storage Co. Ltd.* [1957] A.C. 555.

Members of the British Insurance Association and Lloyd's have a gentlemen's agreement not to enforce their rights of subrogation against employees.

Terms implied by statute

Terms implied into the contract of employment by statute, unlike those implied at common law, operate so as to override anything agreed to the contrary between the parties themselves. Thus, under the Equal Pay Act 1970 the contract of employment is deemed to include an equality clause, which operates where a person of one sex is employed on like work (*i.e.* broadly similar work) with a person of the other sex or on work rated as equivalent under a job evaluation scheme or on work of equal value. In such circumstances the equality clause will operate so as to equalise upwards the terms and conditions of employment of employees involved, irrespective of what has been specifically agreed between employer and employee unless the difference between the two sets of terms and conditions can be shown to be "genuinely due to a material difference other than difference of sex."

In the case of a claim based on "like work" or "work rated as equivalent" a successful defence will be possible only if there is a material or significant and relevant difference (*per* the House of Lords in *Rainey* v. *Greater Glasgow Health Board Eastern District* [1987] A.C. 224) between the woman's work and the man's. For claims based on equal value, however, section 1(3) says that any difference in pay must be "genuinely due to a material factor which is not the difference of sex."

In *Hayward* v. *Cammell Laird Shipbuilders Ltd.* [1988] A.C. 894, the House of Lords held that each distinct contractual provision must be compared, rather than the "total remuneration package."

A woman may claim equivalence with a male employee at her own workplace or at a different location provided that there are common conditions of employment. Under Article 119 of the European Treaty, a comparison may also be made with a male predecessor.

Wages Act 1986

The Wages Act 1986, which came into force on January 1, 1987, *inter alia*, repealed the Truck Acts 1831–1940, thus removing the historical right for a worker to be paid in coin of the realm. The contracts of existing workers at that date can only be altered by negotiated agreement.

Section 1 of the Wages Act 1986 provides that an employer shall not make any deductions from any wages of any worker, or require the worker to make any payment unless the deductions or payment are authorised by a contractual provision or the worker has previously signified in writing his/her agreement or consent to it. Statutory deductions in respect of income tax and national insurance contributions and occupational pension contributions are outside the scope of the Act.

In *Pename Ltd.* v. *Paterson* [1989] I.R.L.R. 195 an employee was given a letter stating "should you wish to terminate your employment then a week's notice must be written out and worked. In the event of a default of the above, a week's wages will be forfeited." The company withheld a week's pay when the employee left without giving any notice but the Employment Appeal Tribunal held that this was contrary to s.1(1)(b). This decision confirms that any such letter should be signed by the employee in order to make it contractually binding. Deductions may also be allowed under the terms of an oral collective agreement permitting fines, provided that it was agreed with the union before the unwarranted conduct occurred and that the employee knew of the provision in advance (*York City & District Travel Ltd.* v. *Smith* [1990] I.R.L.R. 213 E.A.T.).

"Wages" are widely defined in s.7(1) and include any sums payable to the worker by his employer in connection with his employment. However, loans, expenses, pension payments and redundancy pay are not so classified. The Court of Appeal have recently considered the position in relation to "payments in lieu of notice" and distinguished between a claim for wrongful dismissal arising out of a breach of contract, where the employee's contract was terminated without the proper notice and where an employer gave notice but released the employee from their obligation to work out that period. In the latter case, the contract of employment remains in existence, and the claim would be for "wages" within s.7 whereas in the former case the claim is essentially one for damages.

Several exceptions to s.1 exist, notably to reimburse an employer as a result of an overpayment of wages or expenses and on account of a worker taking part in a strike or other industrial action. In this latter case there is no requirement that any deduction should be "fair and reasonable" as was required under the Trucks Acts and there is now no limit to the amount of any fine or deduction, merely the rate of deduction in the case of retail workers for cash shortages, which must not exceed 10 per cent. of the gross amount of wages payable on that day (s.3).

Statutory labour standards

Other statutory enactments, although not operating as implied terms, confer rights upon the employee irrespective of what his contract provides. A large number of such rights are contained in the Employment Protection (Consolidation) Act 1978 and only the most important of these can be briefly noted here.

(i) A right to a guaranteed minimum payment from the employer where the employee is not entitled to contractual remuneration because he cannot be provided with work (ss.12–18).

(ii) A right to remuneration from the employer where the employee is suspended on medical grounds under the health and safety legislation and is not entitled to contractual remuneration (ss.19–22).

(iii) A right to maternity pay from the employer and to return to work within 29 weeks of the date of confinement (ss.33–48).

(iv) A right to time off work (with pay) to carry out trade union duties, to receive ante-natal care or, in the case of a redundant worker, to look for work, and without pay to take part in trade union activities or public duties (ss.27–32).

(v) A right to an itemised pay statement (ss.8–10).

(vi) A right to a written statement upon request of the reason for dismissal (s.53).

Termination of the contract

1. *By notice*

At common law the contract of employment may be terminated

by either party for any reason or for no reason upon giving notice of a reasonable length, unless the contract is one for a fixed term or unless it specifically restricts the reasons for which it may be terminated. Since the ordinary contract of employment is one of indefinite duration and without restrictions upon the reasons for termination, the common law puts the employee in particular in a weak legal position. However, by section 49 of the Employment Protection (Consolidation) Act 1978 the minimum period of notice that must be given by an employer to terminate such a contract is one week if the employer has been continuously employed by the employer for at least four weeks. The notice period rises to two weeks once the employee has two years' continuous employment and increases thereafter by one week for each additional year of continuous employment up to a maximum of 12 weeks' notice. The minimum period of notice required of the employee is one week after four weeks' continuous employment, but it does not thereafter increase. If the reasonable period of notice required of either employer or employee at common law is longer than the statutory minimum, then the common law period will be the operative one, as in *Hill* v. *Parsons (C.A.) & Co. Ltd.* [1972] 1 Ch. 305, where Lord Denning thought that a chartered engineer of 35 years' continuous employment was entitled at common law to at least six months' notice and perhaps even a year. Equally, the contract itself may, and often does, fix periods of notice for either employer or employee that are longer than the statutory minima.

2. *Summary termination*

At common law either party may lawfully terminate the contract summarily, *i.e.* without giving any notice, if the other party has committed a serious breach of the contract. Whether the breach is sufficiently serious to justify summary termination has to be answered in the context of each particular contract and few general guidelines can be discerned from the cases. Gross misconduct will only arise where the whole basis of the contract of employment has been destroyed and where a further working relationship based on mutual trust is impossible.

The ACAS Code of Practice, "Discipline at Work" recommends

that employers provide examples of gross misconduct in their disciplinary rules. The judges have tended to view any suggestion of dishonesty or disobedience on the employee's part particularly strictly. For a pair of contrasting decisions on disobedience, see *Pepper* v. *Webb* and *Wilson* v. *Racher* (see p. 240, *ante*).

The manager of a betting shop openly, but without his employer's knowledge, took £15 out of the till, put in an I.O.U. for the money and used the money to place a bet of his own elsewhere. On the next day he repaid the £15. The manager knew the employer would not have given permission for him to borrow the money. When the employer discovered what had happened he dismissed the manager without notice and was held justified in so doing because the manager's conduct, even if not dishonest, was inconsistent with the continuance of the confidential relationship between them. *Sinclair* v. *Neighbour* [1967] 2 Q.B. 279.

3. *Remedies at common law*

The employer acts in breach of contract if he terminates it by giving shorter notice than the employee is entitled to or if he dismisses summarily in a situation in which he is not entitled to do so, as in *Wilson* v. *Racher*. Only in very rare circumstances will the common law require the employer to reinstate a wrongly dismissed employee because the contract of employment is regarded as one of a very personal nature. The damages remedy at common law is also very limited, as is notably illustrated by the rule that even in the case of wrongful summary dismissal, damages in respect of loss of earnings are limited to earnings during the period of notice required to terminate the contract, on the assumption that the employer would have given the employee proper notice to terminate the contract if he had not dismissed him summarily. Further, the common law has developed no general requirement that the employee be given a hearing before dismissal or the reason for his dismissal, whether the termination is by notice or summarily. Finally, as noted earlier, a dismissal on due notice is generally lawful. To mitigate these defects in the common law Parliament has created the quite separate statutory concept of *unfair* dismissal (as opposed to *wrongful* dismissal) with its own system of remedies.

4. *Unfair dismissal*

By virtue of Part V of the Employment Protection (Consolidation) Act 1978, an employee who is dismissed, whether summarily or by notice, whether in breach of contract or not, may challenge the dismissal before an industrial tribunal on the grounds it was unfair. The definition of dismissal is further extended to include the expiration of a fixed-term contract without its being renewed and termination of the contract by the employee where this is in response to a serious breach of contract by the employer ("constructive" dismissal).

In general, the dismissal, as defined, will be held to be fair only if the employer, upon whom the burden lies, shows that the reason for the dismissal is capable of being considered a fair one. For this purpose s/he must show that the reason related to the employee's capability, qualifications or conduct, or was that the employee was redundant or was that the employee could not continue to be employed without a breach "of a duty or restriction imposed by or under an enactment," or was "some other substantial reason of a kind such as to justify the dismissal of an employee holding the position which that employee held." Some other substantial reason under s.57(1)(b) is intended as a safety net provision and has been labelled the "employer's charter" or "dustbin category" although there must be a genuine reason and an honest belief in the reason. The two statutory reasons are where a worker has temporarily replaced a permanent employee who is either suspended on medical grounds or pregnant or where a dismissal occurs on a transfer of undertaking.

Two other categories which have developed through case law are first, "quasi redundancies" arising through reorganisations where the result is that the worker may lose the statutory redundancy pay to which they would be entitled in a true redundancy situation (see p. 252, *post*) and second, a unilateral variation of contractual terms and conditions, for example in connection with job content, location and night shift working. As John Bowers and Simon Honeyball point out in their *Textbook on Labour Law* at p. 164 (Blackstone Press) "it is ironic that dismissals in these latter circumstances may be adjudged fair, notwithstanding that the breach of contract involved could be unlawful at common law and result in damages for wrongful dismissal." Secondly, the tribunal must consider that in the circumstances of the case it was reasonable of the employer to treat the reason as a sufficient reason for dismissal. The burden of proof on this issue is laid upon neither employer nor employee. Thus, smoking in a forbidden area would be a reason capable of being considered a fair one (as relating to the employee's conduct), but might not in the circumstances justify dismissal if, for example, the employer had in practice condoned smoking in this area on previous occasions. A dismissal might also be treated as unfair on procedural grounds, *e.g.* dismissing an employer without giving him a chance to explain his conduct, or on grounds of bad personnel management, *e.g.* dismissing an employee for bad workmanship without giving him prior warning and a chance to improve his standard of work.

The ACAS Code of Practice entitled "Disciplinary Practice and Procedures in Employment" operates as a minimum standard below which employers will not be held to be acting reasonably. It requires communication of the procedures to the workforce and incremental stages of both oral and written warnings.

Additionally Tribunals require adherence to the rules of natural justice so that, for example, an employee must be informed of the allegation, be given an opportunity to prepare their case and have a right to be represented.

Until 1979 there was a need for an employer to comply strictly with the disciplinary procedures in order to be adjudged fair, but the case of *British Labour Pump Co. Ltd.* v. *Byrne* [1979] I.R.L.R. 94, (subsequently supported by the Court of Appeal in *W. & J. Wass Ltd.* v. *Binns* [1982] I.R.L.R. 283) allowed the employer to successfully defend a claim for unfair dismissal if it could be shown, on the balance of probabilities, that the same decision would have resulted. The "no difference principle" has now been overruled by the House of Lords in *Polkey* v. *A. E. Dayton Services Ltd.* [1988] A.C. 344 thus returning to a consideration of fairness in accordance with s.57(3) of the E.P.(C)A 1978 which provides that:

> "the determination of the question of whether the dismissal was fair or unfair, having regard to the reason shown by the employer, shall depend on whether in the circumstances (including the size and administrative resources of the employer's undertaking) the employer acted reasonably or unreasonably in treating it as a sufficient reason for dismissing the employee, and that question shall be determined in accordance with equity and the substantial merits of the case."

A Tribunal will now be prepared to consider a dismissal fair following a failure to observe the relevant disciplinary procedures only when it was reasonable for the employer to conclude that consultation or warning would have been utterly useless having regard to the circumstances at the time.

Dismissals on the grounds of trade union activities, redundancy, pregnancy or in connection with the transfer of a business (see below) are automatically unfair but if a Tribunal finds that the employer acted reasonably in the circumstances the dismissal can be fair.

Section 11 of the Employment Act 1988 now provides that all dismissals for non-membership of a trade union are automatically unfair. In relation to pregnancy there are two exceptions, first, if the employee "is or will have become incapable of adequately doing the work" or if she cannot continue after the effective date of termination without contravening a statute.

A woman without the necessary two years' continuous service is able to bring a claim under the Sex Discrimination Act 1975 if she can show that a comparable man would have received different treatment.

In certain cases the Tribunal does not have jurisdiction to examine the fairness of the dismissals. This includes situations, where:

(a) at the date of the dismissal the employee has not been employed for a continuous period of two years at the effective date of termination;
(b) on or before the date of dismissal the employee has reached the normal retirement age at his/her place of work or, if there is no normal retirement age, if s/he has reached 65;
(c) the employee under a fixed-term contract of at least one year's duration has waived his right to claim;
(d) the employee under this contract ordinarily works outside Great Britain;
(e) the employer is the husband or wife of the employee; and
(f) at the date of the dismissal the employee was participating in industrial action or the employer was conducting a lock-out.

This last situation has been a controversial one. The rules does not apply where the employer does not treat all the other relevant employees equally. Thus, if not all those on strike at the applicant's establishment at the date of the applicant's dismissal are dismissed or some (but not the applicant) are offered re-engagement, the Tribunal will have jurisdiction to determine the fairness of the applicant's dismissal or failure to be offered re-engagement. Similar rules apply to a lock-out, where the "relevant" employees are all those directly interested in it.

By section 60 of the 1978 Act dismissal on grounds of pregnancy is automatically unfair, unless the employee is thereby incapable of doing her work or her continued employment would be in breach of an enactment.

The general remedies for an employee found to have been unfairly dismissed are as follows. If the employee so wishes and if the tribunal so decides, the tribunal may order that the employer reinstate or re-engage the employee but in 97 per cent. of the decisions, such orders are not made, thus leaving compensation as the only remedy. An employer who does not obey an order for reinstatement or re-engagement is not in contempt of court. S/he can refuse to take the employee back but will be liable to pay him by way of penalty an "additional award" of between three months' and six months' pay in the ordinary case. The employer is not liable to pay the penalty if he can show that it was not practicable to comply with the tribunal's order.

Where the tribunal does not order reinstatement or re-engagement or that order is not obeyed, it must make an award of compensation to the employee. This consists of two main parts. First, a "basic award," essentially equivalent to a redundancy payment (see p. 252, *post*) to reflect the employee's loss of accrued redundancy rights. A worker dismissed for trade union membership or activity is, *prima facie*, entitled to a basic award of not less than £2,650. Secondly, a "compensatory award" designed to compensate the employee for the loss he has suffered as a result of the dismissal. Loss of earnings is not confined to the notice period, as at common law, although there is a ceiling of £198 on the weekly earnings that will be taken into account and an overall limit of £10,000 on the compensatory award.

Loss of wages is calculated net of tax and national insurance contributions from the effective date of termination until the hearing date. The effective date of termination will be either the date on which notice expires or, in the absence of any notice, the date on which termination of the contract takes effect, usually the last day worked. Evidence of future loss of earnings must be proved by the former employee and the tribunal will have regard to the probable length of unemployment, the worker's age and other relevant circumstances, such as local conditions. Other loss of benefits such as holiday pay entitlement, tips, company car or accommodation costs may also be awarded. Pension rights are likely to be the hardest to assess, but the most important to the applicant and a committee of Industrial Tribunal chairs has produced a consultative pamphlet called "Compensation for loss of Pensions Rights."

The manner of dismissal can also be included in so far as it can be shown to have affected the worker's confidence in securing a new job, but there is a duty to mitigate the loss where possible.

A *special* award is available following an automatically unfair dismissal on the grounds of either union membership or indeed non membership, or for taking part in trade union activity. This consists of 104 weeks' pay without the normal upper limit of £198 and cannot be less than £13,180 or more than £26,290.

An *additional* award is payable if the employer unreasonably refuses to comply with a re-employment order made by the Tribunal; the special award will be for 156 weeks' pay, without upper limit and must be at least £19,735. A worker's conduct prior to dismissal will reduce this amount and will also affect the compensatory award.

Unemployment benefit and income support must be deducted from the compensatory award, but the recoupment provisions do not apply if the case is settled before the hearing provided that a single figure is agreed, rather than an itemised claim.

Transfer of undertakings

The Transfer of Undertaking (Protection of Employment) Regulations 1981, S.I. 1981 No. 1794 protects the contract of a worker engaged immediately before a take-over or transfer of the business preserving continuity of employment and passing liability to the new employer.

A dismissal either before or after the transfer date will be unfair if it is connected with the transfer, unless the employer can show it was caused by a change in the workforce when reliance upon regulation 8(2)(b) will be possible if it is for an "economic, technical or organisational reason." Thus the employers will come within s.57(2) of the E.P.(C)A 1978 "some other substantial reason" and the dismissal will be fair if found to be reasonable under s.57(3).

In *Litster* v. *Forth Dry Dock & Engineering Co. Ltd.* [1989] I.R.L.R. 161 the House of Lords considered the effect of the EEC Employee Rights of Transfer of Business Directive 77/187, which gave the impetus for the English rules. In considering regulation 5(3) it was held that where an employee has been unfairly dismissed immediately prior to the transfer, but solely for a reason connected with it, liability for that employee passes to the purchaser.

Regulation 10 of the Transfer Regulations 1981 requires information to be provided to the Trade Union representatives affected by the transfer and consultation where it is anticipated that measures will need to be taken. Section 99 of the Employment Protection Act 1975 applies which is discussed *post* under Redundancy.

Redundancy

Part VI of the Employment Protection (Consolidation) Act provides for payment of lump sums by way of compensation to those dismissed on grounds of redundancy who have at least two years' continuous employment with the employer who dismisses them. Dismissal is defined as for unfair dismissal. Redundancy arises where the employer dismisses because (i) he has ceased or intends to cease to carry on the business for the purposes of which the employee was employed, or (ii) he has ceased or intends to cease to carry on that business in the place where the employee was employed, or (iii) the requirements of the business for employees to carry out work of a particular kind in the place where the employee was employed have ceased or diminished or are expected to do so. The Act also covers in certain circumstances those who are laid-off or put on short time and who as a consequence decide to terminate their employment.

Compensation for redundancy is essentially backward looking. Consequently, unlike unfair dismissal, the amount of the payment in respect of redundancy is not in general reduced if the employee immediately obtains another job. However, if the dismissing employer makes the employee an offer to re-employ him within a certain time-limit either on the same terms and conditions as previously or on suitable alternative terms and conditions and, in either case, the employee unreasonably refuses the offer, then he will not be entitled to a redundancy payment. Where there is a change in the ownership of the business, a concept that has proved very difficult to operate in practice, the new owner of the business is placed in the shoes of the former owner for the purposes of the offer described above. If the employee actually accepts an offer of employment made by the employer within the relevant time limits, s/he is treated as not having been dismissed by the employer, whether the offer was of suitable alternative employment or not (subject to a statutory procedure for a four-week trial period in the new job).

The amount of the redundancy payment, where such is due, is obtained by multiplying the number of completed years of continuous employment the employee has with the employer (subject to a maximum of 20) by the amount of: a half a week's pay in respect of years of employment when aged 18–21; a week's pay (subject to a maximum of £198) in respect of years of employment when aged 22–40; a week and half's pay in respect of years of employment over the age of 40. The Employment Act 1989, section 16 provides that an employee shall not be entitled to a redundancy payment if the employee has reached the normal retirement age within the firm, or the age of 65. This is so for both men and women. The period of continuous employment is calculated for redundancy purposes basically according to the complex provisions of Schedule 13 to the 1978 Act, which indeed is generally used to determine the length of continuous employment where this is necessary under the other provisions discussed in this chapter. The provisions of this Schedule cannot be discussed here in detail, but we may briefly note that it allows certain breaks in employment (*e.g.* on grounds of sickness) to be ignored and occasionally service with previous employer to be aggregated with that with the dismissing employer (*e.g.* on a transfer of the business).

The amount of a week's pay is calculated in accordance with Schedule 14 to the 1978 Act, which again is generally used for this purpose in the provisions discussed in this chapter. The schedule is designed to reflect the employee's pay at the date of dismissal, but differing provisions have to be made for those with normal working hours and those without, those whose pay varies with the amount of work done and those whose pay does not, and so on.

Part VI of the 1978 Act is concerned solely with compensating those who have in fact been made redundant. Part IV of the Employment Protection Act goes further by requiring an employer who is contemplating redundancies to consult in advance with the unions recognised by him as representing the employees affected on the reasons for the proposed redundancies and the methods of selecting the employees to be dismissed. In addition, section 31 of the 1978 Act gives the individual employee the right to reasonable time off from work after having been given notice of dismissal on grounds of redundancy but before the dismissal takes place in order to look for new employment or make arrangements for training for future employment.

Discrimination

Under the Sex Discrimination Acts 1975 and 1986 and the Race Relations Act 1976 it is unlawful (i) to treat a person less favourably than another on sexual, marital or racial grounds, and (ii) to apply a condition or requirement uniformly to all persons if the requirement puts one sex or a racial group at a disadvantage, and if the requirement cannot be justified on non-sexual or non-racial grounds. An example of (ii) with regard to women would be a requirement that all applicants for a job as a bank cashier be six feet tall. Unlawful discrimination may be committed at the point of hiring, during the course of employment, or at its termination. Individual complaints in the employment field are heard by industrial tribunals, which may award compensation and recommend action the respondent should take within a specified period to obviate the adverse impact upon the complainant of the discriminatory act. With regard to dismissal, the remedies under these Acts overlap in a complicated way with the unfair dismissal remedies. The Equal Opportunities Commission and the Commission for Racial Equality have powers to play a broader enforcement role in the employment field.

Restraint of trade affecting contracts of employment

A contract of employment sometimes contains a term prohibiting the employee from engaging in specified activities after termination of the contract. Such a clause is invalid as being in restraint of trade if it is wider than is reasonably necessary for the protection of the employer's justified trade interests. The subject of restraint of trade is treated earlier (see p. 125, *ante*).

The European Dimension

The European influence on employment law and practice has been very significant with directives on equality of treatment regarding: access to jobs; training and promotion; equal pay; pensions and benefits. Part-time female workers have successfully claimed indirect sex discrimination under Article 119 of the Treaty of Rome 1957 in Germany and Denmark.

The Action Programme under the Social Charter contains many more legislative proposals including directives to guarantee both temporary and part-time staff (working over eight hours per week) the same employment rights and benefits, on a *pro rata* basis as full-time staff. Pregnant women would be guaranteed access to paid maternity leave and the right to return to work and disabled workers would be given free transport to and from work. In relation to the contract of employment all employees working over eight hours per week would have the right to receive written confirmation of the main terms and conditions of their employment. It is also possible that the previously blocked directive on parental leave and the reversal of the burden of proof in sex discrimination cases will be resurrected.

Chapter 13

AGENCY

An agent is a person who affects the legal position of another, called a principal, in dealings with third parties. This chapter is mostly concerned with agents making contracts on behalf of their principals but other legal consequences may arise from an agency relationship and some of these will be explained.

Since an agent does not make contracts on his own behalf, it is not necessary that he should have contractual capacity. A minor or a bankrupt may be an agent. The principal, however, must have full contractual capacity; if he does not have it, he cannot make a contract by employing an agent who does.

There are many different types of agents (see p. 278 below) but familiar examples include: directors who are agents of their companies and partners who, in certain circumstances, are each other's agents and agents of their firms (see chapter 14). Apart from these commercial examples, the use of an agent to effect a contract is common too in consumer transactions; a person may book a holiday through a travel agent. However, not all those who describe themselves as "agents" will be considered in law as so being. A car dealer, for example, may be referred to as an "agent" for Volvo motorcars. Such a dealer, however, would buy the cars from the manufacturer and would sell the cars on his own behalf, as a principal, to the customer. A statutory exception can arise in this context when a customer buys a Volvo on hire purchase terms; although there is a contract of sale (of a car) between the dealer and the finance company and another such contract between the finance company and the customer, the dealer is deemed by the Consumer Credit Act 1974, s.56 to be the agent of the finance company as well as being a seller of a car to the finance company (see further chapter 17).

General and special agents

When an agent is employed to act for his principal in all matters concerning a particular trade or business, he is termed a general agent. A special agent is one who is employed to make only a particular contract or series of particular contracts. A managing director of a company is the general agent of the company, but if a man sends a friend to bid for him at an auction, the friend is the special agent of the sender.

Creation of Agency

The power of an agent to affect the legal position of a principal is derived either from the authority vested in the agent or from operation of law, *i.e.* where the law imposes an agency relationship in certain factual situations.

Authority of the Agent

Actual authority

1. Express authority. This type of authority is created by words, either written or oral. It often derives from a contract between the principal and agent, although an agent may act gratuitously. No particular form is required unless the agent is appointed to execute a deed, in which case he must be given authority in a deed, called a power of attorney. Powers of attorney are governed by the Powers of Attorney Act 1971, as amended by the Law of Property (Miscellaneous Provisions) Act 1989, s.1, schedule 1 which dispenses with the requirement for a seal.

2. Implied authority. The agent's implied authority permits him to perform all subordinate or incidental acts necessary to exercise his express authority.

A board of directors whose chairman had assumed the role of managing director, entered into a contract on behalf of the company to indemnify another company. *Held*, the board by allowing the chairman to act as managing director had impliedly authorised him to enter the contract: *Hely-Hutchinson* v. *Brayhead Ltd.* [1968] 1 Q.B. 549.

Implied authority is sometimes divided into:
(a) *Usual authority*. This is a more specific form of implied authority which relates to agents of a certain type acting in the "usual" way of

such agents. Unfortunately, the term usual authority has become confused due mainly to the case of *Watteau* v. *Fenwick*, below.

The defendant had employed H. as manager of an hotel. H.'s name alone, appeared over the bar as licensee. The defendant limited H.'s actual authority by forbidding him to buy cigars. H., however, did order cigars from W. who knew nothing of the existence of the defendant. *Held*, the defendant was liable to pay for the cigars as such purchases were within the usual authority of a hotel manager: *Watteau* v. *Fenwick* [1893] 1 Q.B. 346.

The problem lies with the language used by Willes J. which strongly resembles that used in cases concerning apparent authority. Apparent authority, however, does not arise when the principal is undisclosed as the principal was in *Watteau* v. *Fenwick*. The case has never been overruled but most recently it has been described as "a case which a court should be wary in applying," *per* Bingham L.J. in *Rhodian River Shipping Co.* v. *Halla Maritime Corporation* [1984] 1 Lloyd's Rep 373.

(b) *Customary authority*. Here, an agent's implied authority derives from a locality, market or business usage.

Brokers in cocoa and sugar had acted in their own name and made themselves personally liable to the third party. Held, since there was a custom to act in this way, when they closed certain accounts the principals were liable to the brokers: *E. Bailey Co. Ltd.* v. *Balholm Securities Ltd.* [1973] 2 Lloyd's Rep 404.

Apparent or ostensible authority

"... An 'apparent' or 'ostensible' authority ... is a legal relationship between the principal and the contractor (the third party) created by a representation, made by the principal to the contractor, intended to be and in fact acted on by the contractor, that the agent has authority to enter on behalf of the principal into a contract of a kind within the scope of the 'apparent' authority, so as to render the principal liable to perform any obligations imposed on him by such contract ..." *per* Diplock L.J. in *Freeman and Lockyer* v. *Buckhurst Park Properties* (*Mangal*) *Ltd.* [1964] 1 All E.R. 630.

Apparent authority may arise where there is or was an agency relationship in existence, but unknown to the third party, the actual authority has been limited or terminated.

Apparent authority clearly operates to protect third parties and may arise even where there has never been an agency relationship created between principal, and "agent." Provided the principal represents by words or conduct to the third party that the "agent" has authority to act on his behalf and the third party relies on this representation by entering into a contract, the principal will be prevented or estopped from denying the agency. Normally the principal's representation precedes the contract, but he may be bound by his behaviour subsequent to the contract, *Spiro* v. *Lintern* [1973] 3 All E.R. 319.

Operation of Law

Agency of Necessity

Agency of necessity occurs when a person is entrusted with another's property and it becomes necessary to do something to preserve that property. In such a case, although the person who is entrusted with the property has no express authority to do the act necessary to preserve it, because of the necessity such an authority is presumed. For example, if a horse is sent by train and on its arrival there is no one to receive it, the railway company, being bound to take reasonable steps to keep the horse alive, has been held to be the agent of necessity of the owner for the purpose of sending it to a livery stable for the night (*G.N. Ry.* v. *Swaffield* (1874) L.R. 9 Ex. 132).

The master of a ship in cases of necessity can pledge the ship as security for the cost of repairs necessary to enable her to continue the voyage, provided that (a) there was a reasonable necessity according to the ordinary course of prudent conduct to pledge the ship; (b) the amount was advanced expressly for the use of the ship; and (c) the money was expended on the ship (*Arthur* v. *Barton* (1840) 6 M. & W. 138). If there is an agent of the shipowner on the spot, the master has no such authority (*Gunn* v. *Roberts* (1874) L.R. 9 C.P. 331).

But before any agency can be created by necessity, three conditions must be satisfied—

1. It must be impossible to get the principal's instructions.

Tomatoes were consigned by S. from Jersey to London. The ship delivered them to Weymouth three days late and, owing to a railway strike, the tomatoes could not be unloaded until two days later. When unloaded they were found to be bad and the railway company decided to sell them locally. No communication was made to S. *Held*, the railway company were liable in damages to S., as they should have communicated with him and asked for his instructions as soon as the ship arrived: *Springer* v. *G.W. Ry.* [1921] 1 K.B. 257.

2. There must be an actual and definite commercial necessity for the creation of the agency.

In 1915 and 1916 S., as agent for P., bought skins to the value of £1,900 to be dispatched to P., a fur merchant in Bucharest. P. paid for most of the skins. Owing to the occupation of Romania by the German forces it was impossible to send the skins to P. or to communicate with him. In 1917 and 1918 S. sold the skins, which had increased in value. *Held*, as the skins were not likely to deteriorate in value if properly stored, there was no necessity for the sale, and S. was liable in damages to P: *Prager* v. *Baltspiel Stamp & Heacock Ltd.* [1924] 1 K.B. 566.

Generally, there is no agency of necessity unless there is a real emergency, such as may arise out of the possession of perishable goods or of livestock requiring to be fed (*Sachs* v. *Micklos* [1948] 2 K.B. 23).

3. The agent of necessity must act bona fide in the interests of all parties concerned.

It is not possible to define all the situations in which an agency of necessity arises, but such an agency will be implied more easily when there is an existing agency which requires extending to provide for unforeseen events not dealt with in the original contract, than when there is no such agency (*per* Scrutton L.J. in *Jebara* v. *Ottoman Bank* [1927] 2 K.B. 254). The relevant time for considering whether in particular circumstances there was a necessity or an emergency is the time when the existence of the supposed emergency became apparent: *per* Lord Brandon in *China Pacific S.A.* v. *Food Corpn. of India*; *The Winson* [1982] 1 Lloyd's Rep. 117 at 127.

2. Agency from cohabitation

At a time when the equality of sexes was not as clearly established as today and most wives looked after the common household and did not earn their own living, the common law developed the following principles. In modern times their application may be somewhat doubtful and it may well be that in appropriate cases the court may hold that it is the intention of the wife and the contracting party that the wife has not acted as agent of her husband and has made herself liable to the third party as principal.

At common law when a husband and wife are living together, the wife is presumed to have her husband's authority to pledge his credit for necessaries, judged according to his style and standard of living. The presumption of agency arises from cohabitation, not from marriage. The presumption can, however, be rebutted by the husband proving that:

(a) he expressly forbade his wife to pledge his credit; or
(b) he expressly warned the supplier not to supply his wife with goods on credit; or
(c) his wife was already sufficiently supplied with goods of the kind in question; or
(d) his wife was supplied with a sufficient allowance or sufficient means for the purpose of buying such goods without pledging the husband's credit; or
(e) the order, though for necessaries, was excessive in extent or, having regard to the husband's income, extravagant.

A wife was supplied with clothes to the value of £215 and the husband refused to pay for them. On his being sued by the tradesman, the husband proved that he paid his wife £960 a year as an allowance. *Held*, the husband was not liable (*Miss Gray Ltd.* v. *Cathcart* (1922) 38 T.L.R. 562).

If the husband has been in the habit of paying his wife's bills with a particular supplier, his wife's agency will be presumed and he can only escape liability by expressly informing the supplier that his wife's authority is revoked. If the supplier gave credit to the wife personally and not to the wife as her husband's agent, the husband is not liable. In this connection, it is to be noted that the former rule that if a wife saved money from a housekeeping allowance made by the husband, such money belonged to the husband, has been changed by the Married Women's property Act 1964 with the result that, in the absence of any agreement to the contrary, such money is to be treated as belonging to the husband and wife in equal shares.

Ratification

If an agent has no authority to contract on behalf of a principal or exceeds such authority as he has, the contract is not binding on the principal. The principal may, however, afterwards confirm and adopt the contract so made; this is known as ratification.

The effect of ratification is to render the contract as binding on the principal as if the agent had been actually authorised beforehand. Ratification relates back to the original making of the contract.

A contract can only be ratified under the following conditions:

1. The agent must expressly have contracted as agent. If, having no authority in fact, he merely intended to contract as agent and did not disclose his intention to the other party, *i.e.* if without authority he purports to act for an undisclosed principal (see p. 266, *post*), no ratification is possible.

R., authorised by K. to buy wheat at a certain price, exceeded his authority and bought at a higher price from D. R. bought in his own name, but intended to buy for K. K. agreed with R. to take the wheat at the price, but failed to take delivery. *Held*, K. was not liable to D., as he could not ratify R.'s contract: *Keighley, Maxsted & Co.* v. *Durant* [1901] A.C. 240.

2. The contract can only be ratified by the principal who was named or ascertainable when the contract was made. If the principal was named, he can ratify the contract even if the agent never intended that he should do so, but wanted to keep the benefit of the contract for himself (*Re Tiedemann* [1899] 2 Q.B. 66).

3. The agent must have a principal who was in actual existence at the time of the contract. If, therefore, a person purports to enter into a contract as agent for a company which is not yet formed, then, subject to any agreement to the contrary, he will be personally liable in the contract as if it were his own: s.36(4) Companies Act 1985 (*Phonogram Ltd.* v. *Lane* [1982] Q.B. 938).

4. The principal must have had contractual capacity at the date of the contract and have it at the date of ratification. If the principal was, for example, an enemy at the date of the contract there can be no valid ratification (*Boston Deep Sea Fishing and Ice Co. Ltd.* v. *Farnham* [1957] 1 W.L.R. 1051).

5. The principal must, at the time of ratification, have full know-

ledge of the material facts or intend to ratify the contract whatever the facts may be (*Marsh* v. *Joseph* [1897] 1 Ch. 213).

6. The principal must ratify within the time set or within a reasonable time. (*Bolton Partners* v. *Lambert* (1889) 41 Ch.D. 295. Ratification may be either expressed or implied by the conduct of the principal.

Breach of Implied Warranty of Authority

A person who professes to act as agent, but has no authority from the alleged principal or has exceeded his authority, is liable in an action for breach of warranty of authority at the suit of the party with whom he professed to make the contract (*Collen* v. *Wright* (1857) 8 E. & B. 647). The action is based, not on the original contract, but on the implied representation by the agent that he had authority to make the original contract. Points to note:

1. The action can only be brought by the third party, not by the principal.

2. The agent is liable whether he has acted fraudulently, negligently or innocently, and even if his authority has been terminated, without his knowledge, by death or mental disorder of the principal.

Solicitors were instructed by T. to defend threatened proceedings on his behalf. Before the proceedings started, T., without the solicitors' knowledge, became insane. This revoked their authority (p. 277, *post*). The solicitors delivered a defence and then learnt that T. was insane. The plaintiffs asked for the defence to be struck out and for the solicitors to pay the costs. *Held*, the solicitors, by acting for T., had impliedly warranted that they had authority to do so, and therefore they were liable for the costs: *Yonge* v. *Toynbee* [1910] 1 K.B. 215.

3. The agent is not liable if his lack of authority was known to the third party, or if it was known that he did not warrant his authority or if the contract excludes his liability.

S. signed a charterparty "by telegraphic authority as agents." Owing to a mistake in the telegram the rate of freight offered was wrong, and S. was sued for breach of warranty of authority. *Held*, on its being proved that by mercantile usage the form of signature negatived liability S. was not liable: *Lilly* v. *Smales* [1892] 1 Q.B. 456.

4. If the principal gives ambiguous instructions and the agent acts

on them bona fide and in a reasonable way, he will not be liable in an action for breach of warranty of authority even if he has interpreted them wrongly.

X. sent a telegram to Y. as follows: "You authorise fix steamer prompt loading 3,000 tons coal Newport Cagliari Messina or Palermo 20 shillings." In pursuance of this, Y. let a ship on charter to Z. X. repudiated this on the ground that this authority to Y. was to hire a ship, not to let one. *Held*, if the telegram were ambiguous, (1) Y. had acted bona fide and reasonably in interpreting it as he had done; (2) X. would be responsible to Z. for the interpretation which his agents had bona fide and reasonably placed upon ambiguous instructions; but (3) the actual charterparty entered into was outside the authority in whatever way the telegram was read, and Y. was liable to Z. for breach of warranty of authority: *Weigall & Co.* v. *Runciman & Co.* (1916) 85 L.J.K.B. 1187.

In view of modern communication methods, however, if an agent receives instructions which are ambiguous and he realises or ought to realise this, he may be under a duty to seek clarification (*European Asian Bank A.G.* v. *Punjab and Sind Bank* [1983] 2 All E.R. 508).

5. The agent warrants his authority not only when he purports to contract on behalf of another but also when, purporting to act as an agent, he induces a third party to enter into any transaction with him on the faith of such agency.

One of two trustees of stock standing in the joint names in the books of the Bank of England sold it under a power of attorney, to which the signature of the co-trustee was forged. S., a stockbroker, bona fide acting upon this power of attorney, induced the bank to transfer the stock to the buyer. *Held*, S. had impliedly warranted his authority to the bank, and was therefore liable to indemnify the bank against the co-trustee's claim for restitution: *Starkey* v. *Bank of England* [1903] A.C. 114.

6. Damages for breach of warranty are assessed by reference to the rules laid down in *Hadley* v. *Baxendale* (1854) 9 Ex. 341 for breach of contract (See Chap. 9), except that the liability is limited to the actual damage flowing from the agent's lack of authority and not for the breach of contract. If the agent is sued in tort (deceit or negligence or under the Misrepresentation Act 1967) damages will be awarded according to the rules relating to torts.

Effect of Contracts made by Agents

The effect of a contract made by an agent varies according to the circumstances under which the agent contracted.

Where the agent contracts as agent for a named principal

In this case the agent incurs neither rights nor liabilities under the contract (*Stockton* v. *Mason* [1979] R.T.R. 130).

Exceptions:

1. Where the agent executes a deed in his own name he is liable on the deed (*Appleton* v. *Binks* (1804) 5 East 148). Note: the principal may also be liable.

2. Where the agent signs a bill of exchange in his own name without indicating that he has signed as agent, he is liable on the bill.

3. Where the nature of the contract and the surrounding circumstances make it clear that the agent is liable: *The Swan* [1968] 1 Lloyd's Rep. 5.

4. Where the agent is in fact the principal but contracts as agent he is liable on the contract and can enforce it.

5. Where the custom of a trade makes the agent liable.

It was once thought that an agent contracting on behalf of a foreign principal was personally liable, but it is now settled that there is no presumption of liability on the part of the agent (*Teheran-Europe Co. Ltd.* v. *S.T. Belton Ltd.* [1968] 2 Q.B. 545, below.)

It is possible that a person can be a party to a contract in two capacities *i.e.* as principal and as agent (*The Sun Happiness* [1984] 1 Lloyd's Rep. 381).

Where the agent contracts as agent for an unnamed principal

In this case the agent discloses the existence, but not the name, of his principal. As the agent expressly contracts as agent, he cannot be personally liable on the contract.

A charterparty was made between X. as agent of a shipowner and "J.M. & Co., charterers," and was signed "for and on behalf of J.M. & Co. (as agents), J.A.M." It provided for payment by the "charterers" of demurrage in the event of the ship being detained beyond the stipulated time. X. knew when the charterparty was signed that J.M. & Co. were acting as agents for another, but they did not know who the principals were. In an action by the shipowners against J.M. & Co. for demurrage, *held*, having signed as agents, J.M. & Co. were not liable as principals to pay demurrage, although they were described as charterers in the charterparty: *Universal Steam Navigation Co. Ltd.* v. *James McElvie & Co.* [1923] A.C. 492.

Teheran-Europe was a company incorporated in Iran. Their buying agents in England were Richards Marketing. Richards Marketing negotiated with the defendants Belton for the supply of 12 air compressors, new and unused, "for their clients." Eventually they bought the goods and indicated that they were for shipment to Iran but did not disclose the name of their principals. Teheran-Europe complained that the goods were not in conformity with the contract and claimed damages from the defendants. *Held*, (1) the plaintiffs were unnamed principals and, as such, could sue the defendants directly; there was no rule in modern English commercial law that the principle did not apply if the principal was a foreigner residing abroad; (2) the defendants had not broken the implied condition of section 14(1) of the Sale of Goods Act because, when deciding whether the goods were suitable for the Iranian market, the plaintiffs relied on their own skill and judgment and not on that of the defendants as sellers: *Teheran-Europe Co. Ltd.* v. *S.T. Belton (Tractors) Ltd.* [1968] 2 Q.B. 545.

If, however, the agent does not, on the face of the contract, show that he is merely an agent, he will incur personal liability, and the third party may sue either him or his principal at his option. Descriptive words, *e.g.* on the heading of notepaper or following a signature, such as "broker" or "manager," are not sufficient of themselves to negative personal liability.

Where the agent contracts as agent for an undisclosed principal

In this case the agent discloses neither the existence nor the identity of the principal; he contracts with the third party as if he were the principal. Here:

(a) the undisclosed principal has the right to intervene and claim, and if necessary sue, the third party directly. If he makes use of this right, he renders himself personally liable to the third party; and
(b) the third party, after having discovered the principal, has an option. He may elect to hold liable and sue either the principal or the agent.

If the third party unequivocally elects to hold either the principal or the agent liable he cannot afterwards change his mind and sue the other. Commencement of proceedings against either is prima facie evidence of such election, but if that evidence is rebutted this does not bar subsequent proceedings against the other (*Clarkson Booker Ltd.* v. *Andjel* [1964] 2 Q.B. 775) (followed in *Chestertons* v. *Barons* [1987] 282 E.G. 87). On the other hand, obtaining judgment against either is conclusive evidence, even if unsatisfied, and bars proceedings against the other.

The ordinary rules that an undisclosed principal can intervene and that the third party can elect to sue the principal directly apply also where the undisclosed principal is a foreigner residing abroad; this fact is only one of the elements taken into consideration when determining whether he can sue (*cf.* *Teheran-Europe Co. Ltd.* v. *S.T. Belton* (*Tractors*) *Ltd.*, p. 266, *ante*).

The undisclosed principal may not intervene:

(a) where it is contrary to the terms of the contract (*Humble* v. *Hunter* (1848) 12 Q.B. 310).

(b) where the personality of the principal or agent is a significant factor.

S. tried to get a ticket for the first performance of a play. The theatre manager B. refused to sell him one. S. then sent a friend to buy a ticket. When S. turned up with the ticket, B. refused to admit him. Held, there was no contract between S. and B. B. would not have sold the ticket had he known for whom the agent was acting: *Said* v. *Butt* [1920] 3 K.B. 497.

(c) where the third party made the contract with the agent to obtain the benefit of a set-off (*Greer* v. *Downs Supply Co. Ltd.* [1927] 2 K.B. 28).

Where the rights relating to the undisclosed principal can be duly exercised, the principal can be met with any defence which was available to the third party against the agent before the third party discovered the existence of the principal.

M. employed B. & Co. as his agents to collect a debt from X. To do this B. & Co. properly employed F., who collected the debt. B. & Co. owed F. money, and F., not knowing at the time he was employed that B. & Co. were agents, claimed to set off the debt against money owed him by B. & Co. *Held*, he was entitled to do so: *Montagu* v. *Forwood* [1893] 2 Q.B. 350.

If the third party did not believe the agent to be a principal, he cannot set off any claim he has against the agent against the principal.

C. knew that X., when he contracted in his own name, did so sometimes on his own account and sometimes as agent. X., as agent for D., sold goods to C. without disclosing his agency. *Held*, C. could not set off as against D. a debt owed him by X. because he did not believe that X. was contracting as a principal: *Cooke* v. *Eshelby* (1887) 12 App.Cas. 271.

If an agent borrows money without his principal's authority and applies it in payment of his principal's debts, the lender of the money is entitled to recover the loan as money had and received by the principal to the lender's use (*Reversion Fund and Insurance Co.* v. *Maison Cosway Ltd.* [1913] 1 K.B. 364).

Torts of the agent

The principal is jointly and severally liable with his agent for any torts committed within the scope of his authority. Where the alleged act is performed by an agent acting within his actual authority, it is for the third party to prove that the principal did in fact authorise that particular act. Merely performing an act within the type or class authorised by the principal would not render the principal liable (*Kooragang Investments Property Ltd.* v. *Richardson and Wrench* [1981] 3 All E.R. 65). More often the wrongful act is performed by the agent acting within his apparent or ostensible authority:

L. who owned cottages and money lent on mortgage consulted G. & Co., solicitors. She was seen by S., their managing clerk, who fraudulently induced L. to sign deeds, which in fact transferred the cottages and the mortgage to S. S. realised these assets and absconded. *Held*, G. & Co. were liable for the fraud of S.: *Lloyd* v. *Grace, Smith & Co.* [1912] A.C. 716.

A solicitor acting as a partner in the first case and as an assistant in the second, signed forms of guarantee and undertakings, without actual authority, which resulted in both Banks lending money to fraudulent third parties. *Held* the Banks were reasonable in believing that the solicitor was acting within the firms' authority. Thus both firms were liable: *United Bank of Kuwait* v. *Hammond*; *City Trust* v. *Levy* [1988] 1 W.L.R. 1051.

Rights and Duties between Principal and Agent

Duties of agent

The duties of an agent are:

1. To exercise due diligence in the performance of his duties and to apply any special skill which he professes to have. If he is employed to sell, it is his duty to obtain the best price reasonably

obtainable, and his duty does not cease when he has procured an offer which has been conditionally accepted.

K. employed W. to sell a house. On May 29 W. received an offer of £6,150 from E and communicated it to K., who wrote accepting it "subject to contract." On June 3 D. offered £6,750 to W., who did not communicate this to K., and on June 8 a written contract between K. and E. was signed. *Held*, W. had committed a breach of duty towards K. in not communicating D.'s offer and was liable to pay K. the difference between the two offers: *Keppel* v. *Wheeler* [1927] 1 K.B. 577.

He must disclose to his principal anything coming to his knowledge which is likely to influence the principal in the making of the contract.

H. was employed by P. to sell the lease of P.'s premises. P. had reason to believe that his superior landlord would not consent to the premises being used for a tailoring business. Several tailors were anxious to buy the lease, and H. obtained from the landlords an assurance that they would consent to a tailoring business being carried on. He concealed this from P. and so induced him to sell for a lower figure than he otherwise would have done. *Held*, H. was not entitled to his commission, as he had not properly carried out his duty: *Heath* v. *Parkinson* (1926) 42 T.L.R. 693.

The standard of care owed by a gratuitous agent is an objective standard *i.e.*: "that which may reasonably be expected of him in all the circumstances."

The plaintiff asked the defendant, her friend, to find her a suitable second hand car. She specified that it should not have been involved in an accident. The defendant found a car and recommended that the plaintiff buy it, which she did. The car was unroadworthy. *Held*, the defendant had failed to exercise reasonable care: *Chaudhry* v. *Prabhakar* [1988] 3 All E.R. 718.

2. To render an account when required.

3. Not to become principal as against his employer. This is part of the more general duty that an agent must not let his interest conflict with his duty.

A. employed a stockbroker, J., to buy some shares for him. J. sent a contract note to A. purporting to show that the shares had been bought, but the note was in fact a sham, and J. really sold his own shares to A. *Held*, A. could rescind the contract: *Armstrong* v. *Jackson* [1917] 2 K.B. 822.

4. Not to make any profit beyond the commission or other remuneration paid by his principal. So, for example, an agent is accountable to his principal for any profit which he makes, without the principal's consent, out of

(a) any property with which he has been entrusted by his principal: *Shallcross* v. *Oldham* (1862) 2 Johns & Hem. 609;
(b) a position of authority, to which he has been appointed by his principal: *Reading* v. *Att.-Gen.* [1951] A.C. 507 (see pp. 65–66, *ante*);
(c) any information or knowledge, which he has been employed by his principal to collect or discover, or which he has otherwise acquired for the use of his principal: *Lamb* v. *Evans* [1893] 1 Ch. 218 and *Regal (Hastings) Ltd.* v. *Gulliver* [1942] 1 All E.R. 378, H.L. The reason for this is that such information or knowledge is the property of his principal, just as an invention would be: *Triplex Safety Glass Co.* v. *Scorah* [1938] Ch. 211 and *Sterling Engineering Co. Ltd.* v. *Patchett* [1955] A.C. 534.

An agent is, however, not so accountable when the information or knowledge is not of a special or secret character and he is not dealing with the property of his principal: *Nordisk Insulinlaboratorium* v. *C.L. Bencard* (1934) *Ltd.* [1953] Ch. 430. This is because the agent cannot be prevented from taking advantage of an opportunity of earning money, although it is an opportunity which comes his way because of his employment as agent, provided he does not use his principal's property or break his contract by so doing: *Aas* v. *Benham* [1891] 2 Ch. 244, C.A.

If an agent does make a secret profit, the result is that the principal has the right to do all the following—

(a) The principal may recover the amount of the secret profit from the agent: *Hippisley* v. *Knee* [1905] 1 K.B. 1.
(b) The principal may refuse to pay the agent his commission or other remuneration. In *Hippisley* v. *Knee*, it was held that since the agents had not acted fraudulently they were entitled to their commission.
(c) The principal may dismiss the agent without notice (*Boston Deep Sea Fishing and Ice Co.* v. *Ansell* (1888) 39 Ch.D. 339).

(d) The principal may repudiate the contract.

(e) Where the secret profit amounts to a bribe *i.e.* a payment made to the agent by the third party, the principal has in addition to (b), (c) and (d) above, alternative remedies: *either* for money had and received under which he can recover the amount of the bribe, *or* for damages for fraud, under which he can recover the amount of the actual loss arising from his entering into the transaction in respect of which the bribe was given, but he cannot recover both: *Mahesan S/O Thambiah* v. *Malaysia Government Officers' Co-operative Housing Society Ltd.* [1979] A.C. 374.

If the principal wishes the rescind the contract, he must establish that the third party had actual knowledge or was wilfully blind to the fact that the agent intended to conceal his dealings from his principal: *Logicrose Ltd.* v. *Southend United Football Club Ltd.* [1988] 1 W.L.R. 1256. Where, on discovering the bribe, it is too late to rescind the contract, the principal may bring the transaction to an end for the future: *Armagas Ltd.* v. *Mundogas S.A.* [1986] A.C. 717.

Both the agent and the person paying a bribe are guilty of a criminal offence under the Prevention of Corruption Acts 1906, 1916.

Where a person assumes the character of agent, *i.e.* takes it upon himself to act as if he were the duly authorised agent of another, he is liable to account to that other, as principal, for any profit made out of the property of that other person (*Phipps* v. *Boardman* [1967] 2 A.C. 46).

Before an agent can recover a commission from two principals whose interests are inconsistent he must make the fullest disclosure to each of his principals of his own position, and must obtain the consent of each of them to the double employment (*Fullwood* v. *Hurley* [1928] 1 K.B. 498.).

5. Not to delegate his authority (*Balsamo* v. *Medici* [1984] 1 W.L.R. 951).

The relation between the principal and his agent being a personal one, the agent cannot employ another to do it for him except in the ordinary way of business, as by employing clerks and assistants. Delegation may take place in case of necessity or where it is customary or sanctioned by the principal (*De Bussche* v. *Alt* (1878) 8 Ch.D.

286). An estate agent who has been appointed "sole agent" has no implied authority to appoint a sub-agent: *John McCann & Co.* v. *Pow* [1974] 1 W.L.R. 1643.

6. Not to disclose confidential information or documents entrusted to him by his principal: *Weld-Blundell* v. *Stephens* [1920] A.C. 956. This is part of the agent's general duty of good faith. During the agency the agent must not act against the principal's interest.

A fire broke out in the warehouse of the defendants. They instructed the plaintiffs to act for them in preparing the claim under the fire insurance policy. The defendants gave H., the director of the plaintiffs, confidential information about the policy and allowed him to visit one of their customers whose books were destroyed in the fire but forbade him to disclose certain information relating to their, the defendants', policy. H. disclosed the confidential information to the customers. The defendants terminated their contract with the plaintiffs and claimed damages. *Held*, the defendants were entitled to terminate the contract for breach of confidence and were also entitled to damages: *L.S. Harris Trustees Ltd.* v. *Power Packing Services (Hermit Road) Ltd.* [1970] 2 Lloyd's Rep. 65.

In exceptional circumstances, where the principal fears that he may suffer damage if the agent destroys, or disposes of, confidential information, the principal may obtain an *ex parte* injunction (*i.e.* an injunction granted on the application of one party, the principal, without the other party, the agent, being represented) authorising the principal's representative, usually a solicitor, to enter the agent's premises and to remove the confidential material. Such an injunction is called an **Anton Piller injunction** because it was first granted in *Anton Piller K.G.* v. *Manufacturing Processes Ltd.* [1976] Ch. 55. (See p. 187, *ante*.)

The burden of proving breach of duty by the agent is on the principal (*Gokal Chand-Jagan Nath* v. *Nand Ramm Das-Atma Ramm* [1939] A.C. 106).

Duties of principal

The duties of the principal are:

1. To pay the agent the commission or other remuneration agreed.

The amount of the commission and the terms under which it is payable depend entirely on the terms of the contract between the parties. There is no general rule by which the rights of the agent or the liabilities of the principal under commission contracts are to be determined, but when an agent claims commission from a principal:

(a) When an agent claims that he has earned the right to commission the test is whether on the proper interpretation of the contract between the principal and the agent the "event" has happened on which commission is to be paid.
(b) Once the "event" has happened it must be shown that it was the agent who was the "effective cause" of it (*Cobbs Property Services* v. *Liddell Taylor* [1990] 12 E.G. 104).

The following are examples of such events with the implications. If the agent is to be paid a commission:

(a) on the sale of a particular thing, he is entitled to his commission if the thing is sold to a buyer whom he has introduced, although he may not have negotiated the terms of the sale and although the terms were accepted contrary to his advice (*Burchell* v. *Gowrie and Blockhouse Collieries Ltd.* [1910] A.C. 614). He need not be the first who introduced the buyer (*Nightingale* v. *Parsons* [1914] 2 K.B. 621).
(b) on a sale being completed, it is not enough for the agent acting on behalf of the seller to find a buyer who signs an agreement to purchase but refuses to complete or to pay the purchase money (*Martin* v. *Perry* [1931] 2 K.B. 310). In such an event the seller is not obliged to sue for specific performance to enable the agent to obtain his commission (*Boots* v. *E. Christopher & Son* [1952] 1 K.B. 89). If it is the seller who refuses to complete, this will constitute the breach of an implied term of the agency contract that the principal (the seller) will not fail to perform the contract of sale with the buyer so as to deprive the agent of the commission due to him. (*Alpha Trading Ltd.* v. *Dunnshaw-Patten Ltd.* [1981] Q.B. 290). If the buyer is able and willing to complete but signs an agreement "subject to contract" and the seller refuses to complete, no commission is payable (*Luxor* (*Eastbourne*) *Ltd.* v. *Cooper* [1941] A.C. 108). Neither is it payable if the seller refuses to sign the contract (*Jones* v. *Lowe* [1945] 1 K.B. 73.

(c) if he introduces a person "willing and able to purchase": he is not entitled to commission if he introduces one who is willing to purchase subject to contract or subject to satisfactory survey (*Graham & Scott* (*Southgate*) *Ltd.* v. *Oxlade* [1950] 2 K.B. 257).

(d) if he introduces a person ready, able and willing to purchase: it is payable when a person who is able to purchase is introduced and expresses readiness and willingness by an unqualified offer to purchase, though such offer has not been accepted and could be withdrawn: *Christie Owen & Davies* v. *Rapacioli* [1974] Q.B. 781.

(e) if a "prospective purchaser" is found, the agent is entitled to commission if he finds a person who in good faith seriously contemplates the purchase and makes an offer, though, in the end, he might not be ready, willing and able to purchase (*Drewery and Drewery* v. *Ware-Lane* [1960] 1 W.L.R. 1204).

A contract by which the owner of a house, wishing to dispose of it, puts it in the hands of an estate agent on commission terms, is not (in the absence of specific provisions) a contract of employment in the usual sense; for no obligation is imposed on the agent to do anything. The contract is merely a promise binding on the principal to pay a sum of money upon the happening of a specified event, which involves the rendering of some service by the agent (*Luxor* (*Eastbourne*) *Ltd.* v. *Cooper* [1941] A.C. 108). Nevertheless, the ostensible authority of an estate agent invited to find a purchaser for premises or a lessee for premises does not extend to entering into any contractual relationship on behalf of the person instructing him in respect of the premises (*Hill* v. *Harris* [1965] 2 Q.B. 601).

When property is entrusted to an agent to sell there is, in the absence of any stipulation to the contrary, an implied term that the owner himself may sell or employ other agents to sell the property (*Brinson* v. *Davies* (1911) 105 L.T. 134). But if an agent is employed as "sole agent" no other agent can be employed, although the owner may still sell the property himself without paying commission (*Bentall, Horsley and Baldry* v. *Vicary* [1931] 1 K.B. 253).

Where an estate agent is not the effective cause of the sale, although no commission is payable, he may be entitled to a quantum meruit (*Debenham Tewson & Chinnocks* v. *Rimmington* [1989] 44 E.G. 90).

When an agency has been created for a fixed time, but is revoked before the expiration of that date, the agent is entitled to damages for being prevented from earning his commission if there is an obligation, express or implied, on the part of the principal to continue the agency for that time.

If the employment is one of agency merely, with no service and subordination, and the agent can act for other principals also, there is in general no obligation on the part of the principal to supply the agent with the means of earning his commission; but if the contract is one of service, then the commission is merely intended to be in the place of salary, and the contract cannot be determined without compensation to the servant.

F. was appointed sole agent for the sale of R.'s coals in Liverpool for seven years. F. could determine the contract if R. did not supply 75,000 tons a year and R. could determine it if F. did not sell 50,000 tons a year. After four years, R. sold the colliery. *Held*, there was no implied term that R. should not sell the colliery in the seven years and F. was not entitled to damages: *Rhodes* v. *Forwood* (1876) 1 App.Cas. 256.

G., a shirt manufacturer, employed T. as agent, canvasser and traveller to sell such goods as should be forwarded to him. The agency was for five years determinable by either party at the end of that time by notice. At the end of two years G.'s factory was burned down, although there were other sources of goods available. *Held*, T. was entitled to damages as there was a definite agreement to employ him for five years: *Turner* v. *Goldsmith* [1891] 1 Q.B. 544.

X., a broker, effected a charter for a steamship for 18 months, but after four months of the charter had run the owner sold the ship to the charterer and the charterparty was cancelled. The charterparty provided for payment of a commission of two and a half per cent. to X. on the hire paid and earned under the charterparty. *Held*, X. could not recover commission for the remaining 14 months, as there was no implied term that the owner should not put an end to the charterparty by selling the ship to the charterer: *French & Co. Ltd.* v. *Leeston Shipping Co. Ltd.* [1922] 1 A.C. 451.

If the sale had been made for the express purpose of defeating the agent's right to commission the principal could not have relieved himself from liability. An agreement to pay commission to an agent if a sale is effected at one price does not bind the principal to pay any commission if a sale is effected at a lower price.

In 1920 H., shipbrokers, negotiated a charterparty with K. for five years, one of the terms being that K. could purchase the ship at any time during the charter for £125,000. H.'s principals agreed to pay H. three and a half per cent. commission on the sale. In 1921 K. bought the ship for £65,000, and H. claimed three and a half per cent. on this sum from his principals. *Held*, as the sale had taken place at a different price from that set out in the charterparty, H. was not entitled to any commission: *Howard Houlder & Partners Ltd.* v. *Manx Isles SS. Co.* [1923] 1 K.B. 110.

Commission may be payable even after the termination of the agency. This, however, is exceptional. "Prima facie the liability to pay commission . . . ceases as to future trade with the cessation of the employment in the absence of a reasonably clear intention to the contrary" (*per* McCardie J. in *Marshall* v. *Glanvill* [1917] 2 K.B. 87, 92). An agreement to pay on "repeat" orders may show this intention (*Levy* v. *Goldhill* [1917] 2 Ch. 297). So may an agreement to pay commission as long as the principal does business with the customers introduced (*Wilson* v. *Harper* [1908] 2 Ch. 270). An agent who received an advance on his commission from his principal is normally bound to account for any excess on termination of his contract (*Bronester* v. *Priddle* [1961] 1 W.L.R. 1294).

2. To indemnify the agent for acts lawfully done and liabilities incurred in the execution of his authority.

C. employed X., a broker, to make speculative purchases of cotton for him, and became heavily indebted to X. owing to the fall of prices in the cotton market. X., as he was entitled to do, closed the account by selling the cotton which he had bought for C. X. was personally liable on the contracts and the sale of cotton resulted in a loss. *Held*, X. was entitled to be indemnified by C.: *Christoforides* v. *Terry* [1924] A.C. 566.

The agent loses his right to an indemnity if he acts beyond his authority or performs his duty negligently.

F. asked D., his stockbroker, the price of some stock ex dividend. D. quoted the price, which was cum dividend, but negligently omitted to tell this to F. F., thinking the price was ex dividend, authorised D. to sell. D. sold and, in due course under the rules of the London Stock Exchange, had to pay the dividend to the purchaser. *Held*, D. was not entitled to be indemnified by F.: *Davison* v. *Fernandes* (1889) 6 T.L.R. 73.

Termination of Agency

Agency is terminated by:

(a) the act of the parties; and
(b) operation of law.

By act of the parties

The contract of agency can be terminated by mutual agreement between the parties, but the authority of the agent can be revoked at any time by the principal. If the revocation is a breach of his contract with the agent, the principal will be liable to pay damages for loss of the agent's commission or other remuneration. The power of the principal to revoke the authority of the agent is limited in two directions:

1. If a principal has allowed an agent to assume authority, a revocation of that authority will only be effective as against third parties, if the third parties are informed of the revocation of authority. For example, if B. is the agent of C. to collect debts due to C., and C. revokes B.'s authority and then B., ostensibly on C.'s behalf, collects a debt from X. who has previously paid B. as C.'s agent, the payment will be good as between X. and C. unless X. knew at the time of payment that B. no longer had authority to collect debts.

2. If the principal has given the agent an authority coupled with an interest, the authority is irrevocable. An example of such an authority is where X. sells the goodwill and book-debts of his business to Y. and appoints Y. his agent to collect the debts due to the business. In such a case, as the book-debts form part of the consideration for the sale, X. cannot revoke the authority he has given to Y.

The mere appointment of an agent to collect debts for five years on a commission is not an authority coupled with an interest (*Doward, Dickson & Co.* v. *Williams & Co.* (1890) 6 T.L.R. 316).

By operation of law

The authority of an agent is revoked by the principal—

(a) having died;
(b) becoming bankrupt;
(c) becoming mentally disordered; or
(d) Becoming an enemy.

Although the mental disorder of the principal revokes the

authority of the agent, the principal will be bound by contracts made with third parties who have no notice of that incapacity.

A wife was given authority by her husband to buy goods from D. The husband became mentally disordered, but the wife continued to buy from D., who did not know of the husband's incapacity. *Held*, the husband was liable to pay for the goods: *Drew* v. *Nunn* (1879) 4 Q.B.D. 661.

When the principal becomes an enemy the authority of the agent ceases on the ground that it is not permissible to have intercourse with an enemy, and the existence of the relationship of principal and agent necessitates such intercourse.

S. & Sons were sole agents for a German firm in Great Britain for the sale of machines on a commission basis. *Held*, the outbreak of war between England and Germany terminated the agency: *Stevenson & Sons Ltd.* v. *Akt. für Cartonnagen-Industrie* [1917] 1 K.B. 842.

Types of Agent

Estate agents

The Estate Agents Act 1979 establishes procedures, within the competence of the Director General of Fair Trading, whereby a person can be adjudged and registered as unfit to do "estate agency work" (section 1(1)), and in consequence is prohibited from engaging in such work. An individual's unfitness or otherwise for such work may be determined by a number of criteria including, *inter alia*, his failure: to give complete information on the likely charges and other liabilities at the time the agent is appointed, to disclose any personal interest in the property, to maintain a separate client deposit account, and to cover any clients' money received by him by insurance against his failing to account for it. The Secretary of State may further impose by regulation standards of competence on those engaged in estate agency work (s.22(1)).

Estate agents may receive a deposit from the intending purchaser either as agents of the vendor or in an independent capacity, *e.g.* as stakeholders. The liability of the vendor to return the deposit if the agent is unable to do so arises only if the vendor has authorised the agent to receive a deposit on his behalf. If the vendor has given the agent no actual authority, there would be no liability because the estate agent does not have implied authority to receive a deposit as agent of the vendor.

The vendor is not liable for the return of the deposit, *Sorrell* v. *Finch* [1977] A.C. 728 H.L. Estate agents who mislead buyers may be prosecuted under the Property Misdescriptions Act 1991.

Auctioneers

An auctioneer is an agent to sell goods at a public auction.

On a sale by auction there are three contracts:

1. Between the owner of the goods (the vendor) and the highest bidder to whom the goods are knocked down (the purchaser). This is a simple contract of sale to which the auctioneer is not a party.

2. Between the owner of the goods (the vendor) and the auctioneer. The vendor entrusts the auctioneer with the possession of the goods for sale by auction. The understanding is that the auctioneer should not part with the possession of them to the purchaser except against payment of the price: or, if the auctioneer should part with them without receiving payment, he is responsible to the vendor for the price. The auctioneer has, as against the vendor, a lien on the proceeds for his commission and charges.

3. Between the auctioneer and the highest bidder (the purchaser). The auctioneer has possession of the goods and has a lien on them for the whole price. He is not bound to deliver the goods to the purchaser except on receiving the price in cash; or, if he is willing to accept a cheque, on receiving a cheque payable to himself, the auctioneer for the price. If he does allow the purchaser to take delivery without paying the price the auctioneer can, as he has a special property in the goods, sue in his own name for the full price. If the highest bidder refuses to take delivery of the goods the auctioneer can sue him for the price.

An auctioneer's implied authority is to sell without reserve price, and therefore a sale by him below the reserve will be binding on his principal even if the principal had instructed him not to sell below a definite price. On the other hand if the auctioneer states that the sale is subject to a reserve, but by mistake knocks the article down at a price below the reserve, the sale is not binding on the owner. In the latter case the buyer is informed that there is a limitation on the auctioneer's authority and therefore bids can only be accepted subject to the reserve being reached (*McManus* v. *Fortescue* [1907] 2 K.B. 1). The buyer will be entitled to sue the auctioneer for damages for breach of warranty of authority (p. 263, *ante*) (*Fay* v. *Miller Wilkins & Co.* [1941] Ch. 360).

Mercantile agents

A mercantile agent, also called a factor, is a person who, in the customary course of his business as such agent, has authority either to sell goods, or to consign goods for the purpose of sale, or to buy goods, or to raise money on the security of goods (**Factors Act 1889**, s.1(1)). He has a general lien on goods in his possession and on the proceeds of sale of such goods for the balance of account between himself and his principal. Under the Factors Act, mercantile agents, who are not the owners of goods, can in certain circumstances, sell them and give good title to the buyer. (See Ch. 15, p. 335).

Confirming houses

In the export trade, when a supplier receives an order from a customer abroad, he sometimes asks for confirmation of that order by a person in the supplier's country. The confirmer "adds confirmation or assurance to the bargain which has been made by the primary contractor" and is personally liable to the supplier if the buyer abroad fails to perform the contract.

Turkish buyers placed a considerable order for radio sets with S., and C. confirmed the order. After receipt of part of the consignment the buyers refused to take delivery of the balance. *Held*, C. was liable for damages for non-acceptance: *Sobell Industries Ltd.* v. *Cory Bros. & Co. Ltd.* [1955] 2 Lloyd's Rep. 82.

A confirmer has a particular, but not a general, lien on the goods or documents of title of his overseas principal (*Tellrite Ltd.* v. *London Confirmers Ltd.* [1962] 1 Lloyd's Rep. 236).

If the confirmer fails to pay, the seller has still his claim for the purchase price against the buyer.

Brokers

A broker is an agent who is employed to buy or sell on behalf of another. He differs from a mercantile agent by not having possession of goods, and consequently he has no lien and he cannot sue in his own name on the contract. Brokers who are members of The Stock Exchange or a commercial exchange or other similar institution have an implied authority to make their contracts subject to the rules of such institution, but beyond that they have no implied or presumed authority of any kind. Brokers are not liable to their principal for the failure of a buyer to pay the price.

Del credere agents

A *del credere* agent is an agent employed to sell goods who undertakes for extra commission that purchasers he procures will pay for any goods they take. He only undertakes that he will pay, if the purchasers do not pay, owing to insolvency or an analogous cause. But he does not make himself liable to his principal if his buyer refuses to take delivery (*Gabriel & Sons* v. *Churchill and Sim* [1914] 3 K.B. 1272).

Chapter 14

PARTNERSHIP

Partnership is "the relation which subsists between persons carrying on business in common with a view of profit" (s.1).[1] But the relation between members of any company registered under the Companies Act 1985 as amended by the Companies Act 1989 or incorporated under an Act of Parliament or by Royal Charter is not partnership.

The feature which distinguishes a partnership from a company is incorporation. A company is a legal entity distinct from the members forming the company, while a partnership has no legal existence apart form its individual members. The strictness of this principle is mitigated by the rule that a partnership may sue or be sued under its firm name (Rules of the Supreme Court 1965, Order 81, Rule 1); if the partnership is the plaintiff, the defendant may require it to disclose the names and addresses of all partners (*ibid.* rule 2).

The logical minimum number of partners in a partnership is two. The legal restrictions on the maximum number have changed over recent years. The Companies Act 1948 limited the maximum to 20 and in the case of a banking company, 10, but the Companies Act 1967 permitted this to be exceeded in the case of certain professional and other partnerships. The Companies Act 1985 (ss.716 and 717) now specifically permits partnerships of more than 20 in the case of solicitors, accountants and stockbrokers and those partnerships prescribed by regulations made by the Secretary of State (s.716(2)(d)). Such regulations have been made relating to patent agents, surveyors, auditors, valuers, estate agents, land agents and those engaged in estate management, actuaries, consulting engineers, building designers, and loss adjusters. Earlier restrictions on the number of partners permitted to carry on the business

[1] References in this chapter are, unless the contrary is expressed, to the Partnership Act 1890.

of banking were superseded by the Banking Act 1979 (itself now replaced and substantially repealed by the Banking Act 1987) which introduced a system of recognition of banks and licensing of deposit-taking institutions by the Bank of England. There is no specific reference to banking in ss.716 and 717 of the Companies Act 1985.

A club or society, such as a cricket club, or a social club, or a debating society, is not a partnership because it is not formed to make profit. The members of such institutions are not liable for debts incurred by the committee without their authority, and are not bound to contribute to the losses of the club beyond the amount of their subscription as laid down in the rules (*Wise* v. *Perpetual Trustee Co.* [1903] A.C. 139).

Syndicates are not partnerships because the members do not carry on business "in common" (see p. 306, *post*).

A partnership is formed by contract, either express or implied. The contract may be in writing or verbal or it may have to be inferred from the conduct of the parties. Even where there is no agreement of partnership, a person may incur the liabilities of a partner if he holds himself out, or allows himself to be held out, as a partner. In determining whether a partnership does or does not exist, regard must be had to the following rules:

1. Joint or part ownership does not of itself create partnership whether the owners do, or do not, share any profits made by the use of the thing owned. The differences between co-ownership and partnership are:

(a) Partnership is necessarily the result of agreement, co-ownership is not, *e.g.* X. may by his will leave his house to Y. and Z. jointly. Y. and Z. are co-owners of the house, but not partners, although the rent will be shared equally between them.

(b) Partnership necessarily involves the working for profit, co-ownership does not.

(c) A partner cannot transfer his share of the partnership to a third party without the consent of his partners. One co-owner can transfer his share without the other co-owner's consent.

(d) A partner is the agent of the partnership to bind the firm. A co-owner has no implied authority to bind the other co-owners.

2. The sharing of **gross returns** does not of itself create a partnership, whether or not the persons sharing in the returns have a common interest in the property from which the returns are derived. It is not even evidence of partnership. For example the fact that an author receives a percentage royalty from a publisher on copies of a book sold does not indicate a partnership between author and publisher, *Cox* v. *Coulson* [1916] 2 K.B. 177.

3. The sharing of **profits** is prima facie evidence of partnership, but the receipt of a share of profits, or of a payment varying with the profits of a business, does not **of itself** make the recipient a partner in the business. This means that the sharing of profits, without more, proves a partnership, but this may be rebutted by proving other facts which show that the parties did not intend to be partners. In particular, there is no partnership in the following cases:

(a) Where a person receives a debt or other liquidated amount by instalments out of the profits of a business.
(b) Where a servant or agent is engaged in a business and is remunerated by a share in the profits.
(c) Where a widow or child of a deceased partner receives a portion of the profits by way of annuity.
(d) Where a person has lent money to a person engaged or about to engage in business, and receives a rate of interest varying with the profits or a share of the profits. Such a contract must be in writing signed by or on behalf of the parties thereto.
(e) Where a person has sold the goodwill of a business, and in consideration of the sale receives a portion of the profits.

In cases (d) and (e) above, if the person carrying on business becomes bankrupt, the lender of the money and the vendor of the business are postponed until all the other creditors are paid in full (s.3).

If losses as well as profits are shared, the evidence of partnership is stronger, but it is not conclusive, and in every case the question of partnership depends on the intention of the parties.

A debtor assigned his business to trustees for the benefit of his creditors. The trustees carried on the business with the object of paying off the creditors out of the profits of the business. *Held*, the creditors were not partners in the business: *Cox* v. *Hickman* (1861) 8 H.L.C. 268.

Persons who intend to form a company and are working together prior to its formation are not normally partners; they do not carry on a business in common with a view to profit but are engaged in the preparation of the company's business.

M. and B. agreed to go into business together and to form a limited company which would carry on business in M.'s restaurant. B. ordered certain goods from the plaintiffs; these goods were intended to be used by the company when incorporated. B. was adjudicated bankrupt and the plaintiffs sued M., contending that he was a partner of B. *Held*, M. and B. were never partners because they never intended to carry on business in partnership. All they did was work preparatory to the business to be carried on by the company when formed: *Keith Spicer Ltd.* v. *Mansell* [1970] 1 W.L.R. 333.

Executors carrying on business under the terms of their testator's will are not partners (*Re Fisher & Sons* [1912] 2 K.B. 491).

The term "salaried partner" is not a term of art. It is, however, widely used to describe a person who is held out to the world as being a partner by, for example, including his name with those of the partners on the firm's notepaper but who receives a salary rather than a share of the profits; although he may also receive a bonus or some other sum dependent upon the profits. By holding him out as being a partner, the partners make themselves liable for his acts vis-a-vis third parties as if he were one; but this does not of itself mean that he is a partner vis-a-vis the partners themselves and not just an employee. To decide this one has to look at the substance of the relationship between the parties, not merely the label attached to it: *Stekel* v. *Ellice* [1973] 1 W.L.R. 191.

Creation of Partnership

A partnership is illegal when it is formed for an illegal purpose.

In the case of an illegal partnership, no action can be brought for a breach of it, no account of profits will be ordered, and no proceedings can be brought in respect of it (*Foster* v. *Driscoll* [1929] 1 K.B. 470; see p. 123, *ante*).

Capacity to enter into partnership is governed by the ordinary law of contract. An alien can enter into a valid partnership with a British subject, but if he becomes an enemy owing to the outbreak of war, the partnership is dissolved.

A minor can enter into partnership, and the contract is binding on him unless he repudiates it before or within a reasonable time of his attaining full age. If he repudiates it, he is not liable for partnership debts contracted while he was a minor. (See chapter 5 for the capacity of minors to enter contracts.)

The Firm Name

Persons who have entered into partnership with one another are collectively called a firm (s.4), but the firm name, as such, is only a short way of expressing the names of all partners, and the firm itself has no separate legal existence. The partners, however, may sue and be sued in the firm name.

Brown, Jones, Robinson and Smith may carry on business in partnership as "Brown & Co." or "The City Stationers," but these two titles are merely aliases for the surnames of the four partners.

Business names

If a sole trader, a partnership or a company carries on business under a name other than his or its real name this name is known as a business name. The use of business names is controlled by the Business Names Act 1985. Registration is not required but the use of a business name is subject to the control of the Secretary of State.

Thus, for example, a name must not be used which would be likely to give the impression that the business is connected with Her Majesty's Government or any local authority. Further, a partnership which carries on business under a name not consisting of the surnames of all the partners must:

(a) disclose the name of each partner on all business letters, written orders for goods or services to be supplied, invoices and receipts issued in the course of the business and written demands for payment of debts arising in the course of the business;
(b) display the name and address of each partner in any premises where the business is carried on and to which customers or suppliers have access;
(c) disclose, in relation to each partner, an address within Great Britain at which service of any document relating in any way to the business will be effective.

Non-compliance with these requirements is an offence punishable by a fine. As to civil proceedings, if a firm using a business name has failed to comply with the disclosure requirements and sues, for example, for breach of contract, the claim will be dismissed if the defendant shows that:

(a) he has a claim against the plaintiff arising out of the contract which he has been unable to pursue because of the plaintiff's non-compliance; or
(b) he has suffered financial loss in connection with the contract by reason of the plaintiff's non-compliance.

However, even if the defendant does establish such a defence, the court has power to permit the proceedings to continue if satisfied that it would be just and equitable to do so.

Relations of Partners to Persons Dealing with Them

Every partner is the agent of the firm and his partners for the purpose of the business of the firm. The acts of every partner who does any act for carrying on in the usual way business of the kind carried on by the firm bind the firm and his partners unless (s.5):

(a) the partner so acting has no authority to act for the firm in that matter; and
(b) the person with whom he is dealing either knows that he has no authority or does not know or believe him to be partner.

Subject to the limitation just mentioned, every partner has implied authority to bind the firm by:

(a) selling the goods of the firm;
(b) purchasing on the firm's behalf goods of the kind usually employed in the firm's business;
(c) receiving payment of the firm's debts and giving receipts for them; and
(d) engaging servants for the partnership business.

In **trading firms** a partner may further—

(e) accept, make and issue negotiable instruments in the firm's name;
(f) borrow money on the firm's credit and pledge the firm's goods to effect that purpose; and

(g) instruct a solicitor in an action against the firm for a trade debt (*Tomlinson* v. *Broadsmith* [1896] 1 Q.B. 386).

It was held in *Higgins* v. *Beauchamp* (below) that a trading firm is one which carries on the buying and selling of goods, but it is thought that this is only one example of a trading partnership and that it would be too narrow to confine this concept to those activities.

B. and M. carried on business in partnership as proprietors and managers of picture houses. The partnership deed prohibited a partner from borrowing money on behalf of the firm. M. borrowed money from H. *Held*, the firm was not liable for the debt, because it was not a trading firm, and M. had therefore no implied authority to borrow on the firm's behalf: *Higgins* v. *Beauchamp* [1914] 3 K.B. 1192.

A partner may not, however, bind the firm by deed unless he is expressly authorised by deed, and he may not bind the firm by a submission to arbitration (*Stead* v. *Salt* (1825) 3 Bing. 101).

The firm and all the partners are bound by any act relating to the firm's business done in the firm's name, or in any other way showing an intention to bind the firm, by any person authorised, whether a partner or not (s.6). A partner has not, however, implied authority to bind the other partners in another business.

D. & Co. were a partnership consisting of D., T. and L. and carrying on the business of produce dealers. D. was the only active partner. To cover the possibility of loss, D. asked M., the plaintiff, whether M. was prepared to buy a consignment of potatoes ex s.s. *Anna Schaar* as a joint venture, *i.e.* on the basis of sharing profits and loss, and M. agreed. M. contended that the joint venture was itself a partnership between him and D. & Co., and sued T. and L. for half his share in the profits arising from that venture. *Held*, the contention of M. was correct and the venture was concluded by D. for the partnership and could not be considered as "another" business; consequently, D. bound not only himself but also T. and L.: *Mann* v. *D'Arcy and Others* [1968] 1 W.L.R. 893.

If a partner pledges the credit of the firm for a purpose apparently not connected with the firm's ordinary business, the firm is not bound unless he was specially authorised by the other partners (s.7). The partner himself is personally liable, and his act may subsequently be ratified by the firm. Again, if it has been agreed between the partners that any restrictions shall be placed on the power of any of the partners to bind the firm, no act done in contravention of the agreement is binding on the firm with respect to persons having notice of the agreement (s.8). With respect to persons having no notice, the firm will be bound, notwithstanding the restriction, if the act done is within the ordinary course of business of the firm.

The firm is liable for **torts or wrongs** of each partner if committed in the ordinary course of the firms's business or with the authority of the other partners (s.10).

A partner is a firm, whose business it was to obtain by legitimate means information about the business contracts of competitors, bribed the clerk of a rival to break his contract of service by betraying his masters secrets. The bribe came out of the firm's money, and the profits went into their assets. *Held*, as the partner had done illegitimately that which it was part of his business to do legitimately, the firm were liable for his act: *Hamlyn* v. *Houston & Co.* [1903] 1 K.B. 81.

If a partner acting within the scope of his apparent authority receives the property of a third person and misapplies it, or if the firm in the course of its business receives the property of a third person and, while it is in the firm's custody, a partner misapplies it, in each case the firm is liable to make good the loss (s.11).

The Partnership Act 1890 provides that the liability of each partner in respect of the firm's **contracts** is **joint** (s.9), but this provision must now be read in the light of the Civil Liability (Contribution) Act 1978, s.3, which provides that judgment recovered against any person liable in respect of any debt or damage shall not be a bar to an action against any other person who is jointly liable with him in respect of the same debt or damage. The 1978 Act has virtually made the liability of partners in respect of the firm's **contracts joint and several**. The liability of partners in respect of the firm's **torts** is also **joint and several** (s.12).

Examples—A. and B. are partners. X. sues A. on a contract of the firm and recovers judgment against him, but the judgment is unsatisfied owing to A.'s lack of means. X. can sue B. by virtue of the Civil Liability (Contribution) Act 1978, s.3.

A. and B. are partners. X. sues A. on a wrong for which the firm is responsible and recovers judgment which is unsatisfied. X. can bring an action against B for the unsatisfied balance of his claim, because B's liability is joint and several.

The estate of a deceased partner is liable severally for the debts and obligations of the firm so far as they remain unsatisfied, but subject to the prior payment of his separate debts.

Liability of person by "holding out"

A person may be liable like a partner for the debts of the firm although he is not in fact a partner, if he by words spoken or written or by conduct represents himself or knowingly allows himself to be represented as a partner in the firm. His liability in such a case is only to those persons who have, on the faith of such representation, given credit to the firm (s.14); he is not liable, therefore, for the torts or wrongs of the firm, because such a liability does not depend on giving credit (*Smith* v. *Bailey* [1891] 2 Q.B. 403).

B. carried on business as M.W. & Co., and employed M.W. as the manager of the business. *Held*, these facts amounted to a holding out that M.W. was a partner: *Bevan* v. *The National Bank Ltd.* (1906) 23 T.L.R. 65.

A holding out which makes a person liable as a partner to a third person, does not necessarily establish that he and the person holding him out are, in fact, partners *inter se* though it provides some evidence tending to point to a partnership (*Floydd* v. *Cheney* [1970] Ch. 602).

When a partner dies and the partnership business is continued in the old firm name, the continued use of that name or of the deceased partner's name as part of it does not of itself make his estate liable for any partnership debts contracted after his death (s.14(2)).

M. was a partner in a firm. The firm ordered goods in M.'s lifetime, but delivery was not made until after M.'s death. *Held*, M.'s estate was not liable for the price in an action for goods sold and delivered as there was no debt due in respect of the goods in M.'s lifetime: *Bagel* v. *Miller* [1903] 2 K.B. 212.

Change of Partners

When a person is admitted as a partner into an existing firm he does not thereby become liable to the creditors of the firm for anything done before he became partner (s.17(1)). The new firm may take over the old firm's liabilities, but this of itself does not give the creditors any right to sue the incoming partner. This right may be acquired by novation (see p. 195, *ante*), which is an agreement, express or implied, between the creditor, the new firm and the old firm by which the original contract between the creditor and the old firm is discharged by the acceptance of the liability of the new firm.

A partner who retires from the firm remains liable for the partnership debts contracted while he was a partner. He may, however, be discharged from liability by an agreement between himself, the new firm and the creditors, and this agreement may either be an express one or be inferred from the course of dealing (s.17).

For the debts of the firm incurred *after* his retirement he is liable to persons who (s.36) (a) dealt with the firm before his retirement, unless he has given them notice that he is no longer a partner; or (b) had no previous dealings with the firm, unless he has either given notice of his retirement or had advertised it in the *London Gazette.* He is not liable, however, to persons who had no previous dealings with the firm and did not know him to be a partner.

C. and I. dissolved partnership, but no notice was given or advertisement published. After the dissolution, C. ordered goods from T. using the firm's old notepaper which showed I. as a partner. T. did not know I. was a partner before the dissolution: *Held*, I. was not liable to T.: *Tower Cabinet Co. Ltd.* v. *Ingram* [1949] 2 K.B. 397.

The estate of a partner who dies or becomes bankrupt is not liable for partnership debts contracted after the date of the death or bankruptcy.

A continuing guarantee given to a firm or to a third person in respect of the transactions of a firm is, in the absence of agreement to the contrary, revoked as to future transactions by any change in the constitution of the firm (s.18).

Relations of Partners to One Another

The relations of the partners to one another are usually governed by articles of partnership. If there is no written partnership agreement, their relations are governed by the course of dealing among themselves. In any event, their relations, whether governed by written articles or defined by the Partnership Act, may be varied by the consent of all the partners either given expressly or inferred from a course of dealing (s.19).

The practice of a firm in making out their balance sheets was to treat the loss occasioned by any asset turning out bad as attributable to the year in which it was discovered to be bad. A partner died, and after the balance sheet had been made out various assets were found to be irrecoverable. *Held*, the estate of the deceased partner was entitled to the value of his share as shown in the balance sheet, without any deduction for the losses subsequently ascertained: *Ex p. Barber* (1870) L.R. 5 Ch. 687.

Partnership property

Partnership property must be applied exclusively for the purposes of the partnership and in accordance with the partnership agreement (s.20(1)).

Partnership property is:

(a) property originally brought into the partnership stock;
(b) property acquired, whether by purchase or otherwise, on account of the firm or for the purposes and in the course of the partnership business (s.20); or
(c) property bought with money belonging to the firm, unless the contrary appears (s.21).

William Wray carried on business in partnership with his two sons and T. under the name of "William Wray." On his death, his widow was made a partner and the old firm name was continued. A house was subsequently bought and paid for out of partnership moneys, and was conveyed to "William Wray." *Held*, the house was partnership property, and belonged to the four partners as joint tenants: *Wray* v. *Wray* [1905] 2 Ch. 349.

Where co-owners of an estate in land which is not partnership property are partners as to profits made by the use of that land and buy other land out of the profits to be used in the like manner, the land so bought is not partnership property. Such land belongs, in the absence of agreement to the contrary, to the co-owners in the same shares as they have in the original land (s.20(3)).

Partners in a business borrowed money on the security of freehold premises of which they were tenants in common, and expended the money in adding a part of those premises to adjoining workshops in which the business was carried on, and of which the partners were co-owners. *Held*, the addition to the workshops was not a partnership property: *Davis* v. *Davis* [1894] 1 Ch. 393.

Where land has become partnership property, it is treated as between the partners as personal and not as real estate (s.22). Such land is usually conveyed to the partners (not exceeding four) on trust for sale and to hold the proceeds of sale and the rents and profits until sale as part of the partnership property. On the retirement of a partner, such partner will retire from the trusts and a new partner when admitted will be appointed an additional trustee.

The partnership property is not liable to be taken in execution except on a judgment against the firm. The only remedy of a creditor of a partner in his private capacity, and not as a member of the firm, against the partnership property is to obtain an order charging that partner's interest in the partnership property and profits with the amount of the debt. The creditor may also get a subsequent order appointing a receiver of the debtor partner's share of the profits. When a charging order is obtained in this manner, the other partners may redeem the interest charged, or, if a sale is directed, purchase it (s.23); they also have an option to dissolve the partnership (s.33(2)). The procedure for orders for charging a partner's interest in partnership property is laid down in the Rules of the Supreme Court 1965, Order 81, Rule 10.

Rights and duties between partners

The rights and duties of the partners among themselves, and the interest taken by them in the partnership property, depend on agreement, express or implied. Subject to any such agreement the following rules apply (s.24):

1. All partners are entitled to share equally in the capital and profits and must contribute equally to losses whether of capital or otherwise. The rule is in no way affected by the amount of time given by the partners to the business of the firm.

2. No partner is entitled to interest on capital before the ascertainment of profits.

3. No partner is entitled to remuneration for acting in the partnership business even if the partners have worked unequally.

4. Every partner may take part in the management of the partnership business.

5. No person can be introduced as a partner without the consent of **all** existing partners. This is because a partnership is presumed to be founded on mutual confidence, and an incompetent or dishonest partner may cause heavy loss to his fellow partners. Articles of partnership sometimes contain a provision allowing one of the partners to introduce a new partner, usually his son or near relative. In such a case the consent of the other partners is given in advance by their signing the articles.

Partnership articles between B. and R. gave B. power to introduce into the partnership any of his sons on their attaining 21. His son S. attained 21 and B. therefore proposed to make him a partner. R. refused to consent. *Held*, R. could not prevent S. from being a partner as the clause in the articles operated as a consent: *Byrne* v. *Reid* [1902] 2 Ch. 735.

If under the partnership articles a partner is entitled to nominate by his will a person to succeed him in the partnership, the person nominated cannot enforce the nomination, as he is not a party to the partnership agreement (*Franklin and Swathling's Arbn.* [1929] 1 Ch. 238).

6. Any difference arising as to **ordinary matters** connected with the partnership business may be decided by a majority of the partners; but no change may be made in the **nature of the partnership business** without the consent of all.

The majority of the partners, in exercising their powers, must do so in good faith, and after giving consideration to the views of the minority. It is not competent for a majority to act without consulting the minority.

7. A majority of partners cannot expel a partner unless a power to do so has been reserved by the articles (s.25).

8. A partner is entitled to be indemnified by the firm in respect of payments made and liabilities incurred:

(a) in the ordinary and proper business of the firm; or
(b) in or about anything necessarily done for the preservation of the business or property of the firm.

If, for example, a partner, to save the firm's credit, has paid its debts out of his own pocket, he is entitled to an indemnity.

9. A partner making, for the purpose of the partnership, any advance beyond the amount of capital which he has agreed to subscribe is entitled to interest on that amount at five per cent.

10. The partnership books are to be kept at the place of business of the partnership (or the principal place, if there is more than one) and every partner may, when he thinks fit, have access to and inspect and copy of them. A partner can have the books examined on his behalf by an agent.

Partnership articles provided that proper books of account should be kept. *Held*, any partner was entitled to have the books examined on his behalf by an agent, provided (i) the agent was one to whom no reasonable objection could be taken by the other partners, and (ii) the agent would undertake not to make use of the information obtained except for the purpose of confidentially advising his principal: *Bevan* v. *Webb* [1901] 2 Ch. 59.

In addition to the above, every partner is under a duty to his fellow partners:

(a) To render true accounts and full information on all things affecting the partnership (s.28).
(b) To account to the firm for any benefit derived by him, without the consent of the other partners, from any transaction concerning the partnership, or from any use by him of the partnership property, name or business connection (s.29(1)).

X., Y. and Z. were partners. X. without the knowledge of Y. and Z. obtained for his own benefit the renewal of the lease of the business premises; that lease belonged to the partnership. *Held*, the lease so renewed was partnership property: *Featherstonhaugh* v. *Fenwick* (1810) 17 Ves. 298.

Each partner must also disclose any secret profit made in dealing with the firm, and account for that profit to the firm.

B. and C. were partners, and C. was employed to buy sugar for the firm. C., without B.'s knowledge, sold goods of his own to the firm at the market price and made a considerable profit. *Held*, he must account to the firm for the profit made: *Bentley* v. *Craven* (1853) 18 Beav. 75.

If one partner sells his share of the partnership business to another partner, and the purchaser knows, and is aware that he knows, more about the partnership accounts than the vendor, then the purchaser must disclose his knowledge to the vendor, otherwise the sale is voidable at the vendor's option (*Law* v. *Law* [1905] 1 Ch. 140).

(c) Not to compete with the firm.

Any partner, without the consent of the others, carrying on a competing business must account to the firm for all profits so made (s.30). There is nothing, however, in the absence of an agreement to the contrary, to prevent a partner from carrying on a non-competing business which does not involve the use of the firm's property.

A partner is not entitled to remove partnership documents and other confidential information behind the back of the other partners from the partnership offices for use elsewhere (*Floydd* v. *Cheney* [1970] Ch. 602).

Assignment of share in partnership

If a partner mortgages or assigns his share in the partnership, the mortgagee or assignee is not entitled to interfere in the management of the partnership business, or to require any partnership accounts, or to inspect the partnership books. All he is entitled to is to receive the share of profits to which the assigning partner would otherwise be entitled, and he must accept the account of profits agreed to by the partners (s.31).

A., B. and C. were partners under partnership articles which made no provision for the payment of salaries to any of them. A. charged his share to X. Subsequently, A., B. and C. made an agreement under which, in consideration of their doing more work for the business, they received salaries. *Held*, as the agreement was a bona fide one it was binding on X.: *Re Garwood's Trusts* [1903] 1 Ch. 236.

In the case of a dissolution of partnership, the assignee is entitled to the share of the assigning partner, and, in order to ascertain that share, he is entitled to an account (s.31(2)).

One of two partners mortgaged his share in the partnership to X. Afterwards, without the mortgagee's consent, the partners agreed to a dissolution on the terms that the partner who had mortgaged should sell his share to his co-partner for a sum less than the mortgage debt. *Held*, the agreement was not binding on X., who was entitled to an account on the dissolution of the partnership: *Watts* v. *Driscoll* [1901] 1 Ch. 294.

Dissolution of Partnership

A partnership may be dissolved by order of the court, but there are many cases when dissolution occurs without any order. A dissolution occurs **without any order of the court** by—

1. Expiration or notice (s.32). Subject to any agreement between the partners, a partnership is dissolved:

(a) if entered into for a fixed term, by the expiration of that term;
(b) if entered into for a simple adventure or undertaking, by the termination of that adventure or undertaking;
(c) if entered into for an undefined time, by any partner giving notice of dissolution to the others. Such a partnership is a partnership at will and may be determined at any time on notice. Where the partnership was originally constituted by deed, notice in writing is required (s.26), but in other cases verbal notice is sufficient.

M. and E. were partners under an agreement which provided that the partnership should be terminated "by mutual arrangement only." *Held*, one partner could not terminate the partnership without the consent of the other: *Moss* v. *Elphick* [1910] 1 K.B. 846.

2. Bankruptcy or death (s.33). Subject to any agreement between the partners, a partnership is dissolved by the death or bankruptcy of any partner. Often, however, the partners do not want the death, bankruptcy or retirement of one partner to dissolve the partnership, so it is frequently provided in the partnership deed that in such event the continuing partners shall have the option of purchasing the share of that partner at a valuation.

If one partner sends notice of dissolution to the other partner, and dies before the other partner receives the notice, the partnership is dissolved by death and not by notice (*McLeod* v. *Dowling* (1927) 43 T.L.R. 655).

3. Charge (s.33). If one partner suffers his share to be charged for his separate debt, the others have the option of dissolving the partnership.

4. Illegality (s.34). If an event happens which makes it unlawful for the business of the firm to be carried on or for the members of the firm to carry it on in partnership, the partnership is dissolved.

A., resident in England, and B., resident in Utopia, are partners. War breaks out between England and Utopia. The partnership has become unlawful and is dissolved automatically on the outbreak of war.

On application by a partner **the court** may decree a dissolution of the partnership in the following cases (s.35, as amended):

1. When a partner is incapable by reason of mental disorder of managing and administering his property and affairs (Mental Health Act 1959, s.103(1)(*b*)).

2. When a partner, other than the partner suing, becomes in any other way permanently incapable of performing his duties under the contract of partnership.

3. When a partner, other than the partner suing, has been guilty of conduct calculated to affect prejudicially the carrying on of the business.

C. and E. were partners, and C. was convicted of travelling on the railway without a ticket and with intent to defraud. *Held*, as the conviction was for dishonesty, it was calculated to be detrimental to the partnership business: *Carmichael* v. *Evans* [1904] 1 Ch. 486.

4. When a partner, other than the partner suing, wilfully or persistently commits a breach of the partnership agreement, or otherwise so conducts himself that it is not reasonably practicable for the other partners to carry on the business in partnership with him.

It is a ground for dissolution under this head if one of the partners keeps erroneous accounts and omits to enter receipts, or refuses to submit his dealings to the examination of his co-partners and if there is continued quarrelling between the partners, or such a state of animosity between them that all mutual confidence is destroyed.

5. When the business of the partnership can only be carried on at a loss.

6. Whenever the court thinks it just and equitable to dissolve the partnership. This provision enables the court to decree a dissolution in any case not specifically covered by the first five cases if it thinks it

equitable to do so, *e.g.* when the partnership has reached a deadlock.

W. and R., who had traded separately as tobacco and cigarette manufacturers, agreed to amalgamate and form a private company. W. and R. were the directors and had equal voting power. After a time the relations between them became so strained that neither would speak to the other, communications having to be conveyed between them through the secretary of the company. The company had made and continued to make large profits. *Held*, a deadlock had arisen which would be a clear ground for dissolution in the case of a partnership, and as this was, in substance, a partnership in the guise of a private company, it was just and equitable that the company should be wound up: *Re Yenidje Tobacco Co. Ltd.* [1916] 2 Ch. 426.

On dissolution any partner may give public notice of dissolution, and can compel the other partners to sign the necessary notices of dissolution (s.37). The effect of a dissolution is to revoke the power of each partner to bind the firm, except to complete transactions begun, but not finished, at the time of the dissolution, and to do what may be necessary to wind up the partnership affairs (s.38).

A surviving partner carried on business in the partnership name and continued the partnership banking account, which was overdrawn at the death of the deceased partner, and remained overdrawn until the final winding up of the business. To secure the overdraft he deposited with the bank the title deeds of partnership real estate. *Held*, as the deposit was made for the purpose of winding up the partnership estate, it was binding on the executors of the deceased partner: *Re Bourne* [1906] 2 Ch. 427.

To wind up the partnership, the court may appoint a receiver and manager. A receiver receives the income and pays the necessary expenses, while a manager manages the business with the object, as a rule, of its being sold as a going concern.

Notwithstanding the dissolution of a partnership, where assets remain undistributed, the duty of good faith between the parties continues. Thus, where a leasehold interest had been a partnership asset and the assets of a dissolved partnership remained undistributed, one of the former partners could not acquire the reversion for himself without giving his former partners the opportunity of sharing in the acquisition: *Thompson's Trustee in Bankruptcy* v. *Heaton* [1974] 1 W.L.R. 605.

Application of partnership property on dissolution

1. On dissolution each partner is entitled to have the partnership property, including the goodwill, sold, and the proceeds applied in payment of the debts and liabilities of the firm and to have any surplus assets applied in payment of what may be due to each partner respectively (s.39).

2. In the case of a bankruptcy of one or more (but not all) of the partners:

(a) the partnership will be dissolved, unless the partners had an agreement to the contrary (s.33);
(b) the insolvent partner's share of the partnership will be available for his private creditors;
(c) the firm's creditors will be paid by contribution from solvent parties to the partnership assets as necessary, although the partnership itself and the other partners may be solvent;
(d) as between solvent and insolvent partners the right of solvent partners to recover losses, resulting from additional contributions made by them as a result of a partner's insolvency will be subject to the law on insolvency.

3. As regards insolvent partnership, the position until December 29, 1986 was governed by s.33(6) of the Bankruptcy Act 1914, now replaced by the provisions of the Insolvency Act 1986 as modified by the Insolvent Partnerships Order 1986 (S.I. 2142) under which an insolvent partnership may (subject as therein provided) be wound up as an unregistered company under ss.220 and 221 of the Insolvency Act 1986. Where an insolvent partnership is not wound up as an unregistered company, a petition for bankruptcy orders to be made against all of the partners may be presented, provided all are individual partners and none is a limited partner. In *Re Ashberg (C. & M.) The Times*, July 12, 1990, it was held that the alleged partnership of C. & M. could not be wound up as unregistered company under ss.220 and 221 of the Insolvency Act 1986 as M. was not a *de facto* partner and jurisdiction could not be conferred by estoppel resulting from her conduct in signing cheques and an inland revenue election; C. was in effect a sole trader.

It is provided by Article 10 of the Insolvent Partnerships Order as follows:—

(a) The joint estate of an insolvent partnership is applicable firstly in payment of partnership debts and the separate estate of an insolvent member of the partnership is applicable firstly in payment of that insolvent partner's debts (subject to statutory provisions).
(b) Any surplus remaining after payment of the insolvent partner's debts out of his separate estate is to *be* form part of the joint estate of the partnership and be applied in payment of partnership debts.
(c) Any surplus remaining after payment of partnership debts as above will form part of the separate estate of each partner in proportion to his share in the partnership estate.

4. If the partnership assets are insufficient to discharge the debts and liabilities of the firm, the partners must bear the deficiency in the proportion in which they were entitled to share profits. The order of application of assets to meet losses is:

(a) out of profits;
(b) out of capital;
(c) by the partners individually in the proportion in which they were entitled to share profits (s.44(*a*)).

Apart from this, the assets, including any sums contributed by the partners to make up losses or deficiencies of capital, are applied (s.44(*b*)):

1. In paying the debts and liabilities of the firm to persons who are not partners.
2. In paying each partner rateably what is due from the firm to him for advances as distinguished from capital.

When a partnership was wound up, a partner brought an action against the other partners for the recovery of a loan made by him to the partnership. *Held*, the action was misconceived and had to be dismissed. A partner advancing money to the partnership was advancing some of the money to himself, and the only way in which the money could be recovered was by proceedings for taking the accounts of the partnership, as provided by s.44(*b*)(2): *Green* v. *Hertzog* [1954] 1 W.L.R. 1309.

3. In paying each partner rateably what is due to him in respect of capital.

4. The ultimate residue, if any, to be divided among the partners in the proportion in which profits are divisible.

If the assets are sufficient to pay (1) and (2), above, but insufficient to repay to each partner his full capital, the deficiency in the capital is to be borne by the partners in the proportion in which profits are divisible.

G.M. and W. were partners on the terms that profits should be divided equally. The capital was contributed unequally, G. contributing more than M. On a dissolution, the assets, though sufficient to pay the creditors, were insufficient to repay the capital in full. *Held*, the true principle of division was for each partner to be treated as liable to contribute a third of the deficiency, and then to apply the assets in paying to each partner rateably his share of capital: *Garner* v. *Murray* [1904] 1 Ch. 57.

If one partner has paid a premium on entering into a partnership for a **fixed term** and the partnership is dissolved before the expiration of the term, otherwise than by the death of a partner, the court may order the return of such part of the premium as may be just, having regard to the terms of the partnership and the time it has continued, unless (s.40):

(a) the dissolution is due to the misconduct of the partner who paid the premium; or
(b) the partnership has been dissolved by an agreement containing no provision for a return of the premium.

When a partnership is rescinded on the ground of the fraud or misrepresentation of one of the partners, the partner entitled to rescind is entitled (s.41):

(a) to a lien on the partnership assets, after the liabilities have been discharged, for any sum he has paid for a share of the partnership and for any capital he has contributed;
(b) to stand in the place of any of the firm's creditors for any payments he has made to them to discharge the firm's liabilities;
(c) to be indemnified by the person guilty of the fraud or misrepresentation against all the firm's liabilities.

When a partner dies or retires and the surviving partners carry on the business of the firm without any settlement of account with the late partner or his estate, the outgoing partner or the estate of the deceased partner may:

(a) claim such share of the profits made since the dissolution as is attributable to his share of the assets; or
(b) claim interest at five per cent. on his share of the partnership assets (s.42).

C. and M. carried on business in partnership. On C.'s death the partnership was dissolved, but M. carried on the business for a further period. In an action to decide how the profits earned since C.'s death should be divided, *held*, C.'s estate was entitled to a share in such part of the profits as were attributable to the use of the partnership assets, proportionate to his share in the total partnership assets, and that inquiries should be made to ascertain what part of the profits had been earned otherwise than through the use of the partnership assets, including goodwill, an allowance being made to M. for his management of the business: *Manley* v. *Sartori* [1927] 1 Ch. 157.

R. and A. were partners in selling petrol at a service station in Ceylon. A. gave notice terminating the partnership, but before its termination procured new agreements with the petrol company giving him the sole agency, and after termination continued trading on the partnership property under his own name. R. discovered the new agreements and claimed an account for his share in the profits. *Held*, R. was entitled thereto under section 42 of the Partnership Act 1890 (which applied in Ceylon). Further, R.'s claim was also justified by virtue of section 29 which likewise applied: *Pathirana* v. *Pathirana* [1967] 1 A.C. 233.

Goodwill

Goodwill is the benefit arising from a firm's business connection or reputation. It is defined by Lord Elton in *Cruttwell* v. *Lye* (1810) 17 Ves. 335 as "the probability that the old customers will resort to the old place." This definition is not complete, and must be supplemented by that given by Wood V.-C. in *Churton* v. *Douglas* (1859) Johns. 174: "Goodwill must mean every advantage—every positive advantage, if I may so express it, as contrasted with the negative advantage of the late partner not carrying on the business himself—that has been acquired by the old firm." On a purchase of goodwill the purchaser usually obtains the premises of the old firm and the right to use the name of the old firm and, in all cases, the right to represent himself as the successor of the old firm. Goodwill is a partnership asset and on the death or retirement of a partner it does not pass by survival to the continuing partners, but must be bought by them. If, on a dissolution of partnership, the goodwill is not sold, each of the partners is entitled to carry on business under the name of the old firm, provided he does not expose his former partners to any risk of liability (*Burchell* v. *Wilde* [1900] 1 Ch. 551). For this reason, when there is an agreement that on dissolution the partnership assets, including goodwill, shall be taken by one partner at a valuation, the goodwill must be valued on the footing that the outgoing partner is entitled to carry on a similar business.

The rights and duties between the vendor and the purchaser of goodwill, in the absence of agreement to the contrary, are:

1. The vendor may carry on a similar business to that sold in competition with the purchaser, but he must not use the old firm name or represent himself as continuing the old business.

2. The vendor may not canvass the customers of the old firm or solicit any customer of the old firm to deal with him (*Trego* v. *Hunt* [1896] A.C. 7).

3. The vendor may advertise the fact that he is carrying on business as long as he does not offend the two preceding rules (*Labouchere* v. *Dawson* (1872) L.R. 13 Eq. 322).

B., C. and J.D. carried on a business as J.D. & Co. J.D. retired and B. and C. carried on the business under a new name with the addition of "late J.D. & Co." J.D. formed a new firm carrying on the same kind of business in premises adjoining the old firm's premises in the name of J.D. & Co., and circularised the old firm's customers. *Held*, (1) he could carry on his new business in competition with the old firm and in the immediate vicinity, but (2) although his name was J.D., he could not carry on his new business in the name of J.D. & Co., and (3) he could be restrained by the old firm from canvassing their customers: *Churton* v. *Douglas* (1859) Johns. 174.

4. Unless the right to use the old firm name is expressly assigned, the purchaser of the goodwill must not use that name so as to expose any of the partners in the old firm to liability (*Townsend* v. *Jarman* [1900] 2 Ch. 698).

When a partnership is dissolved on the terms of one partner taking over the assets, the other partners must not solicit the customers of the firm.

A partnership between X. and Y. was dissolved on the terms that Y. retained the "assets." Goodwill was not specifically mentioned. *Held*, the assets included goodwill, and X. would be restrained by injunction from canvassing the customers of the old firm: *Jennings* v. *Jennings* [1898] 1 Ch. 378.

When the deed of partnership provides that on the death of a partner the surviving partner shall acquire the deceased partner's share of the assets, an injunction will be granted to restrain an executor of the deceased partner from soliciting customers of the firm (*Boorne* v. *Wicker* [1927] 1 Ch. 667).

When the assignment of the goodwill of a business is involuntary, as on the sale by the trustee in bankruptcy of the business carried on by the bankrupt, the purchaser cannot restrain the bankrupt from canvassing his old customers (*Walker* v. *Mottram* [1881] 19 Ch. D. 355). Similarly, if a debtor has assigned all his property to a trustee for the benefit of his creditors, he cannot be restrained by the trustee from canvassing his old customers (*Farey* v. *Cooper* [1927] 2 K.B. 384).

LIMITED PARTNERSHIPS

Under the Limited Partnerships Act 1907 limited partnerships, which may be described as a cross between a partnership and a limited company, may be formed. They are not very common, owing to the superior advantages of private limited companies.

The limitation on the maximum number of partners discussed earlier in respect of ordinary partnerships (see p. 282, *ante*) likewise applies to limited partnerships, but at least one of the partners must be a **general** partner and one a **limited** partner. The partnership must be registered by sending to the registrar of companies the following particulars:

(a) the firm name;
(b) the general nature of the business;
(c) the principal place of business;
(d) the full name of each partner;
(e) the term, if any, for which the partnership is entered into and the date of its commencement;
(f) a statement that the partnership is limited and the description of every limited partner as such; and
(g) the sum contributed by every limited partner, and whether paid in cash or otherwise.

Every change in these particulars must also be registered.

A **limited partner** is one who contributes a stated amount of capital or property and who is not liable for the firm's debts beyond that amount. He must not withdraw his capital, otherwise he becomes liable for the firm's debts to the amount withdrawn. The rights and duties of a limited partner are:

1. He may not take part in the management of the partnership business. If he does so, he becomes liable for all the firm's debts and liabilities during that period. He has no power to bind the firm.
2. He may inspect the firm's books and examine into the state and prospects of the partnership business and may advise with the partners thereon.
3. His death, bankruptcy or mental disorder does not dissolve the partnership.
4. He can assign his share with the consent of the general partners.
5. He cannot dissolve the partnership by notice.

Any partner who is not a limited partner is a **general** partner. The general partners manage the partnership business and by a majority can decide differences arising out of the ordinary conduct of the partnership business. They can also introduce a new partner without the consent of the limited partners. A general partner may become a limited partner by registering the change with the registrar and by advertising it in the *London Gazette*. The change is of no effect until it is advertised.

In the event of a dissolution of the partnership, its affairs are wound up by the general partners, unless the court otherwise orders.

Syndicates

The members of a syndicate are liable to third parties only for the amount which they have underwritten (pro rata liability). Syndicates are not partnerships because their members do not carry on business "in common." Consequently, the members are not liable jointly and severally (see p. 289, *ante*), but each member is only liable pro rata for the amount underwritten by him. Unlike a company, a syndicate does not have legal personality.

Syndicates are convenient arrangements for spreading the risk in major commercial transactions. They are mainly used in insurance and reinsurance and in international and domestic finance. Thus, the members of Lloyds of London, the international insurance market, carry on business as syndicates. Further, international bank loans, particularly to sovereign borrowers, such as foreign states or state corporations, are often issued by syndicates of international banks. The flotation of share and bond issues in the home and international market is also often underwritten by banking syndicates.

PART 3: SALE OF GOODS, HIRE-PURCHASE AND CONSUMER CREDIT

CHAPTER 15

THE SALE OF GOODS

A CONTRACT of sale of goods is a contract whereby the seller transfers, or agrees to transfer, the property in goods to the buyer for a money consideration called the price (s.2(1)).[1]

The term "goods" includes all chattels personal, other than things in action and money (s.61). Chattels personal are to be distinguished from chattels real, which are chattels attached to or forming part of the land. Chattels personal, on their part, are subdivided into things in possession and things in action (see pp. 195–196, *ante*). "Goods" are thus all things in possession, with the exception of money used as currency of the realm.

Timber, for example, is not comprised in the term "chattels personal" if it is sold as growing timber, but if it sold as timber severed from the land it is "chattels personal." A ship or aircraft is "goods." "Goods" also includes goods to be manufactured or acquired by the seller after the making of the contract of sale. These are called "future goods."

The consideration for the sale must be money; otherwise the contract is one of barter or exchange. There is nothing to prevent, however, the consideration from being partly in money and partly in goods or some other articles of value, *e.g.* when a dealer, in selling a new car, takes an old car in part exchange.

A contract of sale must be distinguished from a contract for work and materials. A contract of sale contemplates the delivery of a chattel. If, however, the *substance* of the contract is for the exercise of skill and the delivery of the chattels is only subsidiary, there is not a sale of goods. Thus if someone views an already completed painting and then contracts to buy it, the contract is one of sale of goods. If, however, he commissions an artist to paint him a picture, the contract is not one of sale.

[1] References to statutes in this chapter are, unless the contrary is expressed, to the Sale of Goods Act 1979.

G. commissioned R., an artist, to paint a portrait of X. for 250 guineas. R. supplied the canvas and other materials. *Held*, a contract for work and materials and not sale of goods: *Robinson* v. *Graves* [1935] 1 K.B. 579.

A contract for the sale of goods must also be distinguished from a contract of hire.

A price list for "Lucozade" showed the retail price as 2s. 6d. plus 3d. on the bottle. *Held*, the goods which were sold were the contents of the bottles, while the bottles themselves were not sold but merely hired: *Beecham Foods Ltd.* v. *North Supplies* (*Edmonton*) *Ltd.* [1959] 1 W.L.R. 643.

The distinctions are of importance, because a contract of sale of goods is governed by the Sale of Goods Act 1979 while contracts for hire and for work and materials are governed by the Supply of Goods and Services Act 1982 (see pp. 324–326, *post*).

Form of the Contract

A contract of sale of goods may be in writing (whether or not in a deed) or by word of mouth or partly in writing and partly by word of mouth or may be implied by the conduct of the parties (s.4).

Subject-Matter of the Contract

The goods which form the subject of a contract of sale may be either existing goods or goods to be manufactured or acquired by the seller after the making of a contract of sale. Where the property (*i.e.* ownership) in the goods is transferred when the contract of sale is concluded, the contract is called a **sale**; where the property is to be transferred after the conclusion of the contract of sale, the contract is called an **agreement to sell** (s.2(4) and (5)). If, in a contract for the sale of specific goods, the goods have, without the seller's knowledge, perished at the time when the contract was made, the contract is void (s.6). The same result obtains in the case of an indivisible parcel of specific goods if part only of the goods have perished at the time when the contract is made.

X. sold to Y. 700 bags marked "E.C.P." and known as lot 7 of Chinese groundnuts, lying in a specified warehouse. At the time of the sale there were, unknown to both parties, only 591 bags, 109 bags having been stolen. *Held*, the contract was void: *Barrow, Lane & Ballard Ltd.* v. *Philip, Phillips & Co.* [1929] 1 K.B. 574.

The **price** may be fixed by the contract or may be determined by the course of dealing between the parties. In the absence of either of these, the buyer must pay a reasonable price, the amount of which is determined by the circumstances of each particular case (s.8).

CONDITIONS AND WARRANTIES

The distinction between conditions and warranties has already been explained when the **terms of the contract** were considered (in Chapter 3, *ante*). The Sale of Goods Act is, as far as the contract of sale is concerned, founded on this distinction.

A **condition** is a stipulation in a contract going to the root of the contract. It is "of the essence" of the contract. A breach of condition gives rise to a right to treat the contract as repudiated (s.11). A **warranty** is a stipulation which is not of such importance as to go to the root of the contract, but is collateral to the main purpose of the contract, the breach of which gives rise to a claim for damages, but not to a right to reject the goods and treat the contract as repudiated (s.61). Whether a term is a condition or warranty, depends on the construction of the particular contract of sale (s.11(3)).

On a breach of condition the buyer may, if he chooses, bring an action for damages only instead of treating the contract as repudiated (s.11(2)), but he is limited to such an action for damages if the contract is not severable and he has accepted the goods or any part thereof, unless there is a term in the contract to the contrary (s.11(4)).

Stipulations as to time of *payment* are not deemed to be of the essence of a contract of sale, unless a different intention appears from the terms of the contract (s.10; see p. 145, *ante*). Stipulations as to the time of *delivery* will, however, normally be construed as conditions. This is true, not only in respect of stipulations placing an obligation upon the seller as to the date of delivery (or shipment), but also in respect of a stipulation obliging the buyer to do some act (*e.g.* to nominate a vessel) by a stipulated time so as to enable the seller to deliver (*Bunge Corporation* v. *Tradax Export S.A.* [1981] 1 W.L.R. 711, H.L.).

Decisions since the original Sale of Goods Act was passed in 1893 have shown that the division of terms into conditions and warranties is not exhaustive. The same principles apply to contracts of sale of goods as to other contracts (see pp. 33–36, *ante*). Thus, whilst the Sale of Goods Act implies certain conditions into a contract of sale of goods, the breach of a term which is not a condition, could nevertheless give rise to a right to treat the contract as repudiated. Whereas in the case of a condition even a trivial breach gives rise to such a right, in the case of an **innominate term** (*i.e.* something less than a condition) the actual breach must be looked at. If that breach "goes to the root of the contract" or deprives the other party of "substantially the whole benefit of the contract," then the latter is entitled to treat the contract as repudiated.

A written contract to sell fruit pellets contained the express stipulation, "Shipment to be made in good condition." In fact some of the pellets were not in good condition when shipped. However, they were, on arrival, still fit to be used for the purpose the buyer had intended and, although they were worth less than they should have been, they could still have been re-sold at a reduced price. *Held*, the buyers were not entitled to reject the goods. On the facts the sellers were not in breach of either of the conditions implied by section 14 of the Sale of Goods Act as to fitness for purpose and merchantable quality (see below). The express stipulation in the contract was not a condition and the sellers' breach of it had not been serious enough to go to the root of the contract. Therefore the buyers were entitled only to damages: *Cehave N.V.* v. *Bremer Handelsgesellschaft mbH*; *the Hansa Nord* [1976] Q.B. 44.

Implied terms

Several highly important conditions and warranties are implied by the Sale of Goods Act in every contract of sale. These terms are as follows.

1. *Title*

There is an implied condition on the part of the seller that in the case of a sale he has a right to sell the goods and in the case of an agreement to sell he will have such a right at the time when property is to pass (s.12(1)). If, therefore, the seller has no title, he is liable in damages to the buyer.

R. bought a motor-car from D. and used it for four months. D. had no title to the car, and consequently R. had to surrender it to the true owner. R. sued to recover the total purchase price he had paid to D. *Held*, he was entitled to recover it in full, notwithstanding that he had had the use of the car for four months: *Rowland* v. *Divall* [1923] 2 K.B. 500.

If the goods delivered can be sold only by infringing a trade mark, the seller has broken the condition that he has a right to sell the goods (*Niblett Ltd.* v. *Confectioners' Materials Co. Ltd.* [1921] 3 K.B. 387).

There are implied warranties, (a) that the goods are free from any charge or encumbrance not disclosed or known to the buyer before the contract is made, and (b) that the buyer will enjoy quiet possession of the goods (s.12(2)).

In a contract made before May 1970 the seller sold the buyers some road marking machines. Unknown to them, another company was in the process of patenting their own road marking apparatus under the Patents Act which gave them rights to enforce the patent from November 1970. In 1972 this company brought a patent action against the buyers. The buyers then claimed against the sellers for breach of the implied condition as to title and breach of the implied warranty as to quiet possession. *Held*, (i) the seller were not liable for breach of the implied condition because at the time of the sale they had had every right to sell, (ii) the sellers were liable in damages for breach of the implied warranty as to quiet possession because that was an undertaking as to the future: *Microbeads A.C.* v. *Vinhurst Road Markings* [1975] 1 W.L.R. 218.

Section 12(3) governs an exceptional situation, namely where the seller has, or may have, a limited ownership and it is clearly intended that he will transfer only that limited ownership to the buyer. Here there is no implied condition that the seller has a right to sell the goods. This would be the case for example where there is some doubt as to whether the seller has complete ownership in the goods and where the buyer and seller therefore agree that the seller will transfer to the buyer only such ownership as the seller has. The seller may still be liable in respect of the implied warranties relating to freedom from charges and encumbrances and to quiet possession, except that he will not be liable in respect of charges or encumbrances of which the seller had been unaware at the time the contract was made (s.12(4) and (5)).

2. *Description*

Where there is a sale of goods by description, there is an implied condition that the goods shall correspond with the description (s.13 (1)). Goods are sold by description when the buyer contracts in reliance (though not necessarily exclusive reliance) on the description. If the buyer does not see the goods, he must be buying by description. Even if he does see them he may be buying them by description.

G. went to M.'s shop and asked for some men's underwear. Some woollen underwear was shown to him and he bought it. *Held*, a sale by description: *Grant* v. *Australian Knitting Mills Ltd.* [1936] A.C. 85.

A buyer responded to an advertisement describing a car for sale as a "1961" model. He inspected the car before buying it. After buying it he discovered that the car consisted of half a 1961 model and half of an earlier car. *Held*, the seller was liable under section 13, since the buyer had relied at least to some extent on the description: *Beale* v. *Taylor* [1967] 1 W.L.R. 1193.

A sale is not prevented from being a sale by description by reason only that, being exposed for sale or hire the goods are selected by the buyer (s.13(3)). Thus even goods selected by the buyer for himself—for example from the shelves of a supermarket—may nevertheless be bought by description. Reliance by the purchaser on the description is the requirement. If there is no reliance at all by the buyer upon the description, then there is no sale by description and therefore the seller will not be liable under section 13.

The seller, an art dealer, contacted another art dealer informing him that he had for sale two paintings by Gabriele Munter (of the German impressionist school). This resulted in the latter dealer visiting the seller, inspecting the paintings and buying them. The seller, as the buyer knew, had no expertise in the German impressionist school. Subsequently it transpired that the paintings were not by Gabriele Munter. *Held*, the buyer, in deciding whether to buy, had relied not upon the seller's attribution but upon the buyer's own judgment and assessment. Therefore there had not been a sale by description. The court also rejected a claim, under s.14, that the painting was not of merchantable quality; otherwise the buyer could secure via the back door of section 14, that which was denied under section 13: *Leinster Enterprises Ltd.* v. *Christopher Hull Fine Art Ltd.* [1990] 1 All. E.R. 737 (C.A.).

Where there is a sale by description, the buyer can not be compelled to accept goods which do not comply with the description, even though they are not defective in quality. If, for example, the seller could supply only staves varying between half an inch and nine-sixteenths of an inch thick, he should not have contracted to supply staves "half an inch" thick (*Arcos* v. *Ronaasen* [1933] A.C. 470). The question is whether the goods correspond with their description, not whether they are merchantable or of good quality. The key to section 13 is identification.

The sellers, X., supplied herring meal consisting of herrings plus preservative under a contract to sell "herring meal" which was wanted by the buyers, Y., for use as an ingredient in compounding animal feed to be sold to Z. who wanted it to feed to mink. Unfortunately the herrings and preservative together had suffered a chemical reaction making the meal poisonous to mink. *Held*, (1) there had been no addition of goods outside the contract description and therefore the meal supplied corresponded with the description "herring meal"; (2) the feed was not of merchantable quality (see *post*) because it had an ingredient which was toxic. *Ashington Piggeries Ltd.* v. *Christopher Hill Ltd.* [1972] A.C. 441 (for the liability of Y. to Z. see p. 321, *post*).

Where there is a sale of goods by sample as well as by description, the goods must correspond with the description as well as the sample (s.13(2)).

N. agreed to sell to G. some oil described as "foreign refined rape oil, warranted only equal to sample." N. delivered oil equal to the quality of the samples, but which was not "foreign refined rape oil." *Held*, G. could refuse to accept it: *Nichol* v. *Godts* (1854) 10 Ex. 191.

M. sold to L. 3,100 cases of Australian canned fruits, the cases to contain 30 tins each. M. delivered the total quantity, but about half the cases contained 24 tins, and the remainder 30 tins. L rejected the goods. There was no difference in market value between goods packed 24 tins and goods packed 30 tins to the case. *Held*, as the goods delivered did not correspond with the description of those ordered, L could reject the whole: *Re Moore & Co., and Landauer & Co.* [1921] 2 K.B. 519.

In *Reardon Smith Line* v. *Hansen Tangen* [1976] 1 W.L.R. 989 the House of Lords cast doubt on the decision (of the Court of Appeal) in *Re Moore and Landauer*. Even if the decision was correct, it seems (*per* Lord Wilberforce in *Reardon Smith Line*) that, in a contract of sale which is not one for the sale of unascertained future goods, a stipulation in the contract will not be regarded as part of the "description" unless it constitutes a substantial ingredient of the "identity" of the thing sold. A stipulation which is not regarded as part of the "description" is still nevertheless an *express* term of the contract; it would normally be construed, not as a condition, but as an innominate term (see *Cehave N.V.* v. *Bremer Handelsgesellschaft*, p. 314, *ante*).

3. *Merchantable quality*

Where the seller sells goods in the course of a business there is an implied condition that the goods are of merchantable quality (s.14 (2)). The fact that the condition is implied only when the seller sells in the course of a business means that in the absence of an express statement or undertaking a private seller will not be liable in respect of the quality of the goods. The carrying on of a profession and the activities of a government department, a local authority or a statutory undertaking are all regarded as businesses (s.61(1)). There are two further exceptions from the condition as to merchantable quality. The condition is not implied in respect of defects specifically drawn to the buyer's attention before the making of the contract (s.14(2)(*a*)). Similarly, if the buyer examines the goods before the contract is made, the condition is not implied in respect of defects which that examination ought to reveal (s.14(2)(*b*)). In these two exceptional cases, the condition is still implied in respect of defects other than those which were drawn to the buyer's attention or which ought to have been revealed by his examination.

Goods are of merchantable quality "if they are as fit for the purpose or purposes for which goods of that kind are commonly bought as it is reasonable to expect having regard to any description applied to them, the price (if relevant) and all other relevant circumstances" (s.14(6)). Thus it must be asked "What quality is it reasonable to expect in the circumstances?" It is not reasonable normally to expect that the goods will comply with the laws of some foreign country (*Sumner, Permain & Co.* v. *Webb & Co.* [1922] 1 K.B. 55). It is reasonable to expect Coalite not to contain explosive (*Wilson* v. *Rickett, Cockrell & Co. Ltd.* [1954] 1 Q.B. 598). There can be liability under s.14(2) in respect of second-hand goods, for it is reasonable to expect a certain standard of quality—the exact standard depending upon the price and description of the goods in question. A second-hand car with brakes in such a state that they would fail if used in an emergency is not of merchantable quality (*Lee* v. *York Coach and Marine* [1977] R.T.R. 35). A minor repair required to a second-hand car some weeks after the purchase would not indicate that the car had not been of merchantable quality when purchased (*Bartlett* v. *Sydney Marcus Ltd.* [1965] 1 W.L.R. 1013).

The way the statutory definition of merchantable quality works in the case of a motor vehicle (new or second-hand) was set out in *Rogers* v. *Parish* (*Scarborough*) *Ltd.* [1987] Q.B. 933. It works as follows. The definition requires the vehicle to be "as fit for the purpose or purposes for which goods of that kind are commonly bought as it is reasonable to expect." In the case of a vehicle those purposes include, not merely the purpose of driving it from place to place but of doing so with the appropriate degree of comfort, ease of handling and pride in the vehicle's outward and interior appearance. On a vehicle sold as new, the performance and finish to be expected are those of a model of average standard with no mileage. Defects of appearance can render a car unmerchantable. On the other hand, deficiencies which are unacceptable on a car sold as new might be acceptable on a second-hand model. It is a matter of degree.

Unknown to the buyer of a 20 month old Fiat, the car had eight months earlier been totally submerged in water for over 24 hours and had consequently been treated as a "write-off" by its insurer. *Held*, it was not of merchantable quality: *Shine* v. *General Guarantee Finance Co. Ltd.* [1988] 1 All E.R. 911.

The requirement that the goods be of merchantable quality does not mean that they have to be suitable for *all* the purposes for which such goods are commonly used (*Aswan Engineering Establishment* v. *Lupdine*, see below).

The buyer of some heavy duty buckets left them for several days stacked in extreme heat such that the contents reached 70° Centigrade (156° Fahrenheit). The buckets collapsed spilling their contents. *Held*, the buckets, which were suitable for most purposes for which goods of that description are normally bought, were of merchantable quality; *Aswan Engineering Establishment* v. *Lupdine* [1987] 1 W.L.R. 1).

If the goods are still suitable for some of the purposes for which goods of that description are usually used (especially if they could be re-sold for the same or very nearly the same price as if they were suitable for every such purpose), they will remain of merchantable quality.

The buyer of "industrial fabric" found that it was unsuitable for making into dresses but that it was suitable for other industrial purposes; as such it was commercially saleable, though at a slightly reduced price. *Held*, it was of merchantable quality: *Brown (B.S.) & Son Ltd.* v. *Craiks Ltd.* [1970] 1 W.L.R. 752 (and see also *Cehave N.V.* v. *Bremer Handelsgesellschaft mbH*, p. 314, *ante*).

4. *Fitness for purpose*

Where the seller sells goods in the course of a business and the buyer expressly or by implication makes known to the seller any particular purpose for which the goods are being bought, there is an implied condition that the goods are reasonably fit for that purpose (s.14(3)). Like the condition as to merchantable quality, this condition does not apply to the private seller who does not sell in the course of a business. The purpose for which the goods are required need not be expressly made known to the seller if it is impliedly made clear by the circumstances.

A., a milk dealer, supplied F. with milk which F. and his family consumed. Even though A. had taken all reasonable precautions to prevent contamination of the milk, it contained typhoid germs which infected F.'s wife who died as a result. *Held*, the purpose for which the milk was supplied was sufficiently made known to A. by its description; since it was clearly unfit for human consumption A. was liable for breach of condition; *Frost* v. *Aylesbury Dairy Co. Ltd.* [1905] 1 K.B. 608.

Vacwells, who made transistors, bought from B.D.H. some ampoules of boron tribromide which were marked "harmful vapour." Two of Vacwell's chemists washed the ampoules in a sink, to remove the labels. A violent explosion occurred, killing one of the chemists, injuring the other, and causing considerable damage to the premises. The chemical boron tribromide reacted violently to water; apparently one of the chemists had dropped an ampoule in the sink, the ampoule had broken and the chemical had come into contact with water. The dangerous propensity of the chemical was unknown to B.D.H. and the chemists of Vacwells. *Held*, the chemical was not fit for the use for which it was required because the ampoules did not bear labels drawing attention to the danger which would ensue if the chemical was brought into contact with water: *Vacwell Engineering Co. Ltd.* v. *B.D.H. Chemicals Ltd.* [1969] 1 W.L.R. 927.

McAlpines bought four carbon-dioxide fire extinguishers from Minimax. A fire broke out in a timber hut erected by McAlpines on a site. Two of the fire extinguishers were in the hut. When applied to the fire, they exploded, allegedly greatly adding to the damage. *Held*, the fire extinguishers were not fit for the purpose for which they were required: *McAlpine & Sons Ltd.* v. *Minimax Ltd.* [1970] 1 Lloyd's Rep. 397.

Mrs. Griffiths purchased a tweed coat which caused her to suffer dermatitis. She had an unusually sensitive skin and there was nothing in the coat that would have affected anyone with a normal skin. *Held*, since the plaintiff's skin abnormality had not been made known to the seller, the seller was not liable: *Griffiths* v. *Peter Conway Ltd.* [1939] 1 All E.R. 685.

It is possible that there is liability in respect of second-hand goods, although a minor defect will not normally attract liability. This liability may arise under subsection (3) of section 14, just as liability may arise under subsection (2) of this section.

In 1972 the plaintiff paid £390 for a 1964 Jaguar car with 82,000 miles on the mileometer. He drove it 2,000 miles within three weeks of purchase and then the engine seized up. At the time of the sale the engine must have been nearing the point of failure. *Held*, this was not a minor defect and the seller was in breach of the condition that the car should be reasonably fit for the purpose of being driven on the road: *Crowther* v. *Shannon Motor Co. Ltd.* [1975] 1 W.L.R. 30.

If it is clear from the circumstances that the buyer did not rely or that it was unreasonable for him to rely on the seller's skill and judgment, the condition is not implied (s.14(3); *Teheran-Europe Co. Ltd.* v. *S.T. Belton (Tractors) Ltd.* [1968] 2 Q.B. 545 (see p. 266, *ante*)). However, such a situation will not often arise since the courts will generally infer reliance from the fact that a buyer has gone to a particular shop in confidence that the proprietor has selected his stock with skill and judgment (*Grant* v. *Australian Knitting Mills Ltd.* [1936] A.C. 85).

Where the buyer relies on his own skill and judgment in one respect but relies on those of the seller in another respect, the buyer will still be able to rely on the implied condition if the unfitness of the goods relates to the sphere of reliance placed on the seller. Thus it was held in *Ashington Piggeries Ltd.* v. *Christopher Hill Ltd.* [1972] A.C. 441, p. 317, *ante* (where the sellers made the animal food to the specification of the buyers), that the sellers were liable for breach of the condition of fitness for a particular purpose because the unfitness of the goods as feeding stuff for the minks of the buyer arose from an event within the sphere of reliance, *i.e.* as to the quality of the ingredients of the feeding mixture.

5. *Sample*

Where the sale is agreed to be a sale by sample:

(a) the bulk must correspond with the sample in quality (s.15(2)(*a*));
(b) the buyer must have a reasonable opportunity of comparing the bulk with the sample (s.15(2)(*b*)); and
(c) the goods must be free from any defect rendering them unmerchantable, which a reasonable examination of the sample would not reveal (s.15(2)(*c*)). A buyer is not expected to carry out every test that might be practicable. "Not extreme ingenuity, but reasonableness, is the statutory yardstick" (*per* Edmund Davies J. in *Godley* v. *Perry*, see below).

G., a boy of six, bought a plastic catapult from P., a stationer. G. used the catapult properly but it broke in his hands as it was made in an indifferent manner and part of it ruptured G.'s eye. P. had bought a quantity of these catapults from B., a wholesaler, by sample and P.'s wife had tested the sample, before placing the order, by pulling back its elastic. *Held*, G. could recover from P. because (a) the catapult was not fit for its purpose; and (b) it was not of merchantable quality. Further, P. could recover from B. since the defect of the goods could not be discovered by reasonable examination of the sample (s.15(2)(*c*)): *Godley* v. *Perry* [1960] 1 W.L.R. 9.

Exclusion clauses

The provisions of the Unfair Contract Terms Act 1977 have considerably restricted the freedom of the parties to insert exclusion clauses in contracts for the sale of goods. The provisions of that Act are treated earlier (see p. 40, *ante*).

Three further points must be made in relation to the Unfair Contract Terms Act 1977:

(i) A clause which is not rendered ineffective by the Unfair Contract Terms Act 1977 is still subject to the rules of the common law relating to exempting clauses—for example the rule that an express oral warranty may override a printed exemption clause. These rules are likewise explained earlier (see p. 45, *ante*).

In the catalogue at a sale by auction a heifer was described as "unserved." Both the owner and the auctioneer confirmed this in answer to a question by the bidder. The printed conditions of sale excluded liability for misdescription. The heifer was not unserved and died. *Held*, the seller was liable in damages for breach of warranty, the special warranty overriding the printed conditions of sale: *Couchman* v. *Hill* [1947] K.B. 554.

(ii) An order made under the Fair Trading Act 1973, s.22 (see p. 362, *post*) is designed to prevent the giving to the buyer wrong or misleading information about his rights under the Sale of Goods Act. It makes it a criminal offence for someone in the course of a business to display at a place where consumer transactions are effected (*e.g.* a shop or garage) a notice of an exempting clause which is void under section 6 of the Unfair Contract Terms Act 1977. It is similarly an offence for someone in the course of a business to publish such a notice in any advertisement or to supply goods bearing any such notice. Also it is an offence for someone in the course of a business to supply goods bearing any statement about the seller's liability in respect of description, quality or fitness for purpose unless the statement also makes it clear that the statement does not affect the statutory rights of the consumer.

(iii) The Unfair Contract Terms Act also contains provisions relating to exclusion clauses in contracts of hire-purchase, contracts of hire and contracts for services. In relation to hire-purchase the provisions are the same in effect as the provisions which apply to sale of goods contracts (see pp. 40–45, *ante*). Contracts for services and of hire are considered immediately next.

Contracts for services and materials supplied

The Supply of Goods and Services Act 1982 applies to certain contracts which, although they involve a transfer of ownership in goods, do not fall within the definition of sale of goods or of hire-purchase. The intention is to give customers under such contracts rights in relation to title, description, quality and sample similar to those conferred by the Sale of Goods Act upon a buyer under a sale of goods contract. The 1982 Act applies, with certain exceptions, to contracts which are not contracts of sale of goods or hire-purchase but where nevertheless one person transfers or agrees to transfer property (ownership) in goods to another (s.1). Thus, it applies to contracts of exchange or barter (which are not contracts of sale of goods because of lack of a money consideration, see p. 311, *ante*) and to contracts (*e.g.* of repair) where, although some goods are supplied, the *substance* of the contract is the provision of services. A contract to paint someone's house would fall into this category because, although there will be a transfer of ownership in some goods (the paint), the substance of the contract is the doing of the work.

In relation to these contracts the 1982 Act implies terms: as to title, freedom from encumbrances and quiet possession (s.2); as to description (s.3); as to merchantable quality and fitness for purpose (s.4); and as to sample (s.5). These terms relate to the goods supplied and are implied in identical circumstances and are to an identical effect as the terms implied by sections 12–15 of the Sale of Goods Act. An exclusion clause purporting to exclude or restrict liability under one of these implied terms is subject to the same rules as one which purports to exclude or restrict liability under the implied terms as to title, description, quality and sample which are implied by the Sale of Goods Act, sections 12–15, in contracts for the sale of goods (see pp. 40–45, *ante*).

Contracts for services

The Supply of Goods and Services Act 1982 implies a further set of terms into any contract where one party (the supplier) has agreed to carry out any service (whether or not he has also agreed to supply goods). By way of exception, however, these terms are not implied in any contract of employment or apprenticeship. It is clear that these terms are implied not only in contracts where the supply of services is the substance of the contract but also in contracts of hire and sale of goods where, although the substance of the contract is the hire or transfer of ownership in goods, there is nevertheless an undertaking by the seller that he will provide a service, (*e.g.* of installing the goods). These implied terms implied by the Supply of Goods and Services Act 1982 are:

(a) In a contract for the supply of a service where the supplier is acting in the course of a business, there is an implied term that the supplier will carry out the service with reasonable care and skill (s.13).

(b) (i) Where, under a contract for the supply of a service by a supplier acting in the course of a business, the time for the service to be carried out is not fixed by the contract, but is left to be fixed in a manner agreed by the contract, or determined by the course of dealing between the parties, there is an implied term that the supplier will carry out the service within a reasonable time.

(ii) What is a reasonable time is a question of fact (s.14).

(c) (i) Where, under a contract for the supply of a service, the consideration for the service is not determined by the contract, is not left to be determined in a manner agreed by the contract, or determined by the course of dealing between the parties, there is an implied term that the party contracting with the supplier will pay a reasonable charge.

(ii) What is a reasonable charge is a question of fact (s.15).

Whether or not the contract is a sale of goods contract, an exclusion clause purporting to exclude or restrict liability under these implied terms is subject to the rules already explained in relation to exclusion clauses in sale of goods contracts (see pp. 40–45, *ante*). An explanation, however, is required in relation to the term as to reasonable care and skill implied by section 13 of the Supply of Goods and Services Act 1982. This is because a claim for breach of that term is treated by the Unfair Contract Terms Act 1977 (s.1) as a claim for negligence. Thus, as we have seen (p. 40, *ante*), liability for death or personal injury arising from such a breach of contract cannot be excluded or restricted at all; liability for other loss or injury arising from such a breach can be excluded or restricted only in so far as the exclusion satisfies the requirement of reasonableness (U.C.T.A., s.2).

Contracts of hire

A contract of hire is not a contract of sale of goods because it contains no provision for property (ownership) to be transferred to the hirer. The hirer (the bailee) obtains possession but not property. It is a contract of bailment (see Ch. 24, *post*).

Sections 6–10 of the Supply of Goods and Services Act 1982 apply to contracts of hire. The intention behind them is to imply in hire contracts terms similar to those implied in sale of goods contracts by sections 12–15 of the Sale of Goods Act. In fact, the implied terms as to description (s.8), merchantable quality and fitness for purpose (s.9) and sample (s.10) are identical in effect to the corresponding Sale of Goods Act provisions. Section 7 of the 1982 Act contains (i) a condition as to title, namely that the bailor has (or, in the case of an agreement to bail in the future, will have) a right to transfer possession to the bailee for the period of the hire, and (ii) a warranty of quiet possession during the period of the hire except in so far as the bailee's possession may be disturbed by someone entitled of the benefit of any charge or encumbrance disclosed or known to the bailee before the contract.

Exclusion clauses in hire contracts are subject to the same rules as exclusion clauses in contracts for the sale of goods. The Unfair Contract Terms Act 1977 applies, with one small difference, to both kinds of contract in exactly the same way (see *ante*). The difference is that the terms implied by section 7 of the 1982 Act can be excluded or restricted by an exclusion clause which satisfies the requirements of reasonableness.

Transfer of the Property Between Seller and Buyer

It is important to know the precise moment of time at which the property in the goods passes from the seller to the buyer:

(a) in case of the destruction of the goods by fire or other accidental cause it is necessary to know which party has to bear the loss; and

(b) in case of bankruptcy of either seller or buyer it is necessary to know whether the goods belong to the trustee of the bankrupt or not.

The property in the goods means the ownership of the goods, as distinguished from their possession.

Specific goods

In a sale of specific or ascertained goods the property passes to the buyer at the time when the parties intend it to pass. The intention must be gathered from the terms of the contract, the conduct of the parties, and the circumstances of the case (s.17). Specific goods are the goods identified and agreed upon at the time the contract is made. Unless a contrary intention appears, the following rules are applicable for ascertaining the intention of the parties (s.18):

1. Where there is an unconditional contract for the sale of specific goods in a deliverable state, the property passes to the buyer when the contract is made (r. 1 of s.18)). Deliverable state means such a state that the buyer would be bound to take delivery of them.

The defendants bought a carpet from the plaintiffs. When the carpet was delivered to the showrooms where it was to be laid, it was sent away for stitching. It was returned the next day in heavy bales and stolen. *Held*, the carpet in bales was not in a deliverable state. Consequently rule 1 did not apply and the property remained in the plaintiffs. The defendants were not liable for the price: *Philip Head & Sons* v. *Showfronts* [1970] 1 Lloyd's Rep. 140.

Although according to rule 1 the fact that the time of delivery or the time for the payment of the price is postponed does not prevent the property from passing when the contract is made, commercial practice is different in the case of sales in a cash and carry shop or a supermarket; here the intention of the parties is normally that property shall pass when the price is paid.

L. selected goods in C., a cash and carry shop, and placed them into a wire basket. The price of the goods was £185. At the cash desk the till showed only £85 because, if the goods were worth over £100, the price recorded on the face of the till returned to zero. The manager who operated the till did not notice the error and demanded only £85 which L. paid, knowing that it was not the true price and that a mistake had occurred. He was accused under the Larceny Act 1916 of having stolen goods to the value of £100, the property of C. *Held*, L. had to be acquitted. The intention of the parties was that the property in the goods should only pass when the price was paid, but nevertheless the property in the unpaid goods likewise passed to L. when the manager, a duly authorised person, handed them out to L.: *Lacis* v. *Cashmarts* [1969] 2 Q.B. 400. (It should be noted that the Larceny Act 1916 is now repealed and that L. might have been convicted under the Theft Act 1968.)

2. Where there is a contract for the sale of specific goods not in a deliverable state, *i.e.* the seller has to do something to the goods to put them in a deliverable state, the property does not pass until that thing is done and the buyer has notice of it (r. 2 of s.18).

3. Where there is a contract for the sale of specific goods in a deliverable state, but the seller is bound to weigh, measure, test or

do something with reference to the goods for the purpose of ascertaining the price, the property does not pass until that thing is done and the buyer has notice of it (r. 3 of s.18).

4. When goods are delivered to the buyer on approval or "on sale or return," the property therein passes to the buyer:

(a) when he signifies his approval or acceptance to the seller, or does any other act adopting the transaction.

K. delivered jewellery to W. on sale or return. W. pledged it with A. *Held*, the pledge was an act by W. adopting the transaction, and, therefore, the property in the jewellery passed to him, so that K. could not recover it from A.: *Kirkham* v. *Attenborough* [1897] 1 Q.B. 201.

If K., when he delivered the jewellery to W. had done so on the terms that it was to remain his property until settled for or charged, the property would not have passed to W. until either of those events had happened (*Weiner* v. *Gill* [1906] 2 K.B. 574).

(b) if he retains the goods, without giving notice of rejection, beyond the time fixed for the return of the goods or, if no time is fixed, beyond a reasonable time (rule 4 of s.18).

A contract can be a contract for the sale or return of goods within this Rule, whether or not the recipient of the goods under the contract intended to buy them himself or sell them to third parties (*Poole* v. *Smith's Car Sales* (*Balham*) *Ltd.* [1962] 1 W.L.R. 744).

5. Rule 5 of section 18 refers to unascertained goods and is explained in the next paragraph.

Unascertained goods

The property in unascertained goods does not pass until the goods are ascertained (s.16). Unascertained goods are goods defined by description only, *e.g.* 100 tons of coal, and not goods identified and agreed upon when the contract is made. The property in unascertained or future goods sold by description passes to the buyer when goods of that description and in a deliverable state are unconditionally appropriated to the contract, either by the seller with the assent of the buyer or by the buyer with the assent of the seller (r. 5(1) of s.18). The buyer's assent may be either express or implied and be given either before or after appropriation is made.

F., a Costa Rican company, bought from T., an English company, 85 bicycles under a contract providing that T. should ship them in June 1953. F. paid the purchase price in advance. In July 1953 a receiver was appointed for T. and all the assets, including the bicycles, became charged to the receiver. F. alleged that as the bicycles had been duly packed into cases, marked with their name, were registered for consignment, and shipping space was reserved for them in a named ship, this setting aside of the goods constituted an unconditional appropriation to which they had assented by letter and that, by virtue of section 18, Rule 5, the property had passed to them. *Held*, the intention of the parties was that the property should pass on shipment and that, as there was no appropriation within section 18, rule 5, the action failed: *Federspiel* v. *Charles Twigg* [1957] 1 Lloyd's Rep. 240; see p. 409 *post*.

If there is a sale of a quantity of goods out of a larger quantity, *e.g.* of 10 tons of scrap iron out of a heap in X.'s yard, the property will in principle only pass on the appropriation of the specified quantity by one party with the assent of the other. If the buyer has told the seller to send the goods by rail or some other mode of carriage, he will be deemed to have given his assent in advance to the subsequent appropriation by the seller of the goods he has put on rail. Delivery by the seller of goods to a carrier in pursuance of the contract will normally be an appropriation sufficient to pass the property in the goods (r. 5(2) of s.18). When the seller's warehouseman has separated a specified part from bulk and authorises the buyer's collection driver to load that part, that authorisation is an unconditional appropriation of that part and property in it passes to the buyer (*Wardar's* (*Import & Export*) *Ltd.* v. *W. Norwood & Sons Ltd.* [1968] 2 Q.B. 663). If a buyer buys part of an unascertained bulk carried in a ship, *e.g.* 6,000 tons out of a cargo of 22,000 tons, and the cargo exceeding the purchased part (in the example 16,000 tons) is unloaded in intermediate ports, the part remaining on the ship becomes **ascertained goods by exhaustion** and property passes in it to the purchaser (*Karlshamns Olefabriker* v. *Eastport Navigation Corp.*; *The Elafi* [1982] 1 All E.R. 208; see p. 412, *post*).

G. sold to P. 140 bags of rice, the particular bags being unascertained. On February 27 P. sent a cheque for the price and asked for a delivery order. G. sent a delivery order for 125 bags from a wharf, and wrote saying that the remaining 15 bags were ready for delivery at his place of business. P. did not send for the 15 bags until March 25, when it was found they had been stolen without any negligence on G.'s part. P. sued to recover from G. the price he had paid for the 15 bags. *Held*, he could not succeed, because G. had appropriated the 15 bags to the contract, and P.'s assent to the appropriation was to be inferred from his conduct in not objecting. The property in the 15 bags therefore passed to P.: *Pignataro* v. *Gilroy* [1919] 1 K.B. 459.

Sometimes it is the seller who assents to an unconditional appropriation by the buyer. At a petrol station, property in the petrol passes when the petrol is put into the customer's car. If the attendant puts it in, that is an unconditional appropriation by the seller with the buyer's assent (*Edwards* v. *Ddin* [1976] 1 W.L.R. 942). If the customer puts it in (*i.e.* at a self-service garage), that is an unconditional appropriation by the buyer with the seller's assent.

Statutory provisions relating to the reservation of property

The property in goods, whether specific or ascertained,[2] does not pass if the seller reserves a right of disposal of the goods. Apart from an express reservation of the right of disposal, the seller is deemed to reserve the right of disposal in two cases—

1. Where goods are shipped and by the bill of lading the goods are deliverable to the order of the seller or his agent (s.19(2)).

2. Where the seller sends a bill of exchange for the price of the goods to the buyer for his acceptance, together with the bill of lading, the property in the goods does not pass to the buyer unless he accepts the bill of exchange (s.19(3)).

Clauses relating to the reservation of title

Reservation of title clauses have become common in the case of sales of large quantities of industrial goods on credit. This is because of the seller's wish to protect himself against the risk that the buyer, before he has paid the price, goes bankrupt or goes into liquidation. A clause stating that the property shall not pass to the buyer until he has paid for the goods is known as a *simple reservation of title clause*.

[2] Property in unascertained goods cannot pass; s.16; see p. 328, *ante*.

The position is more difficult however, if the buyer, before he has paid for the goods, resells them or consumes them in his manufacturing process and then, perhaps, sells the manufactured products; these clauses are described as *extended reservation of title clauses.*

A contract provided for the sale by a Dutch company to an English company of aluminium foil some of which the English company, the buyers, were going to use in their manufacturing process. The buyers took delivery of the foil but never made full payment. They later became insolvent and a receiver was appointed. At that time the buyers still had possession of some of the foil which was still unmixed (*i.e.* had not been taken into the manufacturing process). The buyers had already resold some of the foil (unmixed) and the receiver kept the proceeds of these sales in a separate account. The Dutch sellers now relied upon a clause (cl. 13) in their contract of sale and claimed therefore to have proprietary rights in priority to the buyer's other creditors. This claim related to the unsold unmixed foil and to the buyers' proceeds of sale on their resale of the unmixed foil. The first part of Clause 13 provided (i) that ownership of unmixed foil would transfer to the buyers only when the buyers had paid all they owed the sellers, and (ii) that the buyers, if so required by the sellers, would store the property in such a way that it was clearly the sellers' property. The second part of clause 13 dealt with mixed foil (*i.e.* foil used by the buyers in a manufacturing process). This provided that the ownership of the sellers would transfer from the foil used in the manufacture to the finished products and that these would remain the property of the sellers until the buyers had paid all they owed the sellers. It also provided that, until the monies owed by the buyers to the sellers were paid, the buyers would keep the finished products as "fiduciary" for the sellers and that the buyers were authorised to sell the finished products on condition that the buyers would, if requested, transfer to the sellers the benefit of those sales. *Held*, on construction of the clause, the provisions in the second part of the clause as to the buyers holding the mixed goods as fiduciary of the sellers and having authority to resell the mixed goods, were intended by the parties to apply equally to that part (the first part) of the clause which dealt with unmixed foil. Therefore the sellers' claim to take priority over the buyers' other creditors (secured and unsecured) was good in relation not only to the unmixed foil still in the buyers' possession but also to the proceeds of sale of the unmixed foil which the buyers had resold. This was because the owner (here the sellers) has a right to "trace," *i.e.* to follow and take the proceeds of sale where the owner's goods are disposed of by someone in a fiduciary position with the owner. When the buyers resold the foil then, as between the buyers and the sub-purchasers, the buyers sold as principals and, as between the buyers and the sellers, the buyers sold as agents of the sellers: *Aluminium Industrie Vaasen* v. *Romalpa Aluminium Ltd.* [1976] 1 W.L.R. 676.

Unsold unmixed goods

Suppose the seller has reserved title in goods until the buyer has paid the price (of £2,000) and that the buyer goes into liquidation without having paid any of the price and without having sold the goods. The seller may then succeed in selling the goods elsewhere for £2,000 in which case the seller is neither in pocket nor out of pocket. Of course, if before the buyer had gone into liquidation, he had paid part of the price, say £500, the seller would have to refund that £500 out of the £2,000 realised from the second sale. If the seller were able to sell the goods elsewhere for more than £2,000, then the seller would be entitled to retain the extra. If, however, he is able to sell them elsewhere only for, say, £1,800, he will deduct that loss (*i.e.* £200) from the amount of the refund he pays to the buyer or, if the buyer had not made any part payment before going into liquidation, the seller would have a claim against the buyer's liquidator for the £200 loss. The above approach was laid down by the Court of Appeal in *Clough Mill* v. *Martin* [1985] 1 W.L.R. 111. That case dealt with the position where the seller's title was reserved in the goods until the contract price was paid. It would be possible for a clause to reserve title to the seller until the buyer had satisfied **all** his liabilities to the seller (*i.e.* under not only this contract but under any *other* contracts that there might be between them). In *Armour* v. *Thyssen* [1990] 3 W.L.R. 811 the House of Lords held that such an "all liabilities" clause would be effective in Scottish law; presumably it would be effective also in English law.

Mixed goods

The cases discussed so far all involved claims in relation to *unmixed* goods (or the proceeds of sale of *unmixed* goods). They leave open the question of whether a claim could succeed in relation to mixed goods or the proceeds of sale of mixed goods. Clearly a clause, which on its wording reserves title in unmixed goods but does not mention mixed goods, gives the seller no rights in relation to mixed goods or the proceeds of sale of mixed goods (*Borden (UK) Ltd.* v. *Scottish Timber Products Ltd.* [1981] Ch. 95). In *Re-Bond Worth* [1980] Ch. 228 it was held that a clause, which reserved to the seller only the "equitable and beneficial" ownership in the goods, did not stop property passing under section 18, rule 1.

It merely created an equitable charge which, since the clause in question reserved the "equitable and beneficial" title in both unmixed and mixed goods, was a charge over fluctuating assets and was therefore a floating charge; the charge was void for lack of registration under the Companies Act 1948, s.95(1). Thus it is clear that the simple reservation of title clause is effective. It seems, however, that a *Romalpa* clause can be effective in relation to mixed goods only if it is registered as a charge (*Re Peachdart Ltd.* [1983] 3 All E.R. 204).

Passing of risk

Unless otherwise agreed, goods remain at the seller's risk until the property has passed to the buyer, after which they are at the buyer's risk, whether delivery has been made or not. But if delivery has been delayed through the fault of either the buyer or the seller, the goods are at the risk of the party at fault (s.20).

Where in a contract of sale which involves sea transit the seller fails to give the buyer sufficient notice to enable him to insure—assuming that the duty to insure does not fall on the seller—the goods travel at the seller's risk (s.32(3)). In contracts for the international sale of goods (Chap. 18, *post*) it is normally the intention of the parties that the risk shall pass on delivery of the goods.

Sale by Person Not the Owner

As a general rule, the sale of an article by a person who is not, or has not the authority of, the owner gives no title to the buyer (s.21(1); *nemo dat quod non habet*). The buyer will be obliged to give the article up to the true owner, generally without any recompense from him. An innocent purchaser will be entitled to be recompensed to the extent that he spent money improving the goods before he discovered they were not his.

B. owned a Jaguar car which he entrusted to S. to do some repairs to it. S. did not do so but instead used it for his own purposes and had a crash in it. Without any authority S. sold the car in its damaged state for £75 to H., an innocent purchaser. H. spent £226 on repairing the car. H. sold it to a finance company. *Held*, B. was entitled to possession of the car but B. had to pay £226 to H.: *Greenwood* v. *Bennett* [1973] 1 Q.B. 195. (It should be noted that the decision as to the payment to H. of a sum representing the value of his work has now been given statutory recognition by the Torts

(Interference With Goods) Act 1977 which provides a statutory mechanism by which the innocent improver is to be reimbursed.)

The rule that a buyer can not acquire ownership from someone who himself has neither ownership nor the owner's authority to sell, is subject to the following important exceptions—

Estoppel

If the true owner stands by and allows an innocent buyer to pay over money to a third party, who professes to have the right to sell an article, in the belief that he is becoming the owner of it, the true owner will be estopped from denying the third party's right to sell (s.21(1), end). This is in harmony with the related doctrine of estoppel by conduct discussed earlier (see p. 107, *ante*).

X., the owner of machinery in Y.'s possession, which was taken in execution by Z., abstained from claiming it for some months, and conversed with Z.'s attorney without referring to his claim, and by those means impressed Z. with the belief that the machinery was Y.'s. Z. sold the machinery. *Held*, X. was estopped from denying that the machinery was Y.'s: *Pickard* v. *Sears* (1837) 6 A. & E. 469.

M., the owner of a Bedford van, wanted to buy a Chrysler car from C., a car dealer, but was unable to pay the deposit. M. and C. agreed that M. should submit proposal forms to the plaintiff finance company according to which M. applied to acquire both vehicles from the company on hire-purchase terms; M. stated in the forms that both vehicles were the property of C. The object of this joint misrepresentation was to use the money obtained on the Bedford van for the payment of the deposit on the Chrysler car. The plaintiff company accepted the proposal for the Bedford van but rejected that for the Chrysler car. *Held*, M. was estopped from denying that C. was the owner of the van: *Eastern Distributors Ltd.* v. *Goldring* [1957] 2 Q.B. 600.

An estoppel can be raised against someone only if he knew of the situation which has given rise to the estoppel and has acquiesced in it. He must further have known that the third party may rely on the (non-existent) authority of the actor to act for the owner.

The plaintiffs were a finance company which owned a car. They let the car under a hire-purchase agreement to M. Before completing his instalments, M. without authority sold the car to the defendant, a motor dealer. The plaintiffs and the defendant were both members of H.P.I., an organisation where finance companies register their hire-purchase agreements so that any dealer member can, before buying a second hand car, check with H.P.I. to see if the car is the subject of a registered hire-purchase agreement. On this occasion the plaintiffs had carelessly failed to register the hire-purchase agreement so that the defendant had been told by H.P.I. that there was no hire-purchase agreement registered in connection with this particular car. The defendant claimed that the plaintiffs were estopped from denying that M. was the owner of the car. *Held*, the plaintiffs were not estopped, because they did not owe any legal duty to join H.P.I. and, having joined, did not thereby come under any legal duty to take care to register their hire-purchase agreements: *Moorgate Mercantile Co. Ltd.* v. *Twitchings* [1977] A.C. 890, H.L. (It should be noted that the ruling might have been different if H.P.I. had had in its terms of membership for finance houses an absolute obligation to register all their hire-purchase agreements.)

Sale by mercantile agent

Under the Factors Act 1889 mercantile agents, who are not the owners of goods, can in certain circumstances sell them and give a good title to the buyer.

A mercantile agent, also called a factor, is a person who, in the customary course of his business as such agent, has authority either to sell goods, or to consign goods for the purpose of sale, or to buy goods, or to raise money on the security of goods (Factors Act 1889, s.1(1)). He has a general lien on goods in his possession and on the proceeds of sale of such goods for the balance of account between himself and his principal.

The owner is bound by the acts of the mercantile agent as follows:

1. If the agent has possession of goods, or of the documents of title to goods, with the consent of the owner, any sale, pledge, or other disposition of them, made in the ordinary course of business is binding on the owner, whether or not the owner authorised it (s.2(1)).

F. owned a motor car and delivered it to H., a mercantile agent, for sale at not less than £575. H. sold the car for £340 to K., who bought in good faith and without notice of any fraud. H. misappropriated the £340 and F. sued to recover the car from K. *Held*, as H. was in possession of the car with F.'s consent for the purposes of sale, K. got a good title: *Folkes* v. *King* [1923] 1 K.B. 282.

S. pledged bills of lading with L. to secure advances. At the request of S., L. handed the bills to S. in exchange for trust receipts, by which S. agreed to sell the goods, represented by the bills, as trustees for L. S. wrongly pledged the bills with B., who acted in good faith, as security for a loan. *Held*, B. had a good title under section 2: *Lloyds Bank* v. *Bank of America Association* [1938] 2 K.B. 147.

If the purchaser from a mercantile agent wishes to claim a good title against the owner it is for him to prove that:

(a) the agent, as such, was in possession of the goods (or documents of title) with the consent of the owner. If a person is in possession of goods only under a hire-purchase agreement, the goods are not in the possession of a mercantile agent "as such" (*Belvoir Finance Co. Ltd.* v. *Harold G. Cole & Co. Ltd.* [1969] 1 W.L.R. 1877, 1881). A vehicle registration book is not a document of title. So it is not sufficient that the mercantile was in possession of the registration document if he was not in possession of the vehicle with the consent of the owner (*Beverley Acceptances Ltd.* v. *Oakley* [1982] R.T.R. 417);
(b) in selling them the agent was acting in the ordinary course of business of a mercantile agent; and
(c) he had not, at the time of the sale, notice that the agent had no authority to make the sale (*Stadium Finance Ltd.* v. *Robbins* [1962] 2 Q.B. 664).

A mercantile agent does not sell a car in the ordinary course of business unless he delivers the registration book with it; but the purported sale of a car with its registration book does not confer a good title on the purchaser if the agent (though having the car with the consent of the owner) obtained the registration book only by larceny or by a trick (*Pearson* v. *Rose and Young Ltd.* [1951] 1 K.B. 275). The sale of a new car sold without the registration document may be within the ordinary course of business of a motor car dealer, if the registration document is in the possession of the appropriate authority for registration or tax purposes: (*Astley Industrial Trust Ltd.* v. *Miller* [1968] 2 All E.R. 36).

2. If the mercantile agent pledges goods as security for an antecedent debt, the pledgee acquires no further right to the goods than the factor has against his principal at the time of the pledge (s.4).

3. If the mercantile agent pledges goods in consideration of the delivery of other goods, or of a document of title to goods, or of a

negotiable security, the pledgee acquires no right in the goods pledged beyond the value of the goods, documents or security when so delivered in exchange (s.5).

4. If the mercantile agent has received possession of goods from their owner for the purpose of consignment or sale, and the consignee has no notice that he is not the owner, the consignee has a lien on the goods for any advances he has made to the agent (s.7).

Sale by seller in possession of goods or documents of title

If a person who has sold goods continues or is in possession of the goods or of the documents of title to them, any sale or pledge by him to a buyer or pledgee who takes the goods in good faith without notice of the previous sale will give a good title to the buyer or pledgee (s.24).

The effect of this is that if X., a shopkeeper, sells, *e.g.* hi-fi equipment to Y. and promises to deliver it, and before delivery sells and delivers it to Z., Z. will get a good title to the equipment, notwithstanding that the property had, before his purchase, passed to Y. This result ensues even if the seller, who retains uninterrupted possession of the goods, does so no longer as seller but as a bailee (*Worcester Works Finance Ltd.* v. *Cooden Engineering Co. Ltd.* [1972] 1 Q.B. 182).

Sale by buyer in possession of goods or documents of title

Again, if a person who has bought or agreed to buy goods obtains, with the seller's consent, possession of the goods or of the documents of title to them, any sale or pledge by him to a buyer or pledgee who takes in good faith and without notice of any lien or other claim of the original seller against the goods will give a good title to the buyer or pledgee (s.25(1)).

X. sold copper to Y. and sent him a bill of lading indorsed in blank, together with a draft for the price. Y. was insolvent and did not accept the draft, but he handed the bill of lading to Z. in fulfilment of a contract for sale of the copper to him. Z. paid for the copper and took the bill of lading without notice of X.'s right as unpaid seller. X. stopped the copper *in transitu. Held*, as Y. was in possession of the bill of lading with X.'s consent, he could give a good title to Z.: *Cahn* v. *Pockett's Bristol Channel Co.* [1899] 1 Q.B. 643.

Section 25 applies not only to cases in which the buyer transfers the actual document of title in his possession with the consent of the seller, for the purpose of this subsection is to protect an innocent person in his dealings with the buyer who appears to have the right to deal with the goods. In such cases the subsection provides that any transfer of the goods or documents of title held by the buyer to a person acting in good faith and without notice of any want of authority on the part of the buyer should be as valid as if expressly authorised by the seller. This position is to be contrasted with that under the proviso to section 47 which relates to the loss by an unpaid seller of his right of lien or stoppage in transit (see p. 346, *post*); that provision applies only where a document is transferred to the buyer and the same document is then transferred by him to the person who takes in good faith and for valuable consideration (*D.F. Mount Ltd.* v. *Jay and Jay (Provisions) Co. Ltd.* [1960] 1 Q.B. 159).

Section 25 was designed to deal with the situation where a seller, S., agreed to sell goods to a buyer and then permitted that buyer, before property had passed to him, to have possession of the goods or documents of title. If the buyer then sold and delivered the goods or documents of title to an innocent sub-buyer, the latter would obtain the title of S. If S. did not in fact have good title, then the buyer cannot get good title. Section 25 confers title only as good as that of S. (*National Mutual General Insurance Association Ltd.* v. *Jones*, see below).

Thieves stole a car and sold it to A. who sold it to C. (a car dealer) who sold it to D. (another car dealer) who sold it to Jones. Jones claimed to have good title by virtue of section 25, thereby defeating the title of the owner from whom the thieves had stolen the car. *Held*, rejecting Jones's claim, section 25 could defeat the title only of an owner who had entrusted possession of his goods (or documents of title) to a buyer. Therefore it could not take title away from the owner from whom the goods had been stolen: *National Mutual General Insurance Association Ltd.* v. *Jones* [1988] 2 W.L.R. 952 (H.L.).

A person who obtains goods under a **hire-purchase agreement** is not a person who has bought or agreed to buy goods within the section (*Helby* v. *Matthews* [1895] A.C. 471, pp. 366–367, *post*).

B. let on hire to M. a motor-car, M. agreeing to pay hire at £15 a month for 24 months. By the hiring agreement, M. could at any time within 24 months purchase the car by making the amount of the hire paid equal to £424. During the hiring M. pledged the car with C. In an action by B. to recover it from C., *held*, M. having only an option of purchase could not give a good title to C.: *Belsize Motor Supply Co.* v. *Cox* [1914] 1 K.B. 244.

Section 25 does not apply to any conditional sale agreement which is a regulated consumer credit agreement (see p. 367, *post*).

If a motor vehicle is under a hire-purchase or conditional sale contract and the hirer or buyer sells it to a private purchaser before the payment of the last instalment, the title of the purchaser who acquires the car in good faith and without notice of the hire-purchase or conditional sale contract is protected by a different provision, namely the Hire Purchase Act 1964, Part III (see p. 385, *post*).

Sale in market overt

Where goods are sold in market overt, according to the usage of the market, the buyer obtains a good title to the goods, provided he buys them in good faith and without notice of any defect or want of title on the part of the seller (s.22(1)).

Market overt means, in the City of London, every shop in which goods are exposed for sale, for such things only as are usually sold in the shop. For example, a sale of jewellery in a men's outfitters' shop is not a sale in market overt. Moreover, the sale must be by and not to the shopkeeper (*Hargreave* v. *Spink* [1892] 1 Q.B. 25). A sale in a showroom to which the general public is not generally admitted is not a sale in market overt (*Clayton* v. *Le Roy* [1911] 2 K.B. 1031). Neither is a sale which takes place other than during the daylight hours between sunrise and sunset (*Reid* v. *Commissioner of Police of the Metropolis* [1973] 1 Q.B. 551).

Outside the City of London market overt means a market held on days prescribed by charter, custom or statute as market days, and is limited to the place where, by charter, custom or statute, the market is held. What is a sale in market overt depends on the custom of the market.

H. had a motor car under a hire-purchase agreement from F. In breach of this agreement, H. took the car to Maidstone market and handed it to auctioneers to sell at the market. The car was not sold by the auctioneers but, later that day, H. sold it to B. *Held*, as the usage of the market allowed sales to be made privately in the market after an auctioneer had failed to sell, the sale was in market overt and B. had a good title: *Bishopgate Motor Finance Corpn.* v. *Transport Brakes Ltd.* [1949] 1 K.B. 322.

Sale by person with voidable title

If the seller has a voidable title to goods and his title has not been avoided at the time of the sale, the buyer acquires a good title to the goods, provided that he did not know of the seller's defect of title and bought in good faith (s.23).

For example, if A. by fraud obtains goods from B., A. has only a voidable title to the goods, and B. can, on discovering the fraud, rescind the contract. If A., **before** B. rescinds the contract, sells **to** C., who buys in good faith and in ignorance of the fraud, C. will get a good title (see *Phillips* v. *Brooks* [1919] 2 K.B. 243; p. 86, *ante*). On the other hand, if A., **after** B. has rescinded the contract, sells the goods to C., the latter does not acquire a good title unless C. is protected by one of the exceptional provisions protecting the purchaser in good faith, such as section 25 of the Sale of Goods Act (p. 337, *ante*) or sections 2 or 9 of the Factors Act 1889 (p. 335, *ante*).

On January 12, 1960, C., the owner of a Jaguar car, was persuaded to sell and deliver the car to a rogue who gave C. a car of much lower value and a cheque. On the next morning C. ascertained that the cheque was worthless and at once asked the police and Automobile Association to recover his car. The rogue sold the car to a person who did not acquire it in good faith, and only on January 15 the car was acquired by a purchaser in good faith. It passed through several hands and eventually was acquired by the Car and Universal Finance Co. Ltd., which acted in good faith. *Held*, that while normally the rescission of a voidable contract must be communicated to the other contracting party, that was not necessary if—as in the present case—the other party, by deliberately absconding, put it out of the power of the rescinding party to communicate. Consequently, C. had rescinded the contract on January 13 and the finance company had not acquired a title to it: *Car and Universal Finance Co. Ltd.* v. *Caldwell* [1965] 1 Q.B. 525.

Performance of the Contract

It is the duty of the seller to deliver the goods and of the buyer to accept and pay for them, in accordance with the contract of sale (s.27). Unless otherwise agreed, payment and delivery are concurrent conditions, that is, they both take place at the same time as in a cash sale over a shop counter (s.28).

Delivery

Delivery is the voluntary transfer of possession from one person to another. It may be actual or constructive. Delivery is constructive when the goods themselves are not delivered, but the means of obtaining possession of the goods is delivered *e.g.* by delivering the key of a lock-up garage where the sold car is kept or the bill of lading which will entitle the holder to receive the goods on the arrival of the ship.

Whether the seller has to send the goods to the buyer or the buyer has to take them from the seller depends on the terms of the contract (s.29(1)). In the absence of any such terms, **the rules as to delivery** are—

1. The place of delivery is the seller's place of business, if he has one, and, if not, his residence. But if the contract be for the sale of specific goods which, to the knowledge of both parties, are in some other place, then that place is the place of delivery (s.29(2)).

2. Where the seller is bound to send the goods to the buyer, but no time for sending them is fixed, they must be sent within a reasonable time (s.29(3)). Delivery must be at a reasonable hour.

3. If the goods are in possession of a third party, there is no delivery until such third party acknowledges to the buyer that he holds the goods on his behalf (s.29(4)). Such an acknowledgment is called attornment.

4. Where the seller is authorised or required to send the goods to the buyer, delivery to a carrier, whether named by the buyer or not, for the purpose of transmission to the buyer is prima facie delivery to the buyer. But the seller must make a reasonable contract with the carrier, otherwise the buyer may decline to treat the delivery to the carrier as delivery to himself. Where the carriage involves sea transit, the seller must give sufficient notice to the buyer to enable him to insure, otherwise the goods will be at the seller's risk (s.32).

5. If the seller agrees to deliver goods to the buyer at a place other than that where they are when sold, the buyer must, in the absence of agreement to the contrary, take a risk of deterioration necessarily incident to the course of transit (s.33).

Similarly, if the seller agrees to deliver goods at the buyer's premises and, without negligence, delivers them there to a person apparently authorised to receive them, and that person misappropriates them, the loss must fall on the buyer and not on the seller (*Galbraith & Grant Ltd.* v. *Block* [1922] 2 K.B. 155).

6. The expenses of putting the goods into a deliverable state must be borne by the seller (s.29(6)).

When the seller is ready and willing to deliver the goods and requests the buyer to take delivery and the buyer does not comply with his request within a reasonable time, the buyer is liable to the seller for:

(a) any loss occasioned by his neglect or refusal to take delivery; and
(b) a reasonable charge for the care and custody of the goods (s.37).

Acceptance

Acceptance is deemed to take place when the buyer (s.35):

(a) intimates to the seller that he has accepted the goods; or
(b) does any act to the goods which is inconsistent with the ownership of the seller;

P. sold barley to B. by sample, delivery to be made at T. railway station. B. resold the barley to X. The barley was delivered at T., and B., after inspecting a sample of it, sent it on to X. X. rejected it as not being according to sample, and B. claimed to be entitled to reject it. *Held*, B.'s act in inspecting a sample and then ordering the barley to be sent on was an acceptance, and he could not afterwards reject it: *Perkins* v. *Bell* [1893] 1 Q.B. 193.

(c) or retains the goods, after the lapse of a reasonable time, without intimating to the seller that he has rejected them.

When goods are delivered to the buyer which he has not previously examined he is not, under the rules mentioned at (b) and (c) *ante*, deemed to have accepted them unless and until he has had a reasonable opportunity of examining them. He is entitled to demand of the seller a reasonable opportunity of examining them (s.34). A buyer is thus allowed a reasonable length of time before he is deemed to have accepted the goods. This means, however, a reasonable length of time to try out the goods generally, not a reasonable length of time in which to discover any defects there might be in them (*Bernstein* v. *Pamsons Motors* (*Golders Green*) *Ltd.*, see below).

The buyer of a new Nissan car had had it for less than three weeks and had made two or three short journeys in it for the purpose of trying it out. The engine seized up because of a, previously latent, manufacturing fault. *Held*, before the seizure, the buyer had already had the car a reasonable length of time for trying it out generally. Therefore the buyer had accepted the car within the meaning of section 35 and was entitled only to damages: *Bernstein* v. *Pamsons Motors* (*Golders Green*) *Ltd.* [1987] 2 All E.R. 220.

Unless the contract is severable, a buyer who accepts the goods or part of them thereby loses any right he would otherwise have had to reject the goods for breach of condition (s.11(4), see pp. 350–351, *post*).

If the seller sends the buyer a larger or smaller quantity of goods than he ordered, the buyer may (s.30):

(a) reject the whole;
(b) accept the whole; or
(c) accept the quantity he ordered and reject the rest.

The contract was for the sale of 4,000 tons of meal, 2 per cent. more or less. The sellers delivered meal greatly in excess of the permitted variation. *Held*, the buyers could reject the whole: *Payne and Routh* v. *Lillico & Sons* (1920) 36 T.L.R. 569.

What the buyer accepts, he must pay for at the contract rate.

Where the contract is for the sale of "about" so many tons, or so many tons "more or less," the seller is allowed a reasonable margin. If, however, he exceeds that margin the buyer cannot be compelled to accept the goods.

If the seller delivers, with the goods ordered, goods of a wrong description, the buyer may accept the goods ordered and reject the rest, or reject the whole (s.30(4)).

Where the contract provides that "each shipment shall be deemed as a separate contract," the seller has an option: he may treat the contract as indivisible or he may make separate deliveries, in which case the contract becomes severable. The seller exercises this option by his mode of performance.

The seller shipped goods from Hong Kong c.i.f. Liverpool, "each shipment under this contract [to] be deemed as a separate contract." He shipped the goods in one ship but under two bills of lading dated the same day, each of these documents relating to half of the consignment. The buyers accepted one half and purported to reject the other. *Held*, there was one indivisible contract and, having accepted part of the consignment, the buyers had lost the right to reject the other: *J. Rosenthal & Sons Ltd.* v. *Esmail* [1965] 1 W.L.R. 1117.

If a buyer has a right under his contract to reject goods, he is not bound to return the rejected goods to the seller, but it is sufficient if he intimates to the seller that he refuses to accept them (s.36).

Instalment Deliveries

Unless he has agreed to do so, a buyer cannot be compelled to take delivery by instalments. When there is a contract for the sale of goods to be delivered by stated instalments which are to be separately paid for, and either the buyer or the seller commits a breach of contract, it is a question depending on the terms of the contract and the circumstances of the case whether the breach is a repudiation of the whole contract or a severable breach merely giving a right to claim for damages (s.31).

If a breach is of such a kind as to lead to the inference that similar breaches will take place with regard to future deliveries, the contract can be at once repudiated by the injured party. For example, if the buyer fails to pay for one instalment under such circumstances as to suggest that he will not pay for future instalments, or the seller fails to deliver goods of the contract description under similar circumstances, the contract can be repudiated.

X. sold to Y. 1,500 tons of meat and bone meal of a specified quality, to be shipped 125 tons monthly in equal weekly instalments. After about half the meal was delivered and paid for, Y. discovered that it was not of the contract quality and could have been rejected, and he refused to take further deliveries. *Held*, Y. was entitled to do so, as he was not bound to take the risk of having put upon him further deliveries of goods which did not conform to the contract: *Robert A. Munro & Co.* v. *Meyer* [1930] 2 K.B. 312.

The tests to be applied are: first, the ratio quantitatively which the breach bears to the contract, and, secondly, the degree of probability or improbability that such a breach will be repeated.

X. bought from Y. Co. 5,000 tons of steel to be delivered 1,000 tons monthly. After the delivery of two instalments, but before payment was due, a petition was presented to wind up Y. Co., and X. refused to pay unless the sanction of the court was obtained, being under the erroneous impression that this was necessary. *Held*, the conduct of X. in so refusing payment did not show an intention to repudiate the contract so as to excuse the liquidator of Y. Co. from making further deliveries: *Mersey Steel & Iron Co.* v. *Naylor* (1884) 9 App.Cas. 434.

A clothing manufacturer contracted to sell 62 suits to a retailer, delivery to be by instalments over an agreed period, the number and size of each delivery to be at the seller's discretion. The buyer informed the seller that the buyer wished to cancel the order. The seller insisted on making deliveries because the seller was already in production. Each of the attempted deliveries because the seller was already in production. Each of the attempted deliveries (five in all) was rejected by the buyer. In defence to the seller's claim for damages for non-acceptance, the buyer claimed that as the attempted deliveries had been one suit short of the total contract quantity of 62, the buyer was entitled to reject all the goods under section 30(1). *Held*, giving judgment for the seller, that section 30(1) which provides that in a case of short delivery the buyer can reject all the goods, does not apply in the case of a severable contract. Section 30(1) was inconsistent with and had to yield to section 31. Applying section 31, the short delivery was not sufficiently serious to amount to a repudiation of the whole contract: *Regent OHG Aisenstadt und Barig* v. *Francesco of Jermyn Street Ltd.* [1981] 3 All E.R. 327.

Rights of Unpaid Seller against the Goods

An unpaid seller of goods even though the property in the goods has passed to the buyer, has (1) a lien for the price, (2) if the buyer is insolvent, a right of stoppage in transit after he has parted with possession of the goods, (3) a limited right of resale (s.39).

A lien

A lien is a right to retain possession of goods, until payment of the price. It is available when (s.41):

(a) the goods have been sold without any stipulation as to credit;
(b) the goods have been sold on credit, but the term of credit has expired; or
(c) the buyer becomes insolvent.

A lien is lost (s.43):

(a) when the goods are delivered to a carrier for the purpose of

transmission to the buyer, without reserving the right of disposal;
(b) when the buyer or his agent lawfully obtains possession of the goods; or
(c) by waiver.

If the property in the goods has passed to the buyer, the unpaid seller has a right of lien as described above. If, however, the property has not passed, the unpaid seller has a right of withholding delivery similar to and co-extensive with his right of lien (s.39(2)).

A right of stoppage in transit

There is a right of stopping the goods while they are in transit, resuming possession of them and retaining possession until payment of the price. It is available when (s.44):

(a) the buyer becomes insolvent; and
(b) the goods are in transit.

The buyer is insolvent if he has ceased to pay his debts in the ordinary course of business or cannot pay his debts as they become due. It is not necessary that he should have committed an act of bankruptcy (s.61(4)).

Goods are in transit (s.45) from the time they are delivered to a carrier for the purpose of transmission to the buyer until the buyer takes delivery of them. The goods are still in transit if they are rejected by the buyer. If goods are ordered to be sent to an intermediate place from which they are to be forwarded to their ultimate destination, the transit is at the end if fresh instructions have to be sent to the intermediate place before the goods can be forwarded, but otherwise the goods are still in transit. The transit is also at an end in the following cases:

(a) if the buyer obtains delivery before the arrival of the goods at their destination; or
(b) if, after the arrival of the goods at their destination, the carrier acknowledges to the buyer that he holds the goods on his behalf, even if a further destination of the goods is indicated by the buyer; or
(c) if the carrier wrongfully refuses to deliver the goods to the buyer.

When the goods are delivered to a ship chartered by the buyer, whether they are in possession of the master of the ship as carrier or as agent for the buyer is a question depending on the circumstances of the case (s.45).

The seller exercises his right of stoppage in transit either by taking possession of the goods or by giving notice of his claim to the carrier in whose possession the goods are. On notice being given to the carrier he must redeliver the goods to the seller, who must pay the expenses of the redelivery (s.46).

Effect of sale by buyer

The seller's right of lien or stoppage in transit is not defeated by any sale or pledge except in any of the following three situations (s.47):

(a) The seller has assented to the sale or pledge by the buyer.
(b) The buyer disposes of the goods in a situation falling within one of the exceptions to the *nemo dat* principle (see pp. 333–334, *ante*).
(c) The buyer transfers to a bona fide purchaser a document of title (*e.g.* a bill of lading) which the buyer has acquired from the seller (s.47 proviso).

X. bought from Y. a shipment of nuts, and Y. sent to X. the bill of lading. X. handed the bill of lading to Z. in return for a loan, and then became insolvent. Y. attempted to stop the nuts in transit, but Z. claimed them. *Held*, Z. had a good title to the nuts, which defeated Y.'s right to stoppage *in transitu*: *Leask* v. *Scott Bros.* (1877) 2 Q.B.D. 376.

A right of resale

The exercise of the right of lien or of stoppage in transit does not rescind the contract or give the seller a right of resale. If, however, an unpaid seller who has exercised either of these rights does resell the goods, the buyer obtains a good title to them as against the original buyer (s.48(2)).

The seller has a right to resell the goods (s.48(3)):

(a) Where the goods are of a perishable nature.
(b) Where he gives notice to the buyer of his intention to resell and the buyer does not within a reasonable time pay or tender the price.

(c) Where the seller expressly reserves a right of resale in case the buyer should make a default.

If the seller should sustain any loss on the resale, he can recover it from the buyer as damages for breach of contract. If he should make a profit on the resale, then he is entitled to keep that profit.

Actions for Breach of the Contract

1. The **seller**, in addition to his rights against the goods set out above, has two rights of action against the buyer.

For the price

An action for the price lies when the property in the goods has passed to the buyer (s.49(1)). When the price is payable on a day certain irrespective of delivery, an action for the price may be brought although the property in the goods has not passed and the goods have not been appropriated to the contract (s.49(2)).

C. sold to O. a quantity of leather f.o.b. Liverpool, the goods being unascertained at the date of the sale. O. instructed C. to send the goods to Liverpool for shipment on the "K." and C. did so. The "K." and other ships substituted could not take the leather, which remained at the docks for two months. C. brought an action against O. for the price. *Held*, as the property in the goods had not passed to O., and there was no agreement as to the price being payable on a day certain, irrespective of delivery, C. could not sue for the price: *Colley* v. *Overseas Exporters* [1921] 3 K.B. 302.

When the property in the goods has not passed, the proper remedy of the seller in the case of a breach of contract is the one following.

For non-acceptance

An action for damages for non-acceptance lies when the buyer refuses or neglects to accept the goods. The measure of damages is the loss resulting from the buyer's breach of contract. This is the loss of profit on the sale when the goods have a fixed retail price and the supply exceeds the demand.

R. contracted to buy a Vanguard motor car from T., who were car dealers. R. refused to accept delivery. There was no shortage of Vanguards. *Held*, T. were entitled to damages for the loss of their bargain, *viz.* the profit they would have made, as they had sold one car less than they otherwise would have sold: *Thompson Ltd.* v. *Robinson* (*Gunmakers*) *Ltd.* [1955] Ch. 177. If the demand of cars exceeds the supply and the car dealer can sell all the cars he can get, he has suffered no loss of profit and the damages are nominal only: *Charter* v. *Sullivan* [1957] 2 Q.B. 117.

A second-hand car does not have a fixed retail price and in such a case the seller cannot recover loss of profit for selling one fewer car than he otherwise would have sold. If he manages to find another purchaser of the car at the same or a higher price he will recover no damages from the first buyer who had backed out: *Lazenby Garages Ltd.* v. *Wright* [1976] 1 W.L.R. 459.

When there is an available market for the goods, prima facie the measure of damages is the difference between the contract price and the market price (s.50(3)).

When the seller is ready and willing to deliver the goods and requests the buyer to take delivery, which the buyer does not do within a reasonable time, the seller may recover from the buyer (s.37):

(a) any loss occasioned by the buyer's refusal or neglect to take delivery; and
(b) a reasonable charge for the care and custody of the goods.

2. The **buyer** has the following actions against the seller for breach of contract—

For non-delivery

This arises when the seller wrongfully neglects or refuses to deliver the goods to the buyer. The measure of damages is, as in the case of the action for non-acceptance, the estimated loss naturally resulting from the breach of contract which is, prima facie, when there is an available market for the goods, the difference between the contract price and the market price at the time when the goods ought to have been delivered or, if no time for delivery was fixed, from the time of the refusal to deliver (s.51).

If the buyer purchased the goods for resale and the seller knew of this, the measure of damages will be the difference between the contract price and the resale price, if the goods cannot be obtained in the market. If they can be obtained in the market, the buyer ought to obtain them there and so fulfil his contract of resale, with the result that the damages will be the difference between the market price and the contract price.

P. bought Russian wheat for delivery on a named date, and before that date resold it to a third party at a profit. The sellers failed to deliver. There was no market for Russian wheat. The sellers knew that P. had bought for resale. *Held*, P. was entitled as damages to the difference between the contract price and the resale price: *Patrick* v. *Russo-British Grain Export Co.* [1927] 2 K.B. 535.

Where delivery is delayed, but the goods are ultimately accepted notwithstanding the delay, the measure of damages is the difference between the value of the goods at the time when they ought to have been and the time when they actually were delivered (*Elbinger Actien Gesellschaft* v. *Armstrong* (1874) L.R. 9 Q.B. 477). A claim for loss of profits, however, can always be brought if that loss was within the rules in *Hadley* v. *Baxendale* (1854) 9 Ex. 341 (see *Victoria Laundry* v. *Newman Industries* p. 175, *ante*).

For recovery of the price

If the buyer has paid the price and the goods are not delivered he can recover the amount paid.

For specific performance

A buyer can only get his contract specifically performed, *i.e.* obtain an order of the court compelling the seller to deliver the goods he has sold, when the goods are specific or ascertained. The remedy is discretionary and will be granted only when damages would not be an adequate remedy. If, therefore, the goods are ordinary articles of commerce which can readily be obtained in the market, specific performance will not be granted; but it will be granted if the goods are of special value or are unique, *e.g.* a picture, a rare book or a piece of antique furniture.

For breach of condition

On breach of condition the buyer is entitled to reject the goods. He cannot reject the goods, however, if (s.11):

(a) he waives the breach of condition, and elects to treat it as a breach of warranty; or
(b) the contract is not severable and he has accepted the goods or part of them.

Merely taking delivery will not amount to acceptance (see p. 342, *ante*).

L., in 1944, bought from I. a picture of Salisbury Cathedral said by I. to be by Constable. In 1949 L. found it was not by Constable and claimed to rescind the contract and recover the purchase price. *Held*, as the picture had been accepted, it could not later be rejected: *Leaf* v. *International Galleries* [1950] 2 K.B. 86.

In all these cases the breach of condition can only be treated as breach of warranty.

In March 1974 a garage sold a second-hand 1967 car for £355 to a buyer who, after using it for some time, discovered that its brakes were in such a poor state that, if the buyer had had to carry out an emergency stop, they would almost certainly have failed. The cost of having the defects put right would be £100. In September 1974 the buyer commenced proceedings claiming to reject the car and to recover the price and claiming also damages. *Held*, because the car was not in a state to be safely driven on the road, it was not of merchantable quality or reasonably fit for its purpose. Therefore the seller was in breach of the conditions implied by s.14 (see p. 318, *ante*). However, as the buyer had not rejected the car until commencing the proceedings in September, she had accepted the car and had thus lost her right to reject it and recover the price. The buyer was awarded damages of £100: *Lee* v. *York Coach and Marine* [1977] R.T.R. 35.

Contracts frequently contain a clause prohibiting the rejection of goods by the buyer. Such a clause has no effect unless the goods are within the contract description.

Timber of different sizes was sold under a contract which provided that "buyers shall not reject the goods herein specified, but shall accept or pay for them in terms of contract against shipping documents." The timber delivered was not, in respect of quantity, the specified timber. *Held*, the buyer could reject the timber as the clause did not operate when the goods tendered were not the specified goods which the buyer contracted to buy: *Green* v. *Arcos Ltd.* (1931) 47 T.L.R. 336. (Today a clause which prohibits rejection of goods for breach of condition may, in any case, fail to satisfy the requirement of reasonableness provided by the Unfair Contract Terms Act 1977 (see p. 43, *ante*)).

For breach of warranty

On breach of warranty, the buyer can either:

(a) set up against the seller the breach of warranty in diminution or extinction of the price; or
(b) maintain an action against the seller for breach of warranty.

The measure of damages for breach of warranty is the estimated loss arising directly and naturally from the breach, which is prima facie the difference between the value of the goods as delivered and the value they would have had if the goods had answered to the warranty (s.53).

N. sold to B. sulphuric acid warranted to be commercially free from arsenic. N. did not know the purpose for which the acid was required. B. used the acid for making glucose, which he sold to brewers for the purpose of brewing beer. Owing to the poisonous nature of the acid the beer was poisonous and killed people who drank it. B. sued N. for damages. *Held*, he could recover (i) the price paid for the acid, (ii) the value of other goods spoilt by being made from the acid, but not (iii) the damages B. had had to pay the brewers, and not (iv) damages for injury to the goodwill of B.'s business: *Bostock & Co. Ltd.* v. *Nicholson & Sons Ltd.* [1904] 1 K.B. 725.

Sales by Auction

The following rules apply to auction sales (s.57):

1. Each lot is a prima facie deemed to be the subject of a separate contract of sale.

2. The sale is complete when the auctioneer announces its completion by the fall of the hammer or in other customary manner. Until such announcement any bidder may retract his bid.

D. sold a motor-car by auction. It was knocked down to K. who was only allowed to take it away on giving a cheque for the price and signing an agreement that ownership should not pass until the cheque was cleared. The cheque was not cleared. Meanwhile, K. sold to S. *Held*, the property passed on the fall of the hammer and the subsequent agreement did not retransfer it from K., so that S. had a good title: *Dennant* v. *Skinner* [1948] 2 K.B. 164.

3. The seller himself or any person employed by him cannot bid, and it is not lawful for the auctioneer knowingly to take any such bid, unless notice is given beforehand that the sale is subject to a

right on the part of the seller to bid. A sale contravening this rule may be treated as fraudulent by the buyer.

4. The sale may be made subject to a reserve price, and a right to bid may also be reserved by the seller.

On a sale by auction announced to be subject to a reserve price, each bid is accepted conditionally on the reserve being reached (*McManus* v. *Fortescue* [1907] 2 K.B. 1).

When an auctioneer sells goods, he impliedly undertakes the following obligations—

1. He warrants his authority to sell.
2. He warrants that he knows of no defect in his principal's title.
3. He undertakes to give possession against the price paid into his hands.
4. He undertakes that such possession will not be disturbed by his principal or himself (*per* Salter J. in *Benton* v. *Campbell, Parker & Co. Ltd.*, below).

Where an auctioneer, disclosing the fact that he is acting as agent but not disclosing the name of his principal, sells specific goods he does not warrant his principal's title to the goods.

B. bought a motor-car at an auction sale conducted by C., an auctioneer. The car was sold on behalf of X., who had no title to it, and the true owner subsequently recovered it from B. B. sued C. for the return of the price. *Held*, he could not recover as he knew C. was an agent, and the sale was a sale of specific goods: *Benton* v. *Campbell, Parker & Co. Ltd.* [1925] 2 K.B. 410.

Subject to contrary agreement, the auctioneer has the following rights (*Chelmsford Auctions Ltd.* v. *Poole* [1973] 1 Q.B. 542):

1. He is entitled himself to sue the purchaser for the price. The purchaser cannot avoid this liability to the auctioneer by paying the vendor direct without telling the auctioneer.
2. He has against the seller a lien over the proceeds of sale for his commission and charges.

Auction sales are usually conducted in accordance with printed conditions contained in the sale catalogue. The conditions frequently contain provisions limiting the liability of the seller in respect of the goods sold (see *Couchman* v. *Hill*, pp. 322–323, *ante*). An express oral warranty given at the time of the sale, however, overrides an exemption clause in the printed conditions of sale

(*Harling* v. *Eddy* [1951] 2 K.B. 739). An exemption clause would in any case be subject to the provisions of the Unfair Contract Terms Act 1977 (see *Southwestern General Property Co. Ltd.* v. *Marton*, (1982) 263 E.G. 1090, see p. 106, *ante*).

Auctions (Bidding Agreements) Acts 1927 and 1969

An agreement by a dealer to give any person any consideration for abstaining from bidding at an auction sale is a criminal offence on the part of the dealer and of the person receiving the consideration. A dealer is a person who, in the normal course of his business, attends sales by auction for the purpose of purchasing goods with a view to reselling them (s.1 of the 1927 Act). The effect of this Act is to make a "knock-out" agreement illegal when it is entered into by a dealer (see *Rawlings* v. *General Trading Co.* [1920] 3 K.B. 30). In case of a conviction the court may order that the convicted person or any representative of him shall not, without consent of the court, enter upon premises where goods intended to be auctioned are on display, or participate in an auction, for a period not exceeding one year in the case of a summary conviction or not exceeding three years on conviction on indictment; contravention of the court prohibition is punishable (s.2 of the 1969 Act).

A civil remedy is provided in favour of a seller whose goods have been sold at an auction to a person who is a party to a prohibited bidding agreement, provided that one of the parties to that agreement is a dealer. Such a seller may avoid the contract and if restitution of goods is not made to him, may recover any loss sustained by him from any party to the prohibited bidding agreement, not only from the buyer (s.3 of the 1969 Act). This remedy is available irrespective of whether a party to the prohibited bidding agreement has been convicted in a criminal court.

A copy of the Act must be affixed in some conspicuous part of any room in which an auction sale takes place.

The Act does not interfere with bona fide agreements to purchase goods on a joint account, where the agreement is deposited with the auctioneer before the sale.

Mock Auctions Act 1961

It is a criminal offence to promote or conduct, or to assist in the conduct of, a mock auction at which one or more lots to which the Act applies are offered for sale. A sale of goods by way of competitive bidding is taken to be a mock auction if during the course of the sale:

(a) any lot to which the Act applies is sold to a person bidding for it, and either it is sold to him at a price lower than the amount of his highest bid for that lot, or part of the price at which it is sold to him is repaid or credited to him or is stated to be so repaid or credited; or
(b) the right to bid for any lot to which the Act applies is restricted, or is stated to be restricted, to persons who have bought or agreed to buy one or more articles; or
(c) any articles are given away or offered as gifts.

The Act applies to any lot which consists of or includes plate, plated articles, linen, china, glass, books, picture, prints, furniture, jewellery, articles of household or personal use or ornament or any musical or scientific instrument or apparatus.

The defendant held a sale and asked his audience who would pay him 30p. for a set of glasses. A number of hands were raised. The defendant chose one of them and then reduced the price to 1p. for that customer. *Held*, the defendant was guilty of conducting a mock auction, since there had been "competitive bidding" as the members of the audience had been competing to buy the one set of glasses: *Allen* v. *Simmons* [1978] 1 W.L.R. 879.

The Trade Descriptions Act 1968

The object of this is to prevent, by way of criminal sanctions, the use of false or misleading trade descriptions. The Act which has taken the place of, and considerably extended the regulation formerly contained in, the Merchandise Marks Acts, does not provide any civil remedies. The Act provides, on the contrary, that "a contract for the supply of any goods shall not be void or unenforceable by reason only of a contravention of any provision of this Act" (s.35). In any case the consumer has extensive civil remedies: they are, in particular, the rules relating to misrepresentation, reinforced by the Misrepresentation Act 1967 (see p. 94, *ante*), and the provisions of the Sale of Goods Act 1979, particularly those on implied terms (see p. 314, *ante*). Although the Trade Descriptions Act does not affect the consumer's civil remedies, the criminal court has power, on convicting an offender, to order him to pay compensation to the victim (Powers of Criminal Courts Act 1973, s.35). This is so irrespective of whether it was the public prosecutor or the victim who brought the prosecution.

The Act of 1968 creates two principal offences, one relating to goods and the other to services.

Goods

Any person who, in the course of a trade or business:

(a) applies a false trade description to goods; or
(b) supplies or offers to supply any goods to which a false trade description is applied,

shall be guilty of an offence (s.1(1)).

A trade description is any indication, direct or indirect, of (s.2(1)):

(a) a quantity, size, or gauge;
(b) method of manufacture, production, processing or reconditioning;
(c) composition;
(d) fitness for purpose, strength, performance, behaviour or accuracy;
(e) any physical characteristics not included in the preceding paragraphs;
(f) testing by any person and results thereof;
(g) approval by any person or conformity with a type approved by any person;
(h) place or date of manufacture, production, processing or reconditioning;
(i) person by whom manufactured, produced, processed or reconditioned;
(j) other history, including previous ownership or use.

The offence under section 1(1) is committed only if the application of the false trade description was associated with the sale or supply of goods (*Wickens Motors* (*Gloucester*) *Ltd.* v. *Hall* [1972] 1 W.L.R. 1418). While most offenders will be sellers, a buyer could commit the offence, *e.g.* a car dealer who when negotiating to buy a second-hand car wrongly informs the seller that it can not be repaired and is fit only for scrap (*Fletcher* v. *Budgen* [1974] 1 W.L.R. 1056).

The trade description is false when it is false to a material degree (s.3(1)).

Under a contract to supply a new car, the manufacturers supplied to the dealer a car which had been damaged in a collision in a compound, which damage had been repaired. The manufacturers were convicted. *Held*, on appeal, the conviction should be quashed because if damage is perfectly repaired making the car as good as new, it is not false to describe the car as "new": *R.* v. *Ford Motor Co. Ltd.* [1974] 1 W.L.R. 1220.

No-one can be guilty of an offence under the Trade Descriptions Act unless he was acting "in the course of a business." Not every transaction connected with a business will necessarily be a transaction made "in the course of a business." A transaction which is not central to the business but which is only incidental to it, will be made "in the course of the business" only if it is of a type which the business makes regularly (*Davies* v. *Sumner*, see below)

The defendant ran a car hire business. As was his usual practice, he sold one of the hire cars when it was no more use to the business. A false indication was given, on the odometer, of the amount of mileage the car had covered. The defendant was charged with an offence under s.1(1)(b). *Held*, he was guilty, since the sale had been in the course of a business, even though the business was not that of a car dealer: *Havering London Borough* v. *Stevenson* [1970] 3 All E.R. 609 (C.A.).

A self employed courier used his car almost exclusively in connection with his business as a courier. He sold the car in part exchange for another vehicle which was also for his business use. The car he part exchanged showed a false mileage reading on its odometer and the courier was charged under s.1(1)(b) with supplying a vehicle to which a false trade description was applied. *Held*, the sale of his old car was not a sale "in the course of a business" since it was merely incidental to the carrying on of his courier's business and he had not got a regular practice of swapping his cars: *Davies* v. *Sumner* [1984] 1 W.L.R. 1301 (H.L.).

It is a defence to a charge under s.1(1)(b) that the defendant displayed a disclaimer which was as bold, precise and compelling as the description itself (*Norman* v. *Bennett* [1974] 1 W.L.R. 1229). A car dealer would be wise to display such a disclaimer adjacent to an odometer, which otherwise will amount to a trade description as to the mileage covered by the vehicle. The disclaimer defence is not available to someone charged under section 1(1)(a) (*R.* v. *Southwood* (1987) 85 Cr.App.R. 272.). This is because someone charged under s.1(1)(a) is charged with having himself applied the false trade description, rather than having supplied, or offered to supply, goods to which a false trade description has been applied by someone else.

Services

Certain false statements relating to " services, accommodation or facilities" are also punishable, although the trader is not guilty unless either he knew his statement was false or else he made the false statement recklessly (s.14).

In November 1979 the defendants displayed outside their Oxford Street shop a notice "Closing Down Sale" and they were still trading there in May 1981. They were charged under section 14 with recklessly making a false statement as to the nature of a facility. *Held*, the defendants were not guilty. Section 14 did not deal with the sale of goods and a reference to a shop sale was not a reference to a "facility" within section 14: *Westminster City Council* v. *Ray Allan* (*Manshops*) *Ltd.* [1982] 1 W.L.R. 383.

The defendant has to have the knowledge or be reckless at the time when the time the false statement is *made.*

Directors of a travel company discovered that one of their brochures contained a false description that the rooms in one of its hotels were air-conditioned. They recalled copies of the brochure. About eight months later a customer booked a holiday, relying on an old copy of the brochure. *Held*, the company had been correctly convicted of making a statement which it knew to be false. A false statement in a brochure is made when the brochure is published and is made again (or alternatively continued) when read at a later stage in an uncorrected form by a member of the public. Thus the defendant company knew the statement was false when it was made, *i.e* when the customer read it at the time of booking the holiday: *Wings* v. *Ellis* [1985] A.C. 272 (H.L.).

Defences

The Act admits certain defences when a prosecution is initiated. In particular, it is a defence for a person to prove (s.24(1)):

(a) that the commission of the offence was due to a mistake or to reliance on information supplied to the defendant or to the act or default of another person, an accident or some other cause beyond his control; and

(b) that he took all reasonable precautions and exercised all due diligence to avoid the commission of such an offence by himself or any person under his control.

Both the requirements under (a) and (b) have to be proved by the defendant if the defence is to succeed.

The defendants sold a car with an odometer reading of 14,000 miles. They made enquiries about the car's history from its previous owner and learnt nothing suggesting that the odometer reading was false. *Held*, the defendants had no defence under section 24 because they had, in failing to display a disclaimer, failed to take all reasonable precautions to avoid the commission of the offence: *Simmons* v. *Potter* [1975] R.T.R. 347.

If a person intends to rely on the defence that the commission of the offence was due to the act or default of another person, he must notify the prosecutor of his intention seven clear days before the hearing (s.24(2)), thus enabling him to prosecute the other person (s.23); the court has power to dispense with that time limit. The shop manager of a company is "another person" within the meaning of section 24(1) and the company can rely on the defence that the contravention was due to his act or default (*Tesco Supermarkets Ltd.* v. *Nattrass*, below).

At one of the defendant's supermarkets a large advertisement stated that Radiant washing powder was 2s. 11d. a packet. In fact some packets marked 3s. 11d. were available on the shelves. A customer took one of these and was charged 3s. 11d. The defendants pleaded that this was due to the default of the store manager in failing to carry out the system laid down by the defendants for the operation of the store. *Held*, the defendants had a good defence since the store manager was "another person" and the defendants had taken all reasonable precautions under section 24(*b*) by devising a proper system for the store and doing all they could to see that it was implemented: *Tesco Supermarkets Ltd.* v. *Nattrass* [1972] A.C. 153.

Another defence admitted by the Act is (s.24(3)):

"for the person charged to prove that he did not know, and could not with reasonable diligence have ascertained, that the goods did not conform to the description or that the description had been applied to the goods."

Misleading Price Indications

The Consumer Protection Act 1987, Part III replaced earlier provisions and creates a widely worded offence. A person commits an offence

"... if in the course of any business of his, he gives (by any means whatever) to any consumers an indication which is misleading as to the price at which any goods, services, accommodation or facilities are available (whether generally or from particular persons)," s.20.

The following are misleading:

(a) an understatement of the price;
(b) the stating of the price without making it clear, if it is the case, that it applies only to cash customers or that it does not apply to part-exchange deals or applies only in certain circumstances or does not apply in other circumstances;
(c) failing to make it clear, if it is the case, that service is charged extra or that some other additional charge is made;
(d) a false indication that a price is expected to be increased or reduced or maintained (whether or not for a particular period);
(e) making a false price comparison, *e.g.* falsely stating that the price is a reduced one, or comparing the price with that of another model without stating that the price for the other model has since been reduced.

There is a code of practice issued by the Office of Fair Trading which gives guidance on avoiding giving misleading price indications. Compliance with the code of practice is not mandatory. Compliance or non-compliance is, however, something that may be taken into account by the court in determining whether an offence under s.20 has been committed (s.25).

There are certain statutory defences including:

1. that the misleading price indication was given, other than in an advertisement, on the media (s.24);
2. that the defendant was an innocent publisher or advertising agency who was unaware, and had no grounds for suspect-

ing, that the advertisement contained a false price indication (s.24);

3. that the defendant took all reasonable precautions and exercised all due diligence to avoid the commission of an offence (s.39).

Misleading Advertisements

The Control of Misleading Advertisements Regulations 1988, implement an EC Directive. They require the Director General to consider complaints about misleading advertisements. If he is satisfied that alternative methods of dealing with the matter (*e.g.* prosecution for a trade description offence) do not cover the problem or are otherwise inadequate, he can apply to the High Court for an injunction to stop the publication of a misleading advertisement.

The Unsolicited Goods and Services Act 1971

The main provision of this Act is that in certain circumstances a person who has received unsolicited goods other than goods reasonable to be used in his trade or business may treat them as an unconditional gift. He may do so if either the sender fails to collect the goods within six months, or if the sender fails to collect the goods within 30 days after the recipient has served on the sender a written statement that the goods were unsolicited (s.1).

The Act also contains provisions regulating the written form for orders relating to entries in trade or business directories (s.3) and making it an offence to send out unsolicited books describing or illustrating human sexual techniques (s.4).

The Fair Trading Act 1973

This Act established the office of Director General of Fair Trading and confers certain consumer protection functions upon the Director General. In conjunction with the Consumer Protection Advisory Committee which also was established by the Act, he can recommend that the Secretary of State for Prices and Consumer Protection makes orders for the control or prevention of consumer trade practices which adversely affect the economic interests of consumers (s.17). The orders so far made by the Secretary of State under this procedure (under s.22) include one prohibiting the display of an exemption clause which is void under s.6 of the Unfair Contract Terms Act 1977 (see p. 323, *ante*). Orders made under the Fair Trading Act do not affect civil rights (s.26). Infringement is a criminal offence. Defences are available similar to those in section 24 of the Trade Descriptions Act 1968 (see p. 358, *ante*).

The Director General has powers in relation to anyone who appears to be persisting in breaking the law (civil or criminal) in a way detrimental to the interests of consumers in respect of health, safety or other matters. He can ask for assurance from the offender as to future conduct (s.34(1)). If that fails to achieve the desired result, he can take proceedings against him in the Restrictive Practices Court (s.35).

(For the functions of the Director General under the Consumer Credit Act 1974, see p. 388, *post*, and for his functions in competition law, see Ch. 20, *post*).

Product Liability

There are three main ways in which a manufacturer may be liable to a consumer who has the misfortune to receive a defective product or to be caused loss or damage by one.

Sale of goods contract

A buyer of goods which are not of merchantable quality can maintain a claim against the seller for both the mere loss of having a defective item and also any consequential damage the item may have caused (*e.g.* if it has caught fire and burnt down his house). However, this claim can be made only by the buyer and only against the seller. If the goods have damaged anyone other than the buyer, that victim can not rely upon the Sale of Goods Act. Furthermore even when it is the buyer who is the victim, he can not sue the manufacturer under the Sale of Goods Act unless he bought directly from the manufacturer.

Negligence

Any consumer, whether or not he was the buyer, who or whose

property is injured or damaged by a defective product can maintain a claim against the manufacturer, providing he can prove that the manufacturer (or one of the manufacturer's employees) was negligent. Such a claim will be difficult since negligence is the failure to take reasonable care and it is quite possible for a product to be dangerous without there having been any failure to take care.

Consumer Protection Act 1987, Part I

This Act implemented an EC Directive. Under this Act, anyone who is injured by a defective product can sue the manufacturer, irrespective of whether the manufacturer was negligent. Damage caused to non-business property can be claimed if it exceeds £275 in value. Damage to business property can not be claimed. Nor can damage to the defective product itself. To succeed in a claim the plaintiff must show four things (s.2):

(a) that a product contained a defect
(b) that the plaintiff suffered damage
(c) that the damage was caused by the defect
(d) that the defendant was, producer, own-brander, or importer into the European Community of the product.

A product is defective "if the safety of the product is not such as persons generally are entitled to expect."

There is an exception for primary (unprocessed) agricultural products and game. Thus there is no liability under this Act for peas or eggs (unless of course they are canned peas, or the eggs have been turned into omelettes before reaching the plaintiff).

There are various defences available (s.4), including:

1. The defect is due to compliance with a statutory requirement or rule of the European Community;
2. The defendant did not supply the product, *e.g.* it was stolen from his premises;
3. The defendant supplied the product otherwise than in the course of a business *and* the defendant did not produce it (or own-brand it or import it into the European Community) with a view to profit. This lets off someone who brings back a souvenir from America and gives it to someone as a present;

4. The defect was not in the product when the defendant supplied it;
5. The "development risks" defence, whereby the defendant is able to show that at the time he put the product into circulation, "the state of scientific and technical knowledge . . . was not such that the producer of products of the same description as the product in question might be expected to have discovered the defect if it had existed in his products while they were under his control." In short, the producer relying on this defence needs to show that the defect was not discoverable at the time he supplied the product. It is thought that drug manufacturing companies might be able to rely on this defence if in the future there were some tragedy akin to the Thalidomide tragedy of some decades ago, where a drug administered to pregnant mothers caused severe deformities in the children subsequently born.

It is not possible to exclude or limit liability arising under Part I of the Consumer Protection Act (s.7).

Consumer Safety

Part II of the Consumer Protection Act 1987 does four things, the first three of which are not new because there was earlier legislation which this Part of the Act replaced:

1. It empowers the Secretary of State to make safety regulations governing the making and supplying of goods. These may require goods to comply with certain standards (*e.g.* of nonflammability or nontoxicity). Regulations cover a wide range of items including such things as children's nightdresses, drip feed oil heaters, electric blankets, lead content of paint on children's cots.
2. It enables a consumer to bring an action for damages against any trader in respect of damage or loss suffered by the consumer because of an infringement by the trader of safety regulations.
3. It enables the Secretary of State to take quick action against the marketing of unsafe products by issuing a "prohibition notice" (to prevent a trader upon whom it is served from

supplying a specified type of goods considered unsafe) or a "notice to warn" requiring the trader upon whom it is served to warn customers about unsafe goods supplied by that trader.

4. It created a new offence for a trader to supply consumer goods which fail to comply with a general safety requirement (s.10). This requirement is that the goods be reasonably safe.

CHAPTER 16

HIRE-PURCHASE

THE HIRE-PURCHASE TRANSACTION

Definition of hire-purchase contract

A **hire-purchase contract** is a contract by which goods are delivered to a person who agrees to make periodical payments by way of hire, with an option of buying the goods after the stated hire instalments have been paid. The goods may be returned to the owner at any time before the option is exercised, on payment of the sum stated in the contract. Until the option is exercised there is no agreement to buy the goods.

The hire-purchase contract thus consists of three parts: a **contract of bailment** under which the hirer obtains possession of the goods, which remain in the ownership of the owner, and is thus enabled to use them before they are fully paid; an **option** in favour of the hirer entitling him, after payment of the periodical instalments and usually for a nominal consideration, to purchase the goods; and, if the hirer exercises the option, a **contract of sale** making him the owner of the goods already in his possession.

Hire-purchase and other instalment sales

The hire-purchase transaction, as described above, is a complex form of instalment sale which is adopted by commercial practice in order to protect the owner's title to the goods if the instalment buyer, in breach of his undertaking, sells them to a third party acquiring them in good faith before the payment of all instalments. A reservation of property would not protect the seller in this case because the Factors Act 1889, s.9, and the Sale of Goods Act 1979, s.25 provide that, if the buyer is in possession of the goods with the consent of the seller and then resells them to a good faith purchaser who has no notice of the original seller's right, the title of the good faith purchaser prevails over that of the original seller. If, on the other hand, the instalment purchaser has possession under a contract of bailment (hire) and is merely given the option of purchasing the goods or returning them, the provisions of the Factors Act and of the Sale of Goods Act do not apply and the original owner can recover them from a good faith purchaser to whom the hire-purchaser has sold them before the payment of the last instalment (*Helby* v. *Matthews,* below).

The owner of a piano agreed to let it on hire, the hirer to pay a rent in monthly instalments, on the terms that the hirer might terminate the hiring by returning the piano to the owner but remaining liable for all arrears of hire; also that the piano should remain the property of the owner but if the hirer had punctually paid all monthly instalments, the piano should become his property. The hirer, after having paid a few instalments, pledged the piano to a pawnbroker. *Held,* the hirer was under no legal obligation to buy but had an option either to return the piano or to become its owner by payment in full; consequently, he had not "agreed to buy" it within the meaning of the Factors Act 1889, s.9, and the owner could recover it from the pawnbroker: *Helby* v. *Matthews* [1895] A.C. 471.

It is important to distinguish between three different types of instalment agreement. First, a **hire-purchase agreement** does not involve the customer in a legal obligation to buy and therefore does not attract the application of the Factors Act 1889, s.9, or the Sale of Goods Act 1979, s.25. Secondly, a **credit sale agreement** does involve the customer in a legal obligation to buy and contains no express provision as to the transfer of property, with the result that property transfers to the buyer at the time the contract is made (Sale of Goods Act, s.18, r. 1; see p. 327, *ante*). Thus, anyone purchasing from the buyer will obtain a good title. Third, a **conditional sale agreement** involves the buyer in a legal obligation to buy but contains an express provision preventing the property from passing to the buyer until he has paid his instalments. At common law, if before completing his instalments under a conditional sale agreement the buyer sold the goods to a good faith purchaser, the latter obtained a good title by virtue of the Factors Act 1889, s.9, and the Sale of Goods Act 1979, s.25. However, these sections no longer apply where the conditional sale agreement is a consumer credit agreement within the meaning of the Consumer Credit Act 1974 (see that Act, Sched. 4; p. 388, *post*). Thus in this case, as in the case of a hire-purchase agreement, the original owner can recover the goods from the good faith purchaser.

In view of the variety of hire-purchase terms which can be arranged, an agreement that "the balance of purchase price can be had over a period of two years" is too vague (*Scammell* v. *Ouston* [1941] A.C. 251, see p. 27, *ante*); such an arrangement does not even indicate whether hire-purchase terms are "to be granted by the [owners] or on the other hand by some finance company acting in collaboration with the [owners]" (*per* Viscount Maugham, *ibid.* at 256).

The social implications of instalment sales have made it necessary for the legislator to intervene, with a view to protecting persons acquiring goods by way of instalment sales because these persons are often members of the economically weaker strata of society. The main enactment is the Consumer Credit Act 1974 (see Ch. 17, *post*).

A different object is pursued where in time of economic need the Government fixes a minimum deposit and other details of the instalment transaction. The aim here is to operate credit restrictions in the interest of the national economy. Contravention of these regulations is punishable but a valid title could pass under a contract contravening them (*Belvoir Finance Co. Ltd.* v. *Stapleton* [1971] 1 Q.B. 210; see p. 143, *ante*). At the time of going to press,[1] no credit restrictions of this kind are in operation; the last of them were removed in 1982.

The finance company

In many instances the owner of the goods does not have the resources necessary to finance his hire-purchase transaction. This is particularly true in the car trade. In these cases the services of a finance company are used which will finance the transaction for a consideration (the finance charges) that is included in the total hire-purchase price and thus has to be borne by the hire-purchaser.

If the services of a finance company are used, the hire-purchase transaction takes on the following triangular form:

1. The original owner of the goods, *e.g.* the car dealer, sells the goods to the finance company under an outright **contract of sale**.

[1] August 1, 1991.

Property is transferred at once to the finance company which becomes the owner of the goods. The finance company pays the cash price of the goods to the original owner. If the goods are a car and the dealer accepts the buyer's car in part exchange, he will give the finance company credit for the car taken in part exchange.

2. The finance company, as owner of the goods, then enters into a **hire-purchase contract** with the person intent on purchasing the goods. The purchaser pays the instalments, which include the finance charges, to the finance company directly and if, after payment of the last instalment, he exercises his option to acquire the goods, title to them will pass from the finance company to the purchaser.

3. No contract of sale or of hire-purchase exists between the original owner (car dealer) and the purchaser. But their relationship might not be entirely devoid of legal effect. It is possible that a **collateral contract of warranty** may exist by virtue of which the original owner has undertaken a warranty relating to the goods to the hire-purchaser in consideration of the latter entering into the hire-purchase contract with the finance company (see pp. 36–37, *ante*, and p. 371 *post*).

The finance company often enters into a **recourse agreement** with the dealer. By such an agreement the dealer agrees to be liable to the finance company if the purchaser defaults on his obligations. The ordinary recourse agreement is in the form of an indemnity (*Goulston Discount Co. Ltd.* v. *Clark* [1967] 2 Q.B. 493, see p. 384, *post*), but it may also take the form of a guarantee. An arrangement similar in purpose but different in legal effect is a **re-purchase agreement** whereby the dealer offers to re-purchase the goods from the finance company if the purchaser defaults. The re-purchase agreement is a unilateral contract subject to certain conditions; two conditions precedent are that the hire-purchase contract is terminated before all the instalments are paid and that the finance company exercises its option to claim the re-purchase within a reasonable time.

Eagle, dealers in aircraft, intended to sell a Vickers Viscount to Orion, one of their customers, on hire-purchase terms. Eagle sold the aircraft outright to United Dominions Trust, a finance company, which granted Orion hire-purchase terms. Eagle also entered into a re-purchase agreement with the finance company whereby they offered to re-purchase the aircraft if the hire-purchase agreement should be terminated before the total hire-purchase price was paid. Orion defaulted on the instalments and the finance company terminated the hire-purchase agreement. The finance company did not call on Eagle to re-purchase the aircraft until nearly five months after termination of the hire-purchase agreement. *Held,* Eagle's offer to re-purchase was in the nature of a unilateral contract and was subject to the implied condition precedent that the call to re-purchase should be made within a reasonable time from the termination of the hire-purchase contract. The call of the finance company was too late and consequently the obligation of Eagle to re-purchase the aircraft never arose: *United Dominions Trust (Commercial) Ltd.* v. *Eagle Aircraft Services Ltd.* [1968] 1 W.L.R. 74.

Under a hire-purchase agreement in which the hirer has only an option to purchase, a guarantor is not entitled, on paying the amount he has guaranteed, to have possession of the article hired (*Chatterton* v. *Maclean* [1951] 1 All E.R. 761).

Refinancing arrangements

An extension of the concept of hire-purchase agreement is the refinancing arrangement. The essence of such an arrangement is that the owner of goods, such as a car, sells them to a dealer who resells them under an outright contract of sale to a finance company which grants the original owner hire-purchase terms.

The validity of this type of transaction is not free from doubt. If the goods never leave the possession of the original owner and only property is transferred to the finance company, the economic effect of the transaction is that the original owner has obtained a loan on the security of goods retained in his possession. This transaction may well infringe the Bills of Sales Acts 1878 and 1882 (see p. 518, *post*) and be void as an unregistered bill of sale.

The courts draw here the following distinction:

1. If all the parties to the transaction, including the finance company, are aware that the real object of the transaction is to provide a loan on the security of goods remaining in the possession of the borrower, the hire-purchase transaction is a sham intended to disguise the true intention of the parties and the transaction is void as an unregistered bill of sale (*Polsky* v. *S. and A Services* [1951] 1 All E.R. 185; affirmed [1951] 1 All E.R. 1063, C.A.). "For acts or documents to be a 'sham,' with whatever legal consequences follow from this, all the parties thereto must have a common intention that

the acts or documents are not to create the legal rights and obligations which they give the appearance of creating" (*per* Diplock L.J. in *Snook* v. *London and West Riding Investments Ltd.* below).

2. If the parties intend the transaction to be a genuine hire-purchase transaction and, in particular, the finance company accepts the proposed hire-purchase transaction unaware of any irregularity, the refinancing agreement is not a sham but is valid (*Stoneleigh Finance Ltd.* v. *Phillip* [1965] 2 Q.B. 537). The original owner is estopped from denying that the dealer had authority to transfer the title in the goods to the finance company (*Eastern Distributors Ltd.* v. *Goldring* [1957] 2 Q.B. 600).

S. bought a new MG car from a dealer for £935. He paid £735 by way of deposit. The balance of £200 was financed by hire-purchase with T. Later S. went to another company, Auto Finance, which contracted with T. to pay off the remaining instalments of £160, and arranged new hire-purchase terms with the defendants who thought that the transaction was a genuine hire-purchase transaction relating to a car belonging to A. A. stated in the proposal form that the cash price which S. was to pay was £800 and that they had received £500 by way of deposit but these figures were fictitious. They received £300 from the defendants of which they paid £160 to T., £125 to S., and kept £15. T. declared themselves to be satisfied and purported to transfer the property in the car to A. which purported to transfer it to the defendants. The defendants entered into a hire-purchase contract with S. who began to pay instalments to them. All the time the car remained in the possession of S. S. defaulted on the instalments and A. seized the car. S. then offered the instalments to A. but they refused to accept them and resold the car for £575. They paid the defendants £280 (which satisfied them) and kept the balance of £295 as their profit. S. sued for damages. *Held* (by the Court of Appeal, Lord Denning M.R. dissenting), (1) the plaintiff was estopped from denying that the defendants had acquired the property in the car; (2) since the defendants were unaware of any irregularity in the transaction, it was not a sham and the hire-purchase contract between the defendants and the plaintiff was valid. The action was dismissed; *Snook* v. *London and West Riding Investments Ltd.* [1967] 2 Q.B. 786.

The liability of the dealer

The normal hire-purchase transaction involves, as has been explained earlier, three parties, the seller, the finance company and the hire-purchaser. In this type of transaction, the hire-purchase contract is concluded between the finance company and the hire-purchaser, and no contract of sale or of hire-purchase exists between the original seller and the hire-purchaser. It follows that if the goods are not fit for the particular purpose for which they are required the hire-purchaser has no claim against the original seller under section 14 of the Sale of Goods Act, his only claims being under the hire-purchase agreement against the finance company (*Drury* v. *Victor Buckland Ltd.* [1941] 1 All E.R. 269).

But if the original seller, *e.g.* the car dealer, gives the hire-purchaser an express warranty, *e.g.* that a second-hand car is in good working order, a collateral contract of warranty is concluded between the original seller and the hire-purchaser. The consideration supporting the warranty is the willingness of the hire-purchaser to conclude the hire-purchase contract with the finance company and to accept liability under its terms. If the original seller's warranty is broken, the hire-purchaser can sue the seller for breach of the contract of warranty (*Brown* v. *Sheen and Richmond Car Sales Ltd.* [1950] 1 All E.R. 1102, applied in *Shanklin Pier Ltd.* v. *Detel Products Ltd.* [1951] 2 K.B. 854, and *Andrews* v. *Hopkinson* [1957] 1 Q.B. 229, see p. 37 *ante*).

Furthermore, the correct measure of damages as between the hire-purchaser and the dealer whose warranty has induced him to enter into the hire-purchase agreement is the whole damage suffered by the hirer, including his liability under the hire-purchase contract, and is not limited to the difference in value between the goods as warranted and as in fact they are (*Yeoman Credit Ltd.* v. *Odgers* [1962] 1 W.L.R. 215).

Quite apart from any express warranty given by the dealer to the customer, there will be a contract between the dealer and the customer if, as part of the arrangements, the dealer agrees to carry out a service, *e.g.* installation of the goods. In such a contract the dealer could be liable under the terms implied by sections 13–14 of the Supply of Goods and Services Act 1982. These terms and the effect upon them of any exclusion clause were explained at pp. 324–325, *ante*.

The liability of the finance company

Under a hire-purchase agreement the creditor can be made liable to the debtor (the customer as hire-purchaser) under the terms of the Supply of Goods (Implied Terms) Act 1973. In the triangular arrangement already described the finance company is the creditor, but where the retailer finances his own hire-purchase agreements the retailer will be the creditor. The effect of the 1973 Act is to extend to the customer acquiring goods on hire-purchase the same protection as is provided for a customer buying for cash. Thus in a hire-purchase contract there are implied terms as to title (s.8), description (s.9), merchantable quality (s.10(2)), fitness for purpose (s.10(3)) and sample (s.11). These terms are virtually identical to those implied in a contract of sale of goods (see p. 314, *ante*). The condition that the goods be reasonably fit for a particular purpose is implied only if that particular purpose for which the goods are required is made known before the contract is made. It is sufficient if the customer makes known to the dealer the purpose for which the goods are required (s.10(3)).

A clause in a hire-purchase agreement which purports to exclude or restrict the creditor's liability under these implied terms is subject to exactly the same rules (including those laid down in the Unfair Contract Terms Act 1977) as it would be in a contract of sale (see pp. 40–45 and 322, *ante*).

It should also be noted that, where in a contract for hire-purchase the *creditor* agrees to carry out a service, *e.g.* installation of the goods, the Supply of Goods and Services Act 1982 (ss.13–15) implies certain terms in relation to the service. These terms and the effect upon them of any exclusion clause were considered at p. 324, *ante*.

The Consumer Credit Act 1974

This Act replaces the Hire-Purchase Act 1965. It is wider in scope and applies to many other agreements besides hire-purchase contracts. In this chapter reference will be made to sections of the Act which are particularly applicable to hire-purchase contracts. However, these contracts are subject to the provisions of the Act as a whole and those are set out in the next chapter. The Act is the main enactment governing hire-purchase, although there are certain others which relate to particular aspects of the subject, namely the Hire-Purchase Act 1964, Pt. III (p. 385, *post*), the Bills of Sales

Acts 1878 and 1882 (p. 518, *ante*) and the Supply of Goods (Implied Terms) Act 1973 (see pp. 372–373, *ante*).

The main definition in the Consumer Credit Act is that of a **regulated consumer credit agreement.** A hire-purchase agreement is such a regulated agreement if it fulfils two conditions; (i) the hirer (termed by the Act, debtor) is not a company or body corporate, and (ii) the amount of the credit does not exceed £15,000 (ss.8 and 9). The credit consists of the capital amount borrowed, not the deposit and not the interest or finance charges. Thus if an individual (or a partnership) enters into a hire-purchase agreement to acquire a car having a cash price of £31,000, the agreement could be a regulated one, *e.g.* if there was an initial payment of £16,000 plus 22 instalment payments of £750 monthly, £1,500 amounting to the interest and finance charges. The amount of the credit here is exactly £15,000, *i.e.* the difference between the initial payment of £16,000 and the amount needed to acquire the car for cash (£31,000). The fact that the subsequent instalments will total £16,500 is irrelevant (see also the example on p. 389, *post*). In this chapter references to regulated agreements are references to agreements which are regulated consumer credit agreements and, unless otherwise indicated, references to sections are references to sections of the Consumer Credit Act 1974.

The Act introduced new terminology. In the past it was customary to refer to the customer, the hire-purchaser, as the "hirer" and to the other party to the hire-purchase agreement (often a finance company) as the "owner." They are termed by the Act "debtor" and "creditor" respectively and that practice will be followed in the rest of this chapter.

The protection provided by the Act cannot be contracted out of (s.173).

Is the dealer an agent of the finance company?

Normally the dealer, when negotiating with the customer or receiving the deposit from him, does so in his own right. Thus at common law he is generally not regarded as agent of the creditor, the finance company. "There is no rule of law that in a hire-purchase transaction the dealer never is, or always is, acting as agent for the finance company or as agent of the customer. In a typical hire-purchase transaction the dealer is a party in his own right, selling his car to the finance company on his own behalf and not as general agent for either of the other two parties" (*per* Pearson L.J. in *Mercantile Credit Co. Ltd.* v. *Hamblin* [1965] 2 Q.B. 242, 269).

Although the dealer is not the agent of the customer, there is a rule of law that normally someone who signs a document is bound by that document even though he may be mistaken about its contents (*Saunders* v. *Anglia Building Society* [1971] A.C. 1004, see p. 83, *ante*). It has been held that this applies to an intending hire-purchaser who signs a hire-purchase proposal form in blank and leaves the dealer to fill in the details. If, after the dealer has fraudulently filled in inflated figures (to which the customer never agreed) in respect of the total price and the size of instalments, the finance company accepts that proposal, the customer is bound by that document and those figures (*United Dominions Trust Ltd.* v. *Western* [1976] Q.B. 513; see p. 84, *ante*).

That is the position at common law. For agreements regulated by the Consumer Credit Act, it is very different. The dealer is regarded as agent of the finance company during the negotiations between the dealer and customer (s.56). Those negotiations include representations made by the dealer to the customer and "any other dealings between them." Thus where the dealer fills in figures different from those agreed to by the customer, the latter is not bound by the document. Furthermore, if on signing the form the customer had paid a deposit to the dealer, he is entitled to recover the amount of that deposit from the finance company because in receiving it the dealer was doing so as agent of the finance company. That is so irrespective of whether the dealer had passed the deposit on to the finance company or not. The fact that representations made by the dealer are made by him also as agent for the finance company means that, in addition to any liability under the Supply of Goods (Implied Terms) Act 1973, the finance company could be liable to the customer for misrepresentation if the goods do not live up to the statements made by the dealer about them (as to liability for misrepresentation see p. 93, *ante*). In the case of a regulated agreement the dealer is also agent of the finance company for the purpose of receiving from the debtor: notice withdrawing an offer to enter the agreement (s.57); notice of cancellation of the agreement (s.69); or notice rescinding the agreement (s.102).

Form and contents of agreement

A regulated agreement must comply with the Act's requirements as to its legibility, information to be given in it, the state of the agreement when signed, and the giving of copies to the debtor. If these requirements are not complied with, the creditor may be unable to enforce the agreement against the debtor (see generally p. 394, *post*).

Right of cancellation

Certain regulated agreements are cancellable (ss.67–73). These rights of cancellation last for only a few days after the agreement has been made and the intention behind them is to provide the victim of doorstep salesmanship with a short period for second thoughts during which he is still free to escape from the agreement at no cost to himself. These rights extend also to regulated consumer credit agreements other than hire-purchase agreements and will be dealt with in the next chapter (see p. 396, *post*).

Termination of agreement

A hire-purchase agreement can either be terminated in accordance with the terms of the agreement or it may be broken. It is terminated in accordance with its terms if the hire-purchaser exercises his option (essential in the hire-purchase transaction of the normal type) to return the goods to the owner. It is broken if the hire-purchaser defaults on his instalments; often the agreement provides that in this case the owner may terminate the agreement by notice to the hirer. Sometimes the agreement provides that the creditor has the right to terminate it on some event other than a breach of it by the debtor (*e.g.* on the debtor's death or bankruptcy or on his being sent to prison).

In the case of a regulated agreement there are restrictions on the creditor's right of termination. If he wishes to terminate the agreement for some reason other than a breach of it by the debtor, he cannot do so without first serving on the debtor a written notice giving at least seven days warning (ss.76 and 98; see p. 401, *post*). Where the debtor's death is the reason for the creditor wishing to terminate a regulated agreement, he probably will be unable to do so at all (s.86; see p. 402, *post*). Where a breach of the agreement by the debtor is the reason for the creditor wishing to terminate a regulated agreement, he cannot do so without first serving a **default notice** giving the debtor at least seven days warning and allowing the debtor in that time to put right his default (s.87; see p. 401, *post*).

For the debtor who is in arrears (by far the most common breach) and whose agreement is a regulated one, there are three ways in which he can escape the undesirable consequences of termination. First, he can bring his payments up to date by paying off his arrears before the expiry date of the default notice. Secondly, after receiving the default notice, he can apply to the court for a time order allowing him extra time to pay (s.129 and see p. 402, *post*). Thirdly, he may be able to take advantage of the protected goods provisions (see p. 382, *post*) thereby forcing the creditor to sue him in order to recover possession of the goods (or a money sum) and, when sued, he can ask the court to make a time order (s.129; see p. 402, *post*). If the court decides to make a time order, it can thereby alter the whole instalment pattern and extend the repayment period (s.130). If the debtor is unable to avoid the consequences of termination, the creditor in addition to recovering possession of the goods will usually claim a minimum payment or damages.

The minimum payment clause

It is customary for a hire-purchase agreement to contain a minimum payment clause whereby the purchaser undertakes to pay the owner a calculable amount in the event of the agreement being terminated or broken. The economic justification of the minimum payment clause is that, if the owner regains possession of the goods, they have often depreciated in value, particularly if he can resell them only as used and no longer as new goods.

Sometimes, however, the sum fixed by the minimum payment clause is excessive. Here the question arises, whether the contractual rules relating to penalties apply (see p. 181, *ante*).

1. If the hire-purchase agreement is terminated by *breach* on the part of the debtor, it is clear that the distinction between penalties

and liquidated damages applies. It may be recalled that if the fixed amount is a genuine pre-estimate of the damages likely to be suffered, it is treated as liquidated damages and can be recovered irrespective of the actual amount of the damages suffered; but if it is a penalty, it is disregarded and only the actual amount of damages can be recovered (see p. 182, *ante*).

It follows that, if the agreement is terminated by breach, a stipulated minimum payment which is inserted *in terrorem* of the debtor, is a penalty and is not recoverable.

B. acquired a Bedford Dormobile from the finance company on hire-purchase terms. The total hire-purchase price was £482. The deposit was £105 which was accounted for by a car given in part exchange to the value of £95 and a cash payment of £10. The monthly instalments were £10 each. The agreement provided in clause 6 that the debtor might terminate the hiring at any time by giving the creditor written notice of termination, and thereupon the provisions of clause 9 should apply. Clause 9 was the minimum payment clause according to which in case of termination the debtor had to pay all arrears of hire rent and as "agreed compensation for depreciation" two-thirds of the hire-purchase price. After eight weeks B. wrote to the finance company apologising that "owing to unforeseen personal circumstances" he would not be able to pay further instalments and returned the Dormobile. The finance company sued him for £206 which were two-thirds of the purchase price, less the payments received from B. *Held,* (1) the letter by which B. informed the finance company of his unwillingness to pay further instalments was not an exercise of his option under clause 6 but was a notification of his intention to break the agreement; (2) since the agreement was terminated by breach, the rules relating to penalties applied; (3) the minimum payment clause provided a penalty which was not enforceable; (4) the case had to be remitted to the county court to determine the amount of actual damages suffered by the finance company: *Bridge* v. *Campbell Discount Co. Ltd.* [1962] A.C. 600.

2. If the hire-purchase agreement is terminated, not by breach, but by exercise of the debtor's option *in accordance with the terms of the contract,* the position is less clear. Older authorities have held that the rules relating to penalties do not apply in this case because their application presupposes a breach of contract (*Associated Distributors Ltd.* v. *Hall* [1938] 2 K.B. 83). The result would be that the debtor is bound by the minimum payment clause even though the stipulated sum is excessive.

The problem was discussed, *obiter,* in *Bridge's* case (above) in the House of Lords. Viscount Simonds and Lord Morton of Henryton thought that the older cases were decided correctly but Lord Denning and Lord Devlin expressed the view that the rules relating to penalties likewise applied to the termination of the contract in accordance with its terms. While the question thus remains open, there is, it is thought, much strength in Lord Denning's observation that, if the present distinction between breach and termination in accordance with the terms of the contract is maintained, the paradox result is that equity "will grant relief to a man who breaks his contract but penalises the man who keeps it."

In any event, a debtor is not to be taken to exercise his option to terminate the agreement unless he does so consciously knowing of its consequences (*United Dominions Trust* (*Commercial*) *Ltd.* v. *Ennis* [1968] 1 Q.B. 54).

A minimum payment clause which escapes the doctrine of penalties, may nevertheless be caught by the provisions of the Consumer Credit Act relating to extortionate credit agreements. These apply not only to regulated agreements but also to credit agreements involving any amount of credit, provided the debtor is not a body corporate (see p. 402, *post*). Furthermore, in the case of a regulated agreement the Act stipulates the amount payable when the debtor exercises an option to terminate (see p. 381, *post*).

The owner's claim for damages

If the hire-purchase agreement is terminated by a breach on the part of the debtor or by notice of the creditor, after the debtor has committed a breach, and the creditor cannot rely on the minimum payment clause because it stipulates a penalty or he does not wish to rely on it, the question arises what is the measure of damages to which the creditor is entitled. Here there are three possible scenarios:

1. If the breach of contract by the debtor amounts to a *repudiation* of the contract which has been accepted by the creditor, the measure of damages is the loss which the creditor has suffered owing to the debtor's failure to carry out the contract; this loss is due to the debtor's repudiation and not to the retaking of the goods by the creditor (*Yeoman Credit Ltd.* v. *Waragowski* [1961] 1 W.L.R. 1124; *Overstone Ltd.* v. *Shipway* [1962] 1 W.L.R. 117).

Such a repudiation takes place, *e.g.* where the debtor fails to pay several instalments and it is clear that he does not intend to be bound by the contract any longer, or where he writes to the creditor that he cannot or will not make any further payments. *Bridge* v. *Campbell Discount Co. Ltd.* (see p. 378, *ante*) was a case of repudiation.

2. Different from repudiation is the case in which the debtor is slightly in arrear with the instalments but has every intention of upholding the contract and carrying out his obligations. If the creditor terminates the agreement in this situation, as he may well be entitled to under its terms, the measure of damages is only the amount of instalments which the debtor has not paid to the date of termination. In this case the principle applies that "when an agreement of hiring is terminated by virtue of a power contained in it, and the owner retakes the vehicle, he can recover damages for any breach up to the date of termination but not for any breach thereafter, for the simple reason that there are no breaches thereafter" (*per* Lord Denning M.R. in *Financings Ltd.* v. *Baldock,* below).

B. agreed to hire a Bedford truck from the plaintiff finance company. The debtor failed to pay the first two instalments amounting together to £56. The finance company terminated the agreement and repossessed the truck. The debtor told them that he would raise the money in the next three days but he could not do so and the finance company sold the truck. They sued B. for £538, claiming this sum as the loss they had suffered owing to the non-execution of the contract. *Held*, in the present case the contract was not terminated by repudiation on the part of the debtor but by notice by the creditor, following the debtor's failure to pay the rentals, a failure which by itself did not amount to repudiation. Consequently, the finance company was only entitled to recover £56: *Financings Ltd.* v. *Baldock* [1963] 2 Q.B. 104.

3. The third possible scenario is that the contract by its express terms makes prompt payment a condition (*i.e.* as opposed to a warranty) of the contract. The contract will do this if it states that prompt payment of any monies due is "of the essence" of the contract. In that case any breach of the duty to pay on time (*e.g.* if just one instalment is paid just one day late), entitles the other party, the creditor, to treat the contract as if it had been repudiated (*Lombard North Central* v. *Butterworth* [1987] Q.B. 527). If the creditor does so treat it, the appropriate measure of damages is that set out in *Yeoman Credit* v. *Waragowski* (above).

Debtor's statutory right of termination

The debtor under a regulated hire-purchase or conditional sale agreement has a statutory right to terminate the agreement by giving notice to the creditor at anytime before the final payment by the debtor falls due (s.99).[2] In that case the debtor must, as well as returning the goods, pay (s.100):

(a) all arrears of instalments due before termination, and
(b) damages for any loss caused by any failure of the debtor to take reasonable care of the goods, and
(c) the smallest of the three following amounts:
  (i) the amount of the minimum payment stipulated in the agreement (if none is stipulated, this figure is zero),
  (ii) the amount necessary to bring his payments up to half the total hire-purchase price (the total hire-purchase price includes the deposit and all the instalments and the option money payable under the agreement),
  (iii) the loss sustained by the creditor in consequence of the termination.

A conditional sale agreement contained an accelerated payments clause providing that if the debtor failed to make punctual payment of any two or more monthly instalments, the creditor could, by serving notice, cause the whole outstanding balance of the sum financed to become payable if 10 days after service of the notice the debtor still had not paid off the arrears owing. Also payable at the same time would be a reduced sum in respect of finance charges (calculated according to a formula in the clause). The debtor paid the initial deposit but failed to pay any instalments. The creditor served a notice under the accelerated payments clause and 10 days later the debtor still had not paid off the arrears. In defence to an action by the creditor claiming the accelerated payment, the debtor claimed to be able to exercise his statutory right of termination and therefore to be able to pay the (lesser) amount payable after a statutory termination. *Held*, giving judgment for the creditor, the statutory right of termination was, on its wording exercisable only "before the final payment falls due" and where the creditor had served notice under the accelerated payments clause, then, unless the debtor paid off his arrears, the final payment by the debtor fell due 10 days after service of the notice. After that the debtor no longer had a statutory right of termination: *Wadham Stringer Ltd.* v. *Meaney* [1981] 1 W.L.R. 39.

[2] The references on this and the following pages are to the Consumer Credit Act 1974.

An alternative method of premature termination is open to the debtor under a regulated agreement who can afford to pay off all his instalments. He has the right to pay them off early and thereby become the owner of the goods that much earlier as well as earning a rebate of some of his interest charges (ss.94 and 95; see p. 400, *post*).

Protected goods

Goods let under a regulated hire-purchase agreement are protected goods if the debtor is in breach of the agreement and has paid or tendered at least one-third of the total hire-purchase price (s.90). The creditor is not entitled otherwise than by court action to recover possession of protected goods from the debtor. If he does recover possession in contravention of that rule, the agreement is terminated and the debtor is released from all liability under it and can even recover all sums which he has already paid (s.91). In two situations the creditor can recover possession of protected goods without court action and without contravening the rule. First, he can obtain possession of the goods with the debtor's consent provided the consent was given at the time of the repossession (s.173 (3), *Mercantile Credit Co. Ltd.* v. *Cross* [1965] 2 Q.B. 194). Secondly, if the debtor has permanently disposed of the goods to a third party or has abandoned them, the creditor will not be in contravention of the rule if he seizes possession of them. This is because the rule prevents him from obtaining possession only "from the debtor" (s.90).

The debtor paid the deposit and a few instalments. After a crash in which the car was damaged, he left it at a garage but gave no instructions for repairs to be effected. He paid no more instalments and nine months later he had disappeared without trace, having on the last occasion he was contacted given a false telephone number. The creditor, a finance company, took the car from the garage where it had been left nine months earlier. *Held*, the debtor had abandoned the car and, although he had paid more than one-third of the total price, the finance company had not contravened the rule against taking possession from the debtor: *Bentinck Ltd.* v. *Cromwell Engineering Co.* [1971] 1 Q.B. 324.

The hire-purchaser of a car had paid more than one-third of the total price but then fell into arrears. The creditor, a finance company, took possession of the car without his consent. A few hours later, realising their mistake, they took the car back and left it outside the debtor's house. The creditor, treating the hire-purchase contract as being still in force, sued for the outstanding instalments and the return of the car. *Held*, that the hire-purchase agreement had been terminated by the creditor taking possession of the car without a court order and without the consent of the debtor and that the debtor was released from his liability; moreover, he was entitled to a return of the moneys paid by him under the agreement. Further on the facts of the case, the debtor was not liable to the creditor in detinue for not returning the car to them: *Capital Finance Co. Ltd.* v. *Bray* [1964] 1 W.L.R. 323.

The creditor is entitled to take court action to recover possession of protected goods, once the agreement has terminated. However, in that case the court may grant a time order allowing the debtor extra time to pay (see below).

The court's powers in relation to a regulated agreement

Any court action brought by the creditor should be brought in the county court and any guarantor should also be made a party to the proceedings (s.141). The creditor's claim will usually be for possession of the goods together with a money claim for the minimum payment or damages. Broadly speaking, the court has three options as to the order it makes. It may decide to give the debtor extra time to pay and therefore grant him a **time order**, very possibly extending the repayment period (s.129). It may decide not to give extra time and therefore make an **immediate return order** requiring the immediate return of the goods to the creditor (s.133). In this case, the creditor may well ask for the minimum payment or damages as well as the return of the goods. The third possibility open to the court is in an appropriate case to make a **transfer order** (s.133). A transfer order is possible if the goods are divisible and the debtor has paid enough of the total price to cover both the cost of a part of them and also at least one-quarter of the rest of the total price. In that case the court can make a transfer order which (i) allows the debtor to keep as his own the part of the goods for which he has paid, and (ii) requires him to return the rest of the goods to the creditor.

Contracts of guarantee

An ordinary recourse agreement between a finance company and a car dealer, by which the latter undertakes to indemnify the former if the hire-purchaser defaults on the hire-purchase contract, is an indemnity and not a guarantee; consequently the finance company can recover from the dealer under such an agreement the whole amount of damages suffered, and not only the equivalent of the instalments with which the hire-purchaser was in arrear before the termination of the hire-purchase contract (*Goulston Discount Co. Ltd.* v. *Clark,* below).

A customer, through the defendant car dealer, entered into a hire-purchase agreement with the plaintiff finance company in respect of a Jaguar car. The total hire-purchase price was £458. The plaintiffs paid the dealer £300 and the latter gave the customer credit for £100 for an old car taken in part exchange. The dealer then signed a recourse agreement in respect of the Jaguar by which he undertook to indemnify the plaintiffs against any loss which they might suffer if the customer did not pay the total hire-purchase price. The customer paid the first two or three instalments and then defaulted. The plaintiffs retook the Jaguar and resold it for £155. They claimed £157 from the dealer under the recourse agreement. If that agreement was a guarantee, they were entitled to claim from the customer only £74, *viz.* the instalments due prior to the termination of the hire-purchase agreement, by virtue of the rule in *Financings Ltd.* v. *Baldock* [1963] 2 Q.B. 104, and the dealer, who would only be liable for the amount recoverable from the customer as principal debtor, would only be liable in that amount. But if the recourse agreement was an indemnity, the dealer was liable for the whole of the £157. *Held,* the recourse agreement was an indemnity: *Goulston Discount Co. Ltd.* v. *Clark* [1967] 2 Q.B. 493.

Where the principal credit agreement (*i.e.* the hire-purchase agreement) is a regulated agreement, certain contracts of guarantee and indemnity are subject to provisions of the Consumer Credit Act. They are those contracts of guarantee or indemnity which are entered by the surety (*i.e.* the guarantor or indemnifier) at the request, express or implied, of the debtor. A recourse agreement would therefore not be affected since it is not entered at the request of the debtor, whereas a contract of guarantee or indemnity entered by the debtor's friend or relative would be. Those agreements that are affected are subject to the following rules:

1. Unless the hire-purchase agreement is in the prescribed form and the contract of guarantee or indemnity is in the prescribed form and unless copies of both have been given to the surety, the contract of guarantee or indemnity can be enforced against the surety only if the court considers it fair and just that it should be (ss.105 and 127, see p. 403, *post*).

2. The agreement cannot be enforced against the surety to any extent greater than the hire-purchase agreement is enforceable against the debtor (s.113, see p. 403, *post*).

Conditional sale and credit sale agreements

The provisions of the Consumer Credit Act 1974 apply to conditional sale agreements in exactly the same way as they apply to hire-purchase contracts. Thus, the debtor's statutory right of termination is the same in both cases, as are the protected goods provisions and court's power to grant time orders, return orders and transfer orders. Credit sale agreements are not treated in the same way. They are subject to most of the Act's provisions, including the formality and cancellation provisions but the debtor has no statutory right of termination and, since ownership is transferred to the debtor at the time the contract is made, the creditor has no right to recover possession of the goods if the debtor falls into arrears. It follows that the protected goods and return order and transfer order provisions have no application to agreements other than hire-purchase and conditional sale agreements. Also it is only with respect to hire-purchase and conditional sale agreements that the court, in making a time order, can allow extra time for the payments which have not yet fallen due (*e.g.* by extending the future instalments to later dates) (s.130).

HIRE-PURCHASE ACT 1964

The provisions of this Act which are not repealed relate to the protection of a private purchaser of a motor vehicle which is subject to a hire-purchase or conditional sale agreement. These provisions apply even if the private purchaser is a company and even if the hire-purchase or conditional sale agreement involved credit in excess of the statutory limit for the application of the Consumer Credit Act.

Protection of private purchaser of motor vehicle

A private purchaser who can claim this protection is a purchaser who is not a car dealer or a car finance house (s.29(2) of the Act of 1964). A car dealer does not obtain the protection even if he is buying the vehicle for his own private purposes and not for his business purposes (*Stevenson* v. *Beverley Bentinck Ltd.* [1976] 1 W.L.R. 483). The protection is available where the debtor under a hire-purchase agreement or conditional sale agreement disposes of a motor vehicle, before the payment of the price and the transfer of property to him, to a private purchaser who acquires it in good faith and without notice of the hire-purchase or conditional sale agreement. In that case the disposition has effect as if the debtor had the title to the vehicle immediately before the disposition; in other words, the title of the purchaser is protected against a claim by the creditor (s.27(2) of the Act of 1964).

The provisions of the Act aimed at the protection of the private purchaser of a motor vehicle do not affect the civil or criminal liability of a debtor who sells the vehicle contrary to the contractual obligations which he has undertaken to the creditor (s.27(6) of the Act of 1964).

Chapter 17

CONSUMER CREDIT

The Consumer Credit Act 1974 was passed in the wake of the Report in 1971 (Cmnd. 4569) of the Crowther Committee on Consumer Credit and it effected a wide-ranging reform of the law. Its scheme is to bring under one Act all forms of consumer credit. Thus, it repealed certain earlier Acts which dealt with particular forms of credit, the Pawnbrokers Acts 1872 and 1960, Money-lenders Acts 1900 to 1927, Hire-Purchase Act 1965 and Advertisements (Hire-Purchase) Act 1967. However, two earlier enactments remain—the Hire-Purchase Act 1964, Pt. III (see p. 385, *ante*) and the Bills of Sales Acts 1878 and 1882 (see p. 518, *post*). Much of the new Act was modelled on the Hire-Purchase Act 1965. It did not so much alter the general structure of the statutory law relating to hire-purchase as improve it and extend it to all other forms of consumer credit. The transactions which are governed by it therefore include: loans by finance companies and banks, bank overdrafts, credit card agreements, *e.g.* Barclaycard and Access, which allow the holder to pay off the debt in instalments, credit sale agreements, conditional sale agreements, hire-purchase agreements, check trading agreements and certain rental agreements, *e.g.* of television sets.

The Act introduces a whole new range of terminology. In particular, the **creditor** is the person who provides the finance and who is to be repaid, *e.g.* the bank or finance company, and the **debtor** is the customer, the borrower, the person who is to do the repaying. Where the terms **owner** and **hirer** are used, reference is being made not to the parties to a hire-purchase agreement but only to the parties to certain rental agreements, termed by the Act consumer hire agreements (see pp. 389–390, *post*).

A framework is provided by the Act, but many details are provided by regulations under the Act. Unless otherwise indicated, references to the Act and to sections are references to the Consumer Credit Act 1974 and to sections of it.

Director-General of Fair Trading

The Director General is given additional functions (s.1). These include administering the licensing system (see p. 392, *post*), superintending the working and enforcement of the Act and keeping under review developments in the field of consumer credit at home and abroad.

Agreements Within the Act

Regulated agreements

Agreements regulated by the Act fall into two categories, **consumer credit agreements** and **consumer hire agreements**. Such agreements, provided they are not exempt agreements (s.16), are **regulated agreements.** A consumer credit agreement is an agreement by which the creditor provides an individual (the debtor) with credit not exceeding a specified figure (s.8). The specified figure was increased to £15,000 for agreements made on or after May 20, 1985. "Credit" includes a cash loan and "any other form of financial accommodation" (s.9(1)). An agreement where the debtor is a company or other body corporate is not a consumer credit agreement because such a body is not an individual. An unincorporated body, *e.g.* a partnership, is treated as an individual (s.189(1)). Consumer credit agreements include all those types of agreements mentioned earlier in this chapter, except for rental agreements (which fall within the definition of consumer hire agreements). However, no agreement is a consumer credit agreement if the credit exceeds the specified figure and for this purpose a distinction has to be made between **fixed-sum credit** and **running-account credit** (s.10). Fixed-sum credit is one where the actual amount of the credit is fixed from the start, *e.g.* a single loan of £100. It is still a fixed-sum credit if it is to be received or repaid in instalments. Thus credit sale, conditional sale and hire-purchase agreements are all examples of fixed-sum credit agreements. A fixed-sum credit agreement is within the specified limit if the *credit* does not exceed the specified figure. The credit is the capital amount borrowed. It does not include anything else, such as the deposit or interest (or "finance") charges on the advance. The latter are part of the total charge for credit (s.20) and are not part of the credit itself (s.9(4)). In the case of fixed-sum credit the relevant figure is the credit, not what it costs to have it.

Example: C. agrees to let D. (an individual) have possession of a car in return for periodical payments. The agreement provides for the property in the goods to pass to D. on payment of a total of £17,500 and the exercise by D. of an option to purchase. The sum of £17,500 includes a down payment of £1,000 and includes also finance charges amounting to £1,500. The price for which D. could have bought the car for cash was £16,000. The agreement is made after May 20, 1985.

This agreement is one which provides fixed-sum credit of exactly £15,000 (*i.e.* £17,500–(£1,500 + £1,000)). It is therefore a consumer credit agreement (Example 10, Schedule 2 to the Act).

A running-account credit is credit the amount of which is not fixed by the agreement, though the agreement may (in fact it usually will) fix a credit limit, *i.e.* a maximum to the amount to which the debtor's debit balance is allowed to rise. An agreement by which a bank authorises its customer to overdraw if he needs or wishes to do so, is an example. Another is the credit card agreement which allows the debtor to keep using his card to obtain credit provided his total indebtedness under the agreement does not exceed his credit limit. A running-account credit agreement is within the specified limit, *i.e.* it is a consumer credit agreement, if the debtor's credit limit does not exceed the specified figure (s.10(3)). If there is a term of the agreement allowing the credit limit to be exceeded merely temporarily, it is disregarded and the agreement is still within the definition (s.10(2)). If there is no credit limit or if the credit limit exceeds the specified figure, the agreement is still within the definition: (i) if there is a limit of £15,000 or less to the amount of credit (ignoring finance charges) that can be drawn on any one occasion; or (ii) if the finance charges become more onerous on the debtor's indebtedness exceeding a figure of £15,000 or less; or (iii) if it is probable that his indebtedness will not exceed £15,000 (s.10(3)).

A consumer hire agreement is one which provides for the hire of goods, is capable of lasting more than three months and does not require the hirer to make payments exceeding a specified figure of £15,000 (s.15). An agreement where the hirer is a body corporate is not within the definition. Neither is any hire-purchase agreement because a hire-purchase agreement falls within the definition of a consumer credit agreement.

A consumer credit agreement or a consumer hire agreement which is an exempt agreement is not regulated by the Act (s.16). By way of exception to that, the court has power to re-open extortionate credit bargains if they are exempt agreements (s.16(7) and see p. 402, *post*). Agreements where credit is secured on land, *i.e.* mortgage agreements, and granted by a local authority or building society, are exempt (s.16(1)). The Secretary of State has made orders exempting land mortgages granted by certain other bodies. These exemptions so far mentioned apply only to mortgage agreements which provide the finance for the buying of land or of dwellings on land already owned (s.16(2)). Also exempt are: certain low-cost consumer credit agreements where the rate of interest is below a certain level; certain consumer credit agreements where the number of repayments does not exceed four; consumer hire agreements for the hire of telephones and gas and electricity meters.

Sub-categories of consumer credit agreement

A regulated consumer credit agreement is either a restricted-use credit agreement or an unrestricted-use credit agreement (s.11). It falls within the latter category if the credit is in fact provided in such a way as to leave the debtor free to use it as he chooses. Thus a bank loan will usually be an example of an unrestricted-use credit unless for example the loan agreement is for the loan to finance a particular transaction and the loan is provided in such a way that it could be used by the debtor only for that transaction. Hire-purchase, conditional sale and credit sale agreements are all restricted-use credit agreements.

A regulated consumer credit agreement is either a **debtor-creditor-supplier agreement** (s.12) or a **debtor-creditor agreement** (s.13). It will fall into the first category:

(a) if it is a restricted-use credit agreement where the creditor and supplier are in fact the same person, *e.g.* where the retailer enters as creditor into a hire-purchase agreement with the customer (the debtor); or
(b) if it is a restricted-use credit agreement "made by the creditor under pre-existing arrangements, or in contemplation of

future arrangements, between himself and the supplier," *e.g.* where a customer buys goods from a shop and, instead of paying cash, makes payment by using his Access credit card; or

(c) if it is an unrestricted-use credit agreement made by the creditor under pre-existing arrangements between himself and the supplier in the knowledge that the credit is to be used to finance a transaction between the debtor and supplier, *e.g.* where the supplier sells the goods directly to the customer for cash but does so only after having put the customer in touch with a firm (the creditor) with which the supplier had a relationship and which agreed to lend the customer the money for this purpose.

Where part of an agreement falls into a category of agreement defined in the Act and part either does not do so or else falls within a different category of agreement mentioned in the Act, the whole agreement is a **multiple agreement**, the two parts of it being treated as separate agreements (s.18).

Example: A. issues to B. (an individual) a credit card for use in obtaining goods or cash from suppliers or banks who have agreed to honour credit cards issued by A. The credit limit is £300.

This is a consumer credit agreement for running-account credit. So far as it relates to goods it provides restricted-use credit and it is a debtor-creditor-supplier agreement. So far as it relates to cash it provides unrestricted-use credit and is a debtor-creditor agreement. It is therefore a multiple agreement (based on Example 16, Sched. 2 to the Act).

The reason for the distinction between debtor-creditor-supplier agreements and debtor-creditor agreements is that the former are agreements where there is some business connection between the creditor and the supplier. In that case the creditor as well as the supplier will often be answerable to the debtor for defects in the goods or services provided by the supplier (see p. 398, *post*).

Further definitions

A **small agreement** is a regulated agreement (other than a hire-purchase or conditional sale agreement) for the provision of credit not exceeding a specified figure of £50 (s.17). The rules for determining whether an agreement is within this limit are similar to those in relation to the £15,000 limit, (see p. 388, *ante*). Thus a fixed-sum credit agreement will not be a small agreement if the amount of *credit* exceeds the specified £50 figure, whereas a running-account credit agreement will not be a small agreement if the *credit limit* exceeds that figure. A **non-commercial agreement** is a consumer credit or consumer hire agreement not made by the creditor or owner in the course of any business carried on by him (s.189(1)). Many small agreements and non-commercial agreements are not subject to certain provisions of the Act, in particular the formality and cancellation provisions (see p. 394, *post*).

Licensing and Seeking Business

Licensing

Part III of the Act (ss.21–42) established a comprehensive system of licensing for those who conduct business dealing with regulated agreements. There are two types of businesses which need to be licensed. They are, first, consumer credit businesses and consumer hire businesses and, secondly, ancillary businesses. Into the first category falls someone who carries on a business which provides under regulated agreements either credit or goods on hire. Thus, not only must finance companies be licensed but so also, *e.g.* must the ordinary retailer who enters into credit sale, conditional sale or hire-purchase agreements with some of his customers, thereby providing them with credit. The second category, ancillary businesses, comprises (s.145(1)) the businesses of credit brokerage, debt-adjusting, debt-counselling, debt-collecting and operating a credit reference agency. Thus, the retailer who does not enter into credit agreements with his customers but who instead arranges finance for them through the familiar triangular transaction (see p. 368, *ante*) must be licensed as a credit-broker, *i.e.* someone effecting introductions of potential customers to someone carrying on a consumer credit business. Mortgage or finance brokers also need to be licensed as credit-brokers. Debt-counselling is giving advice to debtors or hirers about the liquidation of debts due under consumer credit or consumer hire agreements. Thus, solicitors require a licence. Businesses which do more than counselling or advising, which negotiate with the creditor on behalf of the debtor or which will actually take over the debt and pay it off for the customer (usually giving the customer longer time in which to pay them off) need to be licensed as debt-adjusters. Persons carrying on a business of procuring payment of debts due under consumer credit or consumer hire agreements need to be licensed as debt-collectors. Credit reference agencies are businesses which collect and then provide (usually to finance companies) information about the financial standing of individuals. A business is not, however, within the statutory definition of a credit reference agency unless the information it provides about the financial standing of individuals was information collected by the agency for that purpose. Thus, although a bank will provide financial references upon its customers, the bank is not thereby a credit reference agency.

The Director General of Fair Trading is responsible for administering the licensing system. He has powers to vary, suspend, renew and withdraw licences and can thereby clamp down on malpractices. Anyone who without a licence carries on a business requiring one, commits an offence (s.39). A regulated agreement made by an unlicensed business (s.40) or after an introduction by an unlicensed credit-broker (s.149) will generally be unenforceable against the customer. Similarly, any agreement for the services of an unlicensed ancillary business will be unenforceable against the client (s.148). In each of these cases, someone who is unable to enforce agreements can apply to the Director General for an order allowing the agreements to be enforced.

Advertising and canvassing

An advertiser of credit commits an offence if his advertisement:

(a) infringes regulations made under section 44. These regulations are designed to achieve truth in lending and contain detailed provisions in order to ensure that any advertisement either contains a fair and reasonably comprehensive indication of the nature of the credit or hire facilities advertised or else indicates that such information is available;

(b) advertises the supply of goods or services on credit when those goods or services are not also available for cash (s.45); or

(c) is false or misleading in a material respect (s.46). Further offences are: sending someone under 18 a document inviting him to seek information about credit or to obtain credit (s.50); issuing an unsolicited credit-token (*e.g.* a credit card) other than as a renewal or replacement (s.51); infringing regulations as to the contents and form of a quotation of credit terms (s.52); failing to comply with regulations as to information to be displayed at premises of credit businesses (s.53).

It is an offence to canvass debtor-creditor agreements off trade premises (s.49). This is to prevent the doorstep "selling" or ordinary loans and second mortgages. The offence would be committed for example if the canvasser without being requested in writing to do so, deliberately visited someone at the person's home and tried to persuade him to apply for debtor-creditor credit. It is not an offence to canvass debtor-creditor-supplier agreements, provided the canvasser is acting under a licence which specifically authorises that activity (s.23). It is an offence to canvass off trade premises someone to make use of the services of a credit-broker, debt-adjuster or debt-counsellor (s.154).

Rights and Obligations Between the Parties

Section 173 prevents the parties contracting out of the protection provided by the Act for the debtor or hirer.

Formalities

A creditor or owner under a regulated agreement can enforce the agreement only if it satisfies certain statutory requirements (in ss.60–65). Non-commercial agreements, certain small agreements and certain bank overdraft agreements are exempt from the formalities requirements (s.74).

(a) All the terms, other than implied terms, of the agreement must be embodied in the written agreement (or in another document referred to in the written agreement) (s.61(1)(*b*)). All the terms of the written agreement must be readily legible (s.61(1)(*c*)). It must contain details of the debtor's right, if any, of cancellation (s.64)(1)(*a*)). It must comply with regulations as to its form and contents, *e.g.* requiring it to indicate the names and addresses of the parties, the amounts and due dates of payments required of the debtor, the true cost of the credit. Regulations are made under section 60.

(b) The agreement must be signed by the customer (*i.e.* the debtor or hirer) in person and by or on behalf of the creditor or owner (s.61(1)(*a*)).

(c) The customer must receive one copy of the agreement when he is given or sent the agreement to sign (ss.62(1) and 63(1)). If, as is common, the agreement is not actually made when he signs it, then he must be given a second copy later (s.63 (2)). The agreement will not be made on the occasion of his signing it, if it is in the form of a proposal or offer by him which is sent to (or left with) the creditor or owner for him to decide whether to accept it. That is the situation in the common triangular hire-purchase transaction (see p. 368, *ante*). The agreement is made when the offer is accepted, *i.e.* often on the posting of an acceptance addressed to the customer. The second copy must be given to the customer within seven days of the making of the agreement (s.63(2)). In the case of a cancellable agreement it must be sent by post (s.63(3)). In the case of a credit-token agreement (*e.g.* a credit card or trading check agreement) the second copy is given in time if it is given before or at the time the credit-token is given to the customer (s.63(4)). Further, each time a new credit-token is given to the customer, a copy of the agreement must also be given to him (s.85).

(d) In the case of a prospective regulated agreement which is proposed to be secured by a mortgage on land, the customer must receive a copy of the agreement at least seven clear days before he is sent by post the actual agreement for him to sign (s.61(2)). During that time and for a further period of seven days the prospective creditor must stay away from the customer so as to allow him a consideration period free from sales pressure. The only situation in which he may do so is if during the consideration period the customer specifically asks the creditor to contact him. These rules, however, do not apply where the customer wants the credit to buy the land which it is proposed to mortgage or for a bridging loan in connection with the purchase of land.

In an action the court may grant dispensation with most of these requirements if it is just and fair to do so in the light of the degree to which the customer has been prejudiced by the failure to comply with them and the degree of culpability of the creditor or owner (s.127). There are similar requirements as to the contents, form, copies and signatures on security agreements (*e.g.* of guarantee and indemnity) entered by or at the request of the customer (s.105).

Cancellation

Certain regulated agreements are cancellable by the customer (ss.67–73). The object of this right is to allow him a short **cooling off period** to think over the concluded bargain and, on second thoughts, to rescind it. The agreement is cancellable (s.67) if, (i) the antecedent negotiations included oral representations by the creditor or owner or the dealer made in the customer's presence, and, (ii) the customer signed the agreement elsewhere than at certain trade premises (*i.e.* the trade premises of persons such as the creditor or owner or, in the case of a debtor-creditor-supplier agreement, the dealer). Thus, the agreement could be cancellable if the customer signed it in the street, at home or at his own trade premises provided oral representations had been made in his presence. An agreement is not cancellable if it is not subject to the formalities requirements (see p. 394, *ante*) or if it involves a land mortgage or finance to purchase land (or bridging finance for such a purpose).

The cooling off period begins at the time of the customer's signature and lasts until the end of the fifth clear day after he receives his second copy of the agreement (s.68). He cancels the agreement if during that time he gives (or posts) to the creditor or owner (or, in the case of a debtor-creditor-supplier agreement, the dealer) a written notice to that effect (s.69).

The effect of cancellation depends upon whether the agreement was, on the one hand, a debtor-creditor-supplier agreement for restricted-use credit or consumer hire agreement or, on the other hand, a debtor-creditor or unrestricted-use credit agreement. The first category includes all hire-purchase, conditional sale and credit sale agreements. Here the effect is that the customer is entitled to recover payments already made (s.70). He is obliged to return the goods, but he need not take them back; he can wait until they are collected from him in pursuance of a written request (s.72); he has a lien on them for the return of his payments (s.70(2)); he has to take reasonable care of the goods for 21 days after serving his notice of cancellation. By way of exception to what has just been said, the customer is under no duty to return perishable goods, goods supplied to meet an emergency or goods which before cancellation were consumed or incorporated in something else (*e.g.* plants in a garden or spare parts in a car). In two of these cases, namely, where goods or services were supplied to meet an emergency or where the customer has incorporated goods into something else, the customer is liable after cancellation to pay for those goods or services (s.69(2)).

The effect of cancellation is different in the case of an agreement in the second category (*e.g.* an ordinary loan). Here, the customer must repay (usually with interest) any credit he had already received, though he does not have to pay any interest on any of the credit which he repays within one month of cancellation (s.71).

Note that the *Consumer Protection (Cancellation of Contracts Concluded away from Business Premises) Regulations 1987* have created a similar cooling off and cancelling regime for other (*i.e.* cash) contracts made on the doorstep (see generally, p. 29, *ante*).

Credit reference agencies

Someone who is refused credit may wonder if he has been blacklisted by a credit reference agency. Certain courses of action are open (ss.157–159). He is entitled to discover from any creditor or owner to whom he has applied to enter a regulated agreement, the name and address of any credit reference agency consulted (s.157). He is entitled on making a written request and a payment of £1 to demand from any credit reference agency a copy of the file that that agency has on him (s.158). He can then take steps, if necessary, to add a correction to the file (s.159).

Dealer as agent of creditor

A negotiator in antecedent negotiations is deemed in conducting those operations to be the creditor's agent (s.56). There are two such types of section 56 agent. First, there is the credit-broker negotiating with the customer in relation to goods sold or proposed to be sold by the credit-broker to the creditor before forming the subject-matter of a debtor-creditor-supplier agreement. Into this category falls the dealer in the common triangular hire-purchase transaction (for fuller account see p. 374, *ante*). Secondly, there is the supplier negotiating with the customer in relation to a transaction to be financed by a debtor-creditor-supplier agreement. Into this category falls the retailer negotiating with a customer who is proposing to pay with his Access card or Barclaycard. The antecedent negotiations include any representations made by the negotiator to the customer and any other dealings between them (s.56). The effect of the negotiator being an agent of the creditor is to make the creditor liable for misrepresentations made by the negotiator as if the creditor had made them; also any money paid by the customer to the negotiator will be regarded as received by the creditor. The negotiator is also the creditor's agent for the purpose of receiving certain written notices from the customer: notice withdrawing an offer to enter a regulated agreement (s.57); notice of cancellation of the regulated agreement (s.69); notice rescinding the regulated agreement (s.102).

"Any person who, in the course of a business carried on by him, acts (or acted) on behalf of the debtor or hirer in any negotiations for the agreement" is not, unless he falls within the definition of a negotiator in antecedent negotiations, generally agent of the creditor or owner. However, he is the agent of the creditor or owner for the purpose of receiving the notices mentioned in the last paragraph. The customer's solicitor who negotiates a loan for him would, for example, fall within this category.

Liability of creditor for supplier's default

Where the customer acquires goods or services from one person (the supplier) and the credit to pay for them from another (the creditor), the latter can be liable in respect of the supplier's default in two situations:

(i) *Where the creditor himself contracts with the customer to supply the customer with the goods or services.* This occurs in the triangular hire-purchase, conditional sale or credit sale transaction. Here the creditor will himself be liable for breach of implied terms as to title, description, quality, etc., in the hire-purchase agreement or contract of sale (see p. 373, *ante*). He will also normally be liable in respect of misrepresentations made by the dealer to the customer (s.56).

(ii) *Where section 75 applies.* This section applies to debtor-creditor-supplier agreements other than those where the creditor himself contracts to supply the goods or services to the customer. If the debtor has a claim against the supplier in respect of a misrepresentation or breach of contract, he has a like claim against the creditor who with the supplier is jointly and severally liable to the debtor (s.75(1)). Thus, if the customer has used a Barclaycard or Access card to pay for goods or services and has a claim against the supplier, he can also or alternatively bring his claim against the credit card company. However, this rule does not apply to any item to which the supplier had attached a cash price which (a) does not exceed a figure of £100 or (b) exceeds a figure of £30,000 (s.75(3)).

A car dealer introduced a prospective customer to a finance company which made a loan contract with the customer to enable the customer to buy a car from the dealer. The finance company commenced proceedings against the debtor to enforce the loan agreement which was a regulated debtor-creditor-supplier agreement. The customer, the debtor, claimed to have a defence because he claimed first that the dealer had induced him to buy by a misrepresentation that the car was in good condition and secondly that the dealer was in breach of a condition in the supply contract (*i.e.* the contract of sale of goods between the customer and the dealer). The customer claimed that because of the alleged misrepresentation and breach of contract, he had a right to rescind his supply contract with the dealer. He claimed that by virtue of the Consumer Credit Act, s.75 he had a like claim to rescind the loan agreement. *Held*, giving judgment for the debtor, section 75 had the effect that if the debtor had a right to rescind the supply contract, he had a like claim to rescind the loan agreement: *United Dominions Trust Ltd.* v. *Taylor* 1980 S.L.T. 28. (Note, this was a controversial decision on the application of section 75 and it is difficult to understand why the customer did not rely upon section 56 to argue that the dealer, in making a misrepresentation, had been agent of the finance company and that therefore the finance company had, through the agency of the dealer, itself made a misrepresentation.)

Misuse of credit facilities

The general rule is that the debtor under a regulated agreement is not liable for any use of credit facilities by another person who is not the debtor's agent or authorised by the debtor to use them (s.83). That rule does not apply in the case of the misuse of a cheque or other negotiable instrument. A further limited exception applies in the case of a credit-token, *e.g.* a trading check or credit card. Here the holder can be liable up to a maximum of £50 on any occasion when he has lost it, although he is not liable for any misuse occurring after he has given the creditor notice (confirmed in writing within seven days) of the loss of the card (s.84). Also the debtor cannot be made liable for any use (*e.g.* if the credit-token is lost in the post before reaching the debtor) made of a credit-token by any person unless the debtor (or his authorised user) had previously accepted the credit-token by signing it, signing a receipt for it or using it (s.66).

Early and late payment by debtor

A debtor under a regulated agreement has the right, after giving written notice to the creditor, to complete his payments ahead of the due time (s.94). He may then qualify for a rebate of his interest charges (regulations to be made under s.95).

Where he is late making payments under the agreement, he may well in accordance with the agreement have to pay extra interest to take account of the delay in payment. However, he cannot be obliged to pay interest at a rate higher than that payable under the agreement as a whole (s.93).

Consumer hire agreements

These agreements are for the most part subject to provisions governing regulated consumer-credit agreements—hence the frequent use of the expressions "creditor or owner" and "debtor or hirer." However, there are some provisions which do not apply to consumer hire agreements, *e.g.* the extortionate credit bargain provisions (see p. 402, *post*) and sections 93 and 94 dealing with early and late payment. On the other hand, certain sections apply only to consumer hire agreements. Thus after 18 months the hirer has, subject to certain exceptions, a statutory right, after giving notice of either three months or of the length of the shortest interval between his rental payments, to terminate the agreement (s.101).

Also, where the owner recovers possession of goods which have been the subject of a consumer hire agreement, the court can grant the hirer financial relief by excusing him from some payments or even requiring some money to be repaid to him (s.132).

Enforcement of Agreement by Creditor or Owner

Any court action by the creditor or owner to enforce a regulated agreement must be brought in the county court and the debtor or hirer and also any surety (guarantor or indemnifier) must be made parties to the action (s.141).

Default and non-default notices

Where the creditor or owner wishes merely to sue for payments already due, he has an unfettered right to commence proceedings. However, if because the debtor or hirer is in breach of the agreement, the creditor or owner wishes;

"(*a*) to terminate the agreement, or
(*b*) to demand earlier payment of any sum, or
(*c*) to recover possession of any goods or land, or
(*d*) to treat any right conferred on the debtor or hirer by the agreement as terminated, restricted or deferred, or
(*e*) to enforce any security,"

he must serve a default notice on the debtor or hirer (s.87). If the creditor or owner wishes to do one of those things for a reason other than a breach of the agreement by the debtor or hirer and if the agreement is one of specified duration (*e.g.* a hire-purchase agreement) he must serve a notice of his intention (ss.76 and 98). These notice requirements do not apply if the creditor merely wishes to prevent the debtor making further drawings of credit (*e.g.* on his credit card). The notice served under one of the above mentioned provisions must give the debtor or hirer at least seven days notice before the creditor or owner can pursue any of the remedies listed above. In the case of a default notice (s.87), the notice must make clear what, if anything, can be done by the debtor or hirer to rectify his breach and if he then does that, the breach is regarded as never having occurred (s.89).

Time orders

If the debtor or hirer has been served with a default or non-default notice or, if any action is brought by the creditor or owner to enforce a regulated agreement, the debtor or hirer can ask the court for a time order (s.129). The court can in making a time order, allow the debtor or hirer extra time to rectify any breach of the agreement and it can allow him extra time to make payments which have already fallen due. Only in the case of hire-purchase and conditional sale agreements (see p. 377, *ante*) can the court alter the pattern of future payments or allow extra time for them to be made. The court can at a later date revoke, vary or extend a time order.

Extortionate credit bargains

The debtor can at any time ask the court to re-open the agreement as being extortionate (ss.137–140). The court's powers to do so, extend to exempt agreements and also to *any* credit agreement where the debtor is not an incorporated body (*i.e.* irrespective of the amount of credit involved). An agreement is extortionate if it requires payments that are grossly extortionate or if it grossly contravenes ordinary principles of fair dealing (s.138). If it finds the agreement extortionate the court has wide powers to alter its terms, even extending to being able to require the repayment to the debtor of sums already paid.

Death of debtor or hirer

In the event of the death of the debtor or hirer, the creditor or owner cannot terminate the agreement if it is of specified duration (*e.g.* a hire-purchase agreement) and is a fully secured agreement (s.86(1)). If it is of specified duration but is not fully secured, he still cannot do so unless the agreement gives him the power to do so and he is able on an application to the court to show that the obligations of the debtor or hirer under the agreement are unlikely to be carried out (s.86(2)). The object is to enable the deceased's relatives to continue with his hire-purchase agreements and other credit and hire agreements of specified duration if they wish to do so. This right does not extend to agreements of unspecified duration (such as credit card agreements).

Security

The creditor or owner cannot enforce any security given by or at the request, express or implied, of the debtor or hirer, to any extent greater than he can enforce the regulated agreement (s.113). Thus for example a guarantor cannot be made to pay an amount from which the debtor has been excused under the extortionate credit provisions. By way of exception, an indemnifier can be made liable when the only reason that the debtor or hirer is not liable is that he is under 18 (s.113(7)).

PART 4: INTERNATIONAL TRADE

CHAPTER 18

THE INTERNATIONAL SALE OF GOODS

IN the international sale of goods, the use of special trade terms is customary. These trade terms, though universally used, have sometimes a different meaning in various countries with respect to the obligations of the seller and the buyer. In order to avoid a misunderstanding between the parties to the contract and to promote uniformity of law, the International Chamber of Commerce has published "Incoterms," the present edition of which is dated 1990. **Incoterms** apply to a contract of international sale of goods only if the parties have incorporated them into their contract. Incoterms 1990 are frequently adopted by the parties.

The present edition of Incoterms lists the following special trade terms:

ex works (the seller's works, factory or warehouse, where the goods are situate);
free carrier (named point);
f.a.s. (free alongside; named port of shipment);
f.o.b. (free on board; named port of shipment;
c.f.r. (cost and freight; named port of destination);
c.i.f. (cost, insurance and freight; named port of destination);
c.p.t. (carriage paid to; named port of destination);
d.a.f. (delivered at frontier, named place of delivery at frontier. This clause can only be used in terrestrial sales and the two countries separated by the frontier should be indicated);
d.e.s. (delivered ex ship; named port of destination);
d.e.q. (delivered ex quay; duty paid by the seller or duty on buyers account, according to the agreement of the parties);
d.d.u. (delivered duty unpaid; named port of destination);
d.d.p. (delivered duty paid; named port of destination in country of importation).

The trade term "free carrier" under the 1990 Incoterms refers to f.o.b. in ordinary sea transport, f.o.r. (free on rail) for rail transport, and f.o.t. (free on truck) for ordinary truck transport.

The adoption of any of these trade terms indicates at which point the delivery of the goods shall take place. Sometimes the trade terms indicate the calculation of the purchase price and the incidental charges included in it.

F.o.b. contracts

In an f.o.b. contract it is the duty of the seller to place the goods over the ship's rail and to deposit them on board the ship. The contract of carriage by sea has to be made by, or on behalf of, the buyer, and the cost of freight and likewise of insurance has to be borne by the buyer if the buyer wishes to insure the goods.

There are two types of f.o.b. contracts, the strict or classic type and the f.o.b. contract providing for additional services. Under the **strict f.o.b. contract** the arrangements for shipment and, if he so wishes, for insurance are made by the buyer direct. He is a party to the contracts of carriage by sea and marine insurance, if he insures the goods in transit. Under this type of contract the buyer has to name to the seller an effective ship, *i.e.* a ship ready, willing and able to carry the goods away from the port of shipment within the stipulated shipping time. If the buyer fails to nominate an effective ship, the seller cannot make such nomination. In this case the seller's remedy is an action for damages for non-acceptance of the goods but not an action for the price: *Colley* v. *Overseas Exporters* [1921] 3 K.B. 302; *Petraco (Bermuda) Ltd.* v. *Petromed International S.A.* [1988] 2 Lloyd's Rep. 357.

In an **f.o.b. contract with additional services** the parties have agreed that the arrangements for the carriage by sea and insurance shall be made by the seller, but for and on behalf of the buyer and for his account. If after the conclusion of the contract of sale these charges are increased, the buyer has to bear the increase. If the seller has paid the increased charges, he is entitled to have them refunded by the buyer.

In all types of f.o.b. contracts the cost of putting the goods on board ship have to be borne by the seller. Delivery is complete when the goods are put on board ship. The risk of accidental loss under section 20(1) of the Sale of Goods Act 1979 passes to the buyer when the seller has placed the goods safely on board ship. The seller should give notice of the shipment to the buyer so as to enable him to insure; if the seller fails to do this, the goods will be at his risk: *Wimble, Sons & Co.* v. *Rosenberg & Sons* [1931] 3 K.B. 743, holding that section 32(3) of the Sale of Goods Act 1979 applies to f.o.b. contracts.

Unless the parties otherwise agree, the property in goods sold under an f.o.b. contract passes to the buyer when the goods are placed on board ship.

A company in Costa Rica bought from an English company 85 bicycles f.o.b. British port and paid the purchase price in advance. The bicycles were packed into cases, which were marked with the buyer's name and registered for shipment in a named ship that was to load them at Liverpool. The cases containing the bicycles had not yet been sent to the port. A receiver and manager was appointed for the sellers. *Held*, the property in the bicycles had not yet passed to the buyers; *Carlos Federspiel & Co. S.A.* v. *Charles Twigg & Co. Ltd.* [1957] 1 Lloyd's Rep. 240.

Where the seller has taken out a bill of lading, as will always be the case where the contract is on f.o.b. terms with additional services, the common intention of the parties is that property in the goods shall pass on the delivery of the bill of lading unless the facts disclose a different intention as illustrated in *Mitsui & Co. Ltd.* v. *Flota, Mercante Grancolombiana S.A.* [1988] 2 Lloyd's Rep. 208; the Court of Appeal held that according to the intention of the parties, the passing of the property was postponed until the balance of the purchase price was paid.

There is no general rule that, in the absence of a specific provision in an f.o.b. contract, the duty of obtaining an export licence falls on the buyer: the obligation depends in each case on the construction of the contract and the surrounding circumstances and, if there are no indications to the contrary, this obligation will fall on the seller (*A. V. Pound and Co. Ltd.* v. *M. W. Hardy and Co. Inc.* [1956] A.C. 588).

C.i.f. contracts

The central feature of the c.i.f. contract is that this contract is performed by the seller by delivery of the **shipping documents** to the buyer, and not by delivery of the goods. The normal shipping documents are:

(a) the bill of lading, representing the contract of carriage by sea;
(b) the insurance policy or certificate, representing the contract of marine insurance; and
(c) the invoice, representing the contract of sale.

The c.i.f. contract has been described by McNair J. in *Gardano and Giampieri* v. *Greek Petroleum George Mamidakis & Co.* [1962] 1 W.L.R. 40, 52 as a contract in which "the seller discharges his obligations as regards delivery by tendering a bill of lading covering the goods." The c.i.f. price includes the freight and insurance premium. If there is an increase in these charges, the seller must bear them. The cost of unloading and the import duties have to be borne by the buyer. Under the c.i.f. contract, it is immaterial whether the goods arrive safely at the port of destination. If they are lost or damaged in transit, the marine insurance policy should cover the loss or damage and, by the virtue of the transfer of the bill of lading and the insurance policy, the buyer has direct contractual claims against the shipowner or the insurer.

The duties of a seller under such a contract are:

1. To ship at the port of shipment goods of the description contained in the contract.

2. To procure a contract of carriage by sea, under which the goods will be delivered at the destination contemplated by the contract.

3. To arrange for an insurance upon the terms current in the trade which will be available for the benefit of the buyer.

4. To make out an invoice of the goods.

5. To tender, within a reasonable time after shipment, the bill of lading, the policy or certificate of insurance and the invoice to the buyer so that the buyer may obtain delivery of the goods, if they arrive, or recover for their loss, if they are lost on the voyage (Hamilton J. in *Biddell Bros.* v. *E. Clemens Horst Co.* [1911] 1 K.B. 214). The bill of lading tendered must correctly state the date of shipment, otherwise the buyer can reject the goods (*Finlay* v. *Kwik Hoo Tong* [1929] 1 K.B. 400).

Under a c.i.f. contract the buyer has a right to reject the documents and also a right to reject the goods. These two rights are quite distinct.

B. sold goods to K. who were merchants, shipment to be made by October

31. The goods were shipped on November 3. The date of shipment shown on the bill of lading was forged to show a shipment in October, but B. was ignorant of and not a party to the forgery. In ignorance of the forgery K. paid the price and received the documents, but before the goods arrived K. discovered it. K. took delivery, but as the market had fallen was unable to sell the goods. *Held*, (i) the bill of lading, though forged, was not a nullity as the forgery did not go to the essence of the contract; (ii) K., although he had not rejected the documents, still had a right to reject the goods and could recover the difference between the contract price and the market price; *Kwei Tek Chao* v. *British Traders & Shippers Ltd.* [1954] 2 Q.B. 459.

But if the buyer accepts the documents, knowing that they are not in order, he is estopped from later trying to reject them.

P. sold a quantity of Brazilian yellow maize to E. The contract was c.i.f. Antwerp and provided that shipment had to take place from Brazilian ports "during the period of June/July 1965" and that "bill of lading to be considered proof of date of shipment in the absence of evidence to the contrary." The goods were, in fact, shipped on August 11 and 12, 1965 but the bill of lading was antedated and, falsely, gave as the date of shipment July 31, 1965. However, a certificate of shipment issued by a superintendent company in Brazil stated as date of shipment August 10 to 12, 1965, and this certificate was tendered together with the bill of lading. *Held*, by taking up the documents and paying for them, the buyers were aware that the goods were shipped later than provided in the contract and were estopped from complaining of the late shipment or the defect of the bill of lading: *Panchaud Frères S.A.* v. *Etablissement General Grain Co.* [1970] 1 Lloyd's Rep. 53.

The duties of the c.i.f. buyer are:

(a) to pay the price, less the freight, on delivery of the documents. He cannot defer payment until after he has inspected the goods (*Clemens Horst Co.* v. *Biddell Bros.* [1912] A.C. 18);
(b) to pay the cost of unloading, lighterage and landing at the port of destination according to the bill of lading; and
(c) to pay all import duties and wharfage charges, if any.

During the voyage the goods are at the risk of the buyer. This risk will in ordinary cases be covered by the insurance, but if the goods are lost from a peril not covered by the ordinary policy of insurance current in trade, the buyer must nevertheless pay the full price on delivery of the documents.

B. sold to G. 100 bales of cloth on c.i.f. terms. B. shipped the goods insuring them under a policy which did not cover war risks. There was no custom of the trade that the seller should insure against war risks. The ship carrying the goods was sunk by a German cruiser. *Held*, G. was bound to pay the price on tender of the shipping documents, notwithstanding that the policy did not cover the risk by which the goods were lost: *C. Groom Ltd.* v. *Barber* [1915] 1 K.B. 316.

Even if the seller knows that the goods have been lost at the time the shipping documents are tendered, he can still compel the buyer to take and pay for them (*Manbre Co.* v. *Corn Products Co.* [1919] 1 K.B. 198).

The property passes when the documents are taken up by the buyer, but "what the buyer obtains, when the title under the documents is given to him, is the property in the goods, subject to the conditions that they revest if upon examination he finds them to be not in accordance with the contract" (*per* Devlin J. in *Kwei Tek Chao* v. *British Traders and Shippers Ltd.*, *ante* [1954] 2 Q.B. 459 at p. 487). If, however, the goods are not ascertained at the time the documents are taken up, no property in the goods will pass until the goods become ascertained.

Swedish buyers bought 6,000 tons of copra under four identical contracts which provided for delivery c.i.f. Karlshamn, Sweden. The goods were carried in *The Elafi*, which carried altogether 22,000 tons of copra in bulk, 16,000 tons having been sold to other buyers. The 16,000 tons sold to the other buyers were unloaded in intermediate ports (Rotterdam and Hamburg), so that only the quantity bought by the Swedish buyers remained on board *The Elafi*. Part of the cargo purchased by them was damaged on discharge in Sweden by the negligence of the shipowners. The buyers sued the shipowners for the tort of negligence. The shipowners claimed that, at the time of the damage to the cargo, the buyers had no title to the cargo and therfore could not sue in negligence. *Held*, (i) the goods became ascertained by exhaustion when discharge was completed in Hamburg because the buyers could then say that all the copra on board was destined for them; (ii) property had passed on the goods becoming ascertained in Hamburg because in a c.i.f. contract the parties intend that either the property shall pass upon the shipping documents being transferred to the buyer or else, if the goods were not then ascertained, that property shall pass when they later become ascertained. The claim of the Swedish buyers against the shipowners was successful: *Karlshamns Olefabriker* v. *Eastport Navigation Corp.; The Elafi* [1982] 1 All E.R. 208.

As has been seen, under a c.i.f. contract property passes normally to the buyer when the bill of lading is transferred to him. What if, after the risk has passed to the buyer but before property has passed to him, the goods are damaged by the negligence of some third party, such as the carrier? This situation may arise if, for one reason or another, the buyer has not become the holder of the bill of lading. In such a case the buyer, not having had title to the goods at the time of the damage, cannot maintain an action for the tort of negligence against the third party: *Leigh and Sillivan Ltd.* v. *Aliakmon Shipping Co. Ltd.* [1986] A.C. 785. (See p. 624 *post*).

In a c. & f. (c.f.r.) contract the seller is obliged to arrange for the carriage of the goods to the place of destination and to pay the freight, but he need not insure the goods. The buyer may insure them if he is so minded. Sometimes the c. & f. contract provides that the buyer shall be obliged to insure the goods in transit: *Reinhart C.* v. *Joshua Holye & Sons Ltd.* [1961] 1 Lloyd's Rep. 346.

Arrival and ex ship contracts

Under an arrival contract the goods themselves must arrive at the place of destination and it is insufficient that documents evidencing the shipment of the goods to that destination are made available to the buyer. When examining whether a particular contract is a c.i.f. contract or an arrival contract, attention has to be paid to the intention of the parties, as contained in their agreement; the designation of the contract used by the parties is not decisive.

In April 1940 a Belgian company bought 500 tons of La Plate rye from an Argentine company. The terms were c.i.f. Antwerp. The goods were part of a larger consignment, and the documents tendered to the buyers included a delivery order addressed to the seller's agents in Antwerp and instructing them to release 500 tons to the buyer. The buyers paid against the documents, but the ship carrying the goods, the S.S. *Julia*, was diverted to Lisbon because Antwerp had fallen into enemy hands. At Lisbon the goods were sold cheaply. This was one of some 900 transactions concluded by the parties before on similar terms. *Held*, the contract, despite its designation, was an arrival contract because the delivery order, unlike a bill of lading, passed neither possession nor property to the buyers but was merely a note from one agent of the sellers to another. Since, owing to the non-arrival of the goods in Antwerp, the consideration had wholly failed, the buyers were entitled to recover the whole purchase price paid by them from the sellers: *Comptoir d'Achat* v. *Luis de Ridder* [1949] A.C. 293.

When goods are sold ex ship, the duties of the seller are:

(a) to deliver the goods to the buyer from a ship which has arrived at the port of delivery at a place from which it is usual for goods of that kind to be delivered;
(b) to pay the freight or otherwise release the shipowner's lien; and
(c) to furnish the buyer with a delivery order, or some other effectual direction to the ship to deliver.

The goods are at the seller's risk during the voyage and there is no obligation on the seller to effect an insurance on the buyer's behalf: *Yangtsze Insurance Association* v. *Lukmanjee* [1918] A.C. 585.

International sales and the Unfair Contract Terms Act 1977

The Unfair Contract Terms Act 1977 does not normally apply to contracts for the international sale of goods. Such contracts qualify normally as *international supply contracts* and are, as such, exempt from the operation of the Act. An international supply contract is defined in section 26(3) and (4) as follows:

(a) either it is a contract of sale of goods or it is one under or in pursuance of which the possession or ownership passes; and
(b) it is made by parties whose places of business (or, if they have none, habitual residences) are in the territories of different States (the Channel Islands and the Isle of Man being treated for this purpose as different States from the United Kingdom).

In addition, the contract must satisfy the following requirements:

(a) the goods in question are, at the time of the conclusion of the contract, in the course of carriage, or will be carried, from the territory of one State to the territory of another; or
(b) the acts constituting the offer and acceptance have been done in the territories of different States; or
(c) the contract provides for the goods to be delivered to the territory of a State other than that within whose territory those acts were done.

The Uniform Laws on International Sales Act 1967

This Act gives effect on two Conventions signed at a conference at the Hague in 1964, which were designed to achieve some uniformity in the laws which in different states apply to contracts for the international sale of goods. The two Conventions are incorporated in the Act as Schedules. The first Convention, the Uniform Law on the International Sale of Goods, is in Schedule 1 and the second Convention, the Uniform Law on the Formation of Contracts for the International Sale of Goods, is in Schedule 2. The Act is part of English law and whenever a contract of sale of goods is governed by English law as the law governing the contract, the Uniform Law in Schedule 1 will apply to that contract, provided the parties to the contract have expressly chosen the Uniform Law as the law of the contract (s.1(3) and Uniform Laws on International Sales Order 1972 (S.I. 1972 No. 973), art. 2(*b*)).

The Uniform Laws and home transactions

Although the Uniform Laws are conceived of as applying to contracts of international sale, there is nothing to stop the parties to a home transaction expressly adopting them (Sched. 1, art. 4). The only limitation is that the parties cannot in the case of a home transaction avoid the mandatory provisions of English law (Sched. 1, art. 4). The only such mandatory provisions are sections 12–15 of the Sale of Goods Act 1979 (1967 Act, s.1(4), as amended by the 1979 Act, Sched. 2, para. 15). Thus, where in a home transaction the parties expressly adopt the Uniform Laws, the latter will apply except in so far as they are inconsistent with those mandatory provisions of the Sale of Goods Act. Apart from that restriction relating to home sales, the parties are free to contract out of any of the provisions of the Uniform Laws (Sched. 1, art. 3).

The Uniform Law on the International Sale of Goods

The Uniform Law (Sched. 1) contains provisions governing the seller's obligations as to the time and place of delivery, the insurance and carriage of the goods, the conformity of the goods with the contract, and the giving of good title. Other provisions govern the passing of risk and the buyer's obligations as to payment and the taking delivery of the goods. These rules are in several respects different from ordinary English law. In particular, the Uniform Laws do not recognise the concept of the "condition" which exists in English law, for the breach of which the buyer can reject the goods even though the breach causes him no loss. The Uniform Laws instead introduce a concept of "fundamental breach." Thus, in order to determine whether the buyer has the right to reject, one must examine the breach that has actually occurred together with its consequences. The lawyer will be able to reject the goods only if the breach is "fundamental," *i.e.* if a reasonable person in the position of the buyer "would not have entered into the contract if he had foreseen the breach and its effects" (Sched. 1, art. 10).

The Uniform Law does not prevent a contract of a well recognised type, *e.g.* c.i.f. or f.o.b. taking effect as such, or from agreeing on a uniform interpretation of these trade terms, *e.g.* by embodying into their contract Incoterms. The parties are "bound by any usage which they have expressly or impliedly made applicable" (Sched. 1, art. 9).

The Uniform Law on the Formation of Contracts for the International Sale of Goods

Schedule 2, which contains this Uniform Law, applies to the formation of contracts of sale which if they were concluded would be governed by the Uniform Law in Schedule 1. Its provisions relate to offer and acceptance. In particular, it contains the following rules. An offer is in general revocable until the offeree has despatched his acceptance. However, an offer is not revocable if it either states a fixed time for acceptance or else indicates that it is irrevocable (Sched. 2, art. 5). A qualified acceptance will normally be construed as a rejection of the offer and a counter-offer. However, if the qualification consists of additional or different terms which do not materially alter the terms of the offer, it will constitute a binding acceptance unless the offeror promptly objects to the discrepancy (Sched. 2, art. 7). A late acceptance may be treated by the buyer as having arrived in time, provided the offeror promptly informs the acceptor that he regards it as binding. A late acceptance which suffers an unusual delay in transit and which would in normal transit have arrived in time is regarded as being in time unless the offeror promptly informs the acceptor that he considers his offer has lapsed (Sched. 2, art. 9).

The UN Convention on contracts for the International Sale of Goods

On April 11, 1980 this Convention, promoted by UNCITRAL (UN Commission on International Trade Law), was signed in Vienna. The Vienna Convention is a further development of the attempt to unify the law relating to the international sale of goods. The Convention is founded on the two Hague Conventions of 1964, discussed above, and is intended to supersede them. The Vienna Convention combines the topics treated in the two Hague Conventions in one document.

The Vienna Convention came into operation on January 1, 1988 and has been ratified or acceded to by such states as China and the U.S.A. However, at the date of going to press[1] the United Kingdom has not given effect to it.

[1] August 1991.

Chapter 19

THE FINANCE OF INTERNATIONAL TRADE

In the international sale of goods various methods of paying the purchase price are used. The buyer may pay the seller on open account or the seller may allow the buyer credit. The two most common methods are payment under a collection agreement and payment under a letter of credit, also called a documentary credit. In both cases banks are used as intermediaries and the shipping documents are used as collateral security for the banks. In the former case payment is effected by a bank in the buyer's country and in the latter case by a bank in the seller's country.

It is usual in international sales transactions for the seller to draw a bill of exchange, either on the buyer or on a bank. The bill of exchange may be a sight bill, which has to be paid at sight, or a time bill, which is payable usually a certain number of days after sight, *e.g.* 90 days after sight; a time bill requires acceptance.

Collection arrangements and letters of credit are governed by international regulations sponsored by the International Chamber of Commerce and applied by most banks in the world. Collection arrangements are governed by the *Uniform Rules for the Collection of Commercial Paper* (1978 Revision) and documentary credits by the *Uniform Customs and Practice for Documentary Credits* (1983 Revision).

Collection arrangements

If the collection of the price at the buyer's place is arranged, the seller hands the shipping documents, including the bill of lading to his own bank, the remitting bank, which passes them on to a bank at the buyer's place, the collecting bank. The collecting bank then presents the bill of exchange to the buyer and requests him to pay or to accept the bill. When the buyer has done so, the collecting bank releases the shipping documents to the buyer. The buyer thus receives the original bill of lading which enables him to obtain the goods from the carrier on arrival of the ship.

The collecting bank must not release the shipping documents to the buyer unless it obtains finance from him. If it does so contrary to the instructions of the seller, it renders itself liable to him. Sometimes, however, the collecting bank, of which the buyer may be a customer, takes this risk and, notwithstanding the contrary instructions of the seller, releases the bill of lading to the buyer. It will try to protect itself by releasing the bill of lading under a **trust receipt**. This document provides that the buyer constitutes himself a trustee for the bank in three respects: a trustee for the bills of lading, for the goods which he receives from the ship, and for the proceeds of sale, when he resells the goods. He will then pay the original purchase price to the collecting bank and retain the profits which he has made on the resale of the goods. If the buyer, in breach of his obligations under the trust receipt, pledges the bill of lading to another bank as a security for a loan and the second bank accepts the bill of lading in good faith, the second bank acquires a good title to the bill and the goods, by virtue of the Factors Act 1889, s.2(i) and the first bank has lost its title: *Lloyds Bank* v. *Bank of America Association* [1938] 2 K.B. 147. The buyer will be liable to the bank for breach of contract and for conversion of the bill of lading: *Midland Bank Ltd.* v. *Eastcheap Dried Fruit Co.* [1962] 1 Lloyd's Rep. 359.

Letters of credit

Of particular importance are letters of credit. This method of payment applies only if the parties to an export transaction have agreed to it in their contract of sale. The buyer instructs a bank in his country (the issuing bank) to open a credit with a bank in the seller's country (the advising bank) in favour of the seller, specifying the documents which the seller has to deliver to the bank if he wishes to receive finance. The instructions also specify the date of expiry of the credit.

If the documents tendered by the seller are correct and tendered before the credit has expired, the advising bank pays the seller the purchase price, or accepts his bill of exchange drawn on it, or negotiates his bill of exchange which is drawn on the buyer. Whether the credit is a payment, acceptance, negotiation or deferred payment credit, depends on the arrangements between the seller and the buyer.

Types of letters of credit

Various types of letters of credit are used according to the agreement of the parties to the contract of sale. Whether the credit is revocable or irrevocable, depends on the commitment of the issuing bank. Whether it is confirmed or unconfirmed depends on the commitment of the advising bank. These commitments are undertaken to the seller, who is the beneficiary under the credit.

The following are the main types of letters of credit.

1. The revocable and unconfirmed letter of credit. Here neither the issuing nor the advising bank enters into a commitment to the seller. The credit may be revoked at any time. A revocable and unconfirmed credit affords little security to the seller that he will receive the purchase price through a bank.

2. The irrevocable and unconfirmed letter of credit. Here the authority which the buyer gives the issuing bank is irrevocable and the issuing bank enters into an obligation to the seller to pay; this obligation is likewise irrevocable; the bank has to honour the credit. This, from the point of view of the seller, is a more valuable method of payment than a revocable and unconfirmed letter of credit. The seller can claim that the issuing bank honours the credit, provided that he tenders the correct documents before the date of expiry of the credit. If the issuing bank refuses to honour the credit, the seller may sue it in the country in which the issuing bank has its seat. If the issuing bank has a branch office in the seller's country, the seller may in certain circumstances even sue the issuing bank in his own country.

3. The irrevocable and confirmed letter of credit. If the advising bank adds its own **confirmation** of the credit to the seller, the latter has the certainty that a bank in his own locality will provide him with finance if he delivers the correct shipping documents in the stipulated time (*Hamzeh Malas & Sons* v. *British Imex Industries Ltd.*, below). A "reliable paymaster" in his own country has been substituted for the overseas buyer. A confirmed credit constitutes "a direct undertaking by the banker that the seller, if he presents the documents as required in the required time, will receive payment" (*per* Diplock J. in *Ian Stach Ltd.* v. *Baker Bosley Ltd.* [1958] 2 Q.B.

130); the confirmation thus constitutes a conditional debt of the banker, *i.e.* a debt subject to the condition precedent that the seller tenders the specified documents: (*W. J. Allan & Co. Ltd.* v. *El Nasr Export and Import Co.* [1972] 2 Q.B. 189). The buyer need not open the credit as confirmed unless he has undertaken to do so in the contract of sale. A confirmed credit which has been notified to the seller cannot be cancelled by the bank on the buyer's instructions.

U. sold machinery to E. in Calcutta to be delivered by instalments, payment to be made for each shipment as it took place by means of a confirmed credit with E.'s bank in England. E.'s bank told U. that a "confirmed irrevocable credit" was open in his favour. After two shipments had been made and paid for, the bank on E.'s instructions refused U.'s bill. *Held*, the bank was liable in damages, to U. *Urquhart Lindsay & Co.* v. *Eastern Bank* [1922] 1 K.B. 318.

Jordanian buyers bought a quantity of steel rods from British sellers. The goods were to be shipped in two instalments and payment was to be made under two confirmed credits, one for each instalment, to be opened with the Midland Bank, London. After receipt of the first instalment the buyers who had already opened the second credit applied for an injunction restraining the sellers from recovering any money under the second credit. *Held*, the injunction had to be refused because the bank was under an absolute obligation to pay, irrespective of any dispute between the parties to the contract of sale, on tender of the stipulated documents: *Hamzeh Malas & Sons* v. *British Imex Industries Ltd.* [1958] 2 Q.B. 127.

4. The transferable letter of credit. The parties to the contract of sale may agree that the credit shall be transferable. The seller can use such a credit to finance the supply transaction. The buyer opens the credit in favour of the seller and the seller (who in the supply transaction is the buyer) transfers the same credit to the supplier (who in the supply transaction is the seller). The credit is transferred on the same terms on which the buyer has opened it, except that the amount payable to the supplier is made smaller because the seller wishes to retain his profit from the export transaction. Every transferable credit is thus automatically divisible because it is transferred in a smaller amount than the amount in which it is opened by the issuing bank.

The Uniform Customs and Practice for Documentary Credits

(1983 Revision), issued by the International Chamber of Commerce, provide in article 54(e) that a transferable credit can be transferred only once.

The autonomy of the credit

The credit constitutes a separate banking transaction and the issuing and advising banks are, in principle, not involved in the underlying transactions, *e.g.* the contract of export sale.

The Uniform Customs and Practice for Documentary Credits (1983 Revision) express this principle in the *General Provisions and Definitions* article 3, as follows:

"Credits, by their nature, are separate transactions from the sales or other contract(s) on which they may be based and banks are in no way connected with or bound by such contracts, even if any reference whatsoever to such contract(s) is intended in the credit."

The doctrine of strict compliance

The banks which operate the documentary credit act as agents for the buyer who is the principal. If they exceed his instructions, they have acted without authority and he need not ratify their act; the loss would then fall on the bank in question. This has led to the development of the **doctrine of strict compliance** under which the correspondent bank will, on principle, refuse documents tendered by the seller which do not correspond strictly with the instructions. "There is no room for documents which are almost the same or which will do just as well" (*per* Lord Sumner in *Equitable Trust Co. of New York* v. *Dawson Partners Ltd.* below).

D. bought a quantity of vanilla beans from a seller in Batavia (Jakarta). They opened a credit in his favour through E. instructing them to provide finance on presentation of certain documents, including a certificate of experts. E. paid on tender of a certificate by a single expert. The seller was fraudulent and had shipped mainly rubbish but the expert who inspected the cargo had failed to notice it. *Held*, E. had paid contrary to D.'s instructions and could not debit them: *Equitable Trust Company of New York* v. *Dawson Partners Ltd.* (1926) 27 Lloyd's Law Rep. 49.

S. an Italian company, bought a quantity of Chilian fish full meal from M., a New York company. The contract was c. & f. Savona, and provided that the buyers should open a letter of credit with a New York bank. The documents to be presented by the sellers had to include bills of lading issued to order and marked "freight prepaid" and an analysis certificate showing that the fish meal had a content of at least 70 per cent. protein. The documents tendered to the bank were not correct; the bills of lading were not to order and bore the remark "freight collect" instead of "freight prepaid" and the certificate showed only a minimum protein content of 67 per cent. The bank rejected the documents. After the expiry of the credit the sellers made a direct tender of the correct documents to the buyers who rejected them. *Held*, the second tender was irrelevant and had to be disregarded, and the bank had rightly rejected the first tender of the documents: *Soproma S.p.A.* v. *Marine & Animal By-Products Corporation* [1966] 1 Lloyd's Rep. 367.

Article 41(c) states that it is sufficient if all the documents taken together contain the particulars of the bank's mandate and it is not necessary that every document in the set should contain them (*Banque de l'Indoctrine et de Suez S.A.* v. *J. H. Rayner* (*Mincing Lane*) *Ltd.* [1983] Q.B. 711).

Opening of a letter of credit

The credit must be made available to the seller at the beginning of the shipment period (*Pavia & Co.* v. *Thurmann-Nielsen* [1952] 2 Q.B. 84). If the parties have not laid down in their contract a time for opening the credit, it must be opened a reasonable time before the seller has to make shipment (*Sinason-Teicher Inter-American Grain Corporation* v. *Oilcakes and Oilseeds Trading Co. Ltd.* [1954] 1 W.L.R. 935). If an intermediary bank has become insolvent, the buyer or another person involved in the transaction may make direct payment to the seller (*Sale Continuation Ltd.* v. *Austin Taylor & Co. Ltd.* [1967] 2 Lloyd's Rep. 403).

Fraud in letter of credit transactions

Letters of credit have been described by English judges as "the lifeblood of commerce" (Donaldson L.J. and Ackner L.J.J. in *Intraco Ltd.* v. *Notis Shipping Corporation*; *The Bhoja Trader* [1981] 2 Lloyd's Rep. 256, 257). The defence of the bank that it need not honour the credit because a fraud has occurred is therefore admitted only in very limited circumstances. Such a fraud may occur if the shipment of the goods is fraudulent or if the bills of lading tendered under the credit are falsified or forged.

Three cases have to be distinguished here. First, there is only a suspicion—perhaps a grave suspicion—that a forgery has occurred. In this case the bank must pay. Megarry J. said in *Discount Records Ltd.* v. *Barclays Bank Ltd.*: "I would be slow to interfere with bankers' irrevocable credits, and not least in the sphere of international banking, unless a sufficiently grave cause is shown."

D., an English company, ordered records and cassettes from Promodisc, a French company. Discount instructed Barclays Bank to open an irrevocable credit in favour of Promodisc and Barclays Bank passed on these instructions to Barclays Bank International. Discount alleged that on arrival of the goods they found them to be a fraudulent shipment and moved the court for an interlocutory injunction restraining the banks from paying until final judgment or further order. *Held*, no fraud was established and no sufficiently grave cause was disclosed for interfering with the credit; injunction refused: *Discount Records Ltd.* v. *Barclays Bank Ltd.* [1975] 1 W.L.R. 315.

In *Tukan Timber Ltd.* v. *Barclays Bank plc.* [1987] 1 Lloyd's Rep. 171, the fact that two forgery attempts were made before did not support the assumption that on a future third occasion again forged documents would be tendered.

Secondly, it is proved to the satisfaction of the Bank that the documents tendered are fraudulent but it cannot be established that the seller was a party to the fraud or knew of it. In this case, according to the decision of the House of Lords in *United City Merchants* (*Investments*) *Ltd.* v. *Royal Bank of Canada*, (see below), the bank should honour the credit.

Thirdly, it is proved to the bank that the documents are fraudulent and, in addition, that the seller was a party to the fraud or knew of it. In this case the bank should refuse to honour the credit.

Glass Fibres and Equipment Ltd., a British company, sold a glass fibre forming plant to a Peruvian Company. Payment was arranged under an irrevocable letter of credit issued by a Peruvian Bank and confirmed by the Royal Bank of Canada at its London Branch. Shipment was to be made from London on or before December 15, 1976, while the credit was open until December 31, 1976. Shipment of the installation was made on board the *American Accord* on December 16, *i.e.* out of shipping time. The bills of lading were altered and backdated to December 15. The backdating of the bills of lading was, according to the trial judge, carried out fraudulently by an employee of the loading brokers, without the knowledge of the sellers or the assignees of the credit. *Held*, the confirming bank (the Royal Bank of Canada) should have honoured the credit on presentation of the documents: *United City Merchants* (*Investments*) *Ltd.* v. *Royal Bank of Canada* [1983] 1 A.C. 168.

Performance guarantees

Sometimes an overseas buyer arranges with the seller that the latter shall provide a performance guarantee safeguarding the due performance of the contract by the seller. Such a performance guarantee may be given by a bank, an insurance company or a surety company.

There are two types of performance guarantees, conditional and on demand guarantees.

A conditional guarantee is conditional on the buyer obtaining a judgment or an arbitration award against the seller or on the production of a certificate of default on the part of the seller by a neutral person.

A demand guarantee is payable on mere demand on the bank or other guarantor by the buyer. Banks prefer to issue on demand guarantees. In the case of an on demand guarantee the bank or other guarantor must honour the guarantee even if it is manifestly clear that the demand was unfair. The obligations of a bank which has issued an on demand guarantee are similar to those of a bank which has confirmed a letter of credit. The defence of fraud is available to the bank only on the same conditions which would entitle a bank to refuse to honour a confirmed letter of credit.

E., an English company, contracted with Libyan customers to erect greenhouses in Libya. E. had to provide an on demand performance guarantee for 10 per cent. of the contract price. The guarantee was provided by B., an English bank, to the Umma Bank in Libya, which gave its own on demand guarantee to the Libyan customers. The contract further provided that the Libyan customers should open an irrevocable confirmed letter of credit for the benefit of E. The customers failed to open the letter of credit as confirmed by an English bank. Thereupon E. did not perform the contract. Although the non-performance was due to the customer's failure to open the credit in accordance with the terms agreed by the parties, the customers made a demand on the bank under the performance bond. *Held*, B. was bound to pay: *Edward Owen Engineering Ltd.* v. *Barclays Bank International* [1978] Q.B. 159.

PART 5: COMPETITION

CHAPTER 20

MONOPOLIES AND MERGERS, RESTRICTIVE TRADE PRACTICES, RESALE PRICE MAINTENANCE AND OTHER ANTI-COMPETITIVE PRACTICES

PERHAPS one of the most important areas of law developed since the Second World War is the control of anti-competitive practices by business undertakings. In the United Kingdom this development has been piecemeal, and most of the legislation has retained its separate identity, but the overall result has been to create a reasonably comprehensive system of competition law. Putting these rules in their historical perspective, regulation of monopolies was introduced in 1948 (now contained in the Fair Trading Act 1973), control of restrictive agreements and similar practices was introduced in 1956 (now the Restrictive Trade Practices Act 1976), the prohibition of resale price maintenance in 1964 (now the Resale Prices Act 1976) and control of mergers in 1965 (as an adjunct to the monopolies rules); substantial changes to the rules on mergers were effected by the Companies Act 1989, introducing a formal system of advance notification of mergers. Following the Accession of the United Kingdom to the European Communities in 1973, the competition rules of the Treaties establishing the Communities became applicable in the United Kingdom. They are treated in Chapter 21, on p. 449, *post*. Finally, in 1980 the Competition Act was enacted which provides generally for the control of "anticompetitive practices" (defined in terms remarkably similar to those of the relevant provisions of the EEC Treaty) even though they do not fall within the concept of a monopoly or a merger, provided they do not arise from agreements registrable under the restrictive trade practises legislation, which remain subject to the rules of that legislation. New judicial and administrative bodies have been established to apply this legislation: an administrative body, the Monopolies and Mergers Commission, reports on monopoly or merger situations referred to it and on the "public interest" aspects of other anti-competitive practices, whilst a judicial body, the Restrictive Practices Court (see now the Restrictive Practices Court Act 1976), decides whether agreements subject to the restrictive trade legislation are contrary to the public interest and may decide upon exemptions from the basic prohibition on resale price maintenance.

The common thread in the competition law of the United Kingdom, however, is the role of the Director General of Fair Trading and of the Office of Fair Trading established under the Fair Trading Act 1973. The Director may, for example, refer a monopoly situation to the Monopolies and Mergers Commission, he may refer an anti-competitive practice to that Commission, he maintains the register of restrictive trading agreements (see pp. 441–442, *post*), he may institute exemption proceedings in relation to resale price maintenance, and in the context of the competition rules of the European Communities, he and his office act as the competent authority, *e.g.* to accompany Commission officials carrying out investigations in the United Kingdom, to attend hearings before the Commission and to participate in the European Communities Advisory Committee on Restrictive Practices and Monopolies. Hence, in practice, the role of the Director General is of fundamental importance in competition law. The Director General further exercises, by virtue of the Fair Trading Act 1973, certain functions aimed at consumer protection; they are noted on p. 361, *ante*, and as far as affecting consumer credit, on p. 388, *ante*.

Each of the specific areas of prohibition or control will now be considered in turn.

Monopolies and Mergers

The monopolies and mergers to which the relevant provisions of the Fair Trading Act apply are the subject of precise definition. Broadly speaking, a monopoly situation exists where at least one quarter of the market in the supply or export of goods of any description, or in the supply of services of any description, is in the hands of a single firm (or a connected group of firms) or in the hands of several firms which, whether by agreement or not, prevent or restrict the operation of a free market in the goods or services in question. A relevant merger situation exists where it would either lead to or strengthen a monopoly situation or where the gross value of the assets taken over would exceed £30 million (a figure susceptible to amendment by statutory instrument), and there are also special provisions for the control of newspaper mergers.

It should be noted that:

(a) there is no duty to pre-notify mergers, although the Companies Act 1989 introduced a formal mechanism for advance notification of mergers; and
(b) there is no presumption that monopolies or mergers are harmful *per se*; each case is considered on its merits in the light of the public interest. In consequence, control is discretionary and very few of the mergers considered for reference to the Monopolies and Mergers Commission (M.M.C.) are so referred.

The formal mechanism enabling advance notice to be given to the Director General of Fair Trading of proposed arrangements which might result in a merger situation qualifying for investigation was introduced by the Companies Act 1989, adding new sections 75A to 75F to the Fair Trading Act 1973. Following receipt of the notice (and of any fee payable), there begins a period of twenty days for the Director to consider the merger notice. The Director may, and if so required by the Secretary of State shall, extend this period by ten days, and thereafter by a further fifteen days. If no reference to the Monopolies and Mergers Commission is made within that period, then in principle no reference may be made; the effect therefore is to introduce a system of negative clearance for mergers. This is, however, subject to a requirement that the merger be effected within six months of the end of the period for consideration of the notice. Furthermore, during the period allowed for consideration, the Director may reject the notice if he suspects it to be false or misleading or if it does not give prescribed information, and where the period has been extended by fifteen days (*i.e.* the second additional period mentioned above), the Secretary of State may make a reference during the last five of those fifteen days despite the absence of a recommendation from the Director. A reference may also be made, *inter alia*, if the enterprises involved cease to be distinct enterprises during the period for consideration; in effect, therefore, it is necessary to wait until the end of the period before merging if full advantage is to be derived from the advance notification.

The duties of the Director General of Fair Trading include the monitoring of commercial activities in the United Kingdom, so as to ascertain circumstances relating to monopoly and merger situations or uncompetitive practices and, in this connection, the provision of information, assistance and recommendations to the Government (the Secretary of State for Trade). He may require information to be provided to him and whilst only the Secretary of State (on the advice of the merger panel which the Director chairs) may initiate merger references to the Monopolies and Mergers Commission (M.M.C.), the Director General may make monopoly references, subject to government veto where relevant. It is, however, clear from the decision of the House of Lords in *Lonrho* v. *Secretary of State for Trade and Industry* [1989] 2 All E.R. 609 that while the discretion of the Secretary of State should be guided by the advice of the Director General of Fair Trading, it is not fettered by it. His duties also include assistance to the M.M.C., and after report of the M.M.C., obtaining undertakings from the parties if appropriate. The Director General will monitor the observance of such undertakings.

The use of undertakings was broadened by the 1989 Companies Act, which added new sections 75G to 75K to the 1973 Fair Trading Act enabling the Secretary of State to accept undertakings as an alternative to making a merger reference. This possibility arises where the Director General has recommended that a reference be made, and has indicated the particular effects contrary to the public interest which the merger situation might have. The undertakings must provide for action appropriate to remedy or prevent those effects, and must provide for one or more of the division of a business, the division of a group of interconnected bodies corporate, and the separation of businesses which are otherwise under common control. The Director General has the duty of keeping such undertakings under review, and by virtue of a new section 93A civil proceedings may be brought against the person responsible in respect of any failure to fulfil an undertaking. The new section 93A also allows civil proceedings to be brought against the person responsible in respect of any failure to fulfil an undertaking of the type mentioned in the previous paragraph, given after the report of the M.M.C. on a reference.

As regards monopolies and mergers, the establishment of the Fair Trading Office under the Director General means the separation of the investigation or prosecutory function, *i.e.* fact finding, from that of adjudication, *i.e.* providing assessment and advice to the Secretary of State, which remains with the M.M.C.

The M.M.C., which is an independent advisory body with no executive powers, can be required to report to the Government whether the monopoly or merger situation operates against the public interest and to make recommendations. The public interest is defined (s.84 of the Fair Trading Act 1973) with emphasis on the need to promote competition, but this is not necessarily the only element taken into account: in the reports concerning merger proposals relating respectively to the *House of Fraser* and the *Royal Bank of Scotland*, the "Scottish factor" appears to have played an important role. A time limit may be imposed for the production of the M.M.C.'s report, and this is always the case on merger references. The Government may accept an M.M.C. report that the matters on reference have operated in the public interest, but an adverse report is not binding. However, the recommendations in the Commission's report, which is laid before Parliament and published, may be implemented by the Government which may make an order for the purpose of remedying or preventing any mischiefs reported to them by the M.M.C. This power is rarely exercised; in nearly all cases those concerned agree to comply with suitable undertakings at the instance of Government.

Criminal proceedings do not lie for the contravention of such an order. On the other hand, the Crown may enforce it by civil proceedings for an injunction, and an individual injured as a result of the infringement of such an order may institute a civil action.

Furthermore, where a recommendation has been made as to action to be taken by the parties, the Government may at any time refer to the M.M.C. for investigation and report whether it has been complied with.

Apart from the specific monopoly and merger situations referred to above, the M.M.C. may also be required to produce general reports on the effect in the public interest of certain classes of practices, and under section 11 of the Competition Act 1980 the

Secretary of State may make a reference as to the efficiency and costs of the service provided by, or a possible "abuse" of a monopoly situation by, a public sector undertaking. The role of the M.M.C. in considering the public interest aspects of anti-competitive practices in general will be considered below (p. 448, *post*). On the other hand, it should be remembered that the actual conduct of a take-over bid, as opposed to its economic consequences, remains subject for the most part to the self-regulation of the City Code on Take-overs and Mergers. Furthermore, control of even the economic consequences of certain mergers may fall within the jurisdiction of other bodies: under the terms of the European Coal and Steel Community Treaty, mergers between coal and steel undertakings falling within the scope of that Treaty are subject to the exclusive control of the Commission of the European Communities. More generally, it has been held that in some circumstances (see *post* p. 453) a merger may constitute an abuse of a dominant position under article 86 of the EEC Treaty, subject to the control both of the EC Commission and of the national courts, and this has led to the introduction of a formal system of merger control under Council Regulation 4064/89 (O.J. 1989 L395/1), which entered into force in 1990. Arts. 1 and 21 of this Regulation confer on the Commission of the European Communities sole competence to take decisions with regard to "concentrations with a Community dimension," which are defined as those where the aggregate worldwide turnover of all the undertakings concerned is more than 5,000 million ECU and the aggregate Community-wide turnover of at least two of the undertakings involved is more than 250 million ECU, unless each of the undertakings concerned achieves more than two-thirds of its aggregate Community-wide turnover in one and the same Member State. The details of the system are discussed in Chapter 21, but in the present context it may be observed that art. 21(2) of the Regulation prohibits Member States from applying their national legislation to such "concentrations." Member States are, however, entitled under art. 21(3) to protect legitimate interests, defined as including "plurality of the media," by measures compatible with the general principles and other provisions of Community law; this may be of particular importance in the context of the United Kingdom rules on newspaper mergers. Furthermore, by virtue of art. 9 of the Regulation, the Commission may refer a notified concentration to the national authorities with a view to the application of national competition law where it considers that a concentration threatens to create or strengthen a dominant position (see Chapter 21) as a result of which effective competition would be significantly impeded on a market within that Member State which presents all the characteristics of a distinct market, whether or not it constitutes a substantial part of the common market. In effect, therefore, those mergers which produce anti-competitive results at a national rather than a Community level, may be referred back to the national authorities.

Restrictive Trade Practices

The law governing restrictive trade agreements is consolidated in the Restrictive Trade Practices Act 1976.

The Restrictive Trade Practices Act 1956 required restrictive trade agreements to be registered in a public register, except if they referred to exports, in which case they were filed with Government but are now held by the Director General. They are not published. Restrictive trade agreements are agreements under which producers, suppliers or exporters restrict the manufacture, supply or distribution of goods, for example, by arranging minimum selling prices or the same conditions for the supply of goods. The Fair Trading Act 1973 amended the 1956 Act to include restrictive agreements relating to the supply of services within the scope of this legislation. The general rule is that a restrictive trade agreement is presumed to be invalid as being contrary to the public interest, unless the parties can justify the restriction before the Restrictive Practices Court on any one of eight specified grounds (p. 443, *post*).

Duty to register restrictive agreements

Registrable agreements

Any agreement made between two or more persons carrying on business in the United Kingdom must be registered by any of them with the Director General if restrictions are accepted by two or more parties in respect of the following matters (now s.6(1) of the 1976 Act):

(a) the prices to be charged, quoted or paid for goods, supplied, offered or acquired, or for the application of any process of manufacture to goods;

(b) the prices to be recommended or suggested as the prices to be charged or quoted in respect of the resale of goods supplied;

(c) the terms or conditions on, or subject to which goods are to be supplied or acquired or any such process is to be applied to goods;

(d) the quantities or descriptions of goods to be produced, supplied or acquired;

(e) the processes of manufacture to be applied to any goods, or the quantities or descriptions of goods to which any such process is to be applied; or

(f) the persons or classes of persons to, for or from whom, or the areas or places in or from which, goods are to be supplied or acquired, or any such process applied.

Sub-paragraph (b) covers recommended prices for resale, which may well overlap with the contents of sub-paragraph (a). A single manufacturer, however, has freedom to recommend resale prices provided he enters into no agreement with another party as to such prices.

With regard to services, the combined effect of what are now sections 11–13 of the 1976 Act (and see generally Part III, of the 1976 Act) is that the restrictive trade practices legislation which previously applied only to goods, is applied to any agreement:

(a) between two or more parties carrying on business in the United Kingdom in the supply of services brought under control by the Order mentioned below; and

(b) under which two or more parties accept restrictions relating to certain matters, *e.g.* charges to be made for supplying designated services.

The Restrictive Trade Practices (Services) Order 1976 brought all commercial services under control (*i.e.* (a) above), with the exception of certain services already subject to supervision, *e.g.* by the Civil Aviation Authority, or Traffic Commissioners; it further designated all services, (*i.e.* (b) above) as being included into the regulation, except for those specified in Schedule 1 to the 1976 Act, *i.e.* professional services, which may however be reviewed by the Monopolies and Mergers Commission. "Services brought under control" relates to the business of the parties; contrast "designated services" which covers services in respect of which restrictions are accepted. The matters mentioned above which are included in the Order are those listed in section 11(2) of the 1976 Act which resemble (but with necessary changes) those listed in section 6(1) of the 1976 Act.

The Order of March 1976 referred to above required parties to restrictive agreements relating to the supply of services to register their agreements with the Director General by June 21, 1976 or to terminate such agreements. Over 500 service agreements were submitted. Their coverage extends to nearly all commercial services, from finance to sport and entertainment.

Trade associations fall within the legislation, so that restrictions accepted by an association are deemed to be accepted by its members and recommendations made by an association are deemed to be restrictions accepted by the members. Section 16 of the 1976 Act extends the control of the 1956 Act and section 5 of the 1968 Act to trade associations as regards restrictions relating to the supply of services.

As to the definition of services, what is now section 20 of the 1976 Act provides that the term includes all engagements undertaken for gain except for the production or supply or processing of goods. The professional services listed in the First Schedule to the 1976 Act are, however, excluded. See, *e.g. Royal Institute of Chartered Surveyors* v. *Director General of Fair Trading* (March 10, 1981; unreported).

Although comprised in the one consolidating Act of 1976, the legislation applies separately to the supply of goods and services. This means that two parties engaged in the supply of goods only may freely accept restrictions in relation to services and vice versa.

The term "agreement" includes any agreement or arrangement, whether it is or is not intended to be legally enforceable. All that is required to constitute an arrangement not enforceable in law is that the parties to it shall have communicated with one another in some way and that as a result of the communication each has intentionally aroused in the other an expectation that he will act in a certain way (see *Re British Basic Slag Ltd.'s Agreement* (1962) L.R. 4 R.P. 155, and *Re Mileage Conference Group of the Tyre Manufacturers Conference Ltd.'s Agreement* (1967) L.R. 6 R.P. 66).

The phrase "an agreement for the supply of goods" is to be construed as a reference to any agreement whereby one party agrees to supply goods to another, notwithstanding that it may contain agreement on other related or unrelated matters (*Registrar of Restrictive Trading Agreements* v. *Schweppes and Others* (1971) L.R. 7 R.P. 336).

With regard to the obligation to provide particulars of a relevant agreement in due time, section 35 of the 1976 Act provides that if particulars of any registrable agreement are not duly furnished within the time required, the agreement shall be void in respect of all relevant restrictions accepted thereunder and it will be unlawful for any party who carries on business within the United Kingdom to give effect to or to enforce or purport to enforce any such restrictions. It is not a criminal offence to give effect to a void restriction, but the Director General may take proceedings in the Restrictive Practices Court for an injunction restraining the continuance or repetition of any such unlawful action (see also the *Flushing Cisterns* case [1973] I.C.R. 654) and any person who has suffered a loss through the operation of the void restrictions may bring civil proceedings for damages. Particular attention was drawn to this right to sue for damages following the decisions of the Restrictive Trade Practices Court in a group of three price fixing cases in 1991 involving fuel oil supplies in the North East, bus operations in Leicestershire, and steel roofing purlins (May 20, 1991; unreported).

What is now section 21(1)(b) of the 1976 Act gives the Director General a discretion whether to refer to the Restrictive Practices Court for adjudication a restrictive agreement which has been determined (under the Act of 1956 he was under a statutory duty to refer all registered agreements to the Court, whether they had been determined or not). Section 21(2) of the 1976 Act allows the Secretary of State, on the representation of the Director General, to discharge him from the duty of referring agreements to the Court where it is considered that the restrictions are not of such significance (whether on economic or other grounds) as to call for investigation by the Restrictive Practices Court. (Under the Act of 1956 this could only be done where the agreements were considered to be of no substantial economic significance.)

Information agreements

Sections 7 and 12 of the 1976 Act empower the Secretary of State by order to bring agreements for exchange of information within the restrictive trade practices legislation. An information agreement is defined as an agreement between two or more persons carrying on within the United Kingdom any such business as is mentioned in subsection (1) of section 6 of the 1976 Act whether with or without other parties, being an agreement under which provision is made for or in relation to the furnishing by two or more parties to each other or to other persons (whether parties or not) of information with respect to certain matters. These matters are the same as those contained in section 6(1), with the addition of exchange of information as to costs. However, they differ in one other important respect from those matters set out in section 6(1) in that section 6(1) is concerned with restrictions as to future behaviour, *e.g.* the prices to be charged, whereas section 7(1) of the Act of 1976 is concerned with past behaviour as well, *e.g.* the prices charged or to be charged.

Information agreements are not automatically registrable. The Secretary of State may by order call up for registration any class of agreements falling within the definition. So far only one such order has been made; this related to the matters referred to in section 7(1)(a) and (b) of the Act of 1976.

Excepted agreements

Various exceptions to the need for registration are set out in the Restrictive Trade Practices Act 1976 (ss.9 and 18 and Sched. 3). These include agreements containing only restrictions relating exclusively to the goods or services supplied thereunder, agreements expressly authorised by statute, sales agency agreements between two parties, and agreements between two parties for the use of patents, registered designs or trade marks.

Sections 9(7) and 43(2) of the 1976 Act, which provide that a company and its subsidiary are to be treated as a single person, are concerned only with the counting of heads and are not directed to treating the persons to which they relate as the one and the same person so that, for the purposes of section 9(4) of the 1976 Act, it is necessary to look at the agreement as it stands, and if, after counting as one any parties to it which are inter-connected bodies corporate, it is still the case that restrictions relating exclusively to the goods supplied are accepted as between two or more persons by whom the goods are to be supplied, section 9(4) does not apply. This appears from the *Schweppes* case (1971) L.R. 7, R.P. 336, from which it also appears it is not possible to rely within the same agreement on more than one of the exceptions set out in section 9.

In one case X. and Y. undertook to sell their entire production of citrus concentrates to a joint sales company in quota proportions; the parties were held to have accepted registrable restrictions within the 1956 Act. X. and Y. accordingly entered into new arrangements whereby Y. undertook to purchase X.'s production up to a maximum and to compensate X. for any shortfall. Y. might only purchase elsewhere after allowing X. to match a third party's lower price. *Held*, that Y.'s obligation was not a restriction on Y.'s own production. A shortfall might indeed arise through Y.'s own sales but this was no restriction on Y. as to production. It was a restriction relating only to the goods, supplied under the agreement which could therefore be ignored in considering whether the agreement was registrable. Nor was there any implied restriction on Y.'s production to be inferred from X.'s obligation to Y. The agreement did not require registration under the 1956 Act: *Cadbury Schweppes Ltd. and J. Lyons & Co. Ltd.'s Agreement* [1975] 1 W.L.R. 1018.

A further possibility for exemption is contained in section 29(2) of the 1976 Act, which sets out an administrative procedure enabling the Secretary of State to exempt from registration for a specified period any agreement which he considers reasonably necessary to promote the carrying out of a project or scheme of substantial importance to the national economy and the aim of which is to promote efficiency in a trade or industry. The Secretary of State is required to lay copies of any exemption order and of the exempted agreement before both Houses of Parliament and to make them available for public inspection.

Section 30 of the 1976 Act empowers certain government departments to exempt from registration agreements relating exclusively to prices and designed to prevent or restrict price increases so as to secure restrictions in prices. Exempted agreements under this section are also to be made available for public inspection.

Section 9(5) of the 1976 Act extends the scope of the existing exemptions from registration of agreements relating to standards of dimension, design or quality or performance and introduces an exemption for agreements relating to certain arrangements to provide information or advice to purchasers, consumers or users.

Finally, it may be noted that sections 9(1) and (2) of the 1976 Act provide that restrictions in agreements between coal and steel undertakings are to be ignored in determining whether the agreement is one to which Part II of the Act applies. This is in recognition of the fact that the E.C.S.C. Treaty confers jurisdiction with regard to such agreements on the Commission of the European Communities (see *post* p. 449).

Export agreements

These agreements are not registrable with the Director General if all the restrictions relate exclusively to:

(a) the supply of goods by export from the United Kingdom;
(b) the production of goods or the application of any process of manufacture to goods, outside the United Kingdom;
(c) the acquisition of goods to be delivered outside the United Kingdom and not imported into the United Kingdom for entry for home use; or
(d) the supply of goods to be delivered outside the United Kingdom otherwise than by export from the United Kingdom.

Such agreements, however, if all the restrictions relate to the supply of goods by export from the United Kingdom have to be notified to the Director General (s.25 and paras. 6(1) and 9(1) of Sched. 3 to the 1976 Act) and may be referred to the Monopolies and Mergers Commission. References have been made to the Commission to investigate product supply in and export from the United Kingdom (*e.g.* the reference made in July 1974 relating to United Kingdom manufacturers of heavy electric cables).

Administrative and judicial control of restrictive agreements

The Director General of Fair Trading

The Director General's functions in respect of monopolies and mergers have already been discussed (see pp. 430–431, *ante*). In discharging his functions pursuant to the 1973 Act, which remains the authority for his involvement in the field of restrictive trade practices, he retains his independent role. He is appointed by the Secretary of State but is responsible to no minister. He has two main duties: first, to keep the register of agreements subject to registration; and secondly, to bring the registered agreements before the Restrictive Practices Court to declare whether or not they are contrary to the public interest. Both these duties are absolute. He must see that all registrable agreements are put on the register, if necessary using the powers contained in the Act to obtain information; and to bring them before the Court. He has also to enforce orders made by the Court, of which breach is punishable as contempt of court.

The Register

This is kept in two sections, the public section and the special section. The former is open to inspection by anyone on payment of a fee, and copies may be obtained of anything in the register. The special section is secret and contains information the publication of which would be contrary to the public interest, also information about secret processes of manufacture or about the presence, absence, or location of any mineral or other deposits if the Government thinks publication would substantially damage legitimate business interests.

Judicial investigation of registered agreements

The Restrictive Practices Court, which was established by the Act of 1956, is a superior court of record presided over by a High Court judge. The Act provides for both judges and laymen to be members. Laymen are chosen for their knowledge or experience in industry, commerce or public affairs.

The main task of the court is to declare on application by the Director General whether a restriction contained in an agreement is contrary to the public interest, and if so to declare the agreement void in respect of that restriction, and the court may, at the request of the Director General, make an order prohibiting the parties to the agreement from continuing it or making any other agreement to the like effect (now section 2(2) of the 1976 Act). The test as to whether a new agreement is *to the like effect* is whether it is intended to operate in substantially the same way and whether the things it will do or achieve if it is made effective are the same as those which the first agreement would have done or achieved: *Re Black Bolt and Nut Association's Agreement* (*No*. 2) [1962] 1 W.L.R. 75. On the other hand, where the registrability or otherwise of an agreement is in dispute between the Director General and a third party, it will be a matter for the decision of the High Court and not the Restrictive Practices Court.

The onus is placed on the parties to the agreement to satisfy the court that the restrictions are not contrary to the public interest. A restriction will be deemed to be contrary to the public interest unless it satisfies one or more of the following circumstances (commonly known as **gateways**) (now s.10(1)(*a*)—(*h*) and s.19(1)(*a*)—(*h*) of the 1976 Act):

(a) that the restriction is reasonably necessary, having regard to the character of the goods or services, to protect the public against injury;
(b) that the removal of the restriction would deny to the public as purchasers, consumers or users other specific and substantial benefits or advantages;
(c) that the restriction is reasonably necessary to counteract measures taken by a person not party to the agreement;
(d) that the restriction is reasonably necessary to enable the persons party to the agreement to negotiate fair terms with a person not party to it who controls a preponderant part of the trade, business or market in the goods or services concerned;
(e) that the removal of the restriction would be likely to have a serious and persistent adverse effect on the general level of unemployment;
(f) that the removal of the restriction would be likely to cause a reduction in the volume or earnings of the export business which is substantial either in relation to the whole export business of the United Kingdom or in relation to the whole business (including export business) of the trade or industry;
(g) that the restriction is reasonably required for purposes connected with the maintenance of any other restriction accepted by the parties; or
(h) that the restriction does not directly or indirectly restrict or

discourage competition to any material degree in any relevant trade or industry and is not likely to do so.

Even if the Court is satisfied on one or more of these circumstances it must further be satisfied that the restriction is not unreasonable, having regard to the balance between those circumstances and any detriment to the public or to persons not parties to the agreement resulting or likely to result from the operation of the restriction.

The Court has power to vary previous orders it has made if the relevant circumstances can be shown to have materially changed (now s.4 of the 1976 Act). The Court has in several cases accepted undertakings on behalf of the parties to an agreement which it has declared void that they will inform the Registrar, now the Director General, if they intend to make an agreement to the like effect, so that he can apply for an Order before they do so. The Director General can apply to the Court for an Order at any time if parties to an agreement which has been found objectionable continue to operate their arrangements, or to operate new arrangements having the same effect as those condemned.

On a motion on behalf of the Registrar alleging contempt of court the Court imposed fines totalling £103,000 on eight companies members of the Galvanised Tank Manufacturers Association for breach of undertakings given to the Court in earlier proceedings: *Re Galvanised Tank Manufacturers Association's Agreement* [1965] 1 W.L.R. 1074.

Similarly, in *Re an Agreement between the Members of the British Concrete Pipes Association* [1981] I.C.R. 421, a fine of £50,000 was imposed; this case also illustrates the importance of ensuring that the terms of undertakings are brought to the attention of successive holders of managerial posts, since it there appeared that the responsible officer of one firm was unaware of the undertaking which was breached.

A brief analysis of some of the salient features of decisions of the court is set out below.

Section 10(1)(a)

The test to be applied is "whether a reasonable and prudent man who is concerned to protect the public against injury would enforce the restriction if he could" *per* Devlin J. in *Re Chemists' Federation's Agreement* [1958] 1 W.L.R. 1192.

Section 10(1)(b)

"The public as purchasers, consumers or users of goods"—means the public viewed as a collective whole in a specified capacity. "The public as purchasers" denotes collectively all persons who purchased the goods: it is not sufficient that some small class of the public benefits by the restriction, but equally it is unnecessary to prove that the ultimate consumers receive a benefit: *Re Black Bolt and Nut Association's Agreement* [1960] 1 W.L.R. 884.

"Any goods." The respondents may choose the particular kind of goods in respect of which they seek to justify the onus of proof cast upon them: *Re Black Bolt and Nut Association's Agreement, supra.*

"Specific and substantial benefits or advantages." A benefit is specific if it is "explicit and definable." "Substantial" is not a word which demands a strictly quantitative or proportional assessment, nor is it a term the meaning of which the Court has been prepared to define: *Re Net Book Agreement 1957* (1962) L.R. 3 R.P. 246.

Section 10(1)(d)

It is not necessary to show that the preponderant buyer is likely to use his powers to negotiate unfair terms. It is sufficient if, in fact, without the restriction, the suppliers would not be able to negotiate fair terms, *i.e.* giving a reasonable but no more than a reasonable profit but in the hope of getting an occasional contract are likely to tender at an uneconomic price: *Re Water-Tube Boilermakers' Agreement* [1959] 1 W.L.R. 1118.

Resale Price Maintenance

The position is covered by the Resale Prices Act 1976. Arrangements for the collective enforcement of price maintenance arrangements are, on principle, prohibited. Thus, the Act operates so as to prevent manufacturers and other suppliers from imposing conditions for the maintenance of minimum prices at which goods are to be resold and to prohibit enforcement of such prices by withholding supplies from dealers who do not observe them. The Act also prevents, on principle, collective arrangements between suppliers for recommending minimum prices, although an individual supplier is free to recommend minimum prices for his goods.

Certain classes of goods may be exempted by the Restrictive

Practices Court from the general prohibition if they pass through certain gateways but only two exempting orders have been made by the Court, *viz.* in the case of books in 1969 and ethical and proprietary drugs in 1970. The Director General of fair Trading may make an application to the Court with regard to the making or review of an exemption order.

More generally, a feature of the prohibition of resale price maintenance is that under section 25(3) of the Resale Prices Act 1976 a breach of that prohibition is stated to be a breach of a duty owed to any person affected thereby, thus giving rise to an action for breach of statutory duty.

Other Anti-Competitive Practices

Scope

In contrast to the highly specific controls on monopolies, mergers, restrictive trade agreements and resale price maintenance, sections 2–10 of Competition Act 1980 introduced a general control of anti-competitive practices. Under section 2(1) of that Act, "a person engages in an anti-competitive practice if, in the course of business, that person pursues a course of conduct which, of itself or when taken together with a course of conduct pursued by persons associated with him, has or is intended to have or is likely to have the effect of restricting, distorting or preventing competition in connection with the production, supply or acquisition of goods in the United Kingdom or any part of it or the supply or securing of services in the United Kingdom or any part of it." The reference to "restricting, distorting or preventing competition" is redolent of the phrase "prevention, restriction or distortion of competition" in article 85 of the EEC Treaty, but unlike that provision, the Competition Act does not list examples of the practices at issue. Nevertheless, in an explanatory booklet, the Office of Fair Trading has indicated what it cautiously terms "practices . . . which, if adopted in certain circumstances, could be anti-competitive." These are divided into two main groups, relating respectively to pricing policy and distribution policy. The former category includes price discrimination, predatory pricing such as temporarily selling at prices below cost, and vertical price squeezing whereby a firm which controls the supply of a material required both for its own manufacturing processes and those of its competitors raises the price of that material and reduces its own price for the finished product so as to limit, if not eliminate, the profits of its competitors. The latter category includes tie-in sales, requiring the producer of one product to purchase supplies of another product from the same supplier, full-line forcing, whereby a purchaser has to purchase a product range rather than individual items, rental-only contracts, exclusive supply and purchase arrangements, and selective distribution arrangements.

The Competition Act does not, however, impose an outright prohibition on such practices; rather, it imposes a system of control by the Director and the Monopolies and Mergers Commission (see p. 448, *post*), and sanctions are not available unless and until the M.M.C. has reported.

Exemptions

Under section 2(2) of the Act, conduct arising from an agreement registrable under the Restrictive Trade Practices Act 1976 is excluded from the definition of an anti-competitive practice, presumably so as to avoid any conflicts between the separate systems of enforcement. The Anti-Competitive Practices (Exclusions) Order 1980, made under section 2(3) of the Act, further excludes practices carried out by firms with an annual turnover of less than £5 million and with less than a 25 per cent. share of a relevant market, provided the firms in question are not members of a group which exceeds these limits. It may be observed that the market share is numerically the same as the threshold for monopoly or merger references, but the basic criterion appears to be the turnover figure, which may be compared with the £5·75 million turnover used in the definition of a "medium-sized company" for accounting purposes under section 248(2) of the Companies Act 1985.

The Order also exempts certain types or sections of economic activity, notably practices relating to the export of goods, and to international sea and air transport.

Enforcement

The Act introduces a two-tier system of investigation of suspected anti-competitive practices. Under section 32 of the 1980 Act, the Director is empowered to conduct a preliminary investigation with a view to establishing whether a person has been or is pursuing a course of conduct which amounts to an anti-competitive practice, subject to a veto on the part of the Secretary of State. If the Director concludes that a practice is not anti-competitive, no further action is envisaged other than the publication of a report to that effect. If he concludes that a practice is anti-competitive in his report, the Director may accept relevant undertakings from the firms concerned. Subject to specific time limits, however, he may also make a "competition reference" to the Monopolies and Mergers Commission (M.M.C.) under section 5 of the Act where he has not accepted any undertaking, where it appears to him that an undertaking has been breached and he has given notice to that effect under section 4(4)(c), or where under section 4(5) he has required an undertaking to be varied but has not accepted the variation proposed.

On a competition reference, the M.M.C. is required by section 6(5) to investigate not only the existence of the anti-competitive practice but also the question whether that practice operated or might be expected to operate against the *public interest*. This investigation of the public interest is also the role of the M.M.C. in monopoly references and merger references (see pp. 433–434, *ante*), and it will be remembered that in that context section 84 of the Fair Trading Act 1973 defines the public interest with emphasis on the need to promote competition. If the M.M.C. concludes in its report, which must be made to the Secretary of State, that a practice is both anti-competitive and has operated or might be expected to operate against the public interest, the Secretary of State may, under section 9, request the Director to obtain an undertaking from the persons concerned or, under section 10(1)(a), he may make an order prohibiting the practice or remedying or preventing its adverse effects; such an order may also be made where the Director has been unable to obtain an undertaking within a reasonable time or regards it as unlikely that he will obtain such an undertaking, and where such an undertaking has been breached. Just as in the case of undertakings accepted in lieu of making a reference in the context of mergers, the new section 93A introduced by the Companies Act 1989 allows civil proceedings to be brought against the person responsible in respect of any failure to fulfil an undertaking given under these provisions of the Competition Act.

Chapter 21

COMPETITION RULES OF THE EUROPEAN COMMUNITIES

Following the Accession of the United Kingdom to the Treaties establishing the European Communities in 1973, the competition rules of the European Coal and Steel Community (ECSC) and of the European Economic Community (EEC) have become law in, if not of, the United Kingdom. There are considerable differences between these Treaties as to the scope of the rules they contain and as to the enforcement of those rules.

E.C.S.C. Competition Rules

The E.C.S.C. is a sectoral Community concerned with coal and steel (as defined in the E.C.S.C. Treaty) and coal and steel undertakings and associations thereof. The competition rules of that Treaty are therefore triggered by the involvement of coal or steel undertakings and there is no express requirement that trade between Member States should be affected. Article 65(1) prohibits agreements between undertakings, decisions by associations of undertakings and concerted practices tending directly or indirectly to prevent, restrict or distort normal competition within the coal and steel common market, and article 65(4) confers sole jurisdiction on the E.C. Commission to rule whether or not any such agreement or decision is compatible with that provision, subject to review by the European Court of Justice. Hence, in the United Kingdom sections 9(1) and (2) of the Restrictive Trade Practices Act 1976 require restrictions in agreements between coal and steel undertakings which relate to coal and steel not to be taken into account in determining whether an agreement is registrable, and section 34 provides that an agreement which has been authorised under the E.C.S.C. Treaty is exempt from registration. Article 66(1) of the Treaty requires any "concentration" (defined to include mergers) between undertakings at least one of which is a coal or steel undertaking to be authorised by the Commission; hence the Commission has been involved in bids by one United Kingdom company to take over another United Kingdom company as, *e.g.* in Joined Cases 160/73R and 161/73R *Miles Druce* v. *Commission* [1973] E.C.R. 1049.

The E.C. Commission has power to impose fines for breaches of articles 65 and 66 of the E.C.S.C. Treaty.

EEC Competition Rules

Scope

The EEC treaty is not limited to one sector of activity. Its chapter entitled "Rules on Competition" contains provisions governing not only private undertakings but also public undertakings and the grant of state aids, although only the former will be considered here. What is, however, common to all these provisions is that they prohibit anti-competitive practices only in so far as they "may affect trade between Member States," which was held not to be the case where a refusal to supply spare parts for cash registers affected only a firm servicing such case registers in and around London (Case 22/78 *Hugin* v. *Commission* [1979] E.C.R. 1869). Anti-competitive practices affecting only the national market therefore remain subject to national rules, although, if they exist in a legal and economic context of similar practices, they may be regarded as cumulatively affecting trade between Member States, as was suggested in the first *Brasserie de Haecht* case [1967] E.C.R. 407.

Restrictive agreements, decisions and practices

Article 85(1) of the EEC Treaty prohibits "all agreements between undertakings, decisions by associations of undertakings and concerted practices which may affect trade between Member States and which have as their object or effect the prevention, restriction or distortion of competition within the common market." Whilst a detailed examination of the scope of the prohibition must be left to specialist works, a distinction may be drawn between agreements and decisions on the one hand and the looser concept of concerted practices on the other, the latter being defined in Case 48/69 *ICI* v. *Commission* [1972] E.C.R. 619 as "a form of co-ordination between undertakings which, without having reached the stage where an agreement properly so-called has been concluded, knowingly substitutes practical co-operation between them for the risks of competition." It is clear that the prohibition contained in article 85(1) applies both to agreements between potential competitors at the same stage of distribution (horizontal agreements) and to agreements between undertakings at different levels of distribution (vertical agreements); it does not however apply to arrangements within an integrated undertaking or to agreements between a holding company and its subsidiary where the subsidiary has no real economic freedom of action (Case 15/74 *Centrafarm* v. *Sterling Drug* [1974] E.C.R. 1147, 1167). Whether or not an agreement may affect trade between Member States is treated largely as a question of construction of the agreement rather than as a question of the analysis of trade flows. In cases 56 and 58/64 *Consten and Grundig* v. *Commission* [1966] E.C.R. 299, it was held that what matters is "whether the agreement is capable of constituting a threat, either direct or indirect, actual or potential, to freedom of trade between Member States in a manner which might harm the attainment of the objectives of a single market between States." It is now clear that "trade" between Member States comprises not only the movement of goods but also the provision of services, including banking services (Case 172/80 *Zuchner* v. *Bayerische Vereinsbank* [1981] E.C.R. 2021).

Agreements, decisions or concerted practices falling within article 85(1) may be exempted from the prohibition under article 85(3) if they contribute to improving the production or distribution of goods or to promoting technical or economic progress, while allowing consumers a fair share of the resulting benefit, provided they do not impose unnecessary restrictions on the undertakings concerned and do not enable the undertakings concerned to eliminate competition in respect of a substantial part of the products in question. Whilst relatively few individual exemptions are given under this provision, Regulations have been enacted to give general exemptions to certain catagories of agreement, etc., notably Regulation 1983/83 and 1984/83 of the Commission on exclusive dealing agreements, which came into effect on July 1, 1983. They supersede Regulation 67/67. These regulations effectively exempt exclusive sale or purchase agreements to which only two undertakings are party, provided the agreement does not restrict parallel trade in the products concerned. The two Regulations of 1983 deal separately with exclusive distribution and exclusive purchasing agreements.

It was accepted by the European Court in Case 14/68 *Wilhelm* v. *Bundes-Kartellamt* [1969] E.C.R. 1 that the same agreement may be subject both to national competition rules and to EEC competition rules, and in the United Kingdom this is recognised in the Restrictive Trade Practices Act 1976. Broadly speaking, the 1976 Act still applies even though an agreement may be void under article 85(1) or authorised under article 85(3) of the EEC Treaty. But in these circumstances the Restrictive Practices Court, if seised of the matter, has a discretion to decline or postpone the exercise of its jurisdiction (section 5 of the 1976 Act). Alternatively, the Court may review its former decision in the light of the operation of a Community provision, *e.g.* refusal to grant exemption under article 85(3). The Director General may also refrain from taking proceedings before the Court in the light of any authorisation or exemption granted under Community law (section 21(1)(a) of the 1976 Act).

Regulations have been made under section 10(2) of the European Communities Act 1972 under which details of any notification to the European Commission or any Commission, decision or exemption in relation to an agreement or agreements are to be registered with the Director General.

Abuse of dominant position

The other major competition provision of the EEC Treaty concerning commercial undertakings is article 86, which prohibits "any abuse by one or more undertakings of a *dominant position* within the common market or in a substantial part of it . . . in so far as it may affect trade between Member States." A dominant position was defined in Case 27/76 *United Brands* v. *Commission* [1978] E.C.R. 707 as "a position of economic strength enjoyed by an undertaking which enables it to prevent effective competition being maintained in the relevant market by giving it the power to behave to an appreciable extent independently of its competitors, customers and ultimately of its consumers." Since dominance is a relative concept, the definition of the relevant market is here of particular importance; such a market has been held to be constituted by goods of a particular brand, by spare parts for goods of a particular brand

(Case 22/78 *Hugin* v. *Commission* [1979] E.C.R. 1869), or by the raw materials required for the manufacture of certain products (Cases 6 & 7/73 *Commercial Solvents* v. *Commission* [1974] E.C.R. 223), to take a few random examples. Dominance in itself is not prohibited, but only its abuse. Perhaps the most usual example of abuse is refusal to sell to an able and willing purchaser, as in the *Commercial Solvents* case (*ante*), but it has also been held to be an abuse for an undertaking in a dominant position to strengthen that position in such a way that competition on the relevant market is effectively eliminated (Case 6/72 *Continental Can* v. *Commission* [1973] E.C.R. 215); in other words, a merger involving an undertaking already in a dominant position may be subject to the control of EEC law, even though the EEC Treaty contained no express rules on mergers.

A formal system of merger control under the EEC Treaty was introduced by Council Regulation 4064/89 (O.J. 1989 L395/1), which entered into force in 1990. Arts. 1 and 21 of this Regulation confer on the Commission of the European Communities sole competence to take decisions with regard to "concentrations with a Community dimension," which are defined as those where the aggregate worldwide turnover of all the undertakings concerned is more than 5,000 million ECU and the aggregate Community-wide turnover of at least two of the undertakings involved is more than 250 million ECU, unless each of the undertakings concerned achieves more than two-thirds of its aggregate Community-wide turnover in one and the same Member State.

The question whether trade between Member States may be affected is in principle the same as in the case of agreements prohibited under article 85(1), but here it is a course of conduct rather than the terms of an agreement which must be considered, so that there may be more scope for factual analysis.

Enforcement of EEC competition rules

Unlike the E.C.S.C. Treaty, the competition rules of the EEC Treaty confer no exclusive powers on the Commission. Article 87 enables the relevant powers to be conferred on the Commission, and until measures to that effect were adopted, articles 88 and 89 enabled the competition rules to be enforced by the national authorities or by the Commission in co-operation with the national authorities. Power to enforce the competition rules alone was eventually conferred on the Commission in 1962 by Council Regulation No. 17; certain sectors, such as air and sea transport, were however excluded from its scope, so that in these sectors articles 88 and 89 remained in force. Power to enforce the competition rules in the context of sea transport was eventually conferred on the Commission by Regulation 4056/86, and this was done with regard to air transport by Regulations 3975 and 3976/87.

Under Regulation No. 17, the Commission may not only require an infringement to be terminated but may also impose a fine of up to 10 per cent. of turnover in the preceding business year, and article 192 of the EEC Treaty provides that such a fine is enforceable as a civil judgment in a Member State. The European Communities (Enforcement of Community Judgments) Order 1972 makes the decision imposing such a fine registrable in the High Court in England and Northern Ireland and in the Court of Session in Scotland and enforceable as a decision of the court in which it is registered. In investigating alleged breaches of the EEC competition rules, the Commission has the power to carry out on-the-spot inspections without notice, upheld in Case 136/79 *National Panasonic* v. *Commission* [1980] E.C.R. 2033, and in the United Kingdom the Commission's inspectors would normally be accompanied by officials from the Office of Fair Trading.

Irrespective of the terms of Regulation No. 17, however, it has been held by the European Court that "as the prohibitions of articles 85(1) and 86 tend by their very nature to produce *direct effects* in relations between individuals, these Articles create direct rights in respect of the individuals concerned which the national courts must safeguard" (Case 127/73 *BRT* v. *SABAM* [1974] E.C.R. 51). In other words, the prohibitions imposed by articles 85(1) and 86 are regarded as sufficiently clear and unconditional to give rise to correlative rights enforceable by individuals before their national courts; such rights remain enforceable before national courts even if the anti-competitive practice at issue has come before the Commission, although the court may exercise its discretion as to whether or not to stay the proceedings in such a case. In the United Kingdom, the direct effect of articles 85(1) and 86 appears to have been invoked most frequently as a defence as, *e.g.* in *Aero Zipp Fasteners* v. *Y.K.K. Fasteners* (*U.K.*) [1973] C.M.L.R. 819, but it has also been used as the basis for an application for an injunction in *Garden Cottage Foods* v. *Milk Marketing Board* [1983] 3 C.M.L.R. 43. Although in this case the injunction was refused on the ground that damages were an adequate remedy that in itself may be taken to mean that breach of the EEC competition rules may give rise to liability in damages. There is, however, a procedural difficulty in that the House of Lords held in *Rio Tinto Zinc* v. *Westinghouse* [1978] 1 All E.R. 434 that the possibility that the Commission might impose a fine gave rise to the privilege against self-incrimination under section 14 of the Civil Evidence Act 1968. However, it would appear that in practice an undertaking which invokes that privilege will be likely to attract the attention of the Commission's inspectors, as noted in the previous paragraph.

Although the enforcement of the EEC competition rules is not exclusively in the hands of the Commission, article 9(1) of Regulation No. 17 does give the Commission sole power to grant *exemptions* under article 85(3). Under article 4(1) of the Regulation, no exemption may be granted unless the agreement, decision or concerted practice in question has been *notified* to the Commission. There are a number of specific exceptions to the requirement of notification, and group exemptions may be available (see *ante*, pp. 451–452), but if a notifiable agreement has not been notified, then no exemption may be granted, whatever the merits (Case 30/78 *Distillers* v. *Commission* [1980] E.C.R. 2229).

In principle, notification of an agreement to the Commission confers no protection on the parties except with regard to the imposition of fines by the Commission (article 15(5) of Regulation No. 17). In particular, the direct effect of the prohibition in article 85(1) of the Treaty may be invoked against a notified agreement before a national court, as was held in the second *Brasserie de Haecht* case [1973] E.C.R. 77. It was, however, there recognised that, on grounds of legal certainty, there should be protection of notified 'old' agreements, *i.e.* agreements entered into before the enactment of Regulation No. 17, or (presumably) before Accession in the case of agreements relating to new Member States: national courts may not declare such agreements void until the Commission has either taken a decision or, as was held in Case 99/79 *Lancôme* v.

Etos [1980] E.C.R. 2511, indicated that it does not contemplate taking an individual decision on the agreement in question.

Indeed, the practice of the Commission has been to issue very few formal decisions with regard to the agreements, etc., referred to it; the vast majority have been disposed of informally, usually by a "comfort letter" indicating that no further action will be taken. It would appear that in dealing with the initial flood of notifications following the entry into force of Regulation No. 17, the Commission reduced a backlog of 37,014 cases in April 1967 to 2873 cases at the end of December 1972 whilst issuing only 66 formal decisions.

Council Regulation 4064/89 on the control of concentrations between undertakings

Arts. 1 and 21 of this Regulation, which introduces a Community system of merger control, confer on the Commission of the European Communities sole competence to take decisions with regard to "concentrations with a Community dimension" (see p. 453 above). A concentration arises (art. 3) where two or more previously independent undertakings merge, or where one or more persons already controlling at least one undertaking acquire direct or indirect control of the whole or parts of one or more other undertakings, control being defined as rights, contracts or any other means which confer the possibility of exercising decisive influence on an undertaking.

Under art 4. of the Regulation, the relevant concentrations must be notified to the Commission, which must decide whether they are compatible with the common market, by virtue of art. 2. In making this appraisal, the Commission is required to take into account the structure of the relevant markets and the market position of the undertakings concerned. A concentration which does not create or strengthen a dominant position so that effective competition would be significantly impeded in the common market or in a substantial part of it shall be declared compatible with the common market but one which does create or strengthen such a position shall be declared incompatible with the common market.

If a concentration found to be incompatible with the common market has already been implemented, the Commission may, under art. 8(4) require the undertakings or assets brought together to be separated, or the cessation of joint control, or any other action that may be appropriate. Conditions may be attached to a declaration of compatibility, and under art. 14, fines of up to 10 per cent. of the aggregate turnover of the undertakings concerned may be imposed where undertakings breach such conditions. Fines of 100 to 50,000 ECU may also be imposed in relation to failures to notify and in relation to the supply of incorrect or misleading information.

Unlike the United Kingdom legislation, therefore, for the mergers to which it applies, the EEC Regulation imposes a system of compulsory notification backed up by financial penalties, in particular for those who do not obey the Commission's decisions.

It should finally be recalled that, just as with Regulation 17/62, the fact that a Regulation confers exclusive jurisdiction on the Commission does not prevent a trader invoking the direct effect (see pp. 454–455 above) of the competition rules before his national courts. Hence, the case-law holding that arts. 85 to 86 of the EEC Treaty may be used for merger control (see p. 453 above) remains of interest in the context of disputes between traders and undertakings before national courts.

PART 6: NEGOTIABLE INSTRUMENTS

CHAPTER 22

BILLS OF EXCHANGE

A BILL of exchange is an instrument of the class called "negotiable."

The characteristics of a negotiable instrument are:

1. The title to it passes on delivery if it is a bearer instrument, and on delivery and indorsement if it is an order instrument. This distinguishes if from such things as a fire insurance policy, a bill of sale and a right to recover a debt.

2. The holder for the time being can sue in his own name.

3. No notice of assignment need be given to the person liable thereon.

4. A bona fide holder for value takes free from any defect in the title of his predecessors. This quality distinguishes a negotiable instrument from an assignable contract. Choses in action, for example, can be assigned, either at law under section 136 of the Law of Property Act 1925 or in equity, but in each case the assignee takes subject to any defences available against the assignor. In the case of a negotiable instrument, however, the assignee takes free from any such defences.

Examples of negotiable instruments are: bills of exchange, cheques, promissory notes, dividend warrants, share warrants and debentures payable to bearer. On the other hand, postal orders, share certificates, bills of lading and dock warrants are not negotiable.

A **bill of exchange** is—

—an unconditional order in writing
—addressed by one person to another
—signed by the person giving it
—requiring the person to whom it is addressed
—to pay
—on demand, or at a fixed or determinable future time
—a sum certain in money

—to or to the order of a specified person or to bearer (s.3(1)).[1]

The following are common forms of bills of exchange:

Order bill payable on demand

£400 London, *October* 1, 1991
On demand pay John Jones or order the sum of
£400 for value received. WILLIAM SMITH
To Thomas Robinson.

Bearer bill payable at future fixed time

£300 Newcastle, *October* 1, 1991
Three months after date pay bearer the sum of
£300 for value received. WILLIAM SMITH
To Thomas Robinson.

Bill payable 90 days after acceptance

£200 Manchester, *October* 1, 1991
Ten days after sight pay to my order £200 for
value received. WILLIAM SMITH
To Thomas Robinson.

From these forms it will be seen that there are three parties to a bill:

(a) the person who gives the order to pay—the **drawer**;
(b) the person to whom the order to pay is given—the **drawee**;
(c) the person to whom payment is to be made—the **payee**.

In the examples given, "William Smith" is the drawer, "Thomas Robinson" is the drawee, and "John Jones" is the payee. The drawer and the payee may be the same person, as may also be the drawee and the payee. If the drawer and the drawee are the same or the drawee is a fictitious person, the instrument may be treated as a bill of exchange or a promissory note at the holder's option. The holder is the payee or indorsee who is in possession of the bill, or the bearer in the case of a bearer bill.

[1] References in this chapter are to Bills of Exchange Act 1882 unless the contrary is expressed.

Both the drawee and the payee must be named or indicated with reasonable certainty. If the payee is a fictitious or non-existing person the bill may be treated as payable to bearer (s.7(3)). A bill drawn in favour of an existing person may be in favour of a "fictitious" person if the person named was never intended by the drawer to take under the bill.

X., a clerk employed by V., forged Z.'s signature to a bill drawn in favour of P., an existing person with whom V. did business. The forged bill was accepted by V., the drawee; X. forged P.'s indorsement and, on the maturity of the bill, presented it for payment to V.'s bank. The bank paid, and V., on learning of the fraud, claimed that the amount of the bill should not be debited against him by the bank. *Held*, as P. was never intended by X. to take under the bill he was a fictitious person. The bill was therefore payable to bearer, and, as the bank had paid the bearer, V.'s claim failed: *Bank of England* v. *Vagliano Bros.* [1891] A.C. 107.

If, however, the drawer intends the payee to take under the bill, although he is induced by fraud to form that intention, the payee is not fictitious.

M. was induced by the fraud of W. to draw a cheque in favour of K. M., when he signed, intended that K. should take the money. W. forged K.'s indorsement and paid the cheque into his own bank, which received payment. M. sued W.'s bank for the amount of the cheque. *Held*, he was entitled to succeed, because K., being intended by M. to receive the money, was not a fictitious payee, and the cheque was consequently not payable to bearer: *North and South Wales Bank Ltd.* v. *Macbeth* [1908] A.C. 137.

"Cash" cannot be said to be a fictitious or non-existing person and so an instrument made out "cash" cannot be read as payable to bearer. Accordingly, an instrument in the terms "pay cash or order" is not a bill of exchange because it is not to or to the order of a specified person or to bearer; but by virtue of the Cheques Act 1957, s.4, a banker collecting payment on such a document may be protected (*Orbit Mining and Trading Co. Ltd.* v. *Westminster Bank Ltd.* [1963] 1 Q.B. 794).

The bill must be an order, not a request. Accordingly, a document in the terms, "We hereby authorise you to pay on our account to the order of G £6,000," is not a bill of exchange (*Hamilton* v. *Spottiswoode* (1894) 4 Ex. 200).

The order must be unconditional. It must not order any act to be done in addition to the payment of money. If these conditions are not complied with, the instrument is not a bill of exchange. An order for payment out of a particular fund is not unconditional, but an order which is coupled with:

(a) an indication of a fund from which the drawee is to refund himself; or
(b) a statement of the transaction which gives rise to the bill,

is unconditional (s.3(3)).

A bill at the end of which is written "provided the receipt form at foot hereof is signed" is not unconditional (*Bavins* v. *London and South Western Bank* [1900] 1 Q.B. 270).

On the other hand, a dividend warrant which ends with the words, "This warrant will not be honoured after three months from date unless specially indorsed by the secretary," is unconditional, the words merely denoting what the company thinks is a reasonable time for presenting the warrant (*Thairlwall* v. *G.N. Ry.* [1910] 2 K.B. 509).

Similarly, where the words "to be retained" were written on a cheque, it was held that the cheque was unconditional, on the ground that the words merely imported a condition between the drawer and the payee, and did not affect the order on the bankers (*Roberts & Co.* v. *Marsh* [1915] 1 K.B. 42).

A bill is payable on demand if it is expressed to be payable on demand, or at sight, or on presentation, or if no time for payment is expressed (s.10).

A bill is payable at a determinable future time when it is expressed to be payable at a fixed period after date or sight, or after the occurrence of a specified event which is certain to happen, although the time of happening may be uncertain (s.11). For example, an order to pay three months after X.'s death will be a valid bill, but an order to pay three months after X.'s marriage will not. Even though X. does in fact marry, the order will not be a bill Furthermore, where a document expresses the sum to be payable "on or before" a stated date, the option thus reserved to pay at an earlier date than the fixed date creates an uncertainty and contingency in the time for payment and the document is not a bill (*Williamson and Ors.* v. *Rider* [1963] 1 Q.B. 89). It has been held by the Court of Appeal in *Korea Exchange Bank* v. *Debenhams (Central Buying) Ltd.*, [1979] 1 Lloyd's Rep. 548, that a bill of exchange payable at a certain time after "acceptance" was not a bill payable at a determinable future time but the correctness of this decision is respectfully doubted.

A sum is certain although it may be payable:

(a) with interest;
(b) by instalments, with or without a provision that upon default in payment of any instalment the whole shall be due;
(c) according to an indicated rate of exchange (s.9(1)).

If there is a difference between the sum payable as expressed in words and as expressed in figures, the sum expressed in words is the amount payable (s.9(2)).

A bill is **payable to order** when:

(a) it is expressed to be payable to order;
(b) it is payable to a particular person and does not contain words prohibiting transfer, *e.g.* a bill in the form "to pay A.B. £500" is an order bill, but a bill "to pay A.B. only" or "pay A.B. personally £500" is not an order bill;
(c) it is payable to the order of a particular person. In such a case it is payable either to the person in question or his order (s.8), *e.g.* a bill payable to "the order of A.B." is payable either to A.B. or to A.B.'s order.

A bill is **payable to bearer** when it is expressed to be so payable or when the only or last indorsement is an indorsement in blank (s.8(3)).

An **inland bill** is one which is:

(a) both drawn and payable within the British Isles, or
(b) drawn within the British Isles upon some person resident therein.

A **foreign bill** is any other bill (s.4).

A bill which is payable at a fixed period after date may be issued undated. In such a case any holder may insert the true date of issue, and if by mistake the wrong date is inserted, the bill is payable as if the date so inserted had been the true date (s.12). The date on a bill is presumed to be the true date unless the contrary is proved.

A bill may contain words prohibiting its transfer. In such a case it is valid between the parties, but is not negotiable.

D. drew a bill on G. payable three months after date "to the order of D. only" and crossed it "not negotiable." The bill was accepted by G. and indorsed for value by D. to H. *Held*, H. could not sue G. for the amount of the bill, because it was not transferable: *Hibernian Bank* v. *Gysin* [1939] 1 K.B. 483.

Incomplete bills (s.20)

When a bill is wanting in any material particular, the person in possession of it has prima facie authority to fill up the omission in any way he thinks fit.

Acceptance

If the bill is a **sight bill**, *i.e.* if it is payable at sight or on demand, it must be paid by the drawee when seen by him and the question of acceptance of such a bill cannot arise. But different is the position if the bill is a **time bill**, *i.e.* if it is payable at a future fixed time or a fixed time after acceptance. After a time bill has been issued, the holder should present it to the drawee for acceptance to find out whether the drawee is willing to carry out the order of the drawer. If the drawee agrees to obey the drawer's order he is said to accept the bill, which he does by signing his name on the bill, with or without the word "accepted" (s.17). Acceptance is defined as the signification by the drawee of his assent to the order of the drawer. After acceptance, the drawee is known as the **acceptor**. It is not essential for the holder to present the bill for acceptance, although it is to his advantage to do so as he thereby gains the additional security of the acceptor's name and, if acceptance is refused, the antecedent parties become liable immediately. In three cases, however, a bill must be presented for acceptance:

1. When it is payable after sight, presentment for acceptance is necessary to fix the date of payment.
2. When it expressly stipulates that it shall be presented for acceptance.
3. Where it is payable elsewhere than at the place of residence or business of the drawee (s.39).

A bill may be accepted before it has been signed by the drawer or while otherwise incomplete, and even if it is overdue or has been dishonoured by a previous non-acceptance or non-payment (s.18).

The rules as to **presentment for acceptance** are:

1. Presentment must be made at a reasonable hour on a business day and before the bill is overdue.

2. When the bill is addressed to two or more drawees who are not partners, presentment must be made to them all, unless one has authority to accept for all.

3. Where the drawee is dead, presentment may be made to his personal representative.

4. Where the drawee is bankrupt, presentment may be made to him or to his trustee.

5. Where authorised by agreement or usage, presentment may be made through the post (s.41(1)).

On the presentment the drawee may give either a general or a qualified acceptance, or he may refuse an acceptance.

A **general** acceptance assents without qualification to the order of the drawer.

A **qualified** acceptance in express terms varies the effect of the bill as drawn. An acceptance is qualified which is:

(a) conditional;
(b) partial, *i.e.* for part only of the amount of the bill;
(c) local, *i.e.* to pay only at a particular place. An acceptance to pay at a particular place is a general acceptance, unless it expressly states that the bill is to be paid there only and not elsewhere;
(d) qualified as to time;
(e) the acceptance of some of the drawees, but not all (s.19).

The holder of the bill may refuse to take a qualified acceptance and may treat the bill as dishonoured by non-acceptance (s.44(1)). If the holder does take a qualified acceptance, the drawer and indorsers are discharged unless they have assented to it. They are deemed to assent to a qualified acceptance if, after notice, they do not dissent within a reasonable time.

A bill may therefore be treated as dishonoured by non-acceptance when:—

1. The drawee does not, after presentment, accept the bill within the customary time, which is generally 24 hours.

2. The drawee gives a qualified acceptance (s.43(1)).

3. The drawee is dead or bankrupt, or is a fictitious person or a person not having capacity to contract by bill.

4. Presentment cannot be effected, after the exercise of reasonable diligence.

5. Although the presentment has been irregular, acceptance has been refused on some other ground (s.41(2)).

When a bill is treated as dishonoured by non-acceptance, notice of dishonour must be given in the manner stated below, otherwise the holder will lose his right of recourse against the drawer and indorsers.

If the acceptance is procured by fraud, the acceptor is only liable to a holder in due course and not to other holders.

A bill drawn on M. in favour of A. was accepted by M. through the fraud of F. *Held*, M. was not liable on the bill to A.: *Ayres* v. *Moore* [1940] 1 K.B. 278.

Acceptance for Honour

If a bill is dishonoured by a non-acceptance, the holder may nevertheless allow any other person to accept it for the honour of the drawer. The bill itself sometimes has inserted in it the name of a person to whom the holder may resort in case the bill is dishonoured. Such a person is called **the referee in case of need**, but there is no obligation on the holder to resort to the referee in case of need (s.15).

To be valid, an acceptance for honour can only take place after the bill has been protested for non-acceptance and is not overdue.

The acceptance for honour *supra protest* must:

(a) be written on the bill and indicate that it is an acceptance for honour; and
(b) be signed by the acceptor for honour (s.65).

It may state for whose honour the bill is accepted, but if it does not so state it is deemed to be accepted for the honour of the drawer.

The effect of accepting a bill for honour is that the acceptor for honour becomes liable to pay the bill, provided that:

(a) it is presented to the drawee for payment;
(b) it is not paid by the drawee;

(c) it is protested for non-payment; and
(d) he has notice of these facts (s.66).

Every person who has accepted a bill becomes liable to pay it according to the tenor of his acceptance (s.54(1)).

Negotiation

A bill is said to be negotiated when it is transferred from one person to another in such a manner as to constitute the transferee the holder of the bill. It may be negotiated by the holder at any time either before or after acceptance in the following manner:

(a) In the case of a bearer bill, by delivery.
(b) In the case of an order bill, by indorsement followed by delivery. If an order bill is delivered without indorsement, the transferee acquires such title as the transferor had in the bill, and in addition the right to have the indorsement of the transferor (s.31).

Indorsements

An indorsement, in order to operate as negotiation, must be written on the bill itself and signed by the indorser. It must be an indorsement of the entire bill, *i.e.* if the bill is for £100 it is not possible to indorse it as to £25 to X. and as to £75 to Y. Where there are two or more indorsements on a bill, they are presumed to have been made in the order in which they appear on the bill, but the liability of an indorser is not affected if he inadvertently puts his signature above instead of below the indorsement of the payee, provided that it is the intention of the parties that the indorser shall be liable on his signature (*Yeoman Credit Ltd.* v. *Gregory* [1963] 1 W.L.R. 343). Each indorser is in the nature of a new drawer, so far as those taking the bill after his indorsement are concerned.

Indorsements are of four kinds:

(a) in blank;
(b) special;
(c) conditional; and
(d) restrictive.

Blank indorsement

A blank indorsement is effected by the simple signature of the payee on the back of the bill. If the payee's name is wrongly spelt, he may indorse according to the spelling on the bill, adding, if he thinks fit, his proper signature (s.32). A blank indorsement specifies no indorsee and the bill in consequence becomes payable to bearer (s.34(1)).

Special indorsement

A special indorsement is when the payee writes on the back "pay A.B." or "pay A.B. or order," both of these having the same meaning. If a bill has been indorsed in blank, any holder may insert some person's name above the signature and so convert the indorsement into a special indorsement (s.34).

Conditional indorsement

A conditional indorsement is where a condition is attached to the signature, as, for example, where the indorser adds the words "*sans recours*," which has the effect of negativing his personal liability on the bill. When a bill is so indorsed, the condition may be disregarded by the payer and payment to the indorsee is valid whether the condition has been fulfilled or not (s.33).

Restrictive indorsement

A restrictive indorsement is one which prohibits further negotiation of the bill, as, for example, "pay D. only," or "pay D. for the account of X.," or "pay D. or order for collection." This gives the indorsee the right to receive payment of the bill, but no right to transfer his rights (s.35).

A holder transferring a bill after indorsement incurs the liabilities of an indorser as set out below. The transferor of a bearer bill incurs no liability except that he warrants to his immediate transferee for value:

(a) that the bill is what it purports to be;
(b) that he has a right to transfer it; and
(c) that he is not aware of any fact rendering it valueless (s.58).

A bill which is negotiable in its origin continues to be negotiable until it has been:

(a) restrictively indorsed; or
(b) discharged by payment or otherwise (s.36).

Holder in Due Course

The effect of the negotiation of a bill is to give the transferee, if he took the bill bona fide and for value, a good title to the bill notwithstanding any defects in the title of his predecessors. This attribute is the characteristic of negotiability, and it only attaches to a transferee who is **a holder in due course**.

A holder in due course is a holder who has taken a bill:

(a) complete and regular on the face of it;

A bill was drawn in favour of "F. & F. N. Co." It was indorsed "F. & F. N." *Held*, the bill was not complete and regular on the face of it: *Arab Bank Ltd.* v. *Ross* [1952] 2 Q.B. 216.

(b) before it was overdue;
(c) without notice that it had been previously dishonoured, if such was the fact;
(d) in good faith and for value;

Three cheques were written by D. in favour of S., a customer of the plaintiff bank. S. presented the cheques for payment but did not receive payment because D. stopped the cheques. D. stopped the cheques because S., a car dealer, had failed to deliver certain cars to D. The bank manager of the plaintiff bank had in the past credited some other cheques to S.'s account which the manager knew would be dishonoured. Also, the bank manager had delayed debiting some other cheques against S.'s account. The reason was to keep S.'s account in credit. *Held*, when S. became overdrawn on the account to a value in excess of these cheques, the plaintiff bank had a lien on the cheques. However, because of the actions of the plaintiff bank's manager, the plaintiff bank did not become a holder in due course under section 27(3) of the Bills of Exchange Act 1882. The reason was that the plaintiff bank had not acted in good faith as required by Section 27(3) Bills of Exchange Act 1882: *Bank of Credit and Commerce International S.A.* v. *Dawson and Wright* [1987] F.L.R. 342.

(e) without notice, at the time the bill was negotiated to him, of any defect in the title of the person who negotiated it (s.29(1)).

Every holder is prima facie deemed to be a holder in due course. But if in an action on a bill it is established that the acceptance, issue or subsequent negotiation of the bill is affected with fraud, duress or illegality, the burden of proof shifts. This means that to be a holder in due course, the holder must prove that, subsequent to the alleged fraud or illegality, value has in good faith been given for the bill (s.29(2)). In this context fraud means common law fraud. (*Österreichische Länderbank* v. *S'Elite Ltd.* [1980] 2 All E.R. 651).

The original payee is not a holder in due course (*R.E. Jones Ltd.* v. *Waring & Gillow Ltd.* [1926] A.C. 670).

The holder of a cheque who had a lien on it is deemed to have taken it for value to the extent of the sum for which he had a lien. Accordingly, provided such a holder satisfies the other conditions of section 29(1), he can be a holder in due course (*Barclays Bank Ltd.* v. *Astley Industrial Trust Ltd.* [1970] 2 Q.B. 527).

A holder, whether for value or not, who derives his title through a holder in due course has all the rights of a holder in due course as regards the acceptor and all parties prior to such holder if he was not a party to any fraud of illegality affecting the bill (s.29); such a person may be the drawer of a bill which has been dishonoured and returned to him by way of recourse (*Jade International Stahl und Eisen GmbH & Co. K.G.* v. *Robert Nicolas* (*Steels*) [1978] Q.B. 917.

The rights and powers of the holder of a bill are:

1. He may sue on the bill in his own name.

2. Where he is a holder in due course he holds free from any defect of title of prior parties.

(3) Where his title is defective:

(a) if he negotiates the bill to a holder in due course, that holder obtains a good title;
(b) if he obtains payment, the person who pays him in due course gets a valid discharge (s.38).

Valuable consideration

Valuable consideration is presumed in the case of negotiable instruments, but the presumption may be rebutted. Thus, in the case of a cheque the onus is upon the drawer of it to show that it was not for value. The consideration to support a bill is either:

(a) any consideration sufficient to support a simple contract; or
(b) any antecedent debt or liability.

The antecedent debt or liability must be the debt or liability of the drawer. A cheque drawn to pay an existing debt owed by the drawer is accordingly drawn for valuable consideration, but a cheque drawn to pay another's debt is not.

D. owed O. £400 for money lent. When payment was due D. persuaded W. to draw a cheque in favour of O. for £400 to discharge the debt. Before the cheque was cashed, W. countermanded payment. *Held*, W. was not liable to O. as there was no consideration for the cheque: *Oliver* v. *Davis* [1949] 2 K.B. 727.

Where value has at any time been given for a bill the holder is deemed to be a holder for value as regards the acceptor and all parties to the bill who became parties prior to such time (s.27(2)).

Consequently the holder may sue the acceptor and all such parties. Further, there is no requirement that the consideration must have passed directly between one party to the bill and another party to the bill. The requirement of the subsection is met if consideration has been given by a third person.

D. agreed to lend H. £1,650, provided H. undertook to procure a cheque for that amount from G. by a certain date, so that D. would have G.'s cheque in his possession before his own was presented. D. gave H. the cheque but because H. was unable to get in touch with G. in time D. stopped it. Soon after, H. did obtain the required cheque from G. in favour of D., at the same time giving G. his own cheque for the same amount. D. paid in G.'s cheque and authorised payment of his cheque in favour of H. G.'s cheque in favour of D. was dishonoured, and so was H.'s in favour of G. D. sued G., but the latter contended that D. was not a holder for value as no value had passed between them. *Held*, (1) no requirement existed for value to be given *by the holder of the cheque*; (2) on the facts double value had been given: by H. giving G. his own cheque in return for G.'s cheque in favour of D.; and by D. releasing his cheque in favour of H., after having stopped it; (3) accordingly D. was holder for value of G.'s cheque and was entitled to judgment on it: *Diamond* v. *Graham* [1968] 1 W.L.R. 1061.

A payee gives consideration for a negotiable instrument by impliedly agreeing to forgo a debt which is owed to the payee. Even where the debt is owed to others as well as the payee, the payee will still furnish consideration so as to enable the payee to sue the drawer bank where the cheque is dishonoured. (*M. K. International Development Co. Ltd.* v. *The Housing Bank. The Financial Times*, January 22, 1991.)

From the description of a holder in due course it follows:

1. When an overdue bill is negotiated, the holder takes it subject to any defect of title affecting it at its maturity (s.36(2)). A bill payable on demand is overdue when it appears on the face of it to have been in circulation for an unreasonable length of time.

2. When a bill which is not overdue has been dishonoured, any person taking it with notice of dishonour takes it subject to any defect of title attaching to it at the time of dishonour (s.36(5)).

Payment

In order to make the drawer and indorsers liable on a bill it must be presented for payment. But presentment for payment is not necessary to make the acceptor liable when the bill is accepted generally (s.52(1)). Presentment for payment must comply with the following rules:

1. Presentment is made by exhibiting the bill to the person from whom payment is demanded. On payment the holder must deliver up the bill to the payer.

2. When the bill is payable on demand, presentment must be made within a reasonable time from issue to make the drawer liable, and within a reasonable time from indorsement to make the indorser liable (s.45(2)). What is a reasonable time depends on the nature of the bills, the usage of trade with regard to similar bills, and the circumstances of the case.

3. When the bill is not payable on demand, presentment must be made on the date payment is due. Three days of grace must be added to the time of payment, but when the last day of grace is a non-business day, the bill is payable on the succeeding business day. Non-business days are: Saturday, Sunday, Good Friday, Christmas Day, a day declared to be a non-business day by an order made under the Banking and Financial Dealings Act 1971, s.2, and a day appointed by Royal proclamation as a public fast or thanksgivings day (s.92, as amended by the Banking and Financial Dealings Act 1971, ss.3 and 4).

4. Presentment must be made at a reasonable hour on a business day to the payer or some person authorised to make payment on his behalf (s.45(3)).

5. Presentment must be made:

(a) at the place of payment specified in the bill;
(b) if no place is specified, at the address of the drawee or acceptor as given in the bill;
(c) if neither of these are present, at the acceptor's place of business, if known, and, if not, at his ordinary residence;
(d) in any other case, if presented to the acceptor wherever he can be found or at his last known place of business or residence (s.45(4)).

6. Presentment may be made through the post where agreement or usage authorises that course.

7. Delay in making presentation will be excused it if is imputable to circumstances beyond the holder's control, and presentment is effected with reasonable diligence after the cause of the delay has ceased to operate.

Presentment for payment may be dispensed with:

(a) where, after the exercise of reasonable diligence, it cannot be effected;
(b) where the drawee is a fictitious person;
(c) as regards the drawer, where the drawee is not bound as between himself and the drawer to accept or pay the bill, and the drawer has no reason to believe that the bill would be paid if presented. This occurs when the bill is an accommodation bill;
(d) as regards an indorser, where the bill was accepted or made for the accommodation of that indorser, and he has no reason to expect that the bill would be paid if presented;
(e) by waiver of presentment, express or implied (s.46).

If a bill is not paid when it is presented for payment or if, presentment for payment being excused, it is overdue and unpaid, the bill is said to be dishonoured by non-payment and the holder has an immediate right of recourse against the drawer and indorsers (s.47). But whether the bill is dishonoured by non-acceptance or by non-payment, the drawer and indorsers cannot be sued until notice of dishonour is given.

Notice of dishonour

This notice must be given by the holder to the last indorser and to everyone on whom he wishes to impose liability. If he merely gives notice to the last indorser, the latter must give notice to any preceding indorsers whom he may wish to make liable, and they in turn must give notice to their predecessors in title. No particular form of notice is essential. The notice may be verbal or in writing or partly one and partly the other, provided that it is given in terms which sufficiently identify the bill and that it intimates that the bill has been dishonoured by non-acceptance or non-payment (s.49). The return of the dishonoured bill is a sufficient notice of dishonour. The notice may be given as soon as the bill is dishonoured and must be given within a reasonable time.

In the absence of special circumstances, a reasonable time is as follows:

1. Where the parties live in the same place, the notice must be given or sent off in time to reach the recipient on the day after the dishonour of the bill.

2. Where the parties live in different places, the notice must be sent off on the day after the dishonour of the bill, if there be a post on a convenient hour on that day, and if there be none, then by the next post thereafter (s.49(12)).

Non-business days are excluded (s.92). Notice of dishonour which is duly addressed and posted is effective although the letter may be lost or delayed in the post. Further, the notice is effective at the date when it is received, *i.e.* when it is opened or would be opened in the ordinary course of business. The notice must become effective after the bill is dishonoured. If the notice is received before the dishonour of the bill it is bad, but if it is sent out before dishonour and received after that event it is a good notice.

A bill was drawn by Needham Builders on Fir View Furniture. The bill matured on December 31, 1970. It had been accepted by Fir View Furniture and discounted and indorsed to Eaglehill. By December 28, 1970 Eaglehill and Needham knew that Fir View Furniture were in liquidation and that there was no prospect of the bill being honoured on presentation. Eaglehill prepared a notice of dishonour which they intended to send to

Needham; the notice was dated January 1, 1971 and was intended to be posted that day. By a clerical error the notice was posted on December 30, 1970 and arrived at Needhams by the first post on December 31. *Held*, the notice was not vitiated by the fact that it was posted before dishonour and on balance of probabilities, as a matter of fact, it was received after dishonour. It was, therefore, a good notice: *Eaglehill Ltd.* v. *J. Needham Builders Ltd.* [1973] A.C. 992.

Delay in giving notice of dishonour will be excused if it is caused by circumstances beyond the control of the giver of the notice and is not imputable to his misconduct or negligence. But when the cause of the delay has ceased to operate, notice must be given with reasonable diligence (s.50(1)).

The master of a ship at Colombo drew a bill of exchange on his owners for the price of coal supplied to the ship. The bill was dishonoured on a Saturday, and the holders, after making inquiries, learnt that the vessel was in the Tyne. Not knowing what part of the Tyne, they made further inquiries without success, and finally, on the following Thursday wrote a letter giving notice of dishonour to "the master of the 'Elmville,' Newcastle-on-Tyne." *Held*, the delay in giving notice of dishonour was excused under section 49(12) and section 50(1): *The Elmville* [1904] P. 319.

Notice of dishonour is dispensed with:

1. When after the exercise of reasonable diligence, notice cannot be given or does not reach the person sought to be charged.
2. By waiver, express or implied.
3. As regards the drawer, where:

(a) the drawer and the drawee are the same person;
(b) the drawee is a fictitious person or person not having capacity to contract;
(c) the drawer is the person to whom the bill is presented for payment;
(d) the drawee is as between himself and the drawer under no obligation to accept or pay the bill;
(e) where the drawer has countermanded payment.

4. As regards the indorser, where:

(a) the drawee is a fictitious person or a person not having capacity to contract and the indorser was aware of the fact at the time he indorsed the bill;

(b) where the indorser is the person to whom the bill is presented for payment;
(c) where the bill was accepted or made for his accommodation (s.50(2)).

If a bill has been dishonoured by non-acceptance and notice of dishonour is given, it is not necessary to give a fresh notice of dishonour on non-payment of the bill, unless in the meantime it has been accepted.

Where a **foreign bill** has been dishonoured by non-acceptance or non-payment, in addition to notice of dishonour the bill must be **protested**. If it is not protested, the drawer and indorsers are discharged. An inland bill need not be protested.

A protest is a document drawn up by a notary, or, if no notary is available at the place of dishonour, by a householder in the presence of two witnesses, certifying that the bill was duly presented for payment and that payment was refused. It must be signed by the notary making it and must specify:

(a) the person at whose request the bill is protested;
(b) the date and place of protest and the reason for protesting the bill;
(c) the demand made and the answer given, if any, or the fact that the drawee or acceptor could not be found.

The protest must also contain a copy of the bill. It must be made at the place where the bill was dishonoured, except that—

(a) when the bill is presented through the post office and returned by post dishonoured, it may be protested at the place to which it was returned;
(b) when the bill is payable at the place of business or residence of some person other than the drawee and has been dishonoured by non-acceptance, it must be protested for non-payment at the place where it is expressed to be payable.

Protest may be dispensed with by any circumstances dispensing with notice of dishonour. It must be made promptly, but it is sufficient if the bill has been noted for protest within the specified time, and the formal protest may be extended at any time afterwards as of the date of the noting (s.93). A bill may be noted on the day of its dishonour and must be noted not later than the next succeeding business day (Bills of Exchange (Time of Noting) Act 1917); non-business days are excluded.

Payment for honour

If a bill has been accepted for honour *supra protest* or contains a reference in case of need, it must at maturity be presented to the acceptor for payment. If the acceptor dishonours it, it must be protested for non-payment and then presented to the acceptor for honour or referee in case of need. The presentment must be made in accordance with the following rules:

1. Where the address of the acceptor for honour is in the same place as where the bill is protested for non-payment, the bill must be presented not later than the day following its maturity.
2. Where his address is in some other place, the bill must be forwarded not later than the day following its maturity (s.67).

When a bill has been protested for non-payment, any person may intervene and pay it. Such a payment, in order not to operate as a mere voluntary payment, must be attested by a notarial act of honour which may be appended to the protest. The notarial act of honour must declare the intention to pay the bill for honour and for whose honour it is paid. The effect of a payment for honour *supra protest* being made is to discharge all parties subsequent to the party for whose honour it is paid and to subrogate the payer for honour for the holder. On paying the bill and the notarial expenses incident to the protest, the payer for honour is entitled to receive both the bill and the protest. If the holder of the bill refuses to receive payment *supra protest*, he loses his right of recourse against any party who would have been discharged by the payment (s.68).

Liability of Parties

No person is liable on a bill whether as drawer, indorser or acceptor who has not signed it, but the fact of his signing it in a trade or assumed name does not absolve him from liability (s.23). Where a cheque drawn on a partnership account bears the printed name of the partnership and the signature of one partner, the other partners are likewise liable (*Ringham* v. *Hackett* (1980) 124 S.J. 201). A signature by procuration operates as notice that the agent has only a limited authority to sign, and therefore the principal will not be bound unless the agent was acting within the scope of his authority (s.25). Accordingly, if the payee receives payment of a bill drawn by an agent without authority and knows that it is so drawn, he is liable to refund the amount received to the drawer.

T. had a power of attorney to draw cheques on R.'s behalf. He bought a motor car from B. and paid for it by a cheque signed "R. by T. his attorney." B. knew the car was bought by T. for his own use. *Held*, B. must refund the amount of the cheque to R.: *Reckitt* v. *Barnett* [1929] A.C. 176.

If a person signs a bill and adds words to his signature indicating that he signs for or on behalf of a principal or in a representative character, he is not personally liable on the bill; but the words must clearly show that he signs as agent, a mere description of himself as an agent does not negative his personal liability. When it is doubtful whether the signature is that of a principal or of an agent, the construction most favourable to the validity of the instrument is to be adopted (s.26).

Examples: A signature "for and behalf of X. as agent—Y.," Y. is not liable as he has negatived personal liability.

A signature "P. & W., Churchwardens;" P. and W. are liable, the word "churchwardens" being merely a description: *Rew* v. *Pettet* (1834) 1 Ad. & E. 196.

A bill of exchange drawn on the F. company was accepted by the company. It was also indorsed on the back "F. Co., Ltd., A.B. and C.D., directors." In an action against A.B. and C.D. as indorsers, *held*, A.B. and C.D. were liable, the addition to their signatures of the word "directors" being a description only, and not a word excluding their liability: *Elliott* v. *Bax-Ironside* [1925] 2 K.B. 301.

The Companies Act 1985 s.349(4), provides that an officer of a company or another person who signs or authorises to be signed on behalf of a company a bill of exchange, promissory note or cheque in a name other than the proper name of the company, shall be personally liable. Thus, where the directors of the L. & R. Agencies Ltd. signed a cheque for the company by writing "L.R. Agencies Ltd.," omitting the connecting ampersand, they were held to be personally liable (*Hendon* v. *Adelman and Others* (1973) 117 S.J. 631). But the use of the abbreviation "Ltd." or a similar abbreviation for "Limited"—or possibly the use of an ampersand for "and"—does not attract personal liability (*Durham Fancy Goods Ltd.* v. *Michael Jackson* (*Fancy Goods*) *Ltd.* [1968] 2 Q.B. 839).

Goodville Ltd., a company registered in England, traded under the business name "Italdesign," which was registered under the Registration of Business Names Act 1916 (repealed by the Companies Act 1981). Maxform S.p.A., an Italian company, drew bills of exchange on Goodville Ltd., describing the drawee as "Italdesign." The bills were accepted by Mr. Mariani, the sole director of Goodville Ltd. His signature was not accompanied by words indicating his status of director or that he was purporting to sign for and on behalf of Italdesign or Goodville Ltd. *Held*, Mr. Mariani was personally liable: *Maxform S.p.A.* v. *Mariani and Goodville Ltd.* [1981] 2 Lloyd's Rep. 54.

B. supplied goods to R. R. issued certain cheques which were dishonoured on presentation. The cheques were signed with the two personal signatures of the directors of the R. company. These signatures were placed under the printed name of the company. The cheque was a company cheque and the number of R.'s account was indicated on the cheque. *Held*, by virtue of Section 26 of the Bills of Exchange Act 1882 the directors of the R. company were not personally liable: *Bondina Ltd.* v. *Rollaway Shower Blinds Ltd.* [1986] 1 W.L.R. 517.

The court will not allow rectification of such an instrument so as to nullify the effect of the statutory provisions (*Blum* v. *O.C.P. Repartition SA* [1988] BCLC 170).

Further, where the statutory requirements are not complied with, an officer of that company will not be able to rely on the doctrine of estoppel where there is simply no compliance with the statutory provisions (*Lindholst A/S* v. *Fowler and another* [1988] BCLC 166).

This statutory provision (Companies Act 1985 s.349(4)) is entirely consistent with the general law relating to bills of exchange whereby a person who signs a bill of exchange will be personally liable if there is nothing to indicate that the instrument is signed as agent for the company (*Rafsanjan Pistachio Producers Co-operative* v. *Reiss* [1990] BCLC 352).

A person who accepts a bill engages to pay it according to the tenor of his acceptance. He is precluded from denying to a holder in due course the existence of the drawer, the genuineness of his signature or his capacity to draw the bill; also he is precluded from denying the capacity of the drawer or payee to indorse the bill, but not the genuineness of their indorsements (s.54).

The drawer engages that on due presentment the bill shall be accepted and paid according to its tenor, and that if it be dishonoured he will compensate the holder or any indorser who is compelled to pay it, provided that the requisite proceedings on dishonour be taken. He is precluded from denying to a holder in due course the existence of the payee or his capacity to indorse (s.55).

The indorser engages that on due presentment the bill shall be accepted and paid according to its tenor, and that if it be dishonoured he will compensate the holder or a subsequent indorser who is compelled to pay it, provided that the requisite proceeding on dishonour be taken. He is precluded from denying to a holder in due course the genuineness of the drawer's signature and all previous indorsements, and to his immediate or a subsequent indorsee that the bill was at the time of his indorsement a valid bill and that he had a good title thereto (s.55).

A bill purports to be drawn by A. on B. in favour of C. A.'s signature is forged. The bill is indorsed in blank by C. to D. for value and eventually is negotiated to X., a holder in due course. C. is liable on the bill as indorser; B. is only liable if he accepts the bill; D. is under no liability unless X. is his immediate transferee for value.

Any person who signs a bill otherwise than as drawer or acceptor incurs the liabilities of an indorser. If a person has signed a bill as drawer, acceptor or indorser without receiving value therefor, he is known as an **accommodation party**. He incurs full liability on the bill to a holder for value, and it is immaterial whether, when the holder took the bill, he knew the party to be an accommodation party or not (s.28).

The **measure of damages** on a dishonoured bill is

(a) the amount of the bill;
(b) interest from the time of presentment for payment if the bill is payable on demand and from the maturity of the bill in any other case;
(c) the expenses of noting, and, when protest is necessary, the expenses of protest.

When the bill is dishonoured abroad, the measure of damages is the amount of the re-exchange with interest until the time of payment. This is the sum for which a sight bill, drawn at the time and place where the drawer or indorser sought to be charged resides, must be drawn to realise at the place of dishonour the amount of the dishonoured bill and the expenses consequent on its dishonour (s.57).

A claim on a bill may be met with the defence that acceptance was procured by fraud, duress or for a consideration which has failed, but not with a counterclaim for unliquidated damages (*James Lamont* (*James*) *& Co. Ltd.* v. *Hyland* [1950] 1 K.B. 585).

Forged Signatures

If any of the signatures on a bill are forged, the signature in question is wholly inoperative and no person, even if acting in good faith, can acquire rights under it (s.24).

S. carried on business in London, and had a branch in Manchester. X., the manager of the Manchester branch, without any authority from S., drew seven bills of exchange, purporting to do so on behalf of S., and signed them "X., Manchester manager." The bills having been dishonoured, K., a holder in due course, sued S. as drawer. *Held*, (1) the bills being drawn by X. without authority were forgeries and (2) S. was not liable on them: *Kreditbank Cassel* v. *Schenkers Ltd.* [1927] 1 K.B. 826.

Exceptions

1. If a banker pays a bill which is drawn on a banker and payable to order on demand, in good faith and in the ordinary course of business, he is protected from liability for his act if the **indorsement** has been forged or made without authority (s.60).

The person receiving payment will, however, be liable to refund any money received under a forged indorsement to the true owner.

G. drew cheques in favour of X. G.'s clerk forged X's indorsement and negotiated the cheques to C., who took them in good faith and for value. C. received payment of the cheques. *Held*, G. could recover the amount of the cheques from C.: *Goldman* v. *Cox* (1924) 40 T.L.R. 744.

2. If a transferee taking under a forged instrument in a foreign country obtains, by the law of that country, a good title, his title will be treated as good in England (s.72).

A cheque on a London bank was drawn in Roumania in favour of E. The cheque was stolen and the thief forged the indorsement. It was then presented in Vienna to a bank which paid it in good faith and without negligence, and by Austrian law this gave the Vienna bank a good title. The Vienna bank sent the cheque to the Anglo-Austrian bank who obtained payment from the bank on which it was drawn. In an action by E. to recover the amount of the cheque from the Anglo-Austrian bank, *held*, that as their predecessors in title had by Austrian law a good title to the cheque, the Anglo-Austrian bank also had a good title and E. could not succeed: *Embiricos* v. *Anglo-Austrian Bank* [1905] 1 K.B. 677.

DISCHARGE OF THE BILL

A bill is discharged by—

1. **Payment** in due course by or on behalf of the drawee or acceptor. Payment in due course means payment made at or after the maturity of the bill to the holder in good faith and without notice that his title is defective. Payment by the drawer or an indorser does not discharge the bill, but—

   (a) where a bill payable to or to the order of a third party is paid by the drawer, the drawer may enforce payment against the acceptor, but may not reissue the bill;

   (b) where a bill is paid by an indorser, or where a bill payable to the drawer's order is paid by the drawer, the party paying it is remitted to his former rights as regards the acceptor or antecedent parties, and he may, if he thinks fit, strike out his own and subsequent indorsements and again negotiate the bill.

When an accommodation bill is paid by the party accommodated the bill is discharged (s.59).

2. The acceptor of the bill becoming the holder of it at or after maturity in his own right (s.61).

3. **Waiver,** where the holder renounces his rights under it. Renunciation must be in writing, unless the bill is delivered up to the acceptor (s.62).

4. **Cancellation,** where it is done intentionally by the holder or his agent and the cancellation is apparent (s.63).

5. **Alteration** of the bill in a material particular without the assent of all parties liable on it. The following alterations are material: the date, the sum payable, the time of payment, the place of payment,

and, where the bill has been accepted generally, the addition of a place of payment without the acceptor's assent. It is also material to alter an inland bill into a foreign bill. The alteration of the number on a banknote is a material alteration, and avoids the note even in the hands of an innocent holder (*Suffell* v. *Bank of England* (1882) 9 Q.B.D. 555). But if the alteration is made accidentally, the note is not avoided (*Hong Kong and Shanghai Bank* v. *Lo Lee Shi* [1928] A.C. 181).

The effect of a material alteration is only to discharge those who became parties prior to the alteration. The person who made the alteration and all subsequent indorsers are bound by the bill as altered.

If the alteration is not apparent and the bill is in the hands of a holder in due course, the holder may enforce the bill as if it had never been altered (s.64).

An alteration is apparent if it is of such a kind that it would be noticed by an intending holder scrutinising the document which he intends to take with reasonable care (*Woollatt* v. *Stanley* (1928) 138 L.T. 620).

Lost Bill

If a bill is lost before it is overdue, the holder may apply to the drawer to give him another bill of the same tenor, and the drawer is bound to do so on receiving from the holder security indemnifying the drawer against loss (s.69).

Bill in a Set

When a bill is drawn in a set, *i.e.* in duplicate or triplicate, then if each part of the set is numbered and contains a reference to the others, the whole of the parts only constitute one bill. The acceptor should only accept one part, and if he accepts more than one and the different parts get into the hands of different holders in due course, he is liable on each part. On payment, he should require the part bearing his signature to be delivered up to him, because, if he does not do so, he will be liable on it if it is outstanding in the hands of a holder in due course. If the holder indorses two or more parts to different persons, he is liable on each. Except in the cases just mentioned, payment of one part discharges the whole bill (s.71).

Conflict of Laws

The form of a bill is determined by the law of the place of issue, but if a bill issued out of the United Kingdom conforms as regards its form to the law of the United Kingdom, it is valid as between all persons who negotiate, hold or become parties to it in the United Kingdom.

The form and the interpretation of the acceptance, indorsement or acceptance *supra protest* and the interpretation of the drawing of a bill is according to the law of the country where it took place.

A bill was drawn by E.V. in France on K. in London to the order of M.V. It was indorsed in France by E.V. with the authority of M.V. in his own name and without the addition of words to the effect that the indorsement was made on behalf of M.V. Such an indorsement was of no effect in English law (s.32(1)), but gave a good title to the indorsee by French law. *Held*, the indorsee had a good title, as the validity of the indorsement as regards form was governed by French law: *Koechlin et Cie* v. *Kestenbaum Bros.* [1927] 1 K.B. 889.

But if an inland bill is indorsed abroad, the interpretation of the indorsement is according to the law of the United Kingdom. The duty of the holder with respect to presentment for acceptance or payment is determined by the law of the place where it is to be done. The duty of the holder with regard to protest of notice of dishonour is determined by the law of the country where the bill was dishonoured. When a bill is drawn in one country and is payable in another, the time when it is payable is determined by the law of the place of payment (s.72).

Where a bill is expressed in foreign currency, the holder, when suing on it, has a choice: he may either sue in sterling, converting, in the absence of some express stipulation, the foreign currency at the date when the bill matured (s.72(4)), or he may sue in the foreign currency; in the latter case the English court will give judgment in the foreign currency and the judgment debt will be converted into sterling either at the date of payment of the judgment or at the date of execution (*Barclays Bank International Ltd.* v. *Levin Brothers* (*Bradford*) *Ltd.* [1977] Q.B. 270).

CHAPTER 23

CHEQUES AND PROMISSORY NOTES

A **cheque** is

—a bill of exchange
—drawn on a banker
—payable on demand (s.73).[1]

It therefore follows that the law relating to bills of exchange set out in the preceding chapter applies equally to cheques.

A cheque form was filled up "Pay cash or order," the word "cash" being in writing and "or order" printed. *Held*, not a cheque, because it was not payable to a specified person or to bearer but a direction to pay cash to bearer, the printed "or order" being neglected in favour of the written word "cash": *North and South Insurance Co.* v. *National Provincial Bank* [1936] 1 K.B. 328.

A bank is not bound to honour an undated cheque. The holder of such a cheque is authorised by section 20 to fill in the date, but he must do so within a reasonable time (*Griffiths* v. *Dalton* [1940] 2 K.B. 264).

A cheque may be postdated (s.13(2)). A cheque is not usually accepted. Marking or certification is not an acceptance.

A cheque drawn on the B. bank on June 13, postdated to June 20, was certified by the manager "marked good for payment on 20.6.39." The P. bank became holders in due course and on June 20 presented the cheque for payment, which was refused owing to the state of the drawer's account. *Held*, (1) the certification was not an acceptance of the cheque; (2) the manager had no authority to certify postdated cheques; (3) the B. bank was not liable: *Bank of Baroda Ltd.* v. *Punjab National Bank* [1944] A.C. 176.

The holder of a cheque must present it for payment within a reasonable time of its issue, and failure to do this will discharge the

[1] References in this chapter are to the Bills of Exchange Act 1882 unless the contrary is expressed.

drawer to the extent of any damage he may suffer from the delay. Damage will only be suffered when the bank on which the cheque is drawn is unable, for any reason, to honour the cheque.

Y. sent a cheque to W. in payment of his rent. W. received it on a Friday, and on the Saturday he posted it to his bank, which received it on the Monday. The bank sent it to its head office, which received it on the Tuesday, and presented it to Y.'s bank for payment on the Wednesday. That day Y.'s bank stopped payment. The jury found that the cheque was not presented within a reasonable time. *Held*, owing to the unreasonable delay on the part of W., Y. was discharged from liability on the cheque: *Wheeler* v. *Young* (1897) 13 T.L.R. 468.

In such a case the holder of the cheque is a creditor of the bank to the extent of the discharge of the drawer (s.74).

If a bank wrongly dishonours a cheque, it is liable to pay damages to its customer, but only nominal damages can be recovered by persons who are not traders.

R., who had an agreed overdraft of £1,100, had the overdraft extended to £1,500. The bank dishonoured two cheques drawn in favour of third parties, and refused to allow R. to cash a cheque at the bank, even though within the extended overdraft limit. *Held*, he could not recover damages for inconvenience and humiliation. Since he did not allege any specific loss, and since R. was not a trader, he could only recover nominal damages for the breach of contract on the part of the bank: *Rae* v. *Yorkshire Bank Plc* [1988] F.L.R. 1.

The relationship of banker and customer is that of debtor and creditor, with the modification that the banker is only liable to repay the customer on payment being demanded, while the ordinary debtor is under an obligation to pay without any demand being made. The consequence of this is that a banker cannot successfully plead the bar provided by the Limitation Act to any action for money standing to a customer's credit, until six years from a demand of payment has elapsed (*Joachimson* v. *Swiss Bank Corporation* [1921] 3 K.B. 111 and *National Bank of Commerce* v. *National Westminster Bank*, *The Financial Times*, March 16, 1990). If, however, the account has not been operated upon for a number of years, payment may be presumed.

In May 1866 F. deposited £6,000 with the bank. Transactions were recorded until November 1866, after which there was no record of any payment of principal or interest by the bank. F. died in 1893, and in 1927 the deposit receipt was discovered by F.'s executor. *Held*, payment must be presumed: *Douglas* v. *Lloyds Bank Ltd.* (1929) 34 Com.Cas. 263.

Where a deposit account is kept between a customer and a banker, there is not a new contract every time money is paid in (*Hart* v. *Sangster* [1957] Ch. 329).

An unindorsed cheque—like an indorsed one—which appears to have been paid by the banker on whom it is drawn is evidence of the receipt by the payee of the sum payable by the cheque (Cheques Act 1957, s.3).

The authority of a banker to pay a cheque is terminated by:

1. Countermand of payment. An oral countermand is sufficient, but whether oral or written it must actually reach the banker.

C. drew a cheque on his bank and on the same day, after business hours, countermanded payment by telegram. The telegram was put in the letter-box and, owing to the negligence of the bank's servants, did not reach the manager until two days later. In the meantime the cheque was cashed. *Held*, the cheque was not countermanded because (1) countermanding means actual notice to the banker, there being no such thing as a constructive countermand, and (2) the bank were not, although they reasonably might accept, bound to accept an unauthenticated telegram as authority to stop payment: *Curtice* v. *London City and Midland Bank Ltd.* [1908] 1 K.B. 293.

But where a bank, under a mistake of fact, pays a cheque drawn on it by a customer, it is prima facie entitled to recover payment from the payee if it has acted without mandate (*e.g.* if it has overlooked a notice of countermand given by the customer) unless the payee has changed his position in good faith or is deemed in law to have done so (*Barclays Bank Ltd.* v. *W.J. Simms & Son and Cooke* (*Southern*) *Ltd.* [1980] Q.B. 677).

2. Notice of the customer's death (s.75).

3. Notice of a winding up petition against the drawer.

4. Notice of the presentation of a bankruptcy petition against the drawer.

Crossed Cheques

A cheque is a crossed cheque when two parallel lines are drawn across it; in addition to the parallel lines, words may be written across the cheque.

Crossings are of four kinds:

1. General: consisting only of the parallel lines, or with the addition of the words "and company."

2. Special: when the name of a banker is written between the parallel lines.

3. Not negotiable: when these words are written across the cheque, either with or without the name of a banker.

4. A/c payee: when these words are written across the cheque, whether in addition to the other crossings or not.

The use of such words on a cheque imposes no duties upon a banker to its customer.

R. was a customer of the A. Bank and paid various cheques into his account with the A. Bank. Each cheque was made payable to a particular payee. Each cheque was crossed with the words "Not negotiable—account payee only." R. was not the payee. R. alleged that the A. Bank should have advised him as to the risks in putting such cheques into his account. *Held*, there was no duty on the part of the bank to give such advice to its customer: *Redmond* v. *Allied Irish Banks Plc* [1987] F.L.R. 307.

The crossing is a material part of the cheque and must not be obliterated or added to or altered except in the following cases:

1. Where a cheque is uncrossed, the holder may cross it generally or specially.

2. Where a cheque is crossed generally, the holder may cross it specially or add the words "not negotiable."

3. A banker to whom a cheque is crossed specially may cross it specially to another banker for collection.

4. Where a cheque is sent to a banker for collection he may cross it specially to himself (s.77).

When a cheque is crossed it can only be paid to a banker, and if crossed specially, only to the banker named in the crossing. If the banker on whom the cheque is drawn pays it otherwise than in accordance with the crossing, he is liable to the true owner of the cheque for any loss he may sustain owing to the payment (s.79). But if the cheque does not appear to be crossed or to have had a crossing which has been obliterated or to have been added to or altered, and the banker pays the cheque in good faith and without negligence, he does not incur any liability.

When a cheque is crossed "not negotiable," the person taking it does not have and is not capable of giving a better title to the cheque than that which the person from whom he took it had (s.81). Where a non-negotiable cheque is given for an illegal consideration, *e.g.* in exchange for tokens to be used at a casino for gaming, a person to whom the cheque is indorsed has no better title than the person who took the cheque (*Ladup Ltd.* v. *Shaikh* (*Nadeem*) [1982] 3 W.L.R. 172).

W. drew a cheque crossed "not negotiable" in blank and handed it to his clerk to fill in the amount and name of the payee. The clerk inserted a sum in excess of her authority and delivered the cheque to P. in payment of a debt of her own. *Held*, the clerk had no title to the cheque, P. had no better title and W. was not liable on the cheque: *Wilson and Meeson* v. *Pickering* [1946] K.B. 422.

The words "account payee" on a cheque are a direction to the bankers collecting payment that the proceeds when collected are to be applied to the credit of the account of the payee designated on the face of the cheque. If, therefore, the bankers credit the proceeds to different account, they are prima facie guilty of negligence and will be liable to the true owner for the amount of the cheque. This prima facie liability can be displaced on their proving that they made proper inquiry as to the authority of the person, to whose account the cheque was credited, to receive the amount.

A cheque was drawn in favour of "F.S.H. and others or bearer" and crossed "account payee." N., the bearer, paid the cheque into his own account at his bank, and the bank credited him with the proceeds without making any inquiries as to his title to the cheque. N. had no title to the cheque. *Held*, having regard to the crossing, the bank were negligent and liable to the true owner of the cheque: *House Property Co.* v. *London County and Westminster Bank* (1915) 84 L.J.K.B. 1846.

If a bank collects the cheque on behalf of another bank, they are not bound to see that the other bank credits the payee with the amount of the cheque.

X. drew cheques in favour of Y., crossed "account payee only," and sent them to Z., his agent, to forward to Y. Z. forged Y.'s indorsement and paid the cheques into his own bank in Germany, who forwarded them to their London agents, the W. bank, for collection. The W. bank collected the proceeds of the cheques and credited the German bank with the amount received. *Held*, the W. bank were not liable to X., because they were not bound to inquire to whose account the German bank credited the proceeds of the cheques: *Importers Co. Ltd.* v. *Westminster Bank* [1927] 2 K.B. 297.

The duty of the collecting banker must be carefully distinguished from that of the paying banker.

"A crossing is a direction to the paying bank to pay the money generally to a bank or to a particular bank, as the case may be, and when this has been done the whole purpose of the crossing has been served. The paying bank has nothing to do with the application of the money after it has once been paid to the proper receiving banker. The words "Account A.B." are a mere direction to the receiving bank as to how the money is to be dealt with after receipt": *per* Bigham J. in *Akrokerri (Atlantic) Mines Ltd.* v. *Economic Bank* [1904] 2 K.B. 465 at 472.

A cheque crossed "account payee" is still negotiable (*National Bank* v. *Silke* [1891] 1 Q.B. 435), but a bill payable to "payee only" is not negotiable.

Provisions Protecting Bankers

The Bills of Exchange Act 1882 and the Cheques Act 1957 afford bankers special protection from liability when paying a crossed cheque to a banker; or receiving payment of a crossed cheque for a customer; or paying a cheque that is not indorsed. However, no definition is given of a banker save that it *includes* a body of persons, whether incorporated or not, *who carry on the business of banking.*

Characteristics which are usually found in bankers today were identified in *United Dominions Trust Ltd.* v. *Kirkwood* [1966] 2 Q.B. 431, as follows:

(a) they accept money from, and collect cheques for, their customers and place them to their credit;
(b) they honour cheques or orders drawn on them by their customers when presented for payment and debit their customers accordingly; and
(c) they keep current accounts, or something of that nature, in their books in which the credits and debits are entered.

A banker, but not other persons, is protected:

1. If, when there is a forged indorsement, the banker pays

(a) a bill drawn on him payable to order on demand,
(b) in good faith and in the ordinary course of business, he is deemed to have paid the bill in due course (s.60).

X. drew a cheque in favour of Y. or order. Z. stole it and forged Y.'s indorsement. X.'s bankers paid the cheque in good faith, and in the ordinary course of business. *Held*, the bankers could debit X.'s account with the amount of the cheque: *Charles* v. *Blackwell* (1877) 2 C.P.D. 151.

A banker can act negligently although he is acting in the ordinary course of business. "The common aphorism that a banker is under a duty to know his customer's signature is in fact incorrect even as between the banker and his customer. The principle is simply that a banker cannot debit his customer's account on the basis of a forged signature, since he has in that event no mandate from the customer for doing so" (*per* Kerr J. in *National Westminster Bank Ltd.* v. *Barclays Bank International Ltd.*, see below). Where a banker, without acting negligently, pays a cheque on which the signature of his customer (the drawer) is forged, he can recover the amount paid from the collecting bank and the payee.

Commander Robert Bill, who lived in Nigeria, was a customer of the National Westminster Bank at one of their branches in London. One of his cheques was stolen in Nigeria. His signature as drawer was so skilfully forged that the forgery was practically undetectable and the cheque was made payable to Mr. Mohamed Ismail, of Nigeria, who was unaware that it was forged and who gave valuable consideration for it; the cheque was not crossed. Mr. Ismail sent the cheque to Barclays Bank International in London, with whom he banked, and instructed them to collect it by way of special collection. National Westminster, to whom Barclays International presented the cheque, did not discover the forgery and paid Barclays who credited the amount to Mr. Ismail's account. Later the forgery was discovered and National Westminster brought an action against Barclays and Mr. Ismail for the recovery of the £8,000. *Held*, (1) National Westminster had not acted negligently in honouring their customer's cheque, (2) they could recover: *National Westminster Bank Ltd.* v. *Barclays Bank International Ltd.* [1975] Q.B. 654.

Further, if, in the absence of an indorsement or where there is an irregular indorsement, a banker pays

(i) a cheque drawn on him,

(ii) in good faith and in the ordinary course of business,

he is protected (Cheques Act 1957, s.1).

2. If, *when a cheque is crossed*, the banker pays

(a) the cheque drawn on him,
(b) in good faith and without negligence,
(c) if crossed generally, to a banker, and, if crossed specially, to the banker to whom it is crossed,

he is placed in the same position as if he had paid the true owner (s.80).

The drawer is also protected if the cheque has come into the hands of the payee.

3. A banker who receives an unindorsed cheque "for collection" and has given value for, or has a lien on it, has the same rights as if the cheque had been indorsed to him in blank (Cheques Act 1957, s.2).

Section 2 applies even if the cheque is collected not for the payee's account but for another account, but the banker can successfully sue the drawer of an unindorsed cheque only if he gave value for the cheque or had a lien on it; otherwise the cheque must be indorsed to him (*Westminster Bank Ltd.* v. *Zang* [1966] A.C. 182).

4. If, when a customer has no title or a defective title to a cheque, the banker receives payment of a cheque *whether crossed or not crossed*,

(a) for the customer,
(b) in good faith and without negligence,

the banker does not incur any liability by reason only of having received payment (Cheques Act 1957, s.4).

This section (which takes the place of the repealed s.82 of the Act of 1882) applies to cheques and to any document issued by a customer of a banker which, though not a bill of exchange, is intended to enable a person to obtain payment from that banker of the sum mentioned in the document. It therefore applies, *inter alia*, to bankers' drafts, dividend warrants and cheques payable "cash or order." Further, where an agent having a customer's ostensible authority to sign and issue an instrument, the instrument is a document "issued by a customer" even where the agent signs it and puts it into circulation in fraud of his principal (*Orbit Mining and Trading Co. Ltd.* v. *Westminster Bank Ltd.* [1963] 1 Q.B. 794).

A banker is not protected if a cheque ceases to be a cheque by reason of a material alteration (*Slingsby* v. *District Bank* [1932] 1 K.B. 544).

A person becomes a customer of a banker when he goes to the banker with money or a cheque and asks to have an account opened, and the banker accepts the money or cheque and agrees to open an account. The duration of the relationship is immaterial. But mere casual acts of service, such as cashing a cheque for a friend of a customer, do not create the relationship of banker and customer (*Commissioners of Taxation* v. *English, Scottish and Australian Bank Ltd.* [1920] A.C. 683).

A bank may be a "customer" of another bank if it has a drawing account with it (*Importers Co.* v. *Westminster Bank* [1927] 2 K.B. 297).

What amounts to negligence depends on the facts of the particular case and the practice of bankers. In *Marfani & Co.* v. *Midland Bank* [1968] 1 W.L.R. 956, Nield J. formulated four principles which should guide a court in such cases, namely:

1. The standard of care required of bankers is that to be derived from the ordinary practice of careful bankers.
2. The standard of care required of bankers does not include the duty to subject an account to microscopic examination.
3. In considering whether a bank has been negligent in receiving a cheque and collecting the money for it, a court has to scrutinise the circumstances in which a bank accepts a new customer and opens a new account.
4. The onus is on the defendant to show that he acted without negligence.

The principles that should guide a court in deciding whether a bank was negligent were further formulated by Hutchinson J. in *Thackwell* v. *Barclays Bank Plc* [1986] 1 All E.R. 676.

1. It was reaffirmed that in order for a bank to establish a defence under Section 4 Cheques Act 1957, the bank must show that it received payment of the cheque in good faith and without negligence. The onus is on the bank to establish this.
2. In deciding whether a bank has acted negligently, there were two tests that have been applied by the courts.

3. The first test is that based on the ordinary practice of banks. The court must look at the transaction and decide whether the circumstances surrounding the paying in of the cheque in question would have aroused suspicion in a banker's mind so that the bank in question would have made further inquiry. The test is an objective one.

4. Furthermore, it is no defence to a bank, which has been guilty of negligence in the collection of a cheque, to show that had they made further inquiries, then a reassuring answer would have been given to them.

5. In this particular case the court applied the first test.

6. The second test is that based on the practice of banks to protect themselves and others against fraud. A bank should act in a way which furthers this aim.

It is negligence

(a) To open an account without inquiring as to the identity and circumstances of the customer (*Ladbroke & Co.* v. *Todd* (1914) 111 L.T. 43). Among the circumstances to be inquired into are the nature of the customer's employment and the name of his employer.

Lumsden & Co., plaintiff stockbrokers, employed a Mr. Blake as temporary accountant. The practice of the plaintiffs was to draw cheques in favour of their clients in an abbreviated form; thus, where the cheques were payable to Brown Mills & Co., they simply drew them in favour of Brown. Blake, who was fraudulent, opened an account with the defendant bank in the name of a fictitious J.A.G. Brown whose profession he gave as a self-employed chemist. Blake gave the fictitious J.A.G. Brown an excellent reference, describing himself as a "D.Sc., Ph.D." The branch manager of the defendant bank, who thought that he was dealing with two reputable professional men, failed, contrary to his instructions, to make inquiries with Mr. Blake's bank. Mr. Blake then transferred some of the cheques due to Brown Mills & Co. but simply made payable to Brown to the fictitious J.A.G. Brown's account with the defendant bank. *Held*, (1) the defendant bank had acted negligently in opening the account and was not protected by section 4(1) of the Cheques Act 1957; (2) there was contributory negligence to the extent of 10 per cent. on the part of the plaintiffs and the damages to which they were entitled had to be reduced accordingly: *Lumsden & Co.* v. *London Trustee Savings Bank* [1971] 1 Lloyd's Rep. 114.

(b) To receive payment of a cheque for a customer, when the

cheque is drawn in favour of the customer's employer, without inquiring as to his title to the cheque.

U. was the sole director and practically the sole shareholder in U. Ltd. U. had a private account with the L. bank, and the company had an account with the X. bank, but the L. bank knew nothing of this account. Cheques payable to the company were indorsed, "U. Ltd.—U., sole director," and paid into the L. bank to U.'s private account. *Held*, U. Ltd. were entitled to recover the amount of the cheques, because the L. bank were negligent in not inquiring whether U. Ltd. had an account, and, if so, why the cheques were not paid into it: *Underwood Ltd.* v. *Bank of Liverpool and Martins Ltd.* [1924] 1 K.B. 775.

If a cheque payable to a customer in his official capacity is paid into the customer's private account, the bank should make similar inquiries (*Ross* v. *London County, etc., Bank* [1919] 1 K.B. 678). The same applies if the instrument bears a clear indication that it is payable to the customer as agent of another person.

M. was the manager of three farms in Scotland belonging to B.; his duties included the making of applications for and receiving of certain hill sheep subsidies for B. After having left the employment of B., M. paid into his personal account three crossed warrants relating to those hill sheep subsidies and made payable to M. "(for the Marquess of Bute)." *Held*, the bank had not discharged the onus of proving they had acted without negligence, and therefore they could not claim the protection of section 82[2]: *Bute (Marquess)* v. *Barclays Bank Ltd.* [1955] 1 Q.B. 202.

C., the manager of B. bank, was induced to pay out a cheque which, unknown to him, formed part of a species of take-over fraud, whereby those seeking to buy a controlling interest in a certain company stole money from the company in order to pay for their purchase. The circumstances surrounding the tendering of the cheque were unusual and out of the bank's ordinary course of business. Moreover, the amount involved was unusually high. The company to be taken over commenced proceedings claiming replacement by B. bank of the amount of the cheque. *Held*, that a reasonable banker, in the interests of his customer, would have made further inquiries before payment, and the bank was liable: *Karak Rubber Co. Ltd.* v. *Burden (No. 2)* [1972] 1 W.L.R. 602.

(c) To receive payment of a cheque for a customer, when the

[2] This section is now repealed and section 4 of the Cheques Act 1957 is substituted for it.

cheque is drawn by the customer's employer in favour of a third party or bearer, without inquiring as to the customer's title to the cheque (*Lloyds Bank* v. *Savory* [1933] A.C. 201).

(d) To receive payment of a cheque for a customer, when the cheque is drawn by the customer as agent for a third party in his own favour, without inquiring as to the customer's title to the cheque (*Morison* v. *London County, etc., Bank* [1914] 3 K.B. 356).

T. was authorised by a power of attorney to draw cheques on behalf of R. He drew cheques on R.'s banking account signed "R., by T., his attorney," and fraudulently paid them into his own account with the M. bank to reduce his overdraft. *Held*, the bank were negligent, because they had not inquired into T.'s authority to pay the cheques into his own account and were liable to pay the amount of the cheques to R.: *Midland Bank* v. *Reckitt* [1933] A.C. 1.

(e) Where the circumstances would put a reasonable banker on enquiry and the banker does not make any inquiries.

S. paid in two cheques into an account, one after the other. One cheque was made payable to S. and endorsed by S.'s own signature. The other cheque was drawn by J. The payee of this cheque was T. This cheque was forged by S. who forged the signature of T. The assistant manager witnessed the forgery of T.'s signature by S. The assistant manager merely glanced separately at each endorsement on each cheque without noticing the fraud. *Held*, the assistant manager, and hence the bank, were negligent. They could not establish the statutory defence under Section 4 Cheques Act 1957: *Thackwell* v. *Barclays Bank* [1986] 1 All E.R. 676.

(f) Not to notice the account of the customer from time to time and consider whether it is a proper or a suspicious one (*Lloyds Bank* v. *Chartered Bank of India* [1919] 1 K.B. 40).

If an open cheque for a large amount payable to bearer is presented to a bank for payment over the counter, it is not negligence for the bank to pay the cheque without making inquiries "in the absence of very special circumstances of suspicion, such as presentation by a tramp, or a postman or an office boy" (*per* Wright J.).

A bill of exchange for £876, payable to X., was indorsed by X. and handed to W. to take to the bank for the purpose of collecting through the clearing house. Instead of doing this, W. presented the bill for payment over the counter and received cash, which he stole. *Held*, the bank were not liable to X., because such a payment over the counter, though unusual, was made to the bearer in good faith and without notice of any defect in his title: *Auchteroni & Co.* v. *Midland Bank Ltd.* [1928] 2 K.B. 294.

If a banker pays a cheque on the forged signature of his customer he cannot debit his customer with that amount. Similarly, if the amount of a cheque properly drawn by the customer has been fraudulently increased and the banker pays the altered amount, he can only debit his customer with the amount of the cheque as originally drawn. But the customer owes a duty to his banker in drawing a cheque to take reasonable and ordinary precautions against forgery, and, if as the natural and direct result of the neglect of these precautions, the amount of the cheque is increased by forgery, the customer must bear the loss as between himself and the banker.

The firm of M. & A. entrusted to their clerk the duty of filling up cheques for signature. The clerk presented to one of the partners a cheque payable to the firm or bearer. No sum was written in the space for the writing, and the figures "2 0s. 0d." were written in the space for the figures. The partner signed the cheque and the clerk then wrote in the space for writing "one hundred and twenty," and altered the figures accordingly. The bank paid £120 out of M. & A.'s account. *Held*, they were entitled to do so, because M. & A. had been guilty of negligence in signing the cheque in the manner described: *London Joint Stock Bank Ltd.* v. *Macmillan & Arthur* [1918] A.C. 777.

It is not normally a breach of duty on the part of the customer to use reasonable care in leaving a space between the name of the payee and the words "or order" but if the customer abbreviates the name of the payee in a manner which makes forgery more easily possible, that may be contributory negligence (*Lumsden & Co.* v. *London Trustee Savings Bank* [1971] 1 Lloyd's Rep. 114.

T. drew a cheque in favour of A. and handed it to X. to be forwarded to A. A space was left between A.'s name and the words "or order," and X. inserted the words "per X." in this space. X. indorsed the cheque in his own name and received payment. *Held*, (i) the cheque was not properly indorsed, the proper indorsement being "A. per X.," so that the bank was not protected by section 60; (ii) the insertion of the words "per X." was a material alteration avoiding the cheque; (iii) there was no negligence on the part of T. in the manner in which the cheque was drawn: *Slingsby* v. *District Bank* [1932] 1 K.B. 544.

There is no corresponding duty to be careful imposed on the drawer or acceptor of a bill of exchange (*Scholfield* v. *Londesborough* [1896] A.C. 514.

The customer is under a duty to disclose to the bank any forgeries which he has discovered (*Greenwood* v. *Martins Bank* [1933] A.C. 51).

Whilst a customer owes its bank a duty to take care in the drawing of cheques, and a duty to inform the bank of any forgeries of which the customer knows, the customer does not owe a duty to its bank to take precautions in the carrying on of its business so as to prevent its employees committing fraud in relation to the cheques of the company. (*Tai Hing Ltd.* v. *Liu Chong Hing Bank* [1986] 1 A.C. 80).

In modern practice banks use computers to sort out cheques on which the branch and account number of the customers are printed in magnetic ink. Where a customer alters the printed branch to another one by ordinary ink (which the computer cannot read) and then countermands the cheque but the computer dispatches the cheque to the original branch which pays it, the bank might be liable.

B. was a customer of the defendant bank and had accounts at two branches, the Borough and the Bromley Branches. In 1964, many years after the relationship of banker and customer had been established, the bank adopted the system of computer banking and the Borough branch issued B. with a cheque book stating his account number in magnetic ink and informing him that he must not use these cheques for another account. B. altered one of the cheques by making it payable at the Bromley Branch; the alteration was made in ordinary ink which the computer could not read. B. then countermanded the cheque by informing the Bromley branch but the computer cleared the cheque to the Borough branch which, being unaware that it had been stopped, paid it. *Held*, that the bank was liable since the notice on the cheque book had not become part of the contract with B., on the principle in *Chapleton* v. *Barry U.D.C.* However, the position might have been different if the cheque book bearing the notice had been the first issued to the customer on his opening the account: *Burnett* v. *Westminster Bank Ltd.* [1966] 1 Q.B. 742.

Promissory Notes

A **promissory note** is

—an unconditional promise in writing
—made by one person to another

—signed by the maker
—engaging to pay
—on demand or at a fixed or determinable future time
—a sum certain in money
—to or to the order of a specified person or to bearer (s.83(1)).

As to certainty of time of payment, it has been held that a document expressing a sum to be payable "on or before" a stated date introduced uncertainty and so was not a promissory note (*Williamson and Ors.* v. *Rider* [1963] 1 Q.B. 98).

B.K. Ltd. was loaned £10,000 by C. B., who was the principal shareholder in B.K. Ltd., signed a document which stated that the loan was to be paid back in full by July 1, 1983. The question was whether this document was a promissory note within Section 83 of the Bills of Exchange Act 1882. *Held*, the document did not satisfy the requirements of Section 83 since there was no unconditional promise to pay at a fixed or future time. The payer could choose to pay the loan at an earlier date than July 1, 1983: *Claydon* v. *Bradley* [1987] 1 W.L.R. 521.

The following is one form of promissory note:

> Newcastle,
> *June* 1, 1991
>
> I promise to pay on demand A B or order the sum of £100 for value received.
>
> X Y.

An instrument, which is void as a bill of exchange because it is not addressed to anyone, may nevertheless be valid as a promissory note.

A document was in the following form:

"On December 31, 1928, pay to my order the sum of £125 7s. 4d. for value received."

It was not signed, but across the face were the words "Accepted payable at Lloyds Bank Ltd., Highgate Branch, J.H. Lack." *Held*, the instrument was a promissory note on which Lack was liable as maker: *Mason* v. *Lack* (1929) 45 T.L.R. 363.

An instrument in the form of a note payable to the maker's order is not a note unless and until it is indorsed by the maker. A note which is made and payable within the British Isles is an inland note:

any other note is a foreign note. A promissory note is not complete until it has been delivered to the payee or bearer (s.84).

A note may be made by two or more makers, who may be liable on it jointly or severally. If it is payable on demand it need not be presented for payment within a reasonable time to render the maker liable; but it must be presented within a reasonable time after indorsement to render the indorser liable.

Even if it appears that a reasonable time has elapsed since the note was issued, the holder is not, on that account, affected by defects of title of which he had no notice (s.86).

B. gave a mortgage on some property to W., and also a promissory note for the amount of the mortgage. W. transferred the mortgage to X. for the full amount due thereon, and subsequently indorsed the note to G. for value. G. had no notice of the mortgage. A considerable time later, G. sued B. *Held*, although after his transfer of the mortgage W. had no right to sue on the note, G. was a bona fide holder for value and not affected by the defect in W.'s title: *Glasscock* v. *Balls* (1889) 24 Q.B.D. 13.

Presentment for payment is not necessary to render the maker liable, but it is necessary to make the indorser liable. If, however a note is, in the body of it, made payable at a particular place, it must be presented for payment at that place in order to render the maker liable.

The maker of a promissory note by making it:

(a) engages that he will pay it according to its tenor;
(b) is precluded from denying to a holder in due course the existence of the payee and his then capacity to indorse (s.88).

The law as to bills of exchange applies to promissory notes, the maker of a note corresponding with the acceptor of a bill, and the first indorser of a note corresponding with the drawer of an accepted bill payable to the drawer's order. When a foreign note is dishonoured, protest is unnecessary (s.89).

PART 7: COMMERCIAL SECURITIES

Chapter 24

BAILMENT, PAWN AND LIEN

Bailment

In General

Bailment will usually be constituted by a contract of bailment but it may arise by other means, for example by voluntarily taking possession of another's goods.

Bailment is the delivery of goods by one person, called the bailor, to another, called the bailee, on condition that the same goods are re-delivered by the bailee to or on the direction of the bailor. Examples are the deposit of goods in a cloakroom or left-luggage office for safe custody and the loan, pawn or hire of goods; further examples occur when goods are entrusted to a warehouseman or carrier but special rules apply to the latter case. A contract of bailment may also be combined with other types of contract, such as a contract to repair the bailor's goods.

Where there is a contract of bailment, the consideration moving from the bailor is his parting with possession of the goods; that from the bailee, the promise to return them. There may also be the additional consideration of a payment on the part either of the bailor, as in the deposit of goods in a left-luggage office, or of the bailee, as in a contract of hire.

But there need not be a contract for the obligations of a bailee to arise. A person may assume the obligations of a bailee in respect of the goods of another by voluntarily taking possession of them, *e.g.* the finder of goods. Such a bailee, if he fails to return the goods on demand, may be liable for loss or damage to the goods even if this occurred without his fault. (*Mitchell* v. *Ealing L.B.C.* [1979] Q.B. 1).

Where the goods of the bailor, while in the possession of the bailee, are lost or damaged by an event for which a third party is responsible, the bailee can recover damages from the third party but has to hold the amount recovered as trustee for the bailor (*The Winkfield* [1902] P. 42). The bailee can also insure the bailor's goods and has an insurable interest in them but again, if the goods are lost or damaged, has to hold the insurance sum as trustee for the bailor (*A. Tomlinson (Hauliers) Ltd.* v. *Hepburn* [1966] A.C. 451.

Two cases of clocks were shipped from Germany to Australian buyers (the plaintiffs). The ship carrying them was the *Regenstein.* They arrived in Sydney where the defendant stevedores and ship's agents unloaded them in a shed on the wharf under their control. When the plaintiffs wanted to take delivery, one case was missing. *Held*, (1) the absence of a contract of bailment between the plaintiffs and the defendants was irrelevant, (2) the defendants, by voluntarily taking possession of the plaintiff's goods, assumed an obligation to take reasonable care of them, (3) this obligation was the same as that of a bailee, (4) the defendants had become sub-bailees (the shipowners being the main bailees), (5) the defendants were liable: *Gilchrist Watt and Sanderson Pty. Ltd. v. York Products Ltd.* [1970] 1 W.L.R. 1262.

Duty of bailee

The bailee is under a duty to take reasonable care of the goods bailed. The standard of care required of a bailee (whether gratuitous or otherwise) is the standard demanded by the circumstances of each particular case. The burden is on the bailee to show either that there has been no negligence or, if there has that he is not liable by virtue of an exemption clause (*Levison* v. *Patent Steam Carpet Cleaning Co. Ltd.* [1978] Q.B. 69). Thus if he fails to return goods or returns them in a damaged condition it is for him to show that the loss or damage occurred in spite of the fact that he took reasonable care of them. It follows that if the cause or the circumstances of loss or damage to goods are unexplained by a bailee, the bailor's claim against him will succeed as the bailee has failed to discharge the burden of proving that this was not due to his negligence (*Houghland* v. *R.R. Low (Luxury Coaches) Ltd.* [1962] 1 Q.B. 694). For example, if the loss or damage is due to act of God or to robbery with violence, a bailee is not liable, but it is the bailee who has to prove that this was the cause of the loss or damage. If the article bailed is stolen by the employee of a bailee, the latter will be liable if he did not use reasonable care in selecting his employee (*Williams* v. *Curzon Syndicate Ltd.* (1919) 35 T.L.R. 475), but a bailee for reward will also be liable if goods were stolen by an employee to whom they were specifically entrusted, as where a fur coat was given to an employee to clean and he stole it (*Morris* v. *C.W. Martin & Sons* [1966] Q.B. 716).

If, however, the goods are not entrusted to a specific employee and the bailee can show that he had a proper system for looking after them, he is not liable for any loss or damage they may sustain.

B. left some engraving plates with S. as a gratuitous bailee. The plates were stolen from S., but the manner of the theft was unknown. S. proved that the plates were kept in a proper place, under the charge of proper persons and under arrangements which were reasonably sufficient. *Held*, S. was not liable: *Bullen* v. *Swan Electric Engraving Co.* (1907) 23 T.L.R. 258.

But it is not sufficient for a bailee to prove that the loss occurred without any negligence on his part; he must also show that he either informed the bailor or used reasonable care to assist in their recovery.

Some cattle belonging to A. were sent to be looked after by B. Without any negligence on B.'s part, the cattle were stolen. B. did not inform the owner or the police or make any effort to recover them, because he thought it would be useless to do so. *Held*, B. was liable for the loss, unless he could prove that, even if he reported the loss, the cattle could not have been recovered: *Coldman* v. *Hill* [1919] 1 K.B. 443.

The bailee is also under a duty to return the goods bailed in accordance with the terms of the contract of bailment. If he fails to do this, he is liable for their loss or damage, notwithstanding the exercise of reasonable care on his part.

A. delivered books to B. to be bound. He pressed for their return, but B., although more than a reasonable time had elapsed, neglected to return them. A fire accidentally broke out on B.'s premises, and the books were burnt. *Held*, B. was liable for the loss, although he was not negligent, because of his failure to deliver the books within a reasonable time: *Shaw & Co.* v. *Symmons & Sons* [1917] 1 K.B. 799.

The duty of a bailee is generally a duty owed to the bailor, but where the bailor is not himself the owner of the goods bailed the bailee may owe a duty to the owner also.

A., customs and forwarding agents, made one contract with the plaintiffs to clear the plaintiffs' goods through customs and deliver them. A. made another contract with the defendants, transport contractors, to collect the goods from the docks and deliver them to A.'s warehouse. The defendants knew from a period of trading with A. that A. were continuously handling goods owned by their customers, and in the present case the defendants received delivery notes naming the plaintiffs as owners. The defendants' driver collected the goods but left the vehicle unattended, when half the goods were stolen. *Held*, the defendants were bailees for reward of the plaintiffs' goods albeit their contractual duty was owed not to them but to A.; since the defendants knew the goods were the plaintiffs', they owed a duty of care to the plaintiffs in respect of their goods, and since, in the circumstances, the defendants could reasonably have foreseen the loss which in fact occurred they were liable to the plaintiffs for the value of the stolen goods: *Lee Cooper Ltd.* v. *C.H. Jeakins and Sons Ltd.* [1967] 2 Q.B. 1.

Implied terms

Where goods are bailed, terms may be implied into the contract of bailment by the Supply of Goods and Services Act 1982. Thus where there is a bailment by way of hire there will be implied terms (1) that the bailor has the right to transfer possession to the bailee, (2) that the bailee will enjoy quiet possession of the goods, (3) that the goods comply with the description in the contract, and (4) (where the bailment is in the course of a business) that the goods are of merchantable quality, and where the bailee makes known any particular purpose for which the goods are to be used that they are reasonably fit for that purpose. In addition, where the bailment involves the supply of services by the bailee there are implied terms that the bailee will carry out the service with reasonable care and skill and (where the contract is silent on the point) will carry out the service within a reasonable time and for a reasonable charge.

Right of bailee to sell

A bailee has no right at common law to sell the goods bailed even if he has incurred expenses in relation to them. Under the Torts (Interference with Goods) Act 1977, a bailee who has not been paid for services rendered in respect of the goods bailed may sell them. Thus a watch repairer who, in the course of his business, accepts for repair a watch left with him by the owner, may, if the owner fails to pay for the work done and to collect the watch, subject to giving notice and to other conditions of the Act, sell the watch. Out of the proceeds of sale the watch repairer may retain his charges, the balance being payable to the owner. Under the Act the bailee is granted protection against the bailor, but not against the true owner if he is someone other than the bailor.

CONTRACTS OF BAILMENT

Deposit

In the contract of deposit, goods are deposited by the bailor with the bailee for safe custody. The bailee is not, as a rule entitled to use the goods bailed; if he, in breach of his contract, does use them, he is liable for the resultant damage. He is bound to take reasonable care of the goods bailed.

X. entered a restaurant to dine. His coat was taken by a waiter and hung on a hook behind X. The coat was stolen. *Held*, the restaurant proprietor was liable for the loss: *Ultzen* v. *Nicols* [1894] 1 Q.B. 92.

The contract may, however, exempt the bailee from liability for negligence.

R. deposited a motorcar with P., a garage proprietor, for sale on commission, upon the terms of a printed document containing the clause: "Customers' cars are driven by our staff at customers' sole risk." While the car was being sent by P. to be shown to a prospective buyer, it was damaged owing to the negligence of P.'s driver. *Held*, P. was protected from liability by the clause in the contract: *Rutter* v. *Palmer* [1922] 2 K.B. 87.

Exemption clauses are, however, subject to the provisions of the Unfair Contract Terms Act 1977, under which the exclusion clause must be reasonable.

A. took some photographs of a wedding and took the roll of film to the defendants for processing. Most of the photographs were lost. The contract contained a clause limiting damages to the cost of replacing the film, but this clause was held unreasonable and thus ineffective: *Woodman* v. *Photo Trade Processing* see (1981) 131 N.L.J. 933.

However even if the clause is valid it must be apt to cover what has occurred. Thus where a bag was deposited at a railway left luggage office and a term of the contract excluded liability for "misdelivery," it was held that this term did not cover the situation where the bailee deliberately misdelivered by allowing a third party to open the bag and remove goods (*Alexander* v. *Railway Executive* [1951] 2 All E.R. 442).

If the contract is that the goods shall be deposited at one place and they are deposited by the bailee at another, the bailee will be liable for any loss and will not be able to rely on protective terms.

D. contracted to warehouse some drapery goods for L. at Kingsland Road, but warehoused a portion elsewhere. A fire occurred there, without any negligence on D.'s part, and the goods were destroyed. *Held*, D. was liable for the loss: *Lilley* v. *Doubleday* (1881) 7 Q.B.D. 510.

If goods deposited in a warehouse are stolen, the warehouseman is liable unless he can prove that he took all reasonable precautions against theft: *Brook's Wharf* v. *Goodman Bros.* [1937] 1 K.B. 534.

Gratuitous loan for use

Under this arrangement the bailee is entitled to use the goods bailed, and so is not liable for reasonable wear and tear but he must restore the goods in a proper condition and at the proper time. He must not, however, deviate from the conditions of the loan, otherwise he will be liable for any loss of or injury to the goods.

Hire

In a contract of hire there is an implied warranty on the part of the owner that the goods hired are as fit for the purpose for which they were hired as reasonable care and skill can make them. Even when the hirer has inspected the goods, this warranty applies. The hirer is bound to take reasonable care of the goods and only to use them in accordance with the contract.

The owner cannot claim a return of the goods from the hirer except in accordance with the terms of the contract. If, however, the hirer sells the goods, the contract is terminated and the owner may recover the goods from the purchaser, whether or not he knew of the hiring.

A hiring agreement will be subject to the controls of the Consumer Credit Act 1974 (see Chapter 17) if it is not a hire purchase agreement, is capable of lasting three months and it does not require the hirer to make payments totalling more than £15,000.

The main effect is to control the formation and content of the agreement and to control the right of the bailor to terminate the agreement. In particular the bailee, on giving notice under section 101 of the Act, may terminate the agreement after 18 months, whatever the length of the agreement.

Innkeeper and guest

A "common innkeeper" is one who keeps an inn for the reception of travellers. The liability of the innkeeper is largely regulated by the Hotel Proprietors Act 1956. An hotel is defined in section 1(3) as "an establishment held out by the proprietor as offering food, drink and, if required, sleeping accommodation, without special contract, to any traveller presenting himself who appears able and willing to pay a reasonable sum for the services and facilities provided and who is in a fit state to be received."

An hotel proprietor's legal position is similar to that of a common carrier. He is bound to receive all travellers who come to his inn, provided that he has sufficient room, that the traveller is able and willing to pay, and that no reasonable objection can be taken to the traveller's personal condition.

Failure to accept a traveller renders the hotel proprietor liable in damages but if the inn is full, the hotel proprietor is not bound to provide the traveller with accommodation.

Like a common carrier, an hotel proprietor is an insurer of the property brought by the guests to the hotel. Property includes his luggage, but not his motorcar or any property left in it. If, therefore, any of the guest's luggage is lost, damaged or stolen, the innkeeper is liable at common law unless he can prove that the loss was due to:

(a) act of God;
(b) the King's enemies; or
(c) the guest's own negligence.

S. brought jewellery worth £600 to an hotel and locked it in her dressing case. She did not lock her room and this was not the practice at the hotel. The jewellery was stolen. *Held*, the hotel was liable. S.'s conduct not amounting to negligence. (A notice under what is now the Hotel Proprietors Act 1956 was not exhibited): *Shacklock* v. *Elthorpe Ltd.* [1939] 3 All E.R. 372.

The Hotel Proprietors Act 1956 provides that an hotel proprietor shall not be liable for the loss of or injury to any property brought to his hotel to a greater amount than £50 for one article or a total of £100 in the case of any one guest unless:

(a) the property was stolen, lost or damaged through the neglect or wilful default of the hotel proprietor or his servant; or
(b) the property has been deposited expressly for safe custody with the hotel proprietor, in which case he may require them to be deposited in a box fastened and sealed by the person depositing them.

To obtain the protection of the Act, the hotel proprietor must exhibit a copy of the notice set out in the Schedule to the Hotel Proprietors Act 1956 (the effect of which is set out above), in a place where it can be conveniently read by his guests at or near the reception office or desk or, where there is no reception office or desk, at or near the main entrance to the hotel. His liability for articles lost or destroyed up to the value of £50 is the same as at common law.

B. took a bag of jewellery samples worth £1,800 to a hotel and without saying anything handed it to a porter who placed it in the office. The bag was stolen but the hotel was not liable as it had not been deposited **expressly** for safe custody: *Whitehouse* v. *Pickett* [1908] A.C. 357.

An innkeeper has a lien on all goods brought by the guest to his inn for the price of the food and lodging supplied to him except on articles for which he is not responsible in case of their loss or damage, for example there is no lien over a guest's motorcar or any property left therein. Further, the innkeeper has no power to detain the guest himself or to take the clothes from his person. The lien is enforced by detaining the goods and is lost if the innkeeper allows the guest to remove them.

In addition to the right of lien the Innkeepers Act 1878 gives a power of sale over goods deposited or left in an inn where the person leaving them owes money for board and lodging. The power includes the power to sell motor vehicles left by the lodger. The sale can only be effected if the goods have been six weeks on the premises, and the sale has been advertised at least one month before it is due to take place.

Involuntary bailment

A person may be placed in possession of goods without his consent, in which case he is an involuntary bailee. Such a bailee is not liable for negligence, but must not wilfully damage the goods or deliberately sell them. (*Hiort* v. *Bott* (1874) L.R. 9 Exch. 86). He is under no obligation to return the goods but he will be under no liability if he acts reasonably in attempting to do so. Under the Unsolicited Goods and Services Act 1971, where goods are sent to a person without his consent with a view to sale, the recipient may regard them as his own (and thus use or sell them) if the sender fails to collect them within 30 days of being given notice by the recipient, or within six months where no notice is given.

PAWN

Pawn is the delivery of a chattel by one person, called the pawnor, to another, called the pawnee, as security for a loan. The chattel pawned still remains the property of the pawnor, but its possession is with the pawnee. This distinguishes pawn from mortgage, in which the owner, for example of a house, usually remains in possession. It is distinguished from lien, because the pawnee can, in certain circumstances, sell the chattel pledged, whereas in the case of lien there is no power of sale.

The pawnor has the right to redeem the chattel pawned in the stipulated time or, if no time is stipulated, within a reasonable time after demand for repayment has been made. If he does not redeem, the pawnee has the right to sell the chattel and to pay himself the amount of the loan and expenses, the balance being due to the pawnor.

The pawnee is bound to take reasonable care of the chattel pawned, and if it is not forthcoming when an offer to redeem is made, the burden of proof is on him to show that the loss occurred in spite of his taking due care. The pawnee cannot use the chattel pawned.

The Consumer Credit Act 1974, ss.114–122, regulates pawn agreements so long as the credit does not exceed £15,000. The Act provides that it is an offence to take a pawn from a person who is under 18, and to fail to give a pawnor a copy of the credit agreement. In addition the pawnee must give the pawnor a receipt for the pawn.

A pawn is redeemable at any time within six months but, subject to this limitation, the redemption period is that fixed by the parties for the duration of the credit secured by the pledge, or such longer period as they may agree. The imposition of special charges for redemption is prohibited, as are higher charges for safe keeping, after the end of the redemption period. It is not possible to contract out of these provisions. The pawnee is not liable if he gives up the pawn to the wrong person so long as that person has the pawn receipt, nor is he liable for refusing to give up the pawn if he reasonably believes that the bearer of the pawn receipt is not the owner of the pawn or is not authorised to receive it. It is an offence to refuse to allow a pawn to be redeemed without reasonable cause.

If the amount of credit does not exceed £25 and the redemption period is six months, the pawn becomes the property of the pawnee if it has not been redeemed. In other cases the pawnee is entitled to sell the goods, but, first he must give notice of such intention to the pawnor and subsequently inform him of the result of the sale and account for the proceeds. It is not necessary for the sale to be by auction but the pawnor is entitled to challenge the price realised or the expenses incurred and if he does so it is for the pawnee to justify the price or expenses in question.

LIEN

There are three kinds of lien:

(a) possessory lien;
(b) maritime lien; and
(c) equitable lien.

Possessory lien

A possessory lien is a right to retain that which is in the possession of the person claiming the lien until a claim is satisfied. For the creation of this lien possession is essential and must be (1) rightful, (2) not for a particular purpose, and (3) continuous.

H., the owner of a motorcar, agreed with a company that they would maintain and garage her car for three years, on being paid an annual sum by H. H. was entitled to take the car out of the company's garage as and when she liked. The annual payment being in arrear, the company detained the car in the garage and claimed a lien. *Held*, as H. was entitled to take the car away as and when she pleased, the company had no lien: *Hatton* v. *Car Maintenance Co. Ltd.* [1915] 1 Ch. 621.

A possessory lien may be general or particular.

1. A general lien is a right to retain possession of the goods of another until **all** claims against that other have been satisfied. It may arise by (a) a course of dealing, (b) continuous and well-recognised usage, or (c) express agreement.

X. imported frozen meat into England. X. was financed by J., who paid for the meat, and reimbursed himself by drawing a bill of exchange in favour of the bank on X., who accepted it. The bills of lading for the meat were deposited with the bank as security that the bill of exchange would be met. On its arrival in England, the meat was stored with the U. Co. on the terms (general in the trade) that they should have a general lien. X. failed to meet his acceptance, whereupon J. took up the bills of lading from the bank and demanded the meat. The U. Co. claimed a lien on the meat for charges due from X. in respect of other goods. *Held*, the U. Co. could enforce their general lien against J.: *Jowitt & Sons* v. *Union Cold Storage Co.* [1913] 3 K.B. 1.

By well-recognised usage, a general lien exists in the case of solicitors, factors, stockbrokers and bankers. There is no custom of a general lien in favour of "consolidators," that is persons who pack goods from various customers into containers for export: *Chellaram* v. *Butlers* [1978] 2 Lloyd's Rep. 412.

A banker, in the absence of agreement to the contrary, has a lien on all securities in his hands for the general balance owing to him on all accounts of his customer. Although not a right of lien as such—for a debtor cannot have a lien over his own indebtedness to his customer—a banker also has the right, again in the absence of agreement to the contrary, to combine accounts of the customer if the customer is in credit in one account and in debit in another. This right to combine accounts may be limited by special agreement so as to exclude certain accounts of the customer from its operation, although the exclusion ceases to bind the banker on the death, bankruptcy or liquidation of the customer (*Halesowen Presswork &*

Assemblies Ltd. v. *Westminster Bank Ltd.* [1972] A.C. 785, see pp. 149–150, *ante*).

2. A particular lien is a right to retain goods until all charges incurred **in respect of those goods** have been paid. Common carriers have a lien in respect of the freight on goods carried. Innkeepers have a lien on most of the luggage and other property brought to the inn (see p. 512, *ante*).

A person who, at the request of the owner, has done work or expended money on a chattel has a particular lien in respect of his claim.

G. owned a motorcar which was let on hire-purchase to X., who agreed to "keep the car in good repair and working condition." The car was damaged, and X. sent it to A. for repair. The instalments being in arrear, G. terminated the hire-purchase settlement and sued A. for the car. A. claimed a lien for the cost of repair. *Held*, A. had a lien, as X. had G.'s authority to have the car repaired: *Green* v. *All Motors Ltd.* [1917] 1 K.B. 625.

If, in the case just quoted, the agreement had been terminated before the car was sent for repair, the repairers would have had no lien as against the owner (*Bowmaker* v. *Wycombe Motors Ltd.* [1946] K.B. 505).

A particular lien does not arise unless (a) the work has been completed, except when the owner prevents completion, and (b) the chattel has been improved by the work or the expenditure. An agreement to maintain a motorcar does not amount to improving it, so that the person responsible for maintenance has no lien (*Hatton* v. *Car Maintenance Co.*, *supra*).

Enforcement of lien

A possessory lien is enforced only by a right of retention. No claim can be made for storage or for any other expense to which the person exercising the lien may be put. There is no general right of sale.

Under particular statutes, a lien may be enforced by sale in the following cases: repairs of goods or persons accepting goods for treatment, under the Torts (Interference with Goods) Act 1977, and unpaid sellers of goods, under the Sale of Goods Act 1979.

Extinguishment of lien

A possessory lien is extinguished by:

(a) loss of possession of the goods;
(b) payment or tender of the amount claimed;
(c) taking security under such circumstances as to show that the security was taken in substitution for the lien; and
(d) abandonment.

Maritime lien

A maritime lien is a right specifically binding a ship, her furniture, tackle, cargo and freight for payment of a claim founded upon the maritime law. It is distinguished from a possessory lien in two respects:

(a) it is not founded on possession;
(b) it is exercised by taking proceedings against the property itself, *e.g.* by arresting the ship, in the Admiralty Court.

The persons who have a maritime lien are: salvors of the property saved, seamen for their wages, the master for wages and disbursements, the holder of a bottomry bond (which relates to money advanced to the master of a ship to enable a voyage to continue) for the amount of his bond, and claimants in respect of damage caused by collision due to the ship's negligence.

A maritime lien attaches to the ship notwithstanding any sale or transfer of the ship (*The Bold Buccleugh* (1851) 7 Moore P.C. 267), even to a bona fide purchaser without notice of the lien. It remains in existence until payment, release, abandonment or loss or destruction of the ship.

Equitable lien

An equitable lien is a charge upon property, conferred by law until certain claims have been satisfied. It is distinguished from a possessory lien in that it attaches independently of the possession of property.

Upon an exchange of contracts for the sale of land an unpaid vendor's lien arises in favour of the vendor, unless there is something to exclude it in the contract. Further, if a third person advances money in payment for land which another is under contract to purchase, he is entitled by subrogation to the same lien as the vendor would have had if the price remained unpaid, unless there is evidence that the parties intended otherwise (*Paul* v. *Speirway Ltd.* [1976] Ch. 220). Similarly the purchaser of land has a lien on it for the amount of his deposit.

On a dissolution of partnership owing to the death, bankruptcy or retirement of a partner, the retiring partner has a lien on the partnership assets existing at the date of dissolution for payment of all the partnership debts prior to the date of dissolution.

An equitable lien is binding on all persons who acquire the property the subject of the lien with notice of the lien. It is enforced by sale, after a declaration by the court that the lien exists.

Bills of Sale

A bill of sale is "a document given with respect to the transfer of chattels, and is used in cases where possession is not intended to be given" to the transferee (*per* Lord Esher M.R. in *Johnson* v. *Diprose* [1893] 1 Q.B. 512, 515). An example is where A. sells goods to B. but A. retains possession of them. Such a bill is used where the person who has title to the goods needs documentary evidence of his title as he has not got possession, although a bill given on the transfer of goods in the ordinary course of trade is not a bill of sale within the Bills of Sale Act 1878. Where the bill records a simple transfer of property it is called an **absolute** bill and is subject to the Bills of Sale Act 1878.

Sometimes the transaction is for the purpose of securing a debt, for example where B. makes a loan to A. and A., by way of security, assigns the goods to B. on condition that they will be transferred back to A. when the debt is paid. Such bills are called **conditional (or security)** bills and are subject to the Bills of Sale Act (1878) Amendment Act 1882. In addition conditional bills are regulated by the Consumer Credit Act 1974. Bills of Sale are rarely used today as a form of security. Charges and chattel mortgages entered into by a company are not covered by the Bills of Sale Acts but are registrable under the Companies Act 1985, s.395.

A bill of sale, whether absolute or conditional, has to be attested by a solicitor and registered at the Central Office of the High Court within seven days of execution; it has to be re-registered every five years. If an absolute bill of sale is not registered in the prescribed manner, it is void as against the trustee in bankruptcy or liquidator of the grantor, but it is valid between the grantor and the grantee. If a conditional or security bill of sale is not registered, it is void in every respect, and likewise as between grantor and grantee, but even if it is void the money lent (together with reasonable interest) may be recovered as money had and received: *North Central Wagon Finance* v. *Brailsford* [1962] 1 W.L.R. 1288.

CHAPTER 25

GUARANTEE

NATURE OF THE CONTRACT OF GUARANTEE

Guarantee and indemnity distinguished

A contract of **guarantee or suretyship** is a contract by one person to answer for the debt, default or miscarriage of another. Whether a particular contractual promise constitutes a guarantee depends upon the words used to express the intentions of the parties. The use of the word guarantee is not in itself conclusive, for it is sometimes used loosely in ordinary commercial dealings to mean a warranty and sometimes used to mis-describe what is in law a contract of indemnity and not of guarantee. Further, where the contractual promise can be correctly classified as a guarantee it is open to the parties expressly to exclude or vary any of their mutual rights or obligations which would otherwise result under the general law from its being classifiable as a guarantee.

The characteristics of a contract of guarantee are:

1. There must be three parties: the principal creditor, the principal debtor, and the guarantor or surety.

2. There must be a primary liability in some person other than the guarantor; the guarantor must be liable only secondarily, *i.e.* to pay if the principal debtor does not pay.

A. and B. go into a shop. B. says to the shopkeeper, "Let him (A.) have the goods, and if he does not pay you, I will." This is a contract of guarantee, the primary liability being with A., and the secondary liability with B.: *Birkmyr* v. *Darnell* (1704) 1 Salk 27.

The creditor's right to enforce a guarantee may not necessarily involve the guarantor (surety) incurring liability for the total amount of the debt. For example, A. may guarantee B.'s loan to C., by the deposit of the title deeds to his property. In such a case the equitable mortgage becomes the creditor's buffer, *i.e.* in the event of non payment of the debt by the principal debtor and the subsequent enforcement of the guarantee, whilst A. may have to forfeit the mortgaged property, he will not incur personal liability in respect of any difference between the value of his mortgaged property and the outstanding balance of the debt (*Re Conley* (1938) 107 L.J. Ch. 257).

3. The guarantor is totally unconnected with the contract except by means of his promise to discharge the principal debtor's liability if he does not do so.

It is this which prevents a *del credere* agent or a half-commission man employed by a stockbroker from being a guarantor, because each has an interest in the contract by negotiating it.

S. & Co., stockholders, agreed with G. that in respect of clients introduced by G., G. should have half the commission earned as a result of the introductions, and he would pay S. & Co. half of any loss sustained in respect of them. *Held,* the contract was not one of guarantee. Lord Esher M.R.: "The test is whether the defendant is interested in the transaction, either by being the person to negotiate it or in some other way, or whether he is totally unconnected with it. If he is totally unconnected with it, except by means of his promise to pay the loss, the contract is a guarantee; if he is not totally unconnected with the transaction, but is to derive some benefit from it, the contract is one of indemnity": *Sutton & Co.* v. *Grey* [1894] 1 Q.B. 285.

But if a large shareholder in a company promises to pay the company's debt in order to prevent its goods from being taken in execution, it is a guarantee, because he has no legal interest in or charge upon the goods (*Harburg India Rubber Co.* v. *Martin* [1902] 1 K.B. 778).

A contract of **indemnity**, which must be distinguished from a guarantee, differs from a guarantee in all three respects—

1. There are only two parties.

2. The person giving the indemnity is primarily liable and there is no secondary liability.

A. and B. go into a shop. B. says to the shopkeeper, "Let him (A.) have the goods, I will see you paid." The contract is one of indemnity: *Birkmyr* v. *Darnell*, *supra*. *Goulston Discount Co. Ltd.* v. *Clark* [1967] 2 Q.B. 493; see p. 384, *ante*.

3. The person giving the indemnity has some interest in the transaction apart from his indemnity.

The distinction is of practical importance. If the contract is one of guarantee and the principal contract is discharged without further liability on the part of the principal debtor, the guarantor is discharged. Thus, the guarantor is no longer liable if the principal debtor exercises a contractual option to rescind the contract: *Western Credit Ltd.* v. *Alberry* [1964] 1 W.L.R. 945, or if the principal contract is frustrated and the debtor has not to pay compensation under the Law Reform (Frustrated Contracts) Act 1943 (p. 170, *ante*). The position is otherwise in the case of an indemnity, for the person giving the indemnity is primarily and not secondarily liable.

The distinction between a guarantee and an indemnity is of further importance because a contract of **guarantee is required** by the Statute of Frauds **to be evidenced by a note or memorandum in writing**, while a contract of indemnity is not.

The following rules apply to the note or memorandum required by the Statute of Frauds 1677 as evidence of the contract:

1. It need not be made at the time of the formation of the contract, but may be made at any time before action is brought. This is because the memorandum is not the contract itself, but merely evidence of it, the contract being good but unenforceable in the absence of writing.

2. It must contain the names of the parties or a sufficient description of them.

3. The subject-matter must be described so that it can be identified, and all material terms of the contract must be stated.

4. Although there must be consideration for the guarantee, the note or memorandum in writing does not have to include reference to the consideration, Mercantile Law Amendment Act 1856, s.3.

5. It may be comprised in several documents, but they must be connected on the face of them. The correspondence between the solicitors of the parties containing the essential terms of the oral agreement may be a good "note or memorandum in writing" (*Law* v. *Jones* [1974] Ch. 112).

6. It must be signed by the guarantor or his agent. It is only the guarantor and not the creditor who need sign. The signature may be printed or stamped and may be at the beginning, middle or end of the document.

If there is no memorandum the contract cannot be enforced.

By the Statute of Frauds Amendment Act 1828 (Lord Tenterden's Act), no action can be brought in respect of a representation given by one person as to the credit of another to the intent that such person may obtain credit or money, unless the representation is in writing signed by the party to be charged. The memorandum under this statute must conform to the requirements of the Statute of Frauds, except that (1) the consideration need not be stated, and (2) the signature cannot be made by an agent.

Guarantee is not a contract of utmost good faith (*uberrimae fidei*). Disclosure of all material facts by the principal debtor or the principal creditor to the guarantor before the contract is entered into is not required. Fraud on the part of the principal debtor is not enough to set aside the contract, unless the guarantor can show that the creditor or his agent knew of the fraud and was a party to it. When a guarantee is given to a bank there is no obligation on the bank to inform the intending guarantor of matters affecting the credit of the debtor or of any circumstances connected with the transaction which render the position more hazardous (*Wythes* v. *Labouchere* (1859) 3 De G. & J. 593).

G. guaranteed the account of C. with the bank. C. afterwards drew on this account in order to pay off an overdraft he had with another bank. *Held,* the fact that the bank were suspicious that C. was defrauding G., and did not communicate their suspicions to G., did not discharge the guarantee: *Nat. Prov. Bank of England Ltd.* v. *Glanusk* [1913] 3 K.B. 335.

If the guarantee is in the nature of an insurance, as in fidelity guarantee, all material facts must be voluntarily disclosed by the creditor, without being asked to do so, otherwise the guarantor can avoid the contract.

In 1903 G. employed L. as a clerk, and in 1905 L. misappropriated £29 of their money. This sum was made good by L.'s relations and G. agreed to retain L. in their service on having fidelity guarantee. H. gave the guarantee without being informed of L.'s previous dishonesty. In 1909 L. misappropriated £100, and G. claimed against H. under the guarantee. *Held,* the guarantee could not be enforced against H. owing to the non-disclosure of L.'s previous dishonesty: *London General Omnibus Co.* v. *Holloway* [1912] 2 K.B. 72.

Consumer Credit Act 1974

Whether the Consumer Credit Act applies to any given contract of guarantee or of indemnity, will depend upon the contract under which the principal debt is owed. If that contract is regulated by the Act **and** if the guarantee or indemnity was given at the request (express or implied) of the principal debtor, then the contract of guarantee is subject to the provisions of the Act. A recourse agreement between a garage and finance company will therefore not be subject to the Act, since it is not entered into by the garage at the request of the debtor, its customer, see page 384 above. Where a guarantee or indemnity is subject to the Act, the following rules apply:

1. The contract of guarantee or indemnity must be in writing in the form prescribed by regulations made under the Act, s.105.
2. Copies of the principal debtor's regulated agreement and of the contract of guarantee or indemnity must be given to the surety, s.105.
3. When a default notice is served under the Act upon the principal debtor, a copy of it must be served upon the guarantor or indemnifier, s.111.
4. The contract of guarantee or indemnity cannot be enforced against the surety to any greater extent than the principal contract can be enforced against the principal debtor, s.113. Thus in this situation, the indemnity becomes a secondary liability and is the same in effect as a guarantee. However, by way of exception to the general rule in section 113, a contract of guarantee or of indemnity can be enforced where the only reason that the principal debtor's agreement cannot be enforced is that the principal debtor was a minor at the time the principal contract was made, Minors' Contracts Act 1987, ss.2 and 3.

Liability of the Guarantor

The guarantor is a favoured debtor to the extent that he can insist on a strict adherence to the terms of his obligation. The liability of the guarantor will, on the default of the principal debt, become operative. The principal debt will become the responsibility of the guarantor. The creditor need not give the guarantor notice of the principal debtor's default unless either he has expressly agreed to do so or the creditor has served upon the principal debtor a default notice under the Consumer Credit Act (see above). On maturity of the principal debt the creditor may immediately commence proceedings against the guarantor.

If the transaction between the creditor and the principal debtor is void or unenforceable by the creditor, the guarantor is not bound. An exception to that, however, allows the creditor to enforce the guarantee where the reason that the principal debtor cannot be made liable is that at the time he made the transaction he was a minor, *i.e.* under 18, Minors' Contracts Act 1987.

The guarantor is not bound if the principal debtor is discharged, *e.g.* by statute (*Unity Finance Ltd.* v. *Woodcock* [1963] 1 W.L.R. 455).

Any conditions precedent to the guarantor's liability must be fulfilled before recourse can be had to him. For example, if the guarantor agrees to be only one of several co-sureties, he will not be under any liability unless the others execute the guarantee.

B. signed a guarantee to the bank which, on the face of it, was intended to be the joint and several guarantee of A., B., H. and J. J. did not sign, and he afterwards died. The bank never agreed with A., B., and H. to dispense with J.'s signature, and J. was willing to sign, although by an accident his signature was not obtained. *Held,* B. was under no liability on the guarantee: *Nat. Prov. Bank of England* v. *Brackenbury* (1906) 22 T.L.R. 797.

Again, if several guarantors have agreed to become co-sureties for definite amounts, and the creditor allows the amounts to be altered by one guarantor without the consent of the others, the guarantee will not be binding.

A firm of brewers employed C. and required him to execute a bond with sureties for the faithful discharge of his duties. The bond was drawn up with four sureties, N. and E. being liable to the extent of £50 each, and P. and B. to the extent of £25 each. P., B. and E. all signed, but N., who was the last to sign, added "£25 only" to his signature. The brewers accepted the bond so signed. *Held,* none of the guarantors was liable on the bond: *Ellesmere Brewery Co.* v. *Cooper* [1896] 1 Q.B. 75.

If the contract is an instalment contract and it is broken by a wrongful repudiation on the part of the principal debtor, *e.g.* by persistent failure to pay the instalments, acceptance of this repudiation by the creditor does not release the guarantor from liability to pay either the past instalments, due and unpaid before acceptance of the repudiation, or the future instalments, due and payable thereafter (*Lep Air Services* v. *Rolloswin Investments Ltd.* [1973] A.C. 331; *Hyundai Heavy Industries Co. Ltd.* v. *Papadopoulos* [1980] 1 W.L.R. 1129).

Although a guarantor can insist on strict adherence to the terms of the guarantee the court, in construing the guarantee, is not limited to interpreting the terms expressed in the contract document. It may refer to the subject-matter and to the surrounding circumstances. Further, when considering the surrounding circumstances, it may take account of the subsequent conduct of the parties which, according to the circumstances, may be regarded as replacing the original terms of the contract (*Amalgamated Investment and Property Co. Ltd.* v. *Texas Commerce Intl. Bank Ltd.* [1981] 3 W.L.R. 565).

A type of guarantee that is increasingly used, particularly in international business transactions, is the **performance guarantee** or performance bond which has many similarities to a letter of credit. This subject is treated in Chapter 19 on the Finance of International Trade (p. 419, *ante*).

Continuing Guarantees

A guarantee may be intended to cover a single transaction only, or may be a continuing guarantee. A continuing guarantee may be defined as "one which extends to a series of transactions, and is not exhausted by or confined to a single credit or transaction." The liability of the guarantor in such a case extends to all the transactions contemplated until the revocation of the guarantee.

Whether a guarantee is continuing or not depends on the language of the guarantee, the subject-matter and the surrounding circumstances. Where the guarantee is limited in its totality to a specific debt, which is by its very nature fixed and not variable, then it is unlikely that the guarantee will be of a continuing nature.

For example, A. guarantees B.'s purchase of five sacks of flour from C. B.'s debt is payable within one month. Here, A.'s guarantee covers the purchase of a specific quantity of goods, the guarantee is not continuous and as such will not extend to subsequent deliveries, beyond the prescribed maximum of five sacks of flour (*Kay* v. *Groves* (1829) 6 Bing. 276).

When a guarantee is continuing it is not exhausted by the first advance or credit up to the pecuniary limit.

A. guarantees B.'s overdraft up to £100. If B. overdraws up to £100 and then reduces his overdraft to £50 and subsequently increases it to £100 again, A. is still liable if his guarantee is a continuing one.

Guarantor's Rights against the Creditor

The rights of a guarantor against the creditor arise at the time of his becoming guarantor, and not merely when he discharges the obligation of the principal debtor.

"It certainly is not the law that a surety has no rights until he pays the debt due from his principal": Cozens-Hardy J. in *Dixon* v. *Steel* [1901] 2 Ch. at p. 607.

The rights of the guarantor are:

1. On default of the principal debt the guarantor may request the creditor to sue for and collect the amount owed by the principal debtor. There is no compulsion on the part of the creditor to agree to do so, but if he does agree, the guarantor must undertake to indemnify the creditor for the risk, delay and expense that may result (*Wright* v. *Simpson* (1802) 6 Ves. 714).

2. On being sued by the creditor, to rely on any set-off or counterclaim which the debtor possesses against the creditor (*Bechervaise* v. *Lewis* (1872) L.R. 7 C.P. 372).

3. On payment of what is due under the guarantee, to be subrogated to all the rights of the creditor in respect of the debt to which the guarantee relates.

X., the director of a company in voluntary liquidation, guaranteed and paid rates due from the company before the date of liquidation. *Held,* X. was entitled to all the rights of the creditor whose debt he had paid, and consequently he was a preferential creditor of the company for so much of the payment as was in respect of rates due and payable within twelve months of the liquidation: *Re Lamplugh Iron Ore Co. Ltd.* [1927] 1 Ch. 308.

4. On payment of what is due under the guarantee, to have

assigned to him every judgment or security held by the creditor in respect of the debt (Mercantile Law Amendment Act 1856, s.5).

This right to have securities assigned to him extends to all securities, whether known by the guarantor or not at the time when he entered into the contract, whether the creditor received them before, at, or after the creation of the guarantee, and whether they existed at the time the guarantee was created or not.

S. mortgaged leasehold premises and a policy of assurance to W. to secure £200 and interest, F. joining in as surety. Subsequently, S. borrowed further sums amounting to £530 from W. and charged them on the same leasehold premises. F. knew nothing of these further advances. On S. making default, F. paid the £200 and interest, and claimed to have the policy and the leasehold premises assigned to him. W. refused to assign the premises unless G. also paid him the £530. *Held*, on payment of the £200, F. was entitled to have both securities handed to him: *Forbes* v. *Jackson* (1882) 19 Ch.D. 615.

When a guarantor has only guaranteed part of a debt he is, on paying the amount for which he is liable, entitled to all the rights of a creditor in respect of that amount, and to share in the security held by the principal creditor for the whole debt (*Goodwin* v. *Gray* (1874) 22 W.R. 312).

5. On payment of what is due under the guarantee, to all equities which the creditor could have enforced not only against the debtor himself, but also against persons claiming through him.

Goods belonging to C. were sold by D., a broker acting as agent for buyer and seller, to B. & Co. D. gave B. & Co. a delivery order, which B. & Co. indorsed to the bank. B. & Co. stopped payment and D., who was personally liable for the purchase price to C., paid C. and obtained a second delivery order. At the time he paid C., D. had no notice of the bank's title. *Held,* D. was in the position of a surety, and, having paid the vendor, could exercise the unpaid vendor's lien against the goods: *Imperial Bank* v. *London and St. Katherine Docks Co.* (1877) 5 Ch.D. 195.

Guarantor's Rights against the Debtor

Against the debtor, the guarantor has the following rights:

1. Before payment has been made, to compel the debtor to relieve him from liability by paying off the debt. This right can be exercised by one of several co-sureties without consulting the others.

A. and four others guaranteed the T. company's overdraft to the extent of £20,000. A. died and the bank closed the old account and opened a new one. The company's liability at the time of A.'s death was £17,000. A.'s executors, being anxious to wind up A.'s estate, called on the company to pay off the overdraft and relieve them from liability. The company refused. *Held,* A.'s executors could compel them to do so: *Ascherson* v. *Tredegar Dry Dock Co.* [1909] 2 Ch. 401.

But before the guarantor can compel the debtor to pay, the debt must be an ascertained one, and there must be an existing liability to pay on behalf of the guarantor.

M. guaranteed the B. Co.'s overdraft up to £5,000, the guarantee to be determinable on the bank's closing the account and demanding payment by M., and on M.'s giving three months' notice to determine the guarantee. In the absence of either of these steps, *held,* M. had no immediate right to compel B. & Co. to relieve him of his liability: *Morrison* v. *Barking Chemicals Co. Ltd.* [1919] 2 Ch. 325.

Once the debtor's liability has become due as a fixed sum, the guarantor is entitled to ask the debtor to exonerate him, irrespective of whether the creditor, under the guarantee, had to make a demand on the guarantor or not (*Thomas* v. *Nottingham Incorporated Football Club Ltd.* [1972] Ch. 596).

2. After payment has been made, to be indemnified by the principal debtor against all payments properly made.

The right of indemnity may be an express one contained in the instrument of guarantee, in which case the rights of the parties are governed by the express agreement, or an implied one. An implied right of indemnity arises in every case when the guarantee has been undertaken at the request, actual or implied, of the debtor, but not otherwise.

A right to indemnity arises immediately a payment has been made under the guarantee, and on payment the guarantor becomes a simple contract creditor of the principal debtor. He is entitled to recover the amount he has paid with interest, and if he has sustained damage beyond that, he is entitled to recover that damage also.

"If a surety could prove that by reason of the non-payment of the debt he had suffered beyond the principal and interest which he had been compelled to pay, he would be entitled to recover that damage from the principal debtor:" Stirling J. in *Badeley* v. *Consolidated Bank* (1887) 34 Ch.D. at p. 556.

The guarantor cannot recover the costs of an action brought against him on the guarantee from the principal debtor, unless he was authorised by the principal debtor to defend the action, and the defence was based on reasonable grounds (*Mors le Blanch* v. *Wilson* (1873) L.R. 8 C.P. 227).

3. When sued by the principal creditor, the guarantor can issue a third party notice against the principal debtor and claim an indemnity.

Rights of Co-Guarantors among themselves

A guarantor who has paid more than his share under the guarantee is entitled to contribution from his co-guarantors, whether they are bound by the same or different instruments, and whether he knew or did not know of the existence of co-guarantors at the time he became bound. This is because the doctrine of contribution is not founded on contract, but is the result of general equity on the ground of equality of burden and benefit.

To obtain contribution, all the guarantors must have guaranteed the same debt. There is, therefore, no right of contribution:

1. When each guarantor has expressly agreed only to be liable for a given portion of one sum of money.

> A. borrows £100 from B. and X. guarantees one-half of the debt and Y. the other half. There is no right to contribution between X. and Y. If X. and Y. had each guaranteed the £100 there would have been a right to contribution.

2. When guarantors are bound by different instruments for equal portions of a debt due from the same principal, and the guarantee of each is a separate and distinct transaction (*Coope* v. *Twynam* (1823) Turn. & R. 426).

The right to contribution may be enforced before or after the guarantee has been discharged. To enforce the right **before payment** the guarantor should make the principal creditor a party to the action, when he will obtain an order on his co-guarantor to pay his proportion to the principal creditor (*Wolmershausen* v. *Gullick* [1893] 2 Ch. 514).

After payment, the guarantor can recover contribution only if he has paid more than his proportion under the guarantee.

The proportion due from each guarantor is regulated by the number of solvent guarantors.

A., B. and C. guarantee X.'s debt of £150. A. becomes insolvent and B. pays the full amount. He can recover £75 from C.

If the guarantors have not guaranteed equal amounts, contribution can be claimed from each of them in proportion to the amount guaranteed.

Before recovering contribution, the guarantor who has paid the debt must bring into account all securities he has received from the creditor in respect of the debt.

H. and A. guaranteed C.'s debt with D., who had as security three policies on C.'s life. H. later on paid off the debt and took an assignment of the policies. In an action for contribution against A., *held,* B. was entitled to contribution from A., on bringing into account the value of the policies: *Re Arcedeckne* (1883) 24 Ch.D. 709.

Similarly, if a guarantor consented to give the guarantee only on condition of receiving security from the principal debtor, he must nevertheless account for the security if he sues to obtain contribution from his co-guarantors. It is not necessary, in an action for contribution, to join the principal debtor if the rights of the parties can be finally decided in his absence.

Discharge of the Guarantor

The guarantor will be discharged in the following events:

1. If the contract between the principal debtor and the principal creditor is varied without the consent of the guarantor.

X. as surety for Y. joined in a mortgage by Y. of his property to Z. X. guaranteed the loan made by Z. and brought in some of her own property as additional security. Y. later borrowed further sums from Z., who eventually consolidated his advances by a deed in which Y. entered into a fresh covenant for payment of all the sums advanced. *Held,* X. was discharged from liability and her property which she had brought in was released: *Bolton* v. *Salmon* [1891] 2 Ch. 48.

T. owed a bank a considerable amount of money. His uncle A. undertook, in consideration of the bank continuing the existing account with T., to guarantee T.'s liabilities to the bank to the amount of £10,500. Without knowledge and consent of A., the bank opened a No. 2 account for T. and received considerable payments from him on that account. *Held,* the opening of the No. 2 account was, on the construction of the terms of a guarantee, an unauthorised variation of the principal contract and the guarantee and consequently the liability of A. as guarantor was discharged: *National Bank of Nigeria Ltd.* v. *Awolesi* [1964] 1 W.L.R. 1311.

It is immaterial whether the variation be prejudicial to the guarantor or not, the principle being, "If the creditor does intentionally violate any rights which the surety had when he entered into the suretyship, even though the damage be nominal only, he shall forfeit the whole remedy" (*per* Blackburn J.; in *Polak* v. *Everett* (1876) 1 Q.B.D. 669).

2. If the identity of the creditor or the principal debtor is changed, unless the guarantor has agreed to change expressly or by necessary implication. Such change may, *e.g.* occur where the creditor is a company and amalgamates with another company. Such a change in the identity of the creditor or the principal debtor is a variation of the contract between them and, if not agreed upon by the guarantor, discharges him. Stephenson L.J. said in *First National Finance Corporation Ltd.* v. *Goodman*, below: "The basis of this principle was that the guarantor's knowledge of both creditor and debtor might be material to his decision to guarantee the debts of the one to the other, whether those persons were firms, companies or individuals. Where companies amalgamated or where one company was merged with or taken over by another, the same principle would apply again and the effect of the takeover on the existence of a guarantee would principally depend on the terms of the guarantee in question."

In 1970 a company called Apartotel (London) Ltd. was incorporated by G. and a father and son, Messrs. F., to run a holiday business in London. The company obtained a loan from a bank named Cassel Arnez & Co. Ltd. and, to secure the company's borrowings, G. entered in 1970 into a written guarantee in favour of the bank. The guarantee was open-ended, *i.e.* it did not contain a maximum limit. One of the clauses in the guarantee provided that the expression "bank" used in the guarantee to describe the creditor should include "its successors and assigns and any company with which it may amalgamate." On January 1, 1972 Cassel amalgamated with the First National Finance Corporation Ltd. (F.N.F.C.) and thereafter all monetary advances to Apartotel were made by F.N.F.C. In September 1972, when Apartotel owed F.N.F.C. £149,415, G. ceased to be a director and shareholder of Apartotel and his involvement with the company's business ended. But he took no steps to terminate his guarantee. In April 1975 Cassel executed a deed of transfer assigning to F.N.F.C. the benefit of G.'s guarantee. In June 1977 Apartotel was wound up and F.N.F.C. demanded £338,165 from G. under his guarantee. *Held,* G. was liable to pay, as the clause in the guarantee expressly permitted a change in the identity of the creditor on amalgamation: *First National Finance Corporation Ltd.* v. *Goodman* [1983] Com.L.R. 184.

3. If the creditor makes a binding contract to give time to the principal debtor. Mere omission to press the debtor or delay in suing him is not such conduct as to release the guarantor. The contract, to have this effect, must be one which is legally enforceable.

P. and C. guaranteed the performance by D. of his contract with the gas company. Under that contract D. undertook to pay for each month's supply within 14 days. In July the gas company, not being paid within 14 days, took a promissory note from D. *Held,* this was a binding agreement to give time and discharged P. and C. from liability for the July account: *Croydon Gas Co.* v. *Dickinson* (1876) 2 C.P.D. 46.

If the contract is one contract, and not a series of monthly contracts, a binding contract to give time to the debtor will discharge the guarantor from the whole contract.

T. bought from M. a motorcar under a hire-purchase agreement, by which he was to pay £14 a month. N. guaranteed these payments. T. fell into arrear with his instalments, and it was agreed between T. and M. that T. should give a cheque for £20 and pay the rest of the arrears at the end of the month. *Held,* N. was discharged from the whole contract, because M. had agreed to give time to T., and the contract was one contract and not a series of monthly contracts: *Midland Motor Showrooms* v. *Newman* [1929] 2 K.B. 256.

If the creditor, when giving time to the debtor, expressly reserves his rights against the guarantor, the guarantor is not discharged. The effect of this is to leave untouched the guarantor's rights against the debtor and, therefore, if the guarantor is pressed by the creditor, the agreement to give time to the debtor becomes of small value.

If, however, when agreeing to an extension of time, the creditor and debtor agree to an increase in the rate of interest, without the agreement of the guarantor and in the absence of clear words in the guarantee permitting such variation, the guarantor will be discharged (*Burnes* v. *Trade Credits Ltd.* [1981] 1 W.L.R. 805).

4. If the creditor omits to do something which he is bound to do for the protection of the surety. For example, if he omits to take up an award until the time for its performance is past (*Re Jones* (1863) 2 H. & C. 270), or if he omits to register a deed giving security so that the deed becomes inoperative and the creditor unsecured (*Wulff* v. *Jay* (1872) L.R. 7 Q.B. 756).

Unless a security is surrendered, lost, rendered imperfect or altered in condition by the creditor's actions, the guarantor will remain liable for the guaranteed debt. Where the security is, by its very nature, potentially volatile in terms of value, for example, where the security is in the form of company shares and the market value of the shares falls, the creditor is under no duty to sell the shares, even where a failure to do so may render them worthless.

"No creditor could carry on the business of lending if he could become liable to a mortgagee and a surety or to either of them for a decline in the value of mortgaged property, unless the creditor was personally responsible for the decline" *per* Lord Templeton in *China & South Sea Bank Ltd.* v. *Tan* [1989] 3 All E.R. 839.

5. If the creditor relinquishes any security held by him in respect of the guaranteed debt. On payment of the debt the guarantor is entitled to have handed over to him all the securities held by the creditor in respect of the debt in the same condition as he received them. If the creditor, by any act or neglect on his part, is unable to hand over the securities in their unimpaired condition, the guarantor will be, to that extent, discharged.

X. and Y. held partly paid shares in a company and D. and P. guaranteed the payment of their unpaid calls to the company. The company called upon X. and Y. to pay the calls and, on default being made, forfeited the shares under a power given in the articles. *Held,* the company by forfeiting the shares had deprived D. and P. of the lien on the shares to which they would have been entitled had they been compelled to pay the calls, and they were therefore discharged from their liability as sureties under the guarantee: *Re Darwen and Pearce* [1927] 1 Ch. 176.

6. If the creditor expressly or impliedly discharged the debtor. An express discharge of the debtor by the creditor will always discharge

the surety, unless the creditor expressly reserves his rights against the surety. Also, if the creditor does some act which, by implication, releases the debtor from his liability, the surety will be discharged.

X. let some chattels to Y. under a hire-purchase agreement, Z. guaranteeing the instalments payable under the agreement. On the instalments being in arrear, X. determined the contract and seized the chattels; he then sued Z. on his guarantee. *Held,* as X. had determined the contract he could not recover from Z.: *Hewison* v. *Ricketts* (1894) 63 L.J.Q.B. 711.

Similarly, a guarantor for rent payable under a lease is discharged from liability if the lease is determined before the expiration of the term (*Hastings Corpn.* v. *Letton* [1908] 1 K.B. 378).

The bankruptcy of the debtor and his subsequent discharge do not release a guarantor for him, Insolvency Act 1986, s.281(7).

7. If the creditor discharges a co-guarantor or does any act whereby the right of contribution between the co-guarantors is destroyed or prejudiced. The discharge of one guarantor from whom his co-guarantors could have obtained contribution is a discharge of those co-guarantors (*Mayhew* v. *Crickett* (1818) 2 Swan. 185, *per* Lord Eldon L.C.).

W. guaranteed the overdraft of a company, and 12 persons deposited the deeds of their various properties with W. and charged their properties with the repayment to W. of any sum he might pay under the guarantee. X., one of the 12, persuaded W to hand over her deeds to her, and she mortgaged her property to Y. The company went into liquidation and W. paid under his guarantee. *Held,* W.'s action in handing back her deeds to X. had released a property which might have been taken towards the satisfaction of the bank's debt; this increased the burden on the remaining properties and thereby brought about a substantial alteration of the rights of the 11 parties among themselves, and they were therefore discharged: *Smith* v. *Wood* [1929] 1 Ch. 14.

8. If the guarantee is revoked. In the absence of an express provision for revocation in the contract itself, the question whether a guarantee can be revoked or not depends on the question whether the consideration for the guarantee is entire and indivisible and given once for all.

B. appointed X. his agent to collect his rents, and required him to execute a fidelity bond in which C. was surety. C. died. In an action by B. against

C.'s executors, *held,* C. could not revoke his liability under the bond during his lifetime, and consequently his death did not release his estate from liability.

"The right to determine or withdraw a guarantee by notice forthwith cannot possibly exist, in my opinion, when the consideration for it is indivisible, so to speak, and moves from the person to whom the guarantee is given once for all, as in the case of the consideration being the giving or conferring an office or employment upon any person whose integrity is guaranteed" *per* Joyce J. in *Balfour* v. *Crace* [1902] 1 Ch. 733.

A continuing guarantee can be revoked as to future transactions by notice of revocation or by notice, actual or constructive, of the death of the guarantor. In such cases, however, liability for previous transactions remains.

W. let a cottage to X., who was C.'s gardener, and C. thereupon guaranteed the payment of X.'s rent for three months and thereafter from week to week. After four months X. left C.'s employment, and C. gave notice to W. terminating his guarantee. X. remained in the cottage and became liable to W. for rent. *Held,* C. was not liable for the rent which became due after he had revoked his guarantee: *Wingfield* v. *de St. Croix* (1919) 35 T.L.R. 432.

On the bankruptcy of the surety, the principal creditor can prove for the whole amount due at the date of the receiving order notwithstanding that he may, since that date, have received sums on account from a co-surety, provided that he does not receive more than 100 pence in the pound (*Re Houlder* [1929] 1 Ch. 205). On the other hand, on the bankruptcy of the principal debtor, the surety cannot prove unless he has paid off the debt or the principal creditor has renounced his right to prove while preserving his rights against the surety; otherwise there would be a double proof in respect of the same debt (*Re Fenton* [1931] 1 Ch. 85).

PART 8: INSURANCE

Chapter 26

LIFE, FIRE AND ACCIDENT INSURANCE

Nature of Contract of Insurance

The owner of a ship or of a house can never be certain that his ship will not be damaged or lost or his house not damaged or destroyed.

To cover himself, he may enter into a contract called a contract of insurance, providing for a sum of money to be paid upon the happening of such an event. There are two categories of insurance and for a contract to be a contract of insurance three elements must be present.

The two categories of insurance are:

(a) Indemnity insurance, which provides an indemnity against loss, as in a fire policy on a house or a marine policy on a vessel. Within the limits of the policy the measure of the loss is the measure of the payment; and

(b) Contingency insurance, which provides not an indemnity but a payment on a contingent event, as in a life policy or a personal injury policy. The sum to be paid is not measured by the loss but is stated in the policy. The contractual sum is paid if the life ends or the limb is lost, irrespective of the value of the life or limb.

The three elements in a contract of insurance are:

(a) For some consideration, usually but not necessarily by way of periodical payments called **premiums**, the contract gives the assured a right to receive money or money's worth, upon the happening of some event.

(b) The event must be one which involves some degree of **uncertainty**. There must be either uncertainty whether or not the event will ever happen, of if the event is one which is bound to happen at some time there must be uncertainty as to the time at which it will happen.

(c) The uncertain event which is necessary to make the contract

> one of insurance—rather than a wager—must be an event which is prima facie adverse to the interest of the assured. That requirement is expressed by the law stipulating that there shall be an **insurable interest** in the assured at the time of the making of the contract.

Each member of an association paid an annual sum so that if an event occurred which prevented the member from driving, due to disqualification or injury, the member had a right to be provided with a chauffeur, and if necessary a car and chauffeur, for up to 40 hours a week for a maximum of 12 months. The Department of Trade contended that the association was carrying an insurance business and was an insurance company to which the Insurance Companies Act 1958 (then in force) applied. *Held*, there was no difference in substance between the association paying for a chauffeur for a member and its agreeing to pay him the cost of providing himself with a chauffeur; accordingly, the contracts between the members and the association were contracts of insurance; insurance business was being carried on: *Dept. of Trade* v. *St. Christopher Motorists' Assn. Ltd.* [1976] 1 W.L.R. 99.

On the other hand, where the right of a member of the Medical Defence Union, on a claim being made against him, was to have his application for help with that claim properly considered by the Union but not the right to money or money's worth, it was *held* in *Medical Defence Union* v. *Department of Trade* [1980] Ch. 82 that the contract between him and the Union was not a contract of insurance.

Regulation and Protection

Under the Insurance Companies Act 1982 (as amended), persons carrying on insurance business as insurers need the **authorisation of the Secretary of State** who has wide powers of regulation and investigation, but special provisions apply to insurers established in other member states of the EEC, implementing EC Directives on Freedom of Establishment and Freedom of Services.

The Act applies whether a company is established within or outside Great Britain, provided it carries on business within Great Britain. Insurance business is carried on where the contracts of insurance are made and the policies are issued, not where the risks are situated (*Re United General Commercial Insurance Corpn. Ltd.* [1927] 2 Ch. 51). The Act does not apply to insurance business (other than industrial assurance business) carried on:

(a) by a member of Lloyd's; or

(b) by a body registered under the enactments relating to friendly societies; or
(c) by a trade union or employers' association where the insurance business carried on by the union or association is limited to the provision for its members of provident benefits or strike benefits.

It also does not apply to industrial assurance business carried on by a friendly society registered under the enactments relating to such societies.

The carrying on of insurance business by an unauthorised company is a criminal offence. The enforceability of contracts issued by such an insurer is governed by the Financial Services Act 1986, s.132. Under this provision, the insured can elect whether or not to enforce the contract; the insurer cannot enforce such a contract.

The powers of the Secretary of State for Trade and Industry include the power:

> to control entry into the insurance business, needing to be satisfied that the value of the company's assets exceed its liabilities by a certain amount and that every director, controller or manager of a company is a fit and proper person to be in such a position; and
> to intervene in the affairs of a company where he considers it desirable for protecting policyholders or potential policyholders, having regard to what appears to be the financial stability or solvency of the company.

Further protection for policyholders is afforded by the Policyholders Protection Act 1975. The main purposes of this Act are:

> to provide for the protection of policyholders who have been or may be prejudiced because of the inability of authorised insurance companies to meet their liabilities; and to provide for the imposition of levies on the insurance industry in order to finance this protection.

The Policyholders Protection Board is the body which administers the Act.

The extent of the indemnity provided differs according to the type of insurance and other factors. Thus, *e.g.* the Board is required to secure payment of:

the full amount that a company in liquidation is liable to pay to a United Kingdom policyholder in respect of a liability subject to compulsory insurance;
the full amount, to a person entitled to the benefit of a judgment under the Road Traffic Act 1988;
90 per cent. of the amount, to a United Kingdom policyholder, who is an individual or partnership, under a policy which is not one for marine, aviation or transport insurance, reinsurance or under a requirement for compulsory insurance.

Life Insurance

Life insurance is a contract by which the insurer agrees, upon the death of a person whose life is insured, to pay a given sum in consideration of the payment of certain sums called premiums.

The insurable interest

By the Life Assurance Act 1774, s.1, any insurance made by one person on the life of another is null and void unless the person making the insurance has an insurable interest in the life insured. An insurable interest means that the person effecting the insurance will sustain some pecuniary loss on the death of the person whose life is insured. The interest, however, need only subsist when the insurance is effected, and the policy does not become void if it has ceased before the death of the insured. But no more than the amount of the insurable interest at the time of effecting the insurance can be recovered under the policy.

A creditor has an insurable interest in the life of his debtor to the extent of the debt, and the policy money is recoverable even though the debt be paid before the maturity of the policy (*Dalby* v. *India and London Life Assurance Co.* (1854) 15 C.B. 365). A surety has an insurable interest in the principal debtor's life, and so have joint debtors in each other's lives to the extent of half the debt (*Beauford* v. *Saunders* (1877) 25 W.R. 650). A theatrical manager has an insurable interest in the life of an actor engaged by him, and so has a servant engaged for a term of years in his employer's life (*Hebden* v. *West* (1863) 3 B. & S. 597). A person always has an insurable interest in his own life, and one spouse has an insurable interest in the life of the other spouse.

A husband and wife made a contract of insurance whereby the policy money was payable, on the death of either of them, to the survivor. The premiums were paid by them jointly. The wife died first and the husband sued for the policy money. *Held*, it was not necessary for him to prove pecuniary interest in his wife's life: *Griffiths* v. *Fleming* [1909] 1 K.B. 805.

A parent has no insurable interest in his child's life, nor has the child in the life of the parent, unless the parent is supporting the child (*Howard* v. *Refuge Friendly Society* (1886) 54 L.T. 644). Sisters have no insurable interest in each other's lives (*Evanson* v. *Crooks* (1911) 106 L.T. 264).

Whenever one person effects an insurance on the life of another there must be inserted in the policy the name of the person interested therein, or for whose use, benefit or on whose account the policy is made, otherwise the policy will be void (Life Assurance Act 1774, s.2). By the Married Women's Property Act 1882, s.11, a husband or wife may insure his or her own life, and if the policy is expressed to be for the benefit of the other, or for the children, a valid trust of the policy money will be created, and the policy money will not form part of the insured's estate or be liable for his debts.

A husband insured his life for £500, the money to be paid to his wife if living at his death, otherwise to his personal representatives. Under a clause in the policy the husband elected to have the present value of the policy paid. *Held*, as a trust was created in the wife's favour in a certain event, the money could only be paid to the husband and wife jointly: *Re Fleetwood's Policy* [1926] 1 Ch. 48.

Insurance as contract uberrimae fidei

Life insurance, like all other forms of insurance, is a contract *uberrimae fidei*, and therefore full disclosure must be made voluntarily to the insurer of every material circumstance which is known to the insured and which would influence the judgment of a prudent insurer in fixing, or determining whether to take the risk. In the event of failure to disclose any such circumstance the policy is voidable.

In making a proposal for insurance, M., in reply to questions asking whether previous proposals on his life had been made to any other office, and, if so, whether they had been accepted at the ordinary rates, said that he was then insured at two offices at the ordinary rates. He omitted to disclose that his life had been declined by several other offices. *Held*, this was a material failure to disclose and the policy could be set aside: *London Assurance* v. *Mansel* (1879) 11 Ch.D. 363.

Whether the omission to disclose any particular circumstance is material so as to render the contract voidable is a question of fact in each case.

A proposal form asked the name of any physician whom the proposer had consulted in the last five years. The proposer said "none," though in fact, he had consulted a doctor and received tonics, but he had never been away from his work. The insurer's doctor said that if he had known of this he would still have recommended the acceptance of the risk at the ordinary premium. *Held*, there was no material concealment and the policy was not avoided: *Mutual Life Insurance Co. of New York* v. *Ontario Metal Products Co.* [1925] A.C. 344.

If between the date of the proposal and the making of the contract there is a material alteration of the risk, disclosure of this alteration must be made, otherwise the contract will be voidable (*Looker* v. *Law Union and Rock Insce. Co. Ltd.* [1928] 1 K.B. 554).

If the insured makes a statement containing certain information, and the policy contains a term to the effect that the statement is to be taken as the basis of the contract, then the policy is voidable if any part of the statement is untrue, whether it is material or not (*Dawsons Ltd.* v. *Bonnin*, p. 548, *post*).

Under the *Statement of Long-Term Insurance Practice*, promulgated in 1986 by the Association of British Insurers and Lloyd's, insurers have agreed, in respect of non-commercial insurances, *inter alia*, (i) that proposal forms will warn proposers of their duty to disclose material facts, (ii) that proposal forms will not contain "basis of the contract" clauses, and (iii) that they will not reject a claim or avoid a policy for an innocent non-disclosure or misrepresentation.

Return of the premium

If the policy is voidable owing to fraudulent misrepresentation, the insurer can have the policy set aside without having to return the premiums. But if the insurer can have the policy set aside on the ground that it is void *ab initio* from some cause not amounting to fraud or illegality, *e.g.* if the policy if expressed to be void on a misstatement of fact in a declaration which is the basis of the contract, the premiums can be recovered back from the insurer. In such a case no risk is run by the insurer. The policy may, however, contain a term that if the policy is void the premium shall be forfeited, and this term will prevent the premiums from being recoverable (*Sparenborg* v. *Edinburgh Life Assurance Co.* [1912] 1 K.B. 195). If the policy is voidable on the ground of the fraud of the insurer, the insured can recover back the premiums.

If the policy is illegal, whether because there is no insurable interest or from any other cause, no premiums can be recovered back.

The insurer's agent in good faith represented to H. that an insurance effected by H. on his mother's life would be valid. H., relying on the representation, insured his mother's life and paid premiums. In an action to recover the premiums, *held*, the policy was illegal for want of an insurable interest, but, as the representation was made innocently, both parties were *in pari delicto* and the premiums could not be recovered: *Harse* v. *Pearl Life Assurance Co.* [1904] 1 K.B. 558.

Where the parties are not *in pari delicto* the insured, if he is the innocent party, can recover the premiums.

T. effected five policies with the L. company, and then decided not to keep them up. The L. company's agent fraudulently represented to H., who had no insurable interest in the lives insured, that if she paid the arrears on the policies and paid the premiums in the future, she would be entitled to the policy moneys. T. knew nothing of this arrangement. On learning that the policies were illegal, H. sued to recover the premiums she had paid. *Held*, the parties not being *in pari delicto*, H. succeeded: *Hughes* v. *Liverpool Victoria Friendly Society* [1916] 2 K.B. 482.

Assignment of life policies

By the Policies of Assurance Act 1867, s.1, the person entitled by assignment to a policy of life insurance may sue in his own name to recover the policy moneys. The assignment of a policy may be made either by indorsement on the policy or by a separate instrument in the form or to the effect set out in the Schedule to the Act (s.5), but it must be followed by notice in writing to the insurer (s.3). The date on which notice is received by the insurer regulates the priority of all claims under the assignment as between the insurer and the assignees, and the insurer is bound, on the request in writing of the person giving the notice, and on being paid a fee not exceeding 25p, to give a written acknowledgment of the notice (s.6). The notice does not, however, regulate the rights of the various claimants to the policy moneys among themselves, and consequently an assignee who has given notice with knowledge of a prior incumbrance does not thereby obtain priority (*Newman* v. *Newman* (1885) 28 Ch.D. 674). In any action on a life policy a defence on equitable grounds may be relied on (s.2).

If, in the opinion of the board of directors of an insurance company, no sufficient discharge for the policy moneys can be otherwise obtained, the company may pay the moneys into court (Life Insurance Companies (Payment into Court) Act 1896).

Fire Insurance

A contract of fire insurance differs from a contract of life insurance in that it is a contract of indemnity. The contract is to indemnify the assured up to a certain amount from loss or injury by fire to specified property during a specified time. The contract is usually embodied in a policy.

Although the Life Assurance Act 1774 refers in its title to life assurance only, it is not in its terms limited to such insurance. As a result, it has been held to apply, for example, to personal accident insurance. On the other hand, section 4 expressly excludes from its operation insurance on ships, merchandise and goods, goods for this purpose including money.

The P.S. Union took out a policy covering their members against the loss of money collected by them for the Union by burglary. A member sustained a loss by burglary and the Union sued under the policy. *Held*, the money was "goods" and the Union need not have an insurable interest under the Act: *Prudential Staff Union* v. *Hall* [1947] K.B. 685.

It has recently been stated that the Act does not apply to ordinary indemnity insurances of property (*Mark Rowlands Ltd.* v. *Berni Inns Ltd.* [1986] Q.B. 211), but a literal reading of it suggests otherwise and there is a contrasting judicial view in *Re King* [1963] Ch. 459. If the Act does apply to fire insurance then by section 1 a policy is void unless the person for whose benefit it is made has an interest in the subject matter; and by section 2 the name of the person for whose benefit the policy is made must be inserted in the policy.

Usually, when the insured has no insurable interest the policy will be void by Gaming Act 1845 as a wagering contract.

Quite apart from statutory requirements, the nature of fire insurance requires that the insured must have an insurable interest at the date of the loss and that he can recover only to the extent of his interest. An insurable interest means a proprietary or contractual right to the property. The following are examples of persons who have an insurable interest: tenants who are liable to pay rent after a fire; carriers, innkeepers and wharfingers for goods entrusted to them, by virtue of their responsibility for loss, their lien or their possession; a mortgagee; an insurer, who may reinsure and so cover himself against loss. If the policy so provides, a bailee can insure goods for their full value, accounting to the bailor for the proportion of the money received that is surplus to his own loss (*Hepburn* v. *A. Tomlinson* (*Hauliers*) *Ltd.* [1966] A.C. 451).

Since a contract of fire insurance is a contract of indemnity, if the insured suffers no loss as a result of the fire he is not entitled to any money under the contract.

X. agreed to sell his house to Y. Before completion the house was destroyed by fire, and X. received its value from the insurance company. On completion X. also received the price from Y. *Held*, the insurance company could recover from X. the money they had paid: *Castellain* v. *Preston* (1883) 11 Q.B.D. 380.

Any money received by the vendor under a policy of insurance relating to the property sold has to be paid by the vendor to the purchaser on the completion of the contract, but this is subject to (1) any stipulation to the contrary contained in the contract, (2) any requisite consents of the insurers, and (3) the payment by the purchaser of a proportionate part of the premium (Law of Property Act 1925, s.47). The insurers are not under an obligation to consent. By section 83 of the Fires Prevention (Metropolis) Act 1774—a statute which extends to all England and Wales—any person interested in any buildings destroyed by fire can compel the insurer to expend the insurance money in reinstatement of the buildings. Under this Act a mortgagee can insist on the insurance money being used to rebuild the mortgaged premises (*Sinnott* v. *Bowden* [1912] 2 Ch. 414).

Assignment

A contract of fire insurance can be assigned only with the consent of the insurers. If the insurers refuse to consent, the attempted assignment is of no effect.

The policy

In order to effect an insurance, the person wishing to insure fills in a proposal form. This is his offer, and when it is accepted the policy is issued. If the answers to the questions in the proposal form are untrue in a material particular, the policy is voidable at the option of the insurers. Sometimes in the policy it is stated that the statements in the proposal form shall be the basis of the contract. In such a case, if any of the statements are untrue, whether in a material particular or not, the policy may be avoided by the insurers. The statements are warranties, *i.e.* fundamental terms of the contract, as in marine insurance (see p. 568, *post*) and it is irrelevant in law whether there is a causal connection between a breach and a loss.

D. insured his lorry with B. The policy recited that the proposal should be the basis of the contract. One question in the proposal form asked where the lorry was usually garaged, and to this D. replied that it was garaged at his address in Glasgow, whereas in fact it was garaged outside Glasgow. The answer was given inadvertently and had no effect on the acceptance of the risk. *Held*, B. could avoid the policy, as a misstatement, although not material, was a breach of the conditions on which the policy was issued: *Dawsons Ltd.* v. *Bonnin* [1922] 2 A.C. 413.

Warranties are also found in the policy itself, *e.g.* a term to the effect that if the insured fails to notify any increases in the risk, the insurer can avoid the policy. On a breach of warranty, the insurer's only option is to avoid the contract in its entirety. Sometimes, promissory statements as to the risk, whether in the proposal form or in the policy, are construed not as warranties but as terms descriptive of the risk. A breach of such a term does not entitle the insurer to avoid the policy but to repudiate liability for a particular loss if the statement was not being complied with at the time of loss.

On the other hand, as with a warranty, there is no need to prove a causal connection.

A policy effected by the plaintiffs had 12 sections, including ones covering cash in their premises. A term in the policy provided: "Warranted that the secure cash kiosk shall be attended and locked at all times during business hours." *Held*, this term was not a warranty or condition in the strict sense but merely a clause descriptive of the risk. The insurers could repudiate liability for a claim as the term was not being complied with at the time of loss, without having to repudiate the whole policy. It was not necessary for them to prove a causal connection between breach and loss: *C.T.N. Cash & Carry Ltd.* v. *General Accident Fire & Life Assurance Corporation plc* [1989] 1 Lloyd's Rep. 259.

Where a policy makes a particular term a condition precedent to the insured's right to recover, it is for the insurer to prove the insured has not complied with that term.

An insurance policy against loss of or damage to an aeroplane provided that it should be a condition precedent for a claim under it that the pilot had observed all statutory regulations relating to air navigation. The plane crashed and its owners claimed to be indemnified under the policy. *Held*, the burden of proving that the pilot had not complied with the regulations was on the insurers: *Bond Air Services* v. *Hill* [1955] 2 Q.B. 417.

The person making the proposal is also under a duty, as in the case of all insurances, of disclosing to the insurers all facts material to the risk which are likely to affect the insurer's judgment, whether or not any questions are asked on the point in question.

An insured who had convictions for, *inter alia*, robbery, insured his house. He did not disclose his previous convictions and was not asked to give any information for the purposes of the insurance but maintained that, if he had been asked, he would have truthfully disclosed his previous convictions. The house was destroyed by fire. *Held*, as far as the interest of the insured was concerned the non-disclosure of the insured's criminal record constituted a moral hazard which the insurers would have to assess, and the insurers were entitled to avoid the policy on the ground of material non-disclosure: *Woolcott* v. *Sun Alliance and London Alliance Ltd.* [1978] 1 W.L.R. 493.

It is submitted that the Rehabilitation of Offenders Act 1974 entitles, in principle, the insured not to disclose a conviction which is spent within the meaning of the Act. The Act provides that a judicial authority may admit evidence on a spent conviction if justice cannot be done otherwise (s.7(3)). In *Reynolds* v. *Phoenix Assurance Co. Ltd.* ([1978] 2 Lloyd's Rep. 440, 461) Forbes J. referred to "the universal practice of insurance companies" to refuse cover if previous convictions are disclosed and, relying on section 7(3), was prepared to admit evidence of a spent conviction because the insurance was obtained in 1972, when the protective provisions of the 1974 Act were not in operation yet (see also C.A. in [1978] 2 Lloyd's Rep. 22). There is at present no authority which supports the view here expressed and the question must still be regarded an open one.

Under the *Statement of General Insurance Practice*, promulgated in 1986 by the Association of British Insurers and Lloyd's, insurers have agreed, in respect of non-commercial insurances, that, *inter alia*: (i) neither proposal forms nor policies will convert statements on forms into warranties as to present or past facts; (ii) there will be warnings on proposal forms and renewal notices of the duty of disclosure; and (iii) insurers will not repudiate liability for innocent non-disclosure or misrepresentation.

Fire policies sometimes contain an average clause, the effect of which may be illustrated as follows:

A. insures property worth £8,000 with B. for £4,000. If £2,000 worth of the property is destroyed, then under an average clause A. will only be able to recover one-quarter of £4,000 from B. If the whole is destroyed he will recover £4,000.

Risks covered

Fire policies cover loss by fire. Ignition is necessary to fire; heating, unaccompanied by ignition, is not fire. The cause of the fire is immaterial, unless it was the deliberate act of the insured himself or someone acting with his knowledge or consent. Loss by fire caused by the insured's negligence is covered.

H. hid her jewellery in her grate under the coal. Later, having forgotten this, she lit the fire and the jewellery was damaged. *Held*, H. could recover under a fire policy: *Harris* v. *Poland* [1941] 1 K.B. 462.

The usual excepted perils in a fire policy are civil commotion, war and explosion. To recover under a fire policy it must be proved that the loss claimed was proximately caused by fire, that is, that it was actually caused by fire, as where a building is burned down, or that it was the reasonable and probable consequence of fire, as if property is damaged by water in extinguishing a fire or destroyed to prevent the spread of a fire. Consequential loss is not covered, and must form the subject of a separate policy. Such a policy will cover loss of profit from the interruption of a business carried on at premises damaged by fire, standing charges which continue to be payable although the business is interrupted, and increased cost of carrying on the business.

Subrogation

The doctrine of subrogation applies to those contracts of insurance which are contracts of indemnity, *e.g.* fire, motor and contingency insurance covering non-payment of money, but not life or personal accident insurance. The doctrine is a corollary of the principle of indemnity. By requiring any means of reducing or extinguishing a loss to be taken into account it prevents the assured from recovering more than a full indemnity.

Subrogation means that the insurer is entitled to enforce any remedy which the assured himself might have enforced against any third party. This applies to rights both in contract and in tort, and if the assured renounces any benefit or rights of action against third parties, the insurer is discharged to that extent.

S. insured buildings against fire with P. During the currency of the policy the Plymouth Corporation served a notice to treat on S. for the compulsory purchase of the buildings. Thereafter the buildings were destroyed by fire. P. paid S. £925 under the policy. S. subsequently agreed with the corporation to receive a sum which took into account the £925 received from P. *Held*, as the buildings were at the corporation's risk from the date of the notice to treat, S. was entitled to the full purchase-money from them notwithstanding the fire, and as P. were subrogated to S.'s rights, they were entitled to recover from her the £925 they had paid: *Phoenix Assurance Co.* v. *Spooner* [1905] 2 K.B. 753.

The right arises only in so far as the insurer has admitted his liability to the assured and paid him the amount of the loss, although the loss itself may be total or partial. However, it is usual for express terms to vest the right in the insurer before he has indemnified the insured. The insurer can sue in his own name only if there is a formal assignment of the right of action; otherwise he must bring the action in the name of the assured who is under an obligation to permit his name to be used in this way.

An insurer who has indemnified an assured is entitled to sue the wrongdoer to recover not only the loss but also interest on the whole or any part; further, in order to give efficacy to the contract of insurance and to ensure that the assured is not over-compensated for the loss and the insurer is not under-compensated it is necessary to imply a term into the contract of insurance to the effect that the assured can retain any interest which accrued before the date of settlement but that interest awarded in respect of any period subsequent to that must go to the insurers (*H. Cousins and Co. Ltd.* v. *D. & C. Carriers Ltd.* [1971] 2 Q.B. 230).

When construing a policy of insurance regard should be had to the general doctrine of subrogation only if there is ambiguity in the policy: the terms of the policy itself should be considered first and may exclude the application of the doctrine or subrogation (*L. Lucas Ltd.* v. *Export Credit Guarantee Dept.* [1974] 1 W.L.R. 909).

Subrogation will not lie against a co-insured nor against someone who was clearly intended to benefit from the insurance effected by the insured, *e.g.* a tenant where his landlord has covenanted to insure and the tenant has paid some or all of the premium (*Mark Rowlands Ltd.* v. *Berni Inns Ltd.* [1985] Q.B. 211).

Accident, Burglary and Other Forms of Insurance

Burglary insurance resembles fire insurance in that it is a contract to indemnify the assured against loss from the risk insured against. Accident insurance, on the other hand, is not a contract of indemnity, but is an agreement to pay a specified sum of money upon the happening of certain events. The usual form of accident insurance is a contract to pay a certain sum to the executors of the assured in the event of his death by accident, and a smaller sum in the event of his disablement, total or partial, and a weekly sum during his incapacity from following his usual employment.

The principles previously explained in the case of life and fire insurance apply equally to all insurances. In particular, a full disclosure must be made by the assured to the insurer of all facts that are likely to influence the insurer's judgment in deciding whether or not to accept the risk. The fact that the proposal form has a question on any particular point shows that the insurer attaches importance to that point, but the mere fact of there being no question on a point does not dispense with the necessity of disclosing anything material. Examples of things which must be disclosed are:

The fact that another insurance company has declined to accept the proposed insurance. This applies to all classes of insurance except marine insurance. If a partnership makes a proposal for insurance, the non-disclosure by one partner of the refusal of an insurance company to accept his proposal renders the policy voidable.

G. and H. were partners and made a proposal on the firm's behalf with L. for a burglary insurance. G. had been previously refused, but the firm had never been refused. *Held*, the omission to disclose that G. had been refused was a concealment of a material fact, and the policy was voidable: *Glicksman* v. *Lancashire and General Insurance Co.* [1927] A.C. 139.

In a burglary insurance, the non-disclosure by the proposer that he was a Roumanian, although he had been in England since the age of 12, was held to be an omission which entitled the insurer to avoid the policy (*Horne* v. *Poland* [1922] 2 K.B. 364). It is doubtful whether this non-disclosure would be regarded as material today.

In January 1956 a company took out a policy of insurance against loss or damage from whatever cause arising to, *inter alia*, skins and furs. When the policy was effected, the fact was not disclosed that the chairman of the insured company had been convicted and sentenced in 1933 for receiving stolen furs. *Held*, there had been a wrongful non-disclosure of a material fact, *viz.*, the previous conviction of the chairman, and the underwriters were entitled to avoid the policy: *Regina Fur Co. Ltd.* v. *Bossom* [1957] 2 Lloyd's Rep. 466.

Diamond merchants insured their diamonds against all risks. They failed to disclose that their sales manager had been convicted eight years before in America for smuggling diamonds in the U.S.A., since they considered that fact to be immaterial. Later the director of the diamond merchants was robbed of diamonds with violence and the diamond merchants made a claim under the policy. *Held*, the manager's offence and convictions were material facts which should have been disclosed and the claim was dismissed: *Roselodge Ltd.* v. *Castle* [1966] 2 Lloyd's Rep. 113.

The deliberate overvaluation of the property insured will avoid the policy, as also will the valuation of the property on the basis of a reasonable prospect of appreciation, unless the proposer makes it plain to the insurer that the value is not immediate, but speculative (*Hoff Trading Co.* v. *Union Insce. Co. of Canton* (1928) 45 T.L.R. 164). Where an insurance against theft covers jewellery which had been imported into this country with the intention of evading customs duty, the insured cannot claim indemnity from the insurer when the jewellery is stolen because, if he could, he would profit from his illegal act (*Geismar* v. *Sun Alliance and London Insurance Ltd.* [1978] Q.B. 383).

In car insurance the proposer should disclose previous accidents he has had in driving, whether he was driving on his own behalf or on behalf of others (*Furry* v. *Eagle Star and British Dominions Insce. Co.* (1922) W.C. & Ins. Rep. 225).

In a proposal form, false answers which are material make the policy voidable at the insurers' option; if the false answers are not material, the policy will be voidable when the proposer has warranted the truth of his answers, but not otherwise.

Role of agents and brokers

The general rule is that the "agent" who is not an employee of the insurance company, that is an insurance broker or consultant and the like, is not the agent of the company. He is paid a commission on the business he introduces and is supplied with information about the company's terms of business and rates of premiums and also given a supply of insurance forms, but the acceptance or rejection of business he introduces rests with the company. If, as a matter of convenience, he fills up the proposal form he is acting as agent for the proposer. The result is that if he fills in false answers and the proposal form is signed by the proposer without reading the answers, the policy is voidable at the option of the insurer. The same principle applies to agents who are normally agents of the insurer.

The R. Co.'s agent filled in a proposal form for the insurance of N.'s motor-omnibuses. Many of the answers were false, although N. had given the correct answers to the agent. N. signed the form containing the false answers without reading it. *Held*, the policy was voidable, as the knowledge of the true facts by the agent could not be imputed to the R. Co.:

Newsholme Bros. v. *Road Transport and General Insce. Co.* [1929] 2 K.B. 356.

In all matters relating to the placing of insurance, of whatever kind, the insurance broker is the agent of the assured, and of the assured only. It has been contended that while this applies to the placing of the policy, when a claim arises under it the broker who placed it may thereupon become the agent of both parties in some respects. But this contention was rejected by Megaw J. in *Anglo-African Merchants Ltd.* v. *Bayley* [1970] 1 Q.B. 311, when he said: "Even if it were established to be a practice well known to persons seeking insurance—not merely to insurers and brokers—I should hold the view . . . that a custom will not be upheld by the courts of this country if it contradicts the vital principle that an agent may not at the same time serve two masters—two principals—in actual or potential opposition to one another: unless, indeed, he has the explicit, informed, consent of both principals. An insurance broker is in no privileged position in this respect."

But the position may well be different in interim insurance, particularly if it is made orally or over the telephone. In this case the broker, when he accepts the insurance, is acting in pursuance of his implied authority from the insurer and is the agent of the latter. Lord Diplock said in *Stockton* v. *Mason and the Vehicle and General Insurance Co. Ltd.* [1978] 2 Lloyd's Rep. 430, 432: "There must be every day thousands of cases, not only in motor insurance but in other forms of non-marine insurance, where persons wishing to become insured or wishing to transfer an insurance ring up their brokers and ask for cover or ask for fresh cover or ask to transfer the cover from an existing vehicle to another. In every case they rely upon the broker's statement that they are covered as constituting a contract binding upon the insurance company. In that sort of conversation they are speaking, in the absence of any special circumstances, to the broker as agent for the insurance company, and the broker, in dealing with the matter, is acting as agent for the insurance company and not as agent for the person wishing to have insurance."

Insurance brokers have to register under the Insurance Brokers (Registration) Act 1977. The Act has established an Insurance Brokers Registration Council which publishes codes of conduct for insurance brokers and which has a Disciplinary Committee, having disciplinary powers over registered insurance brokers. Only persons duly registered may call themselves "insurance brokers" (1977 Act, s.22). However, "insurance consultants" and others not using the title "broker" are not caught by the Act.

Agents involved in selling life insurance are subject to the regulatory regime of the Financial Services Act 1986.

Risks covered

A burglary policy usually covers loss by burglary, house-breaking and larceny committed on the property described in the policy. A loss from these causes on other property is not covered. An accident policy covers personal injury or death by accident, meaning something not due to natural causes, but brought about by chance. It will include such intentional acts as murder, which is something brought about by chance as far as the deceased is concerned, and also accidents caused by negligence, even of the insured himself.

Accident and burglary policies usually contain a condition that notice of the accident or loss must be given "immediately," "as soon as possible," or within a fixed number of days. Such conditions are almost always conditions precedent to liability, so that there is no liability on the insurers unless the term as to notice is complied with (*Re Williams and Thomas and L. & Y. Accident Insce. Co.* (1902) 19 T.L.R. 82). "Immediately" means "with all reasonable speed considering the circumstances of the case" (*per* Fletcher Moulton L.J., in *Re Coleman's Depositories Ltd. and Life and Health Assurance Association* [1907] 2 K.B. 798). Notice of death by accident is given "as soon as possible" if it is given by the executor of the deceased as soon as possible after they learn that the deceased had an insurance against accidental death (*Verelst's Adm.* v. *Motor Union Insce. Co.* [1925] 2 K.B. 137).

A motor insurance policy which excludes liability if "car is conveying any load in excess of that for which it is constructed" does not prevent the insured from recovering for damage to a private car carrying an extra passenger beyond its ordinary seating capacity (*Houghton* v. *Trafalgar Insce. Co.* [1954] 1 Q.B. 247).

Where a bailee insures the goods of the bailor it is a matter of the interpretation of the policy whether he has insured only his own interest as bailee or the interest of the bailor as owner of the goods (*Petrofina* (*U.K.*) *Ltd.* v. *Magnaload Ltd.* [1983] 1 Lloyd's Rep. 91).

T., carriers, claimed on a policy on goods owned by I.T. The goods were taken to I.T.'s warehouse where they were taken into the charge of I.T.'s night-watchman and were to have been unloaded the following morning, but they were stolen in the night. *Held*, T., as bailees had an insurable interest in the goods, and consequently were entitled to insure them for their full value; they could retain so much as would recover their own interest as bailees; and they would be trustees for the owners for the rest: *A. Tomlinson* (*Hauliers*) *Ltd.* v. *Hepburn* [1966] A.C. 451.

Public policy

In considering a claim under a contract of insurance, a court will consider whether allowing the claim in respect of a particular event would be contrary to public policy, having regard to the nature of that event. The broad principle is that no man should be allowed to profit at another's expense from his own criminal act (see p. 122, *ante*). Thus the murderer *In the Estate of Crippen* [1911] P. 108, and the felonious suicide in *Beresford* v. *Royal Insurance Co. Ltd.* [1938] A.C. 586 (see p. 123, *ante*) or those claiming through them, have had their claims defeated on the grounds that it would be contrary to public policy to assist a personal representative to recover what were in fact the fruits of the crime committed by the assured person. First, the law aims to deter the intending criminal by ensuring that no one shall indemnify him against loss he may incur as a result of his crime. Secondly, it is no part of the court's function to assist those who do commit deliberate crime to recover money to which they can lay claim only by proving the commission of that crime. On the other hand, it was held in *Tinline* v. *White Cross Insurance Association Ltd.* [1921] 3 K.B. 327, that a man who pleaded guilty to a charge of manslaughter arising from the negligent driving of a motor car was entitled to enforce an indemnity against the defendants who had insured him in respect of accidental injury. It was, however, made clear in that decision that if the occurrence had been due to an intentional criminal act on the part of the assured, the policy would not have protected him. Even a deliberate criminal act by the insured will not debar an innocent third party from claiming from the insurers where, as in motor insurance, that procedure is available (*Gardner* v. *Moore* [1984] A.C. 548).

Where death has occurred, the logical test, in the judgment of Geoffrey Lane J., is "whether the person seeking the indemnity was guilty of deliberate, intentional and unlawful violence or threats of violence; if he was, and death resulted therefrom, then, however unintended the final death of the victim may have been, the court should not entertain a claim for indemnity" (*Gray* v. *Barr* [1970] 2 Q.B. 626, see p. 122, *ante*).

Motor Insurance

Liability of insurers to persons other than the insured

Before the Third Parties (Rights Against Insurers) Act 1930, when an injured person obtained judgment against a wrongdoer who was insured, and the wrongdoer then went bankrupt, the injured person had no direct claim against the insurance moneys. He could only prove in the bankruptcy, the insurance moneys going into the pool for the benefit of the general body of creditors. By the Act of 1930 the injured person was given a right against the insurance company. Section 1 says that: "Where under any contract of insurance a person . . . is insured against liabilities to third parties which he may incur," then in the event of the insured becoming bankrupt if he is an individual, or, in the case of the insured being a company, in the event of a winding-up or other insolvency procedure, "if, either before or after that event, any such liability as aforesaid is incurred by the insured, his rights against the insurer under the contract in respect of the liability shall, notwithstanding anything in any Act or rule of law to the contrary, be transferred to and vest in the third party to whom the liability was so incurred."

Under that section the injured person steps into the shoes of the wrongdoer. There are transferred to him the wrongdoer's "rights against the insurers under the contract." As the insurers' obligation under the contract of insurance is to indemnify the insured in respect of what the latter is legally liable to pay the injured third party, the insurers' obligation to indemnify cannot arise until the insured's own obligation to pay the insured third party has been established, either by judgment of a court or by an award in arbitration or by agreement (*Post Office* v. *Norwich Union Fire Insurance*

Society Ltd. [1967] 2 Q.B. 363; *Bradley* v. *Eagle Star Insurance Co.* [1989] A.C. 957).

It is not all the rights and liabilities of the insured under the contract of insurance which are transferred to the third party, only the particular rights in respect of the liability incurred by the insured to the third party. Rights which are not referable to the particular liability of the insured to the particular third party are not transferred. So, insurers are not entitled to set-off against the sum due to an injured party moneys owing to them by the insured as unpaid premium (*Murray* v. *Legal and General Assurance Society Ltd.* [1970] 2 Q.B. 495).

Every driver of a motor vehicle is required to be insured against liability in respect of the death of or bodily injury to any person, including passengers, or in respect of certain damage to property caused by the use of the vehicle on the road. The requirement in respect of property damage can be limited to a sum insured of £250,000 and does not include damage to the vehicle, goods in or on it carried for hire or reward or property in the custody or under the control of the driver. A judgment against the insured in respect of such liability can be enforced against the insurer (Road Traffic Act 1988, ss.151–153). The insurance must not contain a provision that liability shall cease if some specified thing is done or omitted *after* the accident. Further, any restriction on the insurance by reference to the age or condition of the driver, the condition of the vehicle, or the number of persons or weight of goods carried, is void.

If the policy is expressed to indemnify persons driving the motor vehicle with the consent of the insured, such persons, although not parties to the contract or named in the policy as being parties interested, can sue for an indemnity under the policy (s.148(7); *Tattersall* v. *Drysdale* [1935] 2 K.B. 174).

Motor Insurers' Bureau

Over the past 40 years procedures have evolved, outside the terms of any statute, whereby a person injured by a road vehicle or whose property is damaged by a vehicle but who cannot recover damages from the driver of the vehicle, can in certain circumstances and subject to certain conditions recover compensation from the

Motor Insurers' Bureau, if necessary by action in the courts, although he has not given consideration to the Bureau.

In 1937 a Department Committee made recommendations to secure compensation to third party victims of road accidents in cases where, notwithstanding the provisions of the Road Traffic Acts relating to compulsory insurance, the victim was deprived of compensation by the absence of insurance, or of effective insurance. In accordance with an agreement made in 1945 between the Minister and insurers transacting compulsory motor vehicle insurance business the Motor Insurers' Bureau was formed and in 1946 it entered into a further agreement with the Minister to give effect to the recommendations made in 1937.

The 1946 agreement—described by Lord Denning M.R. as being "as important as any statute"—provided for compensation to be payable by the Bureau to a victim who had obtained a judgment which remained unsatisfied in respect of a known driver who had been negligent and ought to have been insured, but was not. The agreement did not, however, cover cases where the negligent driver was not known and could not be traced. As this gave rise to hardship, for many years the Bureau in such circumstances made payments on an *ex gratia* basis. This practice was formally recognised in an agreement in 1969, which also provided for an appeal against the Bureau's decisions in such cases, and in 1971 modifications were made to the provisions relating to compensation in the case of uninsured drivers. Current arrangements are covered by agreements of 1972, 1977 and 1988.

One agreement—*Compensation of Victims of Uninsured Drivers*—provides for payment of compensation, provided judgment is obtained against the driver and the Bureau is informed within seven days of the commencement of proceedings. The agreement was revised in 1988 to include cases of property damage subject to an excess and except where the "victim" recovers from his own insurer. In the notes published with the agreement it is emphasised that there is nothing in the agreement affecting any obligations imposed on a policyholder by his policy. Policyholders are not released from their contractual obligations to their insurers, although the scheme protects third party victims from the consequences of failure to observe them. Thus, the failure of a policyholder to notify claims to his insurers as required by his policy, although not affecting a victim's right to benefit under the scheme, may leave the policy-holder liable to his insurers.

Under another agreement—*Compensation of Victims of Untraced Drivers*—the Bureau accepts liability in this regard but by clause 4 the Bureau will not include in any payment awarded "any amount in respect of any damages for loss of expectation of life or for pain or suffering which the applicant might have had a right to claim under the Law Reform (Miscellaneous Provisions) Act 1934." Applications for a payment under the agreement must be made in writing to the Bureau within three years of the accident giving rise to the death or injury.

It is the publicly declared policy of the Bureau not to rely on the absence of privity of contract.

CHAPTER 27

MARINE INSURANCE

A CONTRACT of marine insurance is a contract whereby the insurer undertakes to indemnify the assured against marine losses, that is to say, the losses incident to a marine adventure (s.1).[1] There is a marine adventure when:

(a) any ship or goods are exposed to maritime perils;
(b) the earning or acquisition of any freight, passage money, commission, profit, or other pecuniary benefit or the security for any advances is endangered by the exposure of insurable property to maritime perils;
(c) liability to a third party may be incurred by the owner of or a person interested in insurable property by reason of maritime perils.

"Maritime perils" means the perils consequent on or incidental to the navigation of the sea, but a marine insurance contract may, by express terms or by usage of a trade, be extended to protect the assured against losses on inland waters (s.2).

Insurable interest

A contract of marine insurance where the assured has no insurable interest is a gaming or wagering contract and is void. Policies are void when they are made:

(a) interest or no interest; or
(b) without further proof of interest than the policy itself; or
(c) without benefit of salvage to the insurer, except where there is no possibility of salvage (s.4).

A person has an insurable interest if he is interested in a marine adventure in consequence of which he may benefit by the safe

[1] References in this chapter are to the Marine Insurance Act 1906 unless the contrary is expressed.

arrival of insurable property or be prejudiced by its loss, damage or detention. The following persons have an insurable interest:

1. The lender of money on bottomry or *respondentia*, to the extent of the loan. Bottomry is a pledge of the ship and freight to secure a loan to enable the ship to continue the voyage. It is named after the bottom or keel of the ship, which is figuratively used to express the whole ship. *Respondentia* is a pledge of the cargo only and not of the ship.

2. The master and crew to the extent of their wages.

3. A person advancing freight to the extent that the freight is not repayable in case of loss.

4. A mortgagor, to the extent of the full value of the property, and a mortgagee for the sum due under the mortgage.

5. The owner, to the extent of the full value, notwithstanding that a third party has agreed to indemnify him from loss.

6. A reinsurer, to the extent of his risk.

Defeasible, contingent and partial interests are insurable.

The assured must have the insurable interest at the time of the loss, although he need not have it when the insurance is effected. If he insures property "lost or not lost" the insurance is good although the property may in fact be lost at the date when the insurance is effected, provided the assured did not know that it was lost. If the assured assigns his interest in the property insured he does not transfer his rights in the insurance to the assignee, unless there is an agreement to that effect.

Disclosure and representations

A contract of marine insurance is one in which the utmost good faith (*uberrima fides*) must be observed, and if it is not, the contract is voidable (s.17). The assured must disclose to the insurer every material circumstance which is known to him, and he is deemed to know everything which he ought to know in the ordinary course of business. A circumstance is material if it would influence the judgment of a prudent insurer in fixing the premium or determining whether to take the risk (s.18). It is not necessary that the prudent insurer would have acted differently if he had known the circumstance, merely that he would have wanted to know of it when making his decision (*Container Transport International Inc.* v.

Oceanus Mutual Underwriting Association (Bermuda) Ltd. [1984] 1 Lloyd's Rep. 476). The following are examples of the concealment of facts, which have been held to be material:

The fact that the ship had grounded and sprung a leak before the insurance was effected (*Russell* v. *Thornton* (1859) 20 L.J. Ex. 9).

A merchant, on hearing that a vessel similar to his own was captured, effected an insurance without disclosing this information (*De Costa* v. *Scandret* (1723) 2 P. Wms. 170).

The nationality of the assured concealed at a time when his nationality was important (*Associated Oil Carriers Ltd.* v. *Union Insce. Socy. of Canton Ltd.* [1917] 2 K.B. 184).

In an insurance on a ship, the fact that the goods carried were insured at a value greatly exceeding their real value (*Ionides* v. *Pender* (1874) L.R. 9 Q.B. 531).

In every case, however, whether a circumstance is material or not depends on the particular facts. The following circumstances need not be disclosed:

(a) Those diminishing the risk.
(b) Those known or presumed to be known by the insurer in the ordinary course of his business.
(c) Those which are waived by the insurer.

If the insurance is effected by an agent, the agent must disclose to the insurer every fact which the assured himself ought to disclose and also every material circumstance known to the agent. The agent is deemed to know every fact which he ought to know in the ordinary way of business or which ought to have been communicated to him (s.19).

In addition to his duty to make a full disclosure, the assured is under a duty to see that every material representation made during the negotiations for the contract is true. If any material representation be untrue the insurer may avoid the contract (s.20).

The policy

The contract of marine insurance is made as soon as the proposal is accepted by the insurer, although the policy may not be issued until later. Before the policy is issued it is usual to issue a document called **the slip** which, when accepted by the underwriter, is a short memorandum of the contract evidencing the date of the commencement of the insurance (s.21). The contract is constituted in the following manner. The broker, who acts as agent of the insured, offers the slip to various insurers, such as underwriting syndicates at Lloyd's, and the agent of each of these syndicates writes "a line," *i.e.* accepts to a limited amount (*pro tanto*), until the full amount stated on the slip is covered. The slip thus constitutes an offer and the signature of each of the underwriters, through their agents, is the acceptance *pro tanto*. Consequently separate binding contracts are concluded by the underwriters when they each accept *pro tanto* and the validity of these contracts is not conditional on the completion of the slip. This legal position becomes relevant when a loss occurs before the slip is fully underwritten. In this case the insured can hold those underwriters who have already written a line liable *pro tanto* but, on the other hand, the insured cannot cancel the contracts concluded with them, if such cancellation would be advantageous to him for one reason or another.

Fennia Patria, a Finnish insurance company, wanted to amend its reinsurance of a particular risk at Lloyd's insurance market in London. The amendment slip was accepted by General Reinsurance for part of the amount stated on it, but before the whole amount was underwritten, a loss occurred and Fennia Patria wanted to cancel the amendment because in the circumstances the unamended cover was more favourable to it. *Held*, a valid contract relating to the amendment was concluded between Fenna Patria and General Reinsurance and Fennia Patria could not cancel it on the ground that insurance on the amendment slip was not completely covered: *General Reinsurance Corporation* v. *Forsakringsaktiebolaget Fennia Patria* [1983] 3 W.L.R. 318.

No action against the insurer can be brought by the insured until the policy is issued; the slip cannot be sued upon, but where there is a duly stamped policy reference may be made to the slip in any legal proceedings (s.89). The policy must be signed by the insurer, or, if the insurer is a corporation, it may be sealed, and must specify:

(a) The name of the assured or of some person who effects the insurance on his behalf;
(b) the subject-matter insured and the risk insured against;
(c) the voyage or period of time or both, as the case may be, covered by the insurance;
(d) the sum or sums insured;

(e) the name or names of the insurers.

The subject-matter of the insurance must be described with reasonable certainty, regard being had to any trade usage. The nature and extent of the assured's interest in the subject-matter need not be specified (s.26).

The Marine Insurance Act 1906 sets out in Schedule 1 the form of a Lloyd's S.G. Policy[2] and Rules for Construction of Policy. As from January 1, 1982 Lloyd's S.G. Policy is no longer used by the practice. It is superseded by the so-called **Lloyd's Marine Policy**, which is supplemented, as required, by the Institute Cargo Clauses A, B or C. The Rule for Construction of Policy still apply, where appropriate.

Lloyd's Marine Policy does not contain any insurance clauses, except the clause "This insurance is subject to English jurisdiction." This clause links the whole policy with the provisions of the Marine Insurance Act 1906. Apart therefrom, Lloyd's Marine Policy is merely the vehicle for the Institute Cargo Clauses, which define the risks covered and the exclusions of liability on the part of the insurers. These documents are called "Institute Cargo Clauses" because they are sponsored by the Institute of London Underwriters.

Policies are of the following kinds:

1. **Voyage policies**, where the contract is to insure "at and from" or from one place to another. The subject-matter is then insured for a particular voyage only.

2. **Time policies**, where the contract is to insure for "a definite period of time" (s.25(1)). A policy for a period of time and not for a voyage does not cease to be a time policy merely because that period may thereafter be extended or curtailed pursuant to one of the policy's provisions. The duration of the policy is defined by its own times and is thus for "a definite period of time" (*Compani Maritime San Basilio S.A.* v. *Oceanus Mutual Underwriting Assn. (Bermuda) Ltd.* [1977] Q.B. 49 (C.A.). By the Stamp Act 1891, s.93, no time policy can be made for a period exceeding 12 months, but by virtue of section 11 of the Finance Act 1901 a time policy may contain a "continuation clause" providing that if at the end of the

[2] "S.G." stands for "Ship and Goods."

period the ship is at sea the insurance shall continue until the ship's arrival at her port of destination or for a reasonable time thereafter. A time policy sometimes contains restrictions as to locality, *e.g.* "from June 1, 1984, to April 1, 1985, no Baltic." A contract for both voyage and time may be included in the same policy (s.25). This is known as a **mixed policy.** The underwriter is only liable under it when the loss occurs within the insured period and while the ship is on the described voyage.

3. **Valued policies**, where the policy specifies the agreed value of the subject-matter insured. In the absence of fraud, this value is conclusive as between the insurer and the assured, whether the loss be partial or total; but it is not conclusive in determining whether there has been a constructive total loss (s.27). Mere over-valuation is not fraudulent unless it is of a very gross nature. Without fraud, over-valuation is not a ground for repudiation as such (*Berger & Light Diffusers Pty.* v. *Pollock* [1973] 2 Lloyd's Rep. 442).

4. **Unvalued policies**, where the value of the subject-matter is not specified, but is left to be subsequently ascertained, subject to the limit of the sum insured. The insurable value is ascertained as follows—

(a) As to the ship, the value includes her outfit, provisions and stores, money advanced for wages and disbursement to make the ship fit for the voyage, plus the charges of insurance on the whole. In the case of a steamship, it also includes the machinery, boilers, coals and engine stores.

(b) As to the freight, the value is the gross freight at the risk of the assured, plus the charges of insurance.

(c) As to the goods and merchandise, the value is the prime cost of the property insured, plus the expenses of and incidental to shipping and the charges of insurance (s.16).

5. **Floating policies**, where the insurance is described in general terms, leaving the name of the ship and other particulars to be defined by subsequent declaration. The subsequent declarations may be made by indorsement on the policy or in other customary manner and must be made in order of shipment. They must, in the case of goods, comprise all consignments within the terms of the policy and the value of the goods must be stated. If the value is not stated until after notice of loss or arrival, the policy must be treated as unvalued as regards those goods (s.29).

Open cover is not a policy, but is an agreement by the underwriter to issue an appropriate policy within the terms of the cover. To this extent it resembles a floating policy.

Reinsurance is where the insurer himself insures the whole or part of the risk he has undertaken with another insurer. In such a case the ordinary law as to insurer and assured applies as between the reinsurer and the insurer. Unless the policy provides otherwise, the original assured has no right or interest in the reinsurance (s.9). When a constructive total loss occurs, the insurer need not give notice of abandonment to the reinsurer (s.62(9)).

Double insurance is where two or more policies are effected by or on behalf of the assured on the same adventure and interest and the sums assured exceed the indemnity allowed by the Act, *e.g.* if X. insures property worth £1,000 with Y. for £750 and Z. for £500, there is a double insurance, because the measure of X.'s indemnity, *viz.* £1,000, has been exceeded. If X. had insured with Y. for £450 and Z. for £550 there would be no double insurance.

Where the assured is over-insured by double insurance he may, unless the policy otherwise provides, claim payment from the insurers in such order as he may think fit, provided he does not recover more than his indemnity. If the policy is a valued policy, the assured must give credit as against the valuation for any sum received under any other policy without regard to the value of the subject-matter insured. If the policy is unvalued, the assured must give credit, as against the full insurable value, for any sum received under any other policy. If the assured receives any sum in excess of his indemnity, he is deemed to hold it in trust for the insurers according to their rights amongst themselves (s.32).

As between the insurers, each is liable to contribute to the loss in proportion to the amount for which he is liable. If any insurer pays more than his proportion he can sue the others for contribution (s.80).

Warranties

In contracts of marine insurance the term "warranty" has a different meaning from that in the Sale of Goods Act 1979. In the Marine Insurance Act 1906 it means that the assured undertakes that some particular thing shall or shall not be done, or that some condition shall be fulfilled, or whereby he affirms or negatives the existence of a particular state of facts. A warranty must be exactly complied with whether it be material or not. The effect of non-compliance is to discharge the insurer from liability as from the date of the breach (s.33). The result is not dependent on the insurer taking a decision (*Bank of Nova Scotia* v. *Hellenic Mutual War Risks Association* (*Bermuda*) *Ltd.* (*The Good Luck*) House of Lords, May 16, 1991), although a breach of warranty may be waived by the insurer.

The following warranties are implied:

1. In a voyage policy, that at the commencement of the voyage the ship is seaworthy for the purpose of the particular adventure insured. A ship is deemed to be seaworthy when she is reasonably fit in all respects to encounter the ordinary perils of the seas of the adventure insured (s.39(1), (4)).

2. In a voyage policy, where the voyage is to be performed in stages, during which the ship requires different kinds of or further equipment or preparation, that at the commencement of each stage the ship is seaworthy in respect of such preparation or equipment for the purpose of that stage.

A ship was insured for a round voyage from the United Kingdom to South America and back. During the voyage the master left Montevideo without enough coal to take the ship to St. Vincent, the next port of call, and in consequence some of the ship's fittings and spars had to be burnt, otherwise the ship would have been a total loss. In an action against the insurers to recover the value of the fittings and spars, *held*, as the vessel was not fit when she left Montevideo to meet the ordinary perils of the voyage, there was a breach of an implied warranty and the policy did not attach: *Greenock SS. Co.* v. *Maritime Insce. Co. Ltd.* [1903] 2 K.B. 657.

3. Where the policy attaches while the ship is in port, that the ship shall, at the commencement of the risk, be reasonably fit to encounter the ordinary perils of the port (s.39(2)).

4. In a voyage policy on goods or other movables, that at the commencement of the voyage the ship is not only seaworthy as a ship, but also that she is reasonably fit to carry the goods to the destination contemplated by the policy.

5. That the adventure is a legal one and will be carried out in a lawful manner (s.41).

There is **no** implied warranty in the following cases:

1. As to the nationality of the ship or that her nationality shall not be changed during the risk (s.37).

2. In a time policy, that the ship shall be seaworthy at any stage of the adventure, but where, with the privity of the assured, the ship is sent to sea in an unseaworthy state, the insurer is not liable for any loss attributable to seaworthiness (s.39(5)).

If the loss is not attributable to the unseaworthiness to which the assured was privy, the insuer will be liable on the policy.

A ship which was insured under a time policy, was sent to sea unseaworthy in two respects; her hull was in an unfit state for the voyage and her crew was insufficient. The assured knew of the insufficiency of the crew but not of the unfitness of the hull. The ship was lost because of the unfitness of the hull. *Held*, the insurers were liable: *Thomas* v. *Tyne and Wear S.S. Freight Insce. Assn.* [1917] 1 K.B. 398.

3. In a policy on goods or other movables, that the goods or movables are seaworthy (s.40(1)).

The voyage

In a voyage policy, if the voyage is altered, the insurer is discharged from liability. If, when the contract is made, the ship is said to be at a particular place, it is not necesssary that it should be at that place, but the voyage must be commenced within a reasonable time (s.42). If the ship does not sail from the place of departure specified in the policy or does not go to the destination so specified or does not prosecute the voyage with reasonable dispatch, in all these cases the insurer is not liable on the policy.

If the ship deviates from the voyage contemplated by the policy, the insurer is discharged from liability as from the time of deviation, and it is immaterial that the ship may have regained her route before any loss occurs (s.46). Deviation, however, is excused in the following cases:

(a) where authorised by the policy;
(b) where caused by circumstances beyond the control of the master and his employer;
(c) where reasonably necessary to comply with an express or implied warranty;
(d) where reasonably necessary for the safety of the ship or subject-matter insured;

(e) for the purpose of saving human life or aiding a ship in distress where human life may be in danger; but not for saving property (*Scaramanga* v. *Stamp* (1880) 5 C.P.D. 295);
(f) where reasonably necessary to obtain medical aid for any person on board the ship; and
(g) where caused by the barratrous conduct of the master or crew if barratry be one of the perils insured against.

When the cause excusing the deviation ceases to operate, the ship must resume her course and prosecute her voyage with reasonable dispatch (s.49).

If the policy specifies several ports of discharge, the ship must proceed to such of them as she goes to in the order designated by the policy; if she does not, there is a deviation (s.47).

Assignment of policy

A marine policy is assignable by indorsement, and the assignee can sue on it in his own name subject to any defence which would have been available against the person who effected the policy. The assignment may be made either before or after loss, but an assured who has parted with or lost his interest in the subject-matter assured cannot assign.

The premium

The insurer is not bound to issue the policy until the payment of the premium. If the insurance is effected through a broker, the broker is responsible to the insurer for the premium. He has, however, a lien on the policy for the premium and his charges. If he has dealt with the person who employs him as a principal, he has a lien on the policy for his general balance of insurance account. When a broker effects the insurance and the policy acknowledges the receipt of the premium, the acknowledgment is, in the absence of fraud, conclusive as between the insurer and the assured, but not as between the insurer and the broker (s.54).

Risks covered

Lloyds' Marine Policy does not contain insurance clauses, except a clause providing for English jurisdiction (see p. 566, *ante*). The risks covered are stated in the Institute Cargo Clauses A, B and C.

Institute Cargo Clauses (A) cover:

all risks of loss or of damage to the subject-matter insured.

Institute Cargo Clauses (B) cover:

1.1 loss of or damage to the subject-matter insured reasonably attributable to
1.1.1 fire or explosion,
1.1.2 vessel or craft being stranded ground sunk or capsized,
1.1.3 overturning or derailment of land conveyance,
1.1.4 collision or contact of vessel craft or conveyance with any external object other than water,
1.1.5 discharge of cargo at a port of distress,
1.1.6 earthquake volcanic eruption or lightning,
1.2 loss of or damage to the subject-matter insured caused by
1.2.1 general average sacrifice,
1.2.2 jettison or washing overboard,
1.2.3 entry of sea lake or river water into vessel craft hold conveyance container liftvan or place of storage,
1.3 total loss of any package lost overboard or dropped whilst loading on to, or unloading from, vessel or craft.

Institute Cargo Clauses (C) cover:

1.1 loss of or damage to the subject-matter insured reasonably attributable to
1.1.1 fire or explosion,
1.1.2 vessel or craft being stranded grounded sunk or capsized,
1.1.3 overturning or derailment of land conveyance,
1.1.4 collision or contact of vessel craft or conveyance with any external object other than water,
1.1.5 discharge of cargo at a port of distress,
1.2 loss of or damage to the subject-matter insured caused by
1.2.1 general average sacrifice,
1.2.2 jettison.

All three sets of Institute Cargo Clauses contain a general average clause and a "both to blame collision" clause. In all three cases the risks covered are subject to a long list of "exclusions," specifying the cases in which the insurer is not liable. This list contains, *inter alia*, a war exclusion clause and a strikes exclusion clause but it is possible to obtain additional cover under the Institute War Clauses and the Institute Strikes Riots and Civil Commotion Clauses. It will be noted that Set A covers "all risks," but excluded from this cover is damage or loss caused by delay, inherent vice or insufficient packing. Set B covers in clause 1.2.3 loss or damage caused by "entry of sea lake or river water into the vessel craft hold conveyance container liftvan or place of storage" but this risk is not covered by Set C.

Burden of proof

Whether the burden of proof is upon the insured or the insurer is often a matter of practical importance in that a case may be determined one way or the other according to where the burden lies owing to the paucity of evidence. Thus, when a plaintiff claims for loss under a policy of marine insurance asserting that the loss was caused by one of the perils of the sea specified in the policy, the onus is on him to prove that the loss was accidental (*Rhesa Shipping Co. S.A.* v. *Edmunds* (*The Popi M*) [1985] 1 W.L.R. 948). Accordingly, if on the available evidence the loss is equally consistent with accidental loss by perils of the sea as with scuttling, the plaintiff fails. It follows therefore that if the plaintiff in such a case does not disprove scuttling on a balance of probabilities, he has failed to prove his loss was caused accidentally and fortuitously by one of the specified risks.

The position is different, however, in the case of a claim under a policy for "loss by fire." The risk of fire insured against is not confined to an accidental fire. Thus, if a ship has been set alight by some mischievous person but without the insured's connivance, the insured will be entitled to recover. The insured cannot, of course, recover if he was the person who fired the ship or was a party to the ship being fired, because of the principle of insurance law that no man can recover for a loss which he himself has deliberately or fraudulenty caused. However, the fact that the insured cannot recover does not prevent an innocent mortgagee from recovering (*The Alexion Hope* [1988] 1 Lloyd's Rep. 311). As to the burden of proof, once it is shown that the loss has been caused by fire, the plaintiff has made out a prima facie case and the onus is upon the defendant to show on a balance of probabilities that the fire was caused or connived at by the plaintiff. Accordingly, if the court comes to the conclusion that the loss is equally consistent with arson as it is with an accidental fire, the onus being on the defendant, the plaintiff will succeed (*Slattery* v. *Mance* [1962] 1 Q.B. 676).

Loss and abandonment

The insurer is only liable for those losses which are proximately caused by a peril insured against.

The fact that the loss would not have happened but for the negligence of the master or crew does not relieve the insurer from liability, but he is not liable for loss attributable to the wilful misconduct of the assured. He is not liable for loss through delay, even though caused by a risk insured against, or for wear and tear, leakage or breakage, or inherent vice of the subject-matter insured (s.55).

A loss may be either **total** or **partial**. A partial loss is any loss other than a total loss. A total loss may be actual or constructive.

An **actual total loss** is where the subject-matter insured is (1) destroyed, (2) so damaged as to cease to be a thing of the kind insured against, or (3) where the assured is irretrievably deprived thereof.

A ship was insured against perils of the sea and not loss from capture. During the Russo-Japanese war she was captured and, whilst being navigated towards a Court of Prize, was wrecked. *Held*, the loss was a loss by capture and not by perils of the sea: *Andersen* v. *Marten* [1908] A.C. 334.

A ship on which dates had been loaded was sunk during the voyage and subsequently raised. The dates still retained the appearance of dates, and were of value for distillation into spirits, but were no longer merchantable as dates. *Held*, there was an actual loss of the dates: *Asfar & Co.* v. *Blundell* [1896] 1 Q.B. 123.

An actual total loss may be presumed if a ship is missing and, after a reasonable time, no news of her has been received (s.58).

A **constructive total loss** is where the subject-matter insured is reasonably abandoned because its actual total loss appears to be unavoidable, or because the expenditure to prevent an actual total loss would be greater than the value of the subject-matter when saved. For example, there is a constructive total loss where a ship has sunk and the cost of raising her exceeds her value when recovered; where a ship is damaged and the cost of repairs exceeds the value of the ship when repaired; where goods are damaged and the cost of repair and forwarding them to their destination exceeds their value on arrival (s.60).

A ship sank in harbour and notice of abandonment was given to the insurers. The insurers, by a large expenditure, raised the ship and claimed that she could then be repaired for less than her value, the loss was only partial. *Held*, the insurers could not, by incurring expenditure which an ordinary prudent and uninsured owner would not have incurred, change a constructive total loss into a partial loss: *SS. "Blairmore" Cō. Ltd.* v. *MacRedie* [1898] A.C. 583.

Where there is a constructive total loss, the assured may either treat the loss as a partial loss, or abandon the subject-matter to the insurer and treat the loss as an actual loss. In the latter case notice of abandonment must be given. No notice of abandonment need be given in the case of actual total loss.

Notice of abandonment may be either in writing or by word of mouth, and may take any form as long as it indicates clearly that the assured abandons unconditionally the subject-matter of the insurance to the insured. If notice is not given the loss will be considered as partial. The notice must be given with reasonable diligence after the receipt of reliable information of the loss, time being allowed to make inquiries in a doubtful case. When notice of abandonment is accepted the acceptance conclusively admits liability for the loss, but if the insurer refuses to accept the notice the assured is not prejudiced if the notice has been properly given (s.62).

On abandonment of the subject-matter the insurer is entitled to take over the interest of the assured in whatever may remain of the subject-matter insured, and consequently would be entitled to any freight earned subsequent to the casualty causing the loss (s.63).

General average (p. 624, *post*)

If a general average loss has been incurred in connection with a peril insured against, the assured may recover the whole amount from the insurer without having recourse to the other parties liable to contribute (s.66). The insurer can recover this amount from the others.

A **particular average** loss is a partial loss of the subject-matter insured, caused by a risk insured against, which is not a general average loss. It gives no right of contribution from the other parties interested in the adventure. Such a loss can be recovered from the insurers if it is caused in connection with a peril insured against.

Measure of indemnity

Marine insurance being a contract of indemnity, the assured is only entitled to recover from the insurer such loss as he actually sustains. In the case of a **total** loss, the measure of indemnity is the sum fixed by the policy in the case of a valued policy, and the insurable value of the subject-matter in the case of an unvalued policy (s.68).

In the case of a **partial loss to the ship** the measure of indemnity is:

1. Where the ship has been repaired, the cost of repairs less the customary deductions which are usually one-third of the cost of new materials replacing old.

2. Where the ship has been partially repaired, the cost of repairs as above, and the amount of depreciation arising from the unrepaired damage.

3. Where the damage has not been repaired, the amount of depreciation from the unrepaired damage (s.69).

In the case of a **partial loss of goods** the measure of indemnity is:

1. Where part of the goods is lost and the policy is valued, such proportion of the fixed value as the value of the lost goods bears to the whole value of the insured goods.

2. Where part of the goods is lost and the policy is unvalued, the insurable value of the part lost.

3. Where the goods have been damaged, such proportion of the fixed value in the case of a valued policy, or of the insurable value in the case of an unvalued policy, as the difference between the gross sound and damaged values at the place of arrival bears to the gross sound value (s.71).

An insurer is liable for successive losses, although the total amount may exceed the sum insured; but if a partial loss, which has not been made good, is followed by a total loss, the assured can only recover in respect of the total loss (s.77).

It is the duty of the assured to take reasonable measures to avert or minimise a loss, and to prevent him from being prejudiced by anything he does to preserve the insured property after an accident, the policy usually contains a "suing and labouring" clause. This provides that it shall be lawful for the assured "to sue, labour and travel for, in and about the defence, safeguards, and recovery of the goods, ship, etc., without prejudice to this insurance." Under the clause the assured can recover from the insurer any expenses properly incurred pursuant to the clause, notwithstanding that the insurer has paid for a total loss (s.78).

Rights of insurer on payment

When the insurer pays for a total loss, he is entitled to whatever remains the subject-matter insured, but if he pays for a partial loss he is entitled to no part of the subject-matter. In both cases, however, he is subrogated to the rights of the assured, *i.e.* he can bring an action in the assured's name against any person responsible for the loss.

Return of premium

Where the consideration for the payment of the premium totally fails, and there has been no fraud or illegality on the part of the assured, the premium is returnable to the assured, *e.g.* if the assured insured goods on the wrong ship by mistake (*Martin* v. *Sitwell* (1691) 1 Shower 156). If the consideration is apportionable, and there is a total failure of an apportionable part of the consideration, a proportionate part of the premium is returnable.

The premium is returnable in the following cases:

1. Where the policy is void or is avoided by the insurer as from the commencement of the risk, if there has been no fraud or illegality on the part of the assured.

2. Where the subject-matter insured has never been imperilled.

But if a ship is insured "lost or not lost," and has arrived safely when the insurance is effected, the premium is not returnable unless the insurer knew of the safe arrival.

A ship was overdue and the insurers reinsured at a heavy premium. At the date of the insurance, the ship had arrived safely, but neither party knew of it. *Held*, the insurer was bound to pay the premium to the reinsurer: *Bradford* v. *Symondson* (1881) 7 Q.B.D. 456.

3. Where the assured has no insurable interest, unless the policy is a gaming or wagering policy.

4. Where the assured has over-insured under an unvalued policy, a proportionate part of the premium is recoverable.

5. When the assured has over-insured by double insurance, a proportionate part of the several premiums is returnable, except when the double insurance was effected knowingly by the assured (s.84).

Mutual insurance

Mutual insurance is where two or more persons agree to insure each other against marine losses. In such a case no premium is usually payable, but each party agrees to contribute to a loss in a certain proportion. The rights and duties between the parties depend on agreement, usually embodied in the rules of an association, and the ordinary law of marine insurance applies, subject to any such agreement.

Protection and Indemnity Associations, usually referred to as **P. & I. Clubs**, are a most common example of mutual insurance. It is a usual practice of shipowners to enter their tonnage in a **P. & I. Club**, contributing to its funds on an agreed basis of mutuality, in return for which the Association, on behalf of its members and within the framework of its rules, undertakes to meet the cost of various kinds of liabilities incidental to shipowning, usually those which would otherwise not be covered by the ordinary form of marine hull insurance policy, *e.g.* liabilities for injuries to passengers and crew, damages to piers, docks and harbours and quarantine expenses.

Frequently the rules of P. & I. Clubs contain a "pay to be paid" clause, the effect of which is that the club is liable to indemnify a member only where the latter has paid the claim against it. The presence of such a clause means that the third party will be unable to use the provisions of the Third Parties (Rights Against Insurers) Act 1930 in the event of the member becoming bankrupt (*Firma C-Trade S.A.* v. *Newcastle Protection and Indemnity Association* (*The Fanti*) [1990] 2 All E.R. 705).

PART 9: CARRIAGE BY LAND, SEA AND AIR

Chapter 28

COMMON AND PRIVATE CARRIERS

Common carriers are not now so numerous as in the past but the law relating to them is of importance as a basis to the understanding of current law and conditions of carriage. A common carrier is one who holds himself out as being ready for hire to transport from place to place, either by land, sea or air, the goods of anyone (or for that matter any passengers) wishing to employ him. He must do it as a business and not as a casual operation. He is bound to carry all goods offered to him by persons willing to pay his hire unless:

(a) he has no room in his vehicle;
(b) the goods offered are not of the kind he professes to carry;
(c) the destination is not one to which he usually travels;
(d) the goods are offered at an unreasonable hour;
(e) the goods are not properly packed; or
(f) reasonable charges are not paid in advance.

If he wrongfully refuses to carry any goods or passengers he may be sued for damages in tort.

The defendants who were common carriers by rail refused to accept "packed parcels" from the plaintiffs who were themselves carriers and who were undercutting the defendants' freight rates. *Held*, the defendants were liable for refusal to carry: *Crouch* v. *London and North Western Ry.* (1854) 9 Ex. 556.

Whether a carrier is a common carrier or not depends on the circumstances. If he holds himself out to all and sundry as being prepared to carry he is a common carrier. If he reserves to himself the right of accepting or rejecting offers of goods whether his conveyances are full or empty, being guided by the attractiveness of the offer and not by his ability to carry (*i.e.* whether his vehicle is already full or not), he is not a common carrier.

B. was a haulage contractor who owned two lorries. With these and others, which he hired when necessary, he carried sugar from Liverpool to

Manchester. At Manchester, he invited offers of goods of all kinds, except machinery, and these he accepted or rejected according as the rate, route and class of goods were or were not satisfactory. *Held*, he was not a common carrier, because he reserved the right to reject goods whether his vehicle was full or not: *Belfast Ropework Co. Ltd.* v. *Bushell* [1918] 1 K.B. 210.

Most carriers nowadays state in their conditions of carriage that they are not common carriers but such a statement is not conclusive (see *Palmer on Bailment* 2nd ed. (1991), Ch. 15). Privately owned parcel companies and bus companies who carry passengers and luggage by road may still be common carriers and the species is not extinct.

H. were carriers of hanging garments. By their advertisements, calendars and circulars to customers they held themselves out as being prepared to carry for all and sundry at standard rates, irrespective of the attractiveness of the offer of business. *Held*, they were common carriers and thus strictly liable for loss or damage whether they were negligent or not: *Siohn (A.) & Co. and Academy Garments (Wigan)* v. *Hagland (R. H.) & Son (Transport)* [1976] 2 Lloyd's Rep. 428.

The organisation of the nationalised transport undertakings is now regulated by the Transport Act 1962 and the London Regional Transport Act 1984. The undertakings set up by the Transport Act 1962 that are still in existence, *viz.* the British Railways Board and the British Waterways Board, are not to be regarded as common carriers by rail or inland waterways (Transport Act 1962, s.43(6)). There is nothing in the London Regional Transport Act 1984 to prevent London Regional Transport from being common carriers of passengers and their luggage. The operators of the Channel Tunnel are not common carriers (Channel Tunnel Act 1987, s.19(2)).

Carriers by water, even if they do not hold themselves out as prepared to carry for all and sundry, are probably by custom of the realm at common law strictly liable for loss or damage *as if* they were common carriers (*Liver Alkali* v. *Johnson* (1872) L.R. 7 Ex. 267, (1874) L.R. 9 Ex. 338) (see Chap. 30, *post*). The liability for loss, damage, injury or death of carriers by air (see Chap. 31, *post*) is largely regulated by statute, but there is no reason, in theory, why carriers by sea or air should not be common carriers and thus be sued for refusal to carry.

Liability of common carriers of goods for loss or damage

A contract of carriage of goods is presumed to be made by the owner of goods with the carrier. The consignor is deemed to be acting as agent for the owner if he is not the owner himself. The consignor as agent must make a reasonable contract; (see, for example, s.32(2) of the Sale of Goods Act 1979). As the ownership of the goods during transit usually is with the buyer/consignee (see s.32(1) and s.18 Rule 5(2) of the Sale of Goods Act 1979 discussed at pp. 409 and 412–413, above) he is the correct person to sue on the contract (*Texas Instruments* v. *Europe Cargo*, Financial Times July 6, 1990).

A common carrier is strictly liable for loss or damage to the goods irrespective of negligence (see *Siohn (A.) & Co. and Academy Garments (Wigan)* v. *Hagland (R. H.) & Son (Transport)*, see p. 582, *ante*).

But to this rule of strict liability there are four common law **excepted perils,** *viz.* the carrier is not liable if the loss or damage is caused by:

(a) an Act of God;
(b) the Queen's enemies;
(c) inherent vice in the thing carried; or
(d) the fault or fraud of the consignor or consignee.

It must be emphasised that the burden of proving these defences falls on the common carrier and that he cannot rely on them if he has been negligent. These common law defences reappear in the modern conditions of carriage of private carriers of goods.

Act of God

An Act of God has been explained as "a mere short way in expressing this proposition. A common carrier is not liable for any accident as to which he can show that it is due to natural causes directly and exclusively without human intervention, and that it could not have been prevented by any amount of foresight and pains and care reasonably to have been expected from him" (*per* James L.J. in *Nugent* v. *Smith* (1876) 1 C.P.D. 423.

The defendant was a common carrier by barge. Without any negligence on his part a sudden tempest blew the barge into a bridge and the plaintiff's goods were lost. *Held*, the defendant was not liable due to an Act of God (*Amies* v. *Stevens* (1716) 1 Stra. 127).

The Queen's enemies

The Queen's enemies means a hostile foreign sovereign or government. Injury to the goods caused by robbers or through a riot is not within the exception, and neither are the acts of terrorists.

Inherent vice in the thing carried

A carrier is not liable for damage caused by something inherent in the nature of the goods carried over which he has no control and against which he cannot guard. Inherent vice is "unfitness for the treatment the contract of carriage authorised or required" (*Albacora S.R.L.* v. *Westcott & Lawrence Line* [1966] 2 Lloyd's Rep. 53, 59).

H. consigned a cask of gin to B., a common carrier. Through no fault of B. the cask leaked in transit. *Held*, B. was not liable; (*Hudson* v. *Baxendale* (1857) 2 H. & N. 575.

The fault or fraud of the consignor or consignee

If the damage is caused by the goods not being properly packed, the carrier is not liable. Similarly, if loss is caused by inaccurate addressing or fraudulent practice by the consignor then the carrier is not liable.

B. hid money in a consignment of tea which he gave to W. a common carrier. The money was stolen. *Held*, W. was not liable as "the plaintiff bought this loss on himself by his own manner of conducting the business" (*per* Tenterden C.J.) (*Bradley* v. *Waterhouse* (1828) 3 C.O.P. 318).

Liabilities of common carriers of passengers

It should be emphasised that, unlike a common carrier of goods, a common carrier of passengers is not strictly liable for the safety of his passengers although he can be sued for refusing to carry.

R. was injured in a railway accident which happened without any negligence on the part of the railway company who were common carriers. *Held*, the railway company were not liable (*Readhead* v. *Midland Ry.* (1869) L.R. 4 Q.B. 379).

Liability of private carriers of goods for loss or damage

A private carrier of goods is a **bailee** and as such is only liable for negligence although in the event of loss or damage the burden of disproving negligence is upon him (see p. 506, *ante*).

A valuable racehorse died in transit. *Held*, the burden fell on the carrier to disprove negligence. As the driver had not regularly inspected the health of the horse during transit he had been negligent and the carrier was held liable. (*Cowper* v. *J. G. Goldner Ltd.* (1986 40. S.A.S.R. 457 (Australia)).

Liability of common and private carriers for delay

It should be noted that common carriers are not strictly liable for delay as they are for loss or damage. Both common and private carriers are liable for delays caused by their negligence only.

T. consigned poultry by rail leaving adequate time for the poultry to reach the market in London in normal circumstances. Transit was, however, delayed by a rail accident caused by the negligence of another railway company over which the defendants had no control. *Held*, the railway company was not liable for the delay even though they were common carriers as there was no lack of diligence on their part and the delay was beyond their control: *Taylor* v. *Great Northern Ry.* (1866) L.R. 1 C.P. 385.

No "Warranty" of roadworthiness or railworthiness

A private or common carrier by land is only liable for negligence at common law and does not warrant the safety of his vehicle or craft (*John Carter* v. *Hanson Haulage* [1965] 2 Q.B. 495).

Modification of common law liability

A common carrier can always be sued for refusal to carry but is not bound to undertake the common carrier's strict liability. He may make a contract either excluding altogether or restricting his strict liability as a common carrier. When his liability is restricted, he still carries as a common carrier subject to the restriction. If, for example, the contract is that he is not to be liable for damage caused by collision, he will be under the full liability of a common carrier in respect of damage caused in other ways, *e.g.* by fire. The conditions of a carrier by land can be challenged on the ground that they do not pass the "reasonableness test" laid down by section 24 of the Unfair Contract Terms Act 1977 (see pp. 43–45 *ante*). Common carriers (but not private carriers) of goods by land as opposed to common carriers of passengers or common carriers by sea or air are subject to the Carriers Act 1830. This Act, now of little practical importance, provides that where "valuables" worth in excess of £10 are delivered to a carrier by land their nature and value must be declared. If they are not the carrier is not liable for them (see *Caswell* v. *Cheshire Lines Committee* [1907] 2 K.B. 499). The Act can lead to injustice, however, and is in need of repeal.

Only the carrier and other parties to the contract can take advantage of any limitation or exemption clauses in the contract (*Scruttons Ltd.* v. *Midland Silicones Ltd.* [1962] A.C. 446, discussed on p. 61, *ante*).

The Carriers Act 1830 only applies to common carriers. The liability of private carriers at common law is unlimited. If they want to limit or exempt their liability for valuables or for anything else they must do so by contract.

Carrier's duties and liabilities

If dangerous goods are given to a carrier for carriage the consignor is deemed to warrant to the carrier and also to the carrier's servants and owners of other goods that the goods are fit to be carried. For a breach of this warranty (which is apparently a form of tortious liability rather than contractual) the consignor will be liable in damages even if he were ignorant of the dangerous character of his goods (*Bamfield* v. *Goole and Sheffield Transport Co. Ltd.* [1910] 2 K.B. 94).

The T. Co. sent by railway some carboys of corrosive fluid and other persons sent some felt hats. During the transit, the fluid escaped from the carboys and damaged the hats. Being common carriers, the railway company were liable for the damage to the hats, and consequently they paid £437, the value of the hats, to their owner. In an action by the railway company to recover this amount from the T. Co., *held*, they were entitled to do so, upon an implied warranty that the carboys were fit to be carried: *Great Northern Ry.* v. *L.E.P. Transport Co.* [1922] 2 K.B. 742.

In addition to any contractual or statutory rights a carrier of goods may have the right to sell goods without consulting the owner. This arises where the carrier is an agent of necessity. For this agency to arise it must be commercially impossible to contact the owner and there must be a real emergency, *e.g.* the goods are perishable.

S. consigned tomatoes to the railway company. The tomatoes were delayed in transit by a strike for which the defendants were not liable and they were sold by the defendants. *Held*, there was no agency of necessity as the tomatoes were still in reasonable condition and the defendants could have contacted the owners for instructions. The defendants were, therefore, held liable: *Springer* v. *G.W.R.* [1921] 1 K.B. 257.

A carrier must obey the orders of an unpaid seller of goods who exercises a right of stoppage in transit under sections 44–46 of the Sale of Goods Act 1979 (see p. 346, *ante*).

A carrier is liable during the period of "transit." Transit is defined in relation to carriage by air by the Warsaw Convention and Hague Protocol. In relation to carriage by land and sea transit at common law begins at the moment the goods are delivered to the carrier or his agent for the purposes of carriage and the carrier accepts them. Transit does not mean movement and goods can be in transit while being stored in a warehouse (*William Soanes Ltd.* v. *F. E. Walker Ltd.* (1946) 79 Lloyd's Rep. 646). Transit ceases when the goods are delivered to the consignee or when the goods are tendered to the consignee. Where goods are "to be collected" transit ceases a reasonable time after the arrival of the goods at the destination. After transit ceases a carrier is certainly liable for negligent loss or damage if he charges for warehousing. If he does not then for a reasonable time he is probably liable for loss or damage caused by his negligence or wrongdoing (*McKinnon* v. *Arcadian Lines* (1978) 81 D.L.R. 484) (Canada).

It is the duty of a carrier to deliver the goods to the consignee at the place to which they are directed. If he delivers them to the consignee he is not liable (*Edmunds* v. *Merchants Despatch* 135 Mass. 283 (1883) (U.S.A.)). The carrier, in the absence of notice to the contrary, is entitled to treat the consignee as the owner of the goods and the consignor as his agent to contract with the carrier. Therefore, the consignee can take possession of the goods at any point in the transit when they can reasonably be got at (*Cork Distilleries* v. *Gt. S. & W. Ry. of Ireland* (1874) L.R. 7 H.L. 269).

Measure of damages

The measure of damages is often controlled by Act of Parliament according to whether the transport is by land, sea or air (see Chaps. 29–31). Alternatively, many contracts attempt to limit the amount of damages payable usually by reference to the weight of the goods. It is also common to exclude liability for "consequential loss." Such clauses can be challenged under the "reasonableness test" in the Unfair Contract Terms Act 1977 (see page 43). The position in the absence of such provisions is however as follows.

Where goods are lost the measure of damages is the value of the goods. If the value has been declared no higher value can be recovered. In other cases the value is the market value at the place to which they were consigned at the time when they ought to have been delivered (*C. Czarnikow Ltd.* v. *Koufos* [1969] 1 A.C. 350). See p. 175, *ante*.

When there is delay in delivery, the measure of damages is the loss reasonably arising from the breach (see p. 175, *ante*). If the delay has caused the goods to fall in value, for example, because they are perishable or seasonable, the damages will be the difference between the value when actually delivered and the value when they ought to have been delivered. If the article carried is a profit-earning machine, damages may be recovered for loss of use. Loss of profit on resale can only be recovered when the circumstances are brought to the carrier's notice.

Carriage of passengers

As stated above, common carriers of passengers can exist and they can be sued for refusal to carry. All carriers of passengers, whether common or private, are at common law liable only for injury to passengers caused by the carrier's negligence. The liability of carrier of passengers by air is largely controlled by statute (see Chap. 31) and carriers of passengers by land are forbidden to exclude liability for death and injury by the Unfair Contract Terms Act 1977 (see Chap. 29). As regards carriage of passengers by sea see Chap. 30.

The burden of proving negligence falls on the injured passenger but sometimes the circumstances so strongly suggest negligence that it will be presumed in the absence of convincing evidence to the contrary by the carrier. This is known as the doctrine of *res ipsa loquitur* (the thing speaks for itself).

G., a passenger on a railway train, put his hand on a bar across the window. The door immediately flew open and G. fell out of the train and was injured, *Held*, negligence on the part of the railway company could be assumed: *Gee* v. *Metropolitan Ry*. (1873) L.R. 8 Q.B. 161.

CHAPTER 29

CARRIAGE BY LAND

GENERAL

A CARRIER of goods by land does not warrant that his vehicle is roadworthy although the standard of care required is high. Breach of statutory provisions such as the Road Traffic Act 1988 is strong evidence of negligence. This is an important difference from the law of carriage of goods by sea where at common law (but not under the Hague-Visby Rules relating to Bills of Lading, see p. 613, *post*) there is an absolute "warranty" of seaworthiness. (See *John Carter Ltd.* v. *Hanson Haulage* (*Leeds*) *Ltd.* [1965] 2 Q.B. 495).

A carrier by land who unjustifiably deviates from the agreed route or mode of carriage deviates from the terms of the bailment and is strictly liable for any loss or damage irrespective of negligence and cannot rely on any contractual term to exclude or limit liability (*London & N.W. Ry.* v. *Neilson* [1922] A.C. 263). This doctrine has survived section 3 of the Unfair Contract Terms Act 1977.

The defendant carriers put the plaintiff's cameras on the same lorry as the goods of another customer and delivered the goods of the other customer first, thus deviating from the direct route. *Held*, this deviation was normal commercial practice and was not unjustifiable. The defendants were not, therefore, strictly liable for a theft that occurred without their negligence (*Mayfair Photographic Ltd.* v. *Baxter Hoare Ltd.* [1972] 1 Lloyd's Rep. 410).

Other unjustifiable acts of a carrier may amount to a deviation from the terms of the bailment and thus lose him the protection of his conditions, *e.g.* giving the goods to a person he ought to know has no right to them; subcontracting without the owner's permission and leaving the goods in an unlocked vehicle in a side street, etc.

CARRIAGE BY RAIL

As the British Railways Board is no longer a common carrier, the Carriers Act 1830 which is unaffected by the Transport Acts no longer applies to carriage by rail. Similarly there is now no legislation controlling the terms under which the Board may carry goods, *e.g.* there is no limit upon their power to restrict or exclude liability for negligence in the carriage or delivery of goods other than the Unfair Contract Terms Act 1977. The **Railway Board's Conditions of Carriage** therefore operate purely as contractual terms. The most important are the General Conditions for the Carriage of Goods (other than Goods for which Conditions are specially provided). These Conditions cover virtually all traffic, the principal exceptions being (a) certain international traffic, and (b) special contracts with individual traders.

International traffic

Certain international traffic is carried under the International Convention concerning International Carriage by Rail 1980, known as COTIF.[1] This Convention is given statutory force by the International Transport Conventions Act 1983. The Convention has two sections. CIM covers contracts for the carriage of goods by rail under a through consignment note over the territory of at least two contracting states. CIV covers contracts for the international carriage of passengers by Rail. Essentially liability under CIM is very similar to that under CMR (see pp. 595–596) but the limit of liability is approximately double that under CMR.

Board's risk conditions

Under Clause 5A of the General Conditions the Board is liable for any loss, or misdelivery of, or damage to merchandise during transit, unless the Board can prove that it has arisen from:

(a) an Act of God;
(b) any consequence of war, invasion, act of foreign enemy, hostilities (whether war be declared or not), civil war, rebellion, insurrection, military or usurped power or confiscation, requisition, destruction of or damage to property by or under the order of any government or public or local authority;
(c) seizure under legal process;

[1] See Cmnd. 8535.

(d) act or omission of the trader;
(e) inherent liability to wastage in bulk or weight, latent defect or inherent defect, vice or natural deterioration of the goods;
(f) insufficient or improper packing;
(g) insufficient or improper labelling or addressing;
(h) riot, civil commotion, strikes, lockouts, stoppage or restraint of labour from whatever cause; or
(j) consignee not taking or accepting delivery within a reasonable time.

The Board can rely on one of these exceptions only where it proves that the Board has not been negligent.

When the trader has suffered loss arising from delay the Board is liable, unless it can prove that the loss was not caused by any negligence on the part of the Board.

The liability of the Board is now limited:

(a) where the loss is of the whole of a consignment, to a sum at the rate of £2,000 per metric tonne on the gross weight of the consignment; or
(b) where the loss is of part of a consignment, to the proportion of the sum calculated under (a) which the actual value of that part of the consignment bears to the actual value of the whole of the consignment.

The Board is not liable where the consignor or consignee has been fraudulent.

It should thus be noted that the Board undertakes a liability for loss, damage or delay somewhere between that of the common and private carriers at common law. As a private carrier it would not, but at common law it would, be liable for the malicious acts of strangers occurring without its negligence. Under these conditions it appears that it would.

Owner's risk conditions

In an owner's risk contract the liability of the Board is more restricted. Clause 5B of the General Conditions (August 1986) provides that the Board shall not be liable for loss, damage, misdelivery, delay or detention "except upon proof . . . that the same was caused by the wilful misconduct of the Board." But the Board is not exempt from any liability which it would have had under Board's risk conditions for non-delivery of the whole of a consignment or of any separate package forming part of it.

Wilful misconduct means "misconduct to which the will is a party," *i.e.* deliberate or reckless wrongdoing and is something much more than negligence. The person concerned must realise the wrongful nature of the act.

B. consigned a large switchback plant to the railway company "at owners risk." The servant responsible made no effort to gauge the goods although it was obvious that they were dangerously large. The goods were damaged when they hit a bridge. *Held,* the railway company were guilty of wilful misconduct and were therefore liable: *Bastable* v. *North British Ry.* [1912] S.C. 555.

It should be emphasised that wilful misconduct is not a doctrine of the common law and arises only under these or similar conditions of carriage.

It is very doubtful whether Clause 5B would pass the "reasonableness test" in section 24 of the Unfair Contract Terms Act 1977 if challenged (see page 43 *ante*).

Dangerous goods

The conditions under which the Board now accepts dangerous goods are contained in clause 20 of the General Conditions of Carriage of Goods (August 1986). The list of dangerous goods is constantly revised by the Railways Board. The conditions, for example, require prior notice to the Board of the intention to consign dangerous goods.

Liability to pay carriage

The conditions provide that the sender is to be liable to pay carriage but that, if the consignment note states that carriage is payable by the consignee, the sender is not to be required to pay unless the consignee fails to pay after reasonable demands have been made.

Termination of transit

The transit is at an end when the goods are delivered or if the transit is determined by the sender exercising his right of stoppage *in transitu* or otherwise prematurely determining it. If the goods are detained to await order or carried to a private siding, the transit ends one clear day after notice in writing is given to the consignee. After the termination of the transit, the Board holds the goods as a warehouseman, subject to its usual charges.

On the termination of the transit, the Board is given by the conditions a lien on the goods for carriages and other proper charges, and also a power of sale. A power of sale is also given in certain cases of emergency, chiefly in connection with perishable goods.

Time for claims

The general conditions provide that notice of a claim must be made within three days of the termination of the transit, and the claim itself within seven days, both to be in writing. If the claim is for non-delivery of the whole consignment or of a separate package forming part of the consignment, the times are 28 days and 42 days from the commencement of the transit. These time limits do not apply if it was "not reasonably possible" for the customer to advise the Board of the loss or damage within these time limits.

Carriage of passengers

The Board is not—because it is no longer regarded as a common carrier—legally obliged to carry any passenger. It is not, however, permitted to impose a term on the carrying of passengers which restricts their liability for death or personal injury resulting from negligence (Unfair Contract Terms Act 1977, s.2(1)).

Apart from this restriction the Railways Board can impose whatever contractual conditions it likes, provided they satisfy the requirement of reasonableness established by the 1977 Act (see p. 43, *ante*). The Standard Conditions of Carriage of Passengers and their Luggage are available for inspection at booking offices.

Carriage by Road

As stated above, most carriers of goods by road are private carriers and as bailees are only liable for negligence at common law.

R.H.A. Conditions

There are no statutory restrictions affecting contracts made by road carriers for the carriage of goods within the United Kingdom. Thus carriers by road can, *e.g.* exclude liability for negligence if they see fit but such terms can be challenged under section 24 of the Unfair Contract Terms Act 1977, if they are unreasonable. Many carriers use the standard **Conditions of Carriage of the Road Haulage Association** (1982). Under Clause 9 of these conditions there are three alternative bases of liability. Firstly the customer may agree in writing that the carrier shall be under no liability. Such an agreement may well fail the "reasonableness test" in the Unfair Contract Terms Act. Secondly, if there is no such agreement the carrier is liable for loss or damage to "valuables" if negligent. Thirdly, as regards other merchandise the liability of the carrier is very similar to that of British Rail under Clause 5A of New General Conditions (see p. 591).

The C.M.R. Convention

The **Carriage of Goods by Road Act 1965** which incorporates the Convention on the Contract for the International Carriage of Goods by Road (CMR) into British law. It regulates the carriage of goods by road between the territories of its signatories if either the country of "departure" or the country of "destination" is a High Contracting Party. CMR has thus been given statutory force in this country and carriers cannot contract out of its provisions.

Basically, under this Convention and CIM the carrier is liable for loss or damage unless he can bring himself within the scope of listed defences. The primary defences are:

(i) Wrongful act or neglect of the claimant.
(ii) Instructions of the claimant.
(iii) Inherent vice.
(iv) Circumstances which the carrier could not avoid and the consequences of which he was unable to prevent (even with the utmost care) (see *Silber* v. *Islander Trucking* [1985] 2 Lloyd's Rep. 243).

It should be noted that in the event of ambiguity the judges can go to the French text of the Convention and interpret the Acts in accordance with it to give effect to the Conventions. Thus, in *James Buchanan & Co. Ltd.* v. *Babco Forwarding & Shipping* (*U.K.*) [1977] 2 W.L.R. 107 the carriers were held liable to pay £30,000 to the plaintiffs who had been forced to pay this sum in excise duty for whisky originally destined for export but negligently lost by the carriers in England. This was despite the wording of the English translation which referred to losses "incurred in respect of the carriage of the goods" (art. 23(4)), which this sum literally was not.

The Carriage by Air and Road Act 1979 provides that the maximum limits of liability of the carrier, which in the CMR are expressed in gold francs, shall be expressed in the Special Drawing Rights of the International Monetary Fund.

Carriage of Passengers

When a passenger is carried by road in a public service vehicle the contract of carriage cannot contain any provision which exempts liability for death or personal injury arising from negligence (Unfair Contract Terms Act 1977, s.2(1)). The Act applies whether the passenger pays a fare or is carried under a free pass.

The Carriage of Passengers by Road Act 1974 should also be noted. It gave effect to an international Convention concerning the international carriage of passengers by road. It has no application to purely domestic transport. However, the Act is not yet in force.

CHAPTER 30

CARRIAGE BY SEA

THERE are two types of the contract of carriage by sea, also called the contract of affreightment. They are:

(a) contracts contained in a charterparty; and
(b) contracts evidenced by a bill of lading.

If a cargo owner requires a whole ship, he will hire it from the shipowner by way of a **charterparty**. If he requires only shipping space in a ship, the terms of his contract with the carrier are normally stated in a **bill of lading**. If the carrier does not carry the goods of the cargo owner under a written contract—which would be a most unusual occurrence—the carrier would be liable as if he were a common carrier.

CHARTERPARTIES

Voyage charters, time charters, charters by demise

A charterparty is a contract whereby the charterer hires the use of a ship from the shipowner. Three types of charterparties are in use:—

(a) voyage charters,
(b) time charters, and
(c) charter by demise or bareboat charters.

Under a **voyage charter** the parties agree that the charterer shall hire a specified ship for the carriage of cargo from a port of shipment to a port of destination for one voyage or several voyages.

Under a **time charter** the charterer is entitled for an agreed period of time to direct within agreed limits how the ship shall be used.

Under a **charter by demise** the ship is leased to the charterer in a manner which, for the time being, transfers the control over her working and navigation entirely to the charterer.

Voyage and time charters give the charterer only the *use* of the ship; the master and the crew are provided by the shipowner who makes their services available to the charterer and the shipowner remains in possession of the ship. Under a charterparty by demise the charterer is in *possession* of the ship may put in his own master and crew. Voyage and time charters are much more frequent than charters by demise.

In voyage and time charters the parties usually use standard forms which they suitably amend. Illustrations of such standard forms are the "Gencon" form for voyage charters and the "Baltime" form for time charters but many more forms are in use. Some of them are sponsored by the Baltic and International Maritime Conference.

A charterparty must be in writing, either with or without a seal. The liability of the carrier for loss or damage depends upon the terms of the charter.

A charter may contain a clause (called a Clause Paramount) embodying the provisions of the Hague Rules or Hague-Visby Rules on Bills of Lading (see p. 613, *post*). Although these Rules are essentially designed for bills of lading and not for charterparties, the effect of such incorporation is to limit the liability of the owner to the charterer in the manner stated in the Rules (*Adamastos Shipping Co. Ltd.* v. *Anglo-Saxon Petroleum Co. Ltd.* [1959] A.C. 133; p. 29, *ante*).

Voyage charters

The voyage

The charter will contain an express term obliging the shipowner to carry the goods from the named port of loading to the destination named in the charter. This is usually expressed as, for example, "The vessel shall proceed to New York."

Sometimes a voyage charter does not name the ports of loading and discharge. In such cases there is invariably a contractual term that the charterer will nominate, *e.g.* "good and safe ports" (see *The Eastern City* [1958] 2 Lloyd's Rep. 153).

Use of ship

The charterer undertakes to engage only in "lawful trades." He further agrees to use only "safe ports." Such clauses also appear in time charters. Sometimes the "safe port" clause is further specified by phrases requiring the ship to be "always afloat" or "always afloat at all times of the tide." A "safe port" clause means that the ship can safely enter the port, lie safely there and safely leave it. Safety refers not only to the political and structural conditions of the port but may also refer to its meteorological conditions.

The *Dagmar*, which was on a time charter, was directed by the charterers to Cape Chat, Quebec, to load timber. While lying there on anchor, the ship was caught by heavy North winds and swell and driven aground. The shipowners claimed damages, alleging that Cape Chat was an unsafe port. *Held*, that the fact that the master had not been warned that he would not receive weather information from the shore and had to rely upon his own resources for obtaining weather forecasts made Cape Chat an unsafe port: *Tage Berglund* v. *Montoro Shipping Corporation Ltd. The Dagmar* [1968] 2 Lloyd's Rep. 563.

The question whether a port is a "safe port," has to be decided according to the conditions prevailing at the time of the nomination of the port by the charterer; subsequent unexpected and abnormal events have to be disregarded: *Kodros Shipping Corporation* v. *Empresa Cubana de Fletes*, *The Evia* (*No. 2*) [1982] 2 Lloyd's Rep. 307.

If the master enters a port or leaves the ship at a port which he knows to be, or can foresee or ought to have foreseen that it might become unsafe, and damage results to the ship, the charterer is not liable.

The common law duties

Under every voyage charter (and bills of lading) there are three basic common law duties:

1. the duty to supply a seaworthy ship;
2. the duty to proceed with reasonable despatch; and
3. the duty not to deviate from the agreed voyage.

1. *Seaworthiness*. The shipowner must not only have done his best to make the ship fit for the voyage, she must actually be fit for the voyage. It is no defence that the shipowner did not know that the ship was not seaworthy. The test of seaworthiness is: would a

prudent shipowner have made good the defect before sending the ship to sea, if he had known of it? If he would, the ship was not seaworthy (*McFadden* v. *Blue Star Line* [1905] 1 K.B. 697).

Seaworthiness is a relative term and means that the ship is fit to encounter the ordinary perils of the voyage." (*Stanton* v. *Richardson*) (1875) L.R. 9 C.P. 390. There is no guarantee that she will survive every calamity.

Lemons were loaded at Naples for London. At Marseilles the ship was required by the French authorities to be fumigated, because she had come from Mombasa, a plague infected port. The fumigation damaged the lemons. *Held*, as the ship was bound to be fumigated at Marseilles, she was not reasonably fit at Naples for the carriage of the lemons and was, therefore, unseaworthy: *Ciampa* v. *British India Steam Navigation Co.* [1915] 2 K.B. 774.

Bad stowage will amount to unseaworthiness if it endangers the safety of the ship (*Kopitoft* v. *Wilson* [1876] 1 Q.B. 377), but not if it merely affects the cargo.

A ship was loaded with casks of palm oil, on top of which were placed bags of palm kernels. On arrival, it was found that the palm kernels had crushed the casks and much of the palm oil was lost. *Held*, the ship was seaworthy and the damage was due to bad stowage: *Elder Dempster & Co.* v. *Zochonis & Co.* [1924] A.C. 522.

A ship is unseaworthy if it is not fitted with the required loading and unloading gear (*Hang Fung Shipping & Trading Co. Ltd.* v. *Mullion & Co. Ltd.; The Ardgroom* [1966] 1 Lloyd's Rep. 511) or if its crew is incompetent and inexperienced (*Hongkong Fir Shipping Co. Ltd.* v. *Kawasaki Kisen Kaisha* [1962] 2 Q.B. 26).

Breach of the obligation to supply a seaworthy vessel does not, by itself, allow a charterer to escape liability under the charter unless the delays involved in making the vessel seaworthy are so great as to frustrate the commercial purpose of the charter (*Hongkong Fir Shipping Co. Ltd.* v. *Kawasaki Kisen Kaisha Ltd.* above.

If the charterer or shipper discovers the unseaworthiness before the commencement of the voyage, he can repudiate the contract unless the ship can be made seaworthy within a reasonable time. In all other cases, or if he does not repudiate, he can recover such damages as he has suffered by reason of the unseaworthiness.

2. *Reasonable despatch.* The ship must be ready to commence the voyage agreed on and to load the cargo to be carried and shall proceed upon and complete the voyage agreed upon with all reasonable despatch. A breach of this duty gives the charterer the right to repudiate the contract if the delay is so serious as to go to the root of the contract, otherwise the remedy is in damages.

3. *Deviation.* The ship must proceed on the voyage without deviation in the usual and customary manner. Departure from the agreed voyage to save life is allowed under a charterparty at common law, but not to save property.

A ship was sailing from Kronstadt to the Mediterranean. On the voyage she sighted a vessel in distress and agreed to tow her into Texel, which was out of the direct course. While going there she was stranded. The jury found that the tow was not reasonably necessary to save life, but was reasonably necessary to save the vessel and cargo. *Held*, the deviation was unnecessary, and the shipowners were liable for the cargo: *Scaramanga* v. *Stamp* (1880) 5 C.P.D. 295.

In bills of lading governed by, or charterparties incorporation, the Carriage of Goods by Sea Act 1971 deviation to save property is also allowed. Deviation is allowable in case of necessity, *e.g.* to avoid hostile capture, pirates, icebergs, or other dangers of navigation. The effect of deviation is to displace the contract of carriage, whether charterparty or bill of lading, and to reduce the carrier to the position of a "wrongful bailee," so that he can no longer rely on the exceptions contained in the contract of carriage.

Goods were shipped under a bill of lading exempting the shipowners from loss through negligence of stevedores. The ship deviated from the voyage. In discharging the ship, the stevedores employed by the shipowners damaged the goods. *Held*, the ship having deviated, the contract evidenced by the bill of lading was broken, and the shipowners were not entitled to rely on the exception: *Joseph Thorley Ltd.* v. *Orchis SS. Co. Ltd.* [1907] 1 K.B. 660.

In addition the carrier becomes strictly liable as a "wrongful bailee" irrespective of negligence (*L. & N.W. Ry.* v. *Neilson* [1922] A.C. 263).

Where the ship loads part of the cargo, then deviates, and the charterer with knowledge of the deviation, loads the remainder of the cargo in another port, he has affirmed the charter and waived the rights accruing to him from the deviation (*Hain S.S. Ltd.* v. *Tate & Lyle Ltd.* [1936] 2 All E.R. 597 (H.L.)).

The preliminary voyage and the cancellation clause

The **preliminary voyage** is the voyage which the ship has to undertake in order to be available at the port of shipment at the agreed time of loading, unless the ship happens to be already at that port. If the shipowner undertakes absolutely "to proceed to (named) port and there to load," this is a condition precedent to the charterer's liability. If this condition is broken, the charterer is released from his obligation to load and to pay the freight. If there is no express clause the shipowner must proceed to the named port of shipment "with all due despatch." This is an intermediate term of the contract (see p. 35). If this implied term is broken, the charterer must load but may claim damages for any loss suffered as the result of the delay unless the delay is so serious as to "frustrate" the venture. In that latter event the charterer may repudiate the contract.

A voyage charterparty usually contains a **cancellation clause**. This clause gives the charterer a contractual right to cancel the charter if the vessel is not at his disposal in the port of shipment at a specified time. This contractual right exists in addition to any common law right of the charterer to rescind the contract. If the ship cannot get to the port of loading by the cancelling date, the ship is still under the primary obligation to proceed to that port. Nor is the shipowner relieved by the fixing of a cancellation date of his secondary obligation in the event of non-performance to pay damages to the charterer for any loss sustained by such non-performance (Diplock L.J. in *C. Czarnikow Ltd.* v. *Koufos* [1966] 1 Lloyd's Rep. 595, 610).

A charterer is not entitled to cancel the charter under the contractual cancellation clause before the cancelling date is due. This is so, even though it is clear that the ship will not arrive at the port of loading in time; a premature cancellation of the charterparty may constitute an anticipatory breach of contract by the charterer (*The Mihalis Angelos* [1971] 1 Q.B. 164).

If the ship is unable to reach the port of loading owing to an excepted peril or to an event which constitutes frustration in common law, neither party is in breach of contract and both parties are discharged.

Port and berth charterparties

It is of great importance to ascertain when the ship is an **arrived ship**. The question is here whether the ship has "arrived" at the place where, according to the terms of the charterparty, it should load or discharge the cargo. The lay days, *i.e.* the days allowed for loading and unloading the cargo, begin to run only if the ship is an "arrived ship" and only after the expiration of the lay days can the shipowner claim demurrage from the charterer.

Some charterparties simply state the port to which the ship should proceed (**port charterparties**). Others state that the ship shall proceed to a specified and actual loading spot, quay or berth in a port (**berth charterparties**). Where the charter provides that the ship shall proceed to a berth to be named by the charterer, the position is the same as if the named berth was actually specified in the charterparty.

In the case of a port charterparty it is not always easy to determine whether the ship is an arrived ship. Sometimes a ship may have to wait at a place of anchorage until a berth becomes free and it can proceed thereto. The "port" includes all areas that are under the fiscal and administrative control of the port authorities. If she is within such an area then the ship is at the immediate and effective disposition of the charterer; it is an arrived ship. But if the customary place of waiting is outside the port, the ship is not an arrived ship until it has entered the port (*The Johanna Oldendorff*, below).

The Johanna Oldendorff carried a bulk cargo of grain from the United States under a voyage charter. The charter was a port charter and the charterers, in accordance with the terms of the charter, nominated Liverpool/Birkenhead as the port of discharge. The vessel arrived at Mersey Bar anchorage on January 2, 1968, but no berth was nominated by the charterers. The following day the ship cleared with customs and was ordered to proceed to anchor at the bar light vessel. This position was about 17 miles away from the berths but still in the port area. The ship lay at anchor at the bar from January 3 to 20, ready, as far as it was concerned, to discharge. The bar was the customary waiting place for bulk grain ships. The shipowners gave notice of readiness to discharge on January 3, 1968. The issue was who was liable to pay for the delay. That depended on whether the ship was an arrived ship. *Held*, the ship, when anchored at the bar, was an arrived ship because it was at the immediate and effective disposition of the charterers at a place within the port area where waiting ships usually lay: *The Johanna Oldendorff* [1974] A.C. 479.

Lay days and demurrage

When the ship is an arrived ship and the shipowner gives the charterer **notice of readiness**, the "lay days" begin to run. Notice of readiness to *load* must always be given, though it may be given orally, but notice of readiness to *discharge* is not required unless so stated in the charterparty.

The **lay days** are the time specified in the charterparty for loading or unloading. If the charterparty does not fix the lay days, the charterer must load and unload the cargo within a reasonable time. The charterparty sometimes specifies as lay days "working days" or "weather working days." (See *Glass and Cashmore*, Introduction to the Law of Carriage of Goods (1989) para. 5.74).

If the lay days are exceeded and the ship is detained longer in the port of loading or unloading than agreed in the charterparty, **demurrage** is payable by the charterer to the shipowner. Demurrage is in the nature of liquidated damages. The rate at which demurrage is payable is laid down in the charterparty, *e.g.* "ten days loading and demurrage at £120 per day afterwards" but sometimes the rate of demurrage is calculated on the tonnage of the ship. If the stipulation on demurrage in the charterparty is unlimited in time, *i.e.* covers *all* delay, no further claim for damages for delay is admitted (*Suisse Atlantique* v. *N.V. Rotterdamsahe Kolen Centrale* [1967] A.C. 361) but if the stipulation for demurrage is limited for a number of days and the delay exceeds this time, damages may be claimed for the excess on normal common law principles.

If the shipowner, contrary to his undertaking in the charterparty, fails to tender notice of readiness at the port of discharge before he begins to discharge the cargo, the lay days run from the (later) date of notice of readiness, and not from the (earlier) date of actual discharge (*Pteroti Compania Naviera* v. *National Coal Board* [1958] 1 Q.B. 469).

If the charterer has agreed to load or unload within a fixed time, his obligation is absolute and he will not be released by delay resulting from the crowded state of the docks, bad weather or a strike of dock labourers (*Budgett* v. *Binnington* [1891] 1 Q.B. 35) unless the charterparty so provides.

Demurrage is usually payable by the charterer. However, the charterparty may provide differently. The charterer may intend to make the chartered ship available to other cargo owner/s and the intention may be that they shall be liable to the shipowner for demurrage and the charterer shall be free from this obligation. The bill of lading issued to the cargo owner must then state this liability clearly, *e.g.* by providing "freight and all other conditions as per charter." In this case the charterparty will often contain the following clause: "Charterer's liability to cease under this charterparty on the cargo being loaded, the master and owners having a lien on cargo for freight and demurrage." The first part of this clause is known as a **cesser clause**, and the second part as a **lien clause**. The two clauses have to be construed together; they mean that the charterer shall be relieved from his obligation to pay demurrage if that obligation falls on others but that in this case the shipowner shall have a lien on such cargo owners' goods (*Fidelitas Shipping Co. Ltd.* v. *V/O Exportchleb* [1963] 2 Lloyd's Rep. 113).

If the currency in which freight and other monetary obligations arising under the charterparty have to be paid is a foreign currency, the English courts have jurisdiction to give judgment for payment of demurrage in foreign currency, even though the contract constituted by the charterparty is governed by English law (*Federal Commerce and Navigation Co. Ltd.* v. *Tradax Export S.A.*; *The Maratha Envoy* [1977] Q.B. 324).

If the charterer loads or unloads the cargo in a period shorter than the lay days, he is sometimes entitled under the terms of the charterparty to a rebate which is known as **dispatch money**.

Cargo and charter hire

The charterer often undertakes to load a "full and complete cargo." If the charterparty so provides, the charterer is obliged to load a full cargo.

The shipowner has an interest in the charterer performing this obligation because normally the charter hire is calculated according to the weight or measurement of the cargo. The charterer is entitled to the full benefit of the use of the ship, and the shipowner cannot impair this benefit by loading more bunker coals than are needed for the voyage (*Darling* v. *Raeburn* [1907] 1 K.B. 846).

If the charterer is obliged by the charterparty to load a complete cargo and does not fulfil his obligation, he is liable for **dead freight**, *i.e.* damages for the unoccupied space payable at the same rate as if the space had been occupied by cargo.

Time charters

The time

In a time charter the ship may be placed at the charterer's disposal at the port of delivery:

(a) from a particular date;
(b) from the day on which the ship arrives at that port; or
(c) alternatively, from a particular date or from the day on which the ship arrives at that port.

In case (a) the contract can be repudiated if the ship is not ready by the date in question; in case (b) the ship must arrive at the port within a reasonable time from the date of the charterparty; in case (c) the charterer cannot be compelled to accept the ship before the named date, but the owner is allowed a reasonable time from the date in which to place the ship at his disposal.

The employment and indemnity clause

The charterparty usually provides that the master shall be under the orders of the charterer as regards employment, agency or other arrangements and that the charterer shall indemnify the shipowner against the consequences of complying with the charterer's orders, in particular, when the master signs bills of lading on the instructions of the charterer.

Although thus the master and crew must comply with the lawful orders of the charterer, they remain employees of the shipowner. The "employment and indemnity clause" obliges the master only to accept the orders of the charterer with respect to the commercial use of the ship. In navigational matters the master is responsible to the shipowner.

Charter hire

The time for the payment of the charter hire is of the essence of the contract of charterparty. If the charterer does not pay the hire punctually the shipowner may invoke **the withdrawal clause** in the charterparty entitling him to withdraw the vessel from the charter. He will do so particularly if the freight market is rising. If the payment falls due on a Sunday or a holiday, payment of the charter hire has to be made on the preceding business day, and not on the day following the Sunday or the holiday (*The Laconia*, below).

In January 1970 the shipowners let the *Laconia* to the charterers on a time charter for three months 15 days. The charterparty required payment of hire "in cash" semi-monthly and gave the owners liberty to withdraw the vessel "failing punctual and regular payment of the hire." The seventh instalment fell due on April 12, a Sunday, when the London banks were closed. On Monday, April 13, at about 3 p.m. the charterer's bank delivered a payment order to the owner's bank which accepted it. On the same day, at 6.55 p.m. the owners' agent informed the charterers that the vessel was withdrawn. *Held*, "punctual payment" should have been made on Friday, April 10, and the owners were entitled to withdraw the vessel: *Mardorf Peach & Co. Ltd.* v. *Attika Sea Carriers Corporation of Liberia. The Laconia* [1977] A.C. 850.

The charterer has until midnight of the day when the hirer is due to effect payment. In order to mitigate the strict rule relating to the payment of charter hire, as laid down in the *Laconia*, the charterparty sometimes contains an **anti-technicality clause**. Such a clause obliges the shipowner to give the charterer notice of a specified short time, *e.g.* 48 hours, that he will withdraw the ship if the charterer does not effect payment during this period of grace. Notice of withdrawal under an anti-technicality clause given *before* the payment of the charter hire becomes due is invalid (*Avovos Shipping Co.* v. *Pagnan. The Avovos* [1983] 1 Lloyd's Rep. 335).

Time charters usually contain an **"off-hire" clause**. The clause usually provides that no hire is payable in the following circumstances:

> dry-docking, other necessary measures to maintain the efficiency of the vessel, deficiency of men or owners' stores, breakdown of machinery, damage to hull or other accident, either hindering or preventing the working of the vessel and continuing for more than 24 consecutive hours.

Redelivery of the ship

Time charters usually provide that the charterer shall redeliver the ship after the agreed time of hire in the same order and condition, fair wear and tear excepted, as when it was delivered to him. As it may not be certain where the ship will be when the charter expires, the charterparty often contains provisions allowing the charterer leeway for the return of the ship. When no permitted leeway is stated, a reasonable period for leeway is implied. During the leeway period the charterer must pay the agreed charter hire. If he delivers the ship after expiration of the leeway period, he is in breach of contract and has to pay damages which may well be higher than the charter hire, if the freight market has risen.

Charter by demise

Under this type of charterparty, known in American law as **bare boat charter**, the charterer obtains possession and control of the ship and may put in his own master and crew, who are his employees. Essentially such a contract is a bailment for reward of a ship (see Ch. 24) and not a contract of carriage and, therefore, will not be discussed here. Such charterparties are not frequently used in the ordinary trade, but they are often used in the oil tanker trade.

Liability of shipowners

The Merchant Shipping Acts 1894 to 1983 provide that an owner of a British ship, a charterer, any person interested in or in possession of such a ship, and in particular any manager or operator of such a ship, shall not be liable for damage unless he is personally guilty of intentional or reckless misconduct in the following cases:

(a) Where goods are lost or damaged by fire on board the ship. Unseaworthiness of the ship causing fire does not destroy the protection given by what is now section 18(1) of the Merchant Shipping Act 1979 (*Louis Dreyfus & Co.* v. *Tempus Shipping Co.* [1931] A.C. 726).

(b) Where gold, silver, watches, jewels or precious stones on board the ship are lost or damaged by reason of theft, robbery, or other dishonest conduct, unless their true nature and value has been declared to the owner or master of the ship at the time of shipment either in the bill of lading or otherwise in writing.

The shipowner is not liable in damages beyond, in the case of damage or loss to goods, an amount equivalent to £45 per ton of the ship's tonnage (s.503 as amended by the Merchant Shipping (Liabilities of Shipowners and others) Act 1958 and the Merchant Shipping (Sterling Equivalents) (Various Enactments) Order 1986). A ship of less than 300 tons is treated as though it were of a tonnage of 300 tons.

Passenger liability

The Merchant Shipping Act 1979 also incorporates into English law the Athens Convention of 1974. Under the Act the carrier is essentially liable for death or injury or loss or damage of luggage caused by his "fault or neglect." Liability for death or injury is limited to approximately £38,000, £2,700 for loss or damage to vehicles, £1,000 for unaccompanied luggage and £680 for accompanied luggage. The carrier cannot rely on these limits if he is *personally* guilty of "intentional and reckless misconduct" (*R.G. Magor* v. *P. & O. Ferries* [1990] 2 Lloyd's Rep. 144).

Bills of Lading

A bill of lading is a document signed by the shipowner or by the master or other agent on behalf of the shipowner, which states that certain goods have been shipped on a particular ship or have been received for shipment. It sets out the terms on which those goods have been delivered to and received by the shipowner. On being signed by or on behalf of the carrier, it is handed to the shipper.

When goods are delivered to the ship, a receipt is usually given, called **the mate's receipt**. This may be qualified, if the goods are in a damaged condition. If it is qualified, it is a claused receipt, otherwise it is a clean receipt. The mate's receipt is not normally a document of title. By local custom it may have that character but not if it is marked "non-negotiable" (*Kum* v. *Wah Tat Bank Ltd.* [1971] 1 Lloyd's Rep. 439).

The qualifications on the mate's receipt are transferred to the bill of lading, and accordingly one distinguishes between **clean bills of**

lading and **claused bills of lading**. In a claused bill the qualification of the statement that the goods are "in apparent good order and condition" refers to the condition of the goods at the time when they are loaded. A notation on the bill that the goods were damaged after they were loaded, *e.g.* by fire on board ship, does not make the bill claused and such bill has to be treated as clean (The *Galatia,* below).

Sugar was loaded in Kandia, India, into the *Galatia.* On the face of the bill of lading, presumably before the signature was put on the bill, a typewritten notation was put which stated "cargo covered by this bill of lading has been discharged Kandia view damaged by fire and/or water used to extinguish fire for which general average declared." *Held*, the bill was a clean bill: *Golodetz & Co. Inc.* v. *Czarnikow-Rionda Co. Inc. The Galatia* [1980] 1 Lloyd's Rep. 453.

A document which is not signed by or on behalf of the carrier is not a bill of lading in the legal sense (*The Maurice Desgagnes* [1977] 1 Lloyd's Rep. 290; a Canadian case). Receipts issued by freight forwarders, although sometimes described as "house bills of lading," do not have the legal character of a bill of lading and, in particular, are not documents of title.

"Negotiable" and non-negotiable bills of lading

The bill of lading is the representation or symbol of the goods to which it refers. Strictly speaking, the bill of lading is not a negotiable instrument. Thus a transferee of a bill of lading gets no better title than the transferor. But the mechanism of negotiability—indorsement and delivery—can be used and such a bill which must be made "to order," is described by businessmen as "negotiable" although, strictly speaking, it is only **"quasi-negotiable."**

The transfer of the bill of lading transfers the right to the possession of the goods in transit, to which the bill relates, from the transferor to the transferee (*Evans* v. *Martell* (1697) 1 Ld. Raym. 272). Whether such transfer also transfers property in the goods, depends on the intention of the parties. Where the seller of goods transfers the bill of lading to the buyer, the intention of the parties will normally be that the title to the goods shall pass to the buyer. If the bill is negotiable, the buyer may then further transfer the bill to a repurchaser, and so forth, and the title to the goods which are in transit, may thus pass from hand to hand by transfer of the bill of lading. But the intention of the parties may also be not to pass property in the goods. A negotiable bill of lading is a bankable document. It may be accepted by a bank as collateral security for a loan. In this case the intention of the parties, when transferring the bill of lading to the bank, is only to create a pledge or lien on the goods in favour of the bank.

It has already been observed that, as the bill of lading is only "quasi-negotiable," in principle the transferee cannot acquire a better title to the goods than the transferor had. But a transfer to a bona fide purchaser of the bill of lading may transfer a better title than the transferor's title if the transferor qualifies as a mercantile agent under the Factors Act 1889 and the requirements of the Act are satisfied (see p. 335, *ante*). Further a transfer of the bill to a bona fide purchaser for value without notice of the insolvency of the transferor defeats the original owner's right of stoppage in transit (*Lickbarrow* v. *Mason* (1794) 3 Term Rep. 683).

In modern practice, if the transaction is an ordinary contract of sale and the buyer does not intend to pass title to a repurchaser while the goods are in transit, **non-negotiable transport documents** may be used. They are non-negotiable bills of lading, blank back bills of lading, data freight receipts, cargo key receipts, waybills, or similar documents. These documents are also used in the container or multi-modal transport. In the commodity trade, on the other hand, where the documents pass from one buyer to the other while the goods are in transit, "negotiable" bills of lading are preferred.

Characteristics of the bills of lading

The bill of lading has three characteristics.

(a) It is a receipt issued by or on behalf of the carrier whereby he acknowledges that he has shipped the goods or received them for shipment.
(b) It evidences the terms of the contract of carriage which is normally concluded earlier.
(c) It is a document of title.

The receipt character

The receipt which the carrier gives the shipper may either acknowledge that he has "shipped" the goods in a named ship, or it may acknowledge that he has "received the goods for shipment."

The carrier can issue a "shipped" bill only if he has actually loaded the goods on board the vessel. In modern container transport where container collection depots are not only at the ports but also at many inland locations, only "received for shipment" bills of lading are issued.

From the point of view of the buyer, a "shipped" bill of lading is more valuable than a "received for shipment" bill of lading because, if he receives the former type of bill, he knows that the goods are in transit to their destination.

It is possible to convert a "received for shipment" bill of lading into a "shipped" bill. When the goods are loaded on board, a notation may be written on the bill confirming that the goods have been shipped. The notation is dated and that date is the date of shipment.

If payment has to be made under a letter of credit, the nominated bank will refuse to accept a "received for shipment" bill of lading, unless expressly instructed by the applicant of the credit to accept such a bill.

Evidence of the contract of carriage by sea

The contract of carriage by sea is normally concluded before the carrier issues the bill of lading. The contract is made when the goods are accepted by agents of the carrier for loading or even earlier, when shipping space is reserved. The bill of lading is issued only when the ship leaves port. But the bill normally contains the terms of the contract of carriage. It is therefore evidence of those terms.

The bill of lading as a document of title

This is the most important characteristic of the bill of lading. Its significance is that the carrier need deliver the goods only if an original bill of lading is presented to him. The bill of lading is thus "the key to the goods." If on arrival of the vessel there is nobody to tender an original bill of lading, the master would be entitled to unload the goods into a warehouse and to sail away.

The function of the bill of lading as a means of transferring possession of and property in the goods in transit, to which the bill refers, has been discussed earlier (on p. 610, *ante*).

Bills issued under the Carriage of Goods by Sea Act 1971

History

An international convention, aimed at reconciling the interests of the shipowners, cargo owners and insurers was promoted with the assistance of the Maritime Law Committee of the International Law Association and became known as the *Hague Rules relating to Bills of Lading* of 1921. Effect was given to these Rules in the United Kingdom by the *Carriage of Goods by Sea Act* 1924. The Hague Rules were amended by the Brussels Protocol of 1968, and, the amended Hague Rules became known as the **Hague-Visby Rules**. Effect was given in the United Kingdom to the Hague-Visby Rules by the Carriage of Goods by Sea Act 1971 which came into operation in 1977.

Application

The 1971 Act applies to contracts which expressly or by implication provide for the issue of a bill of lading or any similar document of title (s.1(4)), where the bill of lading or other document of title relates to the carriage of goods between ports in two different states if:

(a) the bill of lading is issued in a contracting State; or
(b) the carriage is from a port in a contracting State; or
(c) the contract contained in or evidenced by the bill of lading provides that the Hague-Visby Rules or legislation of any State giving effect to them are to govern the contract.

Whatever may be the nationality of the ship, the carrier, the shipper, the consignee or any interested person (Art. X),[1] carriers cannot contract out of the Hague-Visby Rules (Art. III r. 8)

A road-finishing machine was shipped from the Scottish port of Leith on

[1] Reference to Articles is to the Hague-Visby Rules appended as Schedule to the 1971 Act.

board a Dutch vessel, the *Haico Holwerda.* The shipment was destined for Bonaire in the Dutch West Indies. The bill of lading specified that the contract of carriage by sea should incorporate the law of the Netherlands and that all actions should be brought in the court of Amsterdam. The machine was transhipped in Amsterdam into the Norwegian vessel, the *Morviken.* When the machine was unloaded in Bonaire it was damaged, as the owners alleged, by the negligence of the carrier's employees. In the United Kingdom under the Hague-Visby Rules the cargo owners could recover about £11,000, if they could prove their case, but in the Netherlands where at that time the unamended original Hague Rules applied, the maximum liability of the shipowner was limited to about £250. The *Hollandia,* a sister ship of the *Haico Holwerda,* was arrested within the jurisdiction of the English Admiralty Court. The preliminary issue arose whether the English courts had jurisdiction. *Held*, the Hague-Visby Rules could not be contracted out by adopting a foreign law which gave the cargo owners, if they could prove their case, a lower measure of compensation: *The Hollandia* (also reported as *The Morviken*) [1983] 1 Lloyd's Rep. 1.

The Hague-Visby Rules apply also to non-negotiable receipts, such as waybills, if the Rules are expressly stated to apply, as if such receipts were bills of lading (s.1(6)).

Duties of the parties

By Article III(3) of the Rules, the shipper, after delivering the goods into the charge of the owner, charterer, or the master of the ship or other agent, can demand a bill of lading giving the following particulars:

1. The leading marks necessary for identification of the goods, as the same are furnished in writing by the shipper before the loading of such goods starts, provided such marks are stamped or otherwise shown clearly upon the goods if uncovered, or on the cases or coverings in which such goods are contained, in such a manner as should ordinarily remain legible until the end of the voyage.
2. The number of packages or pieces, or the quality or weight, as the case may be, as furnished in writing by the shipper.
3. The apparent order and condition of the goods. Such a bill of lading is prima facie evidence of the receipt by the carrier of the goods therein described, but if the bill is transferred to a third party acting in good faith, it is conclusive evidence (Art. III(4)).

As regards the particulars which he has to furnish in writing, the shipper is deemed to have guaranteed their accuracy and to have undertaken to indemnify the carrier from any inaccuracy, but where carriers issued clean bills of lading, when both parties knew that the goods were not in good order and condition, and the shippers agreed to indemnify the carriers, it was held that the carriers had committed the tort of deceit and the indemnity was accordingly unenforceable (*Brown Jenkinson & Co. Ltd.* v. *Percy Dalton (London) Ltd.* [1957] 2 Q.B. 621). On the other hand, whilst a carrier who delivers without production of the bill of lading does so at his peril, an indemnity given to the carrier in order to induce him to deliver the goods to the consignee without production of the bill of lading is valid and enforceable by the carrier (*Sze Hai Tong Bank Ltd.* v. *Rambler Cycle Co. Ltd.* [1959] A.C. 576).

A statement in the bill of lading that the goods are in apparent good order and condition refers only to their external appearance. Thus, if they arrive damaged, the shipowner is liable on proof:

(a) that the goods were shipped in good condition; or
(b) that the damage resulted from some external cause within the control of the shipowner.

Such a statement estops the shipowner from denying to an indorsee for value of the bill that the goods were in good order and condition externally, if the indorsee acquired the bill in good faith.

Bags of zinc ashes were shipped at Buenos Aires for Liverpool. The upper layers of the bags were wet externally, but the bill of lading stated that the bags were shipped in good order and condition. Owing to the wet the ashes became heated, and had to be discharged and dried. They were then reshipped and arrived in Liverpool three months late. Meanwhile, the price of zinc ashes had fallen. An indorsee for value of the bill of lading sued the shipowners for damages for delay. *Held*, he succeeded, because the shipowners were estopped from denying that the goods were shipped in good order and condition: *Brandt* v. *Liverpool etc., Navigation Co.* [1924] 1 K.B. 575.

Although the bill of lading is only prima facie evidence of the receipt by the carrier of the goods therein named, as far as the shipper is concerned, yet as against the master or other person signing it, it is in the hands of a consignee or indorsee for value conclusive evidence that the goods were shipped notwithstanding that the goods were not shipped (Bills of Lading Act 1855, s.3). As far as a transferee of the bill acting in good faith is concerned, this is now provided in Article III(4). The only way in which the person signing the bill of lading can escape liability is by showing either:

(a) that the holder took the bill with actual notice that the goods were not on board; or
(b) that the mistake was not due to his, the signer's fault, but was due to the fraud of the shipper, holder, or some person under whom the holder claims.

The shipowner is not estopped by the master's signature from proving that the goods were not in fact shipped, or that the master has signed for a greater quantity of goods than has actually been put on board, or that he has delivered all the goods which were put on board. The burden of proving that the bill of lading is false rests on the shipowner. At common law the master has no apparent authority to sign for goods that were never put on board (*Grant* v. *Norway* (1851) 10 C.B. 665). However, in *The Nea Tyhi* [1982] 1 Lloyd's Rep. 606 it was held that a ship's agent who stated in a bill of lading that the goods were carried below deck, while in fact they were carried on deck, had ostensible authority to act for the carrier and rendered him liable on this misstatement. However, under Article III(iv) where the Hague-Visby Rules apply as regards a transferee all statements on the bill are conclusive and bind the carrier. Where the shipowner is not liable because he can prove that the agent signing the bill of lading acted without authority, *e.g.* because he signed for a greater quantity than was actually shipped, the agent himself might be liable for breach of an implied warranty of authority (*V/o Rasnoimport* v. *Guthrie and Co. Ltd.* [1966] 1 Lloyd's Rep. 1).

A shipper has the right, after the goods are loaded, to a "shipped" bill of lading, *i.e.* a bill which says that the goods have been shipped on board and not merely "received for shipment" by the shipowner, and if he has previously received another bill of lading he can ask that it should be exchanged for the "shipped" bill (Art. III(7)).

In all bills of lading to which the Carriage of Goods by Sea Act 1971 applies, the following provisions are implied—

1. An obligation on the carrier, before and at the beginning of the voyage, to exercise *due diligence* to;

(a) make the ship seaworthy. There is no absolute warranty of seaworthiness (s.3) as there is at common law (see p. 599, *ante*);

(b) properly man, equip and supply the ship;

(c) make the holds, refrigerating and cold chambers and all other parts of the ship in which the goods are carried fit and safe for their reception, carriage and preservation (Art. III(1)).

The word "voyage" in this context means the contractual voyage from the port of loading to the port of discharge as declared in the bill of lading. There is, therefore, an obligation on the carrier to exercise due diligence before and at the beginning of sailing from the loading port to have the vessel adequately bunkered for the first stage of the voyage, and to arrange for adequate bunkers of a proper kind at the first and other intermediate ports on the voyage so that the contractual voyage might be performed (*The Makedonia* [1962] P. 190).

If loss or damage arises from unseaworthiness, the burden of proof is on the carrier to show that due diligence has been exercised. The carrier does not discharge this burden merely by showing that the negligence in repairing the ship was that of an independent contractor to whom he delegated the work because it called for technical or special knowledge or experience (*Riverstone Meat Co. Pty. Ltd.* v. *Lancashire Shipping Co. Ltd.* [1961] A.C. 807). The duty is thus non-delegable and personal to the shipowner.

2. An obligation on the carrier, subject to the provision of Article IV, which deals with the excepted perils (see below), properly and carefully to load, handle, stow, carry, keep, care for and discharge the goods carried.

3. Removal of the goods by the person entitled to delivery is prima facie evidence of delivery by the carrier. In the event of loss or damage to the goods, **notice in writing** must be given to the carrier before or at the time of removal, unless at the time of their receipt the goods have been the subject of joint survey or inspection. If the loss or damage is not apparent, the notice must be given within three days. In any event, the carrier is discharged from all liability in respect of the goods unless action is brought within one year after delivery or the date when the goods should have been delivered (Art. III(6)), but for an action for indemnity against a

third party, this time limit is extended by three months, subject to certain conditions (Art. III (6 bis)). Article III(6) does not apply where the carrier misdelivers or steals the cargo (*The Captain Gregos* [1989] 2 Lloyd's Rep. 63).

4. The carrier is not responsible for loss or damage arising from the following **excepted perils**:

(a) Act, neglect or default of the master, mariner, pilot or the servant of the carrier in the navigation or in the management of the ship.

The effect of this exception is that the shipper has to bear risks incident to navigation and management of the ship. The operation of management is not restricted to the period during which the vessel is at sea; it extends to the period during which the cargo is being loaded or discharged (*The Glenochil* [1896] p. 10). A distinction has to be drawn between want of care of the cargo and want of care of the vessel indirectly affecting the cargo.

A ship with a cargo of tinplates sustained damage during the voyage, and had to be kept in dock for repairs. During the execution of the repairs, workmen were frequently in and out of the hold, and the hatches were in consequence left open. Owing to the negligence of the shipowners' servants the hatches were not covered up, and rain fell into the hold and damaged the tinplates. *Held*, the shipowners were liable because (1) they had failed properly and carefully to "carry, keep and care for" the tinplates, and (2) the negligence in the management of the hatches was not negligence "in the management of the ship" so as to protect them from liability but rather neglect of the cargo. *Gosse Millard Ltd.* v. *Canadian Government Merchant Marine* [1929] A.C. 223.

(b) Fire, unless caused by the actual fault or privity of the carrier.

(c) Perils, dangers and accidents of the sea or other navigable waters.

(d) Act of God.

(e) Acts of war or of public enemies. Arrest or restraint of princes, rulers, or people, or seizure under legal process. Quarantine restrictions.

(f) Act or omission of the shipper or owner of the goods or his agent or representative.

(g) Strikes or lock-outs.

(h) Riot and civil commotions.

(i) Saving or attempting to save life or property at sea.

(j) Wastage in bulk or weight or any other loss or damage arising from inherent defect, quality or vice of the goods.

(k) Insufficiency of packing or insufficiency or inadequacy of marks. Insufficiency of packing cannot be relied upon if a reasonable inspection would have disclosed it, and the bill of lading acknowledges the receipt of the goods in apparent good order and condition (*Silver* v. *Ocean Steamship Co.* [1930] 1 K.B. 416).

(l) Latent defects not discoverable by due diligence.

(m) Any other cause arising without the actual fault or privity of the carrier or his servants or agents. The burden of proof is on the carrier to show that neither he nor his servants or agents have contributed to the loss. The carrier is liable for the acts of stevedores if they are acting under his control and supervision but not if they are independent contractors.

H. shipped cloth from Liverpool to Shanghai under a bill of lading governed by the Carriage of Goods by Sea Act 1924. While the cargo was being unloaded at Shanghai, some of the cloth was stolen. *Held*, (1) the shipowner was liable unless he could show that the cloth was stolen by someone who was not his servant or agent; (2) on the probabilities, the stevedores' men had stolen the cloth, and as the shipowner's duty was to discharge the cargo, the stevedores he employed to fulfil that duty were his servants or agents: *Heyn* v. *Ocean SS. Co. Ltd.* (1927) 43 T.L.R. 358.

A consignment of tea was shipped in *The Chyebassa* from Calcutta to Rotterdam under bills of lading incorporating the Hague Rules. When other goods in the ship's hold in which the tea was stowed were unloaded at an intermediate port, the stevedores stole the cover plate of a storm valve and on the further voyage sea-water damaged the tea. The officers and the crew were not negligent in the supervision of the stevedores in the intermediate port. *Held*, the carriers were exempt from their liability because the damage was caused by "any other cause" without the actual fault of the carriers' servants: Art. IV, r. 2(*q*). The stevedores were independent contractors not "servants or agents": *Leesh River Tea Co. Ltd.* v. *British India S.N. Co. Ltd.* [1967] 2 Q.B. 250.

5. The carrier is not liable for any loss or damage resulting from any departure from the agreed voyage to save or attempt to save life or property at sea or any reasonable "deviation." Reasonable deviation is one which is reasonable having regard to the terms of the contract and the interest of all persons concerned in the voyage (*Stag Line* v. *Foscolo Mango & Co.* [1932] A.C. 328, 343).

6. The carrier is not liable for loss or damage to goods exceeding

approximately £500 per package or unit or £1·70 per kilo of the gross weight of the goods lost or damaged, whichever is higher (Art. IV(5)(a)) and Merchant Shipping (Sterling Equivalents) (Various Enactments) Order 1986, unless the nature and the value of the goods is declared before shipment and inserted in the bill of lading. If the nature or value of the goods has been knowingly misstated, the carrier is not liable for their loss or damage in any event.

Where a container, pallet or similar article of transport is used to consolidate goods, the number of packages or units enumerated in the bill of lading as packed in such article of transport is deemed the number of packages or units. If the packages or units are not enumerated in the bill of lading, the article of transport is considered to be the package or unit (Art. III(5)(c)).

The limits of liability, as the other defences provided by the Rules, apply to an action against the carrier in respect of loss or damage to the goods, whether the action is founded in contract or in tort (Art. IV Bis (1)). Under Article IV(5)(e) the shipowner cannot rely on the limits of liability if he is *personally* guilty of intentional or reckless misconduct (*The European Enterprise* [1989] 2 Lloyd's Rep. 185).

7. If goods of an inflammable, explosive or dangerous character have been shipped without disclosure of their nature to the carrier, the carrier may discharge or destroy them without paying compensation. Even if the carrier was told the nature of the goods, they may be discharged or destroyed if they become a danger to the ship or cargo. In such a case the shipper may have a claim to general average (Art. IV(6)).

The carrier may increase his liability or contract out of any immunities given to him, provided the terms of the contract are set out in the bill of lading.

8. A servant or agent of the carrier is entitled to the same defences and limits of liability as the carrier, provided that the servant or agent is not an independent contractor (Art. IV Bis (2)). An independent contractor is not protected by the Rules.

A stevedore engaged as independent contractor by a carrier in the discharge of goods cannot rely on these limitations of liability as he is not a party to the contract of carriage (*Scruttons Ltd.* v. *Midland Silicones Ltd.* [1962] A.C. 446, see p. 61, *ante*).

But a servant or agent of the carrier cannot rely on the limits of liability if he is guilty of intentional or reckless misconduct (Art. IV Bis (4)).

Freight

Freight is the consideration paid to the carrier for the carriage of the goods. It is only payable if the carrier has delivered the goods, or is ready to deliver them but is prevented from doing so by the default of the consignee, unless the contract of carriage by sea otherwise provides. Even if delivery cannot be effected because of the happening of one of the excepted perils, the carrier, though relieved of liability for the goods, cannot recover the freight.

Cement was shipped under a bill of lading which stipulated for payment of freight within three days after the ship's arrival. On arrival, a fire broke out on board and the ship had in consequence to be scuttled. When the ship was raised it was found that the cement was useless. *Held*, the shipowners, not being ready to perform their part of the contract, were not entitled to freight: *Duthie* v. *Hilton* (1868) L.R. 4 C.P. 138.

The fact that the goods can only be delivered in a damaged condition does not prevent the carrier from recovering freight, unless it can be shown that the thing delivered is not the same thing in a business sense as the thing shipped (*Asfar* v. *Blundell* [1896] 1 Q.B. 123). The remedy of the cargo owner must be a separate action for damages and he cannot plead the damage to the cargo as a defence to the action for the unpaid freight (*The Aries Tanker* [1977] 1 Lloyd's Rep. 334).

The carrier is entitled to his freight if the consignee refuses to name a safe port to which the ship can proceed and enter.

Advance freight

Advance freight is freight which under the contract is earned before the delivery of the goods. It must be paid even if the goods are lost by excepted perils after the agreed date of payment.

C. chartered a ship from Liverpool to Archangel, freight payable in Liverpool before sailing on signing bills of lading. Before the vessel was completely loaded, and all the bills of lading signed, fire broke out and the vessel sank with the cargo. *Held*, freight could be recovered from C. for the amount of cargo for which bills of lading had been signed: *Coker & Co. Ltd.* v. *Limerick SS. Co. Ltd.* (1918) 34 T.L.R. 296.

The mere fact that the cargo owner is required to make payments in advance does not always mean that the payment is "advance freight." Such payment may be a mere loan of money (*Gt. Indian Ry.* v. *Turnbull*) (1885) 53 L.T. 325).

When freight is payable on the signing of the bill of lading the charterers must present the bills for signature within a reasonable time, even though the ship has been lost after the goods have been supplied (*Oriental Steamship Co.* v. *Taylor* [1893] 2 Q.B. 518).

Lump sum freight

Lump sum freight is where the charterer agrees to pay a lump sum for the use of a ship. It is payable if the shipowner is ready to perform his contract though no goods are shipped. When goods are shipped, the whole freight becomes payable on delivery of part of the cargo only if the non-delivery of the remainder is due to an excepted peril.

T. chartered a ship to carry a cargo of timber for a specified lump sum, the charterparty containing an exception of perils of the seas. The ship arrived outside the port, but owing to heavy weather was driven ashore and wrecked. Part of the cargo was washed ashore and was collected by the captain and delivered to T. The remainder was lost by the perils of the seas. *Held*, the whole of the freight was payable: *Thomas* v. *Harrowing SS. Co.* [1915] A.C. 58.

Pro rata freight

Pro rata freight is that percentage of freight recoverable by the carrier when he delivers only part of the cargo. Full freight is earned if the shipowner is forced by an excepted peril to deliver at an intermediate port or delivers there at the cargo owner's request. However, if the shipowner delivers at an intermediate port for his own convenience or because the contract is frustrated no *pro rata* freight is payable: *St. Enoch SS. Co.* v. *Phosphate Mining Co.* [1916] 2 K.B. 624.

By whom payable

The person liable to pay freight is prima facie the owner of the goods who is presumed to be the owner of the goods, usually the consignee (*Drew* v. *Bird* (1828) 1 Mod. & M. 156). Additionally the shipper of the goods impliedly promises to pay the freight unless the bill of lading or other contract frees him from this liability, as, for example, when there is a cesser clause (see p. 605, *ante*). In addition, the fact of taking delivery of the goods may be evidence of an implied promise to pay the freight (*Sanders* v. *Vanzeller* (1843) 4 Q.B. 260). The Bills of Lading Act 1855, s.1 provides:

> Every consignee of goods named in a bill of lading, and every indorsee of a bill of lading to whom the property in the goods therein mentioned shall pass upon or by reason of such consignment or indorsement, shall have transferred to and vested in him all rights of suit, and be subject to the same liabilities in respect of such goods as if the contract contained in the bill of lading had been made with himself.

This provision imposes a liability to pay freight upon every consignee of goods named in a bill of lading and every indorsee of a bill of lading to whom the property in the goods has passed by reason of the consignment or indorsement. By section 2 of the same Act, this does not relieve the original shipper or owner of any liability to which he *may* be subject.

Right of suit

Where section 1 of the Bills of Lading Act 1855, which has just been quoted, applies, the right of suit is vested exclusively in the consignee or the indorsee to whom the property in the goods has passed by virtue of the consignment or indorsement. This means that in these cases the consignor, who has concluded the contract of carriage with the shipowner, cannot claim by way of damages the loss which the consignee or indorsee has suffered (*The Albazero* (below)).

The charterers chartered *The Albacruz* from the shipowners. They shipped a cargo of crude oil from La Salina in Venezuela to Antwerp. The carriage was covered by a bill of lading issued pursuant to the charterparty naming the charterers as consignees. *The Albacruz* and her cargo became a total loss owing to breaches by the shipowners of the charterparty. Before the ship and cargo were lost, the charterers had indorsed the bill of lading to the indorsees in whom the property in the cargo was vested at the time of the loss. The indorsees (as cargo owners) had lost their right of action under the bill of lading owing to expiry of the one year prescription period provided by Article III, rule 6, of the Hague Rules. The charterers as "consignors" claimed from the shipowners by way of damages the loss suffered by the cargo owners, and arrested the *Albazero*, a ship belonging to the same shipowners. *Held*, the charterers were only entitled to nominal damages because the goods did not belong to them at the time of their loss; *Albacruz* v. *Albazero; The Albazero* [1977] A.C. 774.

A person who has agreed to buy goods cannot sue in tort or contract for substantial damages if the goods do not belong to him even if the goods are at his risk (*The Aliakmon* [1986] A.C. 785). The correct person to bring the action is the owner and it is irrelevant that he has already been paid for the goods (*The Sanix Ace* [1987] 1 Lloyd's Rep. 465). In such a case the owner receives damages for the benefit of the person at whose risk the goods are. This often happens in bulk cargo cases where no property passes to the "buyers" by virtue of s.16 of the Sale of Goods Act 1979 (see p. 412).

Shipowner's lien

At common law a sea carrier has a possessory lien for freight, that is, he can withhold delivery until he is paid. This lien only attaches when freight is payable on delivery and does not exist in the case of:

(a) advance freight; or
(b) freight agreed to be paid after delivery of the goods.

It can be exercised against all goods coming to the same consignee on the same voyage for the freight due on all or any part of them, but not to goods on different voyages under different contracts. The lien may be waived by accepting a bill of exchange for the freight or by making delivery without requiring payment. At common law there is no lien for dead freight, but such lien may be granted by express agreement. The charterparty and the bill of lading often contain special provisions dealing with liens, and in such a case the common law lien will be modified.

General Average

During the course of a sea voyage there are three interests which are at risk: the ship, the cargo, and the freight. As a general rule any loss which any of these interests sustains must be borne by that interest alone; this is known as particular average, *i.e.* loss to be borne by the particular interest incurring it. If, for example, one the ship's boats is carried away in a storm, this is a particular average loss and must be borne by the shipowner alone. Where, however, extraordinary sacrifices are made or expenditure is incurred for the benefit of the whole adventure, the loss is borne by all in proportion and is known as a general average loss. In such a case the particular interest which has suffered the loss is entitled to contribution, called a general average contribution, from the other interests. The conditions under which a general average contribution can be claimed are:

1. There must have been a common danger. An interest which was never in peril cannot be compelled to contribute.

2. The danger must not be due to the default of the interest claiming contribution; *e.g.* if goods are thrown overboard because they are dangerous their owner cannot claim for general average contribution.

3. The danger must be a real one. Where, therefore, the master of a ship believed that the ship was on fire and caused steam to be turned into the hold to extinguish it and the ship was never in fact on fire, it was held that the resulting damage to the cargo was not a general average loss (*Joseph Watson & Son Ltd.* v. *Fireman's Fund Insurance Co.* [1922] 2 K.B. 355).

4. There must have been a voluntary and reasonable sacrifice of the property in respect of which contribution is claimed. This occurs when cargo is thrown overboard to lighten the ship in heavy weather.

5. The interest called upon for contribution must have been saved.

Extraordinary expenditure incurred by the shipowner for the benefit of the adventure will be the subject of general average contribution. "Extraordinary expenditure must to some extent be connected with an extraordinary occasion. For example, an abnormal user of the engines and an abnormal consumption of coal in endeavouring to refloat a steamship stranded in a position of peril is an extraordinary sacrifice and an extraordinary expenditure (*The Bona* [1895] P. 125). A mere extra user of coal, however, in order to accelerate the speed of the vessel would not be a general average act" (*per* Sankey J. in *Société Nouvelle d'Armement* v. *Spillers and Bakers Ltd.* [1917] 1 K.B. 865).

General average contribution is made by all who have benefited by a general average act. These are:

(a) The shipowner in respect of his ship and the freight payable under the charterparty, if any, and, if not, under the bills of lading.
(b) The charterer in respect of freight payable under the bills of lading, if he uses the ship as a general ship to carry cargo.
(c) The cargo owner in respect of the cargo.

The liability is enforced by the shipowner on behalf of all interests by exercising his lien over the cargo, and if he fails to exercise his lien, he may be sued by those entitled to contribution (*Crooks* v. *Allan* (1879) 5 Q.B.D. 38).

The amount of contribution payable by each interest is settled by average adjusters, and is borne by the owners of each interest rateably. The adjustment is made on the basis of the York-Antwerp Rules 1974, if the parties have adopted them, as they do frequently. If the York-Antwerp Rules are not adopted, adjustment is made according to the law of the country where the port of destination is situated or, if the ship does not reach that port, at the port where the voyage ends.

Chapter 31

CARRIAGE BY AIR

History of statutory provisions

There is substantial uniformity, internationally, in the law relating to the carriage of goods by air. This is because over a period of years there has been international negotiation of international Conventions. The three British statutes, of which the earliest is now repealed, were all related to such agreements.

The **Carriage by Air Act 1932** gave statutory effect in the United Kingdom to the Warsaw Convention of 1929. In contrast with the Carriage of Goods by Sea Act 1924, which dealt only with the carriage of goods, the Act of 1932 dealt with the carriage of persons as well as goods. The 1932 Act applied to all "international carriage" of persons, luggage or goods performed by aircraft and to the air portion of a "combined carriage," *i.e.* a carriage partly performed by air and partly by another mode of carriage, provided the air portion qualified as an "international carriage." The general effect of the Act was to make it relatively easy for a plaintiff passenger, or cargo owner to establish legal liability on the part of the defendent air carrier for loss, damage, injury or death occurring during the carriage by air. This was done by providing that the carrier was liable unless he could establish one or more specified defences. In return for this shift in the burden of proof on to the carrier, *i.e.* to prove that he was *not* liable, the liability of the carrier was subject to maximum limitations, specified in terms of the gold franc.

Over the years it became clear that the Warsaw Convention required amendment, more particularly with regard to the limitation of liability in the event of death of a passenger which was regarded as too low. Amendment was therefore agreed upon at The Hague on September 28, 1955 in the Hague Protocol. The Warsaw Convention, as amended at The Hague, 1955, was enacted in the **Carriage by Air Act 1961** which came into force on June 1, 1967. The 1961 Act repealed the Act of 1932, but by section 10 provision is made to give effect to the unamended Warsaw Convention in applicable cases.

The third stage in the development of the statutory provisions was reached because neither the original nor the Hague Protocol makes it clear whether the "carrier" referred to is the carrier in contractual relationship with the passenger or cargo owner, or whether the "carrier" was the carrier who actually performed the carriage. It was therefore necessary to supplement the Warsaw Convention by a further convention, signed in 1961 at Guadalajara in Mexico. This supplementary convention aims at the unification of certain rules relating to international carriage performed by a person other than the contracting carrier. The Guadalajara Convention was enacted by the **Carriage by Air (Supplementary Provisions) Act 1962**, which applies to carriage governed by the original Warsaw Convention as well as to carriage governed by the Hague Protocol.

The Warsaw Convention was further amended by certain protocols signed at Montreal on September 25, 1975. Effect will be given to these amendments in the United Kingdom by the **Carriage by Air and Road Act 1979**, but this Act is not in force yet.[1]

By virtue of the four statutes and the orders made under them there is a comprehensive, although complex, regulation of reasonable uniformity for the carriage of goods by air, so far as actions in the English courts are concerned. The fact remains however that there are three different regimes, namely:

(a) carriage governed by the original Warsaw Convention;
(b) carriage governed by the Hague Protocol;
(c) "Non-International Carriage."

The basic elements of carrier's liability are common to all three.

Basic elements of liability

The carrier of goods by air is liable for destruction or loss of, or damage to or delay of cargo if it occurs during the carriage by air. "Carriage by air" comprises the whole period during which the cargo is in the charge of the carrier, whether in an aerodrome or on board an aircraft, or in the case of landing outside an aerodrome in

[1] Position: 1991.

any place whatsoever. He has the right to use specified defences if he can, but he cannot contract out of liability. In return for this liability the carrier can rely on the benefit of maximum limits for his liability, and even that liability arises only if the claimant can prove damage to that extent. The maximum limits of the carrier's liability are;

—250 gold francs per kilogram (which under the latest Sterling Equivalent Order (1986) is approximately £14); or

—the value declared by the consignor for which any supplementary charge has been paid.

There is, however, a difference in the calculation of the carrier's maximum liability between the original (unamended) Warsaw Convention and the amended Warsaw Convention. According to the original Warsaw Convention the maximum limit of 250 gold francs per kilogram is calculated with respect to the package lost or damaged, but according to the amended Convention, art. 22(2)(b), when the loss or damage of a package also affects the value of other packages covered by the same baggage check or air waybill, the total weight of the other affected packages may also be taken into consideration to determine the carrier's liability (*Datacard Corporation* v. *Air Express International Corporation* [1983] 2 All E.R. 639).

Under the original Warsaw Convention the carrier loses the limits of liability and defences if he is guilty of wilful misconduct (see p. 627, above). Under the Hague Protocol he loses the limits of liability if he is guilty of intentional or reckless misconduct. For the carrier to be guilty of such misconduct, the plaintiff must prove that (1) the damage resulted from the misconduct and (2) was done deliberately or recklessly (*Goldman* v. *Thai Airways* [1983] 1 W.L.R. 1186). Receipt of cargo by the person entitled to delivery without complaint is prima facie evidence of delivery in good condition.

Who may sue

The question of who can sue the carrier is complex (see *Glass & Cashmere*, introduction to the Law of Carriage of Goods (1989) paras. 6.34–6.36). Essentially, it seems that the consignor or consignee can sue on behalf of the true owner of the cargo even if the cargo does not belong to the consignor or consignee. However, even if he is not the named consignor or consignee the true owner also may sue the carrier (*Gutewhite* v. *Iberias Lineas Aereos* [1989] 1 Lloyd's Rep. 160).

Who may be sued

1. *The contracting carrier,* as a principal, makes an agreement for carriage with the consignor or the consignor's agent. In many cases he will be the first or sometimes the only carrier by air, but he may also be one who merely issues a waybill, or an aircraft charterer, or a cargo consolidator or forwarder. He is liable for the whole of the carriage.

2. *The performing carrier,* by virtue of authority from the contracting carrier, performs the whole or part of the carriage. He is liable only for the part performed by him.

3. *A successive carrier* is deemed to be a party to the original contract of carriage so far as is relevant to the carriage performed under this supervision.

The first carrier, the performing carrier and the last carrier are jointly and severally liable. At the plaintiff's option, written complaints may be made and actions may be brought against either the performing carrier or the contracting carrier or against both together or separately.

Servants and agents of the carrier acting within the scope of their employment can claim the benefit of the limits of liability applicable to the carrier. Acts and omissions of the performing carrier, including his servants and agents, are deemed to be those of the contracting carrier and vice versa.

Defences available

The carrier is not liable if he proves that he and his agents or servants took all necessary measures to avoid the damage or that it was impossible to take such measures. This essentially means that the carrier is liable unless he can disprove negligence (*Chisholm* v. *B.E.A.* [1963] 1 Lloyd's Rep. 79).

If the carrier proves that the damage was caused or contributed to by the negligence of the injured person the court may exonerate the carrier wholly or partly.

Application of the regimes

Carriage of cargo for reward by aircraft or gratuitous carriage by an air transport undertaking is governed by the various regimes as follows.

Original (unamended) Warsaw Convention

When, according to the contract between the parties, the places of departure and destination are located in:

—the territories of two states parties to the Convention; or

—the territory of a single such state with an agreed stopping place anywhere outside that state.

There is a complication when the place of departure is in the territory of a state party to the original Convention (*e.g.* USA) whilst the place of destination is in the territory of a state which is not only a party to the original Convention but has also become a party to the amended Convention (*e.g.* the United Kingdom). In such circumstances, the only obligations which bind both states are those in the original Convention. In addition such carriage to, from or with an agreed stopping place in the USA is subject to American legislation under which the carrier of passengers agrees not to rely on the defence of all necessary measures and agrees to increase the limits of liability to $75,000 in the event of death or injury.

Hague Protocol

When, according to the agreement between the parties, the places of departure and destination are located in:

—the territories of two states both of which are parties to the amended Convention; or

—the territory of a single state party to the Protocol with an agreed stopping place anywhere outside that state.

Non-International Rules

When the carriage of cargo is governed neither by the original nor by the amended Convention, then whatever the place of departure, no part of the contract or agreement for carriage would, as a matter of law, be governed by either of the two Conventions. In an action before the English courts the carriage would be governed by the non-Convention rules, even though the carriage was "international" in the ordinary meaning of the word but not within the technical meaning which is what governs the applicability of the two Conventions. The non-Convention rules are contained in the Carriage by Air Acts (Application of Provisions) Order 1967.

The non-Convention rules also govern:

(a) carriage, wholly within the territory of *any* state, which does not form part of the performance of a Convention contract or agreement for carriage, and without any stopping place outside that state, and regardless of whether that state is a party to either of the Conventions; and
(b) carriage of mail or postal packets.

Each regime involves variation of the basic elements of liability.

Carriage governed by the original (unamended) Warsaw Convention

Document of carriage

The document of carriage is in the British legislation called an air waybill. The carrier has the right to require the consignor to make out an air waybill and to require a separate one for each package, and the carrier is required to accept it. Nevertheless the absence, irregularity or loss of the document does not affect the validity of the contract or the operation of the Convention rules.

If, however, the carrier issues no air waybill or one that does not contain any of the following particulars, then he cannot take advantage of the provisions of the Convention which would otherwise exclude or limit the carrier's liability:

(a) place and date of execution of the air waybill;
(b) places of departure and destination;
(c) agreed stopping places (which the carrier may alter in case of necessity);
(d) name and address of consignor;
(e) name and address of first carrier;
(f) name and address of consignee "if the case so requires" [sic];
(g) nature of the goods;
(h) number of packages, method of packing and the particular marks or numbers on them;

(i) weight, quantity, volume or dimensions of the goods;
(j) a statement that the carriage is subject to the rules relating to liability established by the Convention.

The air waybill and the statements therein are prima facie evidence of the conclusion of the contract, receipt of the goods, the conditions of carriage, the weight, dimensions, packing and number of goods. Statements relating to quantity, volume or condition are not evidence against the carrier unless expressly stated on the air waybill to have been either checked in the presence of the consignor or they relate to apparent condition.

Basic liability

Besides the two basic defences, the carrier of goods is not liable if he can prove that "the damage was occasioned by negligent pilotage or negligence in the handling of the aircraft or in navigation and that in all other respects he and his agents have taken all necessary measures to avoid the damage."

Special rights of consignor and consignee

Unless varied by express provision in the air waybill, the consignor and the consignee have the following rights:

The consignor:

(a) has the right of disposal prior to delivery to the consignee, subject to the production of the consignor's copy of the air waybill to the carrier and payment of all expenses involved; and
(b) may enforce in his own name even if acting in the interests of another, subject to fulfilment of all obligations of the consignor under the contract of carriage.

The consignee:

(a) has the right to require the carrier to hand over goods on production of the air waybill on arrival at the destination on payment of proper charges and compliance with any other conditions set out in the air waybill; and
(b) may enforce rights in his own name even if acting in the interests of another, subject to the fulfilment of all obligations of the consignee under the contract of carriage.

Carriage governed by the Hague Protocol

Document of carriage

The document of carriage is called an *air waybill.* All the provisions of the original Convention relating to the air waybill also apply under the Protocol, with the important exception of the particulars to appear in it and the penalties for omission.

If, **with the consent of the carrier**, cargo is loaded on board without an air waybill or if the air waybill does not contain a notice to the consignor "to the effect that, if the carriage involves in an ultimate destination or stop in a country other than the country of departure, the Warsaw Convention may be applicable and that the Convention governs and in most cases limits the liability of carriers in respect of loss of or damage to cargo," then in either of these circumstances, the carrier cannot take advantage of the limits of liability.

It is stated in the Protocol that nothing in it "prevents the issue of a negotiable air waybill." In practical terms, the speed of air transport has largely eliminated the need for a negotiable document of carriage and waybills are usually printed "not negotiable."

Basic liability

There are no defences other than the two basic ones. The defence of negligent pilotage does not apply. Servants and agents of the carrier enjoy the benefit of the same limits of liability as the carrier. The special rights of the consignor and of the consignee are the same as those under the original Convention.

Non-Convention carriage

The basic system of liability, including limits, is the same as that under the Protocol, but there are no provisions relating to documents of carriage or to what has been described above as special rights of consignor and consignee.

PART 10: TRADE SECRETS, PATENTS, TRADE MARKS, COPYRIGHT

Chapter 32

TRADE SECRETS, PATENTS AND TRADE MARKS

Trade Secrets

Trade secrets form one aspect of intellectual property law, which also includes patents, trade marks, copyrights and designs. In today's competitive business environment, with so many businesses exploiting innovative products, the intangible assets protected by this area of the law are often the most valuable assets that a business owns. Intellectual property rights overlap, protecting different facets of a product, for example the product itself may be patented; its method of manufacture may be protected as a trade secret; sales literature, and software used to run the product, may be protected by copyright; its shape or configuration may be protected by the new design right; and its name by a trade mark.

Elements of an action for breach of confidence

Trade secrets are protected by the civil laws of confidentiality. Criminal law does not really play a part. Three conditions must be satisfied before an action for breach of confidence can succeed:

1. The information must be confidential;
2. The information must have been imparted in circumstances imposing an obligation of confidence; and
3. There must be an actual or threatened unauthorised use or disclosure of the information.

Remedies

The final remedies are the usual civil ones of injunction, damages, account, etc., but interlocutory procedures such as Anton Piller orders and interlocutory injunctions are particularly important, for intellectual property cases rarely go to full trial. An unusual feature of the injunction in these cases is the "springboard doctrine," which holds that a person who has acquired confidential information in breach of an obligation cannot use it to obtain a "head start" on other trade rivals. He is therefore restrained from using the information for the length of time the court judges that it will take the trade rivals to catch up, or for the information to enter the public domain.

Confidential information

The main test for assessing whether information is confidential was given by Sir Robert Megarry in *Thomas Marshall* v. *Guinle* [1978] 3 All E.R. 193, 209. He said that there were four factors which might be of assistance in identifying confidential information in a trade or industrial setting:

1. The information must be such that the owner believes its release would be injurious to him or of advantage to his rivals or others;
2. The owner must believe the information is confidential or secret, *i.e.* not already in the public domain;
3. The owner's belief under the two previous headings must be reasonable;
4. The information must be judged in the light of the usages and practices of the particular industry concerned.

When will an obligation be imposed?

As a general rule, an obligation of confidence will be imposed whenever confidential information is disclosed for a limited purpose. The cases have not limited the range of circumstances in which an obligation can arise. Common situations which give rise to the obligation in a commercial context are pre-contractual disclosures, *e.g.* for the purpose of negotiations; contracts; licences; employment; and the professional relationships lawyers, bankers and accountants have with their clients and customers. In *Coco* v. *Clark* [1969] R.P.C. 41, 48, Megarry J. said that where information of commercial or industrial value is given on a business-like basis, or with some avowed common object in mind, such as the manufacture of articles by one party for another, the recipient will find it difficult to deny that he is bound by an obligation of confidence. The test is whether a reasonable man standing in the shoes of the recipient would realise on reasonable grounds that information was being given to him in confidence.

It is not necessary for the obligation of confidence to be set out in writing, but for evidential reasons, writing is often preferable, and also a written statement can serve as a strong warning to the disclosee that the discloser is serious about protecting his secrets.

Employees and independent contractors

The position of employees and independent contractors warrants special attention. Confidential information acquired by an employee in the course of his employment (or by an independent contractor performing a contract for services) will be protected either by an express undertaking of confidentiality, or by the duty of fidelity which is implied into every contract of employment (or contract for services, as the case may be). Express and implied duties to respect confidentiality can continue even after termination of the contract. Express covenants to respect confidentiality are often combined with agreements not to compete with a former employer, when they are known as covenants in restraint of trade. These are prima facie void as being contrary to public policy, unless they are no wider than is reasonably necessary to protect the employer's interest in terms of the information and activities covered, the geographical area over which the restriction extends, and the length of time it is to last.

While an ex-employee (or independent contractor) should not use or disclose his former employer's trade secrets unless authorised to do so, he is however free to exploit general knowledge and skill acquired in the course of his former employment. It is very difficult to draw the line between general knowledge and skill, and trade secrets. In *Faccenda Chicken* v. *Fowler* [1986] 1 All E.R. 617, a case concerning the duty owed by ex-employees, Neill L.J. said that the following matters must be taken into account,

(a) the nature of the employment: was confidential information habitually, normally or only occasionally handled;
(b) the nature of the information itself: only trade secrets or information of a highly confidential information would be protected;

(c) whether the employer impressed upon the employee the confidential nature of the information;
(d) whether the relevant information could be isolated easily from other information which the employee is free to use or disclose.

Third parties

Third parties can also be bound by an obligation of confidence. For example, if an ex-employee, in breach of an obligation of confidence owed to his former employer, discloses a trade secret to his new employer, the second employer will also be bound to respect the confidentiality of the information. He can be restrained by injunction from using or further disclosing it, or be required to pay damages for use after he has been informed of its confidential nature.

PATENTS

A **patent** is the name given to a bundle of monopoly rights which give the patentee the exclusive right to exploit an invention for a stated period of time. It is important to realise that a patent is a right to stop others; an inventor does not need permission to exploit his invention. The right is a true monopoly giving the patentee the right to prevent another exploiting the invention even though devised independently. A patent lasts for 20 years from the date an application for the grant of a patent is made to the Patent Office.

Originally, a patent was a royal grant in the form of Letters Patent—hence the name—but now the rights granted are purely statutory and are set out in the Patents Act 1977.[1] The rationale of the patent system is to encourage technological development. In return for disclosing the invention, the patentee is granted a temporary monopoly of 20 years, during which period he can, in theory, recoup his investment in research and development through exploitation of the invention. Competitors faced with the patent often seek to design round it, thus achieving further innovation. Patenting is not compulsory and some companies can and do rely on trade secrecy to protect their innovations (see above).

[1] All section references in this part of the present chapter are to the Patents Act 1977.

Applying for a patent

An application for the grant of a patent for an invention must be made to the Patent Office. The application procedure is governed entirely by the Patents Act 1977 and its associated Patent Rules. The application is accompanied by a specification which consists of a detailed description of the invention and a set of claims. The claims define the scope of the invention for which the patentee seeks his monopoly. It is the invention as defined in the claims which is tested for patentability (see p. 643, *post*) and against which alleged infringements are considered (see p. 647, *post*).

The Patent Office carries out a **search** in the relevant technical literature ("prior art") to test for "novelty" and "inventive step." The applicant is sent the result of the search usually within about 12 to 15 months from the date of the application. According to the results of the search the applicant may decide to abandon or modify his application or to request a substantive **examination**. The request for the examination must be made within six months from the date the application is published by the Patent Office. This publication must take place within 18 months from the date of filing the application. This is to give an early warning to competitors that a patent is being sought. If an application is withdrawn in time before the publication date it will not be published, thus preserving for the applicant the secrecy of its contents.

At the examination stage, the application is examined by a technically qualified Patent Office Examiner to see whether it complies with the requirements of patentability and certain other technical requirements laid down by the Act. Fees are payable on the initial application, for the search, for the examination and on grant. The application must comply with the requirements of the Act within the period of 4½ years from the date of filing, otherwise a patent will be refused. Once granted, the patent lasts 20 years from the date of filing (note not the date of grant) provided renewal fees are paid every year from the fourth year onwards.

Priority date

Where two or more applications are made independently for the same or for overlapping inventions, it is necessary to have a system for working out which application is to be granted and which rejected. In the United Kingdom, priority is given to the first to file and not to the first to invent. So, the application with the earlier date of filing will have priority.

As a variant to the application procedure described above, an applicant may file an application accompanied only by a description of his invention. If he files a second application within a year from the first, he may claim as his **priority date** the date of filing the earlier application, even though in the intervening period he has further developed his invention. The only requirement is that his second application be "supported by," *i.e.* reasonably related to, the matter disclosed in the earlier application. It is the priority date which is the relevant date for testing the patentability of an invention.

Where an applicant, who is resident in a country which is a member of the Paris Convention (most are), files an application in that country and within 12 months files an application in the United Kingdom, he may claim as his priority date, the date of filing abroad, provided again that his United Kingdom application is supported by the matter disclosed in the foreign filing.

Ilustration:
A. files an application for an invention in the United States on January 1, 1990.

B. files an application for the same invention in the United Kingdom on May 1, 1990.

A. files a United Kingdom application claiming priority from his United States application on December 1, 1990.

A.'s invention has the earlier priority date and *B.*'s application will be refused.

In practice, of course, the problems are far more complex.

Note that, for security reasons, a U.K. resident must file his patent application in the British Patent Office first. He may then apply for patents abroad.

International application procedures

An application made at the British Patent Office will result in the **grant** of a British patent only. An applicant who wished to obtain patent protection in several countries had, until recently, to file separate applications and pay separate fees in each country in which he sought a patent. Not only was this costly, but it resulted in the application being searched and examined with varying degrees of thoroughness in different countries depending on the competence of the local Patent Office. Two international systems have been devised to minimise the need for separate national applications.

The **Patent Co-operation Treaty** provides for the filing of a single application, designating the countries for which the applicant seeks protection. A single search is carried out and the application is then sent to each of the designated countries for separate examination as a national application according to their local laws. A variant provides for a single search and examination before the application is transmitted to the designated countries which may then carry out a supplemental examination if required. The system is operated under the auspices of the **World International Property Organisation** (WIPO) in Geneva. Some 45 countries, including the United States, the Soviet Union, the United Kingdom and most European States, are members.

The second system is the **European Patent Convention** to which all of the EEC member states plus Austria, Switzerland and Sweden belong. Here an application is filed at the **European Patent Office** and the member states in which the applicant requires protection are specified. The application is searched and examined and if the invention satisfies the requirements of the Convention, separate national patents are granted for the specified countries. Thus a single application results in a bundle of national patents. Apart from a period of the first nine months after grant, when the validity of the European patent can be challenged at the European Patent Office, validity and infringement can be contested only before the separate national courts. The Patents Act 1977 contains provisions for treating European patents (United Kingdom), *i.e.* a European patent which specified the United Kingdom, as being in all respects the same as patents applied for and granted under the Act itself.

Patentability and patentable inventions

Patents are granted only for inventions which fulfil certain criteria. The invention must be new, it must involve an inventive step and be capable of industrial application. Each of these criteria is discussed more fully below.

Curiously, the Patents Act 1977 does not define what is a patentable invention; instead it sets out a non-exhaustive list of what are not inventions for the purposes of the Act. The exclusions are there as a matter of public policy as certain matters should be freely available to all. Non-patentable inventions include:—

(a) discoveries, scientific theories or mathematical methods (s.1(2)(a));
(b) literary, dramatic, musical or artistic works or any other aesthetic creations (s.1(2)(b)). (These are protected by copyright, see Chapter 33, *post*);
(c) schemes, rules or methods for performing a mental act, playing a game, doing business; or a program for a computer (s.1(2)(c));
(d) the presentation of information (s.1(2)(d)).

In addition, a patent may not be granted for any variety of plant or animal nor for an essentially biological process for their production (s.1(3)(b)). However, a patent may be granted for a microbiological process, or for the product of such a process (s.1(3)(b)).

Novelty

An invention must be "new" to be patentable. It is new (or "novel") if it does not form part of the state of the art at the priority date (s.2(1)). The state of the art comprises all matter (whether a product, a process, information about either, or anything else) which has at any time before that date, been made available to the public anywhere in the world by written or oral description, by use or in any other way (s.2(2)). Case law under earlier patent legislation has interpreted the phrase "made available to the public" as meaning disclosure to one person who was free in law and equity to use the information as he pleased (*Humpherson* v. *Syer* [1887] 4 R.P.C. 407, C.A.). Thus disclosure to another under an obligation of confidence (see *ante*, TRADE SECRETS) will not affect patentability.

Where the art is a crowded one, two or more inventors may arrive at the invention at the same time and each file patent applications. To avoid the grant of a patent to two patentees, the earlier application is deemed to be part of the prior art when considering the novelty of the later application (s.2(3)).

Certain prior disclosures will not invalidate a patent. These are:

(a) where the disclosure was made in breach of confidence (s.2(4)(*a*), (*b*)) *e.g.* A. discloses his invention to B. in confidence. B. publishes the information in breach of confidence. A. can still patent his invention providing he files his application within six months of the disclosure (s.2(4));

(b) where the invention was disclosed at an "international exhibition," *i.e.* one falling within the terms of the Convention on International Exhibitions (s.2(4)(*c*)). This exception is very narrow as the Convention excludes trade fairs; or

(c) where the invention is the use of a substance or composition for the treatment of the human or animal body, the fact that the substance or composition is already known may be disregarded if it has not previously been known to have pharmaceutical or veterinary properties (s.2(6)).

Where an invention has been disclosed in the prior art it is said to have been "anticipated." To test for **anticipation** it is necessary to compare the invention as defined in the claims with the alleged prior publication. The prior publication must be interpreted as at its date of publication in the light of the then existing knowledge without regard to subsequent events. The claims must likewise be construed as at their priority date. If the prior publication, so construed, contains a clear description of, or clear instructions to make the alleged invention, or if carrying out the directions contained in the prior publication will inevitably result in something being made or done which, if the patent were valid would amount to an infringement, the claim has been anticipated. (*General Tire & Rubber Co.* v. *Firestone Tyre & Rubber Co.* [1972] R.P.C. 457, *per* Sachs L.J. at 485–486). An anticipation must be clear: "a signpost, however clear, upon the road to the patentee's invention will not suffice. The prior inventor must be clearly shown to have planted his flag at the precise destination before the patentee" (*General Tire, supra, per* Sachs L.J. at 486).

Inventive step

An invention is taken to involve an inventive step if it is not obvious to a person skilled in the art having regard to the prior art (s.3), other than co-pending patent applications which are deemed to be prior art for the purpose of testing for novelty only (s.3). Whether an invention is obvious is the most litigious question of all, as a patentee will not defend his patent if shown a clear anticipation. It is the "nearly but not quite" piece of prior art that is the most troublesome. The issue is particularly difficult to resolve as it is often fought years after the invention was made and the benefit of hindsight must somehow be discounted. "I confess that I view with suspicion arguments to the effect that a new combination, bringing with it new and important consequences in the shape of practical machines, is not an invention, because, when it has once been established, it is easy to show how it might be arrived at by starting from something known, and taking a series of apparently easy steps. This *ex post facto* analysis of invention is unfair to the inventors and, in my opinion, it is not countenanced by English patent law" (Fletcher Moulton L.J. in *British Westinghouse Electric & Manufacturing Co. Ltd.* v. *Braulik* [1910] 27 R.P.C. 209).

The test is directed to a hypothetical addressee: the man skilled in the art. He has been described as "a skilled technician who is well acquainted with workshop technique and who has carefully read all the relevant literature. He is supposed to have an unlimited capacity to assimilate the contents of, it may be, scores of specifications but to be incapable of a scintilla of invention" (Lord Reid in *Technograph Printed Circuits Ltd.* v. *Mills & Rockley* (*Electronics*) *Ltd.* [1972] R.P.C. 346 at 355). The notional addressee is also supposed to have read every piece of prior art which has been diligently unearthed in order to attack the patent. Much will be old, and in obscure languages.

The route by which the European Patent Office assesses obviousness is different from that traditionally adopted by British courts. It is more like the German approach, which uses as a yardstick a person who has only reasonable knowledge of the prior art, but who is capable of original thought. U.K. patents granted or litigated domestically are therefore currently measured by different tests than those coming before the European Patent Office or Board of Appeal.

Infringement

Two main questions arise. Does the scope of the invention as defined in the claims cover the product or process concerned? Does the defendant's act fall within the lists of acts prescribed by the Patents Act 1977?

Construction of claims

The claims must not be construed in isolation from the rest of the specification. The correct approach is to read the specification first, looking to see whether any terms are given a particular meaning, and having understood the specification, the claims must then be construed in the light of the whole specification, including the drawings, if any, (s.125). In order for there to be infringement, all the essential features of the claim must have been taken; inessential features added or omitted do not take a product or process out of infringement. The claims must not be given a purely literal meaning but must be given a purposive construction. The question in each case is: "whether persons with practical knowledge and experience of the kind of work in which the invention was intended to be used, would understand that strict compliance with a particular descriptive word or phrase appearing in a claim was intended by the patentee to be an essential requirement of the invention so that any variant would fall outside the monopoly claimed, even though it could have no material effect upon the way the invention worked" (Lord Diplock in *Catnic Components Ltd.* v. *Hill & Smith Ltd.* [1982] R.P.C. 183 at 243).

The patent claims were directed to a lintel which inter alia had a "second rigid support member extending vertically from or near the rear edge of the first horizontal plate or part to join with the second plate or part adjacent its rear edge." The claim thus called for a 90° angle. The defendants manufactured and sold a lintel where the relevant angle was some 6° or 8° from the vertical. Functionally, the reduction was negligible. It was held that the defendant's lintel infringed the claims: *Catnic Components Ltd.* v. *Hill & Smith Ltd., supra.*

Proscribed Acts

A person infringes a patent if, but only if, while the patent is in force, he does any of the following things in the United Kingdom, without the consent of the proprietor of the patent:

(a) where the invention is a product, he makes, disposes of, uses or imports the product or keeps it for disposal or otherwise (s.60(1)(a));

(b) where the invention is a process, he uses the process or he offers it for use when he knows, or it is obvious to a reasonable person in the circumstances, that its use there would be an infringement, (s.60(1)(b)) or he disposes of, offers to dispose of, uses or imports any product obtained directly by means of that process or keeps any such product whether for disposal or otherwise (s.60(1)(c)).

It is also an infringement for a person to supply or offer to supply "means essential for putting an invention into effect" to a person not entitled to work the patent, when he knows or it is obvious to a reasonable person in the circumstances, that those means are suitable for putting and are intended to put the invention into effect in the United Kingdom, (s.60(2)). This is sometimes referred to as contributory infringement. As an example, suppose there is a patent for a mixture of chemical A with chemical B in a herbicidal composition. The supply of chemical A to a person who, the supplier knows, is going to mix it with B and sell the mixture as a herbicide is an infringement.

There are certain limited exceptions to infringement including acts done for private, non-commercial purposes (s.60(5)(a)), acts done for experimental purposes (s.60(5)(b)), acts done on ships and aircraft temporarily or accidentally within the territorial waters or airspace (s.60(5)(d)(e)(f)). A person who has himself used the invention before the priority date of the patent may do so again or continue to do the acts he did before that date (s.64). Obviously, the prior use must have been secret, otherwise the patent would be bad for lack of novelty. The right to continue the use is personal and may be assigned only with the business in connection with which the invention was used (s.64(2)).

Only a valid patent can be infringed and a defendant may attack validity in the defence and in addition counterclaim for revocation of the patent.

Remedies for infringement

A patentee whose patent is valid and infringed is entitled to an injunction, delivery up of infringing articles and damages or an account of profits. Damages are assessed on a loss of profits or on a royalty basis.

Ownership, assignment and licensing

A patent or an application for a patent is personal property (without being a chose in action) (s.30(1)). Any assignment must be in writing signed by or on behalf of *both* parties to the transaction; otherwise it is void (s.30(6)). A licence may be granted orally and may be non-exclusive or exclusive (*i.e.* excludes even the patentee from working the invention). An exclusive licensee can bring infringement proceedings in his own name without joining the patentee (s.67). All transactions must be registered at the Patent Office (s.32). Penalties for non-registration include loss of priority over subsequent transactions (s.33) and restrictions on the right to recover damages against infringers (s.68).

Employee inventions

Where an invention is made by an employee in the course of his normal duties as an employee, or in the course of duties falling outside his normal ones but specifically assigned to him and, in either case, an invention might reasonably be expected to result from his carrying out those duties, that invention belongs to the employer (s.39(1)(a)). Where an invention is made by an employee who, because of the nature of his duties and particular responsibilities arising therefrom, is under a special obligation to further the employer's business, that invention also belongs to the employer (s.39(1)(b)). All other employee inventions belong to the employee (s.39(2)). Where a patent granted on an employee invention is of outstanding benefit to the employer, the employee may be entitled to a fair compensation (s.40). A contract entered into before the invention was made and which diminishes the employee's rights in his inventions is to that extent unenforceable (s.42).

Trade Marks

Trade marks are protected both under the common law of passing off and under the Trade Marks Acts 1938 and 1984. A trade mark is essentially any word or symbol or combination of both which is used to indicate a connection in the course of trade between the goods or services in relation to which the mark is used and the owner of the mark. Trade names and get-up are also protectable by a passing off action, see p. 654, *post*. The law relating to registered trade marks is about to be changed. At the time of writing, the Government has produced a White Paper on Reform of Trade Marks Law (Cm. 1203). Reference will be made to the proposals in the White Paper, for English law must be amended before the end of 1992 to comply with an EEC Directive (first Council Directive of December 21, 1988); and also to allow the U.K. to ratify as soon as possible the Protocol to the Madrid Agreement Concerning the International Registration of Trade Marks; and move us further down the road towards the establishment of a Community Trade Mark System.

Registered trade marks

The Trade Marks Acts provide a system of registration for certain marks and entitles the owner of the mark to its exclusive use.

Since 1986 marks used in connection with goods and with services can be registered.[2]

Registrability

At the moment the Trade Marks Register is divided into Part A and Part B. It is easier to secure registration in Part B but a more restricted protection is obtained. Under the White Paper it is proposed to combine the two parts of the Register into one single part. Turning to the definition of a registrable trade mark, Article 2 of the Directive states that "A trade mark may consist of any sign capable of being represented graphically, particularly words, including personal names, designs, letters, numerals, the shape of goods or of their packaging, provided such signs are capable of distinguishing the goods or services of one undertaking from those of other undertakings." The inclusion of the "shape of goods or of their packaging" is important, as it removes the anomaly introduced by the House of Lords, that a Coca Cola bottle cannot, however distinctive its shape, be registered as a trade mark (*Coca Cola Trade Marks* [1986] R.P.C. 421).

[2] References in this section are to the Trade Marks Act 1938 (as amended).

Returning to the present position, to be registrable in Part A, a mark must consist of or contain at least one of the following:

(a) the name of a company, individual or firm, represented in a special or particular manner (s.9(1)(a));
(b) the signature of the applicant for registration or some predecessor of his in business (s.9(1)(b));
(c) an invented word or words (s.9(1)(c));
(d) a word or words having no direct reference to the character or quality of the goods, and not being according to its ordinary meaning, a geographical name or surname (s.9(1)(d));
(e) any other distinctive mark, but a name, signature or word, other than those covered by (a) to (d) above, is not registrable except on evidence of distinctiveness (s.9(1)(e)).

There is no similar list of requirements for registration in Part B of the register. The limitations set out in section 9(1)(d) and in Article 2 of the Directive are to ensure that no one trader can monopolise, through his trade mark registration, words which other traders may legitimately want to use in connection with their products, such as descriptive words, or the name of the area in which they trade, or laudatory epithets or phrases. All trade marks must be distinctive, *i.e.* distinguish the goods or services of the trade mark proprietor (owner) from those of other traders. There are differences in this requirement as between Part A and Part B registrations, but once again these are to be swept away in the reforms and will not be considered here.

If the reforms are implemented, it should also be easier to register a trade mark. Currently the onus is on the applicant to show that his mark ought to be registered. However, there is evidence that the law is too strict and prevents the registration of marks which ought to be capable of registration. In future there is to be a presumption that a mark is registrable unless there is some specific objection to it. Objections might be raised if, as under current law, a mark is likely to deceive or cause confusion or would be contrary to law or morality, or contain any scandalous design (s.11). This prevents, *inter alia,* registration of marks which are confusingly similar to existing unregistered marks which by use have acquired some goodwill and reputation. It also prevents registration of marks which would be deceptive in use, such as, for example, the use of

"Orwoola" for non-woollen materials. In addition, under section 12(1) no trade mark may be registered if it is identical with or confusingly similar to a mark which is already registered for the same goods or description of goods or services for which registration is sought. It is proposed to broaden protection under this heading so as also to protect against registration in respect of *similar goods or services*; or in respect of goods and services which are not similar, but where use of the mark by another would take unfair advantage of the reputation of a registered mark or be detrimental to the reputation or distinctive character of the mark. The Registrar may however permit registration where in his opinion there has been honest concurrent use of the two marks in question (s.12(2)). The matter is one for the discretion of the Registrar and factors to be taken into account are: the extent of use in time, quantity and area of trade; the degree of confusion likely to ensue: the honesty of the concurrent use; and the relative inconvenience which would be caused if the mark were registered.

Infringement

The owner of a valid trade mark or service mark has the exclusive right to use that trade mark in relation to the goods or services for which it is registered. That right is infringed by any person who, without permission, uses in the course of trade, a mark identical with the registered trade mark or a mark so nearly resembling it as to be likely to deceive or cause confusion (s.4(1)(*a*)).

In considering whether a mark is confusingly similar, the resemblance of the two marks must be considered with reference to the ear as well as to the eye. Also, the idea conveyed by the mark must be regarded. Thus two marks which, when placed side by side, can be seen to be different may yet leave the same impression on the mind.

The plaintiffs used as their trade mark a drawing of a car in the form of a cat's body with the eyes being the headlamps of the car. The defendants used a detailed head of a cat with its eyes shown as a pair of motor car headlights. It was held that the idea of the marks was the same, although visually they were very dissimilar, and that there was infringement: *Taw* v. *Notek* [1951] 68 R.P.C. 271.

Also, some account must be taken of imperfect recollection. It is not to be supposed that a person has the two marks side by side but whether in view of his general recollection of the one mark he would be likely to be deceived and to think that the trade mark before him is the same as the other, *per* Sargant J. in *Sandow's Application* [1914] 31 R.P.C. 196.

A second type of infringement is by "importing a reference" to a trade mark (s.4(1)(*b*). This type of infringement occurs where an infringer uses the mark not to describe his own goods, but compares his own goods with those of the trade mark proprietor and refers to the latter's goods by the trade mark. Thus comparative price lists issued to the public which set out the trader's own brand and price in comparison with a famous named product and its price will be an infringement under section 4(1)(*b*).

The test for infringement of a Part B mark is the same as for a Part A mark, except that it is a defence for the alleged infringer to show that his use of the mark (or one objectively confusingly similar) was not such as to be likely to deceive or cause confusion (s.10).

Defences to infringement

The defences commonly available are:

(a) that the mark is invalid, *e.g.* for non-use for a period of five years (s.26) or that its registration contravened sections 9–12;
(b) that there is no infringement;
(c) that the defendant used his mark prior to the first use by the proprietor of the mark sued upon or prior to its registration, whichever is the earlier (s.7);
(d) that the defendant is bona fide using his own name or that of his place of business (s.8(a));
(e) that the defendant is using a bona fide description of the character or quality of his goods (s.8(b));
(f) that the defendant is himself the registered proprietor of the mark complained of (s.4(4));
(g) that the plaintiff has no title;
(h) general defences, such as acquiescence, estoppel or that the plaintiff's use of the mark is fraudulent or deceptive.

Remedies for infringement

A successful plaintiff is entitled to bring the usual interlocutory procedures, or to obtain an injunction, damages or an account of profits for infringement and to an order for destruction or modification of the offending material. It is not to be assumed that every article sold by the defendant would have been sold by the plaintiff for some customers may have purchased the defendant's goods for other reasons such as lower price, but the plaintiff may claim damages for the general lowering of his trade reputation if the spurious goods are of a much inferior quality.

Ownership, assignment and licensing

Any person who claims to be the owner of a mark used or intended to be used by him may apply for registration (s.17(1)). Once registered, the mark may be assigned either in connection with the goodwill of the business in which it is used or separately (s.22(1)). Where the assignment is without the goodwill of the business, it does not take effect unless the assignee applies to the Registrar of Trade Marks within six months from the date of the assignment for directions with respect to advertising the assignment in a suitable trade journal (s.22(7)). There are no formal requirements for the grant of licences to use a trade mark, save that some form of quality control should be exercised by the trade mark owner over the licensee's goods or there should be some other connection between them, such as being associated companies, so that a connection in the course of trade is still maintained between the registered proprietor and the goods. There is provision for entry of a licensee as a registered user on the Register (s.28) and a registered user may institute proceedings in his own name if the trade mark proprietor neglects or refuses to do so within two months of being called upon (s.28(3)). The rules relating to licensing are likely to be changed in line with recommendations in the White Paper.

Passing off

The purpose of an action for passing off is to prevent one trader from misappropriating the goodwill and reputation which has been built up by another. What is protected is not a proprietary right in a name, mark or get-up which has been improperly used, but the goodwill in the business in which the name, mark or get-up is used. The basic principle behind every passing off action is that no man is entitled to represent that his goods or his business are the goods or business of another. As Lord Diplock said in *Warninck* v. *Townend* [1980] R.P.C. 31, 93, it is possible to identify five characteristics which must be present in order to create a valid cause of action for passing off:

(1) a misrepresentation,
(2) made by a trader in the course of trade,
(3) to prospective customers of his or ultimate consumers of goods or services supplied by him,
(4) which is calculated to injure the business or goodwill of another trader (in the sense that this is a reasonably foreseeable consequence), and
(5) which causes actual damage to the business or goodwill of the trader by whom the action is brought (or in a *quid timet* action) will probably do so.

Whether or not a trader is guilty of passing off is not necessarily to be decided by reference to precedents. Rather, the tort is capable of development to meet the times and could sometimes be regarded as a remedy against unfair trading actionable at the suit of other traders who thereby suffer loss of business or goodwill. For example, the goodwill may be injured by someone who sells genuine goods of an inferior quality as being goods of a superior quality. Thus, in *Spalding* v. *Gamage,* [1915] 32 R.P.C. 273, Spalding's lower grade footballs were sold by Gamage in such a way as to mislead purchasers into thinking they were buying the higher grade Spalding footballs. Or the goodwill may be injured by someone who falsely applies a trade description to a product. Thus, in *Bollinger* v. *Costa Brava Wine Co.*, [1960] R.P.C. 16, and 116 it was held that a sparkling Spanish wine sold as "Spanish Champagne" was a misrepresentation, as the name "champagne" denoted the sparkling white wine produced in the Champagne region of France and not just any sparkling white wine.

A plaintiff must first establish his reputation in the name, mark or get-up complained of. It is possible, though not common, for a name which ordinarily has a descriptive meaning to acquire a secondary meaning, *i.e.* that it has become distinctive of the goods of a particular trader.

For years Reddaway had sold belting under the name "camel hair belting." It was thought for most of that time to be composed of other fibres but was in fact made of camel hair. Banham sold belting under the name "camel hair belting" and was held to have passed off his belting as being that of Reddaway as the phrase "camel hair belting" did not mean belting made of camel hair but instead meant Reddaway's belting: *Reddaway* v. *Banham* [1896] A.C. 199.

Normally, the court requires a great deal of persuading to accept that a descriptive term has lost its primary meaning and is in fact distinctive of the plaintiff's goods or business.

The misrepresentation may be made not only by using names or marks the same as or confusingly similar to that of the plaintiff, but also by adopting a packaging or get-up which is very close. For example, in *Reckitt & Colman Products Ltd.* v. *Borden Inc.* [1990] 1 All E.R. 873, the defendants were prevented from marketing their lemon juice in lemon-shaped containers which closely resembled those of the plaintiffs, as to do otherwise would cause confusion among consumers as to the origin of the product.

It is not necessary for the plaintiff's and defendant's trade to be identical, provided there is a sufficient similarity for the one to be thought connected with the other. The test is whether there is confusion of a common consuming public.

The plaintiffs ran an exclusive club in Mayfair under the name "Annabel's." The defendant started an escort agency called "Annabel's Escort Agency." It was held that there was a sufficient likelihood that a significant number of members or potential members of the Annabel's Club would assume that the escort service was connected with or approved by the Club and an injunction was issued against the defendant: *Annabel's (Berkeley Square) Ltd.* v. *Shock* [1972] R.P.C. 838.

Defences to an action for passing off

The following defences are commonly raised:

(a) that the name or mark or get-up is not distinctive of the plaintiff, or that it is descriptive and the plaintiff cannot establish a secondary meaning;
(b) that there is no real likelihood of confusion or, if there is

confusion, there is no real likelihood of damage to the plaintiff;

(c) that the defendant has a concurrent right to use the mark or name or get-up;

(d) that the defendant is trading bona fide under his own name;

(e) general defences such as acquiescence, estoppel and delay.

Remedies

A successful plaintiff is entitled to an injunction and to damages or an account of profits and to an order for obliteration or modification of the mark name or get-up complained of. Interlocutory procedures, such as interlocutory injunctions and Anton Piller orders, are also important.

Ownership, assignment and licensing

There is no proprietary right in an unregistered mark, trade name or get-up. What may be assigned is the goodwill of the business in connection with which the name, mark or get-up is used. A licence to use the name, mark or get-up is, strictly speaking, merely an agreed immunity from a passing off action capable of being brought by the licensor.

CHAPTER 33

COPYRIGHT AND RELATED RIGHTS

UNLIKE the monopoly granted by a patent, which enables the patentee to exclude independent but later originators from working the invention, the rights comprised by copyright give protection only against copying. Copyright protects the independent skill, labour and effort which have been expended in producing a copyright work and prevents another from taking a short cut to the end result by helping himself to too liberal a portion of that skill, labour and effort. Copyright is acquired simply by bringing a work into existence which has the appropriate degree of originality and a qualifying connection with the United Kingdom. There is no need and, indeed, no provision for registration.

Copyright is purely statutory and the governing legislation is the Copyright, Designs and Patents Act 1988.[1] This statute codified and amended the law; one of the aims of the legislature was to express existing law in more comprehensible form. There are thus many changes of expression as well as substantive changes over earlier legislation.[2]

Copyright protects literary, dramatic, musical and artistic works, films, sound recordings, broadcasts, cable programmes and the typographical arrangement of published editions. The 1988 Act gives to the copyright owner the exclusive right to do or to authorise others to do so-called "restricted acts." These differ according to the nature of the work protected by copyright and define the scope of the protection afforded to that work.

[1] References in this chapter are to the 1988 Act, unless otherwise indicated. For text of the Act see Current Law Statutes 1988 c. 48. The Commission of the European Community is discussing the harmonisation of various aspects of copyright law within the EC, including computer software and rental rights.

[2] The Copyright Act 1956, as amended by the Design Copyright Act 1968 and the Copyright (Amendment) Acts 1971, 1982 and 1983, the Criminal Justice Act 1982, the Cable and Broadcasting Act 1984 and the Copyright (Computer software) Amendment Act 1985.

Subsistence of copyright

Qualification or "connecting factor"

A work may qualify for copyright protection in the United Kingdom by authorship or by first publication[3]:

Authorship If at the material time[4] the author is a national of, resident or incorporated[5] in the UK, a colony *or* a state belonging to an appropriate Convention, the work will enjoy UK copyright.[6] For literary, dramatic, musical and artistic works and films, the Berne Convention[7] is of paramount importance. This Convention guarantees a minimum level of protection and national treatment of foreign works as between signatory states. Most countries are members either of Berne, or of the Universal Copyright Convention of 1952, or of both. For sound recordings and broadcasts the Rome Convention of 1961,[8] with more limited membership, applies. Typefaces are governed by the Vienna Agreement.[9]

Publication First publication in the UK or another country to which the Act extends or applies will also qualify a literary, dramatic, musical or artistic work, film or typographical arrangement for copyright protection. Broadcasts and cable programmes qualify by transmission. "Published" is defined in s.175 as meaning the

[3] Ss.153–156. There is a view that "first fixation"—creation in the UK—should be a qualifying criterion for sound recording copyright.

[4] For literary, dramatic, musical or artistic works the material time is when the work is made, or published or, if published posthumously, immediately before the author's death: s.154(4). For sound recordings and films the time of making is material; for broadcasts or cable programmes, transmission; for typographical arrangements, publication: s.154(5).

[5] A company may come within the definition of author of a computer-generated work, sound recording, film, broadcast, cable programme or typographical arrangment.

[6] For extension and application of the Act to works connected with other countries see ss.157–161.

[7] The Berne Convention for the Protection of Literary and Artistic Works, 1886 and revisions (Cmnd. 5002, 1972). See Ricketson, 1986, The Berne Convention 1886–1986.

[8] Cmnd. 2425 (1964). Since the Rome Convention was limited to Berne and Universal Copyright Convention members a further Phonogram Convention was adopted in Geneva in 1971.

[9] Cmnd. 5754 (1974).

issue of copies of the work to the public[10] or making certain works available to the public by means of an electronic retrieval system.

A work which is copyright in the United Kingdom will enjoy national copyright protection in other Convention countries.

Crown and Parliamentary copyright are available where a work is made by officers of the Crown or under the direction or control of Parliament[11]; protection is also given to works made under the auspices of certain international organisations.[12]

Literary, dramatic and musical works

Copyright subsists in original works of these descriptions. The meaning of "original" is discussed on p. 661, *post.* A literary work means any work, other than a dramatic or musical work, which is written, spoken or sung. The definition (s.3(1)) includes tables, compilations and computer programs. "Writing" includes any form of notation or code, regardless of the method or medium of recording.[13] There is no requirement of literary merit in order for a work to be protected and such diverse works as street directories, logarithm tables, examination papers, advertising brochures, football pool coupons and series of bingo numbers are entitled to copyright. It is possible for more than one copyright to exist in a work: thus in the case of a published anthology of poetry there will be separate copyrights in the individual poems as well as an additional compilation copyright, and typographical arrangement copyright in the anthology as a whole. "Dramatic work" is defined as including works of dance or mime and "musical work" means a work consisting of music, exclusive of any words or action.[14]

There appears to be a quantitative minimum below which creations of these kinds do not constitute "works." In *Exxon*,[15] that word was held not to be a literary work. Copyright does not exist in literary, dramatic or musical works until they are recorded, in writing or otherwise.[16]

[10] S.175 excludes certain public uses, such as the exhibition of an artistic work, public performances, broadcasts or cablecasts, from the definition of publication, as well as unauthorised acts.

[11] Ss.163–167.

[12] S.168.

[13] S.178.

[14] S.3(1).

[15] *Exxon Corp.* v. *Exxon Insurance Consultants International* [1982] Ch. 119.

[16] S.3(2) and (3). Note that a distinct copyright may subsist in the recording.

Originality

It can be seen that copyright only subsists in "original" literary, dramatic, musical and artistic works. Originality here does not have the same meaning as novel or unique in the sense that an invention must be novel to be patentable. Original merely means that the work must be the product of the independent skill and labour of the author and must not have been slavishly copied[17] or derived from some pre-existing work. Even though a work contains a substantial part derived from earlier material it will still attract copyright provided further independent skill, labour, knowledge, taste or judgment have been expended upon it. However, if a derived work has been made in infringement of another's copyright, it may not be possible to exploit the later work without consent.

Artistic works

This important category includes[18]:

(a) graphic works (paintings, drawings, maps, engravings etc.), photographs (wide definition), sculptures and collages *irrespective of artistic quality*;

(b) works of architecture being buildings (fixed structures or parts) or models;

(c) works of artistic craftsmanship.

The phrase "irrespective of artistic quality" enabled the courts to hold that engineering production drawings were entitled to copyright. Copying a product which had been manufactured from engineering drawings amounted to indirectly copying the drawings. Copyright actions were fought (and won) on production drawings for spare parts for cars,[19] such as exhaust systems, light fittings, solid fuel gravity feed boilers, plastic knock-down drawers for furniture and even lavatory pan connectors. In this respect copyright protection was as valuable, if not more so, than patent protection. Other

[17] As in *Interlego* v. *Tyco Industries* [1988] 3 W.L.R. 678 (P.C.)
[18] Section 4.
[19] In *British Leyland Motor Corporation Ltd.* v. *Armstrong Patents Co. Ltd.* [1986] A.C. 577 the House of Lords resorted to the principle of non-derogation from grant to avert success for the plaintiff in spare parts litigation.

growth areas of copyright litigation included the fashion trade since fashion sketches, cutting patterns and point patterns for knitted garments were protected as "artistic works."

Such use of copyright in two-dimensional works to prevent plagiarism of three-dimensional articles has been curtailed by the 1988 Act. It is still possible for copyright in a two-dimensional work to be infringed by a three-dimensional copy, and *vice versa.* However, where an artistic work[20] records or embodies the design for the shape or configuration of an article which is not in itself an artistic work or typeface, s.51 now permits others to make articles to the design or to copy articles made to the design. Thus copyright in production drawings for a pump component may not be used to prevent others from manufacturing the component. Other forms of protection for designers' artefacts may be available—design right (see p. 676 *post*) or registered designs (see p. 673, *post*). Where the article depicted in a sketch or drawing *is* an artistic work, such as a sculpture, copyright in the graphic work may be used to control copying of the work depicted. The same result may be obtained if the drawing or sketch was not *intended* to be a design drawing.[21] However, once an artistic work is applied industrially in the manufacture and marketing of articles,[22] s.52 limits to 25 years the copyright owner's ability to control manufacture.

Designs for the surface decoration of an article are not affected by s.51, so that copyright in the design document may be used to restrain copying of the design. However, s.52 applies in relation to the surface of articles, although not to truly two-dimensional articles such as calendars or posters.[23]

A work of artistic craftsmanship is not defined and the leading case, *Hensher* (*George*) Ltd. v. *Restawile Upholstery* (*Lancs.*) *Ltd.* [1976] A.C. 64 (H.L.) gives no clear guidance except as to what is *not* a work of artistic craftsmanship. The intention of sub-section 4(1)(c) is to give protection to such works as stained glass, pottery and other forms of artistic endeavour not covered by the previous categories of "artistic work".

[20] Made after commencement of the 1988 Act on August 1, 1989.
[21] See Dworkin and Taylor [1990] 1 E.I.P.R. 33.
[22] More than 50 or continuous length or piece goods: S.I. 1989 No. 1070, para. 2 (the Copyright (Industrial Process and Excluded Articles) (No. 2) Order 1989).
[23] S.I. 1989 No. 1070, para. 3.

Authorship of literary, dramatic, musical and artistic works

Section 9(1) defines the author of a work as "the person who creates it." Usually there is no difficulty in identifying that person.[24] Sometimes two or more individuals collaborate in the creation of the work in such a way that their respective contributions cannot be distinguished; in those circumstances the work is treated as a work of joint authorship.[25] Some works are originated by computers in such a way that no particular human author can be identified. In these circumstances a work may be accorded copyright as a computer-generated work; the person who undertook the arrangements for creating the work is given the status of author.[26]

Films

A film is defined by s.5(1) as "a recording on any medium from which a moving image may by any means be produced." This encompasses celluloid and video recordings. It should be noted that the making of a film very frequently involves the use of other copyright works such as books, scripts, music, for which copyright clearance must be obtained. The sound track of a film is treated under the 1988 Act as a sound recording—a separate work.[27] The author of the film is the person who makes arrangements necessary for its creation—usually the producer, although the director of a film is responsible for its cultural merit. It is the director and not the producer who enjoys moral rights in the film—the right to be named as creator and to object to derogatory treatment.[28] Because film is a species of work recognised by the Berne Convention, films can enjoy copyright virtually worldwide. Copyright does not subsist in a film or part of a film which is copied from a previous film: s.5(2).

Sound recordings

Most sound recordings embody literary, dramatic or musical

[24] If all else fails the work will be treated as one of unknown authorship—s.9(4)—there are special rules for duration of copyright. In practice no-one is likely to be available to litigate such copyright let alone establish a connecting factor with the United Kingdom.
[25] S.10.
[26] Ss.178 and 9(3).
[27] Under the Copyright Act 1956 the sound track was treated as part of the film.
[28] See p. 671, *post*.

works, spoken or performed, and the recording provides a means for reproducing the work in sound. This type of recording is included in the definition of sound recording at s.5(1)(b). The first limb of the definition at s.5(1)(a) embraces reproducible recordings of sound such as birdsong or industrial noise. The definition applies regardless of recording medium or means of reproduction but does not appear to include a computer program capable of generating non-musical sounds *ab initio*.

The author of a sound recording is the person who makes the arrangements necessary for its creation: s.9(2)(a). This probably achieves the same effect in most cases as s.12(4) of the Copyright Act 1956, by which the first owner of copyright in a sound recording was the person who owned the master. Sound recordings do not enjoy copyright if or to the extent that they are copies of previous sound recordings (s.5(2)).

Broadcasts and cable programmes

These "works" enjoy an evanescent existence in the form of electromagnetic waves. The medium through which the waves travel is the criterion for distinguishing between the two types of work. If the signals are sent along a cable, optical fibre or other specially adapted medium, they may constitute a cable programme but not a broadcast. If the signals are transmitted through free space, by "wireless telegraphy,"[29] they may constitute a broadcast but not a cable programme. In each case the purpose and recipients of the transmission establish its status as a work. A broadcast[30] is either capable of lawful receipt by members of the public or transmitted for presentation to members of the public. Lawful receipt of an encrypted broadcast requires use of authorised decoding equipment.[31] There are two types of author of a broadcast—the person making the transmission and the person having responsibility for its contents to any extent. This means that joint authorship and ownership of broadcast copyright are likely to be common. As broadcasting is also a means of infringing copyright, copyright in works

[29] See s.178.
[30] S.6.
[31] S.6(2).

included in a broadcast without consent is likely to be infringed by joint tortfeasors.

The complex definition of "cable programme service" in section 7 confers copyright on transmissions of visual, sound and teletext material. It is designed to include public transmissions for passive reception and to exclude private and domestic transmissions and services internal to a business or media organisation. The definition probably includes transmissions sent to those who consult databases online. The Secretary of State has power to add exceptions to the definition or remove them.

Qualifying broadcasts and cable programmes will enjoy copyright to the extent that they do not infringe copyright in another broadcast or cable programme: ss.6(6) and 7(6). This low threshold of originality means that repeat transmissions attract copyright, the duration of which is tied to that of copyright in the original transmission: s.14(3).

Duration of copyright

Unless a work enjoys Crown or Parliamentary copyright, to which special rules apply,[32] copyright endures as follows[33]:

For literary, dramatic, musical and artistic works, copyright expires 50 years from the end of the calendar year in which the author dies[34]: s.12(1). If an original work has been created by computer in circumstances where there is no human author, copyright expires 50 years from the end of the year of making.

Copyright in sound recordings and films subsists for 50 years from the end of the calendar year in which the work was made; if released during that period, 50 years of copyright run from the end of the year of release: s.13. "Release" includes authorised publication, broadcasting or cablecasting and the public showing of a film and its soundtrack.

[32] Ss.163–6. See also s.168 on the copyright of international organisations.

[33] Sched. 1, para. 12 deals with the duration of copyright in works existing at August 1, 1989.

[34] Or the last of joint authors dies. For lawfully published works of unknown authorship the period is 50 years from the end of the year in which the work was made available to the public: s.12(2). Copyright in unpublished works of unknown authors is indeterminate, but a special defence applies: s.57.

Broadcasts and cables programmes enjoy copyright for 50 years from the end of the year of first transmission: s.14.

Copyright in the typographical arrangement of published editions expires 25 years from the end of the year of publication: s.15.

Infringement

The acts restricted by copyright are spelt out in s.16 and subsequent sections. Copyright is infringed by doing any of the restricted acts in relation to a work without the licence of the copyright owner and by authorising others to do so. For there to be infringement of copyright, there must be a sufficient objective similarity[35] between the copyright work and the alleged infringing work such that the original work or a "substantial" part of it has been reproduced (performed in public, broadcast, etc.) Also the copyright work must be the source from which the infringing work is derived—there must be a causal connection between the copyright work and the infringement. "Substantial" is not necessarily measured in terms of the quantity taken, for a short extract may be a very important part of the work and it is often said that whether a substantial part has been copied depends more on the quality rather than the quantity. Difficult questions arise when a defendant acknowledges that he used the plaintiff's work as a source but says he has taken no more than the idea. There is no copyright in ideas as such because ideas are not literary, dramatic, musical or artistic works. It has been said that copyright is confined to the expression of ideas and it is only if the expression has been copied that there is infringement. In reality most copyright works consist of a detailed interlocking interplay of ideas and if that detailed pattern has been taken then there will be infringement.

If there has been substantial taking it is immaterial whether copying has been direct or indirect or whether intervening acts constitute infringement or not. Infringement by "authorisation" was at issue in *C.B.S.* v. *Amstrad.*[36] The House of Lords held in

[35] Objective similarity and opportunity to copy are often the best available evidence of copying.

[36] [1988] A.C. 1013, [1988] RPC 567.

Amstrad that "to authorise" means "to grant or purport to grant, expressly or by implication, the right to do the act complained of."

The acts restricted by copyright are as follows:—

(a) copying—all works. Section 17 provides that in relation to literary, dramatic, musical and artistic works, copying means reproducing the work in any material form or storing on any medium by electronic means. Copies may be permanent or transient, deliberate or incidental. A two-dimensional representation of a three-dimensional artistic work constitutes a copy and vice versa. Films, television broadcasts or cable programmes may be "copied" by photographing the whole or substantial part of any image. Typographical arrangements are "copied" by making facsimile copies.

Collective licensing schemes exist under which published literary, musical and other works may be reproduced upon the payment of royalties to a central agency.

(b) issue of copies to the public—all works. Section 18 replaces the former restricted act of publication—putting a work before the public for the first time—with a distribution right. The copyright owner gains the right to put a given copy of the work into circulation. Once this has occurred, anywhere in the world, distribution of that copy is no longer restricted by s.18 unless the work is a sound recording, film or computer program. For these species of work, the copyright owner may control the commercial rental[37] of copies. If the copy concerned is an infringing copy,[38] however, commercial importation or dealing may constitute "secondary" infringement (ss.22–24, see p. 668 *post*) where the actor has actual or constructive knowledge that the copies are infringing.

(c) public performance, showing or playing—s.19

Copyright in a literary, dramatic or musical work (but not an artistic work) is infringed by its unauthorised performance in public. Copyright in sound recordings, films, broadcasts and cable programmes restricts their playing in public. It is the person who organises the public performance or playing who infringes, rather than the performer or operator of equipment. Performing rights are administered by collecting societies. It is wise for the occupier of

[37] See s.178 for definition of "rental."
[38] See s.27 and p. 668, *post*, for the definition of "infringing copy."

premises used for public entertainment to ensure that the societies' tariffs have been paid: section 25 renders it tortious to permit premises to be used for an infringing performance unless it is believed on reasonable grounds that copyright would not be infringed. A similar burden is imposed upon suppliers of equipment: s.26.

(d) broadcasting a work or including it in a cable programme service—section 20. These activities are restricted by copyright in all works except typographical arrangements.

(e) adaptations. Section 21 provides that making an adaptation is restricted by copyright in literary, dramatic, musical and artistic works. Modes of adaptation include translation, dramatisation, arrangement and transcription. Where, in the course of running, a computer program is incidentally converted into or out of language, subs. 21(4) spares the translation from infringement. Acts restricted by copyright in the original work are also restricted in relation to an adaptation.

(f) secondary infringement—ss.22–27. An "infringing copy" is one which has been made in the UK in infringement of copyright or has been made abroad but whose manufacture in the UK either would have infringed or would have constituted a breach of exclusive licence: s.27(3). "Parallel imports" may thus be deemed infringing copies, unless made in the EC: s.27(5). Commercial imports, dealings with and possession of infringing copies and non-commercial but prejudicial distributions will infringe if the doer knows or has reason to believe that the copies are infringing. The usual way of fixing an importer or other dealer with actual knowledge is to write a letter before action. It is also infringement with knowledge to provide certain means for making infringing copies.[39] Secondary infringement in relation to performances has already been noted.[40]

Offences

Making or dealing with infringing copies is also a criminal offence

[39] S.24.
[40] pp. 667–668.

if actual or constructive knowledge is present; other offences relate to supplying the means to infringe and to infringing performances.[41] The penalties are not trivial and there are provisions for delivery up and search warrants in the 1988 Act.

Exceptions to infringement—the "permitted acts"

The 1988 Act lists[42] a number of exceptions to infringement in ss.28–76. Some of the more important activities which are permitted notwithstanding the subsistence of copyright are:

(a) fair dealing with a literary, dramatic, musical or artistic work for the purpose of research or private study (s.29); a number of detailed provisions in ss.32–36 provide further scope for using works in education without the copyright owner's consent.

(b) fair dealing with a work for the purposes of criticism, review or reporting current events,[43] providing that sufficient acknowledgement is made (acknowledgement is not required for news reporting by audio, film, broadcast or cable).

(c) use of works for the purposes of judicial and parliamentary proceedings (s.45). A number of other acts are permitted, to smooth the path of public administration (s.46–50).

(d) copying by librarians and archivists is permitted in a number of circumstances (ss.37–44, 61 and 75) whilst scientific and technical abstracts may be used (s.60).

(e) the use of designs embodied in artistic works (ss.51–55; see p. 662, *ante*).

Remedies for infringement

In addition to the usual remedies of an injunction and damages or an account of profits for infringement, a copyright owner may be entitled to additional statutory damages having regard to the flagrancy of the infringement and the benefit the defendant has derived from it (s.97(2)).

[41] S.107.
[42] At ss.28–76.
[43] Except photographs: s.30(2).

"Conversion damages," formerly awarded on the basis that the copyright owner was deemed also to own infringing copies, have been abolished save in actions starting prior to August 1, 1989 for infringements committed before that date.[44] There are now special provisions for delivery up in copyright actions.[45] These, it is submitted, do not affect the court's equitable jurisdiction to order delivery up in support of an injunction, or to grant *Anton Piller* orders.[46]

Ownership, assignment and licensing

The general rule is that the author of a work is the first owner of copyright. The most important exception to this principle is that where a literary, dramatic, musical or artistic work is created in the course of employment under a contract of service, the employer is first owner of copyright. This exception is subject to any agreement to the contrary. In fact copyright may be assigned prospectively, in advance of creation of the work; s.91 operates to vest copyright in the assignee upon creation of the work. Crown Copyright, Parliamentary copyright and that belonging to international organisations fall outside the general rule.

Copyright is transmissible as personal property (s.90). An assignment has no effect unless it is in writing, signed by or on behalf of the assignor [s.90(3)]. The assignment may be complete or partial only [s.90(2)] and may be limited as to the type of rights assigned (reproduction rights, publishing rights which, by custom of the trade are further split into serialisation, paperback and hardback rights, translation rights, performing rights, film rights, broadcasting rights, etc.), as to time and geographically, country by country. In this way there can be a multiplicity of rights all stemming from the original work and all capable of separate assignment or licensing. A licence may be created orally or in writing and may be exclusive or non-exclusive. An exclusive licensee whose licence is in writing may sue for infringement in his own name and be entitled to damages,

[44] Sched. 1, para. 31(2).
[45] Ss.99 and 100. See *Lagenes Ltd.* v. *It's At (UK) Ltd. The Times*, March 12, 1991.
[46] See p. 187, [reference to description of *Anton Piller* orders] *or* [search and seize orders, named after the case of *Anton Piller K.G.* v. *Manufacturing Processes Ltd.* [1976] Ch. 55.]

although the copyright owner must at some stage be joined in the action, either as plaintiff or as defendant (s.102(1)).

Public lending right

The Public Lending Right Act 1979 gives authors of books the right to receive payments from time to time out of a Central Fund in respect of their books lent out to the public by local library authorities in the United Kingdom. A Registrar of Public Lending Right is established; his office is at Stockton-on-Tees. The right applies only to books but not to gramophone records or cassettes. The author's entitlement to public lending right depends on loans of his books over the counter at local libraries. Loans from academic, private or commercial libraries are excluded. The Central Fund is constituted by the Secretary of State and placed under the control and management of the Registrar of Public Lending Right.

Moral rights

In addition to restricting economic control over works to the copyright owner, the 1988 act confers certain "moral" rights upon the authors of literary, dramatic, musical and artistic works and upon the directors of films.[47] Previously a right was given to non-authors to object when works were wrongly attributed. This is retained.[48]

Three new forms of moral right are as follows. The first new right, to be identified as author or director when a work is put before the public, has to be asserted before it is effective. Assertion may be upon assignment or by a separate instrument. The second new right is the right to object to derogatory treatment of a work. This involves actual mutilation of the work by addition or deletion. It is the putting of a mutilated work before the public, rather than the act of mutilation, which is tortious. Both these forms of moral right are subject to catalogues of exceptions. Computer programs are excluded; the moral rights of employees are curtailed. Fair dealing and certain other "permitted acts" may be carried out.

Thirdly the commissioner of private and domestic photographs

[47] These provisions were enacted to comply with the Berne convention; the new rights apply only to "Berne" works; see ss.77–79 and 80–83.
[48] With amendments: s.84.

and films has a limited right of privacy; s.85 restricts the distribution, exhibition, broadcasting or cablecasting of the photograph or film. This was enacted to compensate for repeal of provisions vesting copyright in the commissioner of photographs.

All varieties of moral right may be waived formally or informally, although they may not be assigned. The new moral rights endure as long as copyright in the works in question and devolve after the author's death. The right to object to false attribution endures 20 years after death.

Rights in performances

In the United Kingdom, dramatic and musical performances have been protected since 1925 by penal statutes, which were held in *Rickless* v. *United Artists Corp.*[49] to confer civil rights of action on performers and (after death) their personal representatives. Part II of the 1988 Act introduced express civil rights of action in favour of dramatic and musical performers, those who recite literary works and performers of variety acts (ss.180, 182). Rights are also given to those who enjoy the benefit of exclusive recording contracts with such performers (s.185).

The performer's consent is required (s.182) for the non-domestic recording or re-recording of the whole or a substantial part of a qualifying[50] performance—one given by a qualifying individual or taking place in a qualifying country (s.181). Consent is also required for the live broadcasting or cablecasting of the performance (s.182). Activities of these kinds are actionable by performers as breach of statutory duty (s.194). A former requirement that consent be in writing has been repealed, although written consent is desirable for evidential purposes. It is a defence to a claim for damages that the defendant believed on reasonable grounds that consent had been given (s.182(2)). Public use of an illicit recording without consent is also actionable if the user has actual or constructive knowledge of its illicit status, as is the knowing import (other than for private and domestic purposes), commercial possession or dealing with illicit copies. Damages only are available against an innocent acquirer

[49] [1987] F.S.R. 362.

[50] Ss.181 and 206–208. Performers' rights are governed by the Rome Convention, *ante*, p. 659, at n. 8.

(s.184(3)). There is a list of "permitted acts" (s.189 and Sched. 2) like those in the copyright part of the Act.

Similar rights are granted to persons with exclusive recording rights (ss.185–188). The record companies' rights are infringed where neither they nor the performer consents. Where a performer gives consent to a third party in breach of an exclusive recording agreement, the remedy lies in contract or for the tort of procuring breach of contract but not under the 1988 Act.

Rights in performance subsist for 50 years from the end of the year in which the performance takes place: s.191. The rights as such may not be assigned, but devolve upon the death of the performer and are effectively transferred along with the benefit of an exclusive recording contract: ss.185 and 192(4).

Making, using or dealing with illicit recordings is an offence: s.198; it is also an offence falsely to represent authority to give consent: s.201.

Protection for product design

The original design of a three-dimensional artistic work such as a sculpture or building will be protected by copyright. Any two-dimensional or surface design[51] which is created through the medium of a drawing or other original artistic work will also enjoy protection, by virtue of copyright in the design drawing (see p. 000, *ante*). Prior to commencement of the 1988 Act, copyright in design drawings was also widely used to prevent the plagiarism of three-dimensional product design. Now, where a three-dimensional design has been created after July 31, 1989 for a comparatively mundane product, which is not an artistic work in its own right, the removal of copyright protection[52] by s.51 of the 1988 Act means that protection must be sought elsewhere. Two possibilities exist: design registration and exercise of unregistered design right. Both may protect computer-generated designs as well as those of identifiable human designers.

Registered designs

There exists a system of design registration under the Registered

[51] There is a special regime for typefaces under ss.54–5 of the 1988 Act.
[52] See p. 662, *ante*.

Designs Act 1949, which was overhauled by the 1988 Act.[53] Two- and three-dimensional designs which are new and have eye-appeal may be registered for an initial period of 5 years, plus a maximum of four 5-year extensions. Registrable features are those of shape, configuration, pattern or ornament (s.1(1)). Methods or principles of construction are excluded by s.1(1)(a), which means that a registrable design has to be depicted or defined in detail. Purely functional features are excluded from registration: s.1(1)(b)(i). The design of parts which are made and sold separately may be registered separately—the definition of "article" in s.44 includes such parts—but the "part" registration cannot protect features which are dependant on the appearance of the larger whole: s.1(1)(b)(ii).

A registrable design is one which is applied to an article by any industrial process. Rule 35 of the Registered Designs Rules 1989[54] states that a design shall be regarded as "applied industrially" if it is applied to more than 50 articles which do not constitute a single set, or to goods manufactured in lengths or pieces, not being hand-made goods. Rule 26 excludes designs for certain works of sculpture, plaques, medallions and printed matter of a primarily literary or artistic character, such as calendars or post cards. The appeal of the design to the eye of the consumer must be material, appearance being normally or actually taken into account by acquirers or users: s.1(3). The requirement of novelty relates only to the United Kingdom. If the design or a trade variant has been published[55] or registered in the UK before, it is not "new": s.1(4).

A design is registered for a particular article or description of articles. It is in the proprietor's interest to describe the product in wide terms. If a proprietor wishes to gain protection for the same design as applied to further articles, subsequent applications may be made, but the later registrations cannot outlive the original: s.4.

The registration of a design gives its proprietor the exclusive right commercially to manufacture or to deal in an article for which the design is registered and which bears that design or a design not

[53] Ss.265–273. References in this section are to the Registered Designs Act 1949, as amended unless otherwise indicated.

[54] 1989 S.I. No. 1105. The same definition is used for s.52 of the 1988 Act—see p. 662, *ante*, at n. 23.

[55] In the sense that an article bearing the design has been offered or shown to the public.

substantially different from it (s.7(1)). Thus, in relation to a particular description of article, the proprietor is given an absolute monopoly; there is no need to prove that the alleged infringer copied. The manufacture, supply or assembly of a kit may infringe the registration of a design for an assembled article (s.7(4)). Actual registration is necessary to found an action for infringement: s.7(5). One cannot sue upon an application to register. Both the Chancery Division of the High Court and the Patents County Court[56] have jurisdiction over infringement proceedings. Validity and ownership may be challenged in these proceedings.

All the usual remedies for infringement are available. However, a defendant may not be liable to pay damages if innocence can be shown of the registration; it is always wise to mark articles with the registered design number (s.9). Unjustified threats of infringement proceedings against defendants other than manufacturers or importers are actionable (s.26); care must therefore be taken in drafting any letter before action. Compulsory licences (s.10) and licences of right (s.11A) may be made available. There are provisions for Crown use (s.12 and Sched. 1).

Where a design is created under a commission for value, the commissioner is entitled as proprietor to apply for registration. Otherwise, designs created in the course of employment belong to the employer, whilst the design's author is first owner in the absence of commission or employment (s.2). In the case of a computer-generated design, the person who made arrangements necessary for the creation of the design is regarded as author (s.2(4)). There is no qualification requirement for prospective applicants, but a person who has first applied to register the design in a Convention country[57] may use the date of that earlier application as the "priority date" for the UK application; such a priority date may be up to six months earlier than the date of the UK application.

Registered designs may be assigned, transmitted, licensed, or mortgaged, subject to any such prior interest recorded on the register (s.19).

[56] Created pursuant to s.287 of the 1988 Act.

[57] In particular, a country party to the Paris Convention for the protection of industrial property (1883 and revisions).

Design right

A new system of unregistered rights in three-dimensional designs was introduced by ss.213–235 of the 1998 Act. Provided an original design has been recorded in some way, in a "design document" (s.263(1)), prototype article or model, the design right subsists with no formality (s.213(1)). Design right therefore operates rather like artistic copyright, but free from the requirement of an original artistic work. However, the provisions whereby foreign creations may qualify for design right in the UK (ss.217, 221, 256) are much more limited than those for copyright. Designs qualify for design right if the designer, his or her employer or a commissioner for value is a qualifying individual or other qualifying legal person (ss.218, 219). A design will also qualify if it is first marketed in the UK, EC or another country to which the Act extends by a qualifying person who is exclusively authorised to market in the UK (s.220).

"Design" is defined as meaning any aspect of the internal or external shape or configuration of the whole or part of an article (s.213(2)). As for registered designs, design right is not available for a method or principle of construction (s.213(3)(a). Such principles are to be protected by patent, if at all. Also excluded from protection are features which enable the article to fit in, around or against another article so that either may perform its function—the so-called "must-fit" exclusion of s.213(3)(b)(i)—or which are dependant upon the appearance of another article of which the article in question is intended by its designer to form an integral part—the so-called "must-match" exception of s.213(3)(b)(ii). These exceptions ensure that motor spares are not protected by design right.[58] Subject to the exceptions, however, design right may subsist in functional design; there is no requirement of artistic merit or eye appeal.

The threshold of originality is somewhat higher than for copyright; s.213(4) states that a design is not original if it is commonplace in the design field in question at the time of its creation.

The rules for first ownership of design right mirror those for registered designs; the designer's right is displaced by that of his employer where the design was created in the course of employ-

[58] See *British Leyland* v. *Armstrong Patents* p. 661, *ante*, at n. 19.

ment. Both are displaced by the right of a person who has commissioned the design for value (s.215 and 263(1)). Like copyright, design right may be assigned prospectively, so that it vests in the assignee upon the creation of the design (s.223).

Design right may be assigned or transmitted as personal property (s.222). The assignment may be partial either in the sense of assignment for less than the whole term, or in the sense that the assignment relates to some but not all of the activities reserved to the design right holder (s.222(2)). Assignment of a registered design will carry a presumption that any unregistered design right subsisting in the same design is also assigned, in the absence of contrary intention (s.224).

Design right may be licensed; an exclusive licence in writing and signed by or on behalf of the design right owner gives the licensee rights of action for infringement which are concurrent with those of the right owner (ss.225, 234–5).

The duration of design right may be difficult for third parties to estimate. The right endures for the shorter of 15 years from the recording of the design *or* ten years from first marketing, anywhere in the world, by or with the licence of the design right owner: s.216. During the last five years of design right protection, licences are to be available as of right (s.237). There are also provisions for Crown use (s.240–4) and earlier licences of right when the monopolies and Mergers Commission have reported adversely upon the conduct of the right owner (s.238).

Infringement of design right

Like copyright, design right is infringed by copying without licence—by making articles to the design or by making a design document recording the design for the purpose of making the articles (s.226(1)). The copying can be direct or indirect; it does not matter if the process involves intermediate stages which do not infringe (s.226(4)). The infringing articles may be made exactly or substantially[59] to the design. Primary infringement may be effected either by doing these acts or by authorising[60] another to do them (s.226(3)).

[59] For "substantially" see p. 666, *ante*, on copyright infringement.
[60] For the meaning of "authorise" see *CBS* v. *Amstrad* p. 666, *ante* at n. 36.

Apart from these "primary" forms of infringement, there are also "secondary" infringements—importing or dealing with infringing articles (s.227). Such activities infringe if the actor knows or has reason to believe that the article is an infringing one. An "infringing article" (s.228) is one whose making infringed design right. Where an article has been imported into the UK or its import is proposed, the article is deemed to be "infringing" if its manufacture in the UK would have infringed design right or breached an exclusive licence agreement. Subs. 228(5) ensures that this provision cannot operate in contravention of European Community law. The definition of infringing *article* excludes design documents made in infringement of design right. The rules on subsistence and infringement of design right apply to kits as they do to assembled articles (s.260). The remedies for infringement of design right (ss.229–233) are modelled upon those for infringement of copyright.

It is not an infringement of design right to do anything which is an infringement of copyright (s.236). This provision may give rise to problems where copyright in a design document belongs to one person and design right to another. It would be wise for anyone commissioning a design or taking an assignment to contract for ownership of copyright in design documents or models.

Table 1 summarises the forms of protection which may be available for designs, subject, of course to satisfying the requirements of novelty, originality and connecting factor.

The Commission of the European Community is taking an interest in the harmonisation of design law; further changes to the law can be anticipated.

Table 1: protection for designs.

	Design features	
Article	shape or configuration*†‡	surface pattern/ ornament‡
Not artistic work, no eye appeal	design right	copyright in drawings
Not artistic but has eye appeal	design right, registered design	copyright in drawings, registered design

* not principle/method of construction
† not must-fit/function
‡ not must-match

Article	shape or configuration*†‡	surface pattern/ ornament‡
Artistic work e.g. work of artistic craftsmanship	(as right, plus design right (although copyright infringement takes precedence—s.236)	copyright in design drawings, copyright in article, registered design (if to be applied industrially)

* not principle/method of construction
† not must-fit/function
‡ not must-match

PART 11: BANKRUPTCY

CHAPTER 34

ARRANGEMENTS AND BANKRUPTCY

Introduction

When an individual gets into financial difficulties there are two alternative courses of conduct open to him. First he may seek to make some arrangement with his creditors. Secondly he may be made bankrupt. We will begin by looking at what is meant by an arrangement.[1]

ARRANGEMENTS

What can be done by an arrangement?

The only limit on what may be proposed by way of an arrangement is the limitation of human ingenuity. Some possible examples are

1. Debtor A. explains to his creditors that if he is made bankrupt they will receive nothing (because such assets as he has will be needed to pay the fees of the trustee in bankruptcy). He asks his creditors to accept 20p in the £ on the debts which he owes in full and final settlement of what he owes them.
2. Debtor B. has insufficient assets to pay his creditors, but his father offers to pay 50p in the £ of the debts owed if the creditors will accept such payment in full and final settlement.
3. Debtor C. is a sole trader who makes shoes. He believes that if he can keep paying his suppliers he will be able to trade out of his difficulties. Accordingly he asks his non-supplier creditors (*e.g.* local business rates, electricity, water, etc.) if they

[1] Bankruptcy and voluntary arrangements are governed by the Insolvency Act 1986 and the Insolvency Rules 1986. In this chapter all references are to the Insolvency Act 1986. Procedures referred to but not having a section reference as authority are to be found in the Insolvency Rules.

will allow him to defer paying them and instead to pay the supplier of raw materials to him in full so that he can carry on trading.

Types of arrangement

In any of the above examples, if all the creditors are prepared to agree, the arrangement becomes binding upon all of them and none can renege upon it.

A more formal method of settling financial difficulties is possible under the Deeds of Arrangement Act 1914 whereby an arrangement such as those detailed above could be agreed to. The Act was, however, of very limited use since an arrangement made under it was only binding upon those creditors who expressly agreed to it.

Both the Cork Committee (Cmnd. 8558) and the White Paper, a revised framework for insolvency law (Cmnd. 9175) stressed that there should be an alternative type of voluntary arrangement which could be used by individual debtors wishing to arrive at an arrangement with their creditors with the minimum of formality. Such an arrangement is possible now under the Insolvency Act 1986 and is termed a "voluntary arrangement" in the Act, though in the insolvency world it is generally referred to as an "individual voluntary arrangement" so as to distinguish it from a voluntary arrangement which has been entered into by a corporation.

The proposal

The debtor must prepare a proposal in which he explains the proposed arrangement, why it is believed to be desirable and why his creditors may be expected to agree to it. There must be an account of the assets which are to be included in the arrangement, including any assets to be provided by third parties and an account of the liabilities of the debtor. The proposal must then state how these liabilities are to be dealt with under the arrangement. This proposal must be submitted to an insolvency practitioner, the nominee. If the nominee agrees to act in seeking to get the creditors to agree to the arrangement, he must return a copy of the notice to the debtor endorsed with the date that he, the nominee, received it.

Interim orders

While the proposed arrangement is being negotiated, the debtor may apply to the court for an interim order the purpose of which is to protect his property (ss.253 and 255). The application must be accompanied by an affidavit setting out why the application has been made together with the endorsed copy of the notice of the proposed arrangement which had been given to and returned by the intended nominee. During the time that an application for an interim order is pending, the court may stay any legal process against the property or person of the debtor. Similarly, legal proceedings against him in any court may be stayed or allowed to continue on such terms as the court thinks fit (s.254). An interim order may be made where it will assist the consideration and implementation of the proposals of the debtor (s.255). An order may be made only if the court is satisfied that the debtor intends to make a proposal and that when he made the application he was either in a position to be able to petition for his own bankruptcy or was an undischarged bankrupt (s.255).

So long as an interim order is in force, there can be no bankruptcy petition presented against the debtor, nor can one which has already been presented be proceeded with. Similarly there can be no other legal proceedings or legal process proceeded with unless the court expressly permits. An interim order is essentially a short term expedient and comes automatically to an end 14 days after being made. This period may be extended at the request of either the nominee or the debtor (s.256).

Proceedings after an interim order

The nominee must report to the court at least two days before the expiration of the order. The report must indicate whether the nominee believes that a meeting of the creditors should be called to consider the proposed arrangement (s.256). The report must be placed on the court file and is available for inspection by any creditor. A copy must be sent to any creditor who has presented a bankruptcy petition against the debtor and, if the debtor is an undischarged bankrupt, a copy must go to the Official Receiver. If, after the report has been made, the court is satisfied that a meeting of creditors should be called to consider the proposal, the interim order will be extended so as to enable the meeting to be held. The meeting will take place between 14 and 28 days after the submission of the report by the nominee.

Considering the proposal

Whether or not an interim order has been made, the nominee must file a report in court stating whether or not in his opinion a meeting of creditors should be called to consider the proposal. So long as the court does not direct otherwise, the nominee must call the meeting to be held between 14 and 28 days after the filing of the report. Notice of the meeting must be sent to creditors at least 14 days before the day scheduled for the meeting and must identify the court at which the nominee's report was filed and set out the rules governing majorities at the meeting. Accompanying the notice must be a copy of the proposal and a copy or summary of the statement of affairs of the debtor, the nominee's comments on the proposal and a proxy form. Notice must be given to all creditors identified in the statement of affairs and also to any other creditors of whom the nominee is aware.

The function of the creditors' meeting is to decide whether or not to approve the debtor's proposals. It will usually be chaired by the nominee, though it may be chaired by an employee of the nominee or his firm who is experienced in insolvency matters or a nominated insolvency practitioner. To take effect, the arrangement must be approved by at least three-quarters in value of the creditors present, in person or by proxy, and voting. In the short period leading up to the holding of the meeting there is insufficient time for the creditors to prove their debts. There is obviously a risk in any insolvency proceedings that a creditor will exaggerate what he claims to be owed. Accordingly the chairman has an arbitrary power to admit or reject all or any part of a creditor's claim for the purpose of his entitlement to vote (s.259). The chairman must report to the court on the result of the meeting and a creditor may, within 28 days of this report, appeal to the court in respect of the decision by the chairman to accept or reject any particular claim. If the court is satisfied that what has happened results in unfair prejudice or a material irregularity it may order another meeting to be called or make such order as it thinks fit.

Every creditor who has been given notice of the meeting may vote either in person or by proxy. The amount on which the creditor may vote is usually the amount of the debt as at the date of the meeting. There is generally no entitlement to vote in respect of unliquidated debts or debts whose value is unascertained, though the chairman may allow an estimated value in this case. A secured creditor may vote only in respect of the unsecured part of his claim.

As has been said the proposal must be approved by a majority of threequarters in value of those creditors voting either in person or by proxy. Any other resolutions must be passed by a simple majority. However, a resolution cannot be passed if those persons voting against it include more than half in value of the creditors not associated with the debtor.

It is possible that the scheme may be approved with modifications. These may include the replacement of the nominee with another person who is an insolvency practitioner. A modification cannot be made unless the debtor consents to it. Similarly, there can be no proposal or modification to a proposal which affects the rights of a secured or preferential creditor unless such creditor agrees (s.258).

After the meeting the chairman must prepare a report which must be filed with the court within four days. He must send a notice of the result of the meeting to all persons to whom he had sent notice of the meeting. This must detail whether or not the proposal was accepted and any modifications which were made to it. It must also specify which creditors voted at the meeting and how they voted. If the meeting declines to approve the proposal, the court may discharge any interim order at that time in force (s.259).

The effect of approval

If the meeting approves the proposed voluntary arrangement, it takes effect as from the date of the meeting. Every person to whom notice had been given of the meeting and who was entitled to vote is bound by the arrangement. This is irrespective of how he may have voted (s.260).

In cases where the debtor is an undischarged bankrupt, the court may either annul the bankruptcy or give such directions as to the conduct of the bankruptcy and the administration of the bankrupt's estate as is thought appropriate to facilitate the implementation of the arrangement (s.261).

Within the 28 days beginning with the day on which the report of the creditors' meeting was made to the court, an application may be made challenging the decision. Such application must be on the ground that the arrangement unfairly prejudices the interest of a creditor or that there has been some material irregularity at or in relation to the meeting. The objection can be raised by the debtor, by a person entitled to vote at the meeting, by the nominee or any person who has replaced him, or, if the debtor is an undischarged bankrupt, by either the trustee of his estate or the Official Receiver.

If the challenge is upheld, the court may revoke or suspend the approval of the arrangement or may give such directions as it thinks fit for the calling of a further meeting of creditors to consider any revised proposal. If the court finds that there has been some material irregularity in regard to the meeting, it may direct that the meeting should be reconvened to reconsider the original proposal. If, having ordered that a further meeting of creditors be summoned, the court becomes satisfied that the debtor has no intention of submitting a revised proposal, it will revoke the order for the meeting and also revoke or suspend any approval which may have been given at the previous meeting. When a further meeting is ordered, the court has the power to continue any existing interim order (s.262).

The supervisor

Once a proposal has been approved and is free from the risk of challenge, the nominee becomes known as the supervisor (s.263). He must be put in possession of all assets which are included in the arrangement and, if the debtor is an undischarged bankrupt, the supervisor must discharge all fees, costs and expenses of the trustee and of the Official Receiver. In general terms the supervisor is under the supervision of the court. He may apply to the court for directions in relation to any matter arising under the arrangement. If any person, including the debtor or any creditor, becomes dissatisfied as a result of anything done or not done by the supervisor, he also may apply to the court which may make such order as it thinks fit to remedy the problem complained of (s.263).

The supervisor must keep proper accounts and records of his transactions. At least once every 12 months he must prepare an abstract of all receipts and payments by him, and within two months of this a copy of this account must be sent to the court, to the debtor, and to those creditors who are bound by the arrangement.

Within 28 days of the completion of the arrangement, the supervisor must send a notice to the effect that the arrangement has been fully implemented in accordance with the proposals to the court, to the debtor, to all creditors bound by the arrangement, and to the Secretary of State. The notice must be accompanied by a report summarising all receipts and payments made by the supervisor and explaining any differences which may have occurred as between the proposal which was approved by the creditors' meeting and its actual implementation.

BANKRUPTCY

Introduction

If an arrangement cannot be arrived at, the only other way of resolving a debtor's problems will be bankruptcy. The procedure is today very much simpler than it was under the Bankruptcy Act 1914. No longer is there need to show an act of bankruptcy or to apply for a receiving order. If an application is made by a creditor, he simply serves a statutory demand upon the debtor requiring him to pay or secure the debt owed within 21 days. If the debtor does not do this, the creditor may petition the court for a bankruptcy order.

The bankruptcy petition

Bankruptcy proceedings are commenced with a petition to the court for the making of a bankruptcy order. The petition can be presented by

(a) a creditor,
(b) the supervisor of a voluntary arrangement or any person other than the debtor bound by such an arrangement,
(c) the Director of Public Prosecutions,
(d) the debtor himself (s.264).

These will now be considered in more detail.

A creditor's petition

For a creditor to succeed with his application for a bankruptcy petition, he must establish the inability of the debtor to pay his debts. This can be established by proving either that a statutory demand served upon the debtor requiring him to pay or secure his debt to the satisfaction of the petitioner has not been complied with within the 21 days allowed or that enforcement of a judgment debt owing by the debtor to the petitioner has been unsuccessful (s.268). The petition based upon the statutory demand will allege that the debtor appears either to be unable to pay or to have no reasonable prospects of paying the debts specified in the petition (s.267).

As well as establishing the inability to pay debts, the following conditions must be met if the petitioner is to be successful:

(a) the debtor must be either domiciled or personally present in England and Wales at the time of presentation of the petition (s.265);
(b) the debt must be for at least £750 and the liquidated sum must be payable immediately or at some certain future time (s.267);
(c) the debt must be unsecured (s.269);
(d) there must be no application pending for the setting aside of the statutory demand on which the petition is based (s.267).

There are three circumstances where the court may dismiss a petition:

(a) if satisfied that the debtor is able to pay all his debts;
(b) if the petitioner has unreasonably refused to accept an offer of the debtor made pursuant to the statutory demand. In this regard, refusal by a creditor to agree to an offer of an arrangement does not amount to an unreasonable refusal: *Re A Debtor (No. 2389 of 1989), ex parte Travel & General Insurance Co. plc* v. *The Debtor* [1990] 3 All E.R. 984;
(c) if otherwise the court regards it as appropriate to do so because of some breach of the rules or for any other reason.

Additionally there are three instances when the court must dismiss the petition:

(a) if the statutory demand has been fully complied with;

(b) if the debtor has been able to establish a reasonable prospect of being able to pay the debt;
(c) if the petition should not have been presented under the Act because the debtor did not satisfy the domicile or residence requirements (s.271).

Petition by supervisor of or person bound by voluntary arrangement

There are two grounds on which such a person may petition:

(a) that the debtor has failed to comply with his obligations under the arrangement or has failed to do such things as have been reasonably required of him by the supervisor;
(b) that the debtor has supplied false or misleading information in his statement of affairs or any other document or at a creditors' meeting (s.276).

Petition by Director of Public Prosecutions

The DPP may petition in his capacity as official petitioner under the Powers of Criminal Courts Act 1973. The power is exercisable against a person who has been convicted of an offence where a loss has occurred in excess of a specified amount. Such an application may only be made if it is considered to be in the public interest (s.277).

Petition by the debtor

The debtor may petition only on the ground that he is unable to pay his debts. The petition must be accompanied by a statement of affairs giving full details of his financial position (s.272). Generally a bankruptcy order will follow automatically from such a petition, though in one instance this is not so. If the following conditions are satisfied the making of a bankruptcy order is not automatic:

(a) the debtor's unsecured debts are below the small bankruptcies level (£20,000);
(b) the value of his assets is at least equal to the minimum amount (£2,000);
(c) during the five years prior to the presentation of the petition the debtor had not been adjudged bankrupt or made any arrangement with his creditors (s.273).

If these criteria are satisfied, and if the court thinks it appropriate, it may appoint a qualified insolvency practitioner to look into the debtor's affairs and report on the possibility of a voluntary arrangement. If the insolvency practitioner feels that meetings of creditors should be summoned for this purpose he will go ahead and do so unless directed otherwise by the court. The proceedings then follow those described above for the implementation of a voluntary arrangement (s.274).

The bankruptcy order

On the making of the order, the debtor becomes an undischarged bankrupt. As such he is deprived of the ownership of his property and must give possession of his estate to the Official Receiver. He must do all things which may reasonably be expected of him to protect property not in his possession or to enable such property to be recovered. He must give the Official Receiver such information as may be required of him (s.291). The Official Receiver or the trustee in bankruptcy may apply to the court at any time to question the bankrupt. If he fails to appear the court may order his arrest and the seizure of any books, papers, records, goods or money (s.366). While undischarged, the bankrupt cannot sit in the House of Lords or the House of Commons (s.371).

As a general rule, the Official Receiver becomes the receiver and manager of the estate of the bankrupt pending the appointment of a trustee in bankruptcy as soon as the bankruptcy order is made (s.287). There are, however, a number of instances where this does not apply:

1. in a small bankruptcy, when a certificate of summary administration is issued, the Official Receiver usually becomes the trustee immediately on the making of the order. So long as the debtor's unsecured debts are below the small bankruptcies level (£20,000) and during the five years prior to the presentation of the petition he had not been adjudged bankrupt or made an arrangement with his creditors, the court may issue a certificate of summary administration (s.275). In the case of a small bankruptcy, the duty of the Official Receiver to investigate the affairs of the bankrupt is dis-

cretionary (s.289). Discharge from a small bankruptcy is two years after the making of the order (s.279).

2. In a criminal bankruptcy, the Official Receiver becomes trustee as soon as the bankruptcy order is made (s.297).
3. If, following a debtor's petition, an insolvency practitioner has been appointed to look into the possibility of an arrangement with creditors but such arrangement has not been reached and instead a bankruptcy order has been made, the court will appoint the insolvency practitioner as trustee (s.297).
4. If the bankruptcy order results from non-compliance with an arrangement, the supervisor of the arrangement may be appointed trustee at the time of the making of the order (s.297).

Having taken up post as receiver and manager of the estate of the bankrupt, the Official Receiver enjoys all the powers of a receiver and manager appointed by the High Court. He can sell any goods which are perishable or may diminish in value if not sold. Additionally, he can take all necessary steps for the protection of the property of the debtor. However, he must not incur any expense without consent from the Secretary of State (s.287). While acting as receiver and manager, the Official Receiver must investigate the conduct and affairs of the bankrupt. In this regard he must consider matters before the making of the bankruptcy order as well as after. He need only report on his investigation if he thinks fit. Any report which he does make is prima facie evidence of the matters stated therein (s.289).

A statement of affairs must be prepared by the bankrupt and submitted to the receiver within 21 days of the order. If the bankruptcy order is as a result of the debtor's own petition, this does not apply since, of course, he will have submitted the statement with his petition. It is open to the Official Receiver to dispense with the need for a statement of affairs in appropriate circumstances (s.288).

At any time between the bankruptcy order and the discharge, the Official Receiver may apply to the court for the public examination of the bankrupt. Not only can he make the decision of his own motion, but also creditors being owed more than half in value of the bankrupt's debts can require him to do so. If an examination is ordered, the bankrupt must attend and answer questions relating to his affairs, dealings, property and the cause of his failure. Failure to do so without reasonable excuse is contempt of court. Questions can be asked of him by the Official Receiver, the official petitioner (in criminal bankruptcy matters), the trustee in bankruptcy and any creditor who has proved his debt (s.290).

The creditors may appoint a creditors' committee unless the Official Receiver is to be the trustee in which case the functions exercisable by the committee will be exercised by the Secretary of State (s.301).

The trustee in bankruptcy

The administration of the estate of the bankrupt is done by a trustee in bankruptcy, who must be an insolvency practitioner unless the Official Receiver is acting as trustee.

Appointment of the trustee

In cases where the Official Receiver becomes receiver and manager following the making of the bankruptcy order, he must, within 12 weeks, decide whether to call a creditors' meeting for the purpose of appointing a trustee in bankruptcy (s.293). The meeting itself must be held within four months of the making of the bankruptcy order. If a quarter in value of the creditors request the Official Receiver to call a creditors' meeting, he must do so. Notification of the meeting must be sent to the court and notice must be given to every creditor referred to in the statement of affairs or known to the Official Receiver as at 21 days prior to the date of the meeting. The notice must be accompanied by a proxy form and a form for the proof of debt.

The object of the first meeting of creditors is to appoint a trustee and to set up a creditors' committee. If no such committee is established, the meeting may also consider on what basis the trustee should be remunerated. The chairman of the meeting is the Official Receiver or someone nominated by him. Voting is in accordance with the level of debt owed to a creditor and the chairman may admit or reject all or part of a creditor's claim for the purpose of voting. Before a creditor can vote, he must have lodged a proof of debt which has been admitted by the chairman. A creditor whose debt is unliquidated can only vote if the chairman estimates a minimum value.

Voting is by way of the value of debt owed, and a simple majority in value of those present and voting or voting by proxy is sufficient to pass a resolution. The person appointed as trustee must confirm in writing that he is qualified and willing to act as trustee to the chairman of the meeting. The appointment is then certified by the chairman. The certificate is filed by the Official Receiver in court and it is then returned to him with the date endorsed upon it for handing to the trustee (s.292).

In limited circumstances the appointment of the trustee may be done by the court:

(a) in the case of a summary administration, the court may appoint someone other than the Official Receiver to be the trustee;
(b) where the bankruptcy order follows a report to the court by an insolvency practitioner following a petition by the debtor himself, the insolvency practitioner may be appointed as trustee;
(c) if a bankruptcy order is made at a time when a voluntary arrangement is in force, the supervisor of the arrangement may be appointed (s.297).

In certain instances the Secretary of State may appoint the trustee at the instigation of the Official Receiver:

(a) where no appointment has been made at the creditors' meeting (s.295);
(b) where the Official Receiver is acting as trustee (s.296);
(c) where there is a vacancy in the office of trustee and a creditors' meeting has not been held (s.300).

In a criminal bankruptcy, the Official Receiver is the trustee from the time of the making of the order (s.297).

The role of the trustee

It is the duty of the trustee to get in the estate of the bankrupt and then, having realised it into cash, to distribute it amongst the creditors. The powers enjoyed by the trustee in realising the estate are extremely wide. He has the same power of disposal of property of the bankrupt as is enjoyed by the bankrupt himself (s.311). He can require the production of any books, papers, documents or records relating to the affairs of the bankrupt (s.312). He also has power to apply to the court for an order to force the bankrupt to do any act necessary for the administration of the estate (s.363).

There are certain things which the trustee may do with the sanction of the creditors' committee. These include:

(a) carrying on the business of the bankrupt;
(b) bringing or defending legal proceedings in relation to the property of the bankrupt;
(c) accepting a promise of a future payment following the sale of the bankrupt's property;
(d) mortgaging or pledging assets in order to raise money;
(e) making payments in order to acquire any rights or options for the benefit of creditors;
(f) compromising debts due to the estate (Schedule 5).

Disclaimer of onerous property

Onerous property is any property which is likely to cost more to retain than is likely to be gained by its retention. It includes unprofitable contracts, unsaleable property and property which may give rise to a liability to spend money or perform onerous acts. Disclaimer results in the determination of all rights liabilities and interests of the bankrupt in the property. A person suffering loss as a result of disclaimer can claim and prove against the estate of the bankrupt for the value of the loss sustained (s.315). Where a lease is disclaimed, a copy of the notice of disclaimer must be served upon every person who claims under the bankrupt as a mortgagee or underlessee. That person has 14 days to apply to the court for an order vesting the property in himself or in some other person (s.317).

Removal and resignation of a trustee

Generally removal of a trustee is by order of the court or by a general meeting of creditors called for that purpose.

There are three instances where the power to call a creditors' meeting is limited. In these cases, the meeting may be called only if the trustee agrees, or if the court directs, or if one quarter in value request the meeting. These instances are:

(a) where the Official Receiver is acting as trustee as a result of the failure by the creditors to make an appointment;
(b) where the appointment of the trustee was made by the court other than during the currency of a voluntary arrangement; and
(c) where the appointment was made by the Secretary of State.

A trustee cannot be removed by a meeting of the creditors in the case of a summary administration. A trustee appointed by the Secretary of State can be removed by him (s.298).

A trustee may resign on the grounds of ill health, retirement from practice, conflict of interest or any change in personal circumstances which makes it impracticable for him to continue in office. When he resigns a creditors' meeting must be called. If the release is accepted by the meeting, the chairman must send a copy of the resolution and a certificate to the Official Receiver within three days. If the creditors do not accept the resignation, it is open to the trustee to apply to the court which will then deal with the matter as it thinks fit.

A trustee vacates office if he becomes unqualified to act as a trustee in the bankruptcy. He also vacates office if the bankruptcy is annulled (s.298).

Release of the trustee

The effect of release is to discharge the trustee from all personal liability in respect of anything done or not done in the administration of the estate (s.299). Liability may, however, be imposed upon him for misfeasance, breach of trust or breach of duty (s.304). The Official Receiver is released when he notifies the court that he has been released by a nominee of the creditors or of the Secretary of State. In a case where the trustee has finished his administration of the estate and there is no resolution of the creditors against the release at their final meeting, the trustee is released from the time when he notifies the court of the decision of the meeting.

Assets in the bankruptcy

The Trustee's Title

An object of bankruptcy is to divide the assets of the bankrupt between his creditors. The assets which are available for this purpose are those assets of which he was possessed at the commencement of the bankruptcy. This is the date of the making of the bankruptcy order (s.278). This may be different from the date when the property vests in the trustee, since this occurs only when his appointment takes effect. If the Official Receiver is trustee, the property vests at the time of his becoming trustee (s.306). The vesting of property in the trustee occurs automatically. There is generally no need for any legal formalities to be complied with in connection with the vesting of the property (s.306). Property belonging to the bankrupt and situated abroad may require formalities to be complied with under the overseas law and the trustee can require the bankrupt to take such steps as are necessary to effect the vesting of the property.

Avoidance of dispositions after the presentation of the petition

Any disposition of property by the bankrupt or payment of money by him subsequent to the presentation of the petition is void unless it is approved by the court either before or after it was effected. Should the court not approve the transaction, the person to whom any money has been paid or property transferred will hold it as part of the estate of the debtor. Quite clearly this may cause hardship if a third party deals with the debtor without being aware that a petition in bankruptcy has been presented against him. Accordingly the Act gives protection to such a person so long as he dealt in good faith, for value and without notice that the petition had been presented (s.284). This protection applies only to transactions made prior to the commencement of the bankruptcy. With one exception, it does not apply to transactions after the order. This exception is where the bankrupt has incurred a debt to a banker in circumstances where the banker had no notice of the bankruptcy and it is not reasonably practicable to recover the payment from the person to whom it was made. This means that if the banker of the bankrupt honours a cheque drawn by the bankrupt after the making of the order he may be treated as an unsecured creditor in the bankruptcy (notwithstanding that the payment was made after the order) so long as he was not aware of the bankruptcy order and provided that it is not reasonably practicable to recover the payment from the person to whom it was made (s.284).

Property available in the bankruptcy

The estate available in the bankruptcy consists of "all property belonging to or vested in the bankrupt at the commencement of the bankruptcy" (s.283). Property includes "money, goods, things in action, land and every description of property wherever situated, and also obligations and every description of interest, whether present or future or vested or contingent, arising out of, or incidental to, property" (s.346).

Certain items are excluded from the estate of the trustee. These are the tools, books, vehicles and other items of equipment necessary for him for use personally in his employment or business and also such personal and household items as are necessary to meet the basic domestic needs of the bankrupt and his family. Any property held on trust by the bankrupt is excluded from his estate (s.283).

In the case of any property which the bankrupt may be permitted to retain under these provisions, it is open to the trustee to serve a notice upon him pursuant to which the property will be sold and replaced by a cheaper substitute. Thus if a bankrupt dines from a valuable Chippendale table, the trustee may order the sale of that item. From the proceeds of sale, the first payment must go to obtaining a suitable alternative substitute. The balance goes into the bankrupt's estate.

Income payments order

It is possible that a bankrupt will continue in employment or continue to be self-employed. In either of these circumstances the trustee can request the court to make an income payments order. This will require the bankrupt's employer or the bankrupt himself to make payments to the trustee out of the income of the bankrupt (s.310). The bankrupt must be given notice of the hearing and, at least seven days before the hearing is due, he must be notified that he must attend unless he gives his consent in writing to the order which is sought. Before making an order, the court must ensure that there is sufficient remaining from his income to meet the reasonable domestic needs of both the bankrupt and his family (s.310).

Recovery of property not in possession of the bankrupt

The role of the trustee is to get in the property of the bankrupt for the benefit of his creditors. It has already been seen that the property available to the creditors is that in the possession of the bankrupt at the time of the making of the order. This, however, was complicated by the fact that certain of his property could be retained by the bankrupt himself. Conversely, property which is not in the possession of the bankrupt may be claimed by the trustee for the benefit of the creditors. Property falling under this category will now be considered.

Preferences

A preference is any payment made or security given by a debtor which has the effect of putting a creditor in a better position than he would have enjoyed had that thing not been done. For a trustee successfully to challenge a preference he must show that the debtor was insolvent at the time when it was made and that in making it he was influenced by a desire to put the creditor in the better position just referred to. Any such preference made within the six months prior to the presentation of the petition may be upset at the instigation of the trustee. In the case of the transaction being in favour of an associate of the debtor, the period for setting aside is extended to two years prior to the presentation of the petition. An associate is the bankrupt's spouse or former or reputed spouse and, in relation to such a person, a brother, sister, uncle, aunt, nephew, niece, lineal ancester or lineal descendant, including children of the half blood, stepchildren and adopted children. In this regard illegitimate children are treated as legitimate children (s.435). If a preference is made in favour of an associate, the desire to produce the putting of the creditor in a better position is presumed (s.340).

Transactions at an undervalue

A transaction at an undervalue is one where the bankrupt parted with assets:

(a) as a gift;
(b) in circumstances where he received no consideration;
(c) in circumstances where the consideration he received was significantly less than that which he had provided;
(d) where the transaction was in consideration of marriage (s.339).

If such a transaction was entered into in the five years prior to the presentation of the petition, the trustees can apply to the court for an order which will have the result of restoring the parties to their original positions (ss.341 and 342).

For a transaction at an undervalue to be upset, it must be shown that the debtor was insolvent at the time it was made.

Transactions to defraud creditors

An application may be made to the court for the setting aside of any transaction entered into with the intention to defraud creditors. Two matters must be proved, first that a transaction has been entered into at an undervalue, and secondly that this was done with the intention of putting assets beyond the reach of actual or potential creditors. This is a general power in insolvency not exclusively limited to bankruptcy and an application to the court can be made not only by the trustee in bankruptcy but also by any person prejudiced by such a transaction provided that the consent of the court is obtained for the application (s.424). If such an action is successful the court can order the revesting of the property concerned and order payments to be made by persons who have benefited from the transaction. Proceedings cannot be taken against the third party acting bona fide and for value (s.425).

At first sight these provisions look remarkably like the power to avoid a transaction at an undervalue. However there are significant differences. A transaction to defraud creditors can be satisfied regardless of how long before the petition was entered into. A transaction at an undervalue can be set aside only if entered into within the five years prior to the petition. For a transaction to be set aside as one entered into to defraud creditors, the intention to defraud must be established. There is no need to show a state of mind for the setting aside of a transaction at an undervalue. Persons prejudiced by a transaction to defraud creditors may take proceedings to have it set aside. Only the trustee in bankruptcy can challenge a transaction at an undervalue.

Extortionate credit transactions

The trustee can apply to the court for an order in respect of an extortionate credit bargain entered into by the bankrupt in the three years prior to the making of the bankruptcy order. (Note here that the base line from which he works back is the making of the order, not the presentation of the petition.) As in the Consumer Credit Act 1974 an extortionate credit bargain is one which either is grossly exorbitant or grossly contravenes the ordinary principles of fair dealing. When a challenge is made, there is a presumption that the credit bargain was extortionate. Thus it is for the provider of the credit to establish the acceptability of the transaction. Anything recovered as a result of such an action forms part of the estate of the bankrupt (s.343).

Avoidance of general assignments of book debts

A general assignment of existing or future book debts by a person engaged in a business is void against the trustee in bankruptcy unless:

(a) the debts assigned were paid prior to the bankruptcy petition being presented;
(b) the general assignment was registered under the Bills of Sale Act 1878 as though it were not an assignment by way of security under the rules modifying the 1878 Act;
(c) the assignment relates to debts becoming due under specified contracts;
(d) the assignment was of book debts due at the date of assignment from specified debtors;
(e) the assignment forms part of a transfer of a business, in good faith and for value; or
(f) the assignment was an assignment of assets to the benefit of creditors generally (s.344).

Execution creditors

A creditor who has levied execution against the goods or land of the debtor may not retain the benefit of the execution unless, at the commencement of the bankruptcy, the execution was complete. In other words the proceeds of sale by the sheriff must have been handed over to the judgment creditor. If goods have been taken in execution by a sheriff, and before completing execution the sheriff is notified of a bankruptcy order, he must deliver the goods to the Official Receiver or Trustee in bankruptcy on request. He is entitled to a retention for his costs as a first charge on the subject matter of the execution. Where the sheriff levies execution under a judgment for more than £500 and goods are sold, the sheriff must retain the balance for 14 days. If during that time he is notified of the petition upon which a bankruptcy order is made, he may not dispose of the balance until either the 14 days have expired or for so long as the petition of which he is notified is pending, whichever is the later. If the bankruptcy order is made pursuant to that petition, the balance must be paid to the Official Receiver or the trustee in bankruptcy. Once again this is subject to a retention for the costs of the sheriff (s.346).

Distress by landlords

A landlord or any other person entitled to rent may levy distress for six months' rent due prior to the commencement of the bankruptcy. As a general rule this right can be exercised notwithstanding that the estate has vested in the trustee in bankruptcy. There are two exceptions to this. If the distress is against a lessee in respect of whom there is a bankruptcy petition outstanding and a bankruptcy order is subsequently made, the distress is effective only for rent payable for the six month period prior to the bankruptcy order. Distress for any period after that time is ineffective. Similarly if there are insufficient assets to pay preferential creditors in full, the landlord must surrender goods or money resulting from the distress to the trustee. The person surrendering the goods in this case will rank as a preferential creditor.

If the landlord does not distrain he can, of course, claim as an unsecured creditor, as he can in respect of rent arising outside the period in respect of which the distraint relates (s.347).

The family home

Under the Matrimonial Homes Act 1983, a spouse who is not the legal owner of the matrimonial home enjoys certain rights of occupation which can be registered as a charge against the property. Such a charge can be removed only by a court order. These provisions are extended so as to give a spouse a right of occupation after the bankruptcy of the other spouse.

To seek to realise the interest of the bankrupt in the home, there are five factors to which the court must have regard:

(a) the interests of the creditors;
(b) whether the spouse's conduct has contributed to the bankruptcy;
(c) the needs and resources of the spouse;
(d) the needs of any children of the family;
(e) all relevant circumstances (but not the needs of the bankrupt).

If the application to realise the interest of the bankrupt is made more than a year after the vesting of the property of the trustee in bankruptcy, the interests of the creditors must be paramount.

If the home is jointly owned by the bankrupt and his spouse, any application under s.30, Law of Property Act 1925, to realise the interest of the bankrupt in the home must be made to the court dealing with the bankruptcy and is subject to the discretionary factors just described (s.336).

If the bankrupt has a beneficial interest in his home and there are children living there, he cannot be evicted without an order of the court. The children must be under the age of 18 and have been living at the house both at the time of the presentation of the petition and at the time of the making of the order. The court may also grant an order permitting the bankrupt to reoccupy the home if it happens that he is not in occupation. The rights enjoyed by the bankrupt in this regard are a charge on the share in the home held by the trustee. Once again the powers of the court are discretionary and it may make such order as it thinks "just and reasonable" having regard to

(a) the interests of the creditors;
(b) the financial resources of the bankrupt;
(c) the needs of the children;

(d) all relevant circumstances (but not the needs of the bankrupt) (s.337).

The distribution of the estate

Proof of Debts

As a general rule, any claim by a creditor may be proved as a debt against the estate of a bankrupt. This is so whether a claim is present or future, certain or contingent, ascertained or unascertained.

There are four debts which may not be proved:

(a) any fine imposed for an offence;
(b) any obligation which arises as a result of an order made in matrimonial proceedings;
(c) any obligation which arises pursuant to a confiscation order made under section 1 of the Drug Trafficking Offences Act 1986;
(d) any debt which may not be proved by virtue of any rule of law.

The creditor must submit a claim in writing to the trustee (or to the Official Receiver in a case where he is acting as receiver and manager). The proof must be in a form laid down by the Insolvency Rules. This, however, is not necessary where the creditor is a Minister of the Crown or a Government Department.

The form must

(a) be signed by or on behalf of the creditor,
(b) state the creditor's name and address,
(c) detail the amount claimed, giving particulars of whether this includes any outstanding uncapitalised interest or VAT,
(d) state whether the debt or any part of it is preferential,
(e) give details of how and when the debt was incurred,
(f) identify any security held by the creditor,
(g) give details of any documents which can be referred to for substantiating the claim.

The trustee may require a claim to be verified by affidavit. He may also value any debt the amount of which is uncertain and admit the proof at his valuation (s.322). Where he does this the creditor may appeal to the court (s.303).

Each creditor who has been identified in the statement of affairs must be sent the necessary form for the purpose of proving his debt.

Upon appointment, the trustee will have the Official Receiver hand to him any proofs in his possession. He must then allow them to be inspected by the bankrupt, or by any proving creditor or his representative at all reasonable times on any business day.

The trustee may admit proof for dividend either in whole or in part. If he decides to reject a proof or any part of it he must give the creditor a written statement of his reasons. The creditor has then 21 days from receiving this statement to make an application to the court for a variation of the decision of the trustee. The bankrupt himself also has a right of appeal to the court against any decision of the trustee to admit or reject any proof. This right is also enjoyed by any creditor. In either case the application must be made to the court within 21 days of the bankrupt or the creditor becoming aware of the decision of the trustee.

A proof can at any time be withdrawn or varied by the creditor with the consent of the trustee. It may also be expunged or varied by the court if the trustee can show that the proof was improperly admitted or should be reduced.

Secured Creditors

A secured creditor who has realised his security may deduct the amount so realised and then prove for the balance of the debt. Alternatively, he may surrender the security and then prove for the whole of the debt as though it were unsecured. For the purpose of proof, a secured creditor must value his security though, with the consent of the trustee or the court, he may vary his valuation at any time.

The trustee may at any time give 28 days' notice to the creditor that it is his intention to redeem the security at the value placed upon it by the creditor. When this happens, the creditor has 21 days within which he may make a revaluation.

If the creditor at any time should realise his security, the amount realised must be substituted for the value which was previously estimated by the creditor. For all purposes, the realised value will then be treated as an amended valuation made by the creditor.

The secured creditor may at any time require the trustee to decide whether or not he is going to redeem the security at the creditor's valuation. Where a creditor puts the trustee on election in this way, the trustee has six months in which he must make his decision.

Set-off

In any case where there are mutual debts, mutual credits or other mutual dealings between the bankrupt and a creditor, a right of set-off arises. It is not possible to contract out of the right of set-off, though a debt due to a creditor may not be set-off if at the time that the debt became due the creditor was aware that a bankruptcy petition was pending (s.323).

Distribution of the estate

General Principles

Having called in the estate of the bankrupt, the trustee must then distribute it. The first payment out is the expenses which arise as a result of the bankruptcy (s.324). These include the court fees arising as a result of the bankruptcy petition, any fees due to the Official Receiver, all expenses properly chargeable or incurred by the Official Receiver or the trustee in acting in connection with the estate and the remuneration of any person who has been employed by the trustee.

Payment to creditors is by way of a dividend. Before paying any dividend, the trustee must make allowances for claims which, for geographical reasons, may take some time to reach him. He must also allow for claims which have yet to be determined and disputed proofs. A creditor who proves late cannot upset a dividend which has already been paid (s.325). It is possible for the trustee, with the consent of the creditors' committee, to make a distribution *in specie* in a case where property in the estate cannot be readily or advantageously sold (s.326).

Payment of Dividends

The trustee must give notice to the creditors that he intends to declare a dividend (s.324). This includes all creditors who have yet to prove their claims. These creditors must be given at least 21 days in which to lodge their proofs. The notice must state the intention of the trustee to declare a dividend within four months of the last stated date for submission of proof. The proof of every creditor must then be dealt with by the trustee within seven days of the last date for proof. Any claim lodged after the expiration of the 21 day period can be admitted at the discretion of the trustee.

Notice of the dividend must be given to all creditors who have proved and must give details of realisations, payments made by the trustee, amounts retained by the trustee, the amount to be distributed and the rate of the dividend. There must also be an indication as to whether any further dividend may be expected. This notice may be given at the same time as the dividend is paid, and the payment may be made by post or in any other way which has been agreed with any particular creditor.

It is possible that, following the payment of a dividend, a creditor may increase the amount which he is claiming in his proof. If he does this and the proof is admitted, his increased claim will take priority over other creditors when the time comes for the payment of a further dividend. Conversely if there has been any overpayment to a creditor, this must be returned to the trustee.

The final distribution

When the trustee has done as much as he reasonably can to realise the estate without drawing out the proceedings needlessly he must contact all creditors to notify them either as to the final dividend or to state that there will not be a final dividend paid. This notice must then give a final date for the proof of any claims (s.330).

In any case where the trustee in bankruptcy is not the Official Receiver, there must be held a final meeting of creditors. At this meeting the creditors receive a report from the trustee about the conduct of his administration of the estate and must consider whether the trustee should be released (s.331). This final meeting may not be held if part of the estate of the bankrupt includes an interest in a dwelling house which is occupied by the bankrupt or his spouse and where the trustee has been unable to sell, unless the court imposes a charge on the house for the benefit of the house or the court has refused to impose a charge or the Secretary of State certifies that an application for a charge would be inappropriate (s.332).

Priority of debts

After the payment of the expenses of the estate, the debts are paid in the following order. The debts in a particular class are only payable if the debts in the classes ranking in priority have been paid in full.

Specially preferred creditors

If an articled clerk or an apprentice has paid a fee for his training, the trustee may repay a sum in respect of the unexpired period of training (s.348).

Preferential creditors

The preferential creditors are those entitled to

1. PAYE deductions relating to the 12 months prior to the making of the bankruptcy order;
2. 12 months' deductions of payments in respect of subcontractors in the construction industry prior to the making of the order;
3. VAT owing for the six months prior to the making of the order;
4. car tax, general betting duty, bingo duty, gaming licence duty, amounts of any agents' liability for general betting and pool betting duty in respect of collected stakes for 12 months prior to the making of the order;
5. national insurance contributions for the 12 months prior to the making of the order;
6. state and occupational pension scheme contributions owing;
7. arrears of wages or salary for employees for the four months prior to the making of the order, with an upper limit here of £800 per employee;
8. any accrued holiday pay;
9. any advances by a third party for the payment of salary or wages or holiday pay;
10. any money ordered to be paid for defaults in the Reserve Forces (Safeguard Employment) Act 1985;
11. any other debts which are declared preferential by any other enactment (s.387 and s.386).

If there are insufficient funds to pay all the preferential claims in full, they abate equally.

Ordinary creditors

After payment of the preferential creditors, the ordinary creditors are paid. These include trade creditors, all rates and taxes which are not preferential and in particular all assessed taxes (s.328).

Statutory interest

If any surplus remains after all the claims have been met, interest must be paid as from the date of the making of the bankruptcy order. The rate of interest shall be the greater of

(a) that applicable under section 17 of the Judgments Act 1838, and
(b) the rate of interest the bankrupt would have had to pay in respect of the debt had he not been adjudicated bankrupt (s.328).

Transactions between spouses

If the spouse of the bankrupt has a provable debt which arises as a result of credit provided for the bankrupt, this debt ranks after all other debts have been paid (s.329).

Surplus

Any surplus must then be handed to the bankrupt (s.330).

Duration of the bankruptcy

The bankruptcy lasts from the day on which the bankruptcy order is made and continues until the time of discharge (s.278).

In the case of a summary administration, discharge occurs automatically two years after the making of the bankruptcy order.

In the case of a criminal bankruptcy or in any case where the debtor had been an undischarged bankrupt during the 15 years prior to the making of the present bankruptcy order, discharge can only be obtained by means of a court order. When the bankrupt makes an application for discharge in such a case, he must give notice to the Official Receiver and deposit with him any sum which the Official Receiver may require to cover the costs of the application. At least 42 days' notice of the hearing must be given to both the Official Receiver and the bankrupt and, at least 14 days prior to the date set for the hearing, the Official Receiver must give notice of it to the trustee and also to any creditor who still has an outstanding claim against the estate.

At least 21 days before the date of the hearing the Official Receiver must submit a report to the court detailing

1. any failure by the bankrupt to comply with his obligations under the Act;
2. the circumstances surrounding the bankruptcy in respect of which a discharge is sought and also any previous bankruptcies;
3. the extent to which the bankrupt's liabilities have exceeded his assets in both the present and any previous bankruptcies;
4. details of any distribution made or expected to be made to creditors in the present bankruptcy;
5. any other matters which the Official Receiver feels should be brought to the attention of the court.

At the hearing, the Official Receiver, the trustee and any creditor may appear and make representations and put any questions to the bankrupt as the court may permit. It is open to the court to grant the discharge or to make any other order it thinks fit in relation to the bankruptcy. These orders will include refusing the discharge, the suspension of the discharge, or the granting of the discharge subject to the conditions as to how future income or property must be dealt with (s.280).

In all other cases, the discharge occurs automatically three years after the making of the bankruptcy order. This, of course, applies in the vast majority of cases.

It is possible for this automatic discharge to be defeated if the Official Receiver establishes to the satisfaction of the court that there has been a failure on the part of the bankrupt to comply with his obligations under the Act (s.279).

If the Official Receiver decides to try to prevent the automatic discharge, he must file a report with the court supporting his application and send a copy to both the trustee and the bankrupt at least 21 days prior to the date fixed by the court for the hearing. If the bankrupt intends to dispute any part of the notice, he must file a notice in court specifying the matters which he will dispute at least seven days prior to the date of the hearing. Copies of this notice must be sent to the Official Receiver and the trustee at least four days prior to the hearing.

A bankrupt against whom an order has been made in this regard can apply to the court for the order to be removed. The court will then fix a time and place for the hearing and at least 28 days' notice must be given to the Official Receiver and the trustee, both of whom have a right to attend and be heard. Again the Official Receiver may file a report with the court setting out any information which he feels should be brought to the court's attention, including a statement as to whether any conditions imposed by the court had been satisfied.

When a discharge is granted, the court issues to the bankrupt a certificate of discharge. The actual date of discharge is specified in the certificate.

Effect of discharge

Although as a general rule the discharge releases the bankrupt from all his bankruptcy debts, there are certain liabilities which remain. These are:

1. if the trustee in bankruptcy still has duties which he must perform, he may proceed with performing them;
2. creditors may still prove their debts (though, in accordance with principle, any dividends which have already been paid cannot be disturbed);
3. secured creditors may still realise their security;
4. liability continues in respect of any non-provable debts;
5. the bankrupt remains liable for certain provable debts. These are where the liability it arises from is fraud or a fraudulent breach of trust, where the liability is in respect of any fine, and where the liability is for personal injuries arising from negligence, nuisance, breach of contract, breach of statutory duty or any other duty or arising under

any order made in matrimonial proceedings, unless the court orders to the contrary;

6. the bankrupt remains liable for obligations which arise under a confiscation order made under section 1 of the Drug Trafficking Act 1986.

Annulment

The court may annul a bankruptcy order

(a) if it should not have been made,
(b) if the bankruptcy debts and expenses have all been paid or secured since the making of the order (s.282),
(c) if a proposed voluntary arrangement by an undischarged bankrupt is approved by his creditors (s.261).

Insolvent partnerships

In the case of a partnership becoming insolvent, the winding up is conducted in accordance with the Insolvent Partnerships Order 1986. (See further Ch. 14, p. 300, *ante*). In broad terms the partnership is wound up in the same way as if it were an unregistered company.

PART 12: ARBITRATION

Chapter 35

ARBITRATION

The Arbitration Acts 1950, 1975 and 1979

The statutory regulation of the law relating to arbitration is contained in the Arbitration Acts 1950, 1975 and 1979.

The Arbitration Act 1950 is the principal Act.[1] It also gives effect to two international measures, *viz.* the Geneva Protocol on Arbitration Clauses of 1923 and the Geneva Convention on the Execution of Foreign Arbitral Awards of 1927, appended to the 1950 Act as Schedules 1 and 2. The two Geneva measures are in the process of being superseded by the New York Convention on the Recognition and Enforcement of Foreign Arbitral Awards of 1958, which was promoted by the United Nations.

The object of the Arbitration Act 1975 is to give effect to the New York Convention in the United Kingdom. The 1975 Act came into operation on December 23, 1975 (S.I. 1975, No. 1662). The purpose of the New York Convention is to provide for the enforcement of international arbitration agreements and the enforcement of foreign arbitration awards.

The 1979 Act was introduced strictly to limit judicial intervention in arbitral proceedings, to eliminate the former stated case procedure for judicial review on a question of law and to allow for the parties to exclude any right of appeal in certain types of cases. This is consistent with an international trend towards giving greater finality to arbitral awards.

The Arbitration Acts 1950 to 1979 provide, *inter alia*, for:

(1) the enforcement arbitration agreements;
(2) judicial assistance in the formation of the arbitral tribunal;
(3) judicial assistance during the reference (especially in matters

[1] References in this chapter are to the Arbitration Act 1950 unless the contrary is expressed.

which may affect third parties such as the issue of a subpoena or an order for the preservation of property);

(4) judicial supervision during the reference (*e.g.*, in cases where an arbitrator has misconducted himself);

(5) judicial review of arbitration awards; and

(6) the enforcement of arbitration awards.

Reference to arbitration

A reference to arbitration may be made in one of three ways:

(a) Under order of the court.
(b) Under an Act of Parliament.
(c) By agreement of the parties.

Under order of the court

The court may refer any question arising in any matter before it to an official or special referee for inquiry or report. It may also refer the whole question before it to be tried by an official or special referee if:

(a) all the parties consent;
(b) the case requires prolonged examination of documents or scientific or local investigation;
(c) the question in dispute consists wholly or in part of matters of account.

Under an Act of Parliament

Various Acts of Parliament provide for the settlement of disputes arising out of their provisions by arbitration. These Acts usually describe how the arbitration is to be conducted; but in all other cases the Arbitration Acts 1950 to 1979 apply (Arbitration Act 1950, s.31; Arbitration Act 1979, s.3(5); 7(1)).

By agreement of the parties

A reference by agreement of the parties must originate in an arbitration agreement. Such an agreement may be made verbally or in writing. The Arbitration Acts 1950 to 1979 apply only to written agreements, but an agreement by telex is "an agreement in writing"

(*Arab African Energy Corporation Ltd.* v. *Olieprodukten Nederland B.V.* [1983] Com.L.R. 195). This would presumably apply to communications by FAX. A tacit acceptance of a written quotation which contained an arbitration clause is sufficient to comply with the requirement for an agreement in writing (*Zambia Steel and Building Suppliers Ltd.* v. *James Clark and Eaton Ltd.* [1986] 2 Lloyd's Rep. 225).

An arbitration agreement is defined by section 32 as "a written agreement to submit present or future differences to arbitration, whether an arbitrator is named therein or not."

An arbitration must be distinguished from a valuation. It is an arbitration if the parties intend that any dispute between them shall be settled by an inquiry held in a quasi-judicial manner, usually but not necessarily, after hearing argument or evidence.

On the other hand, it is a **valuation** if the object of the activity of the appointed person is to value or appraise something but no dispute exists between the parties on the facts or the law. Examples of valuers are an architect who certifies the sums payable by the building owner to the builder, as the work performed by the builder progresses; or an accountant who, in accordance with the agreement between shareholders of a company, fixes the "fair value" of the shares sold by one of them to another. A valuer is liable for negligence in the performance of his duties but an arbitrator enjoys the same immunity as a judge and cannot be held liable in negligence.

Mr. Sutcliffe was the building owner of land on which he wished to have built a high class dwelling-house. He employed Mr. Thackrah and his partners as architects and the David Walbank Company as builders. The architects negligently issued interim certificates for the work defectively done by the builders who were paid by the building owner on the strength of the certificates. The builders then became insolvent. *Held*, the architects were liable to the building owner in negligence: *Sutcliffe* v. *Thackrah and Others* [1974] A.C. 727.

Archy Arenson was the controlling shareholder of a private company, A. Arenson Ltd. He had agreed with his nephew Ivor Arenson who likewise held shares in the company to purchase Ivor's shares at a fair value to be determined by the company's auditors. Messrs. Casson Beckman Rutley & Co., a firm of chartered accountants, who were the company's auditors, valued Ivor's shares at £4,916 for which sum they were transferred to the uncle. A few months later Ivor alleged that the transaction showed that the shares which he had sold to Archie were worth six times their value as assessed by the auditors. He brought an action against Archie and the auditors, claiming, *inter alia*, damages against the auditors for negligence. The auditors contended that Ivor's claim against them did not disclose a cause of action and should be dismissed. *Held*, that, if the auditors had acted as valuers, and not as arbitrators, and it was also proved that they had acted negligently, a claim in negligence may lie against them. In the present proceedings the courts did not find any facts from which it could be inferred that the auditors had acted as valuers or that they had acted negligently: *Aronson* v. *Casson, Beckman, Rutley & Co.* [1977] A.C. 405. *Arenson* v. *Casson Beckman Rutley & Co.* [1975] 3 W.L.R. 815.

However, it should not be inferred from the *Arenson* case that an accountant is a valuer in all circumstances; if a dispute on facts or a legal question has arisen and is referred by the parties to their accountant, the latter would act as an arbitrator even if in the course of his arbitration he has to make an appraisal, and he would enjoy quasi-judicial immunity unless he acts fraudulently.

If the parties have agreed that the valuation shall be "final, binding and conclusive," a "speaking valuation," *i.e.* a valuation giving reasons, it can be impugned in court proceedings if it is clear from the reasons expressed in the valuation that the valuer proceeded on a fundamentally erroneous basis (*Burgess* v. *Purchase & Sons* (*Farms*) *Ltd.* [1983] 2 W.L.R. 361).

Effect of Arbitration Agreement

Award to be condition precedent to court proceedings

An arbitration agreement may be framed in such a manner as to prevent any right to court proceedings from accruing under the contract until an award is first made. In such a case an award is a condition precedent to a right to sue. A clause which is framed in such a manner is known as a **Scott v. Avery clause** (below).

A policy of insurance on a ship provided that in the event of loss the amount of the loss should be referred to arbitration. It also provided that the award of the arbitrators was to be a condition precedent to the maintaining of an action. *Held*, until an award was made, no action was maintainable: *Scott* v. *Avery* (1856) 5 H.L.C. 811.

It is provided by section 25(4) that if the court orders that the agreement to refer the dispute to arbitration shall cease to have effect, it may also order that the condition precedent shall cease to have effect.

Power of court to break arbitration agreement

If a party to an arbitration agreement commences proceedings in court, contrary to his undertaking to submit to arbitration, the court, on the application of the other party, may either order a stay of court proceedings, thus allowing the arbitration to proceed, or refuse the application for a stay, thus breaking the arbitration agreement (s.4). If the only point in issue is a point of law, the court may be inclined to refuse a stay of proceedings (*Re Phoenix Timber Co. Ltd.'s Application* [1958] 2 Q.B. 1). It is increasingly rare for a court to refuse to give effect to an arbitration agreement.

Two cases have to be distinguished here: if the arbitration agreement is a domestic arbitration agreement, the discretion of the court to order or refuse a stay of court proceedings is wide (s.4(1)), but if it is a non-domestic arbitration agreement its discretion is limited (Arbitration Act 1975, s.1).

An arbitration agreement is domestic if at the time the proceedings are commenced:

1. it does not provide, expressly or by implication, for arbitration in a state other than the United Kingdom, and
2. all parties to it are:
   (a) United Kingdom citizens or natural persons habitually resident in the United Kingdom; or
   (b) corporations incorporated in the United Kingdom or having their central management and control exercised in the United Kingdom (1975 Act, s.1(4)).

Both conditions must be satisfied for an arbitration agreement to be classified as domestic.

1. *Domestic arbitrations*

A stay of court proceedings **may** only be granted if all the following requirements are satisfied (s.4(1)):

(a) The matter in question must be within the scope of the arbitration agreement;

(b) The applicant must have taken no step in the court proceedings. If he delivers a defence, makes an application to the court, or does anything else of a like nature, he cannot have the proceedings stayed;

(c) The applicant must have been ready and willing from the commencement to do everything necessary for the proper conduct of the arbitration; and

(d) There must be no sufficient reason why the dispute should not be referred to arbitration.

The burden of proof is upon the party opposing the stay to satisfy the court there are strong reasons for proceeding with the action and not granting the stay, because when parties have agreed that their disputes are to be decided by a particular tribunal the court is inclined to hold them to their agreement, unless there is some strong reason why they should not be so held. Factors relevant to the exercise of the discretion to stay court proceedings include: whether there are complex issues of law; the delay and expense that might arise if there are other court proceedings involving the same issues or parties and a multiplicity of proceedings might result if the arbitration is allowed to proceed; and the efficiency and economy generally of court proceedings compared to arbitration in the circumstances of the case. The same principles apply where the parties have agreed on an **exclusive jurisdiction clause**, and not on an arbitration clause. An exclusive jurisdiction clause provides that the courts of a particular country shall have exclusive jurisdiction to decide disputes between the parties.

A cargo of turpentine was loaded at a Russian port into a German vessel. The bills of lading were held by an English company which claimed that the turpentine was contaminated in transit and brought an action against the German vessel in the English courts. The owners of the German vessel applied for a stay on the ground that the bills of lading provided that all disputes should be judged in the U.S.S.R. *Held*, that the stay should be refused because the dispute had little connection with the U.S.S.R. None of the parties had Soviet nationality and virtually all the witnesses and other evidence were to be found in England: *The Fehmarn* [1957] 1 W.L.R. 815.

Egyptian Spring potatoes were carried in the *El Amria*, a ship owned by an Egyptian shipping company, from Alexandria to Liverpool. The bill of lading provided that any disputes should be decided in the country where the carrier had his principal place of business, *i.e.* in Egypt. The plaintiffs, who were the cargo owners, alleged that the cargo was found to be in a deteriorated condition when unloaded. They brought an action in the English courts against the defendant shipowners, claiming damages for breach of contract and for negligence. The defendants alleged that the deterioration of the cargo had occurred as the result of the unreasonably slow discharge and applied for a stay of proceedings in the English courts on the ground that the parties had agreed that the dispute was to be decided by the Egyptian courts. *Held*, the application for a stay of proceedings should be refused and the case should be allowed to proceed in the English courts. The issues raised between the parties relating to the alleged slow discharge solely concerned events which occurred in England and since the plaintiffs had issued a writ against the Mersey Docks and Harbour Co. it would be a matter of great convenience if that action could be tried at the same time as this action. Further, the most important evidence was in England. There were therefore strong reasons for refusing a stay of the English proceedings: *Arata Potato Co. Ltd.* v. *Egyptian Navigation Co. The El Amria.* [1980] 1 Lloyd's Rep. 390.

The court may, in particular, refuse a stay (s.24):

(a) After a dispute has arisen, if the arbitrator is or may not be impartial by reason of his relation to one of the parties or of his connection with the subject referred.

J.A. did work for the B. Corporation under a contract by which disputes were to be referred to the corporation's engineer. Disputes arose involving a probable conflict of evidence between J.A. and the engineer. *Held*, the action must proceed, because the engineer would, in an arbitration, be placed in the position of a judge and witness: *Bristol Corpn.* v. *John Aird & Co.* [1913] A.C. 241.

(b) If the dispute involves the question whether any of the parties have been guilty of fraud, so far as necessary to enable that question to be determined.

2. *Non-domestic arbitrations*

Here the court must order a stay of proceedings, unless it is satisfied:

(a) that the arbitration agreement is null and void, inoperative or incapable of being performed, or
(b) that there is not in fact any dispute between the parties with regard to the matters agreed to be referred (1975 Act, s.1(1)).

A party who wishes the court to stay court proceedings so that the arbitration will proceed, must apply to the court after entering an appearance and before delivering any pleadings or taking any other step in the court proceedings (1975 Act, s.1(1)). That party must prove the existence of an arbitration agreement. The party bringing court proceedings in breach of the alleged arbitration agreement would have the onus of proving that the agreement was null and void (for example, because it was induced by fraud or duress) or that the agreement was inoperative (for example, because arbitral proceedings were not brought within a contractual time limit) or that the agreement is incapable of being performed (for example, because the arbitrator named therein died before the dispute arose).

In 1970 the plaintiffs Nova, an English company, entered into a partnership agreement with the defendants Kammgarn, a German company, whereby the plaintiffs were to supply the defendants with knitting machines. The contract contained an arbitration clause and there was also a separate arbitration agreement. In 1972 the plaintiffs sold 12 machines to the defendants and received 24 bills of exchange for a total of £173,558. The first six of these bills of exchange were honoured by the defendants but the others were not paid on the ground, as the defendants alleged, of fraud. The defendants commenced arbitration proceedings in Germany and the plaintiffs issued a writ in the English courts for service out of the jurisdiction claiming payment of the outstanding bills of exchange. The defendants applied for a stay of the court proceedings. One of the issues was whether the arbitration agreement extended to the claims of the plaintiffs for payment of the outstanding bills of exchange. If this question had to be answered in the affirmative, the court was bound by section 1(1) of the Arbitration Act 1975 to grant a stay of court proceedings. *Held*, however, the arbitration agreement did not extend to claims made under the bills of exchange and the application for a stay of court proceedings on the bills of exchange should be dismissed: *Nova (Jersey) Knit Ltd.* v. *Kammgarn Spinnerei GmbH* [1977] 1 Lloyd's Rep. 463.

Summary judgment procedures are available, even under the Arbitration Act 1975 in relation to international arbitration agreements, where there is no arguable defence to a claim, on the premise that there is not in fact any dispute between the parties with regard to the matters agreed to be referred (*Sethia Linens Ltd.* v. *State Trading Corp. of India Ltd.* [1986] 1 Lloyd's Rep. 31).

Whether the arbitrator can determine the validity of the arbitration agreement

The question whether or not an arbitrator has power to determine the validity of the agreement by virtue of which he has been appointed as arbitrator is determined in accordance with the following principles:

(a) An arbitration clause is a written submission, agreed to by the parties to the contract, and, like other written agreements, must be construed according to its language and in the light of the circumstances in which it is made.
(b) If the dispute is whether the contract which contains the clause has ever been entered into at all, that issue cannot go to arbitration under the clause, for the party who denies that he has ever entered into the contract is thereby denying that he has ever joined in the submission.
(c) Similarly, if one party to the alleged contract contends that it is void ab initio (because, for example, the making of such a contract is illegal), the arbitration clause cannot operate, for on this view the clause itself is also void.
(d) But where the parties are at one in asserting that they entered into a binding contract, but a difference arises between them whether there has been a breach by one side or the other, or whether circumstances have arisen which have discharged one or both parties from further performance, the arbitration clause is binding (*Heyman* v. *Darwins Ltd.*, below).
(e) Where there is an application to the court to stay proceedings, if the agreement is on the face of it perfectly valid and effective, the application will generally be granted as the court will be unwilling to treat the agreement or the submission to arbitration as void until the matter has been decided by a court or by an arbitrator (*The Tradesman* [1962] 1 W.L.R. 61).

"It is not the law that arbitrators, if their jurisdiction is challenged or questioned, are bound immediately to refuse to act until their jurisdiction has been determined by some court which has power to determine it finally. Nor is it the law that they are bound to go on without investigating the merits of the challenge and to determine the matter in dispute, leaving the question of their jurisdiction to be held over until it is determined by some court which had power to determine it. They might then be merely wasting their time and everybody else's. They are not obliged to take either of those courses. They are entitled to inquire into the merits of the issue whether they have jurisdiction or not, not for the purpose of reaching any conclusion which will be binding upon the parties—because that they cannot do—but for the purpose of satisfying themselves as a preliminary matter about whether they ought to go on with the reference or not.": *Per* Devlin J., in *Christopher Brown Ltd.* v. *Genossenschaft Oesterreichischen Waldbesitzen R. GmbH* [1954] 1 Q.B. 8 at 12.

Separability of the arbitration agreement

An arbitration clause constitutes a separate agreement independent of the substantive contract in which it is embedded. It will survive the invalidity or termination of the main contract unless the main contract was void *ab initio* or never came into existence. The arbitrator has jurisdiction to adjudicate on the validity of the main contract unless the (separate) arbitration agreement itself is affected by a vitiating event.

D. Ltd., appointed H. their selling agent under a contract containing a clause agreeing to refer disputes "in respect of this agreement" to arbitration. A dispute arose and H. claimed that D. Ltd., had repudiated the contract. He accepted the repudiation, claimed that the contract was at an end and issued a writ. *Held*, the action should be stayed, as the alleged repudiation only amounted to a breach of contract and therefore left the arbitration clause binding: *Heyman* v. *Darwins Ltd.* [1942] A.C. 356.

Scope of the arbitration agreement

An arbitral tribunal may consider only claims which are encompassed by the wording of the arbitration agreement. An agreement to refer all disputes to arbitration arising "under this contract" will be construed narrowly and will not cover claims in tort. But an agreement to refer all disputes to arbitration arising "under or in connection with this contract" will cover claims in tort (*Ashville Investments Ltd.* v. *Elmer Contractors Ltd.* [1989] 2 Q.B. 488). The words "arising out of this contract" will also be given a wide interpretation and will encompass a plea for rectification of the contract (*Ethiopian Oilseeds and Pulses Export Corporation* v. *Rio Del Mar Foods Inc.* [1990] 1 Lloyd's Rep. 86).

If a contract contains an arbitration clause and a claim is made in negligence—a tort—which is coextensive with a claim for breach of the contract containing the clause, the claim in tort is within the jurisdiction of the arbitrators who can dispose of it (*Woolf* v. *Collis Removal Service* [1948] 1 K.B. 11). The position is the same in other cases in which a sufficiently close connection exists between the tort and the breach of contract.

Charterers thought that they had a claim for damages against the shipowners who had stopped the discharge of goods from the ship. In pursuance of their claim, the charterers arrested the ship. The shipowners claimed that the arrest was wrongful and demanded damages. The charterparty contained an arbitration clause and the arbitrators decided the claim for damages for wrongful arrest in favour of the shipowners. *Held*, (1) the claim for damages for wrongful arrest of the ship was founded in tort, (2) the arbitrators had jurisdiction to dispose of the claim as the arrest of the ship was only the sequel to the claim of the charterers and so closely connected with the alleged breach of charterparty that it was within the scope of the arbitration: *Astro Vencedor Compania Naviera S.A. of Panama* v. *Mabanaft GmbH*; *The Damianos* [1971] 2 Q.B. 588.

Arbitration agreement in apprenticeship deed

An arbitration clause in an apprenticeship deed between a minor and his employer is for the minor's benefit (see p. 70, *ante*), and is binding on the minor (*Slade* v. *Metrodent Ltd.* [1953] 2 Q.B. 112).

Assignment of contract containing arbitration agreement

When a contract is assignable, the benefit of an arbitration clause contained in it is assignable as part of the contract (*Shayler* v. *Woolf* [1946] Ch. 320). But an assignment of all money due under a contract does not include an arbitration clause in the contract.

The Arbitration Agreement

Every arbitration agreement is assumed to include the following provisions, unless a contrary intention is expressed in it—

1. If no other mode of reference is provided, the reference is to a single arbitrator (s.6).

2. If the reference is to two arbitrators, they may appoint an umpire at any time after they are themselves appointed and shall do so forthwith if they cannot agree (s.8(1), amended by the Arbitration Act 1979, s.6(1)).

3. If the arbitrators have delivered to any party or to the umpire a notice in writing stating that they cannot agree, the umpire may enter on the reference (s.8(2)).

4. The parties to the arbitration must submit to be examined on oath before the arbitrator or umpire and must produce all books, deeds, papers, accounts, writings and documents in their possession which may be called for, and must do all other things which, during the reference, the arbitrators or umpire may require (s.12(1)).

5. The witnesses on the reference must, if the arbitrators or umpire think fit, be examined on oath (s.12(2)).

6. The award to be made by the arbitrators or umpire is final and binding on the parties (s.16).

7. The costs of the reference and award are in the discretion of the arbitrators or umpire, who can direct who shall pay the costs and can tax or settle the amount of costs to be paid (s.18(1)). A provision in the arbitration agreement that a party shall pay his own costs in any event is void unless the provision is in an agreement to submit to arbitration a dispute which has already arisen (s.18(3)).

8. The arbitrators or umpire can order specific performance of any contract, except a contract relating to land (s.15).

9. An interim award may be made (s.14).

An arbitration agreement may be altered or amended by consent of the parties, but the arbitrator or umpire has no power to alter it.

The authority of an arbitrator or umpire appointed under an arbitration agreement is irrevocable except by leave of the court (s.1). An arbitration agreement is not discharged by the death of any party to the agreement, and the authority of an arbitrator is not revoked by the death of the party appointing him (s.2). On the bankruptcy of a party, an arbitration clause in a contract is enforceable by or against his trustee in bankruptcy if he adopts the contract (s.3). There is no similar provision dealing with the liquidator of a company. The court may revoke an agreement, after a dispute has arisen, on the ground that the arbitrator is not impartial by reason of his relation to one of the parties to the agreement, or of his connection with the subject referred, or when a question of fraud arises (s.24).

The applicable law

Where an international contract contains an arbitration clause but does not define the proper law of the contract, the presumption is that the law of the place at which the arbitration is to be held is the proper law of the contract (*Tzortzis* v. *Monark Line A/B* [1968] 1 W.L.R. 406) but this presumption may be rebutted by the surrounding circumstances (*Cie Tunisienne de Navigation S.A.* v. *Cie d'Armement Maritime S.A.*, see pp. 207–208, *ante*).

The law applicable to the arbitration procedure, or *lex arbitri*, may be different from the substantive law governing the contract (*Whitworth Street Estates* (*Manchester*) *Ltd.* v. *James Miller & Partners Ltd.* [1970] A.C. 583). The *lex arbitri* which governs the conduct of the arbitration is the law of the place where the arbitration takes place unless the parties expressly and clearly agree that the arbitration is to be subject to the procedural law of some other country. Such a provision would, however, produce a highly complex and possibly unworkable result (*Naviera Amazonica Peruana S.A.* v. *Compania Internacional de Seguros de Peru* [1988] 1 Lloyd's Rep. 116).

The validity, effect and interpretation of an arbitration agreement are determined by the proper law of the arbitration agreement itself. In most cases this will be the same law as the proper (or applicable) law of the substantive contract in which an arbitration clause is embedded. The parties may, however, choose to have the main contract and the arbitration agreement governed by different laws. The arbitration procedure may be governed by a third law. Thus, for example, an arbitration in London would be governed by English procedural law but the arbitrators might have to apply Swiss law to the merits of the dispute and French law to questions relating to the scope of the arbitration agreement. The provision of the Arbitration Act 1950 which gives the court power to extend the time for commencing arbitration proceedings in case of undue hardship (s.27) forms part of the substantive law governing the arbitration agreement and can be invoked if the arbitration agreement is governed by English law even though the arbitration procedure may be governed by a foreign law (*International Tank and Pipe S.A.K.* v. *Kuwait Aviation Fuelling Co. K.S.C.* [1975] Q.B. 224).

Appointment of Arbitrator

The parties may refer their dispute to a single named arbitrator, to two arbitrators—one to be appointed by each party—or to two arbitrators and an umpire or chairman. A High Court judge may be appointed arbitrator or umpire; he is known as a judge-arbitrator or judge-umpire (Administration of Justice Act 1970, s.4).

In the following cases—

(a) where the reference is to a single arbitrator and the parties do not concur in the appointment of an arbitrator;
(b) if the appointed arbitrator dies or refuses to act and the parties do not supply the vacancy;
(c) where the parties or two arbitrators are required or are at liberty to appoint an umpire and do not appoint him;
(d) where the umpire dies or refuses to act and the parties do not supply a vacancy;

any party may serve the others with a written notice to make an appointment, and if the appointment is not made within seven days the court will make the appointment (s.10).

The m.v. *Tanais* was under charter for a voyage between Canada and Italy. The charterparty provided, *inter alia*, for "arbitration to be settled in London." A dispute arose between the shipowners and the charterers and the shipowners requested the charterers to agree on the arbitrator, but the latter refused to co-operate. *Held*, that the dispute should be settled by arbitration and an arbitrator be appointed by the court: *Tritonia Shipping Inc.* v. *South Nelson Forest Products Corpn.* [1966] 1 Lloyd's Rep. 114.

Sometimes the arbitrator or umpire is to be appointed by a third person, *e.g.* by a chamber of commerce or the president of a professional association. If the organisation or person who is to make the appointment, declines or fails to do so, any party to the arbitration agreement may give the organisation or person in question written notice to make the appointment and if it is not made within seven days, the party may apply to the court for the appointment of the arbitrator or umpire (Arbitration Act 1979, s.6(4)).

A clause worded "suitable arbitration clause" in an English contract is not void on the ground of uncertainty but means an arbitration which reasonable men in this type of business would consider suitable, the court being empowered to appoint an arbitrator under the Arbitration Act 1950 (*Hobbs Padgett & Co.* (*Reinsurance*) *Ltd.* v. *J. C. Kirkland Ltd.* [1969] 2 Lloyd's Rep. 547). Where the arbitration clause provides for the appointment of "commercial men" as arbitrators and umpire, a practising member of the Bar cannot be appointed umpire by the arbitrators (*Rahcassi Shipping Co. S.A.* v. *Blue Star Ltd.* [1969] 1 Q.B. 173).

Where the agreement provides that the reference shall be to two arbitrators, one to be appointed by each party, and one party appoints an arbitrator who subsequently dies or refuses to act, such party may appoint a new arbitrator. If he fails to do so or fails to appoint an arbitrator in the first instance, the other party may serve notice on him to make an appointment within seven days, and, in default of such appointment, the arbitrator appointed by the other party will be the sole arbitrator and his award will be binding on both parties. An appointment made under these circumstances may be set aside by the court (s.7). As already observed, the two arbitrators may appoint an umpire and shall do so forthwith, if they cannot agree.

If the agreement for reference is to three arbitrators the award of any two is binding unless a contrary intention is expressed (Arbitration Act 1950, s.9 as amended by the 1979 Act, s.6(2)).

The appointment of an arbitrator is constituted by (1) nominating the arbitrator to the other party, (2) informing the arbitrator of his nomination, and (3) an intimation by him that he is willing to accept the nomination.

The plaintiffs chartered the defendants' motor vessel *La Loma*. The charterparty contained an arbitration clause providing for the appointment of an arbitrator by the claimants within three months from the final discharge of the goods from the ship, and further providing that in the absence of such an appointment the claimants' claim should be absolutely barred. A dispute arose between the parties and the plaintiffs, who were the claimants, indicated the name of their arbitrator to the defendants but failed to inform him of his nomination. After the expiry of the three months from the final discharge the plaintiffs notified the arbitrator and he accepted. *Held*, the appointment of the arbitrator was not completed within the time stated in the arbitration clause and consequently the plaintiffs' claim was absolutely barred: *Tradax Export S.A.* v. *Volkswagenwerk* [1970] 1 Lloyd's Rep. 62.

Removal of arbitrator or umpire

The court may remove an arbitrator or umpire who fails to use reasonable dispatch in proceeding with the reference and making an award. No remuneration is payable to an arbitrator or an umpire who is removed (s.13).

Judicial Review

The Arbitration Act 1979 admits the judicial review of arbitration awards on questions of law, but this review is severely restricted and admitted only subject to stringent conditions. If these conditions are not satisfied the court has no power to review the award on its merits. In certain well-defined cases the parties to the arbitration may even exclude judicial review completely.

Reasoned awards

A party is entitled to an award which contains sufficient reasons to enable the court to carry out a judicial review. If an appeal is brought from the award to the court and the judge is unable to consider any question of law arising out of the award, he may order the arbitrator or umpire to state the reasons for his award in sufficient detail or to supplement the reasons given in the award. The judge can make such an order only if:

(a) a party has notified the arbitrator or umpire before the award was made that a reasoned award is required; or
(b) there is some special reason why such a notice was not given. (1979 Act, s.1(5) and (6)).

The court will be vigilant to ensure that the power to order further reasons is used only for its proper purpose and not as an indirect way of obtaining a review of the merits of an award (*Universal Petroleum Co. Ltd.* v. *Handels- und Transport Gesellschaft m.b.H.* [1987] 1 Lloyd's Rep. 517.)

Judicial review procedure

The procedure for a review of the award by the court is as follows. An appeal may be brought to the High Court on any question of law arising out of the award by any party to the arbitration;

(a) with the consent of all other parties; or
(b) by leave of the court but the court shall not grant leave unless it considers that "the determination of the question of law

concerned could substantially affect the rights of one or more of the parties to the arbitration agreement." (1979 Act, s.1(3) and (4)).

According to the guidelines laid down by the House of Lords in the *Nema* (below), the requirements under (b) should be applied very strictly and leave to appeal should be granted by the court only sparingly, particularly in so-called **"one-off" contracts**, *i.e.* contracts of singular occurrence and not concluded on standard contract forms. "In a 'one-off' case, in the absence of special circumstances, leave should not be given unless on the conclusion of argument on the application for leave the court has formed the provisional view that the arbitrator was wrong and considers that it would need a great deal of convincing that he was right" (*per* Parker J. in The *Kerman* [1982] 1 Lloyd's Rep. 62, 65).

The owners of the *Nema* chartered her to the charterers for seven consecutive voyages to Sorel in Canada. Sorel was at the St. Lawrence River and was icebound for many months of the year. After one round voyage the *Nema* arrived back at Sorel but was unable to load owing to a strike. The owners, who were permitted by the terms of the charterparty to take the *Nema* on one transatlantic voyage, took her to Spain. The main issue between the parties was whether, as the charterers claimed, the *Nema* was bound to proceed from Spain to Sorel and wait there until either the strike ended and she could load or the open water season ended and loading was made impossible. Or whether, as the owners contended, their obligations to make the *Nema* available for the outstanding voyages had ended by frustration. The parties agreed on arbitration by a single arbitrator who decided that the whole charterparty, as far as not performed, was frustrated. On appeal to the court, Robert Goff J. gave leave for judicial review of the arbitration award and held that the charterparty was not frustrated, but his decision was reversed by the Court of Appeal. The charterers then appealed to the House of Lords. *Held*, (i) Robert Goff J. should not have granted leave to appeal from the decision of the arbitrator nor should leave have been given to appeal to the Court of Appeal; and (ii) the arbitrator rightly decided that the whole charterparty, as far as not performed, was frustrated: *Pioneer Shipping Ltd.* v. *B.T.P. Tioxide Ltd. The Nema* [1982] A.C. 725.

The philosophy now adopted by the courts is to prefer finality over legality. It is presumed that the parties intended to take the risk that the arbitrators might make an error in fact or law. The appeal court will grant leave to appeal on a question of law only in a case where the interests of justice to the parties or the integrity of the arbitral process demand that a court consider the question or if a matter of general legal import is involved (*Antaios Compania Naviera S.A.* v. *Salen Rederierna A.B.* [1985] A.C. 191).

An arbitrator cannot refer a question of EEC law to the Court of the European Communities in Luxembourg by virtue of article 177 of the EEC Treaty. But where such a question arises in arbitration, the court will allow an appeal from the award if the point is new, is capable of serious argument, and is potentially of great importance and far-reaching effect (*Bulk Oil* (*Zug*) *A.G.* v. *Sun International Ltd.* [1984] 1 W.L.R. 147).

Preliminary points of law

An application may be made to the High Court to determine any question of law arising in the course of the arbitration. The High Court shall not entertain the application unless:

(a) the determination might produce substantial savings in costs, and
(b) the conditions on which the court may give leave to appeal from an arbitration award under section 1(3) and (4) of the 1979 Act (see above) are satisfied. (1979 Act, s.2(2)).

The application for the determination of a preliminary point of law by the court is made either by a party with the consent of the arbitrator or umpire, or with the consent of all other parties (1979 Act, s.2(1)).

Appeals from the decision of the High Court

Appeals from the decision of the High Court to the Court of Appeal are greatly restricted, both in cases concerning an appeal from the award (1979 Act, s.1(6A) and (7)) and in those concerning the determination of a preliminary point of law (1979 Act, s.2(2A) and (3)).

Appeals to the Court of Appeal are only admitted if—

(a) the High Court or the Court of Appeal gives leave; and
(b) a certificate is given by the High Court that the question of law in issue is either of general public importance or is one

which for some other special reason should be considered by the Court of Appeal.

Exclusion agreements

The parties to the arbitration may in certain circumstances exclude judicial review completely. Where they have done so lawfully, no appeal from the award on a point of law is admitted and the court has no power to determine a preliminary point of law.

Domestic, non-domestic and special category arbitrations

For the purposes of exclusion clauses, arbitrations are arranged into:

domestic arbitrations,
non-domestic arbitrations, and
special category arbitrations.

The definition of domestic and non-domestic arbitrations in this connection is the same as that for the purposes of the Arbitration Act 1975 (see p. 721, *ante*), except that the requirements must be satisfied at the time the arbitration agreement is entered into (1979 Act, s.3(7)), and not, as under the 1975 Act, at the time the arbitration proceedings are commenced.

Special category proceedings concern:

(a) a question or claim falling within the Admiralty jurisdiction of the High Court; or
(b) a dispute arising out of a contract of insurance; or
(c) a dispute arising out of a commodity contract. (1979 Act, s.4(1)).

A commodity contract is defined as a contract:

(a) for the sale of goods dealt with on a commodity market or exchange in England and Wales, which is specified by an order made by the Secretary of State; and
(b) of a description as specified. (1979 Act, s.4(2)).

The Arbitration (Commodity Contracts) Order 1979 (S.I. 1979 No. 754) specifies the commodity markets and exchanges to which these provisions apply. They include, *e.g.* the London Metal

Exchange, the Grain and Feed Trade Association Limited (GAFTA) and the Federation of Oils, Seeds and Fats Association of London (FOSFA).

Domestic arbitrations

In domestic arbitrations parties may exclude judicial review by an exclusion agreement only if the agreement is entered *after* the commencement of the arbitration (1979 Act, s.3(6)).

Non-domestic arbitrations (other than special category arbitrations)

Here the parties may enter into an exclusion agreement *before* or *after* the commencement of the arbitration (1979 Act, s.4(1)).

In these cases it would be possible to combine the exclusion agreement with the arbitration clause in the original contract. The admission of exclusion agreements before the commencement of the arbitration in this class of cases should be of particular value in international "one-off" contracts.

When parties agree on arbitration under the Rules of the Court of Arbitration of the International Chamber of Commerce—as they frequently do in international "one-off" contracts—they are taken to have concluded an exclusion agreement because the ICC Rules provide that "the arbitral award shall be final" (*Arab African Energy Corporation Ltd.* v. *Olieprodukten Nederland B.V.* below).

By a contract of December 30, 1980, Arab African Energy Corporation (Arafenco) sold a quantity of gas oil to Olieprodukten Nederland (O.P.N.). One of the terms of the contract was "English law—arbitration, if any, according to ICC Rules." The contract, which was made orally, was confirmed by two telex messages from O.P.N.'s brokers to the brokers of Arafenco. A dispute arose and the arbitrator made an award. Arafenco sought leave to appeal against the award. O.P.N. claimed that the award was final. *Held*, (1) the arbitration agreement confirmed by the telex messages was in writing and consequently the Arbitration Acts 1950 to 1979 applied; (2) the parties had made an exclusion agreement because article 24 of the ICC Rules of Arbitration (1975 Revision) provided that the arbitral award should be final and that the parties are deemed to have waived their right to any form of appeal: *Arab African Energy Corporation Ltd.* v. *Olieprodukten Nederland B.V.* [1983] 2 Lloyd's Rep. 419.

Special category arbitrations

Here an exclusion agreement is only admitted:

(a) *after* the commencement of the arbitration; or
(b) if the contract is governed by a law other than that of England and Wales. (1979 Act, s.4(1)).

Special category arbitrations will often be non-domestic arbitrations. Nevertheless, they are, at least for the time being (1979 Act, s.4(3)) subject to a special regulation which constitutes an exception to the general treatment of non-domestic arbitrations.

Conduct of an Arbitration

The duty of an arbitrator is to make an award on the matters of dispute or difference between the parties submitted for his decision. An arbitrator or an umpire cannot delegate the powers conferred on him by the agreement.

A lay arbitrator may in a proper case, in the absence of an objection by the parties, hear the arbitration with a legal assessor. In all cases he may employ legal assistance in drawing up his award.

The arbitrator should fix a time and place for the hearing of the arbitration and give notice to all parties. Should one of the parties fail to attend after notice, the arbitrator can proceed with the reference, notwithstanding his absence. The arbitrator can administer oaths to the witnesses appearing before him (s.12(3)), and with respect to their testimony he is bound to observe the rules of evidence. Unless the submission provides to the contrary he should hear the witnesses tendered in the presence of both parties. He has no power to call a witness himself without the consent of the parties (*Re Enoch & Zaretsky's Arbn.* [1910] 1 K.B. 327). An arbitrator may order that pleadings be filed or that there be discovery and inspection of documents but has no power to order security for costs unless specifically granted such power by the parties (*Mavani* v. *Ralli Bros. Ltd.* [1973] 1 W.L.R. 468). A court may order security for costs (s.12(6)) but as a general rule will decline to do so against a foreign claimant in an international arbitration (*Bank Mellat* v. *Helliniki Techniki S.A.* [1984] 1 Q.B. 291).

A commercial arbitrator is entitled to rely on his own knowledge and experience in deciding on the quality of the goods which form the subject-matter of the arbitration, and can also assess the damages, even though there has been no evidence before him as to the amount of the damages (*Mediterranean & Eastern Export Co.* v.

Fortress Fabrics Ltd. [1948] 2 All E.R. 186). But if intending to rely on his own knowledge of the trade, he must not take the parties by surprise but invite them, if he thinks they have missed a point, to deal with it; further, if he has knowledge of facts which do not appear to be known to the parties, he must disclose those facts to them and give them an opportunity to plead to them (*Thomas Borthwick* (*Glasgow*) *Ltd.* v. *Faure Fairclough Ltd.* [1968] 1 Lloyd's Rep. 16).

In commercial arbitrations where an umpire has been appointed the arbitrators can give evidence before the umpire.

A dispute arose between buyers and sellers of meat as to its quality. The buyers sent K. to examine the meat, and on the dispute being referred to arbitration, appointed K. their arbitrator. The arbitrators having failed to agree, an umpire was appointed. *Held*, K. could give evidence before the umpire as to the state of the meat: *Bourgeois* v. *Weddell & Co.* [1924] 1 K.B. 539.

The arbitrator must decide according to the law; the parties cannot give him power to decide according to an equitable rather than a strictly legal interpretation because the adoption of such an extra-legal criterion would make it impossible for the court, when a judicial review is called for, to ascertain whether the arbitrator had fallen into an error when deciding a question of law (*Orion Compania Espanola de Seguros* v. *Belfort Maatschappij Voor Algemene Verzekgringeen* [1962] 2 Lloyd's Rep. 257).

"I have no hesitation in accepting ... that a clause which purported to free arbitrators to decide without reference to law and according, for example, to their own motions of what would be fair would not be a valid arbitration clause.": *Home and Overseas Insurance* v. *Mentor Insurance* [1989] 1 Lloyd's Rep. 473 at 485.

However, a decision by the arbitrators to apply internationally accepted principles of law governing contractual relations in an arbitration subject to Swiss law was not so uncertain as to preclude enforcement of the award by an English court (*Deutsche Schachtbau-und-Tiefbohngesellschaft mbH* v. *Rias Al Khaimah National Oil Co.* [1987] 2 Lloyd's Rep. 246).

The arbitrator has no power to dismiss a case for want of prosecution, even if inordinate and inexcusable delay on the part of the parties occurs in the proceedings before him. But an arbitration agreement, like every other contract, might be terminated by frustration, abandonment by both parties, or a repudiatory breach by one party which is accepted by the other (*Bremer Vulkan Schiffbau und Maschinenfabrik* v. *South Indian Shipping Corporation Ltd.*, below). Frustration of the arbitration agreement does not occur if the parties are in default with their mutual obligation to apply to the arbitrator for directions in order to prevent inordinate delay (*Paal Wilson & Co. A/S* v. *Patenreederei Hannah Blumenthal* [1982] 3 W.L.R. 1149). If inordinate delay occurs, the arbitrator or umpire may make an order and if the parties fail to comply with it, he may apply to the court under section 5 of the Arbitration Act 1979. The court has power under this section to allow the arbitrator or umpire to continue with the proceedings in the same manner as a High Court judge may do. Under this provision the court might empower the arbitrator or umpire to dismiss the case for want of prosecution.

In August 1964 South India Shipping ordered from Bremer Vulkan, German shipbuilders, five bulk carriers. The contract provided for arbitration in London. The ships were delivered in 1965 and 1966. Disputes arose and an arbitrator was appointed in 1972. No step was taken by either party for five years, and in 1977 Bremer Vulkan started proceedings in the English courts asking the court to restrain South India Shipping from proceeding with the arbitration for want of prosecution. *Held*, the arbitrator had no jurisdiction to dismiss the claim for want of prosecution and the court should not order an injunction restraining South India Shipping from proceeding with the arbitration: *Bremer Vulkan Schiffbau und Maschinenfabrik* v. *South India Shipping Corporation Ltd.* [1981] 2 W.L.R. 141.

The Award

The award may be in writing or made verbally, unless the arbitration agreement provides that it must be in writing. To be valid, the award should comply with the following:

1. It must follow the agreement and not purport to decide matters not within the agreement. An award on something outside the agreement is void, and if the void part cannot be severed from the rest of the award, the whole award is void (*Buccleuch* (*Duke*) v. *Metropolitan Board of Works* (1870) L.R. 5 Ex. 221).

2. It must be certain. If it is uncertain it cannot be enforced. For example, an award that A. or B. shall do a certain act is void for uncertainty (*Lawrence* v. *Hodgson* (1826) 1 Y. & J. 16).

3. It must be final. An award, therefore, that a third party shall certify the loss arising from a breach of contract is void for want of finality (*Dresser* v. *Finnis* (1855) 25 L.T.(o.s.) 81).

4. It must be reasonable, legal and possible. An award that one of the parties should do something beyond his power, as to deliver up a deed which is in the custody of X., is void (*Lee* v. *Elkins* (1701) 12 Mod. Rep. 585).

5. It must dispose of all the differences submitted to arbitration. If, however, all matters in dispute between the parties are submitted to arbitration, the award is good if it deals with all matters submitted to the arbitrator, although there may be other differences between the parties.

6. The award must be reasoned in the circumstances explained earlier (see p. 732, *ante*).

An arbitrator has jurisdiction to make his award in a foreign currency where that currency is the currency of the contract (*Jugoslavenska Oceanska Plovidba* v. *Castle Investment Co. Inc.* [1974] Q.B. 292).

An arbitrator is entitled to award interest on the sum he finds to be due (*Chandris* v. *Isbrandtsen-Moller Co.* [1950] 2 All E.R. 618). In a commercial arbitration, interest should always be awarded, except for good reason (*Panchaud Frères S.A.* v. *R. Pagnan & Fratelli* [1974] 1 Lloyd's Rep. 394, 411).

When the award is ready the arbitrator gives notice to the parties, who can take it up on paying the arbitrator's costs. After the award is made the arbitrator is *functus officio*, and cannot alter or vary his award. He may, however, correct any clerical mistake or error arising from any accidental slip or omission (s.17).

For the purposes of the Arbitration Act 1975 and the New York Convention, an award is made at the place where it is signed. If an arbitrator in an arbitration which takes place in England according to English procedural law, decides to sign the award in a different country then it becomes an award made in that country and may only be set aside, if at all, under the law and by the courts of that country (*Hiscox* v. *Outhwaite*, unreported decision of the Court of Appeal, March 11, 1991).

Effect of the award

When an award is made it is final, and no appeal can be made to the courts, except in the limited cases when the judicial review of the award is admitted (p. 732, *ante*) or when the award can be remitted to the arbitrator or set aside by the court (see pp. 742–743, *post*). The agreement for arbitration may provide for an appeal to an appeal committee or other tribunal, but except when it does so, the arbitrator's decision on the facts is final and conclusive, and it is his duty to state the facts, as found by him, in the award; a mere reference to the evidence, *e.g.* to the transcript of evidence is insufficient (*Tersons Ltd.* v. *Stevenage Development Corpn.* [1965] 1 Q.B. 37).

The Costs of the Arbitration

The costs of the arbitration, unless a contrary intention is expressed in the agreement, are in the discretion of the arbitrator (s.18). This discretion must be exercised judicially (*Lloyd del Pacifico* v. *Board of Trade* (1930) 46 T.L.R. 476). In the absence of special circumstances, it is settled practice that the successful party should be awarded costs. If there are special circumstances before the arbitrator justifying the exercise of his discretion in favour of the unsuccessful party, he need not follow the settled practice (*Dineen* v. *Walpole* [1969] 1 Lloyd's Rep. 261). The arbitrator may award a lump sum for costs, or may direct that the costs shall be taxed in the High Court or by himself. The costs include all the costs of the arbitration including the arbitrator's own costs.

The arbitrator may fix the amount of his own remuneration and include it in the award. It is then payable on the taking up of the award. The fees of an arbitrator and an umpire may be taxed, and only so much as is found to be reasonable on taxation need to be paid (s.19). If the reference is to two arbitrators and an umpire and the umpire, owing to the disagreement of the arbitrators, draws up the award, he should include the fees of the arbitrators as well as his own fees, specifying the amount of each (*Gilbert* v. *Wright* (1904) 20 T.L.R. 164). In exceptional cases if it is apparent that the umpire, when settling his own and the arbitrators' remuneration, misunderstood his duties and settled it in a wholly extravagant manner, this might amount to misconduct and the whole award be set aside (*Government of Ceylon* v. *Chandris* [1963] 2 Q.B. 327).

An arbitrator is entitled to reasonable fees but may not insist upon a commitment fee unless it was agreed before appointment. It would be misconduct for an arbitrator to insist upon a commitment fee as a condition of continuing to act in the absence of such prior agreement. It would also probably constitute misconduct for an arbitrator to conclude an agreement as to fees with one party, after appointment, if the other party refuses to join in the agreement (*K/S Norjal A/S* v. *Hyundai Heavy Industries Co. Ltd.*, *The Times*, March 12, 1991) (Court of Appeal).

Enforcement of Awards

An award on an arbitration agreement may, by leave of the court, be enforced in the same manner as a judgment (s.26). Leave will be granted unless it can be shown that the award is a nullity, or is bad on the face of it, or is ultra vires (*Re Stone and Hastie* [1903] 2 L.B. 463).

An alternative method of enforcing an award is to bring an action on it. If the submission is oral, an action is the only method of enforcing the award.

Remission to Arbitrator

In all cases of reference to arbitration, the court may remit the whole or part of the matter for reconsideration by the arbitrators or umpire. When an award is remitted the award must be made within three months of the order of remission (s.22), but the time may be enlarged by the court (s.13(2)).

An award may be remitted for reconsideration on the following grounds:

1. Where the arbitrator has made a mistake with respect to his jurisdiction.

The arbitrator was not given the submission but, thinking he understood the matters in dispute, made an award. When the award was taken up, it was found that it did not deal with the matters in dispute. The arbitrator thereupon read the submission, destroyed his award and made a new one. *Held*, the arbitrator, having made an award, was *functus officio* and had no power to make a new award, but that the case should be remitted to the arbitrator for reconsideration: *Re Stringer and Riley Bros.* [1901] 1 Q.B. 105.

2. Where, since the making of the award, material evidence has

been discovered which might have affected the arbitrator's decision (*Re Keighley, Maxted & Co.* v. *Durant & Co.* [1893] 1 Q.B. 405).

3. Where there has been misconduct on the part of the arbitrator. In such a case the court may either set the award aside or remit it to the arbitrator.

Misconduct, sometimes called technical misconduct, does not imply a moral reprobation. It occurs if the arbitrator has failed "to act fairly and to be seen to act fairly. This is not to say that [the arbitrator] intended to be unfair or was aware that [he] might appear to have acted unfairly. Such cases are, happily, very rare because the commercial community is fortunate in the skill and conscientiousness of those who devote time to the resolution of commercial disputes by arbitration" (*per* Donaldson J. in *Thomas Borthwick (Glasgow) Ltd.* v. *Faure Fairclough Ltd.* [1968] 1 Lloyd's Rep. 29).

The court has an unlimited jurisdiction to remit an arbitral award as a safety net to prevent injustice but it is usually invoked, if at all, in relation to procedural mishaps or misunderstandings (*M.F. King Holdings Ltd.* v. *Thomas McKenna Ltd.*, *The Times*, January 30, 1991) (Court of Appeal). A court has no jurisdiction to remit or set aside an award on the ground of errors of fact or law on the face of the award except in accordance with the appeal provisions of the Arbitration Act 1979 (s.1).

Setting Aside the Award

Where an arbitrator or umpire has misconducted himself, or any arbitration or award has been improperly procured, the court may set aside the award (s.23). An award is improperly procured if it is obtained by fraud or by concealment of material facts.

An award can be set aside for misconduct if the arbitrator has received bribes, or if he is secretly interested in the subject-matter of the dispute. Misconduct, however, may exist where no improper motives are imputed to the arbitrator. It is misconduct, for example, to make an award on an illegal contract (*David Taylor & Son* v. *Barnett* [1953] 1 W.L.R. 562). It is also misconduct to make his award before hearing all the evidence, or allowing a party to finish his case; to examine a witness in the absence of either of the parties; to inspect property, the subject of the arbitration accompanied by only one party (*Re Brien and Brien's Arbn.* [1910] 2 Ir.R. 84); to fail to give notice to the parties of the time and place of meeting (*Oswald* v. *Grey* (1855) 24 L.J.Q.B. 69); or to hear the evidence of each party in the absence of the other (*Ramsden & Co.* v. *Jacobs* [1922] 1 K.B. 640); or where one of three arbitrators signs the award in blank without deliberating with the other arbitrators, but if all three have considered their decision, the arbitrators need not sign the award at the same time (*European Grain and Shipping Ltd.* v. *Johnston* [1983] 2 W.L.R. 241).

Foreign Awards

Foreign awards, as defined in section 35, can be enforced in England either by action or in the same manner as the award of an arbitrator under section 26, provided that the conditions laid down in section 37 are complied with.

One of these conditions is that the award has become final in the country in which it was made. Whether an award has become final in this way is a matter of English law when enforcement is being sought in England and it matters not, for example, if the award could not be enforced in the country where it was made until some further step had been taken, such as an order of the local court (*Union Nationale des Cooperatives Agricoles de Cèrèales* v. *Robert Catterall and Co. Ltd.* [1959] 2 Q.B. 44.

Convention Awards

A Convention award is an award made in pursuance of an arbitration agreement in the territory of a foreign state which is a party to the New York Convention on the Recognition and Enforcement of Foreign Arbitral Awards of 1958. These awards are subject to the Arbitration Act 1975, ss.2 to 6.

A Convention award is enforced in the same manner as an English award (1976 Act, s.3). Enforcement of such an award can be refused only if the party against whom it is made proves:

(a) that a party to the arbitration agreement was (under the law applicable to him) under some incapacity; or

(b) that the arbitration agreement was not valid under the law to which the parties subjected it or, failing any indication thereon, under the law of the country where the award was made; or
(c) that he was not given proper notice of the appointment of the arbitrator or of the arbitration proceedings or was otherwise unable to present his case; or
(d) that the award deals with a difference not covered by the arbitration agreement; or
(e) that the composition of the arbitral authority or the arbitral procedure was not in accordance with the agreement of the parties, or failing such agreement, with the law of the country where the arbitration took place; or
(f) that the award has not yet become binding on the parties, or has been set aside or suspended by a competent authority of the country in which, or under the law of which, it was made (1975 Act, s.5(1)).

The enforcement of a Convention award may also be refused if the subject-matter of the award is not capable of settlement by arbitration or it would be contrary to public policy to enforce it (1975 Act, s.5(3)).

As of 1991 more than 80 countries have acceded to the New York Convention (for a list of these countries see the Arbitration (Foreign Awards) Order 1975 (No. 1709), as amended).

International Investment Disputes

Legal disputes arising directly out of an investment between a state (or a department or agency of a state) and a national of another state may be settled by arbitration under the rules of the International Centre for Settlement of Investment Disputes, established at the International Bank for Reconstruction and Development in Washington. The Centre has jurisdiction only if both parties have consented in writing to submit the dispute to the Centre.

The provisions relating to arbitration over international investment disputes are contained in an international convention of 1965, which is set out in the Schedule to the **Arbitration (International Investment Disputes) Act 1966**. A person seeking recognition or enforcement of such an award is entitled to have the award registered in the High Court (s.1(2)). If the award is in a foreign currency, the currency is converted on the basis of the rate of exchange prevailing at the date when the award was rendered (s.1(3)). The Act came into force on January 18, 1967.

INDEX